Studies in Social and Demographic History

General editors Peter Laslett, R. S. Schofield, E. A. Wrigley

This book is the first in a series to be published by Edward Arnold for the Cambridge Group for the History of Population and Social Structure. The Cambridge Group is a Unit of the Social Science Research Council.

Later books in the series will include:

E. A. Wrigley and R. S. Schofield, *The population history of England 1541–1871. A reconstruction**
R. M. Smith (ed.), *Land, kinship and life-cycle*

* Publication 1980

Earlier publications of the Cambridge Group include:

E. A. Wrigley (ed.), *An introduction to English historical demography* (London, 1966)
A. Sauvy, *General theory of population* (English translation; London, 1969)
P. Laslett and R. Wall (eds), *Household and family in past time* (Cambridge, 1972)
E. A. Wrigley (ed.), *Nineteenth-century society* (Cambridge, 1972)
E. A. Wrigley (ed.), *Identifying people in the past* (London, 1973)

Bastardy and its Comparative History

Studies in the history of illegitimacy and marital nonconformism in Britain, France, Germany, Sweden, North America, Jamaica and Japan

Edited by Peter Laslett, Karla Oosterveen and Richard M. Smith
with the assistance of other members of the SSRC Cambridge Group for the History of Population and Social Structure

Edward Arnold

First published 1980 by
Edward Arnold (Publishers) Ltd
41 Bedford Square
London WC1B 3DQ

British Library Cataloguing in Publication Data

Bastardy and its comparative history. – (Studies in
social and demographic history).
1. Illegitimacy – History
I. Laslett, Peter II. Oosterveen, Karla
III. Smith, Richard M IV. Series
301.41'52 HQ998

ISBN 0-7131-6229-5

Printed by Spottiswoode Ballantyne,
Colchester and London.

Contents

List of contributors vii
Preface ix
1 Introduction: comparing illegitimacy over time and between cultures 1
Peter Laslett
Appendix *James Oeppen, with contributions from Kenneth Wachter* 65

I Britain

2 Illegitimacy and illegitimates in English history 71
Alan Macfarlane
3 Family reconstitution and the study of bastardy: evidence from certain English parishes 86
Karla Oosterveen, Richard M. Smith and Susan Stewart
4 An evaluation of bastardy recordings in an east Kent parish 141
Anthea Newman
5 The social context of illegitimacy in early modern England 158
David Levine and Keith Wrightson
6 The nadir of English illegitimacy in the seventeenth century 176
Keith Wrightson
7 Aspects of sexual behaviour in nineteenth-century Scotland 192
Christopher Smout
8 The bastardy prone sub-society 217
Peter Laslett
Appendix *Richard M. Smith* 240

II Western Europe

9 Illegitimates and foundlings in pre-industrial France 249
Jean Meyer
10 Illegitimacy in France during the nineteenth century 264
Etienne van de Walle
11 Illegitimate births in France from 1740 to 1829 and in the 1960s 278
Yves Blayo
12 Urban and rural illegitimacy in Imperial Germany 284
John Knodel and Steven Hochstadt
13 Illegitimacy in seventeenth- and eighteenth-century east Sweden 313
David Gaunt
14 Illegitimacy and marriage in three Swedish parishes in the nineteenth century 327
Ann-Sofie Kälvemark

15 Illegitimacy and marriage in Stockholm in the nineteenth century 336
Margareta R. Matovic

III North America, Jamaica and Japan

16 Illegitimacy and bridal pregnancy in colonial America 349
Robert V. Wells
17 The long cycle in American illegitimacy and prenuptial pregnancy 362
Daniel Scott Smith
18 Illegitimacy in Jamaica 379
Shirley Foster Hartley
19 Illegitimacy in Japan 397
Akira Hayami

Bibliography 403
Index 417

List of contributors

Yves Blayo, Adjoint au chef du Departement de coopération, Institut National d'Etudes Demographiques, Paris, France.

David Gaunt, docent in history, University of Umeå, Sweden.

Shirley Hartley, Associate Professor of Sociology, California State University, Hayward, California, U.S.A.

Akira Hayami, Professor of Economics, Keio University, Tokyo, Japan.

Steven Hochstadt, Department of History, Brown University, Providence, Rhode Island, U.S.A.

Ann-Sofie Kälvemark, docent in history, University of Uppsala, Sweden.

John Knodel, Associate Professor, Department of Sociology, and Research Scientist, Population Studies Center, University of Michigan, Ann Arbor, Michigan, U.S.A.

David Levine, Associate Professor of History, Ontario Institute for Studies in Education, Toronto, Canada.

Peter Laslett, Director of the Cambridge Group for the History of Population and Social Structure, Reader in Politics and the History of Social Structure, University of Cambridge (Fellow of Trinity College).

Anthea Newman, volunteer research assistant of the Cambridge Group and Head of History Department, Cheltenham Ladies College.

Alan Macfarlane, Lecturer in Social Anthropology, University of Cambridge.

Margarita R. Matovic, University of Stockholm, Sweden.

Jean Meyer, Professor of History, Institut Armoricain de Recherches Historiques, Université de Haute-Bretagne, Rennes, France.

Karla Oosterveen, Research Assistant at the Cambridge Group for the History of Population and Social Structure.

Daniel Scott Smith, Associate Professor of History, University of Illinois at Chicago Circle, Chicago, U.S.A.

Richard M. Smith, Research Officer at the Cambridge Group for the History of Population and Social Structure (Fellow of Fitzwilliam College).

Christopher Smout, Professor of Scottish History, University of St Andrews.

Susan Stewart, volunteer research assistant of the Cambridge Group for the History of Population and Social Structure.

Etienne van de Walle, Director, Population Studies Center, University of Pennsylvania, Philadelphia, U.S.A.

Robert V. Wells, Associate Professor of History at Union College, Schenectady, New York, U.S.A.

Keith Wrightson, Lecturer in History, University of St Andrews.

Preface

This first attempt at a comparative history of bastardy has its own history, which is as follows. The Cambridge Group for the History of Population and Social Structure provided a column for illegitimacy when extraction forms were drawn up to be used by volunteer researchers in the work they had offered to do on parish registers. This was in 1964. The hope was that amongst the 5 or 10 dozen sets of parish returns of totals of baptisms, marriages and burials between the sixteenth and nineteenth centuries, which was the most we expected to receive, some at least would contain records of baptisms marked 'illegitimate'. These figures might go a little way towards relieving our entire ignorance of the numerical extent of illegitimacy in England before 1845. In that year civil registration of that particular began, and statistical information about it is continuous up to the present.

In the event aggregative returns have been sent to us not in dozens but in hundreds. Between a half and a third yield information on bastardy with sufficient consistency to create a usable return for the parish concerned. As early as 1966 a graph of decadal totals for six parishes between the 1580s and the 1800s was drawn up, the earliest form of the English bastardy curve.

It is a notable fact that the shape of this curve was substantially the same as the final version published in this volume as figure 1.2 on p. 18. Since we now know that the reproduction rate follows the curve of illegitimacy in England over the whole of this crucial period, we had arrived at a rough and ready sort of solution of the problem of how fertility had behaved during industrialization. We had done so simply by totting up bastardy figures for six places chosen for their superior bastardy recordings.[1]

We were in no position to make any such assertion when the earliest public discussion of the subject took place at the Center for Advanced Study in the Behavioral Sciences at Palo Alto in California in October 1967. The possibility that an inverse relationship between age at marriage and illegitimacy level might be found in English history was already apparent, however. As age at marriage went up, illegitimacy went down, and vice versa, at least in the one or two parishes from which we then had information. This was one of the intriguing contradictions of established expectation – here that marital deprivation must imply high bastardy – which marked the early years of historical sociology. Such striking and unexpected early results encouraged us to embark on two further enterprises.

1. As this book goes to press I am reminded of the publication of a study by an English local historian just at the moment when Cambridge Group researches began. That study related to a small group of Wiltshire parishes, and in his discussion of illegitimacy trends over the seventeenth and eighteenth centuries the author wrote the following: 'There is a general rise in the numbers of illegitimate births from 1570 to 1600–20, after which there is a fall and a period of few or no illegitimate births until 1700. After this there is a steady rise until the end of the period'. (See C. C. Taylor: 'Population Studies in 17th-Century and 18th-Century Wiltshire', *Wiltshire Archeological and Natural History Magazine*, LX (1965), pp. 107–8.) Our national curve already worked out!

One was the establishment of the suggested English illegitimacy curve as securely as possible. We decided to select as its basis a geographically 'representative' sample of the best documented parishes from the point of view of illegitimacy, each entry to be closely analysed by ourselves. The curve was to be confirmed by checking its figures against the largest possible sample which could be derived from usable aggregative returns, whose entries, of course, we would be unable to examine in detail. The other enterprise was to put the English historical experience into an international context. The general object was to make the illegitimacy file at Cambridge yield the greatest possible enlightenment, on sexual and marital nonconformism on the one hand, and on social behaviour generally on the other.

It was six years before two members of the Group, Karla Oosterveen and Peter Laslett, were able to produce in print that close study of a group of geographically 'representative' parishes of accurate record which we had promised ourselves. 'Long term trends in bastardy in England: a study of the illegitimacy figures in the parish registers and in the reports of the Registrar General' appeared in July 1973 in *Population Studies* (XXVII, 2). To the searching study of these 24 sets of illegitimacy statistics we there added a discussion of the relationship of marriage age to illegitimacy. A rudimentary consideration of regional distribution was also presented, bringing in additional sets of much rougher, less complete figures for the purpose. Furthermore, tentative suggestions were made about the persistence in English communities over time of a *bastardy prone sub-community*, a notion which originated with Karla Oosterveen.

After three more years, in 1977, Peter Laslett published an English curve based on the largest possible number of returns, in which recording was complete enough to be satisfactory. There turned out to be 98 of them. This new graph was set out in chapter 3 of *Family life and illicit love in earlier generations*, a chapter which was otherwise much the same as the article of 1973. The illegitimacy curve presented then, virtually the same as that of 1973 and 1967, is the one reproduced here.

Meanwhile our comparative plans had proceeded more slowly. We had intended to invite our volunteer researchers to make their own analytic contribution to a collective, comparative volume, at least in its English section. We were particularly interested by anything they could establish about the bastardy prone sub-community. Chapter 4 by Anthea Newman and part 3 of chapter 3 by Susan Stewart are essays of this description. The references in chapter 3 to the work of Mrs Joyce Lodey on Hemyock indicate the type of further analytic work we have been able to use. As for our contributors from abroad, these were requested from our friends and correspondents on the following principle.

Studies were elicited which would illustrate broad features of the comparative history of bastardy as it was beginning to make itself apparent, from countries where registration was known to be good. Scotland has been much discussed, and was an obvious choice, as it has had the highest incidence in the British Isles. France had been even more extensively studied over a longer period and bastardy levels were much lower than in England, at least in the eighteenth century and in the countryside. French 'enfants trouvés', moreover, had scarcely any equivalents in British records, nor had the institutions which cared for them, common in Italy and other Latin countries as well. Differentiation by locality, and especially urban/rural differences, were particularly well known for Germany. Sweden, with the tendency for high illegitimacy levels which it has shared with the rest of

Scandinavia, certainly since 1750, is the best documented of all European nations from the point of view of historical sociology.

It was natural that the sexual nonconformism of the Puritan English colonies of North America, along with their successor society, the United States, should be contrasted with that of the originating country. This was especially so since the comportment as to bastardy of its black citizens represents an important variation on the theme. Jamaica is included here for an entirely persuasive reason. This is that the proportion of births outside marriage in that country is now, and as Susan Hartley shows in her chapter, has been as far back as the issue can be studied, the highest in the world. Japan is present as the one non-European, non-Christian society for which some indications of a historical record of illegitimacy have so far been recovered.

The reader must judge for himself whether what follows is an appropriate body of evidence and discussion for the purpose of setting the comparative history of bastardy in motion. A free confession is made in chapter 1 that our horizon has been deliberately limited to the incidence of the practices which interest us. This has had to occupy our attention at the expense of many other features of sexually nonconformist behaviour. They have had to be touched upon rather than discussed.

Reference is made in the introduction, however, to a number of other cultures and cases than those already named. Nearly all of them, it has to be admitted, fall within the boundaries of historic Christian Europe and of its Western provinces, with their daughter societies overseas. We would dearly like to have been able to have included, for example, a comparative historical discussion of illegitimacy in any Islamic country, if we had been able. There are two further features of this book of which the reader should take due note.

One is that none of the contributors from outside Cambridge was aware at the time of composition of what would be in the Introduction. The authors of these chapters, then, have not approved of the use made of their materials, especially the theoretical use. If they find themselves in disagreement to any extent, this is perhaps as it should be. It cannot be the object of a collection of this kind made at the present elementary stage of the collective international enterprise to seek for an agreed theory, or even for an agreed approach, least of all to attempt anything in the way of a general solution to the whole set of problems. Rather it has been our duty to present a comparative compendium of the available evidence, and preserve as many differing points of view about its interpretation as are likely to be found.

Nor could it have been the task of the writer of an introduction to such a volume to content himself with a summary of the contents which follow, placing them as neatly as he could amongst other discussions of the subject. With the first body of comparative evidence before him, he should not shrink from trying to explain as much as he can while doing his best not to subject the materials to a set theoretical framework. This is the sense in which, it is hoped, such suggestive hypotheses as that of variable courtship intensity and of a bastardy prone sub-society will be judged.

The second circumstance of importance to the composition and final structure of this volume has to do with the passage of time. In the early 1960s not only were historical data on illegitimacy sparse before the nineteenth century and in Western Europe, but discussions of them in the long term were virtually absent, discussions that is which would seek to account for secular changes and regional variation. Registration officers had made commonsense inferences about their accumulating materials. Sociologists and psychologists had guessed a little about the immediate past, whilst deliberately imprisoning themselves within the present, and within the confines of their theories of social 'breakdown' and of anomie. These theories presumed that urbanization, industrialization and similar changes in the material environment interfered with social convention and individual control in such a way as to make a rise in illegitimacy figures inevitable when and where such processes were going on.

Since work on this collection began, however, historians themselves have increasingly turned their attention to illegitimacy. Evidence of several kinds, mostly rather fragmentary, has begun to be recovered, for a number of areas and at more distant periods, as is evident in our bibliography. Theories of anomie, of social 'breakdown', of social control of lack of control, were adapted to historical purposes.

They have been developed and refined so as to account for changes over time, as by Edward Shorter, Jean-Louis Flandrin, and also by the company of writers who have contributed to the controversy over sexual revolution and its possible occurrence in the late 1700s and early 1800s. Much has been learnt from the study of youth and the action of peer groups at this and a rather earlier period, as in the revealing work of Natalie Zemon Davies, John Gillis and a number of others. Something like a narrative history of sexual and familial attitudes amongst the literate and socially secure English has been worked out with remarkable skill and gusto by Lawrence Stone for some three centuries before the time of Shorter's much disputed sexual revolution.[2] Stone delivered a version of this absorbing story as Trevelyan lecturer at Cambridge University in 1975. That so senior a scholar should take it up is one more sign that sexual nonconformism seems to be establishing itself at the present time as an approved subject of historical research, both for its intrinsic interest and for the general study of social change.

Rather less than might perhaps be expected is being learnt about the incidence of bastardy from this type of historical enquiry, however.[3] Certainly little has so far appeared about its extent and temporal variation over the periods of time longer than a generation or so in any country. Almost nothing has been done to extend the standard demographic source, Susan Hartley's invaluable *Illegitimacy* (1975), in respect of international, intercultural *comparison* over time.

Furthermore historians seem so far to have hesitated to theorize afresh about illegitimacy as their new evidence has become available to them, to go beyond the boundaries set by the social scientists from whom they have inherited. There is little indication as yet of a willingness to subject that inheritance to fundamental examination, to decide when and where the notions of breakdown, anomie, defeat

2. His first sexual revolution, that is to say, the one discussed in section 5 of chapter 1 below. His second sexual revolution, which is taking place in our own generation, is referred to very little in this volume. Shorter's willingness to generalize boldly, and the force, enthusiasm and learning with which he puts his notions forward, have been of the first importance in opening out this field of enquiry. Everyone engaged in it is indebted to him, if only for the energetic and diverting way in which he tackles the criticisms which have crowded in upon his theorization. His writings, and some of those of the others named above, will be found in the bibliography. But we have not found it possible to list more than a few of the recent contributions to the discussion of the history of such subjects.

3. An exception should be made for Ireland, for which Connolly's useful, if restricted, study appeared as this Preface was being composed. 'Illegitimacy and pre-nuptial pregnancy in Ireland before 1864: the evidence of some Catholic parish registers', *Irish economic and social history* IV (1979). His observations on Irish foundlings and foundling hospitals suggest that the statements made above on this subject may need some modification, as they do to take the London Foundling Hospital into account: see Adrian Wilson, ' "Poor bastards": origins of London foundlings in the 1750s' (1979, mimeograph at the Cambridge Group).

by abrupt circumstantial change of familial and communal regulative mechanisms, are appropriate, and when and where they are inappropriate. No one has seemed prepared to reject them entirely, for a case which they cannot help to explain. An example in this volume might be the puzzling behaviour of those 'rogue' counties whose existence is demonstrated in chapter 1 in several countries in the nineteenth and twentieth centuries.[4] There are even fewer signs, it should perhaps be added, that social scientists, and those concerned with welfare, have begun to take the objective historical record seriously into account.

The marked growth of historical investigation of sexual nonconformism whilst our volume was in gestation has had its effect upon it, of course. Though our original plan remained unchanged, the whole enterprise began to take upon itself the model of *Household and family in past time*. This is a volume published eight years ago by the Cambridge Group, in which '*deliberate aim* was taken at opening up a new field'.[5] Such an object was not in our minds when we originally contemplated a book on comparative illegitimacy. The field was somewhat better known for one thing, especially from the work of registrars, and we did not judge it necessary to arrange a meeting of potential contributors, as we had done for historical studies of the household. This change in the character of our book has perhaps been unfortunate in some ways. The introductory chapter, written last of course, may have grown gradually less appropriate to the rest.

It was not possible within the compass we had to set ourselves to include in that chapter much more than a number of passing references to the expanding research activities of those who have taken to the study of bastardy since our own work began. The extraordinary results obtained for the chapelry of Culcheth in Lancashire in the early 1970s by G. N. Gandy, for example, have not been taken into account. He has shown that the handloom knitters of that settlement abandoned ecclesiastical marriage almost entirely for two decades in the early nineteenth century, behaving in a fashion which looks like an extreme form of the practices noticed in our consideration of the bastardy prone sub-society, but which had other characteristics too.[6]

Nor were the vivid, almost lurid, but illuminating facts published by G. R. Quaife in *Wanton wenches and wayward wives, peasants and illicit sex in early 17th century England* [Somerset] (1979) fully available to us, facts which are confirmatory for the most part but some surprising facts as well. We can, however, venture to set out here what we believe to be the general outcome of the investigation of the comparative history of illegitimacy reported here and that undertaken by others. It would not do to pretend that all of those who have worked in the field would accept the statements about to be made. But we hope that these statements will at least provide an entrée into the discussion of what is going on.

Bastardy and its comparative history, we believe, taken along with other investigations, demonstrates the following tripartite, negative proposition. Sexual behaviour has never anywhere been confined to procreative behaviour, procreative behaviour confined to marriage, and marriage confined to the official

4. See below, chapter 1, section 6: A 'rogue county' is a region which abruptly departs in its established and persistent rank order in relation to other counties in respect of illegitimacy levels, very often in the absence of any known change in its productive, economic or urban/rural ecology.

5. Peter Laslett and Richard Wall, eds., *Household and family in past time – comparative studies in the size and structure of the domestic group in England, France, Serbia, Japan and colonial North America, with further material from Western Europe* (Cambridge, 1972).

6. See his doctoral dissertation (Oxford University, 1978).

celebrations established by society. Of the three clauses, the second is the most important of course and the proper subject of our book.

There may be those who will take the whole proposition as self-evident, certainly the first clause about sexual activity and procreation. But though it may seem obvious after threequarters of a century of psychoanalysis and a quarter of a century of the academic study of sexual behaviour, that procreation is not the only purpose of such behaviour, there still seems to be a lingering wish that the contrary was true.

Hence the remarkable myth, for example, amazing in a society like our own, that the black-out of New York City and its environs in 1965 led to a torrent of births nine months later. This picturesque fallacy (its statistical annihilation is to be found in the American demographic journal *Demography*, 7, 1970, pp. 325–7) is frequently repeated and was recently cited at Westminster in the House of Lords. Part of the explanation no doubt is the continuing influence in an almost entirely secular generation of the Christian doctrine which lays it down that sexual expression is intended to be confined to procreation, and is otherwise sinful. The contents of this book should make it plain that every type of sexual activity is always prevalent at all times, and in all the societies discussed, quite independently of procreation. Christianity was never, anywhere, a full description of what people did.

It is hazardous in view of this to argue from changes in levels of illegitimacy or prenuptial pregnancy to changes in sexual behaviour. To proceed from there to talk of social dislocation seems unjustifiable.

The assertion that unofficial procreative unions, some evanescent but others lengthy and some permanent, have always and everywhere existed alongside official marriage should be equally evident from the studies we publish. Indeed it has been recently urged that marriage, both in our day and in the past, should be regarded as an episode in the procreative career of a mature individual, rather than its full description. Marriage has been and still is the most important phase in an individual's procreative career from the point of view of engendering of children but never the whole of that career. For it may include procreative relationships which are not marital both before, after and during marriage itself.[7]

Once this point is reached, it becomes obvious that the definition of what constitutes an official marriage lies at the heart of our subject. That this is no simple issue is evident from the repeated discussions to be found in the text which follows. One of the complications, and fascinations, of the theme is that in the last resort a stable, long-lasting, non-marital procreative union could attain the status of marriage itself, certainly in most of the places and periods dealt with here. It is even more interesting that, given the uncertainty and the variability of the definition of marriage in time and in place, records if illegitimacy should show such regularity, a point dwelt upon in our introductory chapter. Such seems to have been the case in all the countries where we have been able to demonstrate persistence by locality in levels of illegitimacy.

With these bald statements we must leave the contemporary discussion of these matters in the hope that what we present will serve to encourage and intensify the investigation. It remains only for the editors, and especially myself, the senior

7. See Peter Laslett, 'Illegitimate fertility and the matrimonial market', paper presented to the conference of the International Union for the Scientific Study of Population on 'Nuptiality and fertility, plural marriage and illegitimate fertility in historical demography', Kristiansand, Norway, September 1979. Proceedings in course of publication by Academic Press, London.

editor, to register their thanks to the contributors for their patience and the publishers for their forbearance. I freely acknowledge with deep gratitude that the sample of 98 parishes on which the English bastardy count is based was determined by Roger Schofield, and that all the work on this central file was carried out by him and not by me. I am in debt to Richard Smith for his unwearying efforts in the late and final stages of the preparation of this work: his insight and his command of the technical resources have been of the first importance, not to speak of his painstaking accuracy with the text, tables and figures. My debt to Karla Oosterveen over all the years since 1964 must be quite apparent. We owe, as a group of editors, many debts to many people; for information, for discussion and for criticism. Edward Shorter at one time agreed to collaborate in the volume in his friendly way, and Philips Cutright to oversee some parts of it. It is regrettable that these arrangements were interfered with by the exigencies of composition.

As for our other colleagues, we should particularly like to mention Mr Richard Wall, Mrs Trillia Scoins, Dr E. A. Wrigley and the Group's champion of a secretary, Miss Lesley Pepper. Jean-Louis Flandrin and Susan Hartley should be named as well, but once entered the list is too long to be manageable. It is plain how much is owed to Cambridge Group volunteers; that, in its English part, it is largely their book.

Peter Laslett
27 Trumpington Street
Cambridge

December 1979

1

Introduction: comparing illegitimacy over time and between cultures

Peter Laslett

1 Illegitimacy as a social and a moral problem

Illegitimacy has been called a social problem for the last two centuries and a moral problem from time immemorial. A problem can in principle be solved, and in trying for a solution here moralists, administrators and social scientists have written a very great deal. In this sense illegitimacy can be said to possess a considerable historical literature.

Nearly all the earlier writings were heavily moralistic in tone. The frequency of illegitimate babies was taken by eighteenth-, nineteenth- and early twentieth-century registrars and social commentators as an index of the moral state of a community, and especially of a nation. Increases were a cause for alarm, as being a sign of decadence; decreases a subject for self-congratulation, by government statisticians as well as by the clerics, who have naturally been much preoccupied with the topic. The decline in public morality which a rise in bastardy was thought to reveal was also taken very seriously by historians, of politics and power as well as of manners and of culture. When sexual behaviour supposedly changed for the worse, in the later Roman Empire for example, the state was believed to be on the road to ruin.

With the rise of consciously objective social science two generations ago, the moralizing strain in the treatment of illegitimacy was abandoned, in principle at least. That it was still characteristic of much of the discussion can be seen from the statements made by Kingsley Davis in 1939 when he wrote the essay which can be said to have inaugurated the properly sociological study of bastardy.[1] The adoption of ethical impartiality or indifference meant a break with the earlier writings on illegitimacy and, which was characteristic of the social sciences at the time, a deliberately unhistorical approach. Bastardy was to be understood comparatively, continuing the tradition of the national registration offices, though in a less chauvinistic, more scientific fashion. But the comparative exercise was to go on almost exclusively between contemporary nations and cultures, including of course the 'savage' or 'primitive' cultures which so exercised the social scientists in the middle of the twentieth century.

The procreation of children outside marriage, if it was no longer thought of first and foremost as a moral lapse, was still regarded as deviant behaviour. In this phase of social scientific thinking bastardy was taken as a prime example of something which interrupted the proper functioning of social processes, and revealed a failure of social control, the control of individual behaviour by family

1. 'Illegitimacy and the social structure' (1939); see also his *Human society* (1948). Jonas Frykman, 'Sexual intercourse and social norms: a study of illegitimate births in Sweden, 1831–1933' (1975), describes the moralistic phase in that best documented of all countries, and one with high illegitimacy over a long period. Shirley Hartley, *Illegitimacy* (1975), contains a great deal of useful comparative statistical data, much of it also historical, and a full bibliography.

and kin, by political and educational authority, by all the influences which persuade most people to obey the established norms. The conditions which were associated with high illegitimacy levels in any one locality tended to be thought of as pathological, and the individuals who engendered bastards as in some way victimized, disordered, even mentally abnormal.

To describe a whole body of recent scholarly opinion in such abbreviated terms is inevitably to distort it. Accurate and useful information on this subject grew enormously during the time when, as is now being claimed, functionalism dominated the social sciences. The analysis of nonconforming sexual behaviour in terms of social norms and social control has been of great importance, and appears in many places in this volume. Nevertheless, the conviction has grown over the last decade that, in the treatment of subjects of this kind, social behaviour in the historical context was being wilfully overlooked. What is more, the intellectual problem presented by illegitimacy, for this had now begun to weigh upon the student as heavily as the others, was felt to be insoluble unless the history of the phenomenon could be taken into account. For these and other reasons historical studies of illegitimacy, prenuptial pregnancy and sexual behaviour generally have become quite common since 1970, predominantly in France, but also in other countries, particularly in the United States, Great Britain and Scandinavia. The object of the present volume is to provide a compendium of such studies.

The authors of this book have naturally drawn freely on earlier works where these have been found valuable. In this introductory chapter and for chapter 8 I have myself a debt to register to Albert Leffingwell, the writer in 1892 of what he describes as 'the first treatise in the English language upon the subject' and which has the expected description *Illegitimacy, a study in morals*.[2] In spite of his heavily disapproving tone, and of the racist flavour of some of his generalizations, Leffingwell recognized at the very outset of the study in this country that illegitimacy showed notable persistence by locality; that it was the outcome of a conjunction of causal circumstances and could have no single explanation; that it was not the straightforward outcome of poverty, bad housing, illiteracy; nor was it obviously related to the intensity and content of religious belief; that courtship customs were essential to its proper understanding; that the tendency to produce bastards was transmitted in families, though Leffingwell was apparently convinced that biological rather than social genetics were at issue.

This late Victorian theorist of illegitimacy has to be called a crude positivist. But we hope that in the work we present here, and in the use which we have all made of our predecessors, even our remote predecessors, we have avoided the more obvious pitfalls of positivism, and of functional analysis out of context. We hope also that the notable regularities in illegitimacy over time and in place

2. The title of the volume in which it was published, *Illegitimacy, and the influence of seasons upon conduct*, is misleading, since the consideration of climate and behaviour is an entirely separate work. This short book (the piece on bastardy is less than 25,000 words long) was reissued in 1976. Examples of the use of earlier authors by our other contributors are provided by Etienne van de Walle in chapter 10, who cites Emile Levasseur, *La population française* (1891); by John Knodel and Steven Hochstadt in chapter 12, quoting works by Hindelang, Lindner and Rauhe; and by David Gaunt in chapter 13, quarrying Gustav Sundbärg, *Die Bevölkerungsstatistik Schwedens, 1750–1900; einige Hauptresultate* (1907). The statistical and demographic approach to the comparative history of bastardy did not begin until quite recently, and E. Shorter, John Knodel and E. van de Walle, 'The decline of non-marital fertility in Europe' (1971), is still in many ways the most valuable: much use has been made of it in this introduction. The writer responsible for arousing interest in the history of sexuality as such has been Jean-Louis Flandrin in *Les amours paysannes* (1975), and *Familles, parenté, maison, sexualité dans l'ancienne société* (1976), now translated into English as *Families in Former Times* (1979). Ambitious and suggestive works by Edward Shorter, *The making of the modern family* (1975) and Lawrence Stone, *The family, sex and marriage in England, 1500–1800* (1977), have taken up the strain, and such productions will no doubt continue to appear, as well as specialist studies of the evidence itself.

revealed in these studies will illuminate the discussion of social behaviour generally. Perhaps they may even go some way towards rescuing the social anthropologists from the dilemma in which they seem to find themselves, now that the logical limitations of considering societies in terms of the function of aspects of behaviour viewed in isolation have been recognized.

The records of bastardy have revealed unexpected continuity in social structure over the centuries, especially local social structure, and suggest a view of this phenomenon very different from that put forward by most of the moralists and the functionalists. Though there are formidable difficulties in understanding the causes of illegitimacy and how it is related to the social environment, it is clear that bastardy shows a temporal pattern as regular as that of fertility and mortality, and displays a decidedly more definite regional pattern. Fluctuations in illegitimacy figures do in fact seem to reveal spatial and temporal changes in the efficacy of marriage and of other familial institutions in a quite straightforward way. The insight which this may provide into other types of behaviour will not escape the reader.

But this is only one of the reasons why bastardy and its comparative history should continue to occupy our attention. Every illegitimate birth is a demographic event which could also be called a normative event as well. If the solidarity of the family, in the sense of kinship bonding as well as of the domestic group itself, is of importance in the coherence of society as a whole, then any breach of familial and marital regulation might properly be thought of as a social structural occurrence. This principle apparently lies behind the simplistic statements which have been made about the connection between sexual morals, as shown forth in what was believed to be the record of illegitimacy, and political weakness or strength. But there is a paradox here which has often been commented upon, the paradox that breaches of social rules do not necessarily weaken those rules, and under certain circumstances can even serve to strengthen them. Understanding social regulation, moreover, has to proceed to a large extent by the consideration of what happens when such regulation is defied.

Marriage as a set of practices and as an institution, the processes by which families and domestic groups come into being and by which human reproduction takes place, are all opened to view in the study of the comparative history of illegitimacy. So also are such things as the succession to property and to status, the mechanisms and effectiveness of social control, the relationships of ruling élites with the masses of society, of dominant with dominated classes. This, as we shall see, is not the end of the list. The claim that the recoverable record of illegitimacy and of sexual nonconformism in the past is one of the most important activities which could engage the attention of the historical sociologist might be justified on these grounds alone. But the interest of our subject certainly does not come to an end at this point. If we allowed it to do so, we could be accused of failing in common humanity as well as in sociological imagination.

What about the actors in the story which concerns us, that is above all the women who bore the bastards, along with the myriad histories of contempt, oppression and neglect which such individuals so often underwent? What about the lugubrious fate of the bastard children themselves, whose lives were frequently so very brief, but who, if they did survive, could be objects of such obloquy, and who might harbour such resentment in return? What about bastards in literature? A really illuminating consideration of illegitimacy and its place in the past history of various societies and cultures ought perhaps to take as its theme the attitudes to bastards, literary and otherwise, their treatment and their place in society and especially in the family – if the evidence could only be recovered.[3]

Most of our contributors do find opportunities to discuss these subjects to some extent, especially Alan Macfarlane for the English in the chapter which follows this one. But to have pursued them with any thoroughness would have drawn out the contents of this heavy volume to even greater lengths. At this primary stage of the development of historical sociology our concern has had to be with incidence, and with little more than this. The further horizons and the larger themes must be left to our successors.

In our introductory chapter we shall attempt to define in comparative terms the concept of bastardy within the European cultural tradition. We shall present and discuss illegitimacy statistics for the European area, figures which demonstrate the regularity of the movement of bastardy over time and which illustrate the intimate but also slightly puzzling relationship between marital and non-marital fertility, legitimate and illegitimate births. The statistics for England, which have been previously published, will be here set out again in corrected and more complete form.[4] We shall then investigate the persistence of illegitimacy levels by locality. After an interlude on Scottish illegitimacy as a case study of locality persistence in illegitimacy patterns, we continue with a discussion of the reliability of the evidence. In our final paragraphs we venture on a tentative explanatory hypothesis, a partial one, that is to say, presented in a preliminary fashion.

3. Bastards in literature seem to be dealt with as an element in the commentaries on the literary works in which they appear, but have as yet failed to find a treatment of their own, in English anyway. We have collected some information on the familial position of bastards in English history and can as yet identify no standard treatment of illegitimates in this respect. They are found alone with their mothers in single headed households; in the households of their grandparents, their own parents being absent; in the households of their parents along with legitimate half-siblings; in institutions, along with their mothers or even alone; as solitary lodgers and sometimes alone with their fathers. This may be the order of frequency for this variable, but we are not yet certain, nor is it known how long after birth the stain of illegitimacy clung to the individuals to whom it was attached. It appears that children up to the time of marriage were those most affected in England, but in Poland – one of the two European countries for which we have seen relevant evidence – a grown adult could be described as illegitimate in a list of inhabitants, even a household head or his wife, up to the age of 49. In the Latin list for Dobrego Maiasta, in 1695, 42 persons marked *illegitimus* or *illegitima* are present out of about 3,000, once more in highly various familial positions, though about half were servants (see Boleslaw Kumor, in *Przeszość Demograficzna Polski: materialy i studia*, 1975). Repetitive listings covering the late eighteenth and early nineteenth centuries in Austria, where households were large and complex, and where illegitimacy was high and rapidly rising, show bastards and bastard-bearers apparently wholly integrated into the family and the community, and finally so numerous that their presence modified household composition. See a very important study by Michael Mitterauer, of the University of Vienna, 'Familien Formen und Illegitimität in ländlichen Gebieten Österreichs' (1979). Emmanuel Le Roy Ladurie and Antoinette Chamoux Fauve of Paris inform me that the position of illegitimates in the large households of the Pyrenees, and elsewhere in France, was not dissimilar.

4. The English statistics first appeared in: Peter Laslett and Karla Oosterveen, 'Long-term trends in bastardy in England: a study of the illegitimacy figures in the parish registers and in the reports of the Registrar General, 1561–1960' (1973). The conclusions published there about the course of illegitimacy over time were based on 24 checked sets of bastardy recordings up to the end of the parish register era. These figures and the graph based on them have been reproduced several times (in Flandrin, 1976, p. 179, for example), and are cited by many of the contributors to the volume, all of whose work was completed before a second version of the essay of 1973 was published in Peter Laslett, *Family life and illicit love in earlier generations* (1977), chapter 3. There the original statistics were supplemented by a new set for 98 parishes and by other less reliable sets, the largest relating to 404 parishes. None of the figures in these larger collections has been checked by hand against the originals, as in the case of the first set of 24, but were used only if they met certain minimum standards of reliability of registration. The curve described by these new figures showed only slight differences from the one in the exhaustively checked set of 24.

2 The concept of bastardy and the principle of legitimacy

> The most important moral and legal rule concerning the physiological state of kinship is that no child should be brought into this world without a man – and one man at that – assuming the role of sociological father, that is guardian and protector, the male link between the child and the rest of the community. I think that this generalization amounts to a universal sociological law, and as such I have called it . . . The Principle of Legitimacy.[5]

Although this statement by Bronislaw Malinowski was made as early as 1930, and although its phraseology belongs with the moralistic tradition of analysing bastardy, his principle of legitimacy has dominated discussion of births out of wedlock ever since.[6] Its relevance to illegitimacy as a social problem is quite clear: children born without mature, male protectors were problem children. His position seems never to have been seriously questioned until quite recently, when some of those concerned with the family life of blacks in the Caribbean and in the contemporary United States have recorded their dissent.[7] Malinowski announces the principle as a normative rule, a precept which may or may not be observed by individuals in their conduct. But when he goes on to describe it as 'a universal sociological law', he presumably means that this normative rule is to be found in every society, country and culture, and is by and large obeyed.

Although no justification of these weighty propositions is offered in the passage cited, we may propose our own, in terms of social control, which have now largely replaced the moralistic phraseology. The appearance of children for whom no mature male, permanently allied to the mother, can be held responsible, has to be prevented in order to safeguard the future of the society as a society and of each of its constituent members.

For only if the familial system is maintained, marriage carefully protected, and procreation socially controlled, can the population be kept within the means of subsistence known and seen to be available. Moreover, only if each new person is born into an established family can he be brought up as a bearer of the society's culture, as a reliable, a useful and a valued member of its particular structure. To be a legitimately accepted child within the family of his or her father 'represents a need of universal significance for the normal social and psychological development of the individual, as well as for defining his social status, according to the ideals and values of his culture' (Fortes, 1978, p. 131).

Taking note of the functionalist emphasis of these statements, especially as to marriage and the family, recognizing the implicit claims about upbringing requiring attachment to one or two individuals, and about the inevitability of male superiority, we proceed to their implications for the subject matter of this volume.

5. The words quoted come from the version usually cited in Bronislaw Malinowski, 'Parenthood, the basis of social structure' (1930), pp. 137–8. But Malinowski himself refers to earlier statements in his article on kinship in the 14th edition of the *Encyclopaedia Britannica*, and in his *Sex and repression in savage society* (1927). For subsequent appeals to the principle see William J. Goode, 'Illegitimacy in the Caribbean social structure' (1960), or his *World revolution and family patterns* (1963): also the succession of writings by Shirley F. Hartley, and the reference in her chapter on Jamaica, below p. 379.

6. The most recent discussion known to me is by Meyer Fortes in relation to West Africa, where the desirability of the father himself being legitimate is emphasized, in relation to that area anyway. See 'Parenthood, marriage and fertility in West Africa' (1978).

7. See Derek Gill, *Illegitimacy, sexuality and the status of women* (1977), pp. 242–3; and such books as Robert Staple, *Black sociology* (1976), chapter 5. This black scholar seems to go so far as to imply that comparison between white and black family mores is not allowable.

They seem to be as follows. First, that a category of illegitimacy will be found at every point in the past of every society, as well as in all the present societies which Malinowski seems to have had exclusively in mind. Second, that comparisons of illegitimacy over time and between places are comparisons of like with like. Third, that illegitimacy must always be regarded as a negative, the breach of an established rule, never as belonging to a different mode of sexual and reproductive behaviour, as a positive, in fact.

We cannot attempt to pass a final judgement on these three statements. We shall conclude at the end of this chapter that the principle of legitimacy can hardly be observed in action in the historical arena which we shall have to occupy; it deals in fundamentals which we scarcely ever reach. We shall suggest that there is evidence of a counter-attitude to sex, marriage and procreation, and present in chapter 8 some evidence on those who may have held it. The study of the history of a handful of European societies, and European-descended societies, could scarcely prove anything as to whether or not the principle of illegitimacy is indeed universal. But it is certainly significant that wherever historians and historical demographers have found ways of studying the past procreative behaviour of such societies, they have found illegitimacy. It is perhaps even more significant that in the one entirely non-European instance included here, that of Japan before its 'modernization', illegitimacy was absent. Akira Hayami tells us in chapter 19 that there was not even an expression for bastardy in the whole huge Japanese vocabulary (sets of character combinations). The concept of illegitimacy was introduced along with the rest of the European package at the outset of 'modernization' and showed 'illegitimacy' to be high, though tending to fall to vanishing point as industrialization proceeded, which is scarcely what happened in Europe.

We should do well, therefore, to confine the comparative claims we make here to bastardy in Europe and European-descended or European-dominated societies, except where we refer in contrast to Japan or to other cultural areas, to the Arab world for instance. This is not intended to imply, however, that illegitimacy is or has been confined to this particular cultural sphere, or even that Europe, and especially Christian Europe, has been peculiarly insistent on the principle of legitimacy. It is evident from the work of social anthropologists that births outside the established procreative rules are very widely, perhaps in fact universally, distinguished from those within these rules; that they are almost as widely unwelcome and more or less rigorously disapproved of. Even in Tokugawa Japan, children by non-wives were in a different position from other children until or unless they were adopted into the family line.

The rules of respectability, we have found, are adequate for most of the historical comparisons we can make without resort to the principle of legitimacy. 'Respectable' people amongst Europeans like ourselves procreate only with partners to whom they are wedded at the time of the procreative act. They are married only once, unless their spouses die. They do not copulate with persons other than those spouses even if procreation is entirely avoidable because of efficient contraception. It is only necessary to write out these rules in order to recognize that, though respectability is an important category of esteem in our society, it is a very unreliable guide to what people actually do. The same holds for the outlying positions, as we may call them, of the code of respectability in relation to bastardy: the one, for example, which prefers legitimate birth as well as virginity in a spouse-to-be, thus implying that a bastard, a bastard bearer, or even a bastard begetter will have a lower probability of getting married.

We have established, as might be expected that in the past intercourse outside marriage was widespread everywhere, in all the areas studied by our contributors, that bastard bearers did get married, and also the bastards, if they lived long enough. (See chapters 2 and 3 and, for the middle ages, the appendix to chapter 8.) Given the nature of social conventions this need not surprise us. The point of importance is that these rules of respectability – Western, white, Anglo-Saxon, Protestant, Victorian and post-Victorian, middle-class respectability above all – are much more drastic than the principle of legitimacy requires, and more restrictive than is laid down by the established law of the state and even by the demands of Christian conviction. Hence the disadvantages of European notions of sexual nonconformism as a basis of general comparison. Nevertheless, nearly all the historical comparisons we are able to make are inevitably based on the European standard version of the principle: most of them indeed are comparisons within the European tradition itself.

3 Marriage, illegitimacy and prenuptial pregnancy in European history

Since in the European tradition the regulations, formal and informal, are more restrictive than need be by the legitimacy principle, it follows that the category of illegitimates is relatively wide. Kingsley Davis lists the following nine forms.[8]

Illegitimacy engendered through:
1, fornication between unmarrieds;
2,3,4, adultery: the man, the woman, or both, being married to another or to others;
5,6,7, incest: brother-sister, father-daughter, mother-son;
8, forbidden caste unions;
9, procreation by avowed celibates.

All these classes apply to historic Europe and her daughter societies. The least important numerically have been classes 8 and 9, bastards from prohibited inter-caste unions and those from avowed celibates. Since early medieval times, however, all children of those in orders in the Roman church have been illegitimate, falling into class 9. As for class 8, Pericles passed a law in Athens forbidding the marriage of citizens to non-Athenians, thus bastardizing the offspring of such unions. From classical times all slave children have been illegitimate in our cultural tradition: in the United States therefore until the Emancipation of 1865. In the colonial period of the history of that country, all sexual intercourse between white and black, slave or free, was forbidden, as Robert Wells shows in chapter 16 below. Offspring arising in this way, therefore, were indeed illegitimate since they came from inter-caste unions.[9]

The other classes seem to have been well represented in European history, although classes 3 and 4, those born of wives by men not their husbands, may have been fewer in socially recognized fact than in biological reality. In England,

8. See Kingsley Davis, 'The forms of illegitimacy' (1939). This is a somewhat arbitrary set of distinctions, especially within the categories of adultery and incest.

9. On Athenian bastards see W. K. Lacey, *The family in classical Greece* (1968), pp. 90, 103–4. I owe this reference to Beryl Rawson of the Australian National University. See her 'Roman concubinage and other de facto marriages' (1974), pp. 279–305. Though inter-caste unions have been permissible in most European societies for many centuries, sexual associations between the élite and those outside the élite have frequently been prevented from becoming marriages; hence legitimate status has been denied to the offspring.

anyway, a man seems to have had to accept all his wife's offspring as his legitimate children, except where inaccessibility could be proved, and the conditions under which this was possible were strict. As is to be expected, therefore, bastards of married women are infrequently to be met with in English records, though instances are given in chapters 2, 3 and 4 below, and there may well have been so many born in fact that they make the problem of measuring illegitimacy a very difficult one.[10]

With these qualifications, European society seems always to have classed the largest possible number of children as illegitimate. In Europe, moreover, there has been a whole order of potential illegitimates, conceived in defiance of the rules of European respectability rather than of marriage and procreation. These were, and are, babies begotten before the public celebration and registration of marriage, usually referred to as bridal pregnancies, or prenuptial pregnancies, which will be our usage here.

There are important differences, however, between such births and bastards, and between kinds of prenuptial pregnancy. One of the kinds seems to have only an accidental connection with bastardy, since it arose because the process of marriage took a long time, permitting the parties to copulate well before the ceremony and registration. Most prenuptial pregnancies may have been like this, and many, perhaps most, bastardies may have occurred because some interruption took place between the initiation of the marriage and the wedding date. But there are three other types of prenuptial pregnancy. There is the shotgun wedding type, as we have come to call it, where pregnancy was unintentional and marriage not considered, but forced upon the parties. There is the spouse entrapment type, where one partner, perhaps usually the woman, ensured pregnancy so as to induce the other to marry. Finally there is the fertility testing type, often considered to have been very widespread in earlier generations. These three are much closer to bastardy than a prenuptial pregnancy brought about by intercourse during the marriage process.[11]

The difference between the kind of prenuptial pregnancy represented by these three types, and the more usual kind depends upon the intentions of the partners to the acts in question. Such intentions are almost always inaccessible to the historian. For the most part our studies deal with prenuptial pregnancy, as one phenomenon, as well as with illegitimacy proper. Some sets of statistics, like the current official series for England and Wales, add figures for prenuptial pregnancy to those for illegitimacy to make up totals for extra-marital conceptions. The extra-marital conception rate thus tends to become the measure rather than

10. For an authoritative opinion on when a wife's children were to be taken as spurious, see William Blackstone, *Commentaries on the laws of England* (1796), pp. 456–7. Legitimacy is to be presumed unless access of husband to wife can be proved impossible. In his discussion of bastardy, Blackstone comes close to formulating the legitimacy principle, for he considers that the protection and legitimation of children is the point of marriage as an institution. In France, as is shown in chapter 10, the Code Napoléon assumed that all children born to wives were legitimate, and it seems that there may have been more offspring of doubtful origin in that country than in England in earlier periods.

That bastards born to married woman can be recovered from the records even in the sixteenth century, is shown by Alain Croix, *Nantes et les Pays nantais au XVI siècle* (1974), p. 97, who found 27 cases in 95 illegitimacies (12 of which were due to Catholic priests, class 9) in his 40-odd parishes. An English example might be quoted from the parish of All Saints, Newcastle-upon-Tyne, 1797–1801. There 3 of 37 bastards whose mothers had their marital status recorded were born to married women. Births to married women due to men not their husbands were certainly common by the middle of the twentieth century: 26 per cent of all illegitimate births were found to have occurred to married women in England and Wales in April 1961 (see Laslett, 1977, p. 121, note 15, commenting on the way in which this fact makes the illegitimacy rate less effective as a measure).

11. See Laslett (1977), pp. 128–9.

the bastardy rate, and we shall find ourselves using this concept when we come to what we shall call our courtship hypothesis.

It would be natural to expect that in England and in the European tradition generally, with so highly developed a concept of illegitimacy, marriage itself should be precisely defined, and marriage practice unvarying. For the European, and specifically the Western European, reproductive code belongs with what Professor Goody calls 'divergent devolution'.[12] In this pattern males as well as females inherit from both sexes, and 'both males and females require parental property for the maintenance of their status.' We can see why it should have to be quite clear who was a legitimate successor in such a system, why sexual intercourse should be forbidden before marriage, why monogamy, 'rare as far as human cultures go', should be the rule, and the form of the family nuclear, though concubines might well be found.[13] It would surely be required that there could be no doubt how one person got married to another.

The outstanding paradox of European familial history, however, a paradox which must heighten the interest of any account of the place which bastardy has occupied, is that marriage has not been clearly and consistently defined and has not been unvarying in time and space. We cannot proceed on the assumption that the institution was codified in European prehistory and consistently regulated during the Christian era by the injunctions laid down by St Paul in the New Testament. Even if we confine our evidence to the Scriptures and to Christian doctrine in relation to the known behaviour of such conspicuous figures as royal and noble persons, as Jack Goody seems to do, the conclusion must be that marriage regulations and marriage practice varied from time to time and place to place. Amongst the Europeans who settled in North America and elsewhere, variability is bewildering. Nevertheless, we shall show that the incidence of illegitimacy displays a notable regularity in both dimensions.

These two circumstances, that marriage should be variable, and that bastardy should display well-marked patterning, are surely of great interest in themselves. But our present object is to understand the European concept of illegitimacy and to gauge its usefulness for cross-cultural and cross-temporal comparison, and we cannot, therefore, here pursue the history of European matrimony to any great extent. There are a number of treatises on the vicissitudes in European and American marital history, and it is only necessary to leaf over some of these substantial early twentieth-century books to confirm the variability, even the instability, of the marriage institution.[14]

This being so, it is obvious that definitions of bastardy must have varied locally with varying definitions of marriage, which means that comparing an illegitimacy occurring in one area with an illegitimacy in another area is not comparing like with like, or exactly like with exactly like. Any statement about bastardy being high in one place as compared with another must, therefore, be read with

12. See Jack Goody, *Production and reproduction* (1976).

13. Concubinage, where a man takes a partner other than his wife to ensure an heir, is not characteristic of historic Europe, though cited by Goody from the Old Testament along with examples of medieval royalty and nobility, and found in the Solonic law of Greece. It certainly existed, however, and is openly named in lists of inhabitants, as for example in eighteenth-century Austria. Plain living in sin was sometimes called concubinage. See Mitterauer (1979); Laslett (1977), p. 121; and Croix (1974), pp. 96–7, where the practice shades into consensual unions.

14. They belong to the earlier, evolutionary phase of the history of the social sciences which came to an end at about the time when moralizing began to be superseded in the study of illegitimacy. The most useful for us are Edward Westermarck, *The history of human marriage* (1921); and George E. Howard, *A history of matrimonial institutions* (1904). It is noteworthy how little Howard has to say on bastardy.

circumspection. If it can be shown that the definition of a valid marriage changed in the same country, region or place at a particular time, then some caution has to be exercised in judging whether the incidence of bastardy can be properly compared between dates on either side of the change. Such a possibility can be said to exist in English history in respect of clandestine marriage, which might be held to differ to some extent in definition from publicly celebrated marriages, and which was particularly common in the later seventeenth century. This point has been discussed elsewhere (Laslett, 1977, pp. 131–2), and it was concluded that clandestine marriage may have modified the apparent course of illegitimacy in England during that period, at least to some degree. This cannot be the only occasion when this happened in the history of the societies whose bastardy figures are compared in this volume.

No one acquainted with the details of this difficult and complex subject would maintain, however, that all, or anything more than a very minor part, of the changes over time discussed in this volume could have arisen in this way. The position it seems best to occupy is that marriage and its associated practices did indeed vary from place to place in Christian Europe, enough to ensure that whatever the generally prevalent illegitimacy level, some places would always have higher levels than others. We boldly assume that what counted as illegitimacy to local persons counts as illegitimacy for purposes of comparison, so that changes of definition in marriage at particular places can be disregarded. Stress must be laid, moreover, on the fact that marriage practices must always be held to include all the approaches to marriages – the relationship between eligibles not in courtship with each other, the conventions governing courtship itself, especially how far risking conception was to be contemplated, as well as the actual process of getting publicly united.

The localism of marriage practices is illustrated by what was said in the archdeacon's court of Leicester in 1598, when appeal was made in a marriage case 'to the common use and custom within the county of Leicester, especially in and about the town before mentioned'.[15] It is evident here that a marriage practice could apparently be confined to a county, even to the environs of a particular place. At about the same time Henry Swinburne, the authority on English marriage processes and their vocabulary, found himself making the admission that 'if it be the use and custom of that place to contract matrimony [by the use of certain words], indissoluble matrimony is thereby contracted.'[16] The form of matrimony in question was customary, extra-ecclesiastical marriage by promises in the present tense, in front of witnesses, without benefit of clergy.

That such local custom, in other parts of Europe as well as in England, might have pre-Christian tradition behind it, is certainly possible. In so far as European marriage took over the practices of the ancient world in any area, it may also have been perpetuating localism, for what is becoming known of Greek and Roman attitudes to legitimacy also shows that what the opinion of the community took to be a regular union, was a regular union.[17] As for the notorious localism among the English-speaking inhabitants of North America, where marriage has been entirely secular in character and certainly not always Christian, each state has its own regulations. In his chapter on illegitimacy and bridal pregnancy in colonial

15. See Peter Laslett, *The world we have lost* (1979), p. 150.
16. *A treatise of spousals or matrimonial contracts* (1686, but written half a century earlier and more).
17. Information from Beryl Rawson.

America, Robert Wells describes some of these variations. As for later periods, Leffingwell tells us (p. 47) that in New York in his time, 'if two parties, living together, speak of each other as husband and wife, this public acknowledgement is all that is requisite to constitute their relation in the eyes of the law a perfectly valid marriage. Yet children born from such a union and legitimate in New York, are counted as bastards by every nation of Europe.'

The marital code or codes which sanctioned the European tradition of legitimacy or illegitimacy must not, therefore, be looked on as exclusively scriptural, or Christian. European marriage had a further characteristic in its tendency to vary from area to area, that is the remarkable differences displayed by proportions and ages of persons marrying. Here we find ourselves with clearer information, at least for recent centuries. Demographers have shown that northern and western Europe have differed conspicuously from southern and eastern Europe, indeed from the rest of the world, in the lateness of marriage, especially for women, and in the large proportion of those never marrying. What could be more likely than that northern and western Europe should also be a region marked by high levels of bastardy?

We shall find ourselves wondering whether late marriage is always and necessarily connected with high illegitimacy. However this may be, there can be no doubt of the distinctiveness of the European marriage pattern as it has come to be called after the famous essay by John Hajnal published in 1965,[18] which convincingly demonstrated its presence in the early twentieth century. To find, therefore, strong indications that about the year 1900 a similar, if vaguer, divide existed for bastardy is of considerable interest. This pattern of difference between west and northwest, south and southeast, is delineated in the map of levels of illegitimacy published by Shorter, Knodel and van de Walle in 1971, (p. 387) which is reproduced overleaf.[19] The notable feature of the map is that the western and northwestern European provinces had on the whole lower, not higher, illegitimacy rates than the southern and eastern. The pronounced spottiness of the entire landscape is notable too: more so to the west than to the east. Within the two great regions, individual provinces could evidently differ greatly from their neighbours. Nevertheless, in general the west and the north had noticeably less sexual nonconformism than the east and southeast at the outset of the twentieth century.

There are indications that this difference was scarcely new in 1900 and may have gone back much earlier. We know almost nothing, however, about bastardy in the east and southeast before the nineteenth century and regrettably little has yet been established about the European, the northern and western marriage pattern in previous periods. Nevertheless, striking indications have been found of the existence of the European marriage pattern as early as the thirteenth and fourteenth century in England, which modifies Hajnal's original view that this peculiarity made its appearance in the sixteenth century.

We know enough, in fact, to be fairly confident that it is not justifiable to associate high illegitimacy with the west. Bastardy cannot be added to the list of characteristics recently suggested as attached to the western family over time, along with a brief gap between spouses, a relatively large number of servants and a

18. 'European marriage patterns in perspective' (1965). For some extensions, see R. B. Dixon, 'Explaining cross-cultural variations in age at marriage and proportions never marrying' (1971), pp. 215–33.
19. The measure of illegitimate fertility used on the map (I_h) is described in their text, and is the one employed for all the Princeton fertility studies, which provided the sources for their data.

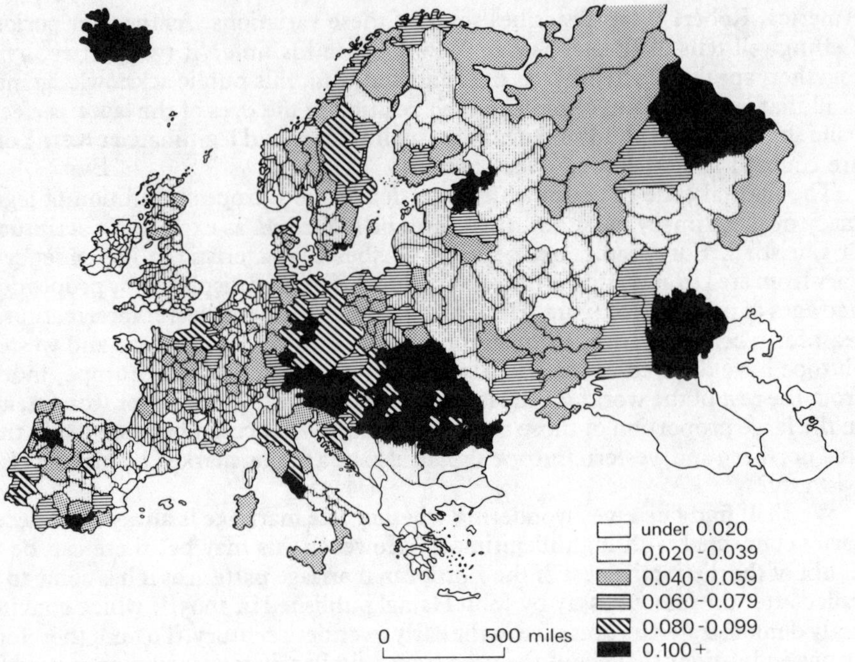

Fig 1.1 Index of illegitimate fertility (I_h), provinces of Europe, 1900 (after Shorter, Knodel and van de Walle, 1971)

pronounced tendency towards simple or nuclear family households, as well as towards late marriage and celibacy.[20] Bastardy, moreover, is not always positively correlated with prolonged celibacy and high proportions never marrying. These facts and circumstances should convince us that no simple explanation is likely to be adequate for these particulars over time and in space.

The main bastardy regions in the west have their counterparts in the east, with the river Danube dividing areas of the highest illegitimacy from areas of the lowest or next lowest. This feature was remarked upon by those who first published the map, and it is obvious that regionality, and persistence by locality, of illegitimacy patterns, may turn out to be its message for the historical sociologist. However, before we turn our attention to regionality, we must look at the evidence for temporal regularity, the shape of change in illegitimacy over time.

4 Legitimate and illegitimate fertility: statistics of variation over time in Britain and in Europe

We begin with figures for the four and a quarter centuries during which bastardy can be reckoned for England and Wales. A record of proportions of baptisms, later births, marked illegitimate for five yearly periods during the four hundred years coming between the 1570s and the 1970s is set out in the three parts of table 1.1. Somewhat unsatisfactory indications for the thirty years before 1570 are also

20. See: Laslett (1977), chapter 1. The thesis will be revised and extended in a forthcoming work on *Family forms in historic Europe*, edited by Richard Wall and Peter Laslett.

included. This lengthy series can be divided between what we call the parish register and the civil register eras. For the first two thirds and more of the time, up until the 1840s, the statistics are derived entirely from the baptismal entries in the parish registers of the Anglican church, our sample of 98 such registers having been used for the purpose and the figures presented in part (a) of table 1.1. The remaining figures represent birth recordings made by civil registrars, and are set out in the two following tables, 1.1(b) and 1.1(c). The year 1838 should mark the transition between the two eras. But the falling away of our ecclesiastical figures in the late 1830s and the failure of the Registrar General to record illegitimacy consistently from the year 1838 and for a few years afterwards, leads to an awkward interlude in the 1830s and the early 1840s, the available figures for which are contained in the second part of our table, 1.1(b).

Fortunately Rickman, the official responsible for the early censuses, interested himself in the ecclesiastical registration of bastardy. He used the authority of the state to require all clergymen in the established church to make the submissions recorded in table 1.1(b) as 'national ecclesiastical returns' for the two years 1830 and 1840, since parsons continued to register baptisms, legitimate and illegitimate, after the state began to record births in 1838. These returns show up a rise in the ratio, from 5.012 per cent to 6.216 per cent between 1830 and 1840, probably the steepest absolute increase over ten years in the whole national series until the twentieth century. Coming at the beginning and end of a decade, when as can be seen from table 1.1(b) our own parish register sample falters and dies, the figures give unexpected confirmation of what our sample suggests.

This is that there was an abrupt rise after 1836, and specifically in the year of the accession of Queen Victoria in 1837 and in the succeeding year 1838 when civil registration began, a leap to a higher level which continued throughout the 1840s and represents the acme of illegitimacy before the First World War. It is undoubtedly possible that the uncertainties of the records throughout these years, especially the complete lack of figures for 1841, 1843 and 1844 are responsible for the impression of an unprecedented increase.[21] But the rise may be perfectly genuine, and of considerable social significance. The new Poor Law of 1834, with its bastardy clauses fastening the responsibility for illegitimates almost entirely on the mother, seems to have come into effect in 1836 and in the three succeeding years.

The illegitimacy ratio is the only measure of bastardy which we have been able to reckon before the 1850s in England and Wales since no more revealing statistics can be derived from the available evidence. After 1850, however, illegitimacy rates are given in the registrars' tables, and are also set down in table 1.1(c). For the first dozen half-decades two such rates are available, a rate for a thousand of the whole population, and a rate for a thousand unmarried women aged 15–44. Only the second of these has been used in more recent times, because of the

21. The whole complex issue is examined in detail by D. V. Glass in *Numbering the people* (1973), pp. 184–7 and 198–202, the second passage, notes on the text, being the more important. Further 'ecclesiastical returns' are shown to have been made, and their figures presented and discussed. The detail becomes a little bewildering, but it is made clear that even closer examination is still necessary and research still in progress.

For the New Poor Law and its bastardy clauses, see U. R. Q. Henriques, 'Bastardy and the New Poor Law' (1967), pp. 103–29. It has to be said that both Laslett and Oosterveen (1973), pp. 206–11, and Laslett (1977) and the reprint of 1978 (see the graph on p. 113 and the tables on pp. 158–9) are in error on detailed points in this complex matter. In 1977 the figures for 1842 and 1845 were accidentally reversed on the graph and in the table and there are other inaccuracies (including the date 1831 for 1830 on the graph), though there is nothing to mislead the reader in a serious way. These errors are corrected in the current (1979) reprint of *Family Life and Illicit Love*.

Table 1.1(a): Illegitimacy ratios by five-year period from our sample of ecclesiastical records, England, 1540s–1830s (98 parishes)

5-year periods	Parishes included	Illegitimacy ratio, %		
1540–44	6–9	[185/4202]	[4.403]	[1540, 1542 only]
1545–9	11–13	[77/2529]	[3.045]	[1540, 1548 only]
1550–54	13–14	[92/3864]	[2.381]	[1550, 1552 and 1553 only]
1555–9	14–25	[31/1596]	[1.942]	[1555, 1559 only]
1560–64	30–41	[135/6844]	[1.973]	
1565–9	43–7	[81/6189]	[1.309]	
1570–74	47–54	127/6541	1.942	
1575–9		197/7726	2.550	
1580–84	56–60	235/8336	2.820	
1585–9		223/7776	2.868	
1590–94	60–68	256/8263	3.098	
1595–9		261/8533	3.059	
1600–1604	71–80	311/9266	3.356	
1605–9		294/9666	3.042	
1610–14	80–85	267/9652	2.766	
1615–19		243/9868	2.462	
1620–24	85–7	239/9607	2.488	
1625–9		257/9930	2.588	
1630–34	87–8	220/10081	2.182	
1635–9		206/10567	1.950	
1640–44	88–9	193/10537	1.832	
1645–9		143/9250	1.546	
1650–54	89–96	87/8661	1.004	
1655–9		82/9048	.906	
1660–64	98	125/8252	1.515	
1665–9		165/11333	1.456	
1670–74	98	132/9650	1.368	
1675–9		116/9405	1.233	
1680–84	98	148/9716	1.523	
1685–9		147/9744	1.509	
1690–94	98	152/9338	1.628	
1695–9		198/9897	2.001	
1700–1704	98	195/10962	1.779	
1705–9		188/10304	1.825	
1710–14	98	199/9710	2.049	
1715–19		239/10948	2.183	
1720–24	98	235/11201	2.098	
1724–9		269/11268	2.387	
1730–34	98	331/12362	2.678	
1735–9		352/13019	2.704	
1740–44	98	344/11900	2.891	
1745–9		360/12794	2.814	
1750–54	98	409/13013	3.143	
1755–9		474/13351	3.550	
1760–64	98	573/14211	4.032	
1765–9		630/14610	4.312	
1770–74	98	672/15620	4.302	
1775–9		764/16623	4.585	
1780–84	98	811/16590	4.888	
1785–9		894/17485	5.113	
1790–94	98	971/19086	5.087	
1795–9		981/19416	5.053	
1800–1804	98	1038/19559	5.307	
1805–9		1144/21466	5.329	

Table 1.1(a) (*cont.*)

5-year periods	Parishes included	Illegitimacy ratio, %	
1810–14	74	1104/21812	5.061
1815–19		1122/24400	4.598
1820–24	74	1504/27564	5.456
1825–9		1334/28893	4.617
1830–34	73–4	1210/29903	4.172
1835–9	18–73	[1667/28549]	[5.839]
1840–44	0		

Note: Except between 1660 and 1804, when the whole sample of 98 parishes is present in the record, the values given along with the illegitimacy ratios are inflated totals for illegitimacy divided by inflated totals for baptisms. These inflated figures represent what we estimate would have occurred if all 98 parishes had been recording. We regard all statistics as unreliable unless the figures from at least half the parishes in the sample could be included, which means that those for the 1540s to the 1560s and for the quinquennium 1835–9 must be regarded as indicators rather than estimates. For some of the years during the 1540s and 1550s no illegitimacies appear along with the baptisms in this sample, and the figures for these years have been omitted from our statistics.

crudity of the first. Even the second, as we have seen, is to some degree problematic in view of the number of children recorded as illegitimates whose mothers are, and were, married women.

But the shortcomings of illegitimacy ratios are notorious. John Knodel and Steven Hochstadt demonstrate in chapter 12 that they can completely obscure the facts when comparisons are made between areas, and as for comparisons over time we may quote a statement made by Etienne van de Walle in chapter 10. 'The ratio is a most misleading indicator of illegitimacy because it is influenced by whatever factor modifies the ratio of illegitimate births to all births – changes in the proportion of single women either by changes in the age distribution or in the proportions married, and changes in the fertility of married women who contribute most to births, as well as changes in the propensity to illegitimacy.' He goes on to say that a fall in marital fertility in nineteenth-century France led to a rise in the national illegitimacy ratio although other measures show illegitimacy to have been fairly stable in the country as a whole. This rise in the ratio took place because fertility was controlled to a larger extent inside marriage than outside it. The claim might be made, of course, that the willingness to complete irregular pregnancies more often than regular ones does represent something like a rise in the propensity towards bastardy. But it certainly seems possible that for reasons of this kind the course of the ratio may underestimate the extent of the drop in illegitimacy in England in the earlier seventeenth century, and also of its rise in the later eighteenth century. Such potential distortions must be borne in mind when we contemplate tables 1.1(a)–(c), and the graphical representation in figure 1.2, along with those arising from erratic registration which we shall discuss in due course.

Nevertheless we have satisfied ourselves that the defects of the illegitimacy ratio as a measure are quite insufficient to deceive us as to the general run of bastardy in our country over the long years during which the reckoning of rates is out of the question for lack of evidence. Rates and ratios can be seen sometimes to move against each other from half-decade to half-decade when they can be plotted together. But the departures from the trend are slight, as is evident from table

1.1(c) and from the figure. It is difficult to resist the conclusion that a different regime, a new order as to bastardy, began in our country early in the twentieth century.

The general shape of the English illegitimacy curve is of some consequence in

Table 1.1(b): Annual illegitimacy ratios from our sample of parish register returns, from national ecclesiastical returns and from civil registration, 1820–49, with rates per thousand of the population in the 1840s

	Ratios	Base of statistics	Rate per 1000 of the population
1820	5.704	74 parishes	
1821	5.851	74 parishes	
1822	5.575	74 parishes	
1823	5.502	74 parishes	
1824	4.714	74 parishes	
1820–4	*5.456*	74 parishes	
1825	4.705	74 parishes	
1826	4.642	74 parishes	
1827	4.811	74 parishes	
1828	4.450	74 parishes	
1829	4.510	74 parishes	
1825–9	*4.617*	74 parishes	
1830	{ 4.829 5.012	74 parishes national ecclesiastical return	
1831	4.189	74 parishes	
1832	4.353	73 parishes	
1833	3.987	73 parishes	
1834	3.570	73 parishes	
1830–34	*4.172*	73–74 parishes	
1835	3.974	73 parishes	
1836	3.770	66 parishes	
1837	[6.047]	20 parishes	
1838	[7.842]	18 parishes	
1839	[6.917]	18 parishes	
1835–9	[*5.839*]	18–73 parishes	
1840	6.126	national ecclesiastical return	–
1841	not available		–
1842	6.721	civil registration	2.2
1843	not available		–
1844	not available		–
1840–44	not available		
1845	7.036	civil registration	2.3
1846	6.728	civil registration	2.3
1847	6.690	civil registration	2.1
1848	6.521	civil registration	2.1
1849	6.803	civil registration	2.2
1845–9	*6.657*	civil registration	

Note: For the national ecclesiastical returns of 1830 and 1840 and the ratios given above (there is an issue over that for 1830), see Glass (1973), pp. 186, 200.

Table 1.1(c): Illegitimacy ratios and illegitimacy rates by five-year periods from civil registration, England and Wales, 1845–9 to 1970s

Period	Illegitimacy ratio	Illegitimacy rates per 1000 of the population	Per 1000 unmarried, widowed and divorced women, aged 15–45
1845–9	6.757	–	–
1851–5	6.591	2.2	18.1
1856–60	6.459	2.2	18.5
1861–5	6.360	2.2	18.8
1866–70	5.844	2.1	17.6
1871–5	5.209	1.8	15.9
1876–80	4.753	1.7	14.4
1881–5	4.80	1.6	13.5
1886–90	4.63	1.5	11.8
1891–5	4.24	1.3	10.1
1896–1900	4.10	1.2	9.2
1901–5	3.95	1.1	8.4
1906–10	4.02	1.1	8.1
1911–15	4.31	1.0	7.9
1916–20	5.392		8.4
1921–5	4.270		6.7
1926–30	4.461		6.0
1931–5	4.347		5.5
1936–40	4.210		5.6
1941–5	6.844		11.4
1946–50	5.487		11.7
1951–5	4.755		10.1
1956–60	5.001		12.8
1961–5	6.9		19.1
1966–70	8.3		22.0
1971	8.4		22.3
1972	8.6		22.1
1973	8.6		19.3
1974	8.8		18.4

Note: Ratios given to three places of decimals where the registration totals have been examined. Otherwise the figure is as in the document concerned. Glass (1973), p. 185, published 'minimally corrected' figures for the illegitimacy rate, 1851–1900; these estimates are sometimes 5 per cent higher than those printed above.

the discussion of regularities in illegitimacy over time.[22] Its conspicuous feature is its double-headedness, one summit just after 1600 and a second just after 1800, decidedly higher than the first. This second summit could itself have been double-headed since, after a little slump between 1825 and 1835, there succeeded the rise to an ever higher level in the 1840s, a rise which may have been so precipitate after 1836. In the 1850s the descent began, quite fast to begin with but slow and

22. See the various curves in figure 3.2 on p. 115 of Laslett (1977): the better the registration, the higher the level about 1600 and about 1800, with the earlier level rising relatively more. As for individual places showing aberrant behaviour, it is made clear in Laslett and Oosterveen (1973) that Colyton itself showed rising illegitimacy when it was falling nearly everywhere else in the late seventeenth century and that many parishes failed to conform at particular periods. Tunstall, Lancs, for example, actually showed a high point of 5.2 per cent baptisms illegitimate in 1641–60, the time of the national low. For the effect on the 'sexual revolution' thesis of the existence of the early high in England, see Richard T. Vann, review of Shorter on the modern family, *Journal of Family History* (1976). The figures printed by Glass (1973), pp. 200–201, giving totals of illegitimacies from ecclesiastical returns for 1830, 1831, 1833, 1839, 1840 and 1841 and contrasting them with civil registration figures in 1842, make it patent that the civil figures were much more comprehensive, though still too low, especially in the cities (see n. 28 on p. 200). More recent work by William Couth on the parish registers of Lincolnshire in the earlier nineteenth century, however, seem to imply that ecclesiastical recorders captured more, not fewer, illegitimacies in that county than the civil ones.

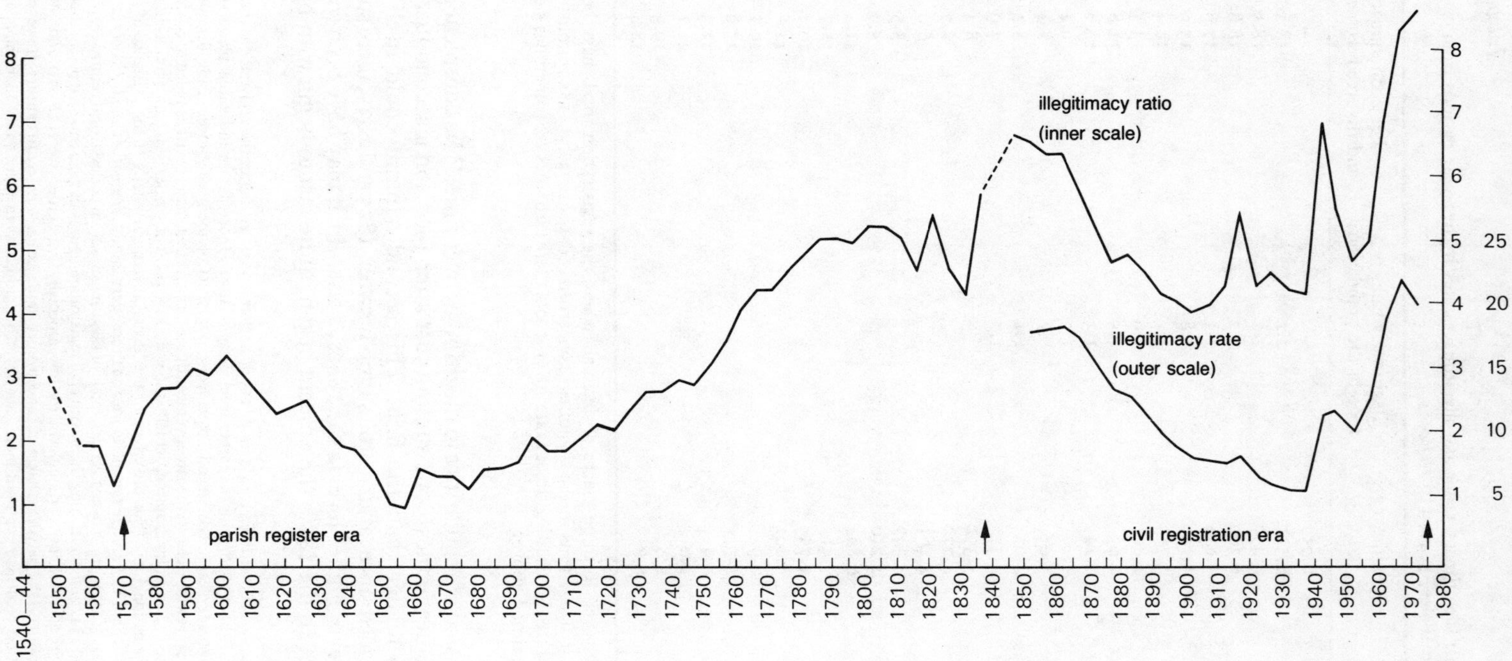

Fig 1.2 Illegitimacy ratios by five-year periods from ecclesiastical records, England and Wales, 1590s to 1830s; rates and ratios from civil registration, 1845–9 to 1970s (data of table 1.1; illegitimacy rate per 1,000 unmarried women, aged 15–44)

steady in the later Victorian decades. Since the First World War, the rapid oscillations of our own period have succeeded, and the peak of the 1840s has been twice surpassed.

A suggestive image for the whole length of the four-century curve might be of successive waves, about two hundred years apart, the first smaller than the second, narrower in its base as well as lower in height. There is a hint of a third major wave coming sooner than it should and rising to an even loftier point in the 1960s and 1970s. A rather different pattern can, however, be seen in the curve. It can be looked upon as describing a secular rise in the proportions of illegitimate births over the four centuries, interrupted by two interludes of decline, in the middle of the seventeenth century and in the later years of the nineteenth and earlier years of the twentieth.

Such an interpretation need have nothing rhythmic about it. Choosing between the two can make a considerable difference to the meaning attached to fluctuations in bastardy levels, in deciding whether revolution, once for all alteration in the social structure, can be supposed to have occurred, for example in the mid- or late eighteenth century. For the moment, however, we shall concentrate on the temporal regularity of the changes which the illegitimacy curve seems to portray.

Especially in the first two hundred and fifty years, illegitimacy moved deliberately, altering its direction only very occasionally and free from rapid oscillation. Care must be taken of course, to distinguish changes at individual places from changes in a number of places taken together. Particular parishes could and did, occasionally show quite sudden and apparently arbitrary fluctuations, against the general trend. Whether or not its behaviour can be described as rhythmic, the movement of the national curve was certainly not random, in spite of the conjectural leap in the 1830s and even though the ups and downs of the twentieth century begin to look a little arbitrary.

Now it is well known to demographers that fertility, general fertility that is, which is for the most part fertility within marriage, behaves in this way, and has itself been called rhythmic. It was suggested in 1973 that the English illegitimacy curve, represented here by the plot of illegitimacy ratios in figure 1.2, pursued the same course as general fertility in earlier centuries. The evidence as to fertility over long periods of time has been confined until recently to a handful of small communities and that earlier suggestion had to be regarded as tentative only.[23] Confirmation of the view that there was a close correspondence between changes in legitimate and illegitimate fertility has recently become available as a result of work carried out at the Cambridge Group for the History of Population and Social Structure on a large sample of 404 parishes. Using a newly developed technique, called population retrojection, or back projection, it has proved possible to estimate the level of the gross reproduction rate in England from the mid-sixteenth century until the beginning of civil registration in 1838.

This fertility measure (female children born to females, net of mortality) underwent wide and regular fluctuations during this long period. Beginning at a very high level about 1550, it fell to a very low level about 1650, only to rise thereafter to a new peak, about 1810, before turning sharply down once more in

23. See Laslett and Oosterveen (1973), p. 265, and Laslett (1977), p. 124, referring to the results of family reconstitution. The suggestion made in these earlier studies that a movement of the illegitimacy level *preceded* a movement of the general fertility level, as it certainly did in England in the nineteenth century, has not been borne out by subsequent investigation at all consistently. Shorter, Knodel and van de Walle first proposed an association between illegitimate and general fertility in their article of 1971.

the last decades before civil registration began in 1838. The coincidence in the timing of major changes in legitimate and illegitimate fertility is well-nigh perfect. When the two curves for five-year intervals are superimposed the correspondence is almost uncanny: when one moves the other moves, usually simultaneously in the same direction and to the same extent.

The synchronism of the two curves helps to confirm our confidence in both sets of estimates. The figures for English gross reproduction rates, soon to be published, will give the impression that illegitimate fertility is a sub-set, so to speak, of fertility as a whole, always a small part of it and varying as overall fertility varied.

This is not the same as saying that movements is general fertility, or in marital fertility which makes up most of it, themselves cause changes in the illegitimacy level. Both may be responding to the same influence, or group of influences, which are responsible for the rhythmic character of demographic processes. Illegitimacy may, presumably, have responded directly to such influences, at least to some extent, as well as being affected as a sub-set of general fertility. It should be noticed, moreover, that a positive correlation between general fertility and illegitimate fertility does not always hold in England. The two seem to have moved in decidedly different directions in the 1840s and the 1850s – the reproduction rate falling rapidly and illegitimacy rising – and there are lesser contradictions in the earlier years of both the nineteenth and eighteenth centuries. Nevertheless, a knowledge of the level of general fertility looks like being of considerable importance when trying to decide how high illegitimacy is likely to have been in a country at any given time.

This rule, of general and illegitimate fertility moving in unison for the most part, might therefore be of value to historical demographers as well as to students of sexual nonconformism. Further interrelations of the same kind along with rather more surprising effects are to be seen in the body of evidence set out in tables 1.2 and 1.3 and illustrated by the curves in figure 1.3. The statistics come from the reconstitution of families, which makes them highly reliable as compared with other figures of a similar kind. But they are less accurate in the sixteenth century, and, for bastardy and prenuptial pregnancy, in the nineteenth.[24] It must be remembered that the samples are small, and differ from table to table. The addition of further parishes would no doubt lead to small changes in the positions of the points on the curves. Nevertheless, the message of these tables and this figure is certainly striking. During the parish register era and in the 17 English parishes covered by the observations, two contrasting sets of movements are shown forth. Prenuptial pregnancy and illegitimacy went up and down together, in quite obvious sympathy with each other. Both reached their nadir in the fifty-year period 1650–99, but diverged somewhat at earlier and later periods. Total fertility, illegitimacy and prenuptial pregnancy, therefore, all followed the same general course.

Age at first marriage, on the other hand, both for men and for women, pursued an almost entirely contradictory pathway. Whilst illegitimacy and the others were falling fast in the early seventeenth century, age at marriage for males was stable, though going down a trifle, and that for females was going up ever so slightly.

24. Sixteenth-century marriage ages are biased slightly downwards in the reconstitution results, and the registrations are in general unreliable before the last two or three decades. Baptisms came so late after births in the nineteenth century that they depress both bastardy and prenuptial pregnancy figures.

Table 1.2: Mean age at first marriage in England by fifty-year periods, 1550–1849

	Females						Males					
	1550–99	1600–1649	1650–99	1700–1749	1750–99	1800–1849	1550–99	1600–1649	1650–99	1700–1749	1750–99	1800–1849
1 Alcester (Warws.)	22.4	25.0	27.2	28.2	24.9	24.2	24.5	29.1	27.8	27.4	27.5	25.3
2 Aldenham (Herts.)	22.0	25.3	26.2	25.8	24.9	22.5	28.6	29.1	29.7	29.2	28.4	25.6
3 Banbury (Oxon)	24.9	25.4	25.8	26.7	25.4	23.8	26.0	27.2	27.4	26.6	26.3	27.0
4 Bottesford (Leics.)	21.9	25.9	26.7	27.4	27.0	25.7	30.3	29.2	27.6	28.7	29.0	26.6
5 Campton & Shefford (Beds.)	24.7	25.5	24.8	24.3	24.0	23.2	28.8	28.0	26.7	26.8	25.6	23.4
6 Colyton (Devon)	26.9	27.3	29.4	28.6	26.3	24.2	27.8	27.4	26.4	26.6	26.4	26.7
7 Earsden (Northumb.)	–	–	22.5	24.8	25.3	24.3	–	–	25.9	26.5	27.6	27.4
8 Gainsborough (Lincs.)	22.1	25.0	25.3	25.5	25.2	24.8	24.0	27.0	27.0	27.5	26.3	26.3
9 Gedling (Notts.)	23.5	27.2	26.4	26.2	24.9	23.7	29.6	29.3	29.4	28.1	26.5	25.1
10 Hartland (Devon)	23.7	27.8	28.4	28.2	26.6	24.7	27.9	28.8	30.7	29.6	27.3	28.0
11 Hawkshead (Lancs.)	–	24.8	27.1	27.4	25.6	27.2	–	27.8	31.0	31.9	28.8	30.6
12 Methley (Yorks.)	25.2	25.7	27.1	26.8	26.8	22.3	24.9	29.9	29.6	29.6	27.6	24.1
13 Shepshed (Leics.)	27.5	28.8	27.1	27.4	25.0	23.3	29.7	29.9	29.2	28.5	25.7	24.3
14 Terling (Essex)	24.5	24.6	23.2	24.4	23.5	22.8	26.0	25.1	25.5	24.7	25.4	24.7
15 Willingham (Cambs.)	22.5	24.8	26.5	24.6	24.2	22.0	25.1	26.7	25.9	25.9	24.8	25.0
Median	23.7	24.5	26.7	26.8	25.3	24.2	27.8	28.1	27.8	28.1	27.3	27.0
Mean (unweighted)	24.0	25.9	26.2	26.4	25.3	23.9	27.2	28.2	28.0	27.8	26.9	26.0

Data: from family reconstitutions, Cambridge Group.

Whilst illegitimacy was rising so swiftly in the later eighteenth century, and prenuptial pregnancy rising too, age at marriage for both sexes was going down almost as fast. It will be noted, moreover, that marriage ages reached their peaks half a century earlier or later than these others reached their lowest points. The inference might be that when age at marriage rises, sexual nonconformism tends to fall, and that when age at marriage falls, sexual nonconformism rises.

That fertility should rise and fall in inverse relation with age at marriage is no surprise; more babies are to be expected if marriage starts earlier, and vice versa. What has also to be accepted is that in England when both sexes were marrying younger more bastards were born, not fewer, and that postponed marriage usually meant less illegitimacy and less prenuptial pregnancy.[25] In Scotland, we are told, the same paradox was present in the nineteenth century when 'generally speaking there was a tendency for lower illegitimacy to go with later marriage.'[26] And in chapter 10 it is stated that in France at the same time 'there seems to be an association between late marriage and sexual restraint before marriage which must be explained by regional customs and attitudes.'

Not all English places show forth the inverse relationship between age at marriage and sexual nonconformism at all periods. In chapter 5 Levine and Wrightson argue for a much more equivocal position in their nine parishes in the seventeenth century and in chapter 14 Ann-Sofie Kälvemark finds no such circumstances in the Swedish parish of Julita.

We shall be returning to these sympathetic and contradictory tendencies in the final paragraphs of this chapter. We may also notice here that preliminary estimates for proportions never marrying in England made by Roger Schofield for the years between 1550 and 1850[27] reveal a relationship with illegitimacy levels which is also problematic, if failure to marry is held to be conducive to bastard births. People born during the earlier seventeenth century, for example, had relatively high expectation of passing through life unmarried. But it was during their lifetime that illegitimacy was so low.

The first summit, or wave, in bastardy coming at about 1600 is the least expected feature of the English illegitimacy curve and the most in need of confirmation or contradiction from the evidence of other countries and areas. No national or even provincial statistics have yet been recovered for any other country earlier than 1600. The closest scholars have come so far is in forty-three parishes of the bishopric of Nantes in western France. Registers were kept in those parishes much earlier than elsewhere in that country and they recorded births, legitimate and illegitimate, from varying dates in the earlier 1500s, some of them from before 1500 itself. As in England there is considerable variation between parish and parish, and considerable doubt about the figures,

25. See Laslett (1977) and note 19, chapter 6, p. 00 below for discussions of the inverse relationship between age at marriage and the illegitimacy ratio.

26. The statement about Scotland will be found in M. Flinn (ed.), *Scottish population history from the seventeenth century to the nineteen thirties* (1977), p. 356 and is repeated by its author in chapter 7 below. Although Levine and Wrightson insist in chapter 5 that the median age at marriage for women cannot be said to display the inverse law for their 9 parishes in the seventeenth century, it will be seen that in our table 1.2 for 15 parishes (not all available when they wrote) the median age moves consistently with the mean, and rather more markedly in inverse relationship with the illegitimacy ratio. If they had extended their analysis of their 9 sets of figures into the eighteenth century they might have had more reason for accepting the inverse principle.

27. Using a technique devised by M. Livi Bacci and presented in R. D. Lee (ed.), *Population patterns in the past* (1977), pp. 318–26. The final figures from 404 parishes when published will show a pronounced effect of this kind, with a nadir in proportions married corresponding to the nadir in illegitimacy and pre-nuptial pregnancy in the middle of the seventeenth century.

Table 1.3: Prenuptial pregnancy in select English parishes by fifty-year periods, 1550–1849

Frequency of prenuptial pregnancy by period	1550–99			1600–1649			1650–99			1700–1749			1750–99			1800–1849			Totals		
Community	Frequency	Total born	%	Frequency	Total born	%	Frequency	Total born	%	Frequency	Total born	%	Frequency	Total born	%	Frequency	Total born	%	nos.		%
1 ALDENHAM (Herts.)	6	27	22	12	75	16	8	48	17	9	45	20	17	51	33	23	63	40	77	309	25
2 COLYTON (Devon)	31	79	39	41	163	25	14	64	22	15	50	30	41	128	32	53	121	44	195	605	32
3 HARTLAND (Devon)	13	48	27	32	138	23	43	176	24	48	153	31	95	207	46	56	132	42	287	854	34
4 EASINGWOLD (Yorks.)	–	–	–	5	26	19	4	41	10	8	62	13	32	108	30	11	38	29	60	275	22
5 ALCESTER (Warws.)	1	6	17	18	75	24	7	80	9	16	89	18	19	82	23	14	73	19	75	405	19
6 BANBURY (Oxon)	10	33	30	23	140	16	8	81	10	43	162	27	73	237	31	0	5	0	157	658	24
7 HAWKSHEAD (Lancs.)	–	–	–	25	116	22	19	95	20	16	70	23	44	97	45	44	95	46	148	473	31
8 EARSDEN (Northumb.)	–	–	–	–	–	–	1	14	7	11	68	16	51	187	27	62	287	22	125	556	22
9 SHEPSHED (Leics.)	3	16	19	5	40	13	3	42	7	10	90	11	64	185	35	116	326	36	201	669	29
10 ASH (Kent)	–	–	–	–	–	–	3	23	13	26	103	25	101	197	51	90	204	44	220	527	42
11 GEDLING (Notts.)	6	15	40	21	54	39	16	79	20	32	131	24	45	150	30	172	294	59	292	723	40
12 WILLINGHAM (Cambs.)	11	25	44	13	56	23	3	23	13	7	26	27	19	45	42	11	20	55	64	195	33
13 GAINSBOROUGH (Lincs.)	11	33	33	60	216	28	27	215	13	45	258	17	125	498	25	21	136	15	289	1356	21
14 CAMPTON & SHEFFORD (Beds.)	2	19	11	17	66	26	12	55	22	24	79	30	49	118	42	68	214	32	172	551	31
15 METHLEY (Yorks.)	3	10	30	8	54	15	8	47	17	5	48	10	28	97	29	8	24	33	60	280	21
16 TERLING (Essex)	9	27	33	7	31	23	1	22	5	12	36	33	13	64	20	34	83	41	76	263	29
Totals	106	338	31	287	1250	23	177	1105	16	327	1470	22	816	2451	33	783	2115	37	2498	8729	29

Data: from family reconstitutions, Cambridge Group.

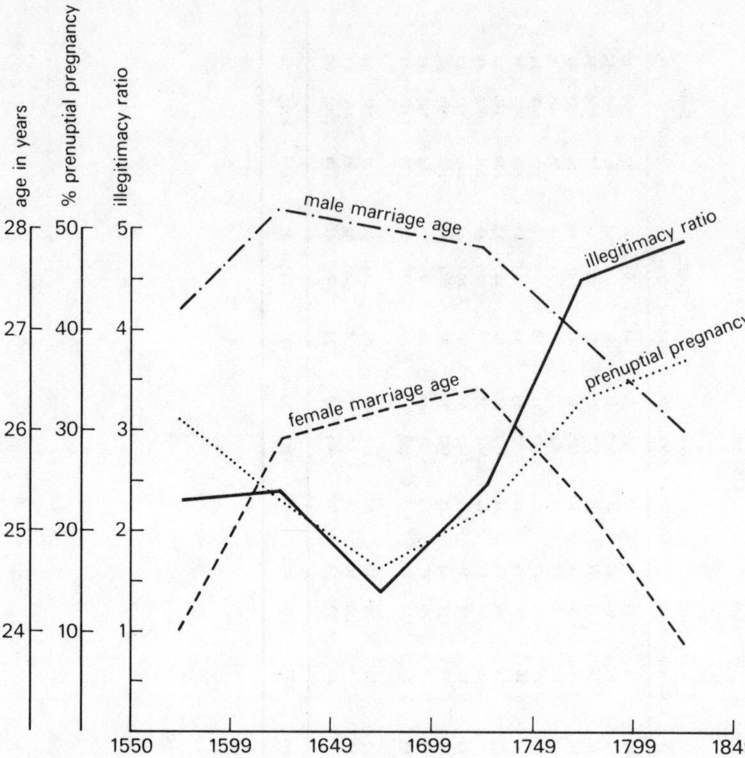

Fig. 1.3 Illegitimacy ratio, percentage prenuptial pregnancy and mean age at first marriage by fifty-year periods, 1550–1849 (data of tables 1.2 and 1.3)

which must be regarded as much below reality. Yet over the whole period 1550–1600, one rural parish, Abbaretz, had an illegitimacy ratio of 4.6 per cent, and an urban one, St Similien, Nantes, one of 3.9 per cent. We are not told whether in general high illegitimacy was, as in England, more frequent towards 1600 than earlier. It so happens that a special register of bastards has survived for St Similien for 1593–1600. The illegitimacy ratio there works out at 7.3 per cent. This is well up with the highest English levels in the later sixteenth century when a median of six parishes selected for their high illegitimacy between 1580 and 1600 is also 7.3 per cent.[28]

28. See Croix (1974), pp. 94–5 and compare Jean Meyer in chapter 9 below. Although 18 of the parishes analysed by Croix (including 5 of the parishes in Nantes) show ratios of 1 per cent or below, and so conform to what has been held to be standard for French rural communities before the eighteenth-century rise, he remarks: 'On comprend que le XVIe siècle ait pu être baptisé "l'ère des bâtards".' The areas where ratios exceed 3 per cent in England before 1600 were mostly in the north and northwest. In Cheshire, Prestbury had a minimum of 6.5 per cent and a maximum of 13.5 per cent, 1561–1600; Eccleshall a ratio of 6.0 per cent, 1561–80, and 7.3 per cent, 1581–1600; Ellastone, Frodsham and Sandbach all exceeded 4 per cent for one twenty-year period while Whittington, Lancashire, showed a ratio of 6.4 per cent for the same decades, 1540–60. But other parts of the country were involved. In Dymock, Gloucestershire, there were 20 bastards out of 505 baptisms, 1539–60, a ratio of effectively 4 per cent. Devonshire, Somerset, Yorkshire and Warwickshire parishes could all attain such levels and in spite of our fragmentary figures it appears that a much wider area than the diocese of Nantes displayed this feature: compare Laslett and Oosterveen (1973), n. 24.

At Talavera in Spain at just this period the illegitimacy ratio had the values which are set out in table 1.4.[29] Such figures as those from France and Spain serve to show that the high levels of the turn of the sixteenth and seventeenth centuries in England were not without parallel elsewhere. Nevertheless, such further data as have come to hand for decades later than this sometimes fail to conform to the shape of the English illegitimacy curve, and sometimes depart from it. The statistics which C. van den Broeke has kindly communicated for the Flemish-speaking region of Belgium begin in the first decade of the seventeenth century with a ratio of under 2 per cent. The subsequent course of the Belgian graph (not shown here) resembles the continuation of that for Talavera. It had its nadir much later than the English, coming well after 1700: and the estimates which van den Broeke has made of the course of prenuptial pregnancy fail to show the close correspondence with illegitimacy which we find in England.[30]

Table 1.4: Illegitimate births at Talavera, Spain, 1570–1609

Period	Total births	Bastard births	% of total births
1570–74	1473	88	6.0
1575–9	1316	87	6.6
1580–84	1227	77	6.3
1585–9	1284	84	6.5
1590–94	1284	67	5.2
1595–9	1230	71	5.8
1600–1604	1291	58	4.5
1605–9	1075	40	3.7

A further possible interpretation of the English illegitimacy curve should perhaps be mentioned now that we have these comparisons with other European countries in front of us. If Keith Wrightson's argument in chapter 6 is accepted, that the very sharp descent of the ratio during the period of the Puritan uprising, and especially the nadir in the decade of their political rule in the 1650s, were probably to a large extent registration artifacts, then it is no longer quite so clear that the lowest point of illegitimacy in early modern times came so much earlier in England than it did in the rest of Western Europe. That there was a descent from the 1620s until the early 1640s cannot be in doubt. Keith Wrightson is confident of the high level in the early 1600s and of a rapid subsequent fall, which is indeed conspicuously illustrated in chapter 5 for the village of Terling, and which is still being confirmed for parish after parish as research continues. But the descent after this point may have been more gradual in the later 1640s than the *allure*, as the French would say, of our present curve suggests.

29. See M. del S. Muñoz, *La poblacion de Talavera de la Reina* (1975), pp. 109 and 196. Compare Frank McArdle, *Altopascio: a study in Tuscan rural society 1587–1784* (1978).

30. Graphique 1 on p. 238 of Flandrin (1975), ratios for 21 parishes in Anjou and for 6 others in France, resembles van den Broeke's graph quite closely, and suggests that a nadir, meaning a fall from already low levels to near vanishing point, in the early eighteenth century may have been characteristic of wide areas of Western Europe. Compare the discussion in A. E. Imhof, *Einführung in die historische Demographie* (1977), pp. 83–5. Pierre Caspard, 'Conceptions prénuptiales et développement du capitalisme' (1974), also finds less correlation with illegitimacy in his detailed study of prenuptial pregnancy at Neuchâtel, Switzerland, 1678–1820. In the late eighteenth century when first handicraft and then factory industry got established in the area, bastardy remained low though prenuptial pregnancies rose markedly.

The rapid rise to a level in the 1660s, close to that of the 1630s may also have to be called dubious, though there is no reason to suspect the reliability of the statistics for those decades. What may have happened is that there were two low points in the course of illegitimacy in seventeenth-century England, the first in the later 1640s and 1650s, the precise extent of which cannot now be determined, and the second in the 1680s, which is much better documented. This second English low is rather closer to that which may have been characteristic of other parts of Western Europe. This point emerges from David Gaunt's discussion of low points in both legitimate and illegitimate fertility in Sweden in the 1680s and the 1690s.

5 Sexual revolution in the late eighteenth century?

Moreover as the eighteenth century proceeds and more and more European countries begin to produce statistics, an extraordinary unison appears in the figures. Every series which has become available, nearly all of them consisting of illegitimacy ratios, shows a peak to correspond with that which we have demonstrated for England between 1800 and 1845. Starting with dates varying from the 1740s to the 1780s, or even later – in France, as our contributors make clear, the upsurge did not get under way for the whole country till the 1790s[31] – all the known series take off, rising from levels often below the English and ending after 1800 at levels often well above them. The peculiarity of England at this period seems to have been that, except in English cities, illegitimacy was initially more common than elsewhere and rose earlier, but not so swiftly and not to such heights. The upward thrust of all the illegitimacy ratio and also of prenuptial pregnancy over all the areas of Europe so far investigated is one of the outstanding discoveries of sociological history and merits all the attention given to it in this collection and by other authorities.[32]

Not every country had bastardy levels which were modest by English standards in earlier centuries. It is particularly important that in the large cities of France, as is demonstrated by Yves Blayo in table 3 of chapter 11 below, the illegitimacy ratio was already over twice that which we have reckoned for all England by the 1740s, at 7.3 per cent, whilst that for the rural areas was below 2 per cent. Yet Iceland, the smallest, most isolated and most westerly of European cultures, lacking urban life entirely, had an illegitimacy ratio of nearly 16 per cent in 1827–30, the highest known for any European area at that period, as distinct from cities like Lyons, Rouen or Paris. It looks as if there had been a recent climb in Iceland, though an authority on that country believes that widespread illegitimacy had been 'the pattern from the beginning of the society eleven centuries

31. See Blayo, chapter 11 below, tables 2 and 3. For comparable figures for Lille, see Alain Lottin, 'Naissances illégitimes et filles-mères à Lille au XVIIIe siècle' (1970), and for St Malo (ratio 5.9 per cent, 1750–99, with foundlings 11.9 per cent) see Meyer, chapter 9 below, note 45. In Paris he shows that the ratio exceeded 10 per cent by the 1730s and 20 per cent by the 1760s; see p. 252.

32. See the relevant chapters below, and especially Shorter (1976), chapter 3. J. W. Shaffer, 'Family, class and young women: occupational expectations in 19th-century Paris' (1978) contains a critique of the revolutionist thesis, a critique developed out of the work of Louise Tilly and her collaborators there cited. Perhaps the conclusive argument against the belief in a revolution of sexual attitudes going with 'modernization' is to be found in Mitterauer (1979), when he confronts the thesis with evidence of an example from Austria. An interesting analysis of the whole issue will be found in Sølvi Sogner, 'Illegitimacy in old rural society; some reflections on the problem arising from two Norwegian family reconstitution studies' (1978). Further Scandinavian figures will be found in R. F. Tomasson, 'Premarital permissiveness and illegitimacy in the Nordic countries' (1976), pp. 252–70, and for Sweden and Denmark see David Gaunt in chapter 13 below.

ago'.[33] Scandinavia, southern Germany and Portugal may also have been more bastardy prone than England before the nineteenth century, and Austria certainly was. It seems, therefore, that some cultural areas, or countries, or ethnic regions – it is difficult to choose the proper term because we know so little about their social structural, as distinct from their political, characteristics – had long term tendencies towards sexual nonconformism markedly different from other cultural areas. But the order of countries may not have changed a great deal, although England, for example, sank pronouncedly in relation to others in the first half of the nineteenth century.

A change of the kind which went forward in Europe at the turn of the eighteenth and nineteenth centuries can scarcely be called revolutionary, if by that is meant an abrupt transition from traditional to non-traditional social structure. This is borne out by the three further circumstances which can be noted in relation to the great rise in sexual nonconformism at that time. In the first place although England, which was the first to industrialize and to concentrate its people in towns and cities, led the way in this development, none of our evidence yet suggests that illegitimacy had much to do with urban or industrial areas in that country. The other European countries, moreover, which so soon joined in the rise of illegitimacy were at very different stages of economic, technical and social structural change. Sweden, where the rise in illegitimacy is certainly known to have been very steep, and where it began as early as it did in England, was scarcely touched by such forces. This was so even by the 1770s and 1780s when the rise became precipitate and the Swedish illegitimacy level began to exceed the English. In France in the 1790s, where the rise was as abrupt as in Sweden, the social structure must still have been more 'traditional' than in England in spite of the Revolution.

The second circumstance is that this was a time of a Europe-wide, even a world-wide rise in population, though the extent to which this increase was due to a rising birth rate rather than to a falling death rate has to be settled for every region. Marked changes in illegitimacy in countries other than England may, therefore, also have been associated with similar changes in fertility. Thirdly, it was not until much later, until the 1880s in fact, that industrialization and urbanization began to affect the structure of most Western European societies. But it was precisely in the 1880s and '90s that bastardy began its prolonged fall all over Europe from the heights attained earlier in the century.

It is simply not true, in fact, that living in towns or even in cities, or migrating to such population centres, has always been directly and positively correlated with illegitimacy, during the so-called sexual revolution, or at any other time. In some countries, as in France (see chapter 11), the positive association was strong, if not universal (see chapter 10): in others, as in Scotland or Germany (see chapters 7 and 12) it was weak or even quite markedly negative. The last was the English case, as we shall see.

The fall in illegitimacy which succeeded the eighteenth-century rise began in the 1850s in our country, as has been noted, rather earlier than elsewhere. In the United States, as Daniel Scott Smith shows in chapter 17, it started even earlier still. Indeed, so prevalent is the notion that each country did have a sexual revolution at some point during the process of *modernization*, a not very fortunate

33. Tomasson (1976), pp. 255–6. He presents evidence to show that medical doctors and lawyers could have half or more of their first children born as bastards in the seventeenth and eighteenth centuries, and that clerical by-blows were also common.

expression taken over from the political scientists, that it apparently makes sense for American historians to debate with each other on the timing of the beginning and end of the sexual revolution in their country. This issue can concern us no further here. We shall have to round off our rapid survey of English and European statistics at the relevant period by looking a little more closely at what actually happened to numbers of births inside and outside marriage at the time when illegitimacy declined, a time which falls well within the civil registration era in most Western countries.

In figure 1.4 below, also reproduced from the article by Shorter, Knodel and van de Walle of 1971 (p. 378), curves for the course of legitimate and illegitimate fertility between 1840 and 1965 are shown. The very different levels of bastardy in these countries should be noticed once again: low in Switzerland and the Netherlands, high in Scandinavia, very high in Austria. As for its relationship

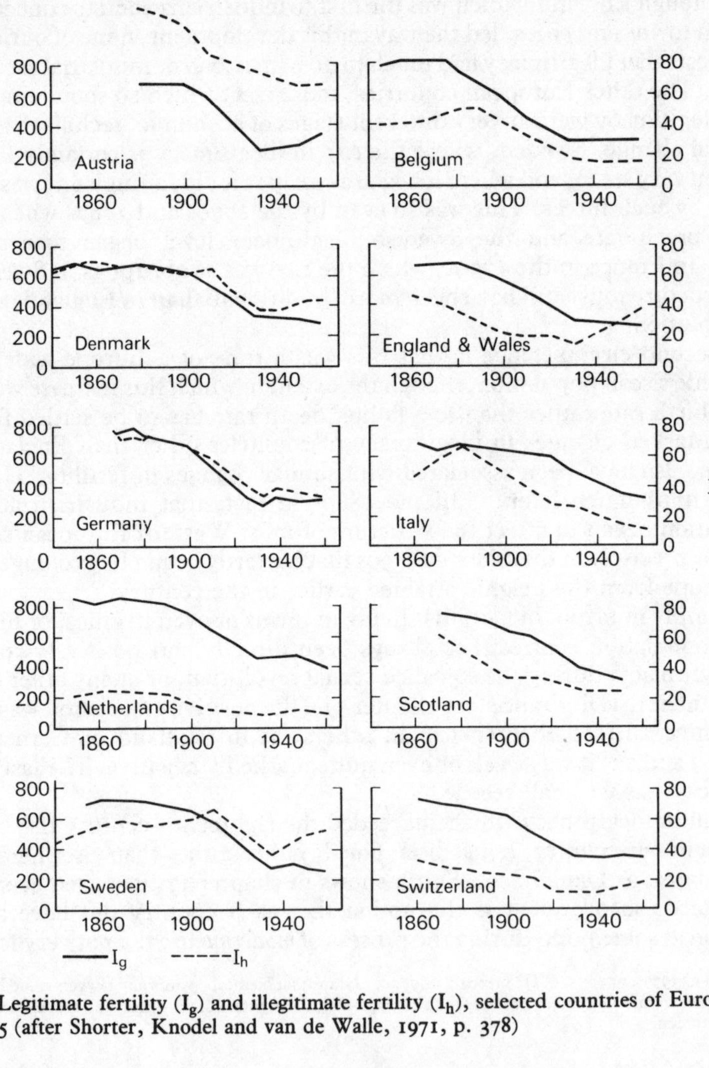

Fig. 1.4 Legitimate fertility (I_g) and illegitimate fertility (I_h), selected countries of Europe, 1840–1965 (after Shorter, Knodel and van de Walle, 1971, p. 378)

with marital fertility, it seems impossible to contemplate the curves for these ten countries without agreeing with the authors of the study that there must have been a connection between the general fall in bastardy and the general fall in all births in late nineteenth and early twentieth century Europe, and, perhaps, though less convincingly, with the growth of contraception in this period. Nevertheless, we cannot overlook the fact which this figure shows up, that in some countries in some periods, as in England and Wales in the 1940s and 1950s, illegitimacy rose when fertility fell, just as it may have done there in the 1840s and 1850s. Now that it is time to add the consideration of regional and micro-regional variation in illegitimacy to its variation over time, we shall find ourselves facing the further disconcerting discrepancies in this relationship to which we have already referred.

6 Regional in relation to temporal variation in illegitimacy

Table 1.5 below lists the first and the last ten or eleven English counties in order of their illegitimacy level for 1842, 1870–72, 1900–1902 and 1972. The illegitimacy ratio, the measure used here by the Registrar General, cannot be expected to be well suited to the fine ordering of counties by rank and its unsuitability for regional comparison has been underlined already. Nevertheless, it is of considerable interest that Nottinghamshire, the North Riding of Yorkshire and Herefordshire retained their exalted places over the whole period of 130 years, while Shropshire was near the top of the table from 1842 till 1902 and the East Riding of Yorkshire from 1870 till 1972. This was so in spite of a series of changes in the structure of English society over this stretch of time, changes which might all be expected to have affected the prevalence of sexual nonconformism, and its distribution between areas of the country. There was a growth of population from under eighteen million to over forty-five million; a continuous expansion of industrial activity and its spread into new regions, its decline in old ones; a transformation of the labour force almost everywhere, in its age composition, its sex composition, the tasks to be performed; the virtual disappearance, where industry did not arise, of a particular form of rural employment often closely associated with bastardy, that is living-in farm service, disappearing much sooner in the southeast than the northwest; a continuous and finally rapid growth of the professional and middle classes, unevenly spread between localities; in later decades a rise in working-class institutions and extensive immigration, again in particular places, from India, Pakistan and the Caribbean.

Further to be reckoned with are the unprecedented ideological changes, changes in the beliefs, opinions, attitudes of the whole mass of the people and not simply of the educated few: of these the decline of religion and the substitution of secular values is only one, if by far the most important. That notwithstanding all these there should have been marked persistence of relative bastardy levels over short periods of time is almost as surprising as such persistence over the total run of years. There was evidently little change in the relative incidence of illegitimacy among districts with traditionally high levels in the last thirty years of the nineteenth century, for example, when bastardy was falling everywhere. This was recognized at the time by Leffingwell and the registration officials themselves. Even the rapid further fall, sharp rise, and succeeding descent recorded for the twentieth century in the English illegitimacy curve left nearly half of the counties undisturbed in the top ten.

Table 1.5: Rank orders of English counties by bastardy ratio 1842–1972

First 10 and last 10

1842	1870–72	1900–1902	1972
1 Cumberland	1 Cumberland	1 Norfolk	1 London
2 Norfolk	2 Shropshire	2 Shropshire	2 Nottinghamshire
3 Shropshire	3 Yorkshire, NR	3 Nottinghamshire	3 Lancashire
4 Westmorland	4 Norfolk	4 Staffordshire	4 Warwickshire
5 Nottinghamshire	5 Staffordshire	5 Cumberland	5 Yorkshire, ER
6 Herefordshire	6 Nottinghamshire	6 Lincolnshire	6 Yorkshire, WR
7 Cheshire	7 Durham	7 Yorkshire, ER	7 Yorkshire, NR
8 Yorkshire, NR	8 Yorkshire, ER	8 Yorkshire, NR	8 Northumberland
9 Suffolk	9 Derbyshire	9 Suffolk	9 Herefordshire
10 Leicestershire	10 Lincolnshire	10 Herefordshire	10 Gloucestershire
	11 Herefordshire		
32 Northamptonshire	32 Warwickshire	32 Dorset	32 Huntingdonshire
33 Durham	33 Kent	33 Rutland	33 Westmorland
34 Kent	34 Dorset	34 Sussex	34 Berkshire
35 Essex	35 Devon	35 Worcestershire	35 Buckinghamshire
26 Huntingdonshire	36 Sussex	36 Hertfordshire	36 Cambridgeshire
37 Warwickshire	37 Hampshire	37 London	37 Worcestershire
38 Devon	38 Somerset	38 Devon	38 Suffolk
39 Cornwall	39 Gloucestershire	39 Gloucestershire	39 Hertfordshire
40 Monmouthshire	40 London	40 Somerset	40 Surrey
41 London	41 Surrey	41 Surrey	41 Rutland

Counties common to various lists

	1870–72		1900–1902		1972	
	Top ten	Bottom ten	Top ten	Bottom ten	Top ten	Bottom ten
1842	5	4	7	2	3	1
1870–72	–	–	9	5	3	1
1900–1902			–	–	4	1

Source: reports of the Registrar General.

Such figures suggest that as the level rose and fell, the counties went up and down in unison, retaining their ordering throughout for the most part, at least in the upper strata, so to speak. Indeed, this is the image we are left with, of superimposed layers of rock such as are portrayed in the geology text books, rising and falling as hill gives way to valley, but always in the same order in relation to each other. The effect was evidently somewhat less at the bottom of the rank order, although it was by no means absent.

But it would be wrong to suppose that every single county always tended to keep at about the same rank order in spite of vicissitudes in social conditions and of changes in the general level. There were planets in this predominantly fixed universe, *rogue* counties, which wandered up or down as period succeeded period, and which might even go right from the bottom to the top. This is exactly what happened with the county of London: forty-first out of 41 in 1842, fortieth in 1870–72, thirty-seventh in 1900–1902, it was first out of 41 in 1972. Warwickshire had a somewhat similar history, though it began its rise earlier and Gloucestershire, twenty-eight in 1842, also climbed up the ranks from the fourth to the first quartile in the twentieth century.[34] Meanwhile Westmorland and Suffolk fell all the way down the table, from the top ten in 1842 to the bottom ten in 1972.

The reasons for the erratic behaviour of some counties in England over the last century and a half obviously invite investigation. The fact that most remained fairly stable in their rank order in relation to all others makes the rogue counties even more intriguing. We can be quite confident that stability in the relative illegitimacy level of localities within national boundaries over time has been, and still is, a feature of many countries and areas. Indeed, we have found it in every set of illegitimacy figures by region and sub-region at different points in time which we have been able to examine. It is true of the first two sets of figures ever worked out for Japan, in 1887 and 1897, and published as table 3 in chapter 19. It is even true of Russia over the period of the communist revolution.

In chapter 12 the authors pronounce on their close and highly expert examination of persistence of illegitimacy levels by administrative areas in Germany in phrases very similar to those we have used for England over the same stretch of time: 'The changes in national governments, the vast economic transformation of Germany and the turmoil of the inter-war years did not greatly alter the regional pattern of illegitimacy.' The similar case made out for the whole of France by Yves Blayo in chapter 11 covers a much longer stretch of time, though he has had to rely on illegitimacy ratios, as we have had to do for England for this purpose up to this point. After comparing the regional distribution of levels of illegitimacy in France in 1790–1829 with the distribution in 1967–9, Blayo concludes that 'the original pattern persisted between the eighteenth and nineteenth centuries' and 'remained almost the same until the latest date for which we have information' (see p. 280 below). France had rogue counties too, he tells us, such as the northerly *départements* which, as his maps reveal, went from the very top to the middle of the rank order during his lengthy period of observation.

7 Stability over time in the relative level of illegitimacy of localities in England

The illegitimacy ratios culled from the registers of a limited number of parishes for the two hundred and forty years before civil registration began, and reported in our earlier studies (Laslett, 1977, pp. 133–47), suggest that there was a certain stability in the relative levels of illegitimacy of various localities in England between the early sixteenth and the early nineteenth centuries. Indeed we know of no reason why such a pattern should not have existed indefinitely.

It has not, of course, been possible to arrange English counties in rank order by illegitimacy during the parish register era. The rank ordering of the five 'bastardy regions' into which, in 1973, we attempted to group the available parishes at successive times between the 1580s and the 1820s would not show significant correlation, using the tests which we shall apply to the complete and superior data sets provided by national statistical offices in the nineteenth century. Nevertheless, the admittedly inadequate material makes it clear that local variation in illegitimacy was present in England from the earliest date of bastardy recording. It is also evident that an approximate rank order persisted in English counties, perhaps even in localities within counties.

34. The figures quoted should not be taken too literally, because successive reports of the Registrar General use different numbers of counties, or county-like districts, which have had to be approximated. In spite of the surprisingly small effect of migration on relative levels of illegitimacy, it seems likely that the rise of London and Warwickshire in recent years must have been associated at least to some degree with the influx of large numbers of people of Caribbean origin, since the Caribbean is an area of such high incidence.

We have even found in the eastern region, and in the particular county of Norfolk, an example of wandering up and down in rank levels before statistical times. The parishes of Norfolk, Suffolk and Essex for which ratios have been recovered had modest figures in the sixteenth and seventeenth centuries, though showing the expected summit about 1600 like the rest of the sample. But their relative values began to increase markedly in the eighteenth century, and by 1842 these three counties, now the Eastern Region of the Registrar General, had the highest illegitimacy levels among the eleven regions into which the country had been divided. Norfolk by then was the second in rank order of the 47 counties.[35] Table 1.5 shows that its illegitimacy ratio was still outstanding at the end of the Victorian era; indeed it was higher than that of any other county in the 1900s. But by 1972 Norfolk had fallen out of the top ten to twenty-first in rank order.

We must now turn from these inexact figures to the full sets of bastardy statistics gathered by officialdom. They are in the form of rates, not ratios, and belong to a period when civil registration was securely established and had developed a critical tradition. It is the manipulation of these data which has convinced us that persistence by locality is more marked in illegitimacy than in any other form of behaviour which the historical demographer and the sociological historian have so far been able to examine. In table 1.6 illegitimacy rates, along with the rates of legitimate births, are set out for each of the 43 English counties at four points in the later nineteenth century, 1870–72 (1871), 1880–82 (1881), 1890–92 (1891), 1900–1902 (1901). Each value is accompanied by a numerical rank order and in the final two columns a variation span as to rank is included for each county for both types of fertility. This is the data set on which our more exact conclusions about persistence by locality of illegitimacy levels in England have been based and which suggested a similar examination for other countries. A glance at the rank order columns makes it clear that there was a pronounced tendency for counties to maintain their place as decade succeeded decade, an impression which is decidedly reinforced by the low values in the variation spans, lower for illegitimate than for legitimate fertility. Precise statistical measures of this tendency to persist by locality are set out in table 1.7, parts (a) and (b). The figures in table 1.7 are for rank order correlations, (see note to table 1.7), and in the case of the illegitimacy rates it will be seen that they are all significant at 0.001 or less. This means that there is only one chance in at least 1,000 that the relationship between any two columns of rank orders, adjacent or otherwise, could have been accidental.

We have decided to call these correlations *locality persistence values*. If each of the figures in the table is squared and expressed as a percentage, the results can be construed in the following way. The rank orders of counties in illegitimacy ratios in 1871 and 1881 would be 94 per cent (0.97 × 0.97 × 100) effective as predictors of each other. Accordingly, we find 92 per cent effective prediction between 1891 and 1871, 82 per cent effectiveness between 1901 and 1871. The corresponding percentages between 1891 and 1881, and between 1901 and 1891, are 81 per cent and 90 per cent.

There is no need to dwell upon the message of such statistics as these. It is evident that the locality persistence value was almost at its maximum for illegitimacy after a lapse of ten years and did not fall below four fifths of its highest

35. See Laslett (1977), pp. 137 and 157–8. Norfolk was the fourth county in the ecclesiastical return of 1830 (see note 21).

possible even after thirty years. But it is notable how much less impressive are the locality persistence values for legitimate fertility. Although these are highly significant for all correlations except that between 1871 and 1881, the locality persistence value could fall as low as 0.44, implying a predictive effectiveness of only 19 per cent. And when we look at the bottom panel of the table, 1.7(c), containing the cross correlations between the two, illegitimate and legitimate, the values are lower still, and more erratic.

There certainly seems to have been a change of some kind which affected the figures for 1881, since so many of the cross correlations involving that year in this part of the table are insignificant. This is a revealing example of how close numerical examination can show up an unsuspected if not major discontinuity in change over time. In spite of this vagary, there are interesting indications in this array of the relationships which we can expect to obtain between irregular and regular births. The rank order of counties by illegitimacy in 1871, for example, was 25 per cent effective as a predictor of the rank order by legitimate fertility in that year, and 36 per cent effective for the rank order by legitimate fertility thirty years later, in 1901. It is puzzling that a higher percentage should obtain in the second correlation than in the first, and that the relationships between the two variables at identical dates, that is, the measures on the diagonal of table 1.7(c), should never rise above 0.62 (38 per cent). But we have already hinted at the traps for the unwary in discussing bastardy in relation to regular births.

James Oeppen of the Cambridge Group for the History of Population and Social Structure, who has done the statistical work, comments on the figures for 1881 as follows: 'This suggests that legitimate fertility became less sensitive in that decade to the forces that produced changes in illegitimate fertility.' We have spelt out the meaning of table 1.7 at some length and as straightforwardly as we could, so as to try to make sure that the results are intelligible to those unfamiliar with exercises of this kind. Along with Kenneth Wachter of the University of California at Berkeley, however, Mr Oeppen has taken the statistical analysis of the variance contained in the values of table 1.6 considerably further. The results will be found in the appendix to this chapter (p. 65), and we shall not go into the details here.

There are three general statements which can be made on the basis of these exercises, all of which bear in an interesting way upon illegitimate fertility, its development over time, its tendency to persist by locality and its relationship with legitimate or total fertility. The first concerns influences from place as compared with influences from time. The figures in the appendix demonstrate that, although locality is consistently significant in relation to both forms of fertility, time is usually more important, often much more important, especially for regular births. Temporal influences, those which are common to the whole country, but vary in strength as the years go by, are stronger in their effect on illegitimacy levels in England than in any of the other countries we have so far studied. Scotland, with Portugal, shows the opposite effect, with locality outweighing time.

The second statement to be made about space-time analysis of variance may sound somewhat technical. It is that an additive model explains the differences in the values for legitimate fertility in table 1.6 rather well, but a multiplicative model suits illegitimate fertility far better. Kenneth Wachter expounds this conclusion by saying that 'we can evidently regard illegitimacy rates as a *product* of some constant, times a multiplier which depends only on the county, times a

Table 1.6: Values of rates of illegitimate and legitimate fertility for English counties, 1870–71, 1880–82, 1890–92, 1900–1902, with rank orders

	1870–72				1880–82				1890–92				1900–1902				Variation span	
	Illegitimate		Legitimate		Illegitimate		Legitimate		Illegitimate		Legitimate		Illegitimate		Legitimate		Illegitimate	Legitimate
	Value	Rank order	Value	Rank order	Value	Rank order	Value	Rank order	Value	Rank order	Value	Rank order	Value	Rank order	Value	Rank order		
London	10.3	41	269.9	44	9.8	41	272.6	43	8.1	38	250.4	39	6.9	38	227.8	24	3	20
Surrey	9.5	42	285.1	37	8.5	43	284.3	31	6.6	42	244.4	41	5.9	42	208.2	42	1	11
Kent	14.7	34	288.8	31	12.1	35	287.6	24	9.3	32	255.6	33	7.5	30	221.2	33	5	9
Sussex	13.7	37	284.6	38	11.5	38	279.2	36	8.7	35	235.9	43	7.2	34	203.3	43	4	7
Hampshire	13.6	38	272.9	42	11.8	36	273.9	41	8.5	36	243.3	42	7.3	31	211.6	40	7	2
Berkshire	16.8	28	294.5	21	13.4	30	290.0	20	10.3	27	257.6	30	8.7	22	219.0	38	8	8
Middlesex	9.4	43	288.0	33	9.4	42	293.6	12	6.5	43	252.3	37	5.9	42	224.1	29	1	25
Hertfordshire	18.4	24	300.0	11	15.3	23	291.7	17	10.4	24	264.0	22	7.0	37	224.8	27	14	16
Buckinghamshire	19.0	20	299.5	12	16.5	16	291.9	16	12.6	15	270.4	11	9.1	19	230.4	20	5	9
Oxfordshire	19.0	20	295.7	20	15.4	22	294.7	11	10.4	24	271.1	9	9.0	21	228.0	23	4	14
Northamptonshire	18.7	22	297.5	14	15.9	19	290.6	19	11.7	18	265.8	19	9.1	19	222.0	32	4	18
Huntingdonshire	19.8	18	302.3	9	14.0	27	274.9	39	12.9	13	262.5	23	10.9	12	236.0	15	15	30
Bedfordshire	21.1	14	296.0	18	18.0	10	283.1	33	11.2	22	256.8	32	8.4	26	219.1	37	16	19
Cambridgeshire	19.3	19	294.3	22	15.6	21	276.6	38	12.4	16	255.0	35	9.6	16	223.9	30	5	16
Essex	16.2	31	293.7	24	12.7	33	300.4	5	9.1	30	270.0	12	7.3	31	238.5	13	3	19
Suffolk	22.0	11	290.2	30	17.8	14	293.6	12	14.0	9	269.5	13	12.0	8	236.5	14	6	18
Norfolk	27.3	4	273.1	41	22.6	2	279.3	35	16.7	2	257.2	31	13.4	1	229.5	21	3	20
Wiltshire	17.1	27	297.9	13	14.7	25	291.6	18	10.3	27	261.3	25	9.2	18	225.1	26	9	13
Dorsetshire	14.2	35	288.8	31	13.1	32	286.8	26	9.6	31	254.7	36	7.2	34	219.2	36	4	10
Devonshire	14.0	36	284.5	39	10.6	40	284.5	30	8.1	38	252.2	38	6.7	39	208.4	41	4	11
Cornwall	16.5	29	294.0	23	14.8	24	287.7	23	11.2	22	262.0	24	8.6	24	219.6	35	7	12
Somersetshire	13.3	39	293.0	26	11.3	39	292.0	15	7.4	41	267.6	16	6.0	41	221.0	34	2	19

Gloucestershire	12.9	40	285.7	34	11.6	37	281.5	34	8.2	37	259.3	27	6.3	40	224.6	28	3	7
Herefordshire	21.4	13	285.6	35	19.0	7	279.2	36	13.4	11	272.3	8	11.2	9	235.0	16	6	28
Shropshire	28.2	2	302.7	8	21.8	3	286.8	26	16.6	3	275.3	6	12.8	2	257.0	6	1	20
Staffordshire	24.6	5	320.2	2	19.4	6	311.1	1	14.5	6	298.7	3	11.2	9	270.1	3	4	2
Worcestershire	16.3	30	296.6	16	13.7	28	288.3	21	9.2	33	268.2	15	7.2	34	239.0	11	6	10
Warwickshire	14.9	33	291.5	29	13.2	31	287.3	25	9.7	30	264.5	20	7.6	29	243.2	9	4	20
Leicestershire	19.9	17	300.6	10	16.1	17	295.0	10	11.4	19	268.4	14	8.6	24	232.7	18	7	8
Rutland	18.1	25	295.9	19	12.7	33	297.9	9	7.9	40	258.5	28	7.2	34	227.5	25	15	19
Lincolnshire	22.3	10	293.4	25	18.5	8	284.1	32	14.2	8	255.3	30	12.2	5	228.3	22	5	10
Nottinghamshire	24.5	6	285.6	35	21.7	4	287.8	22	15.4	4	260.5	26	12.7	3	242.9	10	3	25
Derbyshire	22.5	9	296.6	16	17.7	15	293.2	14	12.8	14	270.8	10	10.0	15	243.9	8	6	8
Cheshire	17.5	26	292.8	28	14.2	26	286.0	28	10.3	27	266.9	18	7.7	28	230.8	19	2	10
Lancashire	16.2	31	297.1	15	13.6	29	285.0	29	10.2	29	264.3	21	7.9	27	233.7	17	4	14
Yorkshire, W.R.	20.4	16	293.0	26	16.1	17	272.7	42	11.4	19	249.3	40	9.4	17	223.0	31	3	16
Yorkshire, E.R.	23.0	8	281.9	40	18.2	9	274.9	39	14.3	7	258.1	29	12.2	5	238.7	12	4	28
Yorkshire, N.R.	27.7	3	313.6	3	20.2	5	304.2	4	15.4	4	274.5	7	12.1	7	260.4	5	4	4
Durham	24.0	7	324.1	1	18.0	10	307.9	3	13.8	10	299.7	2	11.1	11	282.7	2	4	2
Northumberland	21.1	14	313.0	4	17.9	12	300.1	7	12.4	16	290.0	4	10.2	13	266.8	4	4	3
Cumberland	29.2	1	311.8	5	23.9	1	309.7	2	18.6	1	288.6	5	12.3	4	256.5	7	3	5
Westmorland	21.9	12	305.9	6	17.9	12	300.2	6	13.1	12	267.4	17	8.6	24	218.9	39	12	33
Monmouthshire	18.6	23	304.1	7	15.9	19	298.7	8	11.3	21	304.6	1	10.2	13	283.5	1	10	7

Source: reports of the Registrar General.

Table 1.7: Locality persistence values of illegitimate and legitimate fertility, with cross correlations, 43 English counties

Data of table 1.6

Rank-order correlations (Spearman's r_s)

	Illegitimate fertility rates (a) 1871	1881	1891	1901	Legitimate fertility rates (b) 1871	1881	1891	1901
1871–2 (1871)	1.0	.97	.96	.91	1.0	.68	.73	.49
1880–82 (1881)		1.0	.96	.90		1.0	.71	.44
1890–92 (1891)			1.0	.95			1.0	.77
1900–1902 (1901)				1.0				1.0

One tailed test: all significant at 0.01 or less, those in (a) at 0.001 or less.

(c) Cross correlations

		Legitimate fertility rates 1871	1881	1891	1901
Illegitimate fertility rates	1871	.49**	.29	.54**	.60**
	1881	.46	.25	.55**	.58**
	1891	.43**	.19	.51**	.58**
	1901	.36*	.13	.47**	.62**

Two tailed test: * significant at .05
** significant at .01 or less

Note: For Spearman's r_s, see Siegel (1956), pp. 202–13. The statistic measures correlation between two sets of rankings: plus one indicates perfect agreement and minus one perfect reversal of ranks. A value of zero indicates no relation.

multiplier which depends only on the time period.' In the case of legitimate fertility, variation becomes much more understandable when we add or subtract these factors than when we multiply.

Mr Oeppen suggests that this contrast may be due to the fact that the differences between English counties in illegitimacy levels were narrowing over those years, although their rank order was being preserved. Such a conclusion is borne out by the figures which he has calculated for what is called the coefficient of variation; this gets less over time. It may also help to explain why temporal influences predominated more clearly in England than elsewhere. Ours was already a very homogeneous country, at least in respect of overall fertility, by the 1870s, and the persistent differences between counties were no longer narrowing, which makes the additive model more appropriate. This homogeneity in respect of fertility is a feature that distinguishes England from the rest of Europe in the nineteenth century and has recently been noted by Ansley Coale (1979). But this was not yet so much the case with illegitimate fertility; hence the superiority of the multiplicative model in explaining variation in its values.

The third statement is rather more straightforward. Taken together, space and time account for nearly all the differences in the various values in the data set. There is very little room left for two other sources of variation, which might have had to be reckoned as responsible at least in part for the differences between these values; these are random effects and error in recording. The figure for R^2, which in analysis of variance exercises of this kind measures how well the chosen model fits, how little is therefore left to be explained, will be seen from table 1.15 in the appendix to be as high as 0.98 for illegitimate fertility on the multiplicative model, and 0.94 for legitimate fertility on the additive model. Mr Oeppen comments on these values that they 'demonstrate the unexplained element in the figures to be very small'. Indeed a figure of 1.0 would have indicated that nothing whatever was left to be explained after the effect of time and place had been calculated.

To appreciate this statement properly we must recognize how unusual it is to find two sets of influences such as time and place accounting for so high a proportion of the variance. We must also bear in mind the tenour of so many discussions of illegitimacy and its changes over time, its variation by locality. Any modification of familial behaviour in a county would seem likely to affect bastardy and we have referred to some of them already. A flow of migration in or out; a religious revival or decline, confined to a county or group of counties; a depression bearing hard on certain industries in certain places – all these things would be classed as unexplained by the models used in the exercises we have undertaken, unexplained that is to say by time and place and so put down as residual, a random outcome.

So indeed would vagaries in registration. This elementary statistical exercise upon a succession of illegitimacy recordings in a particular country at a time when the efficacy of civil registration was high, but certainly not thought to be perfect, shows that very little can possibly have been missed. This was not a conclusion which we had expected, but it is of considerable significance in view of the widespread disposition of critics to put down the variability of illegitimacy figures to the unreliability of the records.

Our space-time analysis of variance, then, leaves very little room for effects of an error-like character. It directs our attention quite firmly to the generally prevalent level of bastardy as the most important element in elucidating the departure of any illegitimacy figure from the average one way or the other, the generally prevalent temporal trend, that is to say, taken along with the obstinately persistent pattern of localities in respect of sexual nonconformism.

The facts and figures which have been set out and discussed must modify any attempt to account for general developments in bastardy and its comparative history. If, for example, we suppose that the fall in illegitimacy going on in England between 1871 and 1901 was brought about by an intensification of familial control, perhaps with increasing use of contraception by single persons – the temporal trend, then we should have to remember that these influences were modified in such a way that the relative position of all counties in the country remained substantially the same from decade to decade, and over the whole period – the influence from locality. We are, moreover, prevented from supposing that the effect can have been due to decline in the completeness of records. The same set of statements, we remember, might apply to any change in illegitimacy level at any time in the history of our country, and, to a lesser extent, to changes in legitimate or total fertility as well. Other European countries can be similarly examined, with almost identical results. This is made apparent as to locality persistence values in table 1.8, where figures are given for these values in relation to illegitimate fertility for four further countries in the nineteenth and twentieth centuries. They are all of the same high order as for England, and all as highly significant, except only in Italy where there is a marked falling off as the period proceeds. Locality persistence values for marital fertility (not given in the table), though fairly substantial everywhere, are consistently lower than for illegitimate fertility in each of the countries, just as they are for England. This greater persistence by locality in illegitimate fertility, we may remark in passing, is not borne out in Scotland.

Table 1.8: Locality persistence values in illegitimacy rates, various countries in Europe, nineteenth and twentieth centuries

	Sweden, 24 units					Germany, 66 units			
	1811/20	1841/50	1871/80	1901/10		1869/73	1888/92	1908/12	1931/5
1811/20	1.0	.89**	.46*	.34	1869/73	1.0	.90**	.79**	.76**
1841/50		1.0	.56**	.46*	1888/92		1.0	.94**	.91**
1881/90			1.0	.92**	1908/12			1.0	.89**
1901/10			1.0		1931/5				1.0
	Portugal, 18 units					Italy, 14 units			
	1890	1911	1930	1950		1870/72	1900/02	1930/32	1960/62
1890	1.0	.85**	.79**	.73**	1870/72	1.0	.81**	.37	.15
1911		1.0	.97**	.91**	1900/02		1.0	.62*	.11
1930			1.0	.94**	1930/32			1.0	.55*
1950				1.0	1960/62				1.0

One tailed test: * significant at .05 ** significant at .01 or less

Note: The Swedish figures come from Frykman (1975), table 1 (numbers of bastards per thousand of population); those for Germany from Knodel, (1974), appendix table 2–1; those for Portugal and Italy from Livi Bacci (1971), p. 74 and (1977), p. 78. The measure in the three Princeton studies is I_h and the units the provinces referred to earlier. The tables have been abbreviated here, about one third or one quarter of the correlations worked out having been printed: some signs of the effects noticed for England in the 1880s are visible in the full output. The Russian figure (see text) for locality persistence in illegitimacy has been calculated from the data contained in A. J. Coale, Erna Härm and Barbara Anderson (1979). The Russian values for 1926 are approximate only, since the Soviet Union has apparently never issued figures for bastardy.

Corresponding outcomes to those for England arising from a space-time analysis of variance are also presented by Mr Oeppen in the appendix. They conform in general to what has been said about our country as to the temporal component dominating the spatial, about multiplication being suited to illegitimate fertility and addition to legitimate, about the relative unimportance of random effects and of error. With error, of course, variable registration is included. These outcomes must then, along with the similarity in locality persistence values, be taken to provide strong confirmation of the statements we have made for England. Our conclusions could therefore be of general application, at least in Western Europe.

It is astonishing in my view that, in such behaviour as this, Western European countries should resemble each other so closely for so long. The table makes one anxious to find out whether Eastern European countries, or extra-European countries, would show the same results. The single outcome of this kind we can report, as this book goes to the printer, is for Russia. Fifty 'counties' of European Russia had an illegitimacy rank order in 1926 which showed a locality persistence value of 0.381 when compared with the rank of those same 'counties' as they had been in Imperial Russia in 1897 (see note to table 1.8). This is a comparatively low value, lower than most European countries for a similar period, but it is highly significant, at 0.001. The idea that the pattern of fertility itself should show marked localism in European countries is quite a familiar one, and there is a well-known story about a Spanish linguist who mistook a fertility map of his country for a linguistic one. No doubt a map of that country, or of any European country, representing its persistent illegitimacy pattern would also have cultural overtones.

There are differences to be seen in table 1.8, of course, between the English figures and those from elsewhere. The Swedish figures do not conform in every respect and in Portugal both illegitimate and legitimate fertility are best explained by an additive model. Illegitimate rates had not yet begun the process of convergence in Portugal which is evident in England and in other countries. The multiplicative model is, then, associated with a narrowing of the strata, to use our geological metaphor. An entirely novel indicator of 'development' may therefore be extracted from these illegitimacy statistics.

We have said that time and place explain rather more than usual in England. It will be seen from the appendix that R^2 is consistently lower for these other countries than for England, and falls to 0.65 for Germany, still a high value, but leaving considerably more room for random effects and error. We still have to discuss correlations between the two forms of fertility in these countries. But we may first take note of the fact that in every case rogue counties seem to have been present, that is localities (the word county perhaps should not be transferred to other European states) whose illegitimacy levels had histories quite different from the general run.

If a rise or fall of over a third in rank order during the period in question is accepted as a definition, then four such counties qualify for the title in England between 1871 and 1901. Table 1.6 shows that Bedfordshire and Hertfordshire fell 16 and 15 places and Huntingdonshire rose 15 places, while the tiny county of Rutland fell 15 places from 1871 to 1891, then rose the same number by 1901. These are contiguous counties and their strange-looking movement invites investigation. In the course of his time-space analysis of variance, incidentally, Kenneth Wachter concluded that Huntingdonshire, Hertfordshire and Rutland did not conform to the general pattern, and that Norfolk, whose particularity we have already singled out, is classified by him along with others as having higher than expected bastardy. Oeppen makes further interesting comments about English rogue counties, and the quality of their aberrations, in the appendix.

The other countries we have studied show similar rogue-county effects. In Germany, two of the 66 localities moved over a third of the possible range between 1869 and 1935. One of them, the district of Konstanz on the southern border, fell continuously from the beginning to the end, losing 35 places. In Sweden three out of 24 localities, and in Italy two out of 16, qualify as rogue counties over the same stretch of years. Portugal does not provide figures before 1890, but between then and 1950, double the length of time for the other countries, four out of 18 'counties' moved through a third or more of the rank order, two of them through half of it. In European Russia rogue counties seem to have been even more common and five out of the 50 moved 35 places or more between 1897 and 1926. In illegitimacy anyway, the great Russian Revolution did accomplish something.

'Rogue counties' do not seem to have been characteristic of marital fertility in any of the countries surveyed, even in Scotland. A glance at the figures of table 1.6

will demonstrate this for England over the restricted period covered.[36] Longer spans of observation reveal, as might be expected, greater modifications of the rank order in illegitimacy, not all of them in the more recent decades. Here the striking movement of London since 1900 may be misleading. The late nineteenth and early twentieth centuries, a period which we have had to adopt because of the availability of evidence, may not have been a time of marked changes as compared with other times.

A general account of the relationship between legitimate and illegitimate fertility might go along the following lines. As overall fertility changed in response to things like the movement of real wages, so did illegitimate fertility, as a sub-set of general fertility. The determinants of how large that sub-set would be in any locality were the enduring characteristics of its particular social structure, its economic ecology and especially its cultural tradition as expressed in courtship conventions. These in general were associated, in a way we shall try to explain in due course, with more illegitimates when general fertility was high, and less when general fertility was low.

The pattern of local cultural and courtship traditions over the whole country would tend to preserve the rank order of counties by illegitimacy level over time, but with some conspicuous exceptions, the rogue counties. To be acceptable as of general significance, this account would have to work for countries other than England. When and where the birth rate was high, the bastardy rate would have to be relatively high. We would therefore expect the correlation coefficients in table 1.9 to be everywhere significantly positive. While this could well be true of England during the years from the 1870s to the 1900s, in spite of what happened in the 1880s, the relationship between general and illegitimate fertility is far more equivocal in other countries. There they sometimes show contradictory movements similar to those which occurred in England in the twentieth century and may have occurred in the sixteenth. Such divergencies could perhaps be

Table 1.9: Cross correlations between illegitimate and legitimate fertility rates in four European countries

England		Germany		Italy		Portugal	
1870–72	.49**	1869–73	−.03	1870–72	−.49		
1880–82	.25	1878–82	−.15	1880–82	−.45		
1890–92	.51**	1883–7	−.20	1890–92	−.43	1890	−.56*
1900–1902	.62**	1898–1902	−.18	1900–1902	−.28	1900	−.56*
		1908–12	−.26*	1910–12	.14	1911	−.76**
		1923–7	−.32**	1921–6	.13	1920	−.51*
		1931–5	−.11	1930–32	.36	1930	−.62**
				1935–7	.38	1940	−.55*
				1950–52	.63**	1950	−.62**
				1960–62	.51*		
43 counties		66 regions		16 regions		18 regions	

Two tailed test: * significant at .05
** significant at .01 or less

All cross-correlations, Spearman's r_s by rank order of localities.

36. Modal rank change 3 for illegitmate, 16 for legitimate fertility; medians 4 and 14. Twenty counties moved 14 ranks or more in legitimate fertility, so that a rogue county has no meaning here.

explained by the development of the courtship intensity model which will be briefly and crudely expounded in the conclusion to this chapter. But much more information and analysis will have to be undertaken before we can put forward a confident view of how legitimate and illegitimate fertility responded to each other and to the influences at play on both of them.

8 Scotland as a case study

Scotland can perhaps be called the classic country in the study of illegitimacy, at least in the English speaking world. When the Registrar General in London addressed himself in Victorian times to the bastardy figures of Great Britain as a whole, he found Scotland an embarrassment because illegitimacy was so high. Scottish administrators, men of affairs and ministers of the kirk were made exceedingly uncomfortable by the 'moral condition' of a country where religiosity and respectability were so much regarded. Hence much literature, which began in the 1840s and continues to the present day.

Christopher Smout's chapter on Scotland is a contemporary contribution to the perennial discussion and its references explore the writings referred to. There are other very recent studies, of which the most important from the point of view of the data is the definitive volume on *Scottish Population History* by Michael Flinn and others.[37] Scotland has the peculiarity that bastards born to couples subsequently marrying are thereby legitimated. What is more some authors, including Ian Carter (see note 37) take the view that registration varied from place to place along with the concept of marriage. But others deny this point, and it seems probable that Scottish bastardy is directly comparable with bastardy elsewhere. Like England and Wales, the cities of Scotland had lower illegitimacy than the countryside for most of the period we shall review. In this interlude in our introduction to the subject of bastardy and its comparative history, Scottish illegitimacy in the later nineteenth century will be used for exemplary purposes.

The comparative figures show that the 'national shame' of Scotland was an exaggeration. As Shirley Hartley's international table makes quite clear (1975, pp. 38–9), that country was never at the top of rank order in Europe as a whole. After the 1880s Scotland's record of illegitimacy was scarcely conspicuous as compared with that of Iceland, Austria, Portugal, Sweden and other Scandinavian countries. In any case after what has been said in the preceding section, there should be no particular surprise that one of the British countries should have persistently, and consistently, had higher illegitimacy than the others, or than Western Europe generally. The actual extent of variation between localities in Scotland was, we shall see, evidently larger than in England but smaller than in Ireland and much smaller than in Portugal. Nevertheless, we fasten our attention here on the persistent pattern of variation in illegitimacy levels in nineteenth- and twentieth-century Scotland because it is so intriguing.

Our discussion will not be burdened with tables since those containing the Scottish evidence are so readily accessible and the calculations we have done upon

37. Part 5, section 4 is a full and informative essay on Scottish illegitimacy since the eighteenth century. Also of great importance to the present text is a chapter in the as yet unpublished Princeton study on *Fertility decline in Britain*, by Michael S. Teitelbaum (1st draft dated September 1977). I am extremely grateful to Mr Teitelbaum for permission to refer to his draft and to quote from it. A lively essay, by Ian Carter, arising out of Christopher Smout's work, appeared in 1977 in the first volume of the *Scottish Journal of Sociology*, pp. 125–35, with a reply by Smout in volume 2, pp. 98–103. Finally Derek Gill reports on a research enquiry into schoolchildren of Aberdeen born in the early 1950s and develops a general position on the topic in *Illegitimacy, sexuality and the status of women*.

them are identical with others set out at length in the preceding paragraphs. The major source is a very detailed body of illegitimacy ratios for each Scottish county for every five-year period starting in 1855 and ending in 1939. This data set is printed as table 5.4.1 on pp. 350–51 of *Scottish Population History* and we have added details of Scottish illegitimacy rates by county in the years 1920 and 1973 published by the Registrar General for Scotland. These are the sources used for the illegitimacy maps of Scotland at four points in time (figure 1.5 (a) (b) (c)). Along with them we have included a diagram (figure 1.6) drawn up in 1860 by one of the participants in the prolonged altercation over Scottish bastardy, which we hope may give something of the flavour of that literature, and set the scene as it was at

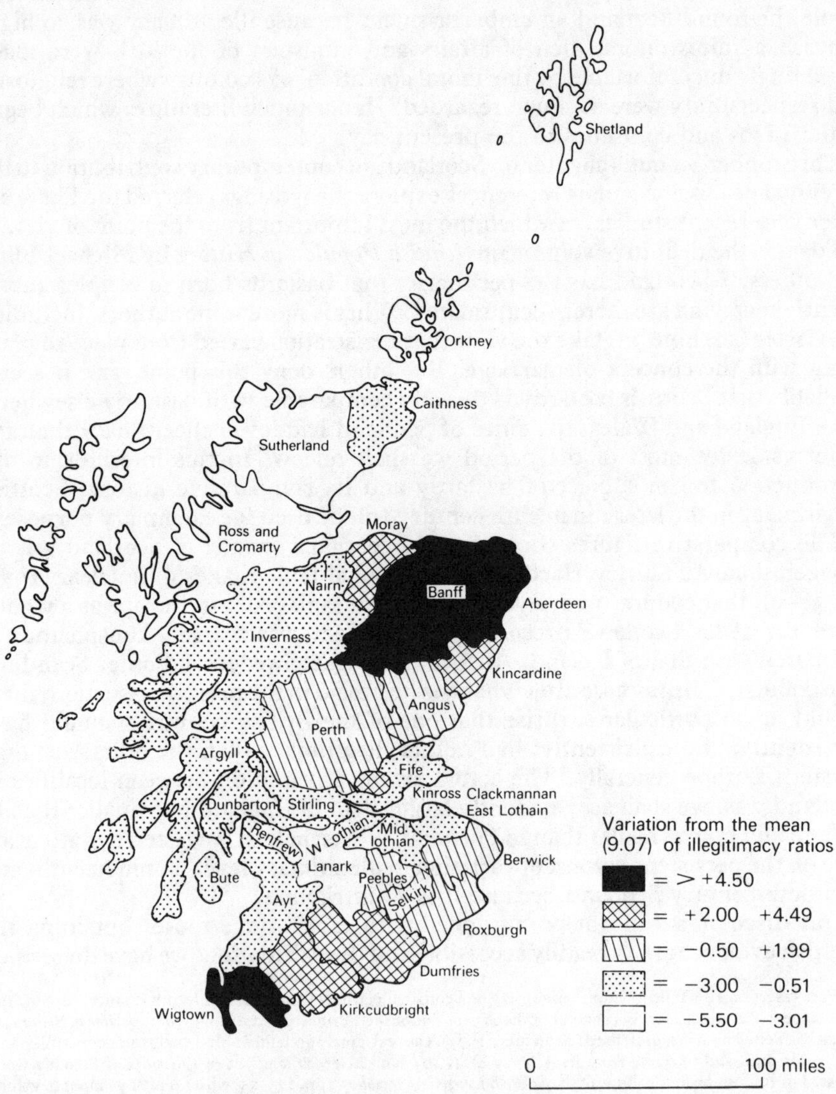

Fig. 1.5 (a) Illegitimacy ratios, Scotland, 1855–60

the time of the first of our maps. These maps may serve to place locality persistence values in a realistic context and warn us against exaggerating their message. There is a fair amount of movement of counties in relative illegitimacy level between 1855 and 1973, and some between each of the points of reckoning. Nevertheless, the locality persistence values which can be derived from the 578 entries in the Scottish table are impressive enough, in spite of the crudity of the ratio as a measure. They represent the most detailed set of such statistics which we have been able to work out for any country over so lengthy a lapse of time. Every one of the 136 locality persistence values comparing rank orders at various dates between the 1850s and the 1930s is significant at 0.01 or less, excepting only that

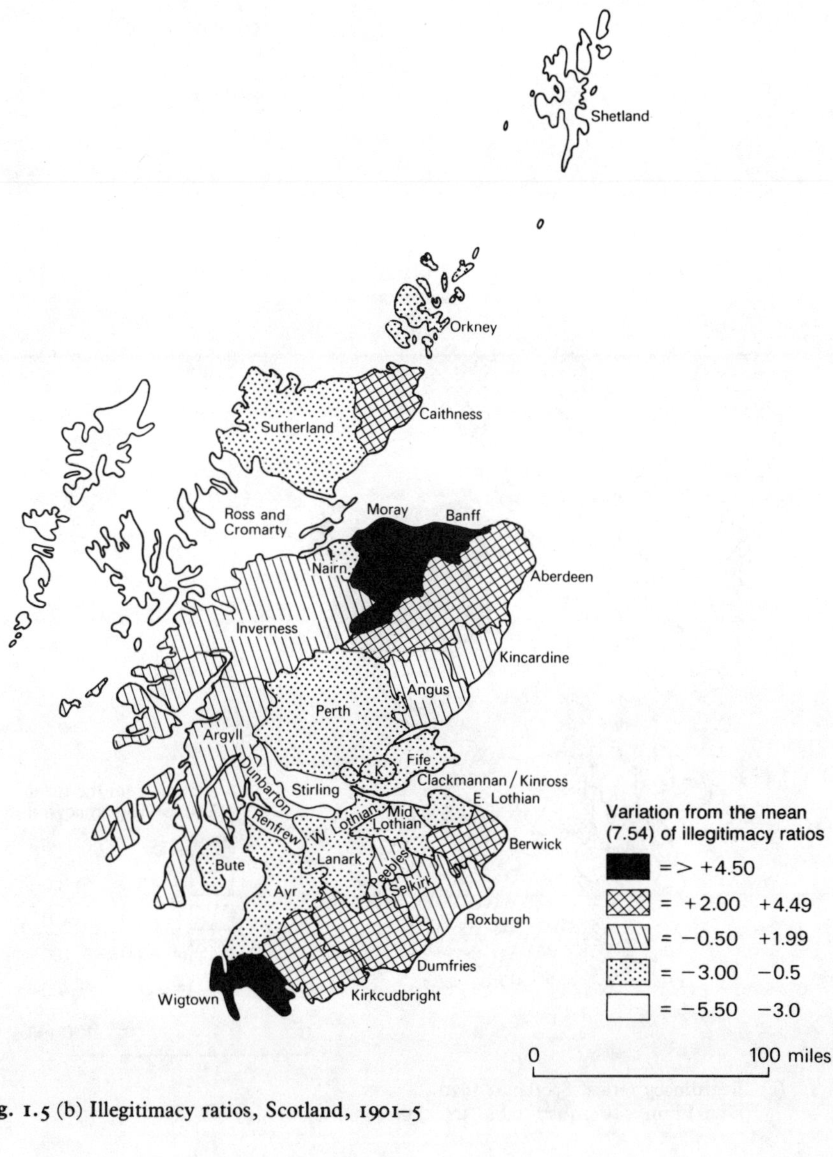

Fig. 1.5 (b) Illegitimacy ratios, Scotland, 1901–5

relating to the two furthest separated from each other in time, that is 1856–60 and 1936–9: this is significant at 0.05. No less than 117 of the locality persistence values exceed 0.70, that is imply rank orders which are at least 50 per cent efficient in predicting each other. The locality persistence value for rates between 1920 and 1973 is 0.36, also significant at 0.05.

Although there was some wavering in the 1920s, these are very striking results. They amplify and confirm for Scotland what we hope can be regarded as established for England and the other countries we have examined. This is that local patterns of illegitimacy survived all the changes or urbanization and industrialization going on in the late nineteenth century, and even in the earlier twentieth

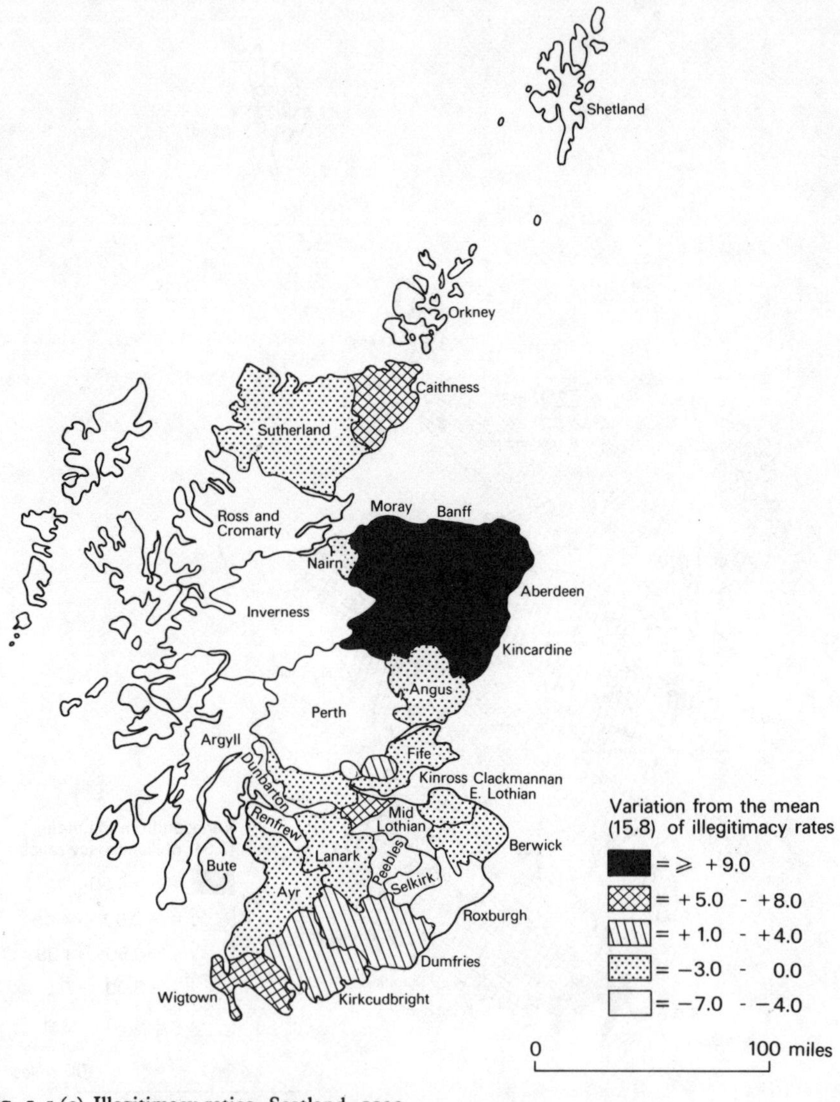

Fig. 1.5 (c) Illegitimacy ratios, Scotland, 1920
(after Flinn *et al.*, 1977, table 5.4.1, pp. 350–1)

century. Local differences were narrowing nevertheless. Hence, as the appendix shows, the multiplicative model suits its figures best. Furthermore most of the differences are associated with temporal and spatial influences, very little with interaction between them and with error or uncertainty.

Scotland was, however, different from England and other countries in two particulars. The spatial variable was more conspicuous than the temporal in the space-time analysis of variance and locality persistence values were higher for legitimate than for illegitimate fertility. Indeed, legitimate fertility was more stable by locality over time than anywhere else. Once more our ignorance as to the relationship between these two variables makes it impossible to suggest why this

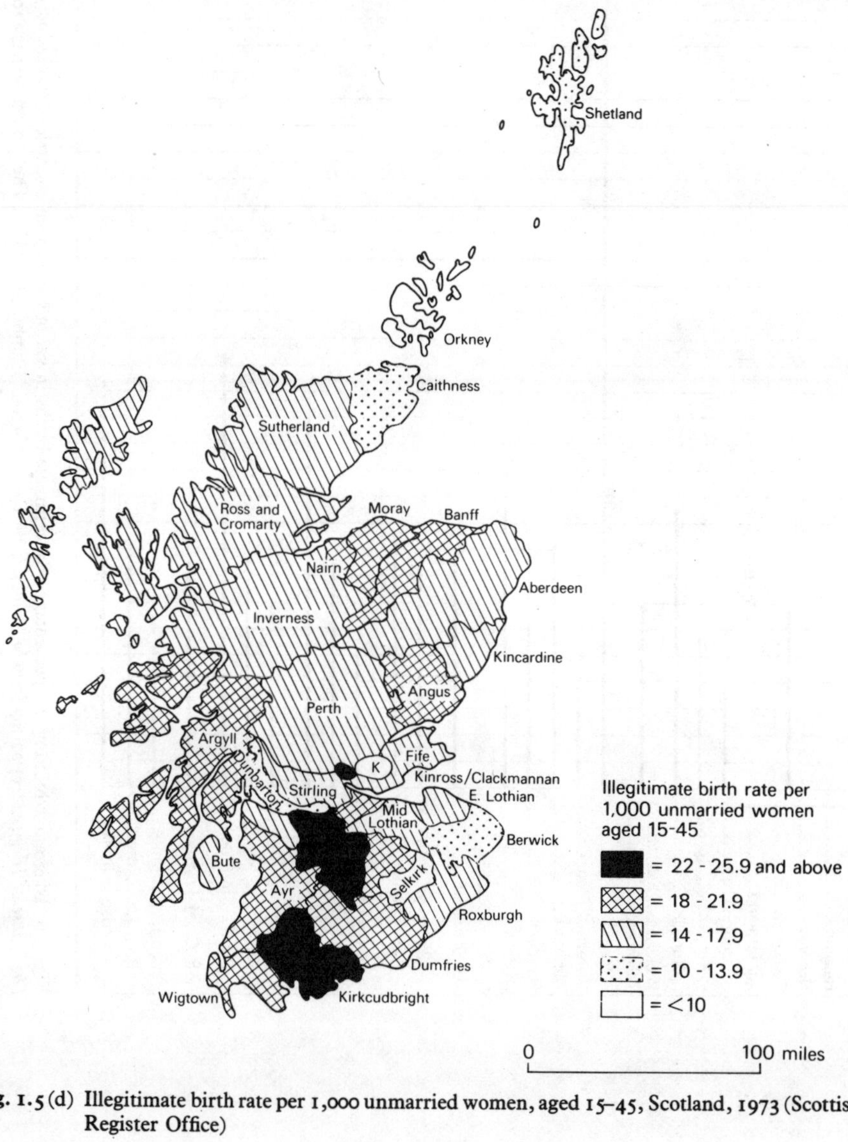

Fig. 1.5 (d) Illegitimate birth rate per 1,000 unmarried women, aged 15–45, Scotland, 1973 (Scottish Register Office)

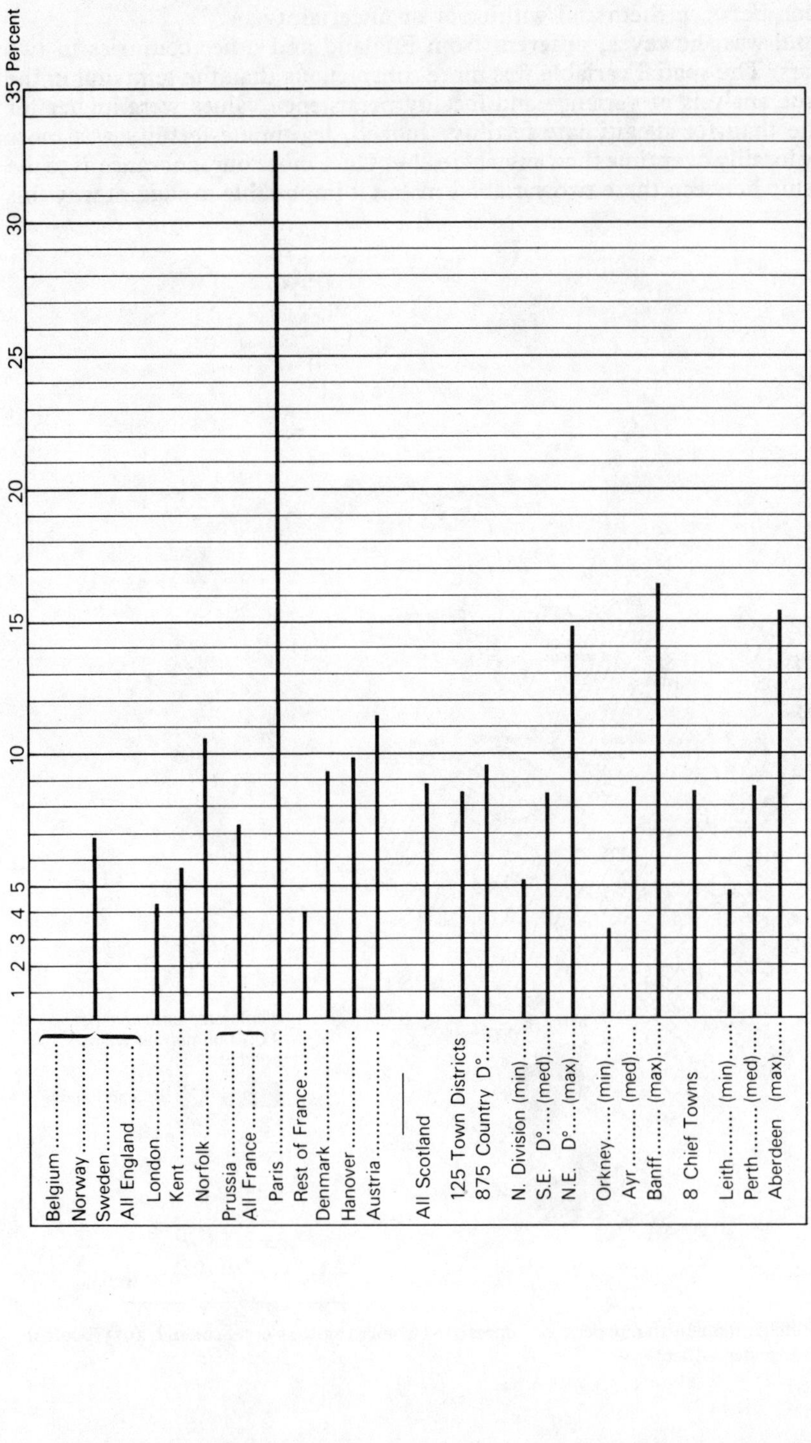

Fig. 1.6 'Diagram exhibiting the percentage of illegitimate births in various European countries', reproduced from *The Cause of Illegitimacy, particularly in Scotland*, by George Seton (Edinburgh, 1860). The passage on page 10 shows that many of the illegitimacies belonging to Leith were attributed to Edinburgh.

difference existed. It seems to have been part and parcel of the demographic individuality of Scotland. In the view of Michael Teitelbaum, the historian of Scottish fertility in the British Isles (see note 37), the border between Scotland and England, the political boundary, that is to say, has been in some respects a boundary for demographic behaviour as well.

Scottish counties can be small in area as will be seen in the maps, and small in population too. Caithness, Nairn and West Lothian had only a few thousand inhabitants in the 1860s and their numbers had not grown a very great deal at the later dates. Yet the contrast between these little areas and their neighbours is often very pronounced, certainly as striking as the perduring large area, or provincial pattern in bastardy in Scotland. This provincial pattern separates low values to the north and west (the Western Highlands and Islands) from high values to the south and east, an overall division which is paralleled in Germany, as Knodel shows, and in many other countries. In the province of high illegitimacy there are very pronounced peak levels on the peninsula to the upper right – the counties of Moray, Banff and Aberdeen, and on the opposite peninsula to the lower left, Wigtown, Kirkcudbright and Dumfries. Very high levels persisted in these counties all the way through from the 1850s to the 1970s, though with some variation.

Enduring micro-localism as distinct from provincial difference is well illustrated by the counties situated at its waist. We take this as a line running east-west through Glasgow and Edinburgh. These are the two major Scottish cities which throughout this period and especially towards the end contained most of the population of the country. The six counties on this line can be seen to have had very varying illegitimacy, which persisted tenaciously over time. In spite of the fact that the two great Scottish conurbations were perpetually growing during the century and a quarter, this process failed before our own day to obliterate the original close-set illegitimacy pattern of the region in which they are situated.

But it has to be added that in the most recent decades Glasgow has behaved like London. In the 1850s the ratio in Glasgow was the sixth in order out of those for the eight largest towns, and below the national average. Illegitimacy in that city has become so high in this century, however, that, considering its relative size, most of the bastards now being born in Scotland may originate there. This does not of itself affect the regional pattern elsewhere.

Even more interesting in some ways is the position and history of the little county of Caithness at the top of the peninsula otherwise consisting of the much larger (geographically larger) counties of Sutherland, and Ross and Cromarty. Though there are intriguing possibilities of differences in genetic inheritance in the population of Caithness, it cannot be claimed that its economic ecology departed in any notable way from that of the rest of the peninsula. Yet Caithness had an illegitimacy ratio pronouncedly higher than that of the rest of the peninsula, from the 1850s up to the year 1915, frequently twice as high. This county, or its operative areas from the point of view of illegitimacy, was still above the others in the late 1930s.

After this time there was a reversal, for Caithness became what we call a rogue county, falling in its illegitimacy rate through 24 places in the rank order (from sixth to thirtieth) between 1920 and 1975. We may well ponder what it was that kept this little enclave so much higher for so long, and what has supervened in recent years to bring its level down so markedly, apparently independently of the history of its neighbours.

Such persisting illegitimacy frontiers marking off small populations can be found elsewhere in the British Isles, and by inference they must have existed in other European regions. Similar conspicuous changes of level between small areas certainly existed in Ireland at the same time as we have traced them in Scotland. This is in spite of the fact that the rate of Irish illegitimacy was then, and still is, one of the lowest in Europe, though it has risen in the present century.[38]

England and Wales had a pattern similar to those of the other British countries, with an overall division northwest/southeast. But it was, and is, a not very conspicuous pattern, and there are only a few signs of the sort of thing which has been described for Caithness and which might be called micro-insularity. Taken without Wales, England itself is the least interesting of the British countries in these respects. Nevertheless Nottinghamshire, a county of consistently and persistently high level in a region of middling ones, would seem to show micro-insularity to some extent. There are also some rogue counties in England, as we have seen.

Germany and Belgium had coefficients of variation of the order of the Scottish at about the same time, but Portugal by the 1960s had a very much higher one. This may well imply micro-insularity in all three countries and certainly shows that the character of illegitimacy in Scotland was by no means exceptional in the European world, in spite of its conspicuousness in the literature on bastardy.

9 Reliability and meaning of the records

Little, indeed nothing, persuasive would follow from what purports to be an analysis of the comparative incidence of illegitimacy unless we are aware of how far the records used can be taken as reliable. Before we attempt a brief conclusion to this introductory chapter we must tackle a problem facing all students of the subject, the problem of deciding how far the changes observed were changes in the habit of registering illegitimate births rather than changes in their frequency. In doing so attention has to be fastened on the only file of evidence which can be well enough known to an Englishman for the purpose at issue, that is the English record itself.

In 1538 Thomas Cromwell, Henry VIII's Vicar-General, required the keeping of 'a register wherein he shall write the day, and the year of every wedding, christening and burying' in every parish in the kingdom. No mention whatever was made of the status of babies to be baptized, legitimate or illegitimate. Yet in the register of Branfield in Suffolk it is recorded at the end of the year following, in 1539, that 14 children were christened, 'whereof men children 11, whereof bastards 2, women children 3'. This is a bastardy ratio of no less than 14 per cent, but the sex ratio is odd enough for us to wonder whether it is a genuine, exhaustive reckoning. Bastardy certainly interested the early sixteenth-century parson at Branfield, whatever the government intended by its decree.[39]

38. For Irish illegitimacy see the figures in Teitelbaum (1977), showing high regional (provincial) differentiation and high locality persistence in spite of low absolute levels. Sean Connolly, of the New University of Ulster, in a typescript in course of publication, 'The chastity of the Irish reconsidered', gives figures for illegitimacy ratios and for prenuptial pregnancy for a small group of Irish parishes going back into the eighteenth century. They confirm a relatively modest level in both series, but not the complete absence of sexual irregularity often supposed.

39. The quotations are from J. C. Cox, *The parish registers of England* (1910), pp. 2 and 72. It is not yet possible to say how many English registers recorded bastardy and when they began to do so. We may be able to decide these things by means of an enquiry through our volunteers.

No subsequent registration ordinance of the British government in relation to ecclesiastical registration seems ever to have mentioned illegitimacy, certainly not by way of commanding the recorder to describe bastards as bastards. Nevertheless, by the end of the sixteenth century, and perhaps almost as soon as the process of registration got fully established, baptisms were being classified by legitimacy in very many parishes and the practice was fairly generally accepted as the regular thing. It is a little puzzling that recording of bastardy never became universal, but this does not of itself imply that where it was carried out it was incompletely done. Perhaps the contrary.

We can take the voluntary character of the recording of illegitimacy as a pointer to the importance to the recorders, and to the local societies where they belonged, of the status of the newborn and hence of the likely reliability of what they set down. This almost instantaneous development coming after the institution of registration in the mid sixteenth century in England makes very dubious the supposition that at previous periods no stigma at all attached to bastard bearers or to bastards, a supposition which is often confidently repeated.[40]

It is true that we have little knowledge of the precise attitude to illegitimacy of the ordinary villagers of England before 1538. We cannot be certain how far spurious offspring were noted, or whether bastardy proneness marked out the repetitive offenders, their offspring and descendants in the way which is hinted at in chapter 8. But we can be confident that officials, secular and spiritual, disapproved of bastardy. Church court records going back to the fourteenth century recite the whippings and humiliations inflicted on errant mothers; irregular children could not inherit at any social level, not as of right that is, and the manorial fine of *childwyte* proclaimed that extra-marital procreation was punishable in medieval English villages. 'Bastard' and 'whoreson' were terms of opprobium from before 1500, for they are Middle English expressions.

It seems likely that it was the notorious who got themselves into trouble with the church and the law, rather than the unfortunate victims of broken courtships. For it was the representatives of village opinion, the churchwardens, who did the reporting. At much earlier periods in the history of our island, in Anglo-Saxon times, it is possible that there was a more indulgent attitude. But I have yet to see convincing evidence to show that the earliest English people went so far in that direction as the Japanese. In the late thirteenth-century Pyrenees, where extra-marital intercourse and bastards were commonplace, even homosexuality between consenting males, and where the village priest seemed to heighten his status by his amours with his parishioners, illegitimacy still brought shame with it.[41] Since bastardy mattered, although if the degree to which it mattered could have varied from class to class, time to time and place to place, then there was a motive for distinguishing legitimates from illegitimates when baptisms came to be recorded. This was so even in cases where the bastard bearer was regarded in the village as simply unfortunate.

40. See, for example, Gill (1977), p. 204, quoting Ivy Pinchbeck, 'Social attitudes to the problem of illegitimacy' (1954).

41. On *childwyte* see the appendix to chapter 9 (p. 242) and its references, and on medieval Pyrrenean society see E. Le Roy Ladurie, *Montaillou, village occitan de 1294 à 1324* (1975), translated in a shortened form as *Montaillou* by Barbara Bray (1978). Prenuptial pregnancy was punished by conscientious parsons until the 1640s in England and in Scotland until much later, once more probably in scandalous cases only, though we have no information on this point from before the sixteenth century. It is not easy to see how far bastardy was a matter of reproach among the Anglo-Saxons from such discussions of medieval marriage as that by Jean Scammell, 'Freedom and marriage in medieval England' (1974), pp. 523–37.

The sanction for the accuracy of our figures, therefore, is that body of local opinion which had to be respected by the parson or the clerk when it required that the shame of bastardy be allocated fairly. We have to suppose that this was done reasonably consistently between parishes and over time but not necessarily always so as to catch every illegitimacy. We must notice, however, that the relationship between the efficiency of recording and the extent of the practice being recorded may be paradoxical.

For we usually have no means of knowing, from the register itself, whether a higher proportion of baptisms marked as of bastards was due to the larger number of such events to record or to greater conscientiousness in the recorder. This is a concern which we should expect would go with a determination to stamp the practice out. Our difficulties do not end here because registration, lax or severe, careless or meticulous, is not itself the final issue: it is rather consistency or inconsistency of registration. Such inconsistency, moreover, would have to affect the ratio of illegitimate to all births; irregularity in registering baptisms as such is not in question.

If under-recording in this sense had been consistent everywhere and at all times, the effects described in this volume would still remain. But if varying degrees of under-recording of illegitimates in interplay with varying incidence of the offence produced the patterns which are here presented, our statistics would not be of much value as evidence of social behaviour. Although it certainly cannot be demonstrated in principle that the results set out in this introduction, for example, did not arise in this entirely artificial manner, common sense seems to dictate otherwise.

Let us consider for a moment what we should be obliged to believe if this had not been so during the late eighteenth century. Almost every parish clerk in England would have had to find himself compelled by conscience or community opinion, or by both, to set down as illegitimate more and more each year of those births which were in fact of that description. They would have had to have acted in unison, so as to produce that national increase which we have found, not only in England but all over Europe. In the early seventeenth century they would all have had to have done the opposite, omitting to record illegitimacies as such in the same progressive, but downwardly progressive fashion. At both periods, moreover, they would have had to have done all these things in such a way as to bring about that measured and regular movement over time which has been described.

The deliberate course of the bastardy curve does much in itself to inspire confidence that changes in behaviour are at issue, rather than vagaries in recording. For these would surely have given rise to a much more erratic graph. The correlations, positive and negative, which have been established with other changes decidedly confirm this impression. Is it likely that degrees of negligence in recording can have produced the relationships which we have worked out between figures for illegitimacy and those for prenuptial pregnancy, age at marriage and so on during the English parish register era? The minute amount which had to be left for error in analysing variance in our chosen samples of illegitimacy figures from the civil registration era in a number of countries makes such improbabilities seem even greater.

The sensible assumption would seem to be that registration was in general, over groups of places and decades of time, capturing a good proportion, though by no means all, of the numbers of children born outside marriage. This is not of course to suppose that at particular places and at particular times the real totals of events we should so much like to have were actually put down, or that the proportion which were recorded never varied as parson succeeded to parson, clerk to clerk, generation (and state of opinion) to generation (and state of opinion). Nor does it mean that changes in national policy as to the recording of births, marriages and deaths had no effect on the illegitimacy ratios which can be calculated from them.

A ratio, of course, is less susceptible to variation in the totals put down in the register than figures for births or baptisms themselves: more or fewer of these may be set down, but the clerk may still be marking those which are spurious. Nevertheless, on the two occasions when an act of the English parliament had the effect of tightening up recording, the so-called Marriage Duty Act passed in 1694 and Hardwicke's Marriage Act of 1753, there was a perceptible jump in the annual number of bastards contained in our 98-parish sample. Anthea Newman has found this happening at Ash in 1754, as she states in chapter 4. When we look at the graph of five-yearly totals in figure 1.2 a distinct lump is evident in the late 1690s, but the ratio seems already to have been rising so fast in the 1750s that no such effect is visible. These events, in fact, seem to have interrupted the long-term temporal trend, but not to have determined its pace or direction. This may also encourage us to suppose that, whilst there was persistent, perhaps reasonably consistent, under-registration, it need not be thought of as affecting, in a sample like the one we have used, more than a fairly small proportion of the bastardies.[42]

An assumption that our figures measure a good part of the incidence of illegitimacy should not be taken, of course, to mean that they also indicate anything like the same proportion of sexual intercourse outside marriage, or do so with the same very rough consistency. This last question has been much discussed. The general opinion seems to be that such registrations constitute a rough guide to the varying extent of illicit love, but only when the proper allowances are made. These allowances are differences in the chances of impregnation, due to age and experience, to physiological condition, that is health, diet and so on, and

42. It seems doubtful whether such considerations as those set out above will convince such a determined sceptic as Christopher Hill (review of *Family life and illicit love, Economic History Review*, 1978, pp. 451–3). He assumes an extraordinary naiveté in the users of figures derived from the parish registers as indicators of illegitimacy, or indeed of any demographic change. But he shows a remarkable obtuseness in his own handling of the many discussions of parochial registration which he cites. None of the authors rejects such materials entirely, as Hill seems to want to do, and all of them end by accepting such figures within the limitations which they attempt to specify and allow for.

It might not seem worthwhile to pursue such offhand and peremptory criticisms any further, but the misleading character of Hill's assertions requires some comment, since statements of this kind are often influential. He bases part of his case on a phrase from Laslett (1977), pp. 56–7, as if it referred to illegitimacy figures, which it most decidedly does not. He quotes P. E. Razzell (*Population Studies* XXVI, 1972) as suggesting that 'up to one third of all births were never recorded in the parish registers', as if the whole parish register era were in question. In fact only the late eighteenth- and early nineteenth-century interlude was intended by Razzell, whose extreme claim about registration of baptisms at that time does not survive E. A. Wrigley's article on the topic in the same journal in 1975. The known inferiority of recording during those years can have affected only that part of our English bastardy curve when illegitimacy was at its highest. But this will have happened, as we have seen, only if the *ratio* of illegitimate to all baptisms was downgraded or upgraded when baptisms in general were incompletely recorded. This is a point which Hill does not seem to appreciate.

A statement in Laslett (1977), p. 115, that the shape of the graph then published 'can be accepted as representing with rough and ready accuracy the objective story of bastardy levels at least from the 1580s to the 1800s' appears as follows in Hill's text. Laslett 'writes as though the *pronounced dip in the number of registered illegitimate births between 1643 and 1660* represents "with rough and ready accuracy the objective story of bastardy levels in England" ' (my italics). This looks like wilful distortion. As for the attribution to me of a view which I do not hold, that it was the Puritans who brought about the fall in illegitimacy in the middle of the seventeenth century, this can be left to the statements on the subject made by Alan Macfarlane in chapter 2, and by Keith Wrightson in chapter 6. Macfarlane's discussion of the completeness of parish register recordings of illegitimacy when checked against other sources, like those of the church courts, is relevant in this context.

even to the season of the year. Even if all this could be effectively done, there remains a further question, a question of some complexity, as to what precisely these entries in the registers can be taken to record, especially in the case of bastardy. For proportions of such entries go to make up measures of the extent to which people were willing to allow a whole series of things to happen, mostly to themselves, rather than measures of the frequency with which acts risking irregular impregnation in fact occurred. Here we begin to realize that issues of registration are not distinct from issues of nonconforming behaviour: they involve each other.

There was a succession of stages between initiation of sexual contact and the writing down of the tell-tale words in the book, a succession which was the same within marriage and without. Nearly all these happenings were subject to the choice of the parties, at least to some degree. They could choose on each occasion in the first place whether there should be intercourse, and in the second whether it should be completed without some form of avoidance of conception. They could further resolve whether the pregnancy, if intercourse occurred often enough and regularly enough for it to come about, or if they were 'unlucky', should be allowed to proceed, or be interfered with. If the pregnancy continued, they had to make up their minds whether to get married, if they were free to do so. They, or rather she, since the woman so often acted alone, could also choose whether to dispose of the child after birth. She had to make the further decision as to whether to submit to baptism in a church where she was known, or to baptism at all. This was always provided that the baby lived long enough, at a time when legitimate infantile mortality was so severe and illegitimate often twice as high.

Up to this point all decisions were made by the individual or individuals concerned, none by authority. It must certainly be said that in a high proportion of all cases of illegitimacy and prenuptial pregnancy, not in every one by any means when attitudes to courtship are considered, the first in order of these decisions, the decision to copulate outside marriage, was made in clear disregard of established codes of conduct.

To this extent, but only to this extent, does it seem justifiable to look upon recorded illegitimacy and prenuptial pregnancy as measures of failure in social control, or in morality, to use an older vocabulary. To accept such records as exhaustive accounts of nonconforming acts of procreation begs all the questions about permissible courtship practices and about probabilities of conception. Moreover, it takes no account of the whole series of decisions which came after the first, in the succession which we have spelt out. These further choices had to be made in the negative sense if a bastardy or a prenuptial pregnancy was to get into the register and be counted by the investigator.

The temptation to try to avoid conception had to be overcome, or to try to bring about abortion or infanticide. The mother had also to resist the inclination to abscond, or to evade baptism of the child. Now these subsequent negative decisions were taken in compliance with conscience and the law, not in defiance of them. The evidence of the studies in this book makes it difficult to believe that choices of this kind lacked all reality, that established authority, familial and neighbourhood opinion would always force the intimidated and often helpless girl to conform to the canons of correct behaviour, even though she had gone against them in the first place. This is quite apart from the fact that strategy was at play, husband-getting strategy, which, in disregard of the official rules, might have been the main reason for the decision to risk pregnancy and to refrain from doing anything to interrupt the progress towards public baptism. It is true that freedom to do one thing rather than the other was much less than it is for a woman in our day. But such freedom certainly existed even in the absence of efficient contraception and adoption. If these choices were all being made in the conformist direction, we reach the paradoxical possibility that the more baptisms of bastards set down in the parish register to unmarried girls, the more socially and morally conforming can the parish be said to have been.

Only the last act in the series, that of inscribing the baptism as irregular, could be said to be that of the community. Even this was an act of choice, made by an official subject to opinion and persuasion. Setting down this final outcome of a series of eventualities and decisions seems to be quite distinct from marking out a record of extra-marital intercourse. We can be quite positive, moreover, that such a record is not that of irregular sexual behaviour itself, which takes on such a bewildering variety of forms. Homosexuality, feminine or masculine, bestiality, fetishism and so on are completely unrepresented. There is no evidence to show that the prevalence of such practices varies positively or negatively with the level of illegitimacy or prenuptial pregnancy.

The considerations we have set down apply with modifications to civil as well as to ecclesiastical registration. Civil registration must have been more effective in general, and the case for its exhaustiveness in late Victorian England has already been made. But this is by no means certain for the earlier nineteenth century, and we have seen that civil recorders have made mistakes, mistakes which, as in the case of bastards to married women (see note 10 above) have taken a very long time to disentangle. At the present moment, moreover, it looks as if political authorities will gradually cease to record illegitimacies altogether, for praiseworthy motives of social policy. We may perhaps allow ourselves, as we leave the issue of registration, to express our gratitude to the English ecclesiastical authorities who recorded illegitimacies so faithfully and for such a long time, and have been so frank and free in allowing historical sociologists to consult and analyse them.

10 Understanding illegitimacy in view of its comparative history

Records of illegitimacy and of prenuptial pregnancy, therefore, are records belonging for the most part to courtship and to marriage; hence the slight element of ambiguity in our evidence itself. By way of conclusion we shall develop in a preliminary fashion the suggestion that it is in terms of courtship and marriage, their variations between period and period, cultural tradition and cultural tradition, locality and locality, that we should begin to understand illegitimacy in the light of its comparative history.

This suggestion is decidedly not original with the present writer, and it is owed to a considerable degree to the work on sexual nonconformism of Keith Wrightson and David Levine. In chapter 6 indeed Wrightson expounds the hypothesis in a form quite close to the one we shall try to articulate, though he talks of it strictly in terms of village controls and makes no claim for its wider application. There, and in this chapter with David Levine, are set out most of the considerations which we shall bring forward in support of the hypothesis. Even here, however, we shall not present it as a generalization for the whole of the evidence about sexual nonconformism, not all of which arose during the approach to marriage. This is true at least of European countries to which, for the present anyway, it would be wise to confine our tentative explanatory theory, and to England in particular. The courtship model, I am informed, seems somewhat unlikely to fit the French or the Austrian evidence. Moreover it is very much of a macro-theory, as social scientists say, explaining what happens to whole areas or groups, and tells us very little about what individual persons did and do. The four sets of considerations which can be brought forward in its favour from the historical analyses contained in this volume are as follows.

The first is that pattern of locality persistence which has already been described. The second is the probability that a high proportion of all spouses at all times and in all places had had sexual intercourse before marriage. The third is the fact that extra-marital conception characteristically took place between persons of an age and status to be wedded to each other. The fourth is the inverse relationship which could obtain between age at marriage, an indicator of intensity of courtship, and the level of extra-marital conception. Prenuptial pregnancy is by definition an incident of courtship and much of illegitimacy is regarded as having arisen in the same way.

Marriages, therefore, according to this explanatory venture, had to be paid for in irregular conceptions, bastardies among them. It is the sum of the two which is the important variable from our point of view, a total which went up and down from time to time over the whole population. We cannot yet estimate a cost per marriage, nor explore its regional or temporal variability. Nor can we dwell upon differences in the 'price' of marriage between the mass of the people and the élite. Localities, cultural regions and countries seem to have varied in the proportion of the 'price' paid in prenuptial pregnancies and the proportion paid in bastardy. This proportion may also have changed from time to time.

Notwithstanding the complexities, we shall take the first set of considerations, about courtship patterns and locality persistence in illegitimacy, as already established. The demonstration that illegitimacy varied locally and that such variations obstinately persisted over time, in spite of change in the marital environment, makes it entirely possible that custom in the form of courtship practice was a controlling variable in sexually non-conforming behaviour. Recalling that the extent of differences from place to place diminished as the nineteenth century wore on in England, diminished but did not disappear, let us proceed with the second set.

A general notion of how widespread sexual experience in the bridal pair has always been in England can be gathered from converting illegitimacy ratios, that is proportions of all births which were spurious, into percentages of first births. Estimating for our parish register era that one quarter of all registered births were first births, this multiplies the illegitimacy ratio approximately by four.

We can reckon, therefore, using the figures of table 1.1, that the course of the illegitimacy ratio in England during the two and a half centuries of the parish register era implied an average proportion of 14 per cent of all first born as births of bastards, with a minimum of 4 per cent in the 1650s and a maximum of 22 per cent in the 1800s. To these proportions we have to add those for prenuptial pregnancy set out in table 1.2, so as to make a first approximation of the notional 'price' we have been discussing. About 15 per cent seems to be the lowest general rate for a period of years indicated there, something like 25 per cent the median, and about 38 per cent the highest likely to be found. When we do the addition we see that roughly a fifth (15 per cent + 4 per cent) of all first conceptions in England may have been extra-marital, that the proportion was usually much more like two fifths (25 per cent + 14 per cent) and could easily reach three fifths. It is also obvious that it might be difficult to find any number of years in an English parish when these figures were nil.

These are estimates for one European country only, and they are very crude. Not all bastard births were first births, as we shall see when we come to discuss repetitive bastard-bearing in chapter 8, and we already know that not all conceptions outside marriage occurred to unmarried women. What is more, we should allow for something in respect of women who both had bastards and then married when pregnant. Ann-Sofie Kälvemark's figures in her table show that this proportion could be 3 per cent, which would lower our proportions somewhat. A slightly better set of estimates would allow for these possibilities and take into account the very modest levels which have been found in the eighteenth-century French countryside and the higher ones recorded in the nineteenth century in many places. These suggest a lower bound of some 10 per cent, a higher bound of about 50–55 per cent, with most of the distribution between 20 per cent and 40 per cent.[43]

An approximate idea of how much sexual intimacy took place before marriage is not all we ought to have to make our case.[44] We should also like to know what proportion of all such associations occurred between potential spouses rather than between other, differently situated people. Here we can only make an informed guess – that this proportion must have been high. If it had been otherwise, if every sexually mature individual had been as likely as every other to procreate a bastard, then numbers of them would have been persons very unlikely or in fact unable to get married. Since marriage came so long after maturity in the societies we are concerned with, it would surely have been the case that the procreation of illegitimates would have been common at all relevant ages for both sexes, and most common at the time when fewest were married, that is in the late teens and early twenties.

This brings us to our third set of considerations about the closeness of the connection between bastard begetting and courtship, those to do with ages of parents of illegitimates and with the social symmetry between them. As for ages, we shall have to content ourselves here with the evidence presented in these studies (see especially chapter 3) and elsewhere, which makes it plain that the engendering of bastards was not concentrated between 16 and 25 in women and 17 and 28 in men. These are the approximate intervals separating mean age of sexual maturity from mean age at first marriage in the two sexes. It seems to me a remarkable and significant circumstance that the expected age for a woman to produce a child outside marriage was very much the same as the age at which she would produce her first child within marriage. Not quite so clear cut, but also persuasive in my view, is the fact that most, though by no means all, illegitimacies

43. These allowances are probably too generous, so that the above proportions can be taken as minimal.

44. More accurate estimates of experience before marriage depend upon better knowledge of fecundability as well as upon the extension of the evidence. The regularity and frequency of intercourse is also important. It is clear for example that most of the recorded prenuptial pregnancies must have meant pretty regular association over most of at least one menstrual cycle. If isolated acts are allowed for, especially those occurring close to the wedding, then the evidence permits the supposition, though it certainly does not imply it, that very high proportions of brides were experienced even when prenuptial pregnancy was low. Christopher Wilson is working at the Cambridge Group on these needling problems.

were the outcome of relationships between persons who might have chosen each other as spouses quite apart from age.[45]

The minority of bastardies which arose in situations of social asymmetry, that is from victimization, especially of woman servants, from the keeping of mistresses and from casual encounters between ill-assorted people often strangers to each other, are prominent in the evidence. They have tended to dominate the discussion of it, and their existence is of considerable significance to the understanding of illegitimacy in any society as well as of personal and class relations. But these events must not be allowed to obscure the facts about the great bulk of the births we have to deal with. The English studies in this volume make it clear that the biggest group of illegitimates must be attributed to associations between men and women servants who, in this society, made up a large part of the marriage queue; they were in a sense all waiting for the opportunity to marry each other. The evidence of other countries points in a similar direction. When at last in 1851 we can get figures by county of proportions of servants in England, they show a significant correlation with the bastardy ratio: a county with more servants had more bastards.[46] Even a pregnancy arising from a relationship of a servant girl with her master may be attributable to frustrated courtship: many masters, especially widowers, did marry their women servants, who had often been their concubines. Associations between 'sons of the house' among the families of the Victorian bourgeoisie and the serving maids may have been a different matter, but they account for a very small portion of our evidence. Strong as is the association between service and illegitimacy, its importance is not so much that servant girls, and the men servants with whom they consorted, were likely to produce bastards, as that they were representative of those in the mass of the population who engaged in courtship. It is well known that illegitimacy could be high when servants were few, as in parts of Scotland for example.

There have been commentators, especially those in the Scandinavian countries, who have gone so far as to suppose that 'in old peasant society the arrival of a child seemed to have been the occasion for official marriage.'[47] Otherwise a marriage would not take place. Eilert Sundt, the pioneer of studies of this kind in Scandinavia and in general, certainly made such suppositions as early as the 1850s.

We may regard this as an extreme version of the view that marriage was always literally celebratory, a public declaration and legitimation of an already established fact. Since we have learned to expect considerable difference between countries, something like this might have been true in Norway, but such a

45. See the relevant tables in chapters 2–7 below on age at bastard-begetting, as well as David Levine, *Family formation in an age of nascent capitalism* (1977), p. 137, table 9.1 and Cissie Fairchilds, 'Female sexual attitudes and the rise of illegitimacy' (1978), p. 661, appendix 1, table 4. For social symmetry and asymmetry in bastard bearing couples, see J. Depauw, in R. Forster and O. Ranum, *Family a d society: selections from 'Annales'* (1976), a translation of an article of 1972, and Fairchilds, appendix 2, table 1, etc., with her references, to which must be added her exchange with J. L. Flandrin on these topics in *JIH* IX, 2, pp. 309–21. There are numerous difficulties with the figures and with levels of fecundability at early ages, quite apart from deciding on social asymmetry in partners. For age at sexual maturity in the past, see Laslett (1977), chapter 6.

46. Anne Kussmaul, 'Servants in husbandry in early modern England' (1978) has calculated farm servants as a proportion of the agricultural labour force in 1851 by county (table II.2, p. 45). The rank order shows a significant relationship with the rank order of counties by illegitimacy ratio in 1845, and a positive relationship, though no longer significant, with that in 1871, 1901 and even 1972. This may have the interesting implication that the local bastardy pattern and the presence of servants seem to have been correlated with some more general regional characteristic.

47. Sogner (1978), p. 64. The relationship between customary unions and official marriage, ecclesiastical and civil, appears to have been particularly complex in Norway.

statement would certainly go too far for England. The view is gaining ground, however, that onset of union was often distinguished from date of wedding in that country, more so at some times than at others. In support of this is the interesting fact that seasonality in date of marriage, a fairly pronounced pattern and continuing over time, is only weakly correlated with date of first baptism.[48]

We do not have to suppose from this that pregnancy or the suspicion of it, or the decision that it must be brought about, was a necessary preliminary to marriage. The complications which have been so extensively discussed, as for example in chapter 11 below, about the legitimation of pregnancies and of bastards already born by subsequent marriage, can concern us only in relation to our fourth set of considerations, those to do with the relationship between age at marriage and intensity of courtship.

The assumption here is that when courtship activity became more intense, because earning prospects were improving, or felt to be so, and for other reasons too no doubt, more people succeeded in marrying quickly. The result was a fall in marriage age, and the associated effects of the changes going forward at times when courtship waxed and waned may have been widespread in the society. The intenser the wooing, it would appear, the greater the number of brides pregnant at the altar. This may have arisen to some extent because of what are called compositional effects. Younger women were more often involved in courtship and marriage, and young women had slightly higher prenuptial pregnancy rates than older ones. The same is true of proletarian women, who may also have married more frequently at times of high courtship intensity than at other times.

The more courtships, the more disappointments in courtship, and hence a rise in the numbers of illegitimates. When the climate changed and marriage prospects were felt to be worsening, courtship fell off, age at marriage went up, and sexual nonconformism lessened. In order to demonstrate these effects we may refer once more to the startling opposition evident in figure 1.2: age at marriage for both sexes on the one hand moving against illegitimacy and prenuptial pregnancy on the other hand. It would seem that intensity of courtship, age at marriage and sexual nonconformism all varied together in relation to the prevailing climate of expectations, especially of economic expectations. In England as we have seen, for long periods of time anyway, overall fertility varied in the same way and illegitimacy in close correspondence with it. To make these assertions may therefore help us to understand the whole problem of demographic variation over time, including perhaps the occasional divergence between the course of total and of illegitimate fertility.

But it is important to recognize that this does not imply that numbers of marriages correspond at all closely to numbers of illegitimacies. This is because marriages intervene to prevent prenuptial pregnancies from becoming bastardies, and there are other complications as well. A complete anatomy of the whole process would have to take account of proportions of never-marrying persons and of remarriage, both of which could vary independently, quite apart from vagaries

48. Work of Christopher Wilson, see note 44 above. Sogner, like Tomasson, appears to follow Sundt in supposing that all illegitimacy can be explained in this way and to imply that the object of courtship was fertility testing. This seems inappropriate to England, where the facts appear to have been as follows, at least at the lower social levels. Courtship very frequently implied full intercourse, and when pregnancy was the result marriage was the expected outcome. This allows for courtship not accompanied by intercourse and for pregnancies which did not give rise to marriage.

of marriage registration.[49] The presumed connection, as has been said, is between age at marriage as an indicator of courtship intensity and the proportion of first conceptions which were extra-marital, and this connection cannot yet be investigated in any detail.

To assume that something like avoidance between persons of marriageable age, and otherwise 'eligible', was common when times were felt to be unfavourable to marriage, does not mean of course that the marriage process was interrupted for everyone. Those with secure expectations, those who were lucky in inheritance, those for whom a 'slot' opened at the right time, married and set up their establishments in the ordinary way. The economically secure and superior, especially the landowning, would be largely immune to the unfavourable influences which might inhibit courtship among those below them in the social scale.

These privileged persons were undoubtedly subject to the vicissitudes of the marriage market, which was of enormous significance to them, as I have tried to show elsewhere (see Laslett, in Wachter, Hammel, Laslett and others, 1978, chapter 7). It played an important part in the maintenance of their class superiority over time. We can think if we wish of privileged young men and women in a traditional European society as being in a state of perpetual courtship, which is how they are portrayed in the literature of their group and of their era: always on the lookout for a spouse, always eligible, always liable to make amatory approaches or susceptible to them. So clear and effective were the rules of sexual conduct amongt the élite, however, that this condition of perpetual courtship did not give rise to many illegitimacies, except amongst one particular set of persons. In chapter 8 we call these persons libertines.

But marriage was not an ever-present possibility for young men and women who had no secure expectation of property, and whose chances of founding an establishment were so much affected by economic vicissitudes. It is among these people, the great majority, that the principle of intermittent courtship intensity must be held to have been in operation to the greatest extent. They were not bound so closely to the rules of respectability, nor was the risk of a birth outside marriage anything like as consequential in respect of property. It was because this was the case in the mass of the population, we may suppose, that the relationship between age at marriage and extent of sexual nonconformism could be inverse. When we reach the proletariat, those with no property whatever and very uncertain expectations of settled married life, we may suppose that courtship was scarcely a part of the pattern of behaviour. When a climate set in which favoured courtship generally, however, even the proletariat seem to have played their part, and the number of births outside marriage coming from this source seems, as we shall see, to have increased enormously. No doubt marriage went up too among the proletarians.

Being deprived of sexual expression in the form of courtship did not mean of course that other sexual outlets, as they are called by the experts, were also closed. Masturbation, homosexuality, bestiality, and all the other practices which they have identified, were no doubt present, though subject, we may expect, to a great complication of conventions and traditions, which themselves perhaps varied by

49. No significant temporal correlations between numbers of marriages and numbers of illegitimacies have been found in the English file, with or without lag, though Sundt and others have tried to discover them elsewhere. Some negative correlations have, however, been established between the trade cycle and bastardy levels in the late nineteenth century, with a time lag of three to four years. See D. S. Thomas, *Social aspects of the trade cycle* (1925).

locality. It would seem right to suppose that such flouting of the rules of respectability was perennial. It was linked therefore to age at marriage and proportions marrying only in so far as all overt sexual expression in single persons is an offence against these rules when strictly interpreted. It seems to me to be rather hazardous to judge of the relative prevalence of sexual deviation from changes in the tone of admonitory literature, confessional handbooks, or any source emanating from the respectable themselves, especially the ecclesiastics.[50]

The claim being advanced, then, is that sexual and marital deprivation cannot have been the important reason for the existence of bastardy, and that its variation over time explains very little of the variation in sexual nonconformism. This seems to be the inescapable conclusion from the evidence surveyed, and if a further illustration is wanted, we need only turn to the Irish in the early twentieth century. Marriage was being postponed among them for longer than for any other European people yet investigated, but illegitimacy was lower than anywhere else. The Irish seem to have done it by avoidance, avoidance of courtship.[51]

The range of variation in emotional and sexual attitudes and practices in humans is enormous. If Freud and Jung are to be followed, the whole of cultural life is informed by such manifestations. There are accordingly myriad ways in which the nubile but unmarried can be reconciled to celibate life, or to sexual and marital deprivation, if indeed such terms are justifiable. The contingent, intermittent character of courtship has been only one among them, the social distance maintained between young individuals who were not at any one time 'going with the boys' or 'going with the girls', as they say, or used to say, in English adolescent company. We cannot now go over the intriguing field of courtship practices, imperfectly known as yet for the English but better documented for the Anglo-Saxons in America and for other European societies.[52] What is important from our point of view is that sexual advances did not take place until or unless the conventional cues were given, the cues for courtship. At all other times contact was rare, excessively rare considering the opportunities offered by the crowded conditions under which the two sexes did their work by day and slept at night.

Since the occasions, the character and the content of courtship were so much a matter of the custom and conventions of a country, a county or even a village, we can begin to see how it might be that local cultural patterns could do much to account for persistence by locality in levels of illegitimacy. We may suggest, though we can certainly go no further than this at present, that complementary features of the individual outlook of national societies determined whether concentrations of population should have high illegitimacy, whether that is to say urban levels were above or below rural ones. Micro-localism raises the possibility,

50. Flandrin and such writers as André Burgière, ' "De Malthus à Max Weber": le marriage tardif et l'esprit de l'entreprise' (1972), pp. 1128–38, propose a different view from the above, particularly in respect of France between the sixteenth and eighteenth centuries. This they take to be a time of increased sexual repression because age at marriage had gone up from its low level in the middle ages. On this interpretation, unpersuasive from several points of view, see R. M. Smith, 'Some reflections on the evidence for the origins of the European marriage pattern in England' (1979). For homosexuality in English history, the prevalence of which is as yet hardly broached by historians, see Laslett (1977), n. 148, and Stone (1977), especially pp. 492–3.

51. In 1911 74 per cent of Irish males and 56 per cent of Irish females were single between the ages of 25 and 34 (compare 38 per cent and 36 per cent in England and Wales), yet in 1910 I_h was 0.010, the lowest out of 14 European countries (mean of 0.048). See R. E. Kennedy, *The Irish* (1975), p. 145 and figures in Teitelbaum (1977). I owe to E. A. Wrigley the suggestion of something like avoidance of courtship occasions being characteristic of societies with low nuptiality.

52. See, for example, Shorter (1975), chapter 4 and references; Orvar Löfgren, 'Family and household among Scandinavian peasants' (1974): 'bundling' or 'night courtship' seems to fascinate the commentators.

of course, that a town itself could have its own illegitimacy characteristics, as perhaps Cambridge did in contrast to Cambridgeshire.

We shall return to these questions in our final paragraphs. But courtship attitudes and practices alone may well be thought inadequate as an explanation of what happened amongst the truly nonconforming parts of the population, where women could have groups of illegitimate children born from different men, and where, as will be suggested in chapter 8, something like a market in sexual services may have existed. It is scarcely obvious that variations in the intensity of courtship over time could explain variations in the number of bastards arising in this way. Controls of a different description must have been at issue.

This brings us to the last of the questions we can touch upon in this sketch of a partial interpretation, the question of how far the comparative study of the history of illegitimacy does reveal a system of social control. It is always disconcerting to discover that a special effect due to local circumstances would have happened at that place anyway because something similar was happening everywhere else at the same time. This is implied by the analysis presented here and it has to be accepted that a rise in illegitimacy is not always a reliable indicator of social breakdown, of anomie, of disturbance in familial control, the ability or willingness of the local élite to supervise the doings of the local people, and so on. Nevertheless, the case studies presented here do portray the workings of such mechanisms in individual cases. What is more the temporal regularity of incidence of illegitimacy, and the marked conformity of localities to the national trend, modulated by their own persistent traditions, reveals a general coherence in social structure, an articulated system of internal control, often resistant, as we have seen, even to rapid change.

If social control is interpreted as the exacting of obedience from the whole population to a set of regulations imposed by the ruling ideology, then the issues complicate themselves. We have to decide to begin with how much conformity with the official, in Europe with the supposedly Christian, code of rules, should be expected in order to pronounce control to be complete.

Here cross-cultural comparison does enlighten us to some degree. Nowhere in the European historical record, east or west, was illegitimacy as rare as it is reported to have been in Egypt since the 1940s, for example, where the bastardy ratio never exceeded 0.1 per cent (see Hartley, 1975, table 7, p. 55). To this extent, then, the comparative historical record shows discipline to have been relatively lax in Europe, east and west, and the Christian church, even in alliance with the civil power, far less effective in controlling sexual behaviour than Islam. A great deal more will have to be known, of course, about the definition of illegitimacy in the Arab world, its history, the reliability of its registration and methods by which it has been kept down before this conclusion can be confirmed. The Western European record makes social control so absolutely successful rather difficult to believe in.

The matter does not end here, however. For we have further to decide about illegitimacy and social control·how far that control was a question of maintaining a code of behaviour accepted by everyone, superior and inferior, and how far it was a question of imposing unwelcome regulations on an unwilling population. Whatever may be the situation in contemporary Egypt, it is evident that keeping to the established marital rules in historic Europe was not always obedience to internal promptings, the conscientious adherence to a faith which was universally shared. Under these circumstances having a bastard may have been something of an act of defiance, defiance of authority and of class superiors, even though it may also have been felt as a lapse from virtue. This last is a point of importance. For we must not end by failing to take account of religious conviction, however imperfect ecclesiastical regulation may be as a guide to actual conduct. When it comes to the more markedly deviant, the chronically nonconformist and bastardy prone, the question of suppression becomes more evident, suppression here perhaps of a different, if only slightly different, code of sexual and marital behaviour (see chapter 8, section 5, p. 231).

The meaning in terms of social control of any change in the incidence of sexual nonconformism requires a knowledge of the type of social control in question. This difficult decision has to be made on each occasion and it is peculiarly awkward for the historian, since the men of the past seem scarcely to have been aware of the issues. A courtship theory of illegitimacy, like most of the many others which have been advanced, implies a high degree of opacity in the social structure, of unawareness on the part of most people, even of educated commentators, of what was actually going forward.

Such witnesses never seem to have had any doubt that only one type of control ever had to be considered – control by personal morality. When illegitimacy increased, in their view, it could only have been due to individuals falling short in their religious duty, failing to obey their consciences. Apparently they could not bring themselves to see that what was happening might have been normal to the social structure, that it had occurred before and would occur again. The opaqueness of social relations was evidently strong enough to prevent them from recognizing that social imposition and class control might have to be considered. They interpreted what they saw as a threat to the only possible code of sexual and marital conduct, and as a threat to society itself. The literature about bastardy is full of predictions of the end of the family and of all settled familial relations, even of the decline of the state, because integrity was disappearing from public as from private life.

We may see this, if we wish, as a historical origin of that tradition of interpretation which sees illegitimacy as always being a symptom of a slackening of social regulation, finally of disintegration and decay. Nevertheless it is not difficult to understand why men should be disposed to talk in this way in Paris in the years after 1780 (illegitimacy ratio over 30 per cent), or in the Styrian province of Catholic Austria from the 1830s to the 1860s (ratio of above 50 per cent), or why they might have done so even in the English village of Prestbury in the 1570s (ratio of 13.8–16 per cent).[53] There is something extraordinary in such instances of virtually entire loss of control by the official ideology, when all is said in favour of the general explanations which have been put forward. Even the courtship hypothesis lacks complete conviction when we attempt to account for the fact that in later eighteenth-century England, as Christopher Wilson has shown, the peak of prenuptial conception began to take place further from the marriage day than it had done before. All these difficult issues have to be left open here, including the possible effects in southern Germany and Austria of prohibitions upon the

53. For Styria, W. H. Hubbard, paper to the Social Science History Association, October 1977; for Prestbury, Laslett (1977), p. 145. The highest illegitimacy ratio yet discovered for England is for the parish of St Paul in the Bale just outside the close of Lincoln Cathedral. There between 1800 and 1827, 176 bastards were baptized out of a total of 541 baptisms, a ratio of some 33 per cent: work of Mr William Couth, who points out that most of the illegitimates came from the 'House of industry', which no doubt contained bastard-bearers from outside the parish. I owe to Mr Couth a number of interesting points about illegitimacy between the 1800s and 1870s, especially for the counties of Lincolnshire and Nottinghamshire.

marriage of the poor. But of one thing we can at least be fairly confident. This is that the social and political catastrophes so freely prophesied by men at the time never seem to have come about in fact.

Such must be our final judgement on social control, if only a preliminary and provisional one, and what goes for social control in particular also goes for Malinowski's principle of legitimacy in general. In comparative European history, such as it has been possible to explore in this volume, social survival was apparently scarcely ever in question, in spite of what contemporaries declared, either in terms of perpetuation of the population or in terms of the continued identity of European cultures. It may be true that popular standards of living often went down at times when sexual nonconformism was very high, and that this brought the proletarians to the edge of subsistence. But he would be a bold man who would look on these two as cause and effect. Kinless, homeless, 'undesirables' must have grown in number as bastardy went up but we cannot say what proportion of these elements was due to illegitimacy.

The principle of legitimacy turns out in fact to be too drastic for the historical record, however appropriate it may still appear to be in the comparative anthropological one. We may suppose that its sanctions did perhaps exist in the background, so to speak, did reinforce the imperatives which parson and magistrate, élite opinion and conscientious scruple exercised over individual behaviour. Possibly when Europe was still what we call an undeveloped society, and at times of really desperate shortage, illegitimacies were felt to be a dangerous liability by everyone, and not to be tolerated. Moreover the ideology of the property-owning, as Ann-Sofie Kälvemark so rightly insists, is bound to interpret any threat to succession as menacing its property rights, and illegitimacy is indeed a threat to the transfer of property between succeeding members of a property-owning class. It is easy to see, therefore, why the property-owner should feel that illegitimacy imperils the society, and why he should wish to invoke the legitimacy principle. But in reality it was the rules of respectability, of praise and blame for people's conduct, which were at play for the most part during the comparative history of bastardy, rather than the rules for survival.

No student of the subject can fail to find himself amazed at the capacity for disapproval which everyone displays. He may see here a vindication of the principle referred to at the outset, the principle that breaches of a social norm provide opportunities to demonstrate and confirm its social import. Nevertheless, the story of bastardy is a sadly impressive record of human censoriousness, a great deal of which maintained itself in ignorance, often it would appear in wilful ignorance, of the social facts. As you read the elaborate and frequently repeated numerical analysis of illegitimacy made by the official statisticians, you are astonished by how little they seem to have entered the awareness of the men supposed to attend to them, of the moralists who yearned over the wickedness of their coevals, or of the subsequent students of control, deviance and breakdown.

Persistence of misapprehension of fact shows itself in the extraordinary difficulty which has been found in disposing of the belief that bastardy in the town must everywhere and always be higher than bastardy in the countryside. So strong is the tradition that cities have been the perpetual corrupters of morals, movement to the city the inevitable cause of breakdown in familial control, living in the city an unceasing source of anomie, that every succeeding study of the problem of bastardy seems to start out with these assumptions. Let us end this introductory chapter by citing some of the facts about rural and urban illegitimacy in the history of one country since the 1840s. Here the historical sociologist can be confident of his ground, in demonstrating with finality that what has always tended to be taken as a necessary relationship is only one more social variable.

In 1845, when bastardy in England and Wales was at its highest before the twentieth century, and the illegitimacy ratio was 7.0 per cent for the whole country, the Registrar General ranked his 323 registration districts in bastardy order (8th *Annual report*, 1849, pp. 78–80). The first in this dishonourable competition was the rural district of Brampton and Longtown in Cumberland, with 17.4 per cent; the second Wigan, the large Lancashire town, with 16.5 per cent; the third a knot of rural villages in Radnorshire in Wales with 15.0 per cent. The City of London was last, 323rd in order, with 1.0 per cent; seven districts in east London were placed between 312 and 322 with 1.9 per cent to 2.9 per cent; Liverpool was 291st with 4.0 per cent; Manchester 207th with 6.4 per cent; Newcastle-upon-Tyne 177th with 7.0 per cent, right on the national average. However important demographically the border may have been, England and Wales shared with Scotland a pronounced tendency for bastards to be more common in the countryside than in the cities. Even if, like Susan Stewart, you compare Banbury with Hartland in the parish register era, a bustling market centre at the crossroads of England with a sleepy and isolated market village, you find that the second has the higher illegitimacy. As we look at the successive figures for much larger places at a later period in table 1.10, we may recall what was stated earlier about the span of variation reducing itself as the nineteenth century proceeded.

Here we can follow the districts which were singled out above in the 1840s decade by decade in the succeeding *Reports*. National rank orderings, unfortunately, were never again provided and we have substituted a rank order for the eleven districts themselves in this table. Locality persistence is evident again, and micro-local variation too. In the county of Nottinghamshire, for instance, whose pre-eminent illegitimacy has been remarked upon already, the town of Nottingham itself had a lower bastardy level than its rural hinterland. And about the general inferiority of the urban population in illegitimacy level there can be no

Table 1.10: Rank order by illegitimacy ratio, eleven select districts, England and Wales, 1859–1912

	1859		1881		1912	
England and Wales	6.5%		4.9%		4.3%	
City of London	1.6%	(11)	2.5%	(11)	4.2%	(6)
East London districts [(a)]	4.5%	(10)	3.0%	(10)	2.8%	(11)
Bristol, Somerset	4.0%	(9)	5.1%	(7)	3.8%	(9)
Liverpool, Lancs.	7.0%	(6)	5.1%	(6)	3.5%	(10)
Manchester, Lancs.	5.3%	(8)	4.1%	(9)	4.1%	(7)
Newcastle-upon-Tyne, Northumberland	7.1%	(5)	5.6%	(5)	4.1%	(8)
Cambridge, Cambs.	6.9%	(7)	4.4%	(8)	4.3%	(5)
Norwich, Norfolk	10.9%	(4)	6.2%	(4)	5.4%	(3)
Wigan, Lancs.	11.8%	(3)	8.6%	(3)	5.0%	(4)
Wigton, etc. [(b)] Cumberland	17.0%	(1)	10.6%	(1)	5.4%	(2)
Presteigne, N. Wales (Radnor)	12.0%	(2)	11.3%	(1)	7.1%	(1)

[(a)] Shoreditch, Bethnal Green, Whitechapel, Stepney, Poplar, Lambeth, Camberwell.
[(b)] Adjacent to Brampton and Longtown.

doubt at all, throughout the Victorian and Edwardian era. It may seem unbelievable, so strong is the conviction about immorality and family breakdown in the slums, that Whitechapel, or Bethnal Green, or Manchester could all have been below the national average throughout the social upheavals of the nineteenth century. But the recognition that it must have been so grows as *Report* succeeds *Report*, registration becomes more and more efficient, and registrars more critical and experienced. The Registrar General recognized himself that recordings of urban illegitimacy were faulty, at least up to 1874. In his 17th report he admitted that in the large towns it appeared that bastards 'are not registered, or are indistinguishable'. Nevertheless, neither in our table nor in the evidence he published in such plenty is there much to show that illegitimacy had become more conspicuous in urban areas by 1881, or by 1912.

As for town and country since 1912, we know that up to 1930 rural districts always had the highest bastardy rate per thousand of the population in England and Wales. When, in about that year, the rural districts lost their pre-eminence in bastardy, as they had already lost their major share of the population, it was the county boroughs, the cities that is to say, which outdistanced them. But London, as we have seen, was still near the bottom of the scale.[54]

Only in the middle of the twentieth century did the cities of the British Isles begin to conform to the cities of France, of Hungary, of Russia and of some other parts of Europe in respect of bastardy. By then, of course, the population of the British countryside had become a remnant, and the rural-urban comparison a comparison with little meaning.

It is surely time we thought again about town and country in relation to personal and to social behaviour, about what 'culture' really means for the society and individual alike, and about how and why some things change rapidly over time and some things change slowly, or remain unchanged. It is time too that we went over our preconceptions about familial conduct and personal conduct, about how and why and when courtship takes place at every social level, and about discipline, sexual and otherwise, ideological or religious discipline and class discipline as well, and all of this in respect of the larger social and political processes. We should reflect in addition on what it means to be born and brought up in a particular place, with its own individual collective experience and cultural traditions, its own peculiar attitude to the relationship between the sexes, to courtship and to marriage – all this in relation to its material conditions and surroundings, its economic and productive history, in relation to them but distinct from them as well.

Which means of course recognizing that society and societies are plural as well as singular, in geography as well as in structure, federal as well as unitary in their composition. The questions raised by the study of illegitimacy and its comparative history go deep indeed, and the figures which that study puts in our hand make an examination of fundamentals an open possibility. This is the second occasion on which the historical sociologist has found himself pleading with the

54. The 1930 *Annual report*, table XCV, shows England and Wales with 1.02 illegitimate births per thousand population, county boroughs 1.09, rural districts with 1.07, other urban districts with 0.96 and London with 0.89. When the figures are broken down into the Registrar General's areas of the country and individual years are compared, it appears that up to 1930 anyway rural Wales had the highest levels, the rural north the second highest, the northern cities the third highest with the urban areas of the Midlands the lowest, for London had begun the rise which was to put the city at the head of the table at last in the 1960s. The rural South was near to the bottom all through the period in the early nineteenth century, showing that difference by area may have been a sharper divide than the urban/rural one.

established body of the social scientists to go back to the beginning of an important area of enquiry and face its fundamentals. What has been found to apply to illegitimacy and to household composition may finally apply to a great deal else besides.

Appendix: space-time analysis of variance in levels of legitimate and illegitimate fertility, England and other countries

James Oeppen, with contributions from Kenneth Wachter

The locality persistence values calculated for legitimate and illegitimate fertility in England and Wales between the 1870s and the 1900s in table 1.6 (p. 34) revealed one consistent source of variation in the rates for both, namely that there were relatively stable differences between counties. At the same time, the table shows that the national rates for both types of fertility were declining steadily, suggesting a second source of consistent variation. One way to formalize this joint hypothesis and to assess the relative importance of the two sources of variation is to regard the table as having a base value (the grand mean across all counties and time periods) which is then modified by appropriate locality and temporal effects to produce an estimate for a particular year and county which differs from the observed value by some residual amount. In its additive form this model can be expressed as:

$$\text{Data Value} = \text{Grand Mean} + \text{Locality Effect} + \text{Temporal Effect} + \text{Residual.}$$

The model can be fitted by the standard two-way analysis of variance, which produces estimates of the locality effect for each county which are constant over time and estimates of the temporal effect for each year which are constant over localities. Thus for illegitimate fertility in the county of London in 1880–82 the estimated model is

$$9.8 = 13.70 - 4.93 + 1.79 - 0.76.$$

London therefore tends to be 4.93 per thousand below the expected value of 13.70, but over all counties the period 1880–82 tends to be 1.79 per thousand above the expected value. The residual terms show that the estimate for 1881 is 0.76 per thousand above the observed value of 9.8. Using the analysis of variance technique the sum of the squared differences between each value and the grand mean (or total variance) can be separated into sub-totals attributable to locality, temporal and residual effects. The results for English illegitimate fertility between the 1870s and the 1900s are set out in table 1.11. The F-ratios relate the explained mean squares to the residual mean square and are both significant at the 0.001 level or less, although the temporal effects dominate the spatial ones. It can be concluded that temporal changes are more important than regional differences in the data

Table 1.11

Source of variation	Degrees of freedom	Sum of squares	Mean square	F-ratio
Locality	42	1851.0	44.1	22.1
Time-period	3	2398.6	799.5	401.5
Residual	126	250.9	2.0	
Total	171	4500.5		

Table 1.12

Source of variation	Degrees of freedom	Sum of squares	Mean square	F-ratio
Locality	42	25247.3	601.1	10.2
Time-period	3	100781.1	33593.7	569.6
Residual	126	7431.7	59.0	
Total	171	133460.1		

set, although the latter are nevertheless highly significant. The same process applied to the legitimate rates yields the results set out in table 1.12. The same conclusion holds for legitimate fertility as for illegitimate, except that the temporal dominance is even greater.

As an indicator of the explanatory power of the additive model we may use a squared multiple correlation coefficient, calculated by analogy with the multiple correlation coefficient in regression. The R^2 for illegitimate fertility works out to be 0.94 and that for legitimate fertility at 0.94 also. These high values show that residual elements in the data set are very small, so that the simple notions of stability in spatial and temporal ordering have a great deal of explanatory power. What is more, if we examine the residual effects a number of interesting conclusions emerge.

Table 1.13 represents the results of ranking the residuals for each data value and arbitrarily selecting the top five, representing under-prediction (Residual = Observed − Expected), and the bottom five, representing over-prediction. These tables show primarily that the 'rogue' counties do not move contrary to the overall trend for a

Table 1.13

Residual ranks, illegitimacy

		1870	1880	1890	1900
	1	Yorkshire, NR	Bedfordshire	London	Surrey
	2	Shropshire	Nottinghamshire	Surrey	London
Under-prediction	3	Cumberland	Cumberland	Middlesex	Middlesex
	4	Norfolk	Herefordshire	Dorsetshire	Hampshire
	5	Durham	Norfolk	Huntingdonshire	Sussex
	39	Dorset	Kent	Shropshire	Norfolk
	40	Gloucestershire	Berkshire	Norfolk	Yorkshire, NR
Over-prediction	41	Surrey	Surrey	Yorkshire, NR	Westmorland
	42	Middlesex	London	Bedfordshire	Shropshire
	43	London	Huntingdonshire	Rutland	Cumberland

Residual ranks, legitimacy

		1870	1880	1890	1900
	1	Rutland	Bedfordshire	London	London
	2	Yorkshire, NR	Hertfordshire	Cumberland	Surrey
Under-prediction	3	Hertfordshire	Somersetshire	Huntingdonshire	Huntingdonshire
	4	Bedfordshire	Worcestershire	Buckinghamshire	Middlesex
	5	Westmorland	Gloucestershire	Cornwall	Monmouthshire
	39	Dorset	Yorkshire, NR	Wiltshire	Leicestershire
	40	Cornwall	Devonshire	Somersetshire	Cumberland
Over-prediction	41	Surrey	Wiltshire	Bedfordshire	Bedfordshire
	42	Middlesex	Yorkshire, ER	Oxfordshire	Westmorland
	43	London	Huntingdonshire	Rutland	Hertfordshire

period and then conform, but pursue paths that are fundamentally different from other counties in the country. This is well exemplified by Surrey, Middlesex and London which tend to have low rates on both measures at the start of the period, but have higher than predicted rates at the end.

A detailed examination of the residuals shows that where locality and time-period effects are both positive, or both negative, the estimate is too low and where the effects are of opposite signs, the estimated value is too large. This is suggestive of multiplicative interaction and is confirmed by plotting the residuals against the following model of interaction:

$$\frac{\text{Locality Effect} \times \text{Temporal Effect}}{\text{Grand Mean}}.$$

The plot is approximately linear with unit slope and the model can be extended to the form

$$\text{Data Value} = \text{Grand Mean} + \text{Locality Effect} + \text{Temporal Effect} + \frac{\text{Locality Effect} \times \text{Temporal Effect} + \text{Residual}}{\text{Grand Mean}}.$$

This can be fitted by analysis of variance on the logs of the original data to produce table 1.14 for illegitimate fertility. This model gives an R^2 of 0.98 which is a small improvement on the additive model. (For legitimate fertility there is no such improvement.) Examining the residuals again shows that Surrey, Middlesex and London change over time from large negative to large positive residuals, with most of the major shifts taking place between 1880 and 1890.

We may therefore conclude that illegitimacy can be regarded as made up of some constant times a factor that depends only on locality times a factor that depends only on time-period. In contrast legitimate fertility is taken as a constant plus a locality effect plus a temporal effect. However, for both types of fertility, period is more important than locality in explaining the rate even though locality is still significant. The success of the model-fitting procedure indicates that there is relatively little random variation in the data and that the fertility rates can be represented by a simple ordering in time and space.

Table 1.14

Source of variation	Degrees of freedom	Sum of squares	Mean square	F-ratio
Locality	42	1.91	0.5	57.27
Time-period	3	2.48	0.83	1040.49
Residual	126	0.10	0.0008	
Total	171	4.50		

The analysis of the fertility data described above was also extended to that for the other countries discussed. Selecting either an additive or a multiplicative model by deciding which gives the better value for R^2 for each country, we can produce table 1.15. The results generally confirm those found for England. The temporal effects tend to dominate the locality effects, although the latter are still significant and multiplicative models are more appropriate for illegitimate fertility, generally giving higher R^2 values than the additive models found to be appropriate for legitimate fertility.

Table 1.15

Country	Type of fertility	Model	Locality effect	Temporal effect	R^2
England	Illegitimate rate	Multiplicative	57.27*	1040.49*	.98
	Legitimate rate	Additive	10.19*	569.56*	.94
Germany	Illegitimate (I_h)	Multiplicative	120.4*	222.1*	.95
	Legitimate (I_g)	Additive	5.6*	66.8*	.65
Italy	Illegitimate (I_h)	Multiplicative	13.7*	69.4*	.86
	Legitimate (I_g)	Additive	14.4*	59.7*	.85
Portugal	Illegitimate (I_h)	Additive	45.2*	5.2*	.87
	Legitimate (I_g)	Additive	20.8*	73.2*	.88
Scotland	Illegitimate ratio	Multiplicative	84.0*	13.4*	.84
	Crude birth rate	Multiplicative	101.1*	504.8*	.94
Sweden	Illegitimates per person	Additive	19.7*	0.1	.69

* Significant at .01 level or less.

I Britain

Ac Alcester, Warwickshire
Ad Aldenham, Hertfordshire
As Ash-next-Sandwich, Kent
Ba Banbury, Oxfordshire
Bf Bottesford, Leicestershire
Bp Bolton Percy, Yorkshire
Bu Burnham on Crouch, Essex
C Colyton, Devon
Ca Canterbury, Kent
Cs Campton and Shefford, Bedfordshire
Cw Clayworth, Nottinghamshire
Ec Earls Colne, Essex
Gb Gainsborough, Lincolnshire
Ge Gedling, Nottinghamshire
H Hawkshead, Lancashire
Ha Hartland, Devon
Hy Hemyock, Devon
Le Lesbury, Northumberland
M Myddle, Shropshire
Ri Rickinghall, Suffolk
Ro Rochdale, Lancashire
Sh Shepshed, Leicestershire
T Terling, Essex
Yo York, Yorkshire

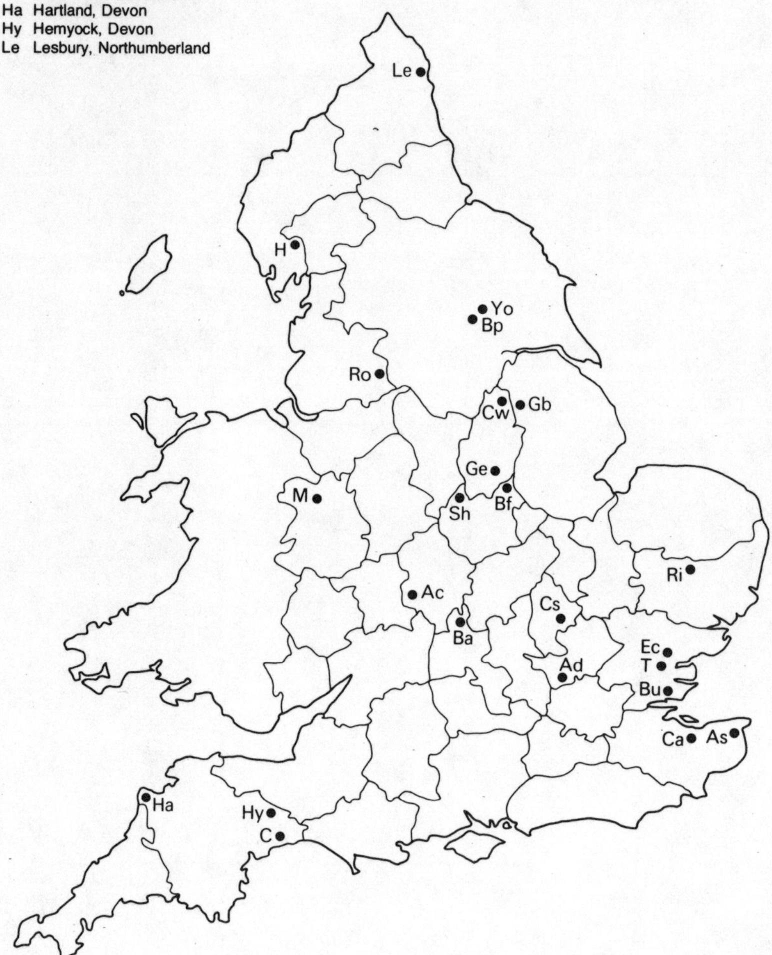

English place names mentioned in Part I

2

Illegitimacy and illegitimates in English history

Alan Macfarlane

'The bastard, like the prostitute, thief and beggar, belongs to that motley crowd of disreputable social types which society has generally resented, always endured. He is a living symbol of social irregularity.'[1] Thus commences one of the classic sociological analyses of the types of illegitimacy, and it immediately poses three problems for the anthropologist and the historian concerned with this topic in Britain. What was the rate of illegitimacy in our country before civil registration began? What was the attitude to those who bore and begat bastards? What was the attitude to the bastards themselves?

The first of these questions has been given a preliminary answer for England in the figures contained in Peter Laslett's introductory chapter. In this initial study in the British section of the book I want to tackle the other two questions. I shall, however, consider at some length the incidence of illegitimacy in a particular parish, Earls Colne in Essex, in relation to the overall estimates of births and baptisms of bastards contained in the figures published by the Cambridge Group for the History of Population and Social Structure. Sources for the study of bastardy other than the registers makes such an assessment possible, and it is from these sources also that we can begin to try to answer our two further questions.

'Try', because as the reader will notice, research into the minute details of social life in Earls Colne is still in progress.[2] Most of our statements, particularly about the sociology of bastardy in English historical development, will take the form of queries rather than conclusions, and the reader may turn to the chapters which follow with a questionnaire in his mind. On one of the recurrent themes of this section, however, he will have a preliminary body of evidence provided for him, and this is the possibility of a bastardy prone sub-society, which has already been referred to in chapter 1 and which is the subject of chapter 8.

For the social anthropologist interested in the family life of people in the past and in the present, the outstanding feature of the English historical record is that so many people had to wait for so many years between sexual maturity and fully sanctioned sexual intercourse within marriage. Some of them indeed, particularly perhaps the servants and the younger children in families, may never have been able to marry at all. How then is this reflected in the bastardy rates and in the

1. Kingsley Davis, 'Illegitimacy and the social structure' (reprinted 1964), p. 21.

2. The Social Science Research Council and King's College Research Centre, Cambridge, have provided support for the collection and analysis of the local records relating to the parish of Earls Colne described in this chapter. I am most grateful to them, and to my colleagues, Cherry Bryant, Sarah Harrison, Charles Jardine, Tim King, Iris Macfarlane and Jessica Styles, who have all assisted in many ways. A fuller account of the sources used and the methods employed is contained in Alan Macfarlane, Sarah Harrison and Charles Jardine, *Reconstructing historical communities* (1977), and a further discussion of sexual behaviour in Earls Colne in the late sixteenth century in 'Historical Anthropology' (1977). The original essay upon which this chapter is based was more than twice this length; I would like to thank Peter and Janet Laslett for encouragement and help in reducing and improving it.

attitude to illegitimacy? Was it permissible to have bastards, although one could not marry? Is there evidence from the number of bastards that extra-marital sexual intercourse was frequent? The topic is of special interest and importance for two reasons. Firstly, because it illustrates a clash between the accepted morality and actual behaviour, and hence is used by many commentators as a 'social strain guage', and index of 'anomie' or social breakdown. There are, as we shall see, dangers in doing this. Nevertheless, bastardy rates reflect indirectly many other features of the society. Again, bastardy is so visible an offence, leaving its mark in the shape of a child needing provision, that it appears very much more often in the records than other offences.

Incest and bestiality may abound and not be noticed. But, with certain exceptions, such as the aborting or killing at birth of bastards, acts of intercourse leading to illegitimate births are very much more likely to be recorded. Moreover, while brides pregnant at marriage can be traced in two sources only – the parish registers and ecclesiastical court records – illegitimacies will appear in a wider range of records. Economic provision for the child was of direct concern to parish officials and to justices of the peace, so that quarter sessions files, accounts of overseers of the poor, wills and other documents will all throw light on the attitude to and the maintenance of bastards.

Cases of bastardy can therefore be used to test the outlook on sexual offences as well as their incidence. Furthermore, they are a useful check on the difference of attitude of different sets of people: local villagers, churchwardens, court officials, justices of the peace. It is possible to study not only specific cases, but also, at the statistical level, the actual incidence and distribution of a particular offence over time and between different social groups.

Except indirectly, in their general study of kinship and paternity, anthropologists have not contributed greatly to the problems surrounding the topic of illegitimacy. They have shown that the attitude differs from society to society, for though illegitimate children are nearly always penalized, as Malinowski has pointed out,[3] there are societies where illegitimacy carries little stigma.[4] With inadequate data, anthropologists have been unable to produce any numerical estimates of the extent of bastardy, and hence any theories concerning change over time, or differences between sub-groups in the population. Sociologists have been much more interested in the topic and have not only provided some interesting comparative rates but have also tried to devise various frameworks to analyse types of illegitimacy: thus Goode distinguishes fourteen major kinds of illegitimacy, from consensual unions and concubinage to various types of incestuous association.[5] The historical data, when assembled, should be useful in refining and developing their hypotheses.

In England bastardy has been studied for some considerable time. In the last century Leffingwell attempted to analyse the geographical and social distribution of illegitimacy.[6] But, with the exception of an interesting essay on bastardy in a Warwickshire village by A. W. Ashby in 1912,[7] relatively little progress has been

3. B. Malinowski, *Sex and repression in savage society* (1960), pp. 212–13.

4. For example, in parts of Nepal, C. von Fürer-Haimendorf, *Sherpas of Nepal* (1964), p. 41; or Sri Lanka, E. R. Leach, *Pul Eliya: a village in Ceylon* (1961), p. 91.

5. W. J. Goode, *The family* (1964), p. 23; chapter 3 summarizes much of the relevant sociological literature, particularly the work of Kingsley Davis.

6. *Illegitimacy and the influence of seasons upon conduct* (1892).

7. 'One hundred years of Poor Law administration in a Warwickshire village'.

made until recently, when the research undertaken at the Cambridge Group for the History of Population and Social Structure began to be published.

2 The legal situation relating to bastardy

There was great ambiguity and conflict in the legal definition of bastardy in England in the past, which makes it impossible to give a simple summary of the position. One of the crucial distinctions was between what was termed 'general bastardy', where the parents did not marry after the birth of the child, and 'special bastardy' where, espoused or not at the time of the birth, they later married.[8] When 'general bastardy' was disputed, it could be tried in the ecclesiastical courts as such, but 'special bastardy' could only be tried in the common law courts, for it was not recognized as 'bastardy' by the church (Burn, I, p. 112).[9]

By the law of the church all those born of parents who married, no matter when the marriage took place, were legitimate (Burn, I, p. 112). According to the thirteenth-century Bishop Grosseteste, there had been an earlier custom that any children born before marriage were placed beneath the care-cloth at the wedding service and were held to be legitimate.[10] Another disagreement between different branches of the law was over inheritance by bastards. On the one hand, by canon law and common law, bastards received no automatic inheritance in land. In manorial law generally, in theory 'a bastard can never be heir unto any man, nor yet have heir unto himself but his children.'[11] On the other hand, 'the Parents of a Bastard may by Deed executed in their Lifetime, or by last Will, give or devise their Lands to their Bastards.'[12] It is clear that both the legal and *de facto* position, and particularly the treatment of bastards in wills, needs further analysis and investigation.

Another ambiguity lies in the treatment of parents. The 'bastard' was clearly penalized by disadvantages in inheritance and other spheres, but how were the offenders themselves punished? A curious fact, pointed out by Ashby (p. 84), emerges here, namely that 'the begetting or conceiving a so-called illegitimate child were acts not punishable under English law.' The position in the secular code is illustrated by the statute of 7 James, cap. 4 (1610), which stated that:

> Every lewd woman which shall have any bastard which may be chargeable to the parish, the justices of the peace shall commit such woman to the house of correction, to be punished and set on work, during the term of one whole year [Burn, I, p. 120].

But this only applied to those who had a bastard 'which may be chargeable to the parish'. If the paternity was acknowledged, and the father could provide maintenance, the offence would not come before the civil courts at all. The very considerable material concerning the punishment of parents and provision for bastard children arises therefore out of the need to assure maintenance and to

8. See the discussion in Richard Burn, *Ecclesiastical law* (1788) I, pp. 117–19.
9. Burn, I, p. 112; the relations between secular and ecclesiastical courts are complex and only an over-simple account of the changing legal position can be given here.
10. Cited in G. C. Homans, *English villagers in the thirteenth century* (1941), p. 172.
11. *The order of keeping a court leet and court baron*, 1650 (1914), p. 41.
12. Henry Swinburne, *a briefe treatise of testaments and last willes* (1728), p. 288. On pp. 350–55 Swinburne discusses three major kinds of illegitimacy and the rules concerning executorship and legacies concerning illegitimates.

prevent the bastard 'falling on the parish'. It was ordered, for example, that midwives at childbirth should try with every means in their power to extort the name of the genitor out of the unmarried woman.[13]

The actual 'punishment', if there was no problem of maintenance, was on a par with other sexual offences, namely public penance in church during a service. It is not even clear whether the father was meant to undergo the same penance as the mother. It appears that the time at which the church punishment was to take place was at the 'churching' of the woman after childbirth. Thus in the articles for York Province issued by Archbishop Sandys in 1578 it was enquired:

> Whether your minister do church any unmarried women after they have been delivered of their children begotten unlawfully, before they have acknowledged their faults openly according to the order prescribed by the Ordinary or his deputy?[14]

Overall, the impression is that bastardy was treated by the church courts as the logical outcome of, and morally equivalent to, fornication. Only a detailed comparison of sources, for instance to see whether bastards registered in the parish registers were also presented at the ecclesiastical court, will begin to tell us what happened in practice.

There are many other difficult points of law and definition to decide in relation to bastardy. If a couple married and it was subsequently discovered that the marriage had to be annulled because of some bar, precontract or affinity, for example, were their offspring illegitimate? The position seems to have been that both by canon and common law, as long as they had a full church wedding, and it could be shown that at least one of the partners could be proved to have been in ignorance of the obstacle to marriage, then the children were still legitimate though the parents were not really married.[15] These were known as 'putative' marriages.

Again, if the husband had been absent from his wife for a number of years, and she had a child in his absence, was it a bastard? According to Coke, as long as the father was alive and in England, the child was his and legitimate (Burn, I, p. 110). Or, what was the position of a woman impregnated by one man who then proceeded to marry another man and the child was born after the wedding to the latter? It was apparently believed that the child was legitimate and must be accepted as his by the man who married the pregnant woman.[16] If there was doubt about the paternity, but both 'paters' were legitimate, when a husband died and the wife remarried, for example, then the child could choose which husband was to be his lawful 'father' (Burn, I, p. 110). Thus there seems to have been an attempt to ensure that the child had a legally recognized father wherever possible, even though it might be well known that he was not the genitor.

The situation is quite different in certain African societies where the physical genitor is of very little importance and where illegitimacy in the European sense is

13. Articles for 1575 for Winchester, for example, containing such instructions are in the Bodleian Library, Oxford, Vet. Al. e. 38, article 46.
14. Reprinted in W. P. M. Kennedy, ed., *Elizabethan episcopal administration* (1924), p. 95. An 'Ordinary' was the bishop or bishop's deputy.
15. G. E. Howard, *A history of matrimonial institutions* (1904) I, p. 356. Chapter 7 of Howard's essential work summarizes the complex legal position concerning the church's view of legitimacy and marriage.
16. E. Chamberlayne, *The present state of England* (1673), p. 333.

practically impossible since the child is always welcome and always belongs to somebody.[17] In these societies bastards are not regarded as a 'burden'. But in England during our period, bastard children, rather than being greeted with delight, were seen as an economic problem, likely to be a drain on scarce communal resources. The quarter sessions of every county are filled with examinations and orders concerning the maintenance of bastards. By an act of 1576 (18 Elizabeth c. 3), it was ordered that bastards should be supported by their putative fathers, though bastardy orders in the quarter sessions date from before this date.[18] If the genitor could be found, then he was put under very great pressure to accept responsibility and to maintain the child.

3 The attitude to illegitimacy

The attitude to bastards and bastardy is best approached indirectly: through the way bastards were treated, through the subsequent marriage expectations of their parents, and so on. The evidence suggests that there was little emphasis on virginity of brides in traditional English society, at least among the people at large. Although Dr Johnson noted that the chastity of woman was 'of the utmost importance, as all property depends upon it',[19] in theory at least, we do not know whether, in practice, the bearing of a bastard child carried a stigma for a woman. In Germany, according to Fynes Moryson, those who lost their virginity found it difficult to get a husband,[20] and the contemporary medical belief that all later children would take after the first (the mother's womb being like a mould), would hardly encourage men to marry women who had borne a bastard.[21] Though the studies which follow show that men and women who had engendered bastards did get spouses, even some of those who had more than one bastard, it seems likely that their marriage chances were significantly lower than for others of the same class and background. It could well be that the mothers of bastards were often servants or younger daughters and at a socio-economic level where marriage was less likely in any case but especially at the average marrying age. In the later eighteenth century a form of illegitimacy resembling the common law unions of contemporary South America was coming into existence and might almost be regarded as a normal institution. These points are discussed further in chapter 8.

A brief survey of seventeenth-century English sources tends to give the impression that bastardy, though its ascription might be libellous,[22] was not greatly disapproved of, as long as the child was maintained. Thus one vicar described how a neighbour had a maid who produced four successive bastards, 'yet because she was a good work woman he kept her still.'[23] Gervase Holles recorded, more with fond indulgence than indignation or horror, that one of his uncles was very enamoured of women and begat several illegitimate children.[24] It seems quite

17. For instance, in the classic Nuer case, E. E. Evans-Pritchard, *Kinship and marriage among the Nuer* (1951), p. 120.
18. An order from a year before the act is in the Essex Record Office, County Hall, Chelmsford (hereafter ERO), Q/SR/49/27.
19. Quoted in Christopher Hill, *Puritanism and revolution* (1962), p. 384.
20. Fynes Moryson, *An itinerary* (1908) IV, p. 299.
21. This belief, which William Harvey seems to have adopted, is known technically as 'telegony'; there is a brief discussion of it in Richard Lewinsohn, *A history of sexual customs* (1958), pp. 204–6.
22. An example of a bastardy libel is in *Historical Manuscripts Commission Report* III, appendix, p. 119a.
23. T. Worthington Barlow, *Cheshire: its historical and literary associations* (1885), p. 152.
24. A. C. Wood (ed.), *Memorials of the Holles family, 1493–1656* (1973), p. 192.

likely that sympathy with the plight of the mother and general tolerance of bastardy as a frailty, but not a sin, continued at least until the nineteenth century. Even in that century there are indications of such tolerance in two of the classical accounts of rural life at that time, *Lark Rise to Candleford* and *Forty Years in a Moorland Parish.*[25] It is possible that the situation was similar to that observed in other societies, where there may be a scandal at the time, but afterwards the child, mother and father are accepted back into normal social relations and the affair does not cause shame.[26]

Yet there are also indications that the picture of tolerance and indulgence can be overstressed, especially when it comes to bastardy itself, as is insisted by Keith Wrightson in chapter 6. Lawrence in his diary of the later seventeenth century warned people to avoid the danger of the 'staine of bastardy' on their coat of arms,[27] and there is some evidence that the women involved felt considerable shame. Thus in a Colchester deposition in the early seventeenth century we learn of a woman who had had one bastard and who said that 'she would never come to shame againe' and proceeded to take ratsbane poison in an attempt to kill herself. But this is the only case I have come across where bastardy led to attempted suicide, and the woman involved proceeded to tell the man in the affair, who gave her an emetic. Perhaps she was trying to force his hand rather than to kill herself from shame. Further indications of the actual attitudes will only emerge in the actual treatment of bastard children and their parents, and in the degree to which people were willing to go to the length of bringing irregular pregnancies to an end before birth.

4 Abortions of illegitimate children

One way of trying to assess the attitude to bastards at the local level is to examine the life expectation of bastards (this is attempted in a preliminary way by Karla Oosterveen and Richard Smith in chapter 3, below). But even before livebirth, the bastard child might be discriminated against in that the abortion of the foetus was attempted. The success and frequency of abortion is not as yet known for periods in the past, but it is clear that attempts were made to abort illegitimately conceived children. Thus a Colchester woman who was made pregnant in the mid seventeenth century took 'savin' and other 'phisick', but neither was successful. When she again conceived illegitimately, her lover, an amateur physician, 'by phisick often assayed to destroy the same child within her', but again unsuccessfully.[28] Curiously enough it was exactly the same herb that had been used half a century earlier in Essex: the rector of Leaden Rothing in 1574 was supposed to have made a woman pregnant and, she suspecting the same, he 'brought her from London a rough herbe, which he called saven willing her to use it in drink for hindering the child if she should have any'. She proceeded to have a premature child which died 'not having either hair nor nails'.[29] In this case the herb was clearly effective.

25. Flora Thompson, *Lark Rise to Candleford* (1945), pp. 129–30; Rev. J. C. Atkinson, *Forty years in a moorland parish* (1891), p. 5.
26. For example, Geoffrey Gorer, *Himalayan village: an account of the Lepchas of Sikkim* (1967), p. 173.
27. G. E. Aylmer (ed.), *The diary of William Lawrence* (1961), p. 6.
28. The whole extraordinary set of depositions is contained in a set of examinations taken on 12 November 1638, in the Colchester Examination Book for 1619–45, at County Hall, Colchester. I am grateful to Mr J. A. Sharpe of the University of York for the reference.
29. The case is in the Consistory Court of London Correction Book for that date, now deposited at the London County Record Office, unfoliated.

A few years earlier an accused witch at Hatfield Peverel in the same county had confessed that, being pregnant by a man who refused to marry her, and the man dying, she 'willed Sathan [her cat familiar] to destroy it, and he bad her take a certayne herbe and drinke it, whych she did, and destroyed the child forthwyth.'[30] Obviously, in the accusations and cross-accusations of a trial which might well end in a death sentence, we have to treat this sort of evidence with caution. The cases we have considered, however, suggest that abortifacients were fairly widely known and used, and more especially when a foetus was going to be born as a bastard.

Contemporary doctors also believed that abortions were possible. Andrew Boorde stated that there were certain 'medicines' (i.e. laxatives) which caused an abortion, and went on to suggest that 'light women' might use such medicines if he described them.[31] Other methods were also employed. Modern sociologists have pointed out that it is not too difficult to induce abortion by wearing an over-tight belt, and a sixteenth-century case is alluded to where a priest's mistress who was pregnant, 'tightened her girdle & performed exercises with a rolling pin in order to destroy the foetus'.[32]

It would seem that people felt sufficiently opposed to the birth of an illegitimate child to resort to such practices. The problem is that, if abortion was widely and successfully used, the baptism registration in the parish registers would be a less accurate index than might be supposed, thus adding considerable difficulties to the statistical study of illegitimacy.

5 Infanticide of illegitimates

If the foetus did survive to termination of pregnancy, it might still be destroyed at birth. Again, infanticide is extremely difficult to assess. But there is more chance here, since infanticide is recognizably murder, and there was a much larger body to dispose of. That we might well expect a considerable number of bastard children to be murdered at birth is implied by an act passed in 1624 (21 James I, cap. 27), 'to prevent the murthering of bastard children'. The wording is as follows:

> Whereas many lewd women that have been delivered of bastard children, to avoid their shame, and to escape punishment, do secretly bury or conceal the death of their children, and often, if the child is found dead, the said women do allege, that the said child was born dead. . . . Be it enacted . . . in every such case the mother so offending, shall suffer death as in the case of murther, except such mother can make proof by one witness at the last that the child . . . was born dead.

Certainly, illegitimate children are destroyed in a number of societies. The Colchester deposition previously alluded to (see note 28) contains several infanticides by the same mother: she buried one, poisoned another, smothered a third. When a neighbour encountered scruples in the mother as to killing one of them, the neighbour replied: 'Tush, it was not the first she had made away.'

30. The pamphlet is reprinted in C. L. Ewen (ed.) *Witch hunting and witch trials* (1929), p. 318.
31. Andrew Boorde, *The breviarie of health* (1575), fol. 8.
32. R. A. Houlbrooke, 'Church courts and people in the diocese of Norwich, 1519–1570' (1970), p. 160. I am grateful to Dr Houlbrooke for permission to quote from his unpublished thesis.

Since it was a capital offence to murder an infant, it is in the assize courts principally that we encounter infanticide. It should be possible to obtain some idea of the distribution of indictments in different periods and counties from the extensive assize files of the period. But it is in the depositions, occasionally in the quarter sessions papers, but more often in the unique Northern Circuit depositions for the latter half of the seventeenth century, that one obtains a really close insight into the circumstances of illegitimate births.[33]

An example of quarter sessions examinations occurs in Essex in 1645 (ERO, Q/SBa/2/61), where there are depositions of various persons 'concerning the murdering of a bastard child born on the body of Margaret Cumplin'. The gist of the examinations was that after the birth, the mother and a man (the presumed genitor?) rode up to London from Burnham, and there the man took the infant, saying he was going to place it with a nurse in 'Thames Street', and she never saw it again. How frequent the use of London was as a dumping ground for illegitimate children in this period we do not know. Certainly, there are many descriptions of bastards being abandoned in the city,[34] and an examination of foundling hospital records in the following centuries may show some interesting features.

6 Illegitimacy statistics

The figures for England summarized in chapter 1 and those given in other chapters of this book on illegitimacy in Europe before the age of statistics all come from entries of baptisms in the parish registers. Although the researches at the Cambridge Group have insisted on the limitations of such statistics and the problems which have to be recognized if they are to be used as measures of variations in extra-marital sexual relations,[35] little has yet been done to estimate their reliability. No investigation has been made, for example, of contemporary theological opinion as to whether bastards should be baptized at all, and Eversley (1966, p. 62) has written that 'many illegitimate births must have been ignored, because only strong religious convictions would lead one to baptize the child.' It is true that in a proportion of English registers, not yet determined but certainly not negligible, no illegitimates appear in the baptismal registers at certain periods, and in many parishes, especially in the years around 1640, decades go by without a baby being marked as a bastard when it seems very unlikely that none was born. Obviously a great deal more investigation is called for.

The ecclesiastical injunctions of the reign of Queen Elizabeth undoubtedly concerned themselves with the question of bastard bearers. The article already cited ordered that a woman should not be churched after illegitimate child bearing until she had made an open confession in church. But if a woman remained unrepentant, would her child be baptized? A hint that the bastard's religious status was extremely dubious occurs in Thomas Becon's works, where he cites the old law that bastards should not be allowed to enter the congregation of the faithful.[36]

33. The relevant class is in the Public Record Office, Assizes 45. Very interesting depositions are, for example, in no. 7, file 78 and no. 3, file 17. A recent survey of the eighteenth-century evidence is R. W. Malcolmson, 'Infanticide in the eighteenth century' (1977).

34. Cases are given in T. R. Forbes, *Chronicle from Aldgate* (1971), pp. 32–3.

35. For example, P. Laslett, *Family life and illicit love in earlier generations* (1977), pp. 108–9.

36. Thomas Becon, *Workes* (1560), DCLII.

Since baptism was the first step into the congregation, it may well be that there was a widespread view that bastards should not be christened. Their parents may also have been excluded: thus a man of Great Totham was presented at the archdeaconry court in 1612 'for incontinency and bastardy for which cause he hath not beene admitted to the holy communion this last Easter' (ERO, O/ACA/34/90ᵛ). There is certainly evidence that Puritan clergy felt worried about how the children of unmarried women, especially notorious prostitutes, should be dealt with. Thus a meeting of ministers at Dedham debated the problem of what was to be done with the child of a 'strumpet' brought into the church secretly.[37] The general problem of baptism of unbelievers' children was discussed by Ralph Josselin, the vicar of Earls Colne in Essex in the 1640s and he concluded that unbelievers' children and therefore presumably bastard children should be baptized.[38]

7 Earls Colne, Essex

Let us then take the parish of Earls Colne as a test case for the accuracy of the registration of bastards, both before the Interregnum of the 1650s and during those troubled years. On the face of it, there would have been no reason for rejecting this register for the kind of analysis which the Cambridge Group has undertaken: the baptisms are complete from 1560, except for a short gap from 1605 to 1609, and continue (with births rather than baptisms) throughout the Interregnum. How accurate would be our impression of bastardy, based on this one source?

While very many of the bastards recorded in the parish register are described in the archdeaconry court records, only six ecclesiastical presentments of Earls Colne women for bastardy before 1640 are not mirrored in the register. In at least two of the cases, in 1587 and in 1603, moreover, the bastard births may have occurred some years before, at a time when the woman lived elsewhere. Thus it may well be that only in two or three cases was there no baptism or burial entry at all. The ecclesiastical courts, then, provide a valuable check for the years up to 1640, but in the subsequent years of the Interregnum the courts disappeared, and after 1660 they did not regain their position as a tribunal for sexual offences. We are therefore forced to use more patchy evidence, and this is especially unfortunate since the assumption has been that this was a time of a sustained low level in the English bastardy ratio all over the country. This low level is also apparent in the parish registers of Earls Colne, but since it may merely betray a decline in the recording of illegitimates, it would be helpful to have some independent insight into the accuracy of bastardy registration there. Clues to the situation in the parish are furnished by two sources: Ralph Josselin's diary as vicar from 1641 to 1683, and the quarter sessions records.

If we look first at the period 1640–59, we find that the parish register indicates that five bastards were born or died: one each in 1642 and 1643 and three in 1656. There are hints, however, that other cases occurred which were not mentioned in the parish registers. Two instances are fairly certain. One is to be found in the quarter sessions (ERO, Q/SR/355/30) when Joan Price of Earls Colne was presented for having had a bastard child since the last sessions. The presentment was

37. R. G. Usher (ed.), *The Presbyterian movement in the reign of Queen Elizabeth* (1905), p. 37. On the Puritans and baptizing the children of the reprobate, see also chapter 6.

38. Alan Macfarlane (ed.), *The diary of Ralph Josselin, 1616–1683* (1976), p. 101, under 26 August.

in January 1653, yet no bastard or child of this name appears in that year in the register. Nor is there any bastardy recorded in 1645 to correspond to the following account by Josselin (p. 39, 27 April):

> Mary Grant a bold wench whose mother had 6 or 7 bastards. Her flesh rotted from her arms, complained she was gotten with child. Oh Lord keep all thine from this scandalous wickedness, humble us for no such abomination ought to benamed among us; the fellow she accused, John Besse run away.

Josselin failed to record whether Mary gave birth, nor did he set down the possible outcome of an adulterous affair described by him as follows (pp. 51–2, 14, 22 and 24 December):

> This weeke acquainted with the scandal of Edward Potter in soliciting the chastity of the widow Ward. Lord this ought not to be named among Christians . . . Edward Potter bound to his good behaviour for abusing the widow Ward, he put in sureties to discharge the town . . . In conclusion the justices had so much against him as to send him to gaol.

Whether a child was conceived we do not know, but the fact that Potter was bound to discharge the town, presumably of the cost of a bastard, suggests that there was a fear that this might happen. Josselin mentions three other bastardy cases, but we would expect none of them to appear in the parish register.

One of these cases does, however, give us a valuable glimpse of the attitude to bastardy:

> This weeke John Read's maid went away with child, and accuseth him for father. This man was once a great professor, admired for his parts. But his base corruptions grew too strong, he fell to drunkeness, to neglect God in ordinances. . . . God may make him to awake by this great fall, which as a crack may amaze him but he keeps out of mans sight in regard of the shame.

The following month John Read's goods were sold up and he left the town (Josselin, pp. 139–40, 2 October; a 'professor' was one who professed the true religion, a godly or devout person).

Unfortunately Josselin cannot be used as a reliable index of bastardy cases since he appears not to have shown much interest in the subject after about 1650. There is no mention in the diary of any of the three cases of bastardy in 1656, though Josselin himself must have noted vital events in the parish register.[39] Nor is the other major source, quarter session records, likely to prove an accurate guide to happenings in the bastardy field.

Of the 68 bastardy cases noted either in the parish registers or the church courts in the period 1560–1639, only five are also recorded in the quarter sessions. The quarter sessions only add one new case where the woman is definitely stated to be of Earls Colne. Even in this case it is not certain that a bastard was actually born, for the women merely confessed that she was great with child (ERO, Q/SR/80/35). Yet, while the quarter sessions are no sort of index of bastardy ratios, they do give us a few more cases after 1640 against which to check the parish register.

39. When Robert Kendall, a bastard, was buried on 3 July 1656, Josselin was away seeing his daughter and preaching in Colchester.

Leaving on one side the four cases where it is only certain that the man was of Earls Colne, we find that there are only two instances of an Earls Colne woman being brought to court in connection with bastardy between 1640 and 1700. The first of these, in 1653, we have already seen was not noted in the parish register. The second was in 1688 when a Bocking man was to answer to give security for keeping a bastard child begotten of Mary Wiseman of Earls Colne (ERO,Q/SR/460/43). There is no record of this bastardy either. This gives a slim impression that after 1650, at least, bastards were not always registered, and it may partly help to account for the long gap in bastards in the parish register between 1662 and 1692. It also accords with the conclusions of chapter 6 as to the very low level of recorded illegitimacy in the middle of the century being largely a matter of registration.

Several conclusions may be drawn from the discussion above. The first is that up to 1640, when ecclesiastical courts provide a check, the parish register appears to have accurately recorded bastardy: perhaps less than one tenth failed to be registered in their home parish. From the 1640s onwards there is evidence from Josselin's diary and from the quarter sessions records that bastardy was not always registered, though the parish register seems to have continued to be well kept until about 1660. Thereafter, bastards may well have failed to be registered at all; throughout the period, quarter sessions records only picked up a tiny fraction of the bastardy cases. Nevertheless, the evidence does not completely destroy the hypothesis that there was a significant change in bastardy ratios in the first half of the seventeenth century. In Earls Colne the change would certainly appear to have been occurring in the late 1620s and 1630s. The bulge in bastardy of the Jacobean period faded away before the Puritans came formally to power, which is what should perhaps be expected from Keith Wrightson's discussion of that period in chapter 6.

8 The sociology of bastardy and the bastardy prone sub-society

To progress towards some idea of why bastardy rates fluctuated, we have to move to the micro-level of actual cases and personalities. Who were the men and women involved and how did they differ from the rest of the population? Is it in fact possible to find out about such people, or were they part of the 'invisible poor', the highly mobile and record-less section of pre-industrial society? The answers to these questions cannot be given for our village of Earls Colne until a full reconstruction is completed, but a few hints at the type of questions to be asked and some preliminary, tentative conclusions of current research may be provided.

Although there has been practically no investigation of the socio-economic level of those involved in illegitimacy, it is usually tacitly assumed by historians that bastardy was a phenomenon mainly connected with the lowest, or at least the lower, part of pre-industrial society. Thus, for example, the conclusion of the Norwich authorities in 1570, that the poor bring forth many bastards, is approvingly quoted.[40] Let us look in more detail at the Earls Colne bastard bearers. Is there anything we can find out about the wealth of those who begat and bore illegitimates, their occupation, their ownership of land and houses, their geographical mobility, their demographic history and their position in the family?

40. I. Pinchbeck, 'The state and the child in sixteenth-century England' (1956), p. 283.

Scattered evidence on these and other points will be found in the studies which follow, and in chapter 8 the whole set of issues is considered in a preliminary way in relation to the hypothesis of a bastardy prone sub-society existing over time in traditional English villages. There are indications that such a society may have been present in the early seventeenth century in Earls Colne, where the evidence seems to resemble that for another Essex village, Terling, only ten miles away to the southeast, discussed by David Levine and Keith Wrightson in chapter 5. The peak of bastard births over the period 1560–1640 occurred between 1600 and 1627, and this was also the time when a number of women had three or more bastards. Of the 33 definite bastards recorded in Earls Colne, no less than 13 were borne by three women only, as follows: Mary Grant, six bastards; Lidia Paine four bastards; Margaret Bunting, three bastards. It was also during these years that another phenomenon, the bastard-begetting male, appears: William Catt begot four bastards and Thomas Allen (on Mary Grant), another four. We may well wonder whether these women were village prostitutes and what sort of women and men these people were in other respects.

We begin with Margery Bunting, daughter of John, baptized in April 1588. Her father seems to have been moderately poor, though he rented a few acres of land at the south of the parish in 1598. He died in 1620 and his wife, Joan, in 1626: thus both were alive during practically the whole of Margery's bastard-bearing career. She appears to have been the eldest of the children; her siblings Nathaniel, John, William, Sara and Joan were baptized in the years 1590–99 and of these William married in 1622 when aged 24 and Joan in 1620 when 21 (both after their father's death). None of them seems to have been accused of sexual offences, but their father may have had a tolerant attitude to bastardy since he was presented in the church court in 1592 because it was noted 'that he keepeth a base child in his home and the father thereof not known' (ERO, D/ACA/20/227). He was excommunicated for non-appearance.

A similar impression emerges of Lidia Paine who was having bastards at almost exactly the same time: namely, that she was from a poor, but not destitute, village family. Lidia was baptized in May 1596, one of the children of Edward Paine who probably married in 1592 and who is said to have been a weaver. This man appears to have been a different sort of deviant since he was frequently presented in the ecclesiastical courts for not receiving communion. His daughter Lidia seems to have had bastard children at two- to three-year intervals between the ages of 23 and 31. After this there is a complete gap in the records, which may suggest that she left or married away from the parish. Certainly there is no record of a burial and Josselin, who mentioned other notorious livers, does not mention her in his diary.

Margery Bunting's bastards were evidently fathered by several men, but Lidia Paine seems to have had several by one man, Thomas Allen alias Grant. She showed forth what may have been a widespread feature of bastardy, where it bordered on consensual unions. Why the pair did not marry it is difficult to say as yet, but the issue could be further explored in the best documented of these cases, that of Mary Grant. There was clearly a close connection between these two women, for the begetter of Lidia's bastards was, in fact, the illegitimate son of Mary Grant. The double surname or alias frequently seems to denote uncertainty or 'double' parentage arising from an earlier bastardy, and hence marks out a bastard strain through time.

Mary Grant's employment as a spinner puts her into the group described by Roger Harlakendon, the lord of the manor in 1595:

> The parish of Earls Colne and divers other parishes thereabouts being much charged with great numbers of poor people, the said people have of a long time been set on work by spinning certain wool of Dutchmen, which they have delivered to the said poor people at the town of Earls Colne aforesaid, and there received the same from them againe being spun, whereby many of the said poor people have been and yet are relieved and maintained in good sort [ERO, Q/SR/130/42].

In this same year, 1595, Mary Grant had her first bastard baptized in June. Nine months earlier Lawrence Gilott and Mary had been presented for incontinency together, and three months before the baptism she alleged that 'Lawrence Gilott of Earls Colne is the father of her child, wherewith she is with child.' She was excommunicated for non-appearance, as was Gilott, a man whose house we can locate at the furthest end of the village and who came from a poor, but not from the poorest, level of society, and whose brother was also involved in sexual offences.

The accusation against Gilott may not have been sustained for in June Mary Grant was excommunicated again for not appearing to answer the suspicion of being impregnated by another man, Richard Coggeshall of Earls Colne, probably a passing inhabitant as little is known of him. Between 1600 and 1610 Mary proceeded to produce a string of bastards: three of them appear in the baptismal register in 1600, 1604 and 1610 and from ecclesiastical court evidence it is clear that another was born in 1606. (At this time the parish register was defective.) There is a long gap after 1610, but then, in 1620, Mary Grant was again accused of incontinent living. Thus her career had lasted for 28 years. The fact that the head of the household in which she lived was summoned to appear in the first case suggests that she was fairly young when she started to produce illegitimate children. Supposing that she was eighteen in 1592, she would have been 46 at the last recorded instance and 64 when she died in 1638.

There are many issues to be explored in this intriguing case,[41] but it is worth stressing one of them here, namely the continuity of bastardy in families. Thomas Allen, alias Giggers, who was the father of most of Mary Grant's children, may have himself come from a family associated with bastardy, since he had the telltale 'alias' in his name. We have seen the checkered career of Mary's first child, Thomas Allen, alias Grant, who gave bastards to Lidia Paine. Mary's second child, as we may recall from Josselin's note on her, was the 'Mary Grant a bold wench whose mother had six or seven bastards, her flesh rotted from her arms, complained she was gotten with child.' At this time, the daughter Mary was over 40 years of age and still unmarried. The construction of Josselin's comment leaves it open as to whether it was mother or daughter who was probably suffering from venereal disease.

9 Reasons for fluctuations in bastardy ratios

Until a much deeper examination has been carried out of village life in general, with particular emphasis on sexual mores, the structure of kinship and marriage,

41. Only about a quarter of the material relating to Mary Grant has been mentioned here; the complex web of relationships between the people involved in different cases will have to be explored on another occasion.

we cannot hope to understand the reasons for the changes in the incidence of bastardy and in the attitudes towards it. A number of hypotheses have been put forward. It is worth listing them briefly.

An obvious suggestion is that bastardy in England was a reaction to sexual frustration, and more directly to the comparatively late age at marriage. In the sixteenth century Stubbes argued that compulsorily to raise the age at marriage would lead to an increase in bastards.[42] It is likely correct to suppose that a negative correlation is more probable, namely that bastardy ratios increased in the late sixteenth and in the late eighteenth centuries when age at marriage may have been dropping. To decide the question finally, we would need to know much more about who the bastard-bearers and their partners were, and whether many of them were part of the never-to-be-married group.

Another view is that bastardy is related to a general economic change in the society. It may be argued either that women in times of prosperity are able to earn enough to support children without having to marry or, conversely, that in times of depression a 'crisis of subsistence' breaks down all social norms and sends up the level of bastardy. The second argument which finds no particular support in the evidence we have examined so far, is also attacked by P. Goubert (1960, p. 51). Another view looks at the problem from the other end: the mechanisms of social control and the mechanisms of segregating the sexes. Thus, for example, M. Drake (1969, p. 145) suggests that illegitimacy was high where male and female servants were lodged together in outhouses. Smout discusses the same possibility for Scotland in chapter 7. Again, there is not much support for such an hypothesis in the English material, but until further work is done on the persons involved in bastardy and on sleeping customs, it is difficult to be certain. Yet another suggestion is that illegitimacy is related to the failure of social control by kin.[43] Certainly there has, as yet, been no evidence that parents, though often alive, disowned or rejected their bastard-bearing daughters and there is some support for the belief that there was a minority ethic which did not condemn the practice.

Undoubtedly the major sanctions against sexual deviance during the period in which we are interested were informal – the treatment of past offenders and attitudes to deviance at the local, non-judicial level. The problem of deciding whether there was a permissive attitude to bastardy is made more difficult by two further facts. Firstly, that in a stratified society those in one stratum may not see bastardy as a frightful offence, while those in other strata may condemn it fiercely. Secondly, that most of our evidence comes from court records, where the handling of this offence and the degree of severity of the punishment may have borne little relation to the actual feelings at the local level. Nevertheless, it is important to see what treatment was meted out to bastard-bearers, and to try to estimate the proportion of cases which were brought to court at all.

In the studies which follow in the British section, some light is thrown on some of the questions raised in this chapter. But it has to be confessed that they leave us with very little general, reliable and systematic knowledge. And there is a further series of questions which they scarcely touch upon. The first concerns the provision which was made for the economic needs of those bastards who survived. I have already alluded to the somewhat contradictory evidence concerning the

42. Philip Stubbes, *The anatomie of abuses* (1585), fol. 55^{v}.
43. W. J. Goode, *World revolution and family patterns* (1963), p. 185.

testamentary position of bastards. Did they inherit land or goods and hence did they remain in the community? Scattered evidence from the sixteenth century and earlier shows frequent bequests to bastards in wills. A detailed study of manorial records and wills for Earls Colne should make it possible to discover what happened to the bastards in that village: for example, how frequently do wills mention them, as did the will of John Kendall on 22 February 1600? It should be possible to trace the life history of at least some of the bastard children. We ought to be able to find out whether they migrated, married or stayed single. Were they doomed to economic poverty or did some grow rich? Did they follow certain occupations, usually being bound apprentice early in life?[44] To give meaning to these analyses, comparison with matched groups of non-bastards is necessary and this would require a complete reconstitution of a particular parish.

It should also be possible to get an idea of the way bastards were regarded from the names conferred upon them. In Earls Colne they were given quite ordinary names, except for the years 1625 and 1626 when 'Repentance' Clarke, daughter of Mary, and 'Repent' Sparrow, son of Jane were baptized. Whether this reflected godly or church attitudes we do not know. Another clue to changing opinion would lie in the use of the word 'bastard' as a term of abuse in libels. An analysis of libel cases in the ecclesiastical courts should throw some light on this. One of the problems here is that changing attitudes to bastardy are intimately related to the numbers of bastards. As has been pointed out, the registration and prosecution of bastards may well reflect the attitude to the offence as much as its incidence.

These then are some of the issues which the reader may have in mind as he proceeds to the detailed studies of bastardy which are contained in the next few chapters of the volume. We may not yet be able to answer in any definite fashion the innumerable questions which have come to the fore in the close examination of illegitimacy in our particular village early in the period which most of these studies cover. But it is hoped that to have pointed out both the difficulties and the merit of using legal and other records and the very great amount of interesting material in local archives will be of value. Some knowledge of the legal, administrative and social background is clearly necessary in order to interpret the statistics which have been extracted with great dedication and labour from parish registers.

44. As had, for example, been suggested by Marie Hartley and Joan Ingilby, *Yorkshire village* (1953), p. 72.

3

Family reconstitution and the study of bastardy: evidence from certain English parishes

Karla Oosterveen, Richard M. Smith and Susan Stewart

1 Introduction

Richard M. Smith

One of the exercises performed by Laslett and Oosterveen in their original study of 1973 was to collate bastard births with the bastard-bearing mothers. Their aim was to establish the relative contribution of women who were known to have produced more than one bastard while residing in the parishes concerned. This simple variant of nominative linkage produced an intriguing, if somewhat shadowy pattern. It appeared, on the basis of data from these places (Colyton, Wem and Bolton Percy) that as the bastardy ratio went up the proportion of women producing more than one bastard went up at an even faster pace. What is more they produced evidence to suggest that these repetitive bastard-bearers were related to each other by kinship.

The pattern was clearly detectable in Colyton and Wem but not at Bolton Percy. Reference was made to work in progress on additional registers which it was suggested would be likely to substantiate the interpretation and give it greater regional representativeness.

In this chapter a summary account is given of these researches. It is the object of the first section to review some of their general outcomes and to comment on publications by other authors which have appeared, bearing on these aspects of the history of illegitimacy, especially in respect of geographical movement of bastard-bearers. Our remarks are confined for the most part to six parishes where family reconstitutions had been completed by 1974. Although rather inconclusive in the evidence they provide for the blood and marital relationships of bastardy-linked individuals, these studies have proved especially important in throwing light on three distinct but clearly interrelated issues:

(a) The degree to which the repetition of bastard-bearing took on the pattern Laslett and Oosterveen suggested.
(b) The extent to which bastard-bearers could be distinguished from the total parochial population concerning their migratory behaviour.
(c) The age patterns of illegitimate in relation to legitimate fertility.

1 The pattern of repetitive bastard-bearing over time and over space

We may begin with the development of what we call 'repeaterdom': in this discussion a 'repeater' is a woman who is known to have given birth to more than one bastard child, and a 'singleton' a woman with only one to her credit. In table

3.1 data are set out and arranged in terms of what have been called the 'early high', 'low' and 'late high' periods of illegitimacy on the percentage of bastard-bearers recording two or more bastards (Laslett and Oosterveen, 1973, p. 283). The patterns they display clearly do not go as far as Laslett and Oosterveen expected in clarifying the hazy picture which they had encountered in their early work. In fact, the weight of evidence would seem to run counter to the idea of a high level of repetitive bastard-bearing followed by a low level in the mid-seventeenth to mid-eighteenth centuries. In five of the twelve parishes a trend of that kind can be detected but it is founded on differences that are not easy to test statistically, based, as all of the percentages for the early periods are, on a very small number of cases even when aggregated for periods of fifty to a hundred years. Of the nine additional parishes only three showed the pattern of high percentages of repeaters in the late sixteenth and late eighteenth centuries as identified in Colyton and Wem.

During the 'later high', however, the repeater effect was decidedly confirmed. In all the parishes the highest percentages of repeating bastard-bearers were to be found in the period of highest bastardy ratios, that is the late eighteenth and early nineteenth centuries. Nonetheless, the sharpness of this rise was far less apparent in the three small middling-sized market towns (Gainsborough, Banbury and Alcester) in this sample.

The most important study of these aspects of the history of sexual nonconformism to appear since 1973 has undoubtedly been that of David Levine (1977, chapter 9). He analyses repeaterdom in a number of English villages of contrasted social structure and development. In Shepshed, a proto-industrial Leicestershire framework knitting village, he finds that nearly 18 per cent of all unmarried mothers after 1750 were repeaters, producing 35 per cent of the bastard births. Here, he claims (p. 142), the proto-industrial environment left 'no hiatus between adolescence and economic maturity' and from this evidence he attempts to

Table 3.1: Percentages of unmarried mothers producing two or more bastards in 12 parishes

	Periods of illegitimacy			
Place	'early high' 1540–1639	'low' 1640–1739	'late high' 1740–1839	
Colyton	11.4[1]	2.1[2]	24.7	after Laslett and Oosterveen (1973)
Wem	11.1[3]	5.0[4]	21.4[5]	
Bolton Percy	1.8[6]	2.5	11.0[7]	
Alcester	11.6[8]	7.0	11.6	
Aldenham	3.0[9]	8.0	16.1	
Banbury	3.0[10]	11.1[11]	13.4[12]	
Campton/Shefford	0.0[13]	9.3	15.1	
Gainsborough	1.0[14]	10.2	11.1	
Gedling	9.7[15]	5.1	13.9	
Hartland	10.6[16]	7.6[17]	22.8[18]	
Hawkshead	1.5[19]	4.2	16.5	
Hemyock	8.3[20]	12.5	17.6	

[1] 1590–1639
[2] 1640–89
[3] 1581–1640
[4] 1641–1720
[5] 1721–1812
[6] 1570–1639
[7] 1740–1812
[8] 1561–1639
[9] 1561–1639
[10] 1561–1640
[11] 1641–1720
[12] 1721–1838
[13] 1540–1639
[14] 1540–1639
[15] 1558–1639
[16] 1561–1640
[17] 1641–1720
[18] 1721–1838
[19] 1586–1639
[20] 1610–39

generalize a more widely applicable pattern. He draws a distinction between two purely agricultural villages (Bottesford in Leicestershire and Terling in Essex) where repetitive bastard bearing was comparatively infrequent, with around 8 per cent of all mothers so classed, and more industrialized communities such as Shepshed and Colyton. Levine thinks it unlikely to be accidental that in the two villages where women could find work outside the household[1] repetitive bastard-bearing was comparatively common, with many couples living in consensual unions and subsequently going on to marry. Attractive though this distinction is, the evidence in table 3.2 does not rest comfortably with Levine's argument. Repetitive bastard-bearing appears to have been highest in the isolated north Devon village of Hartland where no craftwork for women has been traced, while Colyton comes second in the rank ordering, an effect, Levine claims, of women being engaged in lace-making. The next highest levels are to be found in villages (Campton-with-Shefford and Aldenham) where the principal livelihood was market-oriented agricultural production. The village closest in character to Shepshed, Gedling, located on the forest edge of Nottinghamshire with quarrying and basket-making and framework knitting, is one of the parishes with the lowest proportion of repeaters in the eighteenth century. Very similar in this respect to Gedling were the middling sized market towns of Gainsborough, Banbury and Alcester – the last mentioned with a needle-making industry. It may well be that the regionalism of bastard-bearing behaviour commented on in chapter 1 had as much to do with this pattern as differences in community economic character. It also suggests a need to take into account the geographical size of the parishes involved. In addition, it suggests a need for further research into courtship customs and their local variations.

Table 3.2: Percentage of unmarried mothers producing two or more bastards in ten English parishes, 1690–1789

Place	No. of unmarried mothers	No. producing 2+ bastard births	%
Alcester	96	7	7.3
Aldenham	68	13	19.1
Banbury[1]	189	21	11.1
Campton/Shefford	102	22	21.6
Colyton	179	40	22.3
Gainsborough	275	37	13.5
Gedling	89	9	10.1
Hartland[2]	180	42	23.3
Hawkshead	132	18	13.6
Hemyock	84	13	15.5

[1] 1721–1800 [2] 1721–1800

2 Migration and the unmarried mother

Answers to another set of questions concerning the reason for this somewhat structureless pattern as to repeaterdom in the late eighteenth and early nineteenth

1. It is not absolutely clear why Levine refers to work 'outside the household' for it is generally considered that proto-industrial work was a form of household economy (see H. Medick, 'The proto-industrial family economy: the structural function of household and family during the transition from peasant society to industrial capitalism', 1976), although he may be referring to work for women other than as servants in husbandry or domestic servants.

centuries could be pursued with the evidence of the family reconstitutions. This technique can be fruitfully employed in the field of migration analysis and migratory movements may have considerable bearing on 'statistics' concerning repetitive bastard-bearing. The methods by which this problem can be approached will be pursued at greater length in this section. In the process of this analysis we may also learn something of the social and economic distinctiveness of those women responsible for such births.

David Souden (1980) has recently subjected the data from sixteen parish family reconstitution studies to intensive scrutiny in an attempt to ascertain their individual migration profiles and to discover whether any long term trends common to all or the majority of these parishes can be detected. This study provides a valuable backcloth against which to set a similar appraisal of the registration characteristics of bastards and bastard-bearers and their kin.

In sections 2 and 3 of this chapter we present material concerning these characteristics from six parishes that can be compared with a much larger body of individuals not known to have been distinguished by a bastardy connection. The results of analysing by place of birth women producing children within marriage and outside it are presented in table 3.3. It is obvious from the first column in the table that it is usually possible to link married women with baptisms in the parish only relatively rarely, about one time in five. The data in the table are not, however, totally without structure. The two market towns of Banbury and Alcester, both centres of in-migration, stand out with the lowest proportions of wives who were known to have been indigenous to the parish in which they were married. Colyton, too, where as we have seen, textile manufacturing co-existed with an intensive style of pastoral farming, appears as a distinctly 'open' type of parish with low levels of home-produced brides.

At the other extreme we have Hartland in north Devon, geographically a large parish but isolated from its neighbours and as a consequence displaying a high level of geographical marital endogamy among its womenfolk. In addition Aldenham, a Hertfordshire rural parish with a well developed form of capitalist agriculture and deeply embedded into the migration pathways leading into London, experienced a large outmovement of its women after birth. Hawkshead, an upland Lancashire parish, stands fractionally apart from these very mobile female populations with nearly a third of its women marrying in the parish of their birth – a pattern, however, that subsumes steady change over time as the community experienced striking economic developments in the eighteenth century.

Table 3.3: Place of baptism of married women and unmarried mothers in six English parishes, 1600–1789

Place	Married women[1] % baptized in parish	Unmarried mothers[2] % baptized in parish
Alcester	18.0	29.4
Aldenham	21.9	43.2
Banbury	16.9	42.6
Colyton	17.3	42.3
Hartland	50.6	51.3
Hawkshead	28.6	33.9

[1]1600–1780 based on Souden (1979)   [2]1600–1789

Did the bastard-bearing women merely show forth the migratory behaviour of all other women in these parishes? The second column of table 3.3 shows that in certain minor respects similarities do appear to have existed between the two groups. For instance, women who were natives of the parishes in which their bastards had been registered were relatively most frequent in Hartland and least visible in the market town of Alcester: a pattern mirroring that for the married women. Yet any further similarities are difficult to discover. Bastard-bearers in Hawkshead, for instance, are definitely more mobile than in Colyton and Banbury. Indeed, table 3.3 reveals the far lower level of mobility among women producing bastards than that exhibited by the female population at large: between one third and one half of such women were natives of the parish in which they baptized their bastards.

Do these patterns both with respect to married women and unmarried mothers remain stable over time? David Souden's work on sixteen parishes shows a very striking tendency for female mobility levels to decline in the late seventeenth century. In four of the six parishes considered in table 3.4 – Alcester, Hartland, Aldenham and Hawkshead – this pattern is strongly suggested. In Banbury it is less evident. Migration out of and into all six parishes with the notable exception of Hartland appears to have been far more marked in the eighteenth century than the later seventeenth century. This pattern is by no means as clear in its appearance among bastard-bearing women as table 3.5 suggests. The bastard-bearers of Hartland and Aldenham in the late seventeenth century appear increasingly as native-born members of the parish. Elsewhere, we do not find this course of change; indeed, the direction of the trend looks more inclined to be opposite to that of the female population at large. In the later eighteenth century, when the

Table 3.4: Place of baptism of female marriage cohorts in six English parishes, 1591–1800

	% in parish			
	1591–1640	1641–90	1691–1740	1741–1800
Alcester	20.7	30.9	25.1	15.4
Aldenham	32.3	42.6	33.7	24.2
Banbury	24.1	20.7	20.8	20.3
Colyton	30.2	33.0	28.1	28.9
Hartland	36.3	53.3	43.8	43.9
Hawkshead	33.7[1]	53.2	30.3	23.5

[1] 1601–40

Table 3.5: Place of baptism of unmarried mothers, 1600–1789

	% in parish			
Place	1590–1639	1640–89	1690–1739	1748–89
Alcester	29.4	16.6	26.7	31.8
Aldenham	20.8	53.8	58.3	46.4
Banbury	40.5[1]	38.1[2]	39.2[3]	40.4[4]
Colyton	40.5	33.3	42.5	52.2
Hartland	41.4[1]	59.3[2]	51.3[3]	70.1[4]
Hawkshead	5.9[5]	7.4	17.8	55.2

[1] 1601–40 [2] 1641–80 [3] 1681–1720 [4] 1721–60 [5] 1586–1639

repeater phenomenon is seen to have grown in importance, the two trends look to be more clearly at odds. In five of the six parishes bastard-bearers were between two and three times more likely to have been native born than married women appearing on the family reconstitution forms; in four of these parishes this chance increased considerably as the eighteenth century progressed. Furthermore, when in the four parishes in which it is presently possible we compare the registration characteristics of the repeaters with those who were singletons, the pattern is found once again but considerably intensified (see table 3.6). Nearly 60 per cent of the Colyton and 66 per cent of the Hawkshead repeaters were born in the parish in which they gave birth out of wedlock.

This evidence leaves a strong suspicion that bastard-bearers in the second half of the eighteenth century were becoming less mobile. Repeaters, it would seem, were generally more stationary than singletons. Were they immobile because they were repeaters or were they repeaters because they were immobile? Or, are we observing the effect of an institutional involvement in the mobility process such that women conceiving outside their parish of birth were moving back into their birth places to bear and to register their illegitimate offspring? The causal relationships are difficult to unravel.

Table 3.6: Place of baptism of unmarried mothers: repeaters and singletons

	% in parish 1740–89[1]	
Place	Repeaters	Singletons
Alcester	40.0	31.6
Aldenham	41.7	51.2
Colyton	59.1	50.0
Hawkshead	66.7	46.9

[1] Before this period the numbers of bastard-bearers producing two or more bastards and linkable with a baptism are too small to produce meaningful statistics.

We can be reasonably certain that the general trends in migration identified by Souden were not unduly influencing the index of repetitive bastard-bearing worked out in chapter 8 (see table 8.2). For if this was so, the times when the index might be expected to have been highest were those when immobility was most widely prevalent, that is the late seventeenth and early eighteenth centuries. However, unmarried mothers producing more than one birth were generally most frequent when mobility was relatively high as in the later eighteenth century.[2]

We are still left with the problem of why bastard-bearers, both those producing one and more than one child *appear* to have been less mobile in the late eighteenth century. The absence of good evidence on the family economic background of unmarried mothers is clearly a hindrance in this matter, for if it were the case that economic groups most clearly associated with bastardy grew in size at this date then we could be witnessing the statistical manifestation of a compositional change.

2. It should be noted that David Souden does encounter a number of places whose populations became increasingly less mobile in the later eighteenth century, especially in landlord-dominated agricultural parishes with sizable concentrations of agricultural labourers. It is most likely that the immobile bastard-bearers in the parishes we have considered in this chapter came from similar economic groups and we could well be observing among these individuals the pattern more widely found in other local populations.

Yet, conventional views are that labourers were likely to have been the most transient members of society, sending their children away from home early rather than late, thereby minimizing their chances of conception out of wedlock in their parishes of birth. We would therefore expect fewer unmarried mothers registering their bastards' baptisms in their parish unless they were coming back home to have these children.

Alternatively, the turnover rates of these groups may have been declining and if the expectations of women within them as regards their own marriage had been rising over time but were thwarted by a decline in real wages, which set in during the later part of the eighteenth century, in such a way as to produce a number of incomplete or, in Levine's phrase, 'frustrated' courtships, then this pattern of bastardy may have been the outcome. Furthermore, we must take seriously the possible impact of institutional forces at work sending women back perhaps to the parishes where they may have had a settlement in the event of them becoming pregnant and constituting a charge on the poor rates.[3]

We know from a not inconsiderable number of settlement papers that pregnant, unmarried women were certainly removed from parishes under these circumstances.[4] If it was a relatively frequent practice and if it represented a change of policy it might help to explain the apparent 'immobility' of women bearing bastards at this period. If this evidence does nothing else it raises a number of questions about the precise mechanisms responsible for this statistical artefact of the bastardy recordings. Two interesting possibilities are raised. One is that bastard-bearers became immobile because they entered into courtship early in their natal parishes. The other, more likely, is that their migration horizons were temporarily restricted by the Poor Law authorities of neighbouring or more distant parishes. Both these effects could, of course, have been present simultaneously.

3 The ages of married women and unmarried mothers

In no way can the above findings be seen to conflict with the evidence in sections 2 and 3 of this chapter regarding the other demographic attributes of bastard-bearers, particularly those concerning their ages and their marriage chances. For clearly, these activities, influenced as they were by varying migratory patterns, were closely linked with the forces at work determining fertility levels in all of these four communities. We should note the data presented in tables 3.14, 3.15, 3.16, 3.30 and 3.31 of this chapter where the ages of unmarried mothers appear strikingly similar to the ages of married women both when the distribution of those ages and their pattern of change over time are considered.

It is worth noting, however, that David Levine has put forward a case for a changing relationship between these two elements when the seventeenth and eighteenth centuries are compared. He argues that the age of unmarried mothers in the seventeenth century tended on average to be close to a year or so above that of women at marriage. Levine's explanation for this apparent difference is based on the persistence of 'traditional' forms of sexual behaviour into the seventeenth

3. It is not quite clear if this forced movement was occurring why a woman's place of settlement should have been her place of birth. Furthermore, underpinning this pattern is the possibility of changes in the definition of a place of settlement. I am grateful to David Souden for raising these points.

4. See for example cases involving the movement of pregnant women for early nineteenth-century Hartland: Devon Record Office 1201 A/1/PO/736 and 1201 A/1/PO/743.

century at a time when marriage was being increasingly postponed, with illegitimate births ensuing. This relationship between the two ages, he found, was reversed in the eighteenth century, especially in villages which were likely to have provided women with work outside the household.

Although table 3.14 below appears to sustain Levine's view it would be dangerous to accept this interpretation unequivocally. One reason for this scepticism is the fact that in his analysis the number of unmarried mothers whose ages can be determined before the eighteenth century is exceedingly small, growing rapidly, however, in the eighteenth century. Furthermore, table 3.14 is in part misleading because it contains a very high proportion of cases from Colyton where this pattern was first detected by Levine. In fact, before 1749 well over 50 per cent of all the evidence in table 3.14 comes from Colyton cases. It is not until the later eighteenth and early nineteenth centuries that Colyton's share of the evidence falls to a level of 30 per cent or less.

We are in no position, moreover, to control for the occupational background of all those who produced bastards and of those who produced them in their parishes of birth so that their ages could be established. We may, therefore, be observing a temporal effect produced by a growing proportion of bastard-bearers coming from those groups of people who married, and were increasingly marrying at an early age. What is needed in an ideal data set is age evidence on unmarried mothers and married women from similar social and economic backgrounds.

These qualifications need not, however, detract from Levine's forcefully argued case that economic opportunity, family formation and sexual anticipation of marriage were all critically interrelated in directing the course of bastardy levels over time. The association of bastard-bearing with a particular type of 'relations of production' is far from clear. From an admittedly small sample we can say that the median age of unmarried mothers rose over the course of the seventeenth century and fell steadily in line with the median marriage age over the eighteenth century. Meanwhile we now know that general fertility was rising rapidly, the gross reproduction rate moving in a lagged relationship with increasing real wages. The data for these conclusions does not come from the handful of reconstitutions to which we have had to confine ourselves here, but from a sample of no less than 404 English parishes.

2 Bastardy and the family reconstitution studies of Colyton, Aldenham, Alcester and Hawkshead

Karla Oosterveen and Richard M. Smith

The reconstitution studies of the parish registers of Colyton (Devon), Hawkshead (Lancashire), Alcester (Warwickshire) and Aldenham (Hertfordshire), carried out under the direction of the SSRC Cambridge Group for the History of Population and Social Structure in the context of a detailed analysis of English demographic behaviour from the middle of the sixteenth to the early nineteenth century, have provided us with a considerable body of data for the study of bastardy. Because the data are by-products from reconstitution analysis, this particular study must take on a distinctly demographic appearance. No systematic attempt has been made to marshall evidence from other contemporary sources likely to give additional insight into the behaviour patterns, the social and economic backgrounds of the bearers, begetters and immediate kin of bastards or of the attitudes of the local communities, the civil and ecclesiastical authorities to the actions of the offenders. For these reasons this exercise must be seen primarily as a discussion of the extent to which bastardy can be studied through the figures and patterns that are derived solely from the parish register.

The four parishes have been chosen not on the basis of any sampling procedure but on the availability of their registers as reconstituted data sets. They are, however, representative of a wide range of pre-industrial communities. Colyton parish contained the principal settlement of Colyton, a small market town, and a number of hamlets of which Colyford was the largest and most distinct. Agriculture persisted as the dominant means of livelihood along with service trades and industries typical of such settlements, but textile manufacturing, as in many areas of east Devon was at times important. Hawkshead, on the Lancashire borders with Westmorland and Cumberland, was a large though not very heavily populated upland parish with a predominantly agricultural economy, but with some mining in the Coniston area and domestic weaving in the eighteenth century. It also had a small market. Aldenham was a relatively large parish in a mixed farming area of Hertfordshire and possessed a fairly well developed capitalist agricultural economy with a sizable majority of the male population employed as agricultural labourers. Alcester, a small Warwickshire parish with a market throughout the seventeenth and eighteenth centuries, was located in the pre-industrial era in an area of mixed farming. A considerable growth in the size of its industrial population, particularly miners and nailers, in the eighteenth century gave it some of the characteristics of a proto-industrial community with agricultural labour being of relatively limited significance in the overall employment structure.

Some ancillary data are also presented for four other parishes which are not dealt with in great detail in this chapter. They are Gedling in Nottinghamshire, Campton with Shefford in Bedfordshire, Gainsborough in Lincolnshire and Hemyock in North Devon. Gedling was predominantly an agricultural parish in the sixteenth and seventeenth centuries, but the eighteenth century saw the emergence of a framework knitting industry and by the early nineteenth century it could be classed as an industrial parish. The bulk of the labour force of Campton with Shefford worked as agricultural labourers on a number of relatively large estates, although the 1811 census suggests that a sizable proportion of the working population was engaged in retailing and handicrafts. Gainsborough was a typical moderately large market town in the midst of a mixed farming area and had in 1811 a population of nearly 6,000 persons, while Hemyock was an agricultural parish of some 5,000 acres in the Culm valley among the Blackdown Hills on the Devon-Somerset borders.

The registers of the four principal parishes in this study, Colyton, Hawkshead, Alcester and Aldenham, differ in quality and in the period of time they cover. The Colyton register starts in 1540, the Alcester and Aldenham registers in 1561 and the Hawkshead register not until 1572 with the registration remaining poor for the first fifteen years. The reconstitution and the bastardy study of Hawkshead do not therefore start until 1586 and cover a period of 250 years as against 275 for Alcester and Aldenham and 300 for Colyton.

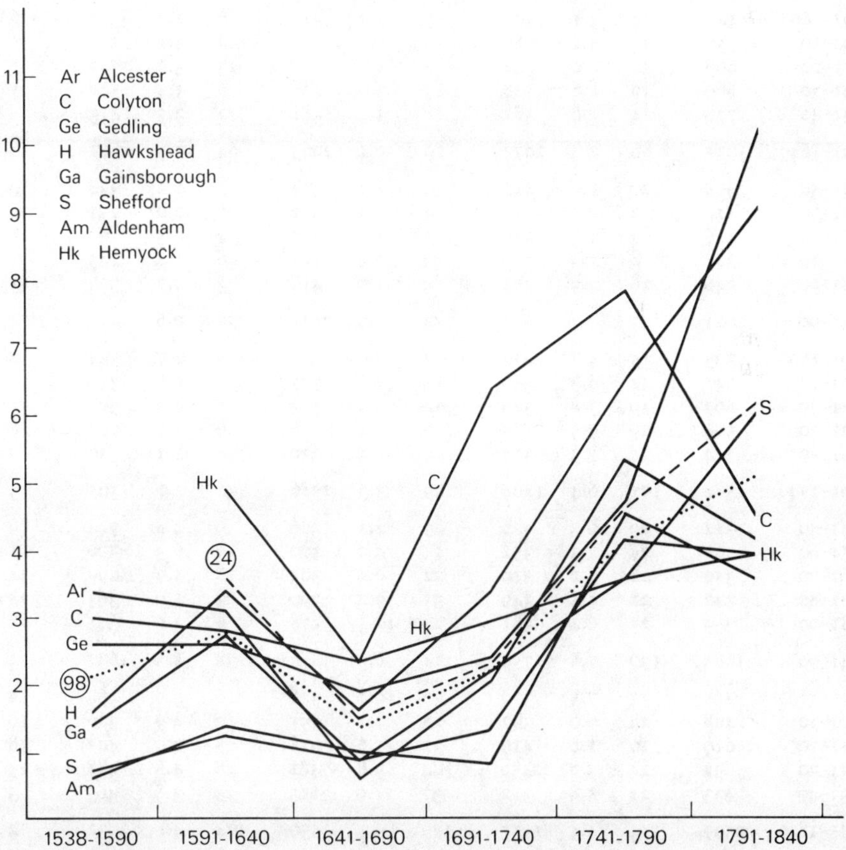

Fig. 3.1 The trend in illegitimacy ratios in eight English parishes, 1538–1840

1 Bastardy trends

Figure 3.1 and table 3.8 chart the course of illegitimacy over almost three centuries from the middle of the last half of the sixteenth century to the end of the third decade of the nineteenth century for the eight parishes. Certain phases in the period from 1540 to 1840 follow closely the trend of the bastardy ratio for both the 24 selected English parishes analysed by Laslett and Oosterveen (1973) and the revised pattern based on a much larger sample of 98 parishes considered by

Table 3.8: Legitimate and illegitimate baptisms in eight English parishes, 1538–1840

Decades	Colyton 1538–1837 Baptisms	Colyton Bastards	Colyton %	Hawkshead 1568–1837 Baptisms	Hawkshead Bastards	Hawkshead %	Alcester 1561–1840 Baptisms	Alcester Bastards	Alcester %	Aldenham 1559–1839 Baptisms	Aldenham Bastards	Aldenham %
1538–50	365	4	1.1									
1551–60	290	4	1.4									
1561–70	283	8	2.8				115	0	0.0	339	2	0.6
1571–80	408	20	4.9	550	9	1.6	213	6	2.8	333	2	0.6
1581–90	472	19	4.0	334	5	1.5	347	17	4.9	364	3	0.8
1538–90	1818	55	3.0	884	14	1.6	675	23	3.4	1036	7	0.6
1591–1600	427	13	3.1	404	15	3.7	343	16	4.7	353	6	1.7
1601–10	550	28	5.1	316	16	5.1	411	17	4.1	366	5	1.4
1611–20	609	12	2.0	444	8	1.8	407	13	3.2	347	7	2.0
1621–30	669	19	2.8	428	13	3.0	421	6	1.4	328	3	0.9
1631–40	776	14	1.8	481	18	3.7	481	12	2.5	413	5	1.2
1591–1640	3031	86	2.8	2073	70	3.4	2063	64	3.1	1807	26	1.4
1641–50	465	20	4.3	412	10	2.4	428	1	0.2	334	2	0.6
1651–60	440	2	0.5	315	3	0.9	462	0	0.0	271	2	0.7
1661–70	426	7	1.6	320	5	1.6	382	2	0.5	232	8	3.4
1671–80	344	8	2.3	229	2	0.9	421	6	1.4	245	1	0.4
1681–90	346	10	2.9	263	4	1.5	418	3	0.7	319	1	0.3
1641–90	2021	47	2.3	1539	24	1.6	2111	12	0.6	1401	14	1.0
1691–1700	323	15	4.7	273	7	2.6	300	8	2.7	324	2	0.6
1701–10	348	22	6.3	256	12	4.6	327	2	0.6	310	1	0.3
1711–20	263	10	3.8	329	14	4.3	303	8	2.6	308	2	0.6
1721–30	306	29	9.5	288	7	2.4	326	6	1.8	273	8	2.9
1731–40	344	25	7.3	318	9	2.8	330	8	2.1	350	0	0.0
1691–1740	1584	101	6.4	1464	49	3.3	1586	32	2.0	1565	13	0.8
1741–50	311	29	9.3	326	7	2.1	206	9	4.4	344	6	1.7
1751–60	326	24	7.3	352	14	4.0	300	19	6.3	300	11	3.7
1761–70	359	26	7.2	346	22	6.4	305	18	5.9	299	14	4.7
1771–80	327	28	8.5	349	31	9.2	390	23	5.9	363	25	6.9
1781–90	359	23	6.4	381	40	10.5	278	9	3.2	341	18	5.3
1741–90	1682	130	7.8	1754	114	6.5	1479	78	5.3	1647	74	4.5
1791–1800	435	31	7.1	379	38	10.0	326	16	4.9	368	18	4.9
1801–10	468	28	6.0	397	28	7.1	391	19	4.9	366	10	2.7
1811–20	629	10	1.6	419	32	7.6	618	18	2.9	405	18	4.4
1821–30	634	24	3.8	450	44	9.8	582	28	4.8	488	13	2.7
1831–40	433	21	4.8	312	37	11.9	613	23	3.8	405	13	3.2
1791–1840	2599	114	4.4	1957	179	9.1	2530	104	4.1	2032	72	3.5
1538–1840	12735	533	4.2	9671	450	4.6	10444	313	3.0	9488	206	2.2

Laslett (1977, chapter 3). The various trends are to be seen in figure 3.1. Two features in particular appear to be encountered in all the series. All seem to fall to a low in the years 1640–89. Most places with the exception of Aldenham show a tendency for the bastardy ratio to pick up in the fifty-year period 1690–1739. The magnitude of the growth in the ratio at Colyton during this phase is particularly noticeable. Aldenham and Campton-with-Shefford report such low bastardy ratios in the early fifty-year periods that no real trend is detectable. Whether the

Table 3.8 (*cont.*)

	Southill/Campton 1541–1840			Gainsborough 1564–1812			Gedling 1558–1837			Hemyock 1610–1837		
Decades	Baptisms	Bastards	%	Baptisms	Bastards	%	Baptisms	Bastards	%	Baptisms	Bastards	%
1538–50	212	2	0.9									
1551–60	135	0	0.0									
1561–70	191	0	0.0				122	4	3.3			
1571–80	367	1	0.3	821	12	1.5	165	5	3.0			
1581–90	417	6	1.4	562	7	1.2	136	2	1.5			
1538–90	1323	9	0.7	1383	19	1.4	423	11	2.6			
1591–1600	391	3	0.8	564	15	2.7	132	1	0.7			
1601–10	450	4	0.9	770	29	3.8	187	4	2.1			
1611–20	432	7	1.6	796	22	2.8	214	8	3.7	74	3	4.1
1621–30	475	6	1.3	765	19	2.5	198	3	1.5	56	3	5.4
1631–40	452	5	1.1	951	18	1.9	202	8	4.0	113	6	5.3
1591–1640	1900	25	1.3	3846	103	2.7	933	24	2.6	243	12	4.9
1641–50	283	5	1.8	876	17	1.9	179	7	3.9	85	3	3.5
1651–60	332	3	0.9	929	6	0.6	189	2	1.0	213	3	1.4
1661–70	384	4	1.0	814	10	1.2	198	3	1.5	238	8	3.4
1671–80	432	2	0.5	827	3	0.4	208	4	1.9	227	4	1.8
1681–90	428	2	0.5	900	7	0.8	218	3	1.4	152	3	2.0
1641–90	1859	16	0.9	4346	43	0.9	992	19	1.9	915	21	2.3
1691–1700	424	4	0.9	856	17	1.9	179	4	2.2	257	3	1.2
1701–10	446	8	1.8	752	21	2.8	183	4	2.2	285	11	3.9
1711–20	443	4	0.9	936	16	1.7	167	3	1.8	263	10	3.8
1721–30	371	9	2.4	1010	15	1.5	190	4	2.1	244	8	3.3
1731–40	444	5	1.1	1196	36	3.0	226	8	3.5	375	10	3.8
1691–1740	2128	30	1.3	4750	105	2.2	945	23	2.4	1424	42	2.9
1741–50	467	8	1.7	1038	39	3.8	211	14	6.6	245	8	3.3
1751–60	491	19	3.8	1142	41	3.6	248	10	4.0	258	14	5.4
1761–70	465	24	5.1	1253	43	3.4	332	16	4.8	357	8	3.6
1771–80	577	21	3.6	1380	44	3.2	388	8	2.1	248	6	2.4
1781–90	541	31	5.7	1558	56	3.6	445	28	6.3	256	15	5.9
1741–90	2541	103	4.1	6371	223	3.5	1624	76	4.7	1364	51	3.7
1791–1800	532	27	5.1	1669	61	3.6	555	55	9.9	249	22	8.8
1801–10	558	11	1.9	2221	93	4.2	660	64	9.7	315	28	8.9
1811–20	625	22	3.5				768	81	10.5	296	15	5.1
1821–30	731	30	4.1				846	79	9.3	389	19	4.9
1831–40	756	35	4.6				676	82	12.1	311	11	3.5
1791–1840	3202	125	3.9	3890	154	3.9	3505	361	10.3	1560	95	6.1
1538–1840	12953	308	2.7	24586	637	2.6	8422	514	6.1	5506	221	4.0

decline in the middle of the seventeenth century and the low level of the ratio persisting into the eighteenth century followed by a general increase is more the product of changes in the quality of registration than of real changes in the relative importance of bastardy is a question that we cannot attempt to answer here.

It is impossible to be certain that the earliest decades in our series exhibited a trend, and for two reasons: first, because the ratio figures were derived from different combinations of years for each parish, thereby making comparison very difficult and, second, because the quality of registration may have been highly variable. Furthermore, by aggregating the evidence into fifty-year periods certain of the short-term trends are lost. Nevertheless table 3.8 shows in many of the communities a period of relatively high bastardy ratios either in the very late sixteenth or early seventeenth centuries. Likewise, the last fifty-year period in the time series, 1791–1840, is difficult to evaluate with four of the eight parishes exhibiting declines and four increases. Too much should not be read into these patterns, partly because of the deterioration in the quality of registration which could easily account for a few percentage points of change. Another influence is probably also at work.

The bastardy figures in the eight parishes have been derived not just from baptismal evidence but also from references to bastards in the burial registers and occasionally also in the marriage registers. After Rose's Burial Act of 1812 the information on individuals was reduced considerably because of the format of the new printed registers which made it very difficult to include ancillary details, such as whether the dead person had been a bastard. For this reason the number of reported bastards in the burial registers falls off. Indeed, at Colyton where the effect is most marked, if we produce a time series based solely on the number of baptisms, the observed decline in the period 1790–1840 is reduced by over 50 per cent. Deterioration in the quality of baptismal registration could quite easily have accounted for part of the remaining decline. Furthermore, the level of prenuptial conceptions, which throughout the eighteenth century at Colyton had followed the bastardy ratio, continued to rise, as it did in other places, and then displayed a similar decline throughout the early decades of the nineteenth century, therefore casting considerable doubt on the likelihood of a real decline in the bastardy level.

David Levine (1977, p. 140) has offered explanations for an observed decline in the level of bastardy ratios in these years in his study. He believes that the practice of supplementing the income of the village poor became common in the Napoleonic Wars and had the effect of tying them even more tightly to their place of settlement. As a consequence, this led to a stabilization or a drop in illegitimacy because marriage was an assumed, even a taken-for-granted condition by the labouring poor. It became associated with a marked rise in the level of bridal pregnancy as Levine believes the level of premarital sexual activity rose – a situation, it is claimed, that existed until the Poor Law Amendment Act of 1834. This interesting argument is never proven empirically at the scale of the individual communities concerned. Furthermore, it is unclear whether it has a wider application outside of the southern, eastern and east Midland counties and it is certainly debatable whether such an argument would apply to all or any of the data sets in our study. Additionally, in our evidence the relationship between an ascending rate of prenuptial pregnancy and declining illegitimacy in the early nineteenth century is not consistently encountered.

Table 3.9 indicates the frequency with which mothers are seen to have had just one or more than one bastard birth. In these calculations the number of birth events have been used rather than the total number of bastards. For the whole period repeating bastard-bearers accounted for just over 8 per cent of Gainsborough mothers of bastards, but rose as high as 15 per cent of those in Colyton. These aggregations hide interesting variations, if somewhat complex and difficult to interpret, from place to place and over time. Only three of the communities had more than 10 per cent of their mothers bearing more than one recorded bastard before the period 1691–1740, and in all three this was encountered in the period ending in 1590. Some caution must be exercised in interpreting these trends as the repeating bastard-bearer has been located in the period in which the first bastard birth occurred: doubtless the repeating time straddles two periods in a number of instances. It is quite clear from these data that the frequency of repeating grows considerably in all communities during the eighteenth century. Indeed, there are cases in Hawkshead, Campton with Shefford and Gainsborough of individuals having six and even eight bastard-birth events in the period 1740–89. Whether these were all fathered by the same man or by different men is difficult to say.

It would seem therefore that, as the bastardy ratio rose in the latter half of the eighteenth century, so did the relative importance of women producing more than one bastard. Figure 3.2 shows the relationship between the bastardy ratio

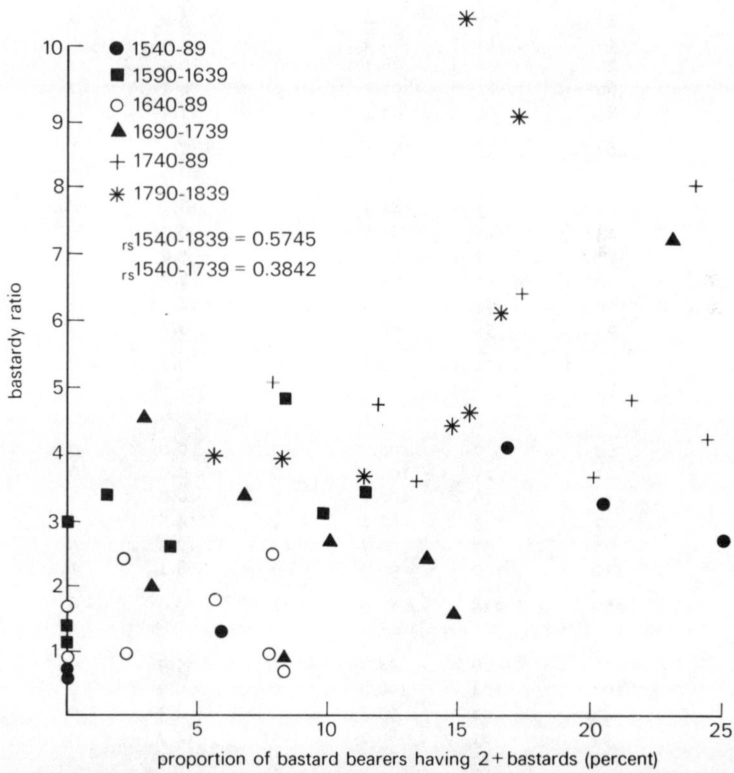

Fig. 3.2 The relationship between the illegitimacy ratio and repetitive bastard-bearing, eight English parishes

Table 3.9: Bastard births per bastard-bearing mother in eight English parishes, 1540–1840

	Bastard-bearing mothers	1 birth per mother	%	2 births per mother	%	3+ births per mother	%
Colyton							
1540–89	44	37	84.1	6	13.6	1	2.3
1590–1639	79	72	91.1	5	6.3	2	2.6
1640–89	48	48	100.0	0	0.0	0	0.0
1690–1739	87	69	79.3	14	16.1	4	4.6
1740–89	92	70	76.1	15	16.3	7	7.6
1790–1839	102	86	84.3	10	9.8	6	3.9
1540–1839	452	382	84.5	50	11.1	20	4.4
Hawkshead							
1586–1639	68	67	98.5	0	0.0	1	1.5
1640–89	27	27	100.0	0	0.0	0	0.0
1690–1739	45	42	93.3	3	6.7	0	0.0
1740–89	87	72	82.8	9	10.3	6	6.9
1790–1837	150	126	84.0	20	13.3	4	2.7
1586–1837	377	334	88.6	32	8.5	11	2.9
Alcester							
1561–89	18	15	83.3	1	5.6	2	11.1
1590–1639	51	46	90.2	3	5.9	2	3.9
1640–89	13	11	84.6	2	15.4	0	0.0
1690–1739	30	29	96.7	0	0.0	1	3.3
1740–89	66	61	92.4	3	4.5	2	3.1
1790–1839	89	76	85.4	11	12.4	2	2.4
1561–1839	267	238	89.1	20	7.5	9	3.4
Aldenham							
1561–89	6	5	83.3	1	16.7	0	0.0
1590–1639	24	24	100.0	0	0.0	0	0.0
1640–89	13	12	92.3	1	7.6	0	0.0
1690–1739	12	11	91.7	1	8.3	0	0.0
1740–89	56	44	78.6	7	12.5	5	8.9
1790–1839	62	55	88.7	6	9.7	1	1.6
1561–1839	173	151	87.3	16	9.2	6	3.5
Campton/ Shefford							
1540–89	7	7	100.0	0	0.0	0	0.0
1590–1639	25	25	100.0	0	0.0	0	0.0
1640–89	16	16	100.0	0	0.0	0	0.0
1690–1739	27	23	85.2	4	14.8	0	0.0
1740–89	75	57	66.7	13	17.3	5	16.0
1790–1839	110	100	90.9	9	8.2	1	0.9
1540–1839	260	228	87.9	26	10.0	6	2.3
Gainsborough							
1540–89	17	16	94.1	1	5.9	0	0.0
1590–1639	104	104	100.0	0	0.0	0	0.0
1640–89	43	42	97.7	1	2.3	0	0.0
1690–1739	94	81	86.2	11	11.7	2	2.1
1740–89	181	157	86.7	19	10.5	5	2.8
1790–1812	135	124	91.9	10	7.4	1	0.7
1540–1812	574	524	91.3	42	7.3	8	1.5

Table 3.9 (*cont.*)

	Bastard-bearing mothers	1 birth per mother	%	2 births per mother	%	3+ births per mother	%
Gedling							
1558–89	8	6	75.0	2	25.0	0	0.0
1590–1639	23	22	95.7	1	4.3	0	0.0
1640–89	17	16	94.1	1	5.9	0	0.0
1690–1739	22	21	95.5	1	4.5	0	0.0
1740–89	67	59	88.1	8	11.9	0	0.0
1790–1837	308	264	85.7	44	14.3	0	0.0
1558–1837	445	388	87.2	57	12.8	0	0.0
Hemyock							
1610–39	12	11	91.7	1	8.3	0	0.0
1640–89	17	14	82.4	3	7.6	0	0.0
1690–1739	39	35	89.8	2	5.1	2	5.1
1740–89	45	36	80.0	8	17.7	1	2.3
1790–1837	74	62	83.8	8	10.8	4	5.4
1610–1837	187	158	84.5	22	11.8	7	3.7

Note: Multiple births are counted as one.

and the proportion of events accounted for by repeaters.[5] There may well be a correlation between these two variables in the eighteenth century and onwards, but before that date the existence of any such relationship is weak and ambiguous.

Table 3.10 presents the information it is possible to obtain from the parish registers relating to the bastards born in their respective parishes. These data serve to underline the caution needed in the interpretation of 'statistics' relating to bastards and bastard-bearers extractable from the parish registers. For example, on a superficial viewing of table 3.10 it would be plausible to suggest very high rates of mortality among bastards. Column 6 of table 3.10 gives a count of the proportion of bastards whose dates of baptism and burial can be linked and who die before they reach three years of age. However, this is not a true indicator of the level of infant deaths among bastards for two reasons. It does not take account of those who are registered as buried only, that is, those who have died before baptism;[6] and it ignores those who remain in the parish but acquire a new name, perhaps because their mothers marry or perhaps because they are adopted by their putative fathers[7] (probably a very small number). Again, out-migration of bastards subsequent to having been baptized further reduces the true size of the

5. Although there appears to be a hint of a correlation ($r_s = 0.5745$ significant at 0.001 level, $t = 4.7$), this apparent relationship must be treated with caution. Indeed, if the period before 1690 is treated separately, the correlation coefficient falls to 0.3842 (significant at 0.1 level, $t = 1.86$), suggestive of a much weaker association.
6. See E. A. Wrigley, 'Births and baptisms: the use of Anglican baptism registers as a source of information on the number of births in England before the beginning of civil registration' (1977), on the problem of decreasing accuracy of baptismal registers over time and the means by which this can be overcome.
7. The late Mr Hartley Thwaite, who was undertaking a reconstitution of the parish of Birstall in the West Riding of Yorkshire before his death, had found examples of this problem. He informed us of one, John Bedford, who married Martha Hepworth in 1735. No baptism entry could be located for John but, 22 years earlier, Matthew Bedford had fathered a bastard, John, on Elizabeth Broadhead and the possibility arose that he could have been the 1735 bridegroom, John Bedford. John Bedford named his first child after his mother-in-law and his second after his father-in-law. On discovering that John called his third child Matthew, Mr Thwaite felt certain that he had located the bastard son of Matthew Bedford now bearing his putative father's surname.

Table 3.10: Registration characteristics of bastards in eight English parishes, 1540–1840

	Total no.	Baptized or buried	Baptized & buried	Baptized & married	Baptized, married & buried	Buried within 3 yrs of baptism	
Colyton							%
1540–89	54	34	14	2	4	10	71
1590–1639	90	60	26	1	3	13	50
1640–89	49	33	15	0	1	13	87
1690–1739	112	68	34	4	6	19	56
1740–89	125	79	27	9	10	17	60
1790–1839	118	88	21	7	2	15	71
1540–1839	548	362	137	23	26	87	64
Hawkshead							
1586–1639	71	65	6	0	0	6	100
1640–89	27	26	1	0	0	1	100
1690–1739	48	40	6	1	1	4	67
1740–89	111	93	17	1	0	10	59
1790–1837	181	152	27	2	0	24	89
1586–1837	438	376	57	4	1	45	79
Alcester							
1561–89	25	14	10	0	1	6	60
1590–1639	62	39	19	1	3	17	89
1640–89	15	10	5	0	0	4	80
1690–1739	32	19	11	1	1	11	100
1740–89	75	60	9	4	2	9	100
1790–1839	106	77	23	5	1	20	87
1561–1839	315	219	77	11	8	67	87
Aldenham							
1561–89	7	5	2	0	0	1	50
1590–1639	26	17	8	1	0	5	62
1640–89	14	12	2	0	0	1	50
1690–1739	13	8	5	0	0	4	80
1740–89	77	52	23	2	0	21	91
1790–1839	72	62	9	1	0	8	89
1561–1839	209	156	49	4	0	40	82
Campton/ Southill							
1540–89	9	9	0	0	0	–	
1590–1639	25	19	6	0	0	5	20
1640–89	16	15	1	0	0	1	100
1690–1739	31	27	4	0	0	4	100
1740–89	103	87	16	0	0	14	88
1790–1839	125	112	13	0	0	11	85
1540–1839	309	269	40	0	0	35	88
Gainsborough							
1564–89	18	17	1	0	0	1	100
1590–1639	106	85	21	0	0	19	90
1640–89	44	32	9	1	2	6	67
1690–1739	112	58	49	3	2	44	90
1740–89	223	120	97	6	0	91	94
1790–1812	150	111	39	0	0	39	100
1564–1812	653	423	216	10	4	200	92

Table 3.10 *(cont.)*

	Total no.	Baptized or buried	Baptized & buried	Baptized & married	Baptized, married & buried	Buried within 3 yrs of baptism	
Gedling							%
1558–89	11	8	1	0	2	0	0
1590–1639	24	20	2	1	1	1	50
1640–89	19	18	0	1	0	0	0
1690–1739	23	17	4	1	1	3	75
1740–89	76	59	10	3	4	10	100
1790–1837	361	334	44	10	1	39	89
1558–1837	514	456	61	16	9	53	87
Hemyock							
1610–39	13	10	2	1	0	2	100
1640–89	20	15	4	1	0	4	100
1690–1739	45	39	5	1	0	2	40
1740–89	55	49	3	2	1	1	33
1790–1837	92	79	9	3	1	7	78
1610–1837	225	192	23	8	2	16	69

population at risk. Indeed, it can be stated that in the majority of cases the only reason why we do obtain both a baptism and a burial reference to a bastard is because he or she dies very soon after birth.

Attempts to estimate the tendency of bastards to stay in their parish of birth to marry are hampered by exactly the same problems (see table 3.10). All that can be said is that bastards appear to have had a low expectation of life, possibly lower than the population as a whole,[8] but the size of the difference between the two groups cannot be estimated in a very meaningful way. Likewise, it would seem from the small number of marriages of bastards linkable with an earlier baptism that bastards who did not die in childhood were a highly mobile group in the population, as indeed were their mothers. Generally well under 10 per cent of bastards are known to have married in the parish of their baptisms and even fewer stayed on to leave a full record of their marriages and burials.[9] In Colyton, where we have the largest number of cases, we can obtain an assessment of the frequency with which the children of bastards were prenuptially conceived. The figure of 22.9 per cent of births of bastards prenuptially conceived seems very similar to the level that prevails among the population at large (see below, p. 109).

2 Identifying and describing the parents of bastards

The search for information on the parents of bastards through the use of parish registers and the conclusions it permits us to draw are particularly rewarding. There seems to have been very little consistency in the frequency with which both mothers and fathers of bastards are identified. As might be expected, mothers are recorded much more often than fathers although there is considerable variation from parish to parish. In Colyton, for instance, fathers of bastards are not named

8. In the late nineteenth and early twentieth centuries rates were generally over 100 and often over 200 per 1,000. See Wrigley (1977), p. 305.
9. For comparisons with the wider parochial populations see Souden (1979), and see below p. 89.

at all in the first 150 years of the record. The mother's name is therefore the principal means of identifying the bastard (see table 3.11). On the other hand, the Alcester register frequently names the fathers throughout the period, although the mothers were still between two and three times more likely to have their names recorded. In Hawkshead, between 1586 and about 1640, both the mother's and the father's surnames were nearly always given by implication by means of the *alias* device, for example, Isabel Sandes *alias* Rigge. It has been assumed that the first surname is the mother's, the second the father's, though the register would appear not to have been entirely consistent in this: we find Isabel Sandes *alias* Rigge in the baptism register, but Isabel Rigge *alias* Sandes in the burial register a few months later. It should be noted that apart from an occasional

Table 3.11: Information on the names of parents of bastards in four English parishes 1540–1839

	Fathers of bastards		Mothers of bastards	
	Named	By implication	Named	Not named
Colyton				
1540–89	0	0	44	0
1590–1639	0	0	75	5
1640–89	0	0	48	0
1690–1737	0	1	83	3
1740–89	1	6	92	1
1790–1839	2	21	99	0
1540–1839	3	28	441	9
Hawkshead				
1586–1639	5	42	12	18
1640–89	19	7	7	13
1690–1739	23	1	31	15
1740–89	38	0	81	6
1790–1837	4	4	149	0
1586–1837	89	54	280	52
Alcester				
1561–89	19	0	14	4
1590–1639	37	0	48	3
1640–89	10	0	9	4
1690–1739	12	2	29	1
1740–89	15	6	65	1
1790–1839	14	10	89	0
1561–1839	107	18	254	13
Aldenham				
1561–89	5	0	5	1
1590–1639	19	0	23	1
1640–89	13	0	13	0
1690–1739	4	4	11	1
1740–89	33	3	56	0
1790–1839	21	5	62	0
1561–1839	95	12	170	3

Note: Father named by implication means that the bastard child was given the father's surname as a second Christian name. It will be noted that this occurs mostly in the later periods. But in Hawkshead, particularly in the years 1586–1639, the father's surname is nearly always implied by an alias, e.g., Isabel Sandes *alias* Rigge. This also explains the large number of mothers not named during the early years.

recurrence in the burial register these *alias* children disappear completely: there is no further mention of them in the registers. In Hawkshead, Aldenham and Alcester the tendency is for less nominative information to be forthcoming, particularly after 1689. Whether this change in registration reflects a change in attitude in the community towards bastardy is a matter for speculation. However, when the father was known he was frequently forced by the overseers of the poor to contribute towards laying-in and maintenance expenses; a lump sum of between £1 and £2 and a weekly contribution of 1 to 2 shillings. Only infrequently is the name of a bastard's mother lacking. For example, in Colyton only in nine cases is there no record of the mother's name: these are most likely foundlings, like the baby discovered in Christopher Brown's doorway, William St Andrew, found on St Andrew's day at the Hare and Hounds in a basket, and Dionisius, son of an Irish travelling woman.

When we delve further into the background of mothers of bastards we find that for the whole period there is no baptism, burial or marriage registration for almost half the total number of mothers in Colyton, a little over half in Alcester and in Aldenham, and almost two thirds of the total numbers of Hawkshead, with some variation over the course of the time period. Before much can be said with great confidence about the distinctiveness of the bastard-bearers in these matters it would be necessary to have comparable information of all women baptizing children in the parishes concerned. Many of the mothers seem to have been immigrants but that should not surprise us given the high mobility of English pre-industrial rural populations. Other, frequently servants, tended to conceive and give birth out of wedlock at a phase in their adult life cycle when they were geographically most mobile. Indeed, they are occasionally dubbed 'sojourner', 'traveller', or 'peregrina', although surname evidence suggests that they came from and moved to the surrounding parishes (see below, p. 107 for a discussion of these issues in greater depth). The practice whereby marriage tended to take place in the bride's home parish would partially account for the lack of information on subsequent marriage, if it occurred.

Table 3.12 indicates the number of bastard-bearers whose age at marriage can be established because they were born, baptized and married in the place in which they were known to have given birth to at least one bastard child. This clearly cannot be used to assess the likelihood of a bastard-bearer marrying at all, only of her marrying in her place of birth. Also it should not be used to argue for a distinctive set of marriage probabilities obtaining among the bastard-bearers. Indeed, a noticeable feature of marriage from the reconstitution studies so far undertaken is the relatively high level of marital exogamy in pre-industrial English parishes. Often it was well over 60 per cent for women. For this reason calculations of marriage ages are almost always confined to a minority of the population. Indeed, often a mere 30 per cent of all marriages can be used to calculate a female age at marriage because no baptismal entry relates to the women involved.[10]

Any statement concerning the distinctiveness of bastard-bearers marrying *vis à vis* other females marrying should be made with care. The evidence about the likelihood of mothers of bastards marrying is confusing. Of those women who

10. Even in Hartland, a large and remote Devon parish, square in shape with the sea on two sides, where migratory movements were less intense than in most parishes, only 41 per cent of the brides' ages at first marriage could be established over the period 1600–1850. See E. A. Wrigley, 'Age at marriage in early modern England' (1976) and R. M. Smith, 'Population and its geography in England 1500–1730' (1978), pp. 222–3.

Table 3.12: Registration characteristics of mothers of bastards in four English parishes, 1540–1839

	Total no.	No. registered	Baptized only	Buried only	Baptized & buried	Married only	Baptized & married	Married & baptized	Baptized, married & buried	Total married
Colyton										
1540–89	44	22	3	5	2	3	0	4	5	12
1590–1639	80	39	11	8	4	3	4	4	7	18
1640–89	48	27	7	3	9	1	0	0	1	2
1690–1739	86	34	14	18	15	1	1	2	1	5
1740–89	93	39	11	7	15	7	8	4	6	25
1790–1839	99	44	23	5	6	8	9	0	4	23
1540–1839	450	205	69	49	44	23	22	14	24	83
Hawkshead										
1586–1639	68	63	2	1	0	0	0	1	1	2
1640–89	27	22	1	1	2	1	0	0	0	1
1690–1739	45	27	4	6	1	2	2	1	2	7
1740–89	87	47	15	8	7	1	4	4	1	10
1790–1837	149	77	42	1	6	6	13	3	1	23
1586–1837	376	236	64	17	16	10	19	9	5	43
Alcester										
1561–89	18	13	0	2	0	1	0	2	0	3
1590–1639	51	30	7	6	4	1	0	3	0	4
1640–89	13	7	2	1	2	0	0	1	0	1
1690–1739	30	17	2	2	1	2	4	1	1	8
1740–89	66	36	8	5	6	6	6	1	4	17
1790–1839	89	54	16	4	2	11	0	2	0	13
1561–1839	267	157	35	20	9	21	10	10	5	46
Aldenham										
1561–89	6	4	0	0	1	0	0	0	1	1
1590–1639	24	16	6	1	0	0	0	0	1	1
1640–89	13	5	3	0	3	1	0	0	1	2
1690–1739	12	4	5	0	1	0	0	1	1	2
1740–89	56	27	6	1	1	7	9	1	4	24
1790–1839	62	43	4	2	0	3	8	1	1	13
1561–1839	173	99	24	4	6	11	17	3	9	40

gave birth to bastards, between 13 per cent and 23 per cent either stayed or survived to marry in the parish, and of this sizable minority between 42 per cent and 65 per cent also possessed a baptismal entry in the parish register, permitting a marriage age to be calculated. This is a much higher proportion with both baptismal and marriage records than that for women as a whole when basing our calculations on the reconstitution studies. We must not too readily argue for immobility among bastard-bearers since it is clear that a majority, just as among all women, must have left to marry and/or to die elsewhere.

It is possible that the pattern we observe could be the combined effect of two factors: one of these factors being that female endogamy levels might well have displayed a tendency to vary with social and economic status and that the small proportion of all women represented among the bastard-bearers whose age at marriage can be calculated, some 17 per cent in all four parishes, came disproportionately from groups who were in general immobile. Also, it may well be that contained in the ranks of those who stayed long enough to marry was a high proportion of the mothers of those bastard children who survived the precarious days and months of early childhood, thereby giving them or local authorities some means of cajoling the putative fathers into marriage. Both these issues would require more refined work stemming from reconstitution analysis.

The frequency with which women married the fathers of their bastard children is difficult to gauge but some minimum levels can be guessed from this small number of reconstitution studies. The difficulties in deriving the data stem from the inconsistency and infrequency with which the names of the fathers of bastards appeared. In Aldenham, where this naming was more frequent, 23.7 per cent of those women married the father of the bastard in the same parish in which their bastard was baptized. If the mother of a bastard married, there was a relatively high probability of her marrying the father of the child. In order to get the full numbers we would need to add to these instances the cases of fathers marrying, who remain hidden in the records because they were not named at the bastard's baptism. Marriages taking place outside the parish, which were particularly likely if the mother was a girl away from her home parish and in service when she became pregnant and gave birth, would also have to be recovered. Notwithstanding these remarks we can detect one trend that is compatible with the arguments concerning the migratory behaviour of unmarried mothers over the course of the eighteenth century. It would seem that a far higher proportion of women producing bastards went on to marry in their community of birth at this time than ever before in the parish register era – a quarter of those at Alcester and Colyton and nearly 40 per cent at Aldenham. This is a feature of behaviour linked in with changes in the character of English fertility in this period which are an integral part of what we come to next.

The data arranged in table 3.13 are of interest, bearing as they do on the age at first birth of the mothers of bastards. Levine and Wrightson (below, chapter 5, p. 161), while suggesting that there is no clearly defined inverse relationship between the age at first marriage for women and the proportion of bastard births, also claim to have evidence that the age at which women bore their first illegitimate child may have responded to the same factors which influenced the age at marriage. They show that the bastard-bearers were neither markedly younger nor older than their contemporaries who married before the birth of their first child during the periods 1600–1649 and 1650–99. Data from the four parishes of this study would seem to confirm this pattern when the median age of women at first legitimate birth is compared with the median age of women at first illegitimate birth.

Table 3.13: Median ages of women at first legitimate and first bastard birth in Colyton, Hawkshead, Alcester and Aldenham, 1550–1849

	Median age of women at birth of 1st bastard	Age of married women at birth of 1st child (mean of medians)
1550–99	25.3 (n = 19)	24.4
1600–1649	26.0 (n = 46)	25.0
1650–99	26.3 (n = 26)	27.4
1700–1749	24.5 (n = 56)	26.9
1750–99	23.6 (n = 111)	24.7
1800–1849	23.1 (n = 115)	24.3

Table 3.14: Ages of mothers at birth of first bastard in four English parishes, 1538–1839 (for those mothers for whom date of birth and/or baptism is known)

	ages														
	20		20–24		25–9		30–34		35–9		40–44		45		Total
	no.	%	no.	%	no.	%	no.	%	no.	%	no.	%	no.	%	no.
Colyton 1538–1839	10	6.3	59	37.1	59	37.1	15	9.4	9	5.7	5	3.1	2	1.3	159
Hawkshead 1586–1837	22	9.3	38	33.3	32	28.1	18	14.0	5	4.4	1	0.9	0	0.0	114
Alcester 1561–1839	4	5.9	30	44.8	21	31.3	9	13.4	2	2.9	1	1.7	0	0.0	67
Aldenham 1561–1839	15	4.2	30	48.4	9	14.5	7	11.3	1	1.6	0	0.0	0	0.0	62

Although absolute or actual ages are not directly similar it would seem that mothers had their first bastard children considerably later in the latter half of the seventeenth century than they did in the latter half of the eighteenth century and early nineteenth century, when both the bastardy ratio and the 'repeater' effect were greater. Clearly, the pattern identifiable among the married women follows the same approximate trend. Tables 3.14 and 3.15 relate to the distribution of ages of bastard-bearers at births of first bastard and ages of women at first marriage. Indeed the modal age class was in all four parishes 20–24 for both data sets, and the second most important, with the marginal exception of Aldenham, was the age class 25–9. Both these sets of evidence seem to support the argument offered by Wrightson (below, chapter 6, p. 190) that many illegitimate first births may have been conceived in the process of courtship which had not resulted in marriage.

Further corroborative evidence would appear to come from the data in table 3.16 which records the pattern of prenuptial conceptions which is closely related in its overall trend to the bastardy ratio and the long-term movement in marriage ages in all four parishes, both bastardy ratio and prenuptial conception being highest in the later eighteenth and early nineteenth century, and female marriage age being lowest at that period. Conversely bastardy ratios and prenuptial conceptions were generally lower in the late seventeenth and early eighteenth centuries while female marriage ages were highest.

Table 3.15: Ages of women at marriage in four English parishes, 1538–1839 (all women)

	ages														
	20		20–24		25–9		30–34		35–9		40–44		45		Total
	no.	%	no.	%	no.	%	no.	%	no.	%	no.	%	no.	%	no.
Colyton 1538–1839	61	10.1	209	34.6	177	29.3	91	15.1	35	5.8	24	3.9	7	1.2	604
Hawkshead 1586–1837	67	11.8	204	36.0	160	28.3	87	15.4	33	5.8	9	1.6	6	1.1	566
Alcester 1561–1839	61	13.5	163	36.1	126	27.9	70	15.5	28	6.2	2	0.4	2	0.4	452
Aldenham 1561–1839	101	19.1	240	45.4	115	21.7	37	7.0	17	3.2	11	2.1	8	1.5	529

Table 3.16: Frequency and percentage of first live births less than nine months after marriage in ten English parishes 1550–1849 (all ages)

	Colyton			Hawkshead			Alcester			Aldenham		
	Prenuptial preg-nancies	Live births	%	Prenuptial preg-nancies	Live births	%	Prenuptial preg-nancies	Live births	%	Prenuptiual preg-nancies	Live births	%
1550–99	31	79	40	0	0	0	1	6	17	6	27	23
1600–1649	41	163	26	25	116	22	18	75	24	12	75	16
1650–99	14	64	22	19	95	20	7	80	9	8	48	17
1700–1749	15	50	30	16	70	23	16	89	18	9	45	20
1750–99	41	128	33	44	97	45	19	82	23	17	51	34
1800–1849	53	121	44	44	95	46	14	73	19	25	63	40
1550–1849	195	605	33	148	473	31	24	405	19	77	309	25
	Gedling			Terling			Ash			Gainsborough		
1550–99	6	15	40	9	27	33				11	33	33
1600–1649	21	54	39	7	31	23				60	216	28
1650–99	16	79	20	1	22	5	3	23	13	27	215	13
1700–1749	32	131	24	12	36	33	26	103	25	45	258	17
1750–99	45	150	30	13	64	20	101	197	51	125	498	25
1800–1849	172	294	59	34	83	41	90	204	44	21	136	15
1550–1849	292	723	40	76	263	29	220	527	42	289	1356	21
	Easingwold			Earsdon								
1550–99												
1600–1649	5	26	20									
1650–99	4	41	10	1	14	7						
1700–1749	8	62	13	11	68	16						
1750–99	32	108	30	51	187	27						
1800–1849	11	38	29	62	287	22						
1550–1849	60	275	22	125	556	22						

Data: from the family reconstitution tabulations of the Cambridge Group.

When the parents of bastard-bearers are considered, the impression of considerable mobility is further emphasized. For example, if we look at the minority of bastard-bearers for whom we have baptismal dates, close to one in five of their mothers have no baptism, marriage and burial reference in the parish (see table 3.17). In Colyton close to one in two leave no reference point and those whose baptism is locatable range from approximately 7 per cent in Hawkshead to 25 per cent in Alcester. However, it would be unwise to assume that the bearers' parents displayed a greater tendency to be mobile than any other section of society in these communities until more work has been done linking the reconstitution results to other social and economic evidence. Indeed, it is possible to interpret this limited evidence on the parents of bastard-bearers in a markedly different, although definitely speculative fashion. In chapter 4 below (p. 146), Anthea Newman considers that bastardy may well have occurred more often in families where the distinction between legal and illegal marriage remained uncertain. Close to one half and often far fewer of all mothers and fathers of bastards whose own baptisms can be traced had parents for whom no recorded marriage in the parish existed. Geographical mobility could account for a great deal of this phenomenon, but it is feasible that some proportion of these couples could not have been formally married.

3 The economic background of bastard-bearers

When we come to consider the economic background of bastard-bearers the task becomes daunting with few if any clear-cut answers. The inconsistency with which occupations are given in the registers for husbands of bastard-bearers adds to these difficulties. This type of information certainly improves in the late eighteenth and early nineteenth centuries, when much more occupational information is provided in the registers. It means that we have to restrict our discussion of this particular issue to the period after 1789. In order to know whether certain occupational groups are more likely to have female children who give birth to bastards or male children who beget bastards, we need to have some idea of the overall employment structure of the parish concerned. Without periodic parochial censuses with information on occupation we have to resort to a number of surrogate assessments.

Firstly, we can look at the pattern of occupations recorded in the parish registers during the period and assume it to be representative of the employment structure of the parish. Also, as most of this information comes from the marriage registers, we must assume that there is relatively little significant difference in the proportions marrying or in the marital fertility of the different occupational groups. In addition we can employ the earliest census enumerations giving occupational characteristics and compare this with the occupational data on bastards from the registers. Neither is an exact measure and both would be made worthless if there were wholesale occupational mobility, that is, if the economic status of a bastard-bearer's father changed dramatically from the time when she was born to the time when she was known to have given birth to her first bastard.

If we compare the proportions of occupational groups connected with bastardy on parish register evidence in the period 1790–1839 with the occupational structure of the parish portrayed in the 1831 census some quite marked differences do appear. One particular feature for Aldenham, Alcester and Colyton is clear. A

Table 3.17: Registration characteristics of parents of mothers of bastards in four English parishes, 1540–1839

	no. of registrations	Baptism only	Burial only	Baptism and burial	Marriage only	Baptism and marriage	Marriage and burial	Baptism, marriage and burial	Total marriage
Colyton 1540–1839									
Total no. of unmarried mothers 450									
Total no. of baptisms 159									
Fathers of unmarried mothers	49	1	25	12	5	9	34	24	72
Mothers of unmarried mothers	68	2	17	0	22	5	24	21	72
Hawskhead 1586–1837									
Total no. of unmarried mothers 376									
Total no. of baptisms 104									
Fathers of unmarried mothers	20	5	11	3	16	6	28	15	65
Mothers of unmarried mothers	25	0	16	0	27	5	29	2	63
Alcester 1561–1839									
Total no. of unmarried mothers 267									
Total no. of baptisms 56									
Fathers of unmarried mothers	11	1	6	5	8	4	15	6	33
Mothers of unmarried mothers	9	1	13	3	10	3	14	6	33
Aldenham 1561–1839									
Total no. of unmarried mothers 173									
Total no. of baptisms 56									
Fathers of unmarried mothers	7	1	16	5	1	5	8	11	25
Mothers of unmarried mothers	13	0	18	1	6	2	12	2	22

much greater number of bastard-bearers seem to have been the children of labourers, or of married people known to have been labourers or servants, than those groups constituted of the whole population (see table 3.18). Unless this group was particularly immobile, thereby making it possible to obtain a link between a baptism and a marriage or a baptism and a reference to a bastard birth, then it seems that these groups were the most bastard prone. It has to be noted, of course, that in general they were the largest occupational group in the male working population by these dates.

This finding can be substantiated in the case of Colyton, where analysis of occupations in the registers during these periods tends to confirm the pattern as

Table 3.18 (a) and (b): Occupational information on bastards and their families in four English parishes, 1586–1839

Table 3.18(a): Occupations in the Colyton parish register 1765–79 and 1813–19 and occupations of bastards, husbands of bastards, husbands and fathers of mothers of bastards, 1740–89 and 1790–1839

	1765–79 All occupations	1740–89 Occupations of bastard-linked persons	1813–19 All occupations	1790–1839 Occupations of bastard-linked persons
Agriculture	436	11	75	6
Agricultural labourer	1	1	124	9
Quarrying	3	0	3	0
Building	81	4	92	1
Dealing, retail service, transport	52	2	33	0
Industry	237	11	86	5
Religion, education, law, medicine	18	0	18	0
Gentlemen	4	0	6	0
Others	0	0	0	0
Total	833	29	437	21

Source: Wrigley (1977)

Table 3.18(b): Occupations of bastards, husbands of bastards, husbands and fathers of mothers of bastards, Alcester and Aldenham

	Alcester		Aldenham	
	Total male employment 1831 census	Occupations of bastard-linked persons 1790–1839	Total male employment 1831 census	Occupations of bastard-linked persons 1790–1839
Agricultural occupiers (with & without labourers)	14	1	22	3
Labourers (agricultural & non-agricultural)	105	11	222	19
Manufacture	89	8	0	0
Retail/handicraft	225	5	80	7
Capitalists etc.	39	0	18	0
Servants 20+	19	3	23	6
Others	8	0	15	2
Paupers		1		23

Table 3.18(c): Occupations of bastards, husbands of bastards, husbands and fathers of mothers of bastards, Hawkshead, 1586–1837

Gentry/householder	10	Swiller/hooper	3
Farmer/husbandman/labourer	43	Butcher	3
Servant/gardener	5	Carpenter	3
Waller/stonemason	6	Innkeeper/fidler	3
Miner/collier	3	Gaiger	1
Slater-getter/dresser	12	Schoolmistress	1
Weaver/webster	7	Pauper/poor/poorhouse	43
Taylor/hatter	5	Stranger/soldier	11
Shoemaker/sadler	2		

derived from the census. For example, in Colyton in the years following Rose's Burial Act, 1813–1819, labourers constituted 28 per cent against 25 per cent in the 1831 census and 29 per cent in 1851.[11] Bastards coming from the families of labourers accounted for over 50 per cent of the total in the years 1790–1839. The tendency then for bastards to be particularly liable to come from the lower-paid group is suggested in the data, and is partially confirmed by the evidence from individuals in receipt of poor relief which is also detectable in the record.

At Aldenham 23 out of 58 and at Hawkshead 20 out of 94 were in receipt of poor relief. We are a little clearer on this matter in this parish where the reconstitution has been undertaken in conjunction with an analysis of the Poor Law accounts. It appears that there were large numbers associated with the workhouse or the almshouse. Throughout the period many, especially the labourers, were either all their lives or at some stage in their lives in receipt of assistance from the overseers of the poor.[12] In Aldenham in the late eighteenth and early nineteenth centuries bastardy was most clearly associated with the labouring classes and the labourers were almost without exception the poor of the parish.

4 The family patterning of bastardy

In table 3.19 we have attempted to give some indication of the size of the various name sets based on the number of family reconstitution forms; the prevalence of bastardy within the name set based on the number of mothers and/or fathers of bastards (we have used only those name sets that supported four or more mothers and/or fathers of bastards), and in the last column the name sets with which the particular name set was in any way linked in bastardy. We will try to give some substance to the figures by the presentation of a few selected case histories.

In Colyton all the 'families' under the name Baker *alias* Tucker in the period 1540–1839 numbered 150. They claimed 10 mothers of bastards between 1636 and 1789 but there is no information about 8 of them except that they had one bastard each; the ninth had two bastards in 1727 and 1737. The interesting one is Elizabeth Baker (also called Bakon) for whom we have no baptism date; she had one bastard son, Solomon Newberry Bakon, baptized 6 March 1745, buried 9 March 1745. She then married Solomon Newberry, 27 February 1747; they had one legitimate son, baptized 14 July 1747, five months after the wedding. The Newberrys (35 families) claimed five mothers of bastards between 1725 and 1782

11. See E. A. Wrigley, 'The changing occupational structure of Colyton over two centuries' (1977).
12. See W. Newman-Brown, 'The receipt of poor relief and the life-cycle in Aldenham, Hertfordshire 1630–1680', in R. M. Smith (ed.) *Land, kinship and life-cycle* (forthcoming).

Table 3.19: Links between bastard-bearing families in four English parishes, 1540–1839

Surname	No. of name sets	No. of mothers/fathers of bastards	Bastardy family links
Colyton			
Abrahams	26	3	Cawley, Davis Mitch
Baker/Tucker	150	10	Halse, Newberry
Bolle	42	4	Bolle, Green, Snell
Bonfield/Rode	25	3	Hellyar, Letherland, Restorick, Roade, Weeke
Carpenter/Rawlyn	18	2	Bawdon, Evans, Stevens
Davi(e)s	9	2	Abrahams
Domett	28	3	Abbott, Gould, Hallett
Edwards	50	5	Anscomb, Bennett, Stevens, Tirpyn
Greene	48	6	Bole, Bull, Hallett, Holcomb, Loveridge, Russe, Salsbery, Smith, Wattes, White
Hallett	6	3	Domett, Green, Hoare
Hoare	75	6	Abbott, Colmer, Hallett, Hicks, Osborn, Saleer, Webber
Hooper	75	5	Green, Pearse, Sweetland, Turle, Underdown, White
Long	43	5	Barrett, Reed
Loveridge	48	4	Batt, Greene, Hatherstone, Oates, Wishlade
Marwood	76	4	Banckes, Cox, Darke, Farbey, Hodge, Oxenbeer
Newberry	35	5	Baker/Tucker, Record, Summers, Wilson
Newton	119	3	Carpenter/Rawlyn, Dunster, Sweetland
Roost	36	6	Seller, Watts
Seaward	78	6	Russell, Wood
Seller	38	4	Rocket, Roost
Smith	100	3	Anning, Clarke, Cross, Greene, Halse, Leighton, Perry, Turner
Snell	43	4	Bennett, Bole, Cockram, Cross, Mayne
Stevens	19	2	Annscomb, Carpenter/Rawlyn, Edwards, Pulman, White, Willis
Sweetland	43	4	Blampin, Guppy, Hooper, Manfield, Power, Strawbridge, Sweetland
Turle (Tyrolle)	51	8	Edwards, Harner, Hooper, Putham, Smith, Vye
Whicker	54	4	Bawden, Collyer, White
White	136	9	Cox, Green, Halse, Hooper, Paddon, Rutter, Spiller, Stevens, Whicker, Woodrow
Wishlade	30	4	Loveridge, Skinner
Hawkshead			
Addison	11	4	Walker
Alexander	5	3	Knype, Cooper
Benson	67	8	Dodgson, Holme, Huddleston, Jackson, Rigge
Birket	40	8	Brockbank, Nicholson, Park, Walker
Braithwait	246	19	Atkinson, Benson, Hill, Holme, Long, Mackreth, Mowson, Rigge, Smith
Bowness	16	4	Clappan, Tennant
Brockbank	36	4	Birket, Dixon, Thwaites, Turner

Table 3.19 (*cont.*)

Surname	No. of name sets	No. of mothers/fathers of bastards	Bastardy family links
Hawkshead – cont.			
Coward	24	5	Foster, Garnet, Hartlowe, Pool, Satterthwait
Dixon	88	9	Atkinson, Brockbank, Hodgson, Keen, Mackreth, Nicholson, Satterthwait
Dodgson	34	7	Jackson, Mackreth, Marr, Martin, Sands
Harrison	43	8	Barrow, Studdart
Hodgson	68	4	Dixon, Jackson, Turner, Wilson
Holme	97	12	Addison, Barker, Benson, Braithwait, Grigg, Knype, Rigge
Jackson	86	12	Benson, Bibby, Cloudsdale, Dodgson, Kirkby, Ture
Kirkby	45	11	Collinson, Fleming, Fountaine, Jackson, Nichols, Rigg, Hisburn (of Kendal)
Knype	56	14	Adamson, Alexander, Carter, Dawson, Denison, Gilpin, Holme, Jackson, Robinson, Scales, Smith, Storie, Vickers, Ward
Mackreth	80	6	Braithwait, Dixon, Dodgson, Grigge, Richardson, Rigge
Martin	16	7	Backhouse, Coleman, Dodgson, Knype, Robinson, Wilson
Nicholson	38	8	Birket, Bushby, Hutton, Kirkby, Long, Martin, Satterthwait
Park	42	6	Birket, Rigge, Shacklock, Usher
Rigge	165	19	Allatson, Benson, Braithwait, Bushby, Fisher, Holme, Kilner, Kirkby, Little, Mackreth, Park, Raven, Rigg, Sands, Walker
Robinson	52	6	Beck, Holliday, Johnson, Knype, Martin, Wallace
Sands	66	8	Dodgson, Pepper, Strickland, Townson
Satterthwait	120	21	Clark, Coward, Crosfield, Green, Gurnell, Holme, Jackson, Nicholson, Peares, Tyson
Sawrey	79	4	Ashburner, Tomlinson
Scales	40	6	Knype, Mason
Smith	15	4	Braithwait, Huddleston
Strickland	37	5	Sands
Taylor	101	6	Dawson, Dixon
Thompson	25	5	Tomlinson
Townson	49	4	Borwick, Keene, Magson, Sands
Tyson	47	11	Bell, Braithwait, Dixon, Garnet, James, Pierce, Wilson
Walker	118	8	Addison, Birket, Grigg, Pearson, Postlethwait, Rigg
Warriner	12	1	Waterson
Waterson	18	1	Warriner
Wilson	108	14	Braithwait, Hall, High, Hodgson, Mawson Sharp, Suart, Turrell, Tyson, Woodend
Woodend	5	4	Banks, Hartley, Wilson
Yerkess	1	1	Satterthwait (1782–94 – 5 bastards)
Alcester			
Crow(ley)	32	4	Allen, Clark, Smith
Dyson/Dislin/ Lambert	16	4	Lambert, Waldern

Table 3.19 (*cont.*)

Surname	No. of name sets	No. of mothers/fathers of bastards	Bastardy family links
Alcester – cont.			
Field/Holtam	29	5	Field, Ingram, Pursell
Goo(u)ld	10	2	Field, Gould, Ingram, Westwood
Green/Ellis/Lye/ Painter	66	5	Berricke, Jillworth, Lorrimore, Sexton, Taylor
Hall/Sawyer	21	4	Greaves, Harton, Parr
Harris/Harrison/ Harrinton	61	7	Ford, Harrison, Homes, Ison, Morris, Parker, Pratt, Stanton, Vixon
Hemming/Harper	51	6	Davis, Edkins, Eglinton, Harris, Holloway, Peck
Moor/Stuttesbury	35	3	Benjamin, Johnson, Lorrimore, Petters, Raven, Sexton, Tayler, Whorley
Okeley	9	2	Hannes, Moor/Stuttesbury, Smith, Wood
Robbins/Tyers	23	4	Harris/Harrison, Tyers
Search/Segge/ Page	19	5	Bartlett, Crofts, Kiffin, Page, Rastell/Stiles
Smith/Court/ Richard(son)	108	10	Crow, Goold, Quinton, Smith, Steepsons, Westwood
Ealdern(dron)	35	2	Dislon/Lambert
William/Davis	50	3	Grafton/Ingram
Aldenham			
Burgess	11	3	Bonnicastle, Francis, How, Larkin, Musson, Tyler
Cook	12	5	Adderley, Dollermore, Eames, Evans
Francis	13	3	Brugess, Carpenter, Larkin, Musson
Hawkins	12	3	Baldwin, Elborn, Hawtree, Robinson, Russell, Wright
Herrington	19	3	Copelin, Donner, Durrant, Elborn, Leach, Nash, Puddifoot, Seagrave
King	15	5	Barton, Eales, Gibbs, Ironmonger, North, Smith, Tapster
Larkin	12	3	Burgess, Francis, Mole, Musson, Quelch
Plat	22	4	Grubbe, Morgan, Nichol, Oxden, Snite
Smith	80	5	Cockman, Eales, Hopkins, King, Lawford, North

Notes:

1 In the main only the surnames of those who could claim four and more mothers and fathers of bastards have been listed: where there was clear evidence of family links those with fewer than four have been included.

2 As fathers of bastards are mentioned so rarely in Colyton, only the number of mothers have been included under the second heading. For Hawkshead, Alcester and Aldenham both fathers and mothers have been included under this heading, giving much higher numbers.

3 For Hawkshead, Alcester and Aldenham the total number of surname sets is equal to the total number of family reconstitution forms (FRFs) and includes the families married in the parish and those married out of the parish but whose children were baptized in the parish church.

4 For Colyton the total number of families has been taken from the computer print-out (CPO) which gives every name on each FRF. There may be some duplication in cases of remarriage or when the name of the husband's father has been entered on the FRF, and consequently an over-estimation of the number of name sets.

and had family links with the Records, Summers and Wilsons as well as with the Bakers *alias* Tuckers. The latter families married into the Anning, Collins, Hallett, Long, Sweetland and White families. The White surname covering 136 families had nine bastard-bearers between 1569 and 1764. The Whites in their turn had family links with the Cox, Green, Halse, Hooper, Paddon, Rutter, Spiller, Stevens and Whicker families.

It needs only a perusal of the names in the last column of table 3.19 to convince us of the existence of certain blood relative networks linking those families where bastardy occurred throughout the period 1538–1838. In each of these families some of the women produced one or more bastards. If they married, their marriage partners frequently came from these families and the same applied to their bastard children if they married. The males too, often chose their brides from those families where bastardy was tolerated and so we find bastards appearing through two or three generations. There are a number of instances of sisters producing bastards; in some families we note both bastards and prenuptially conceived children. But in other families a bastard was never or rarely produced. The Spillers, for example, were a large Colyton family going back to 1540. But it was not until 1825 that Mary Spiller produced a base son, James Shepherd Spiller. The impression given by such an incidence is that the young daughter of a 'respectable' family, often in her late teens or early twenties, had one and only one base child by 'mistake'. Quite often there is no marriage or burial date for the mother and it may well be that she was disowned by her family and left the parish.

In Hawkshead there are a greater number of large name sets than in Colyton; the individual name sets too are much larger. The Braithwaites are easily the largest with 246 families, followed by the Rigges with 165. The Dixons, Holmes, Jacksons, Mackreths, Satterthwaits, Sawreys, Taylors, Walkers and Wilsons were each represented by close to 100 families. Members of these families were married both within and without the parish and persisted in the district during the whole 250-year period. Each of these sets could claim a significant number of bastard-producing mothers and fathers ranging from the Satterthwaits with 21 to the Sawreys with 4. Of course, the whole of these sets cannot be classed as bastardy prone; it is more likely that there were families within the set who had bastard-bearing proclivities and who were linked with bastardy ties to members of other families with similar tendencies. See chapter 8 below, p. 237, where some of the methodological difficulties of the name set for the study of bastardy are discussed. Nor is it possible to associate bastardy with members of the family living in a particular part of the parish or with members of the family belonging to a certain class such as the paupers, although there were undoubtedly a number of bastard-bearers who were poor or who lived in the poorhouse. But on the whole the evidence seems to show that bastardy cuts across social and geographical boundaries. We should remember too that it is a minority of the mothers who were baptized in the parish and about whom we have information. But in Hawkshead we do know the names of fathers of bastards, at least for the first half of the period; this information should extend the bastardy links and add to our knowledge of the family network.

Of the large name sets, we single out the Satterthwaites with 120 families. Between 1586 and 1828, 81 married in the parish. Five Satterthwaites fathered bastards of the Clark, Coward, Green, Peares and Tyson families; 16 Satterthwaite women produced bastards. We instance two sisters: Agnes, spinster of Colthouse, born 10 April 1786, eldest of four children of Braithwait Satterthwait of

Oxenfell, slater, had one bastard son, born 11 March 1806, buried 13 September 1807. She married Birket Nicholson of Town, labourer, 6 June 1808; they had two children, the first baptized 1 January. Mary of Sawrey, the youngest of Braithwait Satterthwait's children had one bastard daughter.

It requires but little further study of the list of names in the last column of table 3.20 to gain the impression that in Hawkshead as in Colyton certain families were drawn together in an inter-familial web of bastardy. Atkinson, Benson, Birket, Braithwaite, Brockbank, Coward, Dixon, Dodgson, Holme, Jackson, Kirkby, Knype, Mackreth, Martin, Nicholson, Park, Sandes, Satterthwait, Scales, Taylor, Turner, Tyson, Walker, Wilson, are the names that constantly recur. It has already been stated that some of these name sets were very large indeed, but it is clear that within the sets there were families where bastardy occurred and was tolerated. Indeed, in Hawkshead bastardy seems to have been a close family affair. There are numerous instances of sisters producing bastards and bastard daughters again producing bastards. In these families the men also often fathered bastards.

In Alcester the frequent use of an *alias* complicates the study of bastardy links. We have, for example, the name set of Green *alias* Ellis *alias* Lye *alias* Painter, 66 strong, persisting through the centuries. The most interesting case is that of Alice Painter, baptized 26 April 1565, second of three children of John and Mary Painter who had a bastard son, John, baptized 30 March 1600, buried 12 March 1601, by Robert Lorrimore. Robert had married, 6 July 1590, Alice's younger sister, Elizabeth. She gave him three children and died just after the third was born (4 January 1599). He then married Ann Sexton, 24 October 1599, (the bastard son by Alice was baptized 12 March 1601). Ann gave him three children between 13 February 1601 and 23 November 1606; she was buried 26 November 1614 and Robert married a third time, 9 May 1615, Joan Taylor, who survived him. Robert's second daughter, Elizabeth, baptized 22 February 1595, married 17 November 1621, Pithias Dixon. She gave him nine children, the last being stillborn. The second child, a son, Thomas (baptized 27 June 1623) fathered a bastard son Pithias when he was just 16 years old.

In Aldenham the *alias* custom was not as marked and the name sets associated with bastardy were on the whole very much smaller. By far the largest group numbered less than 20, many indeed had less than 10 members. The links between these sets, especially the smaller ones may be seen quite clearly from table 3.20. And the links were often effected by the men who fathered bastards on two or three different women. The registers and records of the overseers of the poor also show beyond doubt that in this parish bastardy was associated with large families and the labouring poor. We cite only the case of Susanna Burgess, eldest of five children of Joseph and Susanna Burgess, who had a bastard son in 1760. Her younger brother, Joseph, labourer and servant, married Sarah Tyler in 1758; their only child, Sara, had a bastard son in 1780, the reputed father, William Bonnicastle. She married in 1784 William How, servant and labourer; they had six children. Sara died after the birth of the last child in 1786; the husband was buried from the workhouse in 1835. Susanna's youngest brother, John, married in 1778 Arabella Francis, who had had two bastard children, in 1772 by Robert Larkin and in 1774 by Joseph Musson. Robert Larkin married Ann Mole in 1774 and they had ten children. Earlier in the century Sara Francis, last but one of six children of William Francis and Phoebe Carpenter, had a bastard daughter. William and Phoebe had a son just before they were married.

Within these parishes we have been able to find a small number of indigenous families where natural children were not frowned upon. In these families some of the women, often sisters, produced one or more bastards; if they married their marriage partners frequently came from these families and the same applied to their bastard children if they married. Indeed there was considerable intermarrying, and bastardy was sometimes carried over into the second and third generations, although its persistence over more distant generations is difficult to detect.

Yet we should beware of trying to hive off these families into a separate community or strata living geographically or socially apart. The scant evidence we have does show that bastardy was quite often connected with the farming community. In Aldenham and to a lesser extent in Hawkshead also bastardy was associated with the poor but by no means exclusively. In Aldenham, Colyton and Alcester the labourers seem to have been disproportionately involved in bastardy. The gentry, trades, crafts, professions all show some individuals bearing or begetting bastards. Bastard-bearing families did not congregate in one particular part of the parish, though the Colyton registers did often show Colyford as a place of residence and the Hawkshead registers frequently named Far and Near Sawrey, but bastardy was certainly not confined to these districts. It would seem that in most of these places bastardy on occasions cut across social and geographical boundaries.

We can only speculate on the attitude of ordinary folk to bastardy and on possible changes in that attitude over the years. Throughout the three centuries there seems to have been no difficulty about having these base children baptized and from this one might argue that they were generally accepted. But against this stands the fact that many mothers must have had their bastards baptized out of their own parish. Whether this was out of a sense of shame or because they were living with the father in his parish or were away from home in service at the time of the child's birth, it is impossible to ascertain. It will be remembered that some of the mothers who had more than one bastard had them registered at different places of residence within the parish and named a different father at the baptism of each child.

This leads us to look again at the bastardy registration in Colyton, Alcester, Aldenham and Hawkshead. In Colyton the father's name was rarely given, the mother's always, and one might deduce that in the southern parish of Aldenham the responsibility was assumed to be the mother's. But in the northern parish of Hawkshead until the mid-seventeenth century the bastard children were mostly baptized with their own Christian names and both fathers' and mothers' surnames linked by an *alias*. Until the mid-eighteenth century too the putative father was frequently mentioned and his part in the act at least acknowledged. And here a sense of shame does sometimes creep in, as in the case of the 'young tradesman and gentleman of Fortune and Credit desirous to conceal such scandal'. But in Hawkshead in the last hundred years the responsibility was, as in Colyton throughout the three hundred years, solely the mother's. In Aldenham and Alcester the picture is different again in that we have more information for the first hundred years about the fathers of bastards than in the other two parishes. Here only do we have evidence of the same man fathering bastards on different women and of a married man with a wife still living fathering a bastard.

And what of the bastard child? We are on even more uncertain ground in trying to interpret the tantalising glimpses the registers and other parish documents afford us. Many bastard children died in infancy, many disappeared from the parish together with their mothers. Some, only a very few, were married and buried in the parish and, one assumes, absorbed into the community. Very occasionally the bastard child was accepted into the father's family. In Colyton we know of one whose mother married a thatcher and when the bastard son married his occupation too was given as thatcher. In Hawkshead we learn of the three natural children of William Braithwaite, Gent, who must have lived in his household at Briers and were remembered in his will alongside his three legitimate children. It should be noted too that in all four parishes the bastard child was often given the name of his maternal grandfather or grandmother and one would suspect, was accepted by them. In Hawkshead, Aldenham and Alcester the church wardens and overseers of the poor were very active in forcing the father, when he was known, to pay maintenance money to mother and child. But these were always the exceptions, the very small minority.

We end, finally, with some tentative suggestions for the further study of bastardy using nominal linkage with such records as parish registers, Poor Law accounts and settlement certificates and examinations. There is clearly a need for a regional reconstitution in which it might be possible to trace individuals who moved over parish boundaries to give birth to their bastards and also to follow the fortunes of mothers who moved after their bastard was baptized from one parish to a neighbouring one. We might then begin to obtain more precise evidence on the mortality of bastards than we have at present. Likewise, we might discover whether what may have been common law marriage unions in one parish between a man and a woman inclining the local incumbent to register their offspring as base in the register necessarily produced a similar response from a neighbouring incumbent if the couple crossed parish boundaries. Perhaps it will also be possible to employ mothers of bastards as a test group to investigate the effect of Poor Law administration on short- and medium-distance migration of a particular economic group. In addition we might be able to clarify those processes responsible for unmarried mothers increasingly in the second half of the eighteenth century having been born in the parish and also marrying in the parish where their bastards were baptized.

Acknowledgements

The analysis of the registers of Hemyock has been carried out by Mrs Joy Lodey. We are very grateful to Mrs Lodey for making the results of her interesting bastardy study available to us.

The reconstitutions of the other seven parishes together with the preliminary work on bastardy have been carried out under the direction of the SSRC Cambridge Group for the History of Population and Social Structure by the following persons:

Gedling: Mrs Janet Young;
Campton with Shefford: Mr John Asteraki;
Gainsborough: Mr and Mrs Clarke;
Alcester: the late Mrs Peggy Ford. We deeply regret that she has not lived to see the results of her work;
Aldenham: Mr Newman Brown. The value of his work has been greatly enhanced by his analysis of the records of the overseers of the poor;

Colyton: Dr E. A. Wrigley;
Hawkshead: Karla Oosterveen with the assistance of the late Mrs Kathleen Leonard of Hawkshead, who has also listed the papers in the Hawkshead parish chest and has extracted references to bastardy cases from the accounts of church wardens and overseers of the poor.

We have to thank Dr John Marshall of the University of the Lancaster for making available to us a collection of Hawkshead wills.

3 Bastardy and the family reconstitution studies of Banbury and Hartland

Susan Stewart

Banbury, a market town in the centre of England, and Hartland, an agricultural parish in a remote corner of Devon, offer interesting contrasts as communities in which to investigate extra-marital sexual behaviour in the past. The Banbury register runs without a break from 1558, and throughout the period from the late 1560s to 1840 generally gives information of the kind essential for demographic purposes.[13] The occupations of the men are stated fairly continuously and, in the burial register, relationships, occupations and, after 1813, ages are given so that major problems of identification arise only occasionally, given the size and complexity of Banbury families.

The parish registers of Hartland are continuous from 1561, but the quality of registration varies, deteriorating in the late seventeenth and early eighteenth centuries, but not enough to prevent reconstitution. Occupations are given only intermittently. Relationships are fairly well defined, but in Hartland a few enormous families – name sets in our terminology – in particular the Prusts and the Heards, almost defeat in their complexity the ingenious reconstitutor. They survive in some strength to the present day. Bastardy, however, is clearly indicated in the registers, bastard children usually being registered in their mothers' names. A collection of affiliation orders, which have served mostly to confirm and amplify the data from the registers, have also been used.

Banbury, in North Oxfordshire, is situated in the heart of Midland England, on the intersection of north-south and east-west routes. It received its charter of incorporation on 26 January 1554. At that time its population was about 1,500. It had long been a market town for the surrounding countryside, with its corn-, beef-, hog-, sheep-, and horsemarkets. After a period of stagnation and slow recovery in the seventeenth century, the town began to grow again, largely by drawing in new blood from the surrounding villages. By 1801, the population in the borough had grown to 2,755, plus 1,055 in the surrounding hamlets of the parish. The town had become an industrial centre of considerable distinction with 400 looms at work making jersey and plush. The Oxford and Birmingham canal, cut in 1769–70, ran through the town, adding boatbuilders and boatmen to the list of Banbury occupations. In the early nineteenth century the population rose steeply, in 1831 reaching 3,737 in the borough and 2,685 in the hamlets, a total of 6,422.

13. The volume of the baptism register which runs from 1558 to September 1683 seems to have been regularly and well maintained. A paper register exists which was used as a rough copy, and the entries were written from time to time in the parchment register. Both are extant and both were used in the transcription. However, the bastardy entries for the period are few and this may be accounted for by the incumbency of William Whateley, who was vicar of Banbury from 1610 to 1639. Whateley was a noted Puritan divine and became the vicar of Banbury in 1610. He was a notable preacher in Banbury and the surrounding countryside and it was his practice to set apart days of humiliation for his family and to have sessions of fasting and penitence. Perhaps William Whateley by his Puritan fervour actually discouraged bastard-bearing, or perhaps bastard-bearers were reluctant to bring the evidence of their shame to him for baptism.

Banbury, then, lies in the heartland of England, but Hartland was, and still is, remote and isolated; it was thoroughly agricultural and relatively stable socially. A squire, a fair smattering of yeoman farmers, a few craftsmen practising the crafts associated with agriculture, a number of husbandmen, small tenant farmers and a numerous labour class made up the population of Hartland through the centuries. In 1811 its population numbered 1,734. Hartland parish covers 27 square miles, in the form of a rough rectangle six miles by four and a half miles. On two sides the Atlantic beats against rock and cliff, on the other two rough and uninhabited moorland stretches inland. For contact with the outside world Hartland looked seaward. Hartland Quay, near Hartland Point itself, was a busy port of call for coastal vessels and shipping across the channel from Wales, until storm damage and neglect in the 1880s destroyed it.

Table 3.20 and figure 3.3 attempt to give an impression of the course bastardy ran in Banbury and in Hartland over nearly three centuries. For the whole period from 1561 to 1838, divided in the first place into decades which have then been grouped into seven forty-year periods, the bastardy ratio, that is, the number of bastards expressed as a percentage of the total number of baptisms, follows very roughly the direction of the long-term bastardy trend of 24 and 98 selected English parishes (Laslett and Oosterveen, 1973, p. 267; Laslett, 1977, chapter 3). But there are marked differences between our two places. Banbury, the expanding urban parish, has for the whole period 1561–1838 a ratio of 2.9 per cent; Hartland, the settled rural community, a ratio of 5.9 per cent, more than twice as high.

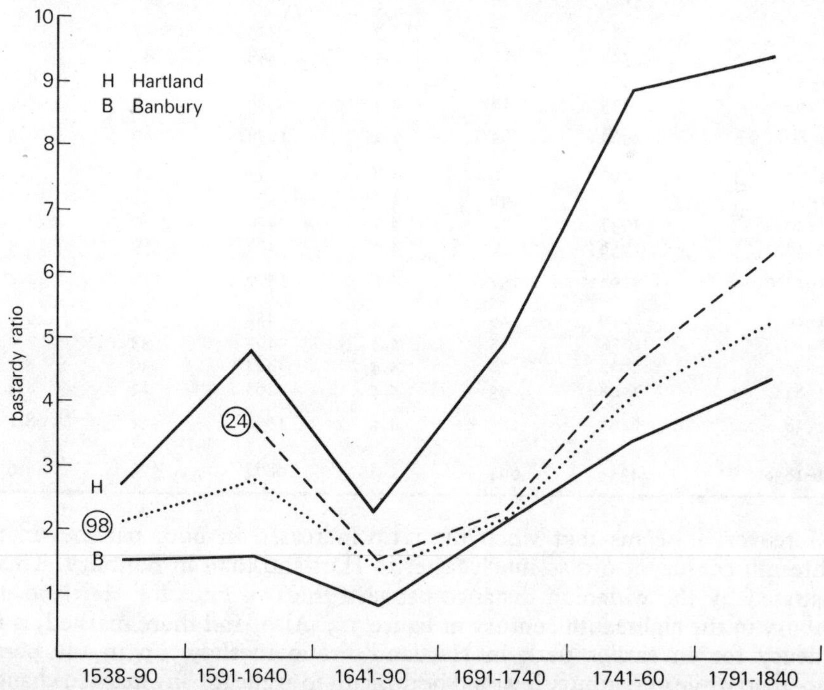

Fig. 3.3 Illegitimacy ratios, Hartland, Banbury and Cambridge Group samples, fifty-year periods, sixteenth to nineteenth centuries

Table 3.20: Legitimate and illegitimate baptisms in Banbury and Hartland, 1561–1838

Decades	Baptisms	Banbury 1561–1838 Bastards	%	Baptisms	Hartland 1561–1838 Bastards	%
1561–70	523	2	0.4	406	6	1.5
1571–80	500	16	3.2	384	15	3.9
1581–90	612	17	2.8	346	10	2.9
1591–1600	723	30	4.1	343	16	4.7
1561–1600	2358	65	2.7	1479	47	3.3
1601–10	828	8	1.0	400	27	6.7
1611–20	886	8	0.9	373	23	6.2
1621–30	796	10	1.2	323	11	3.4
1631–40	855	12	1.5	369	10	2.7
1601–40	3365	38	1.1	1465	71	4.7
1641–50	694	9	1.3	358	8	2.2
1651–60	632	2	0.3	301	7	2.3
1661–70	667	9	1.3	334	8	2.4
1671–80	649	2	0.3	254	9	3.5
1641–80	2642	22	0.8	1247	32	2.7
1681–90	709	5	0.7	288	4	1.4
1691–1700	640	19	2.9	302	6	2.0
1701–10	671	21	3.1	283	13	4.6
1711–20	717	17	2.4	330	18	5.4
1681–1720	2737	62	2.3	1203	41	3.4
1721–30	782	15	1.9	325	17	5.2
1731–40	721	17	2.4	343	23	6.7
1741–50	686	15	2.2	270	22	8.1
1751–60	775	18	2.3	338	18	5.3
1721–60	2964	65	2.2	1276	80	6.3
1761–70	790	30	3.8	375	28	7.5
1771–80	909	39	4.3	387	39	10.1
1781–90	1037	42	4.1	400	50	12.5
1791–1800	1056	46	4.4	408	59	14.5
1761–1800	3792	157	4.1	1570	176	11.2
1801–10	1079	49	4.5	456	41	9.0
1811–20	1676	73	4.3	469	33	7.0
1821–30	2032	70	3.4	444	36	8.1
1831–8	1708	93	5.4	265	22	8.3
1801–38	6495	285	4.4	1634	132	8.1
1561–1838	24353	694	2.9	9874	579	5.9

Moreover, it seems that when the ratio increased in both parishes in the eighteenth century it did so much faster in Hartland than in Banbury. This is illustrated by the widening distance between the two lines for Hartland and Banbury in the eighteenth century in figure 3.3. Also, and more marked, is the tendency for an earlier peak in Hartland's ratio to show up in the period 1591–1640 while in Banbury it would be difficult to argue for any marked changes in the eighty-year period from 1560 to 1640. Nevertheless, a closer consideration of the figures in table 3.21 would seem to suggest some fall in the ratio at Banbury

Table 3.21: Bastard births per bastard-bearing mother in Banbury and Hartland, 1561–1838

	Bastard-bearing mothers	1 birth per mother	%	2 births per mother	%	3+ births per mother	%
Banbury							
1561–1600	62	60	96.8	2	3.2	0	0.0
1601–40	37	36	97.3	1	2.7	0	0.0
1641–80	21	20	95.2	1	4.8	0	0.0
1681–1720	51	44	86.3	3	5.9	4	7.8
1721–60	57	52	91.2	3	5.3	2	3.5
1761–1800	132	116	87.9	13	9.8	3	2.3
1801–38	236	201	85.3	25	10.5	10	4.2
1561–1838	596	529	88.7	48	8.1	19	3.2
Hartland							
1561–1600	46	45	97.8	1	2.2	0	0.0
1601–40	58	48	82.8	7	12.1	3	5.1
1641–80	27	23	85.2	3	11.1	1	3.7
1681–1720	39	38	97.4	1	2.6	0	0.0
1721–60	67	59	88.1	5	7.5	3	4.4
1761–1800	113	79	69.9	18	15.9	16	14.2
1801–38	101	79	78.2	14	13.9	8	7.9
1561–1838	451	371	82.3	49	10.9	31	6.8

Note: Multiple births are counted as one.

during the early decades of the seventeenth century from a moderately high level. At Hartland the early seventeenth-century ratio was much greater in relation to the preceding decades and the subsequent ones, through to the middle and late eighteenth century. Banbury does not display such an unambiguous change until the late eighteenth century, although it does, like so many English parishes, show a very low level of bastardy in the 1650s. This is a feature which Keith Wrightson (below, chapter 6, p. 184) suggests may be due to a deterioration in the quality of registration at the time, although this development is not visible to the same extent in Hartland. One other feature which the aggregations in figure 3.3 tend to camouflage is the difference between the two places at the beginning of the nineteenth century. In Hartland, although bastardy was still at a very high level, the ratio is seen to fall considerably compared with Banbury, where the increase initiated in the eighteenth century continues into the following century. Why this should have been is difficult to establish. It is of interest that the prenuptial conception level, which usually follows the bastardy ratio very closely, shows no sign of falling at that time (see below, p. 132).

Table 3.21 breaks down the numbers of bastard-bearing mothers into those who produced one bastard only and those who produced two, three or more than three bastards each. Following the pattern of the bastardy ratio, repeating bastard-bearers accounted for a higher proportion of the total in Hartland than they did in Banbury. Indeed, 36.5 per cent of all bastards born in Hartland were the offspring of repeating mothers, while in Banbury exactly a quarter of bastards were so characterized. The aggregated figures conceal considerable variations over time. A clearly identifiable feature can be seen in the original data: in the course of the eighteenth century the relative importance of repeating bastard-bearers increases in both communities. This is also the period when the bastardy ratio climbs quite sharply.

Indeed, in Hartland, in the period 1761–1800, the peak period of the illegitimacy ratio, more than half, 54.3 per cent, of bastards were born into repeater groups. In Banbury over the same period just over a quarter of the bastards were born into repeater groups, 40 out of 156, but it should be noted that one group of 8 is included in this figure (seven of whom shared the same father) and would over-influence the figure considerably. Nonetheless, figure 3.4 would seem to show an identifiable link between the bastardy ratio and the importance of repeater groups ($r_s = 0.599$ significant at 0.001 level $t = 18.7$). However, the relationship does not seem to appear until the early eighteenth century ($r_s = 0.006$), suggesting that the high rank correlation coefficient for all time periods may well be spurious. Table 3.22 presents information about those bastards for whom the date of both baptism and burial is known. At first glance the data would seem to suggest excessive infant and child mortality among bastards. Probably levels were high, but it must be added as a caution that the number of bastards at risk is impossible to assess, considering that such a high proportion seem to have moved off to another parish soon after birth. Indeed, nearly 50 per cent of those that we pick up in the records after baptism in Hartland are known about only because they die in infancy, probably in the first few days and weeks of life, before their mothers shifted elsewhere. In Banbury the figure is 70 per cent. These proportions probably tell us more about the mobility patterns of bastards than about their mortality, for

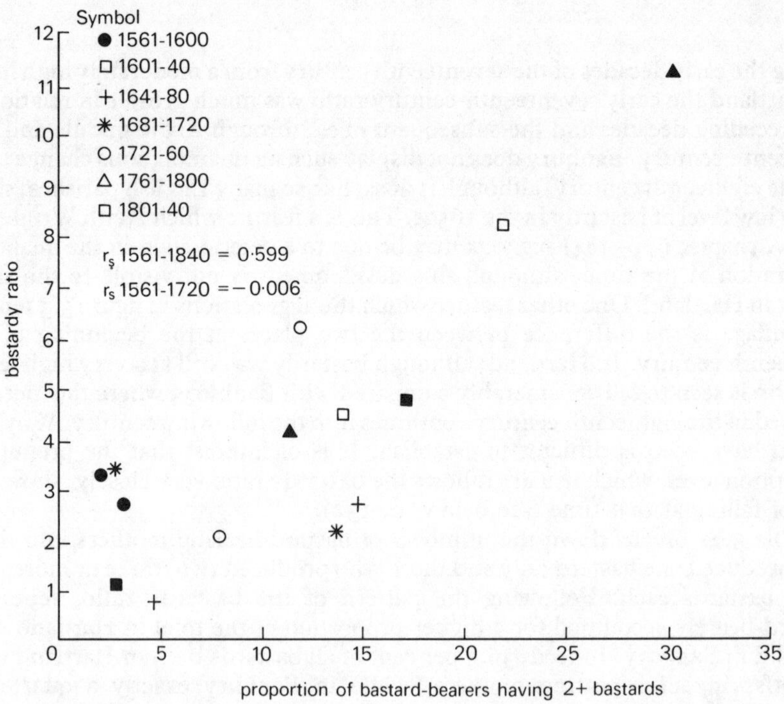

Fig. 3.4 The relationship between the illegitimacy ratio and repetitive bastard-bearing, Banbury and Hartland, 1561–1840

clearly, even in a remote, rural parish like Hartland, the majority did not remain to become part of their community of birth.

Table 3.22: Survival of bastards in Banbury and Hartland, 1561–1838

	Banbury		Hartland	
	No.	%	No.	%
Total no. of bastards	694		579	
No. whose baptism & burial registered	122	17.6	95	16.4
Buried under age 1	85	69.6	46	48.4
Survived to age 1	26	21.3	24	25.3
Survived to age 5	6	4.9	10	10.5
Survived to age 10	2	1.6	5	5.3
Survived to age 20	1	0.8	4	4.2
Survived to age 30	1	0.8	4	4.2
Survived to age 30+	1	0.8	2	2.1

1 Identifying and describing the parents of bastards

Tables 3.23 and 3.24 deal with the parents of bastards, and in essence this means the mothers. Indeed, there seems to have been little consistency in the frequency with which both mothers and fathers were named. In Hartland both were more likely to be named in the sixteenth century and in Banbury in the late seventeenth and eighteenth centuries, although in both instances still in a minority of cases. In both places the bastards were practically always baptized with the names of their mothers. In Hartland only 10 bastards over the whole period were recorded with no parents at all – *enfants trouvés* – and in Banbury 16. In Banbury, of the 578 mothers of bastards named, 45 (7.8 per cent) were stated to be married or

Table 3.23: Registration of parents of bastards in Banbury and Hartland, 1561–1838

	Fathers of bastards	Mothers of bastards	
	Named	Named	Not named
Banbury			
1561–1600	21	56	6
1601–40	9	36	1
1641–80	2	18	3
1681–1720	4	45	6
1721–60	1	57	0
1761–1800	2	130	2
1801–38	0	236	0
1561–1838	39	578	18
Hartland			
1561–1600	1	43	3
1601–40	4	55	3
1641–80	1	27	0
1681–1720	12	36	3
1721–60	14	66	1
1761–1800	35	113	0
1801–1838	15	101	0
1561–1838	82	441	10

Table 3.24: Registration of mothers of bastards in Banbury and Hartland, 1561–1838

	Total no.	No. registered	Baptisms only	Burials only	Baptized & buried	Marriage only	Baptized & married	Married & buried	Baptized, married & buried	Total marriages
Banbury										
1561–1600	62	49	1	2	1	2	4	0	3	9
1601–40	37	20	12	1	1	0	0	1	2	3
1641–80	21	12	6	1	1	0	1	0	0	1
1681–1720	51	27	12	3	4	0	4	1	0	5
1721–60	57	25	6	5	8	0	3	4	6	13
1761–1800	132	71	21	2	3	4	24	0	7	35
1801–38	236	134	53	3	5	4	33	0	4	41
1561–1838	596	338	111	17	23	10	69	6	22	107
Hartland										
1561–1600	46	33	5	3	0	0	3	0	2	5
1601–40	58	30	19	0	1	2	3	2	1	8
1641–80	27	10	10	0	2	1	2	0	2	5
1681–1720	39	18	12	0	0	0	1	1	7	9
1721–60	67	15	24	0	9	2	5	3	9	19
1761–1800	113	28	34	2	12	0	20	2	15	37
1801–38	101	35	43	0	3	3	17	0	0	20
1561–1838	451	169	147	5	27	8	51	8	36	103

widowed and we must therefore assume that the remainder (533 or 92.2 per cent) were single. In Hartland the number of married or widowed named was very small, 13 or 2.9 per cent of a total of 441 mothers' names, leaving an even larger majority of bastard-bearers who were single (428 or 97.1 per cent).

When we attempt an assessment of the background of mothers of bastards based on the extent to which they are identifiable in the baptismal, marriage and burial registers (see table 3.24), we find that in Banbury over the three centuries, more than half (56.7 per cent) have no baptism, marriage nor burial reference. In Hartland, geographically a much more isolated community, we find that only about 38 per cent are unaccounted for in this way.

The evidence of a baptism in the parish is the clearest indicator as to whether the individual was a member of the local community, although there is always the possibility that a girl returned home to have the baby which may have been conceived in a foreign parish. Table 3.25 charts the extent to which this characteristic varied over two and a half centuries and shows that the two parishes displayed quite different patterns. Indeed, it would seem that in Banbury, excluding the period 1561–1600, close to 40 per cent of mothers of bastards had been baptized in the town from 1600 to 1840. In Hartland the pattern is more variable and uncertain, but a trend is detectable. For close to two thirds of the eighteenth century a very high proportion of the mothers of bastards were indigenous to the parish. These proportions from Hartland are emphatically the highest that have so far been derived from any of the, admittedly, small number of English parishes on which this type of analysis has been undertaken. We may interpret this phenomenon in several ways. In general the girls may have moved only a short distance from their home parish; those girls in service who became pregnant may have returned to their home parish because they knew that the bastard child would be tolerated there; or the 'host' parish may not have wanted to bear the cost of supporting transient mothers and their children. It was probably a combination of all three factors. At any rate, it is clear that for much of the late eighteenth century, in contrast to earlier periods, Hartland mothers of bastards were likely to be members by birth of the local community (see above, pp. 89–90, where similar evidence relating to Hawkshead, Aldenham, Alcester and Colyton is presented).

The marriage behaviour of these mothers is even less easy to interpret. Tables 3.26 and 3.27 indicate the number of bastard-bearers whose age at marriage can be established because they were born, baptized and married in the parish in which they were known to have given birth to at least one bastard child. It should be obvious that this cannot be read as an indicator of the marriage chances of a

Table 3.25: Mothers of bastards baptized in Hartland and Banbury, 1561–1838

	Hartland		Banbury	
	No.	% of total	No.	% of total
1561–1600	10	21.7	9	14.5
1601–40	24	41.4	15	40.5
1641–80	16	59.3	8	38.1
1681–1720	20	51.3	20	39.2
1721–60	47	70.1	23	40.4
1761–1800	81	71.7	55	41.7
1801–1838	63	62.4	95	40.3

bastard-bearer. It would, however, seem that an unmarried mother possessed a better chance of marrying in the parish in which she had a bastard in the later eighteenth century than in any other period. This feature is common to both Banbury and Hartland. In Hartland, the bastard-bearers marrying were also mostly recorded as having been baptized in the parish as well.

Table 3.26: Mothers of bastards baptized and married, Hartland and Banbury, 1561–1838

	Hartland		Banbury	
	No.	% of total	No.	% of total
1561–1600	5	10.9	7	11.3
1601–40	4	6.9	2	5.4
1641–80	4	14.8	1	4.8
1681–1720	8	20.5	4	7.8
1721–60	14	20.9	9	15.8
1761–1800	35	31.0	31	23.5
1801–38	17	16.8	37	15.7

Table 3.27: Mothers of bastards marrying, Hartland and Banbury, 1561–1838

	Hartland		Banbury	
	No.	% of total	No.	% of total
1561–1600	5	10.9	9	14.5
1601–40	8	13.8	3	8.1
1641–80	5	18.5	1	4.8
1681–1720	9	23.1	5	9.8
1721–60	19	28.4	13	15.8
1761–1800	37	32.7	35	26.5
1801–38	20	19.8	41	17.4

It is worth considering whether the increase in the proportion of bastard-bearers marrying in the parish in which they bore their bastard is simply the result of a general increase in the levels of parochial endogamy for females in the eighteenth century. In Hartland, where we have figures on the number of all marriages for women linkable with a baptism so that we can derive a marriage age, the level remained quite stable over the period (see table 3.28), oscillating but not very erratically around 40 per cent. It would seem that the mothers of bastards had narrowed their geographical marriage horizons quite considerably by the end of the eighteenth century, or perhaps other factors had intervened to inhibit their movement in search of a spouse.

The data arranged in table 3.29 are noteworthy as they relate to the age at first birth of mothers of bastards. They are aggregations of data over the whole time period from 1560 to 1840 and as such mask a great many variations. When data for all Hartland women on age at marriage are aggregated for this period (see table 3.31), the overall distribution is very similar to that for the ages at which women had their first bastards. Superficially, it would seem that women were having their first bastards in Banbury rather earlier than in Hartland and certainly earlier than women in Banbury as a whole were marrying. However, it should be borne in mind that of the women for whom age at birth of first bastard could be calculated, 66.6 per cent came from the period 1761–1838, precisely when marriage age was

Table 3.28: Proportion of women at Hartland for whom a marriage age can be calculated, by fifty-year periods

	Total marriages	Total women marrying with baptism in Hartland	%
1600–1649	458	141	30.8
1650–99	498	223	44.8
1700–1749	422	190	45.0
1750–99	460	205	44.6
1800–1849	452	169	37.4

Table 3.29: Ages of mothers at birth of first bastard, Banbury and Hartland, 1561–1838 (for those mothers whose date of birth and/or baptism is known; given in numbers, with per cents in parentheses)

	Ages							
	below 20	20–24	25–29	30–34	35–39	40–44	45–49	Total
Banbury 1561–1838	51 (23.7)	76 (35.3)	48 (22.3)	23 (10.7)	10 (4.6)	5 (2.3)	2 (1.1)	215
Hartland 1561–1838	29 (11.2)	93 (36.0)	71 (27.5)	41 (15.9)	21 (8.1)	1 (0.4)	2 (0.8)	258

also much lower than it had been earlier. In Hartland 55 per cent of the cases where age at birth of first bastard could be determined came from the same period. This would suggest that the apparent differences between the two distributions might be the product of the excessive amount of information pertaining to the period 1761–1838.[14] The findings in tables 3.29 and 3.30 confirm the idea that many illegitimate first births may well have been conceived within courtship, courtship which had not resulted in marriage.

This claim is supported to some degree by the evidence in table 3.31 which sheds light on the other aspect of extra-marital sex, prenuptial conceptions. In Banbury the numbers of prenuptially conceived children, expressed as a percentage of first live births, follows the development of the illegitimacy ratio quite closely, starting high at 30 per cent, then, during the seventeenth century, dipping first to 16 per cent, then to 10 per cent, and rising during the eighteenth century to 27 per cent and 31 per cent. In Hartland, except in the first period when it was 28 per cent, prenuptial conceptions run at a consistently higher level and a more even course.

Table 3.30: Ages of women at first marriage, Banbury and Hartland, 1561–1838

	Ages							
	below 20	20–24	25–29	30–34	35–39	40–44	more than 45	Total
Banbury 1561–1838	72 (10.3)	297 (42.6)	192 (27.5)	102 (14.6)	27 (3.8)	3 (0.4)	4 (0.8)	697
Hartland 1561–1838	69 (7.1)	336 (34.5)	312 (32.0)	161 (16.5)	65 (6.7)	25 (2.6)	7 (0.6)	975

14 The mean age at marriage for women in Hartland in the period 1750–99 was 26.6 and in 1800–1849 was 24.7. In Banbury it was 25.4 and 23.8 respectively. See Wrigley, 'Age at marriage in early modern England'.

Table 3.31: Frequency and percentage of first live births less than nine months after marriage (all ages) in Banbury and Hartland, 1550–1849

	Banbury			Hartland		
	Total live births	Less than 9 months	%	Total live births	Less than 9 months	%
1550–99	33	10	30	48	13	28
1600–49	140	23	16	138	32	24
1650–99	81	8	10	176	43	25
1700–49	162	43	27	153	48	31
1750–99	237	73	31	207	95	46
1800–49	–	–	–	132	56	43
Total	653	157	24	854	287	34

2 The economic background of bastard-bearers

Attempting to assess the economic background of women who bore bastards is a frustrating, though not an entirely fruitless task. Occupations are not given consistently in the parish registers for the fathers of bastard-bearers nor for the men whom they subsequently married, although this type of information improves in the later eighteenth century. We are fortunate with the Banbury parish register in having a document in which occupations are given very regularly. In order to know whether men in certain occupational categories had bastard-bearing children or married women who had previously borne bastards, we need to have some notion of the overall employment structure in the parish. A different approach to this problem has been adopted for the two parishes, taking into account the available documentation. In Banbury the assumption will be made that the evidence given in the parish register on all occupations is representative of the total male employment structure. In table 3.32 the relative distribution of bastardy-linked individuals within the occupational groupings between 1760 and 1840 are compared with the distribution of all individuals in the occupational groupings compiled from all the evidence in the parish registers

Table 3.32: Occupations of fathers of bastards and fathers of mothers of bastards in the parish register, Banbury, 1760–1840

	All occupations in parish register 1750–1840		Occupations of bastardy-linked individuals in the parish register 1760–1840	
	No.	%	No.	%
Industry	1270	36.2	63	39.1
Government services	127	3.6	–	–
Tertiary trades and services	127	3.6	–	–
Dealing and retailing	431	12.3	17	10.5
Transport	127	3.6	4	2.5
Building	146	4.2	9	5.5
Quarrying	7	0.1	–	–
Agriculture	205	5.9	3	1.9
Gentlemen	43	1.2	1	0.7
Wanderers and paupers	26	0.7	1	0.7
Labourers and servants	998	28.5	63	39.1
Total	3507	100.0	161	100.0

after 1750. It should be noted that we are comparing the occupational pattern of the 161 bastardy-linked individuals with that of 3,507, so any divergences should be treated with considerable scepticism. To a remarkable extent the data in table 3.32 would seem to imply that bastardy-linked individuals from whom we have some occupational information (and as such may be somewhat a biased group) are broadly distributed in the same occupational groupings as the population as a whole. There is one very notable exception – the labourers and male servants who make up nearly 40 per cent of the bastardy-linked individuals and only 28 per cent of the total population.

The Hartland parish registers do not consistently yield occupational evidence. We are obliged to use the occupational information in the 1831 census which can be compared with the occupations of bastardy-linked individuals between 1761 and 1840 given in the parish registers. On the basis of the data presented in table 3.33 it would be foolhardy to claim that bastardy-linked persons came disproportionately from any one occupational grouping.

Table 3.33: Occupations of fathers of bastards and fathers of mothers of bastards in the parish register, Hartland, 1761–1840

	Male employment structure in 1831 census		Occupations of bastardy-linked individuals in the parish register 1761–1840	
	No.	%	No.	%
Agricultural occupiers with and without labourers	116	20.5	15[a]	31.9
Labourers (agricultural and non-agricultural)	304	53.8	22	46.8
Manufacture	–	–	5	10.6
Retail/handicraft	93	16.4	3	6.4
Capitalists	10	1.8	–	–
Servants over 20	–	–	–	–
Others	42	7.5	2	4.3

(a) Includes 5 gentry.

3 The family background to bastard-bearing

The discussion so far has concentrated on the overall trend in bastard-bearing and the demographic background of the mothers and their illegitimate offspring. In this final section an attempt is made to fill out this impression with some case samples from individual families. In particular it will be considered whether there is a basis for suggesting the existence of a bastardy tolerant sub-society. However, to place all individuals connected with bastardy into a group accepting this particular behaviour trait as normal would be quite incorrect. Indeed, it is obvious that a number of different circumstances could lead logically, even predictably, to an illegitimate birth.

For example, in Banbury between 1750 and 1837, there is evidence of four wives who had bastards while their husbands were still alive. One of these wives had been deserted by her husband and another appeared to be in desperate straits while her husband, a sergeant in the 52nd Regiment, was away on duty in Ireland.

The Banbury registers name 38 widows who had bastards. Where we have the baptism date of the widow, the marriage date and the burial date of the husband, we can establish that most of these women were widowed young, their marriages had usually lasted less than ten years, they almost all had young families. The interval between the death of the husband and the birth of the first bastard was in a few cases very short; usually the gap ranged from three to six years, occasionally it was as much as nine or eleven years. Sometimes the widows remarried though not necessarily to the fathers of their bastards. The registers name seven widows who produced two bastards and one, Jane Baldwin, who had three.

In certain cases it would appear that we are observing bastard-bearers who belong to families where the distinction between legal and illegal marriage remained uncertain. They are difficult to spot but an unusual Christian name, a chance remark jotted in the register gives the clue. In Hartland, in 1611, English May had an illegitimate daughter, Tamisine. In 1615 she bore a bastard son, named Peter. In 1618, Peter Adams, son of Samuel and English Adams was buried. Samuel and English Adams increased their family: twins in 1620, singletons in 1622, 1625 and 1629. It is possible that Samuel and English were married in another parish between 1615 and 1618 and that Samuel gave the two children, registered as bastards, his name; he may even have been their father. But it is also possible that this was a customary marriage.

In both parishes we can discern hints of a web of relationships which may indicate that there were some families where bastardy was more prevalent than others. This becomes clear when we attempted to unravel the tangle of bastardy relationships associated with the marriage of Katherine, daughter of John Bull, labourer, and Thomas Essex on 28 April 1700 at Broughton, a village just west of Banbury. Katherine herself seems to have had a blameless life, but her younger sister had a bastard son in 1707; both mother and child died in 1708. Katherine's cousin, Amy, bore a bastard of unrecorded sex who was baptized on 27 April 1700. Amy married William Adams, a gardener, in June 1701, and in ten years of marriage bore him nine children. The fifth child, Ann, baptized in 1706, having produced a bastard, married first Samuel Austin and then John Handley. To return to Thomas and Katherine: they had four daughters between 1701 and 1717. Hannah, baptized in May 1701, had a bastard by Henry Austin whom she later married; after his death she married Richard Taylor. The second daughter, Eliza, baptized in March 1705, had two bastards, the first by Nathaniel Bloxham, the second father unknown. The third daughter, Sarah, also had two bastards, the first by William Dawkes, the second, father again unknown.

Hartland was much smaller than Banbury; its population remained fairly stable in numbers, and, because of its geographical isolation there was little movement of people into and out of the parish. These factors combined with the fullness of information provided by the parish registers have made it easier to trace family relationships and to make the correct linkages with reasonable certainty. In table 3.34 we have attempted to give some indication of the size of various name sets, based on the number of family reconstitution forms, both for those families where the marriage date is known and where it is not known; the prevalence of bastardy within the name set based on the numbers of mothers and/or fathers of bastards (we have used, in the main, only those name sets with four or more parents of bastards); and in the last column the other name sets with which the particular name set was in any way linked in bastardy. We have further grouped the 'family sets' into various categories and given the proportion each category bears to the total number. It is, admittedly, a crude method, but it does show that the bastardy network was very broadly based.

Table 3.34: Links between bastard-bearing families in Hartland, 1561–1838 (based on 4+ mothers or fathers of bastards)

Surname	Total no. of families (from FRFs)	No. of mothers & fathers of bastards	Inter-family bastardy links
Ashton	27 (1727–1793)	4	Branton, Buse, Colwell, Daymon, Dennis, Harris, Heard, Lewis, Metherel, Mugford, Prust, Score, Short, Way, Westlake
Bagelhole	67 (1597–1812)	10	Ashton, Buse, Cloutmar, Cook, Downing, Littlejohn, Mugford, Nicol, Prust, Rowe, Snow, Trick, Wakely, Way
Beare	36 (1642–1822)	7	Ashton, Bragg, Buse, Chapman, Cholwel, Daymon, Down, Eliot, Heard, King, Marshal, Nicol, Prust, Shutt, Small, Tib, Trick, Wakely, Way, Williams
Beriman	22 (1719–1837)	6	Downing, Littlejohn, Prust, Trick
Bond	29	4	Bagelhole, Blight, Braginton, Cook, Downing, Eddy, Folly, Heard, Jeffery, Littlejohn, Mugford, Nicol, Shut, Trick, Westlake
Braginton/ Branton	28 (1749–1820)	7	Ashton, Colwill, Cloutman, Downing, Gowman, Nicol, Prout, Score, Trick, Williams
Brown	20 (1768–1885)	4	Bragg, Clatworthy, Cook, Mugford, Snow, Walter
Buckler	9 (1728–1805)	5	Bragg, Burman, Evans, Metherel, Prout, Trick
Burnard	13 (1644–1815)	5	Buse, Coul, Heard, Lane, Littlejohn, Neal, Popham, Prust, Rowe, Short, Williams
Buse	26 (1656–1823)	4	Bagelhole, Bond, Brown, Burnard, Cloak, Coul, Eddy, Fish, Galsworthy, Jenking, Metherel, Reed, Trick
Can	25	1	Ashton, Bagelhole, Cook, Dennis, Furshewer, Kinsman, Mugford, Nicol, Prust, Rowe, Trick, Way, Westlake, Williams
Clatworthy	4 (1726–1811)	4	Friend, Holoford, Wakely
Cloak	11 (1728–1827)	4	Buse, Cann, Cook, Metherel, Trick
Cloutman	17 (1717–1770)	4	Baglehole, Braginton, Deyman, Down, Fish, Harris, Holloford, Hooper, Marshall, Mugford, Prust, Row, Snow, Way, Westlake
Coffin	8 (1782–1829)	4	Buckler, Ching, Colwell, Cook, Coul, Eliot, Jeffery, Heard
Coule alias Curtis	74 (1582–1807)	9	Baglehole, Beer, Berriman, Bishop, Bond, Burnard, Can, Coffin, Cook, Curtis, Davy, Deyman, Evans, Forshewer, Galsworthy, Harris, Hatherly, Hooper, Jenkin, Littlejohn, May, Mountjoy, Mugford, Nichol, Pitton, Prust, Row, Snow, Trick, Tucker, Wakely, Walter, Way, Westlake, Wilcock

Table 3.34 *(cont.)*

Surname	Total no. of families (from FRFs)	No. of mothers & fathers of bastards	Inter-family bastardy links
C(h)olwell	43 (1765–1827)	15	Baglehole, Beere, Buse, Bragg, Braginton, Chope, Coffin, Dayman, Downe, Heard, Hooper, King, Lock, Marshall, Metherell, Mountjoy, Mugford, Pitton, Prouse, Prust, Short, Thomas, Trick
Cooke	73 (1647–1834)	19	Baglehole, Bartholomew, Bond, Bragg, Buckler, Buse, Cann, Ching, Cloak, Colwell, Coul, Harris, Hathery, Hearn, Holeman, Hooper, Jeffery, Jenkin, King, Lock, Mabin, Nichol, Prouse, Prust, Rowe, Saunder, Short, Snow, Trick, Wakely, Waldon, Walter, Waye, Westlake
Downing	20 (1634–1786)	7	Bagelhole, Braginton, Heard, Holman, May, Prouse, Rowe, Trick, Williams
El(l)iot	15 (1774–1833)	7	Baglehole, Beare, Coffin, Galsworthy, Grills, Hopper, Jeffrey, Nichol, Prouse, Souch, Williams
Evans	9 (1669–1805)	6	Baglehole, Braginton, Buckler, Buse, Chope, Eliot, Heard, Souch
Forshewer	21 (1590–1798)	5	Baglehole, Burnard, Can, Davy, Deyman, Galsworthy, Gowman, Hamlyn, Heard, Holman, Jeffery, Littlejohn, Prust, Score, Short, Snow, Stambury, Walter
Galsworthy	37 (1730–1821)	3	Bond, Buse, Cook, Deyman, Forshewer, Hambly, Heard, Kinsman, Littlejohn, Martin, Mountjoy, Nichol, Prouse, Prust, Row, Souch, Stambury, Trick, Wakely, Waldon, Westlake, Williams
Hamlin(bly)	19 (1766–1782)	2	Bear, Buse, Eliot, Forshewer, Galsworthy, Jeffery, Jenkin, Martin, Metherel, Mountjoy, Porington, Prust, Rowe, Tucker, Westlake
Harris	36 (1598–1780)	3	Baglehole, Burman, Chapman, Cloutman, Cook, Coul, Curtis, Deyman, Downing, Eddy, Gowman, Grills, Heard, Jenkin, Metherel, Mugford, Nichol, Short,
Heard	106 (1610–1830)	18	Bartholomew, Bear, Bishop, Bond, Branton, Buse, Ching, Cholwell, Chope, Clapman, Coul, Davies, Dayman, Down, Downing, Evans, Folly, Forshewer, Galsworthy, Hamlin, Harris, Hooper, Jeffery, King, Kinsman, Littlejohn, Marshall, Martin, Mountjoy, Mugford, Nicol, Pitton, Prout, Prust, Rowe, Snow, Stambury, Tucker, Waldon, Walker, Williams

Table 3.34 *(cont.)*

Surname	Total no. of families (from FRFs)	No. of mothers & fathers of bastards	Inter-family bastardy links
Holeman	30 (1631–1743)	4	Baglehole, Blagdon, Burman, Chapman, Ching, Cook, Coul, Forshewer, Prust, Row, Snow, Stambury
Hooper	15 (1590–1821)	4	Blagdon, Bond, Cloutman, Coul, Deyman, Eliot, Heard, Jenkin, Trick
Jeffery	39 (1594–1787)	6	Bear, Bond, Cann, Chope, Coffin, Cook, Eliot, Folly, Forshewer, Galsworthy, Godman, Grills, Hambly, Heard, Jenkin, Martin, Metherel, Methrin, Mountjoy, Rowe, Souch, Trick, Tucker, Wakely
Jenkin	26 (1734–1795)	3	Bear, Buse, Chapman, Clatworthy, Cook, Deyman, Gowman, Hamlin, Heard, Hooper, Jeffery, Pitton, Trick, Way, Williams
Littlejohn	32 (1686–1782)	5	Baglehole, Beriman, Bond, Breckler, Burnard, Coule, Fish, Forshewer, Galsworthy, Grills, Heard, Johns, Mountjoy, Pitton, Prust, Rowe, Slowman, Snowe
Mugford	46 (1600–1807)	8	Ashton, Baglehole, Bond, Can, Cholwell, Coul, Cloutman, Davie, Deyman, Grills, Hamlin, Harris, Heard, Holoford, Jollife, Kinsman, Marshall, May, Nicol, Prust, Snow, Stambury, Trick, Wakely
Nicol	59 (1634–1750)	4	Baglehole, Beare, Bond, Bragg, Branton, Can, Ching, Cholwell, Cook, Curtis, Deyman, Galsworthy, Gifford, Hatherly, Heard, Holoford, King, May, Mountjoy, Mugford, Prust, Short, Snow, Stambury, Trick, Witesh
Prust	87 (1593–1831)	6	Ashton, Bagelhole, Bishop, Bragg, Branton, Burnard, Buse, Can, Ching, Cholwell, Cloutman, Cooke, Coul, Deyman, Downe, Fish, Forshewer, Galsworthy, Hambly, Harris, Heard, Holeman, Hooper, Kinsman, Littlejohn, Marshall, Mountjoy, Mugford, Nicol, Prouse, Row, Saunders, Snow, Trick, Wakely
Rowe	66 (1696–1799)	6	Baglehole, Beare, Bond, Bragg, Burnard, Can, Cloutman, Cook, Curtis, Deyman, Downe, Downing, Fish, Galsworthy, Grills, Hambly, Heard, Holeman, Littlejohn, Metherel, Mountjoy, Mugford, Pitton, Prust, Short, Westlake, Williams
Saunder	19 (1558–1797)	5	Cooke, Hatherly, Heard, May, Prust, Rowe, Trick, Wilcock

Table 3.34 *(cont.)*

Surname	Total no. of families (from FRFs)	No. of mothers & fathers of bastards	Inter-family bastardy links
Snow	46 (1614–1737)	4	Baglehole, Bartholomew, Braginton, Buse, Cloutman, Cooke, Couche, Coul, Downing, Harris, Hatherly, Holman, Husband, Littlejohn, Mabin, Mugford, Nichol, Prust, Trick, Walter, Williams
Souch	9 (1603–1832)	5	Downe, Eliot, Evans, Galsworthy, Jeffery, Westlake
Trick	48 (1572–1813)	12	Baglehole, Bartholomew, Beare, Beriman, Bishop, Bond, Bowman, Bragg, Branton, Buckler, Buse, Cann, Cloak, Cook, Deyman, Downing, Fish, Galsworthy, Hooper, Marshall, Mountjoy, Mugford, Nichol, Prust, Saunders, Short, Snow, Wilcock
Tucker	17 (1615–1742)	3	Fish, Hambly, Heard, Mountjoy, Nicol, Prust, Rowe
Wakely	29 (1714–1822)	11	Bagelhole, Beer, Bond, Cooke, Coul, Forshewer, Evans, Galsworthy, Gowman, Hamlyn, Jeffery, Kinsman, Marshall, Mugford, Prouse, Prust, Tucker, Westlake
Westlake	18 (1716–1807)	4	Bond, Can, Cloak, Cook, Coul, Deyman, Douse, Galsworthy, Hambly, Marshall, Nichol, Row, Souch, Wakely
Wilcock	21 (1781–1829)	3	Bagelhole, Coul, Deyman, Nicholl, Poppam, Saunders, Trick, Walter
Williams	34 (1721–1819)	4	Bear, Burman, Burnard, Cann, Coul, Downing, Eliot, Galsworthy, Heard, Hopgood, Jenkin, Metherel, Prouse, Prust, Row, Short, Snow, Westlake

Note: Hartland (Devon) – family sets

	No.	% of total no.
1 Total no. of family sets	537	
2 No. of family sets containing mothers and/or fathers of bastards	181	33.3
3 No. of family sets showing prenuptial conceptions	200	37.2
4 Total no. of family sets either containing mothers or fathers of bastards, or showing prenuptial conceptions, or both	257	46.0
5 No. of family sets showing neither mothers nor fathers of bastards nor prenuptial conceptions, *but* marrying into families containing mothers or fathers of bastards	156	29.1
6 No. of family sets of 1 FRF only that *do not* contain either mothers or fathers of bastards or prenuptial conceptions and *do not* have connections with families containing mothers or fathers of bastards	79	14.8
7 No. of family sets of 2 FRFs and over as above (6) (the largest family set is the Sincock family, with 10 FRFs)	7	1.4
8 No. of family sets with only FRFs without marriage date (where it is therefore impossible to detect either prenuptial conceptions or the marrying into families containing mothers or fathers of bastards) and no bastard-bearers	38	7.1

Hartland seems to have been a village in which families were frequently interrelated because of the relatively low level of out-migration. Certain families forged and maintained closer links among themselves than with other groups of families in the parish. This would probably have been due to the fact that Hartland was not nucleated but was made up of scattered settlements. If the registers had added residence to their entries we might have been able to trace a geographical pattern of relationships.

Interconnections established by the use of surname evidence alone does not justify the assertion that there was a sub-society of the bastardy prone. However, some examples given here are indicative of the strong possibility of such a group existing. The Wakely and Coul families of Hartland and their connections are particularly good examples of this possibility. We observe this behaviour first with Grace Coul who bore a bastard, Phillip, in 1712 and in 1714 married Peter Wakely. They had seven children and while Grace was producing the family, Peter fathered a bastard on Mary Barns, baptized in 1725. Margaret Wakely, sixth child of the union of Peter and Grace, in 1756, at the age of 28, bore a bastard to Thomas Tarraway, a labourer. In 1760 Thomas married Elizabeth Prust, who some years earlier, in 1737 and 1745, had had two bastard sons. Elizabeth Wakely, Peter's sister, bore a bastard son in 1714, and then married William Coul, another cousin to Grace in 1719. Jane, another sister of the Elizabeth and Peter Wakely, bore a bastard in 1719. Others of this family married into the Ahton and Forshewer families, where bastardy also existed.

Elizabeth Wakely's bastard son, Samuel, married a Bagelhole, very much a bastardy family; one of their daughters, Ann, produced two bastards in 1775 and 1781. A granddaughter of John Wakely and Elizabeth Coul had two bastards, Sarah in 1774 and John in 1777. She then married John Friend, the bastard son of Phillippa Friend who, on the same day in 1754 that her son was baptized, married John Clatworthy, supposedly the child's father, who was the eldest of three bastards of Joan Clatworthy. Sarah Wakely continued the line of bastard-bearers by having two in 1799 and 1806, the first by John Kinsman whose mother was a Wakely. He had already fathered a bastard on Ann Evans. His two sisters had bastards in 1798 and 1801.

Wakelys and Mugfords were also closely related. Elizabeth Wakely, a niece of Elizabeth, Jane and Peter, had a bastard son in 1732. Her youngest sister, Margaret, married Thomas Mugford and their daughter, Sarah Mugford, married back into the Wakely family by taking as husband in 1738 Thomas, son of Samuel Wakely and a grandson of Peter Wakely and Grace Coul. Sarah and Thomas were thus second cousins. They had eight children, six boys and then two girls, Grace and Ann. Ann, at age 33, had a bastard in 1822 and Grace, at age 17, had one in 1803. The father of Grace's son was John Grills, whose cousin had a bastard and whose widowed sister, Honor Grimes, alias Grills, had three bastards: John Sage, baptized 24 March 1793, the father James Sage of Hartland; Honor Sage, baptized 2 August 1795, buried 27 May 1818; Charles, baptized 1 July 1798. Their mother, Honor, née Rowe, baptized 6 October 1765 married as follows: first Grimes, 13 July 1787, no children, no burial date for the husband; second John Clatworthy alias Friend, 2 February 1805, one child, baptized 12 April 1805, and thus prenuptially conceived; no burial date for the husband; third, John Parsons, 16 April 1817, no children.

It needs but a perusal of the column headed 'Inter-family bastardy links' in table 3.34 to see the name sets of Hartland which recur: Bagelhole, Beare, Cooke,

Coule alias Curtis, Cholwell, Forshewer, Galsworthy, Heard, Mugford, Prust, Rowe, Trick, Wakely. Central to this network were the Tricks with twelve bastardy connections; Wakelys, eleven; Mugfords, eight; Couls, nine; and from the smaller name sets, Evans produced six; Forshewer, five; Friends alias Clatworthy, six; and Kinsman, two. Great caution must be exercised in interpreting these links (see chapter 8, pp. o–oo, where a similar problem relating to the network analysis of bastard-bearers and begetters is discussed). In a relatively immobile community with a fairly high level of marital endogamy, it would be expected that links such as these would have to exist. Indeed, it is an intractable issue as to whether the links existed because of bastardy or in spite of it.

4

An evaluation of bastardy recordings in an east Kent parish

Anthea Newman

Bastardy recording in English parish registers is often baffling: references to 'base', 'natural', 'illegitimate' are scattered through baptism and burial records with tantalizingly little explanation or supporting detail. What did society, or the parish priest, mean when drawing attention to a child in this way? Was the same thing meant in all periods and in all parishes? Very often the key descriptive words were not used in the parish registers, and bastardy must be inferred, more particularly from the circumstance that the child at baptism was given the mother's rather than the father's surname. Yet there are many gradations in behaviour which may result at one end in bastardy, explicitly recorded, and at the other in prenuptial conception. It is a large assumption that the line for bastardy was drawn in the same place on all occasions.

The following examples indicate to what extent a vicar may choose to ignore or draw attention to the conception of a child outside marriage. On 25 June 1771 the vicar of St Dunstan's, Canterbury, recorded the baptism of a child in the usual way; the marriage register shows that on the same day he joined the parents in matrimony. Another vicar entered the marriage of Esther Carpenter to William Hougham in the register on 2 December 1839. A year later on 6 December 1840 he recorded the baptism of George, son of William and Esther Hougham, and on the same day, the baptism of Emily, daughter of Esther Carpenter, single woman. It would seem probable that Emily was at least a year old.

Is there then a core of cases which was regarded as unacceptable in all centuries by all parish priests? Behind this question lies the much larger issue of how far accepted patterns of behaviour changed over time, and whether bastardy recordings reflect the contemporary structure of society.[1] One method of suggesting answers to these questions is by the detailed investigation of particular cases. The conclusions from one such micro-study are presented here. The emphasis of this chapter is on the characteristics and reliability of bastardy recordings, with the implications such an evaluation has for the study of this social phenomenon.

The evidence for the study is drawn chiefly from a collation of bastardy recordings with the family reconstitution carried out for the parish of Ash-next-Sandwich in east Kent for the period 1654–1840.[2] The article by Laslett and Oosterveen on 'Long-term trends in bastardy in England' (1973) is used as a basis for comparison, as it is the first study of illegitimacy for this country, and its

1. P. Laslett and K. Oosterveen, 'Long-term trends in bastardy in England' (1973), pp. 282–4, and P. Laslett, *Family life and illicit love* (1977), chapter 3, suggest that there may be a 'bastard prone' sub-society whose fertility, at times of generally rising fertility, rose disproportionately and so exaggerated the cyclical variations in the bastardy figures. This sub-society would have importance in the analysis of social structure, see chapter 9 below.

2. The reconstitution of the Ash parish registers was undertaken, with the assistance of the SSRC Cambridge Group for the History of Population and Social Structure, by an evening class of local residents. My debt to their untiring patience and care can only be indicated here. Unless otherwise stated, all material is drawn from this reconstitution file.

general findings are tested against the detailed record. Using the family reconstitution techniques of nominal record linkage, the mothers of bastards have been traced where possible to their families of origin and to their own marriages.

The evidence of bastardy is taken to be firstly, an outright declaration by the parish priest, in one form or another: for instance, the comments, 'singlewoman', 'her husband beyond the seas for more than four years', 'two unhappy violators of the law of God', 'the father impenitent, the mother believed a true penitent', and similar censorious or explanatory declarations which are clear enough evidence, as well as the more common expressions, 'base', 'natural', or 'illegitimate'. Secondly, the recording of the mother's name only, or of the mother's full name in addition to the father's: 'Elijah the son of Lydia Elgar and Thomas Hogben' (a couple whom the vicar had attempted to make repent their sins) is considered unequivocal evidence of bastardy. Finally, the record of the child of a widow where the registers show her husband died a year or more before the baptism concerned is also taken as evidence of bastardy.[3] The inclusion of the second and third type of *'undeclared'* bastardy makes a big difference to the total figures, as table 4.1 illustrates.

Table 4.1: Declared and undeclared bastardy in Ash, 1654–1840

Period	Total no. of baptisms	Declared bastards	Undeclared bastards	Total no. of bastards	Illegitimacy ratio %
1654–1700	1672	11	8	19	1.1
1701–25	971	11	4	15	1.6
1726–50	1185	18	5	23	1.9
1751–75	1296	37	0	37	2.8
1776–1800	1340	27	50	77	5.7
1801–25	1795	105	24	129	7.0
1826–40	996	48	14	62	6.2
1654–1840	9255	257	105	362	3.9

For the overall period, 1654–1840, the level of undeclared bastards is 30 per cent; there is, however, one period, 1776–1800, when the vicars of Ash frequently forbore to enter specific comments in the registers. For this quarter century the illegitimacy ratio would appear too low by as much as two thirds if the registers were not searched for the bastards 'by implication', though at all periods the numbers so included raise the ratio significantly.

The general trend in bastardy figures which table 4.1 indicates is in obvious agreement with the national figures set out by Laslett and Oosterveen. In Ash the late seventeenth and early eighteenth centuries produced a low bastardy ratio; the upward trend is not marked until 1750; then, at the end of the eighteenth century the ratio jumped dramatically and remained at a higher level than at any point in the previous hundred years. This is the period of Laslett's second major wave of illegitimacy, a 'high' which persisted well into the second half of the nineteenth century. In Ash the ratio for 1801–25 is indeed 1 per cent higher than for the aggregated figures for the 24 parishes used by Laslett, so that the upward trend is even more marked. Particularly important is the evidence that in Ash the crucial turning point occurred in the years 1825–40, when the upward trend of the

3. These are the same conventions set out by Laslett and Oosterveen (1973) where 'inferred' is the term used for what is here called 'undeclared'.

previous 150 years was reversed; due to deficiencies in the data this period has been omitted from detailed consideration by Laslett (1977, p. 112 and references), who demonstrates the downturn from the Registrar General's data after 1850.

Can one parish be regarded as in any way typical? Ash, it is true, was a large village, with a population of over 1,000 in 1700 and over 2,000 in 1821, so that the twenty-five-year averages of baptisms and bastards are not so small as to show large random fluctuations. The overall size of the place may not, however, be the critical factor: the country seems to be naturally divided into regions which display their own characteristic levels of illegitimacy. Situated in east Kent, Ash comes into the southern region (Laslett and Oosterveen, 1973, p. 277, table 5). However, stretching from Cornwall to Kent, the region exhibits a wide range of values for the bastardy ratio, and only Sittingbourne represents east Kent in the aggregated figures. Here, as in Ash, the ratios are rather higher in the late eighteenth century than in the region generally. It seems that Ash may not be untypical of east Kent, an arable and market-gardening area with no significant large-scale industrial employment.

Table 4.2: Bastardy ratios in selected English parishes

	1661–1720	1721–1820	1781–1820
Total 24 sets	1.8	4.8	5.9
Southern region	1.4	4.0	4.5
Range	0.4–2.7	2.2–6.5	1.2–8.1
Sittingbourne	2.1	5.7	6.4
	1654–1725	**1726–1825**	**1776–1825**
Ash-next-Sandwich	1.2	4.6	6.5

The simple calculation of the bastardy ratio does not, of course, take account of such factors as repetitive bastard-bearing by certain women, which may influence the ratio to a disproportionate extent. In periods of high fertility, do the bastard prone increase their illegitimate fertility commensurately? Women who bear more than one bastard have been dubbed 'repeaters', and in Ash in the period of rising and high bastardy ratios, there is without doubt evidence of more 'repeaters'. Nonetheless, they do not of themselves account adequately for the rise in bastardy. Table 4.3 examines the position of repeaters in the overall numbers.

At the beginning and end of the period the number of repeaters will be underestimated, since there will be an unknown number of incomplete groups, where the mother may have borne further bastards outside the years under consideration. This tends to make the number in the last short period (1826–40) in particular, too low. If the years 1801–40 are combined, the percentage of children in repeater groups becomes 32, and the proportion of repeaters amongst all the bastard-bearers becomes 15. The majority of repeaters had no more than two children, of which two instances were twins, and the mean number of children in such, apparently fatherless groups varied only between 2.0 (1701–25) and 3.0, despite the one or two outstanding families illustrated in table 4.4. The number of women bearing bastards increased faster than the number of repeaters, markedly so after 1800, so that while repeaters accounted over the whole period for over a third of the bastard children (143 out of 358), they were only part of a social phenomenon of the time.

Table 4.3: Bastardy and repeaters in Ash, 1654–1840

Period	No. of women bearing bastards	Proportion of repeaters No.	Proportion of repeaters %	Bastards in groups of 2 or more %
1654–1700	16	2	12.5	26
1701–25	12	2	16.6	27
1726–50	19	2	10.5	23
1751–75	25	7	28.0	51
1776–1800	50	17	34.0	64
1801–25	88	20	22.7	43
1826–40	59	2	3.4	8

Note: Where groups overlap periods, all children are placed in the period in which the first child was born.

Table 4.4: Frequencies of repeated bastard-bearing in Ash, 1654–1840

Period	No. of women bearing 2 or more children / No. of children								
	2	3	4	5	6	–	8	–	12
1654–1700	1	1							
1701–25	2								
1726–50	1	1							
1751–75	5	1			1				
1776–1800	11	2	2	1			1		
1801–25	15	3		1					1
1826–40	1	1							
Totals	36	9	2	2	1		1		1

Examination of the cases of repeated bastard-bearing throws into relief the major problem of interpreting bastardy data, that is how far parish priests were consistent in their recordings. In the case of repeaters, while it is clear that the same girl is involved, on some occasions the bastard is declared and on others it is not. In this respect the priest was not always consistent, as may be seen from the following examples:

1 Baptized, 24 September 1817, John Gibson, illegitimate son of Jemima Court (declared)
Baptized, 16 November 1817, Robert Courtenay, son of Jemima Court (undeclared)

2 Baptized, 16 August 1778, John, illegitimate son of Mary Dilnot (declared)
Baptized, 4 July 1784, Henry Hopkins, son of Mary Dilnot (undeclared)

With regard to the second example it is interesting to note that five and a half years later Mary Dilnot married one Henry Hopkins, whom one suspects of being the father of the second child. The marriage was not, however, delayed until 1790 because Henry Hopkins was not free to marry: he seems to have been widowed in 1768.

Inconsistency in the recording of bastardy may also be noted in the baptism recording of children of what appear to be stable unions. There is little doubt that the amazing family of 12 bastards was the result of a stable union between Michael Becker, a prominent citizen of the parish, the lessee of the Guilton tithes, overseer of the poor, and Hannah Solly. A letter, dated 3 December 1937 from George Christopher Solly, in private possession, mentions Michael Becker's long-standing liaison with Hannah Solly. The same evidence suggests that no real stigma attached to the children. All but two of the children were given their father's name. But the ninth child of the series was baptized 'Emily Becker, daughter of Hannah Solly, singlewoman'. The vicar commented sadly, 'unhappy violation of the seventh commandment', leaving no doubt as to who was committing adultery. But although the vicar refused to draw a veil over the relationship in the church registers, the census enumerators in 1841 and 1851 listed the whole family as though it were legitimate.

Further evidence that vicars or rectors were not inclined to dissemble the facts is provided by the rector of Wickhambreux who, in 1592, showed himself particularly conscientious when he buried a 'child of a soldier who brought his wife to Wickham where she was delivered of the said child, att the house of Will Lewes, which said Clyffrth showed a testimonial that she was his lawful wife and were married att Norburn by the vicar there'. The same rector remarked tartly when registering a baptism a few years later, 'begotten in fower months'.[4]

As a general rule legitimate children at their baptism were given both a christian name and their father's surname, but it was not invariably the case that the bastard child was known by its mother's surname, although this was the more usual practice. When Frances Roby, the illegitimate daughter of Elizabeth Hammond, presented her bastard twins, Norris and Frederick Fasham, for baptism, she was recorded as Frances Roby, not Frances Hammond. The distinctive surname here enabled the link to be traced. Is this, perhaps, a hint of a stable union, so that Frances could reasonably think of herself (and be known) as Roby, not Hammond?

Another complication in establishing linkages was the practice of baptizing the child, and more particularly the bastard child, with both the father's and the mother's surname, joined frequently by an alias. Thus in Ash, Hannah Solly's children were apparently known as 'Becker Solly', so that an American descendant of the family today still preserves the recollection of a double surname. The association of the term 'alias' with illegitimacy has also been made by J. R. Harrison in his study of Prestbury, Cheshire (Laslett and Oosterveen, 1973, p. 281), while Karla Oosterveen (see chapter 3, above) has found that in Hawkshead (Lancashire), between 1586 and 1645 the surnames of the mother and the father of the bastard are nearly always given by implication by means of the alias device.

On close examination of legitimate and illegitimate recordings side by side, however, bastardy recordings turn out to be far more wayward than so far suggested, and the priest's attitude to stable unions was unpredictable. Inherently the subject is difficult to explore, but some few cases have left a clue which suggests that, throughout the period studied, stable unions might occasionally

4. Canterbury Cathedral Library.

produce evidence of bastardy which most often passed unremarked, as for example:

Baptized, 4 September 1715,	Elizabeth, daughter of Robert and Elizabeth Anderson
Buried, 22 October 1715,	Elizabeth 'Ye Baster' of Robert Anderson.

There are no other Robert Andersons in the registers at this time, though it may be noted that Robert's sister, Katherine, had had a bastard in 1702.[5]

Other examples could be cited. In 1691 Alice, 'natural' daughter of Alice Tilly and Christopher Renold was baptized. In 1692, 1695, 1696 and 1698 four more children of Christopher and Alice Renold were baptized, not labelled 'natural'. It is, of course, possible that the couple was married out of Ash between 1691 and 1692. At the same period a similar case was that of Martha, 'natural' daughter of John and Mary Carter. Here the mother's surname is not even given so that it seems likely that the two were commonly linked like a married couple. Again there is no record of a marriage in Ash; a second child, three years later, is not called illegitimate.[6] Henry and Hannah Saffery baptized three children, in 1798, 1800 and 1802 successively. In 1805 a twin boy and girl were baptized, 'the children of Henry Saffery and Hannah Marsh'. In 1810 another daughter of Henry Saffery and Hannah Marsh was baptized. The chronology of the events, the legitimate baptisms preceding the illegitimate, would suggest that Henry Saffery had not married Hannah Marsh between the dates of the 'illegitimate' and the 'legitimate' recordings. This is the only Saffery in the registers at this time. It is just possible that Henry Saffery was married to one Hannah and then formed a liaison with another Hannah, but the multiplication of similar cases makes this a rather far-fetched explanation. In the early part of the eighteenth century Thomas Hodgman was married twice; he had two children from the first marriage and none from the second, since the wife died within months of the marriage. Then Hodgman, a widower, is recorded as bringing first a bastard boy and then a bastard girl to baptism. Finally, although there is no record in Ash of a third marriage, Thomas and Ann Hodgman baptized a boy. It is unusual for the father to be presenting the children for baptism: perhaps he had a housekeeper. Figure 4.1 presents an illustration of the Hodgman sequence of events.

The most remarkable set of events concerns the families of John Prior and Elizabeth May, again illustrated in diagrammatic form (figure 4.2). Although there is no record in Ash of the marriage of John Prior, the baptisms of four children, all boys, of John and Elizabeth Prior, were registered in the usual way. Between the time of the first and second Prior baptisms, John Prior is named as the father of a bastard daughter borne by Elizabeth May, who three years earlier had had a bastard, no father named. There would have been no reason to suppose Elizabeth Prior and Elizabeth May were one and the same person were it not for a burial of 'Elizabeth Prior alias May', aged 45, only one day after the baptism of the last, apparently legitimate, child of John and Elizabeth Prior. The clue of the burial reveals that there were really six, not two bastards, though a stable union clearly existed. Was it the same John Prior whose wife, Mary, was given a settlement certificate in 1775 to Boughton-under-Blean, on the far side of

5. St Dunstan's, Canterbury, Canterbury Cathedral Library.
6. Ash parish registers; all the examples used are taken from the Ash parish registers, unless otherwise stated.

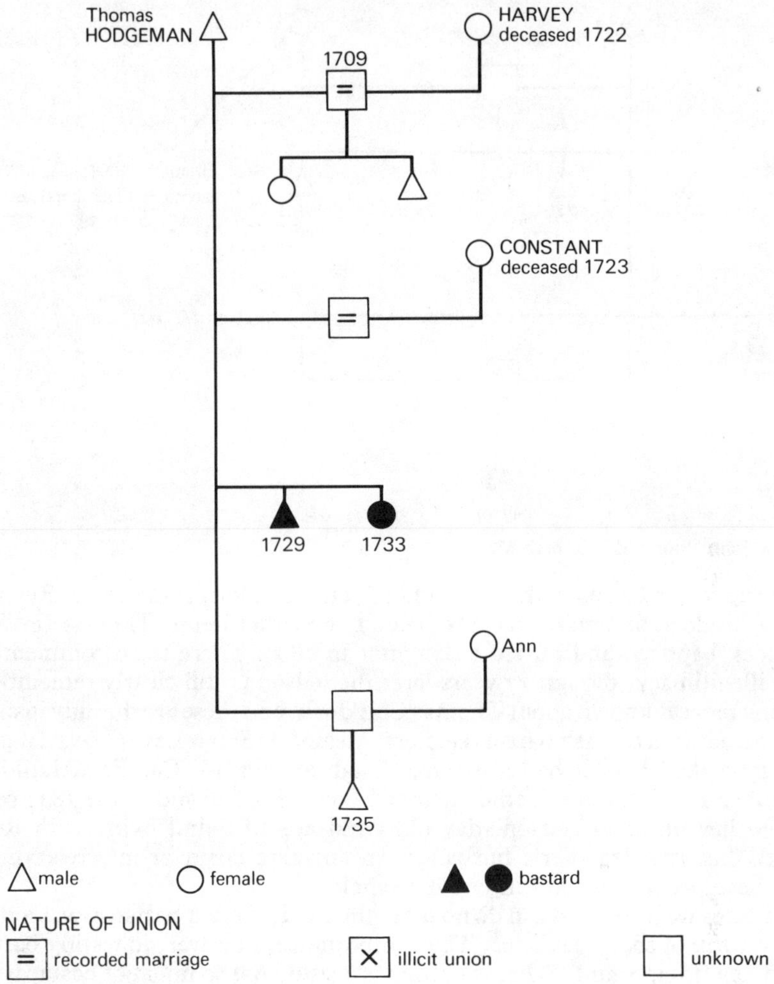

Fig. 4.1 Thomas Hodgeman

Canterbury? It seems probable that she was living in Boughton but was liable to become a charge on the poor rate, unsupported as she may have been by her husband, so that the parish of Ash was asked for the requisite certificate. If this is so, then there could be little doubt that John Prior's situation was widely known.

One last example of the same type of situation revealed through studying an alias may be cited: if all aliases could be investigated it seems likely that more would come to light. The succession of events in this case is as follows: Sarah Lawrence baptized an illegitimate daughter in 1797; in 1817 'Sarah Chiddock otherwise Lawrence' married one Robert Cooper. Despite the long gap between the baptism, in 1797, and the marriage, in 1817, all the evidence points to the two Sarah's being a correct nominal linkage. Sarah had no children after her marriage to Robert Cooper, and her age at burial in 1839 tallies with the baptism date in 1776 of Sarah Lawrence, making her 21 when the illegitimate daughter was born. But the interesting point here is the reference at marriage to the alias 'Chiddock',

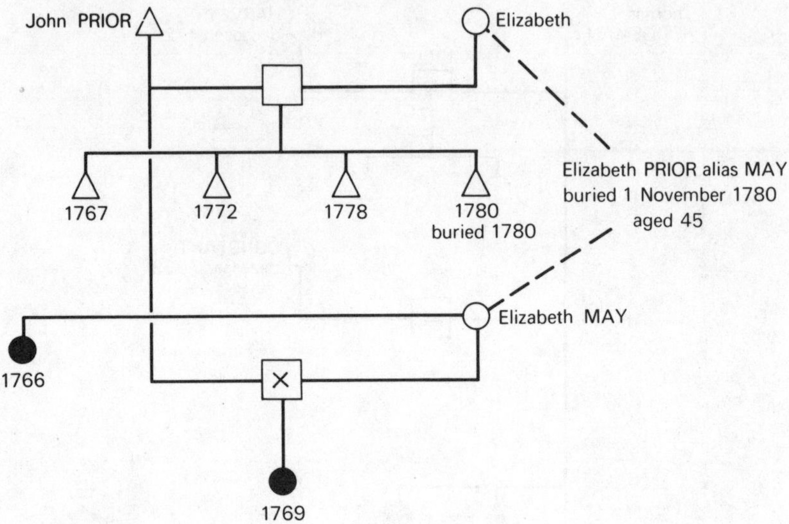

Fig. 4.2 John Prior and Elizabeth May

which suggests a liaison with one Chiddock but not a formal marriage. Reference to the Chiddock file, moreover, produced two further items: Thomas and Sarah Chiddock baptized and buried a daughter in 1800. There is no comment here about illegitimacy, though 17 years later the liaison is still clearly remembered. Nothing more is known about Thomas Chiddock, and these are the only instances of the surname in the Ash parish registers. Meantime Sarah Lawrence's daughter, born 1797, had herself had a bastard daughter in 1816, Caroline Matilda. In December 1840 Caroline Matilda married James Bushell and in the 1841 census she and her husband and one-day old child are all found living with Robert Cooper, her grandmother's husband! An amazing chain of interrelationships links these people together in one household.

The cases we have cited can do no more than suggest that bastardy was a clearly defined form of social deviance. Their importance, however, in testing bastardy recordings is important. What is needed is a study not so much of bastardy as of marriage. How many 'apparent' couples were never married? The marriage rate is the most significant piece of information to be put alongside bastardy recordings. In Ash the marriage rate was generally low, thus yielding high baptism to marriage ratios. These are set out in table 4.5.

The low marriage rate[7] might have been related to hard economic circumstances or simply to a tendency to marry in other parish churches, but it may also indicate the existence of a proportion of unions not celebrated in church, which was indeed what contemporaries thought when Hardwicke's Marriage Act was introduced in 1754. At the same time society must up to that time have been tolerant of such unions. It is very noticeable that the numbers of bastards recorded jump after 1754 (long intervals for aggregating statistics mask such sudden changes in trends), though the single decade 1721–30 saw a remarkably high number of bastards, perhaps related to a particular vicar's outlook on the social scene. While the new marriage act seems to have produced for the next fifty

7. D. E. C. Eversley, 'Exploitation of Anglican parish registers by aggregative analysis' (1966), suggests that a rate of 8 marriages per thousand is the minimum for a reasonable level of registration.

Table 4.5: Marriage rates, numbers of bastards and smoothed fertility ratios in Ash, 1660–1840

Decade	Crude marriage rate	No. of bastards	Fertility ratio
1661–70	4.9	5	
1671–80	7.3	5	5.3
1681–90	6.5	2	
1691–1700	6.2	6	5.5
1701–10	4.9	5	
1711–20	4.3	4	5.4
1721–30	6.1	15	
1731–40	4.5	0	6.8
1741–50	5.5	4	
1751–60	6.7	6	6.8
1761–70	8.1	20	
1771–80	9.1	28	4.7
1781–90	7.6	30	
1791–1800	8.1	30	4.0
1801–10	8.1	48	
1811–20	6.5	56	6.0
1821–30	6.4	47	
1831–40	6.3	40	5.9

Note: The crude marriage and fertility ratios are calculated from the data obtained from an aggregative analysis of the registers. The base population figures are obtained from the Compton Census, the 1705 listing of the parish (KAO/QCTz2) and the censuses 1801–41. Between 1705 and 1801/11 the resident population grew very little, though natural increase was considerable, and this with the agreement of the Compton Census and listing figures makes for a reasonably confident calculation of the population base figures. Between known dates the figures are calculated from an exponential growth rate. The smoothed marriage ratio is calculated by taking the number of baptisms in a 20-year period and dividing them by the number of marriages in a 20-year period commencing 5 years earlier, since the major period of childbearing relative to each marriage should thus be captured in the averages. See Eversley (1966), p. 75.

years more marriages in church, and consequently lower fertility ratios, it might be concluded that only a minority of those previously using common law forms of marriage were persuaded to come to church, though at the same time tighter regulations pinpointed more of the irregular unions.

Indeed, marriages could escape church registration for a number of reasons: before the Civil Wars there was the small Catholic minority, there was some clandestinity, there was the 'risk associated with the state of health and the state of mind of the incumbent, or of his deputy. After 1642, the disruption caused by the wars, the proliferation of sects, and the sequestration of clergy, demand that greater care be taken in the interpretation of the parish registers.'[8] The origins of any tendency to marry outside church must not be sought only in seventeenth-century history; nonetheless following the Commonwealth period it may have been difficult for clergy to know who had been properly married and who not, since it was felt at the time that many technicalities could invalidate even those marriages where the couples concerned had attempted to conform correctly with the requirements of the 1653 Marriage Act (McLaren, 1974, p. 322). This, together with the general disruption, might well have made clergymen hesitant in passing judgement on unknown couples bringing children to baptism and go some way to account for the low level of bastardy recordings in the Restoration period (Laslett and Oosterveen, 1973, p. 257).

8. D. McLaren, 'The Marriage Act of 1653' (1974), p. 320.

A further important factor in preventing clergy from always being able to distinguish the properly married from the less properly is migration. The chances of starting a new life by simply moving to another parish were greatly enhanced by the uncertainties of registration. Migration in pre-industrial periods may have been seriously underestimated. If migrants lived in a 'half world' of their own, and were frequently on the move, the chances of under-registration are obviously much increased, but so too is the chance that the parish priest took at its face value a couple's statement as to their condition, and registered the baptism accordingly.[9]

Poor communications would also have made it difficult for the zealous priest to check up on couples. That people did in fact exploit this situation is revealed in the case of John Feakins. A removal order for him, his wife Elizabeth and one child, aged five years, from St Dunstan's, Canterbury, to Ash was appealed against. At quarter sessions the removal order 'was confirmed as to the said John Feakins and quashed as to Elizabeth his reputed wife and their child John, it now appearing that the said John Feakins has a former wife living' (removal and settlement papers, Ash parish chest). Former wife! Poor Law records would yield further examples of 'reputed' wives.

The same situation is occasionally also revealed when objections to marriage banns are recorded. In 1776, for example:

> The banns were forbid after the first publication by one Susannah Godden, who gave two reasons: one that Mary Brown [the bride to be and described in the banns as a widow] had an husband living, ye other that she herself was with child by John Petley [the potential bridegroom] and that he had promised her [Susannah Godden] marriage. Mary Brown made oath before Mr Hey that her husband had been absent from ten or eleven years, and that about two years ago she was told he was dead. Susannah Godden had no evidence that he promised her marriage, therefore ye publication was continued. No regular certificate was sent to the curate of Ickham [where Mary Brown was said to be resident], but an account of the whole proceeding [Ash marriage register].

In other cases banns were called in Ash but no marriage appears to have taken place. If objections were made, they were not recorded. Thus an illegitimate child of William Page and Ann Andrews was baptized on 25 October 1835, despite the fact that the banns had been called for the third time on 6 September 1835. As the parents were described as 'two unhappy violaters of God's holy law', and William Page came from some miles away, from Upper Hardres, he had perhaps tried to escape from an unhappy marriage. At least three further similar instances have been noted when banns linked a pair who subsequently presented an illegitimate child for baptism.

Some idea of the frequency of non-ecclesiastical unions may be deduced by comparing the numbers of couples baptizing children in Ash for whom there is a record of a marriage with those for whom there is no record of a marriage. It will of course be obvious that many of these couples married outside the parish. In the period 1813–37 a search has been made for all these 'missing' marriages.[10] There

9. P. Clark, 'The migrant in Kentish towns, 1580–1640' (1972), p. 154.
10. Mr Gandy, Trivia, Whitstable, has compiled an index to Kentish marriages in this period, which he most generously allowed us to use.

were 302 marriages in Ash in this period, and 211 different couples (for whom there was no recorded marriage) baptized children between 1814 and 1837 (inclusive). Those baptizing children in 1813 were omitted so as to give a reasonable birth interval from the date for which marriage information was available. Even so a further allowance has to be made for the couples whose first child or children were born before the move to Ash, and for whom a year is therefore too short an interval for the marriage to be picked up in the years searched. Of the 211 'non-married' couples', more than half (110) were indeed found to have been married in surrounding parishes. This leaves a residue of potentially unmarrieds of 101 or 20 per cent of all couples.

It is not suggested that the figure of 20 per cent stands as the level of common law marriages. Some unions, it is true, will be missed because they were childless; on the other hand childless marriages are included in the proportions because they are recorded in the marriage register. Allowance must be made for marriages occurring a considerable distance away, and for marriages missed through the hazards of nominal record linkage, where the form or spelling of the surname has prevented a link being made. When these factors are taken into account, it seems possible that a proportion of up to 15 per cent for non-church unions might be reasonable at this time. It may be significant that in 1834 there was a sudden rush of marriages in Ash, possibly stimulated by the Poor Law Commission's enquiries and the act. From the usual decadal average of 11–13 marriages a year, with a maximum of 19, there were 27 marriages in 1834. The comments in the registers on 'unhappy violaters' and other remarks in similar vein, all occur in the nineteenth century.

Does this evidence suggest that society was becoming more censorious and drawing the boundaries round legitimacy more tightly? It could be that some of the rise in the bastardy recordings is a feature of better communications, more conscious attempts to control the poor because of the rise in poor expenditure, and higher standards on the part of the registration officers, that is, the clergy. In the late seventeenth and eighteenth centuries the number of couples not married in church may well have been considerably higher than this evidence for the nineteenth century indicates.

If it was not uncommon for couples to move in order to escape notice, so leaving broken marriages behind, and if also common law marriage was a deep-rooted tradition amongst a section of the population, this would go far to explain why illegitimacy in England is in general a rural phenomenon. In the town the sheer numbers of people and the shifting mobility of town populations would make it hard to recognize the illegitimate in many cases. It also explains why legitimate and illegitimate fertility move in concert.[11] When general fertility rises, so too does the fertility of non-ecclesiastical marriages, some of which will be noticed and registered as bastardy. These non-church marriages may, indeed, be seen as culturally determined (Knodel *et al.*, 1971, p. 388)[12] the 'bastard prone' sub-society of which Laslett speaks would naturally be more liable to be noticed for contravening the church's doctrine, even if it represented a long-established customary form of marriage.

Contemporaries were aware of this aspect of society. Patrick Colquhoun at the

11. E. Shorter, J. Knodel and E. van de Walle, 'The decline of non-marital fertility in Europe, 1880–1940' (1971), pp. 375 ff. traces the correlation in various European countries from 1840.

12. Southeast Europe north of the Danube had such high illegitimacy levels (in 1900) that they could only be explained as a function of stable consensual unions.

turn of the century commented on the many 'lewd and immoral' women in the metropolis, including in the category 'the prodigious number among the lower classes who cohabit together without marriage'.[13] A hundred years later, 'those living together unmarried – "living tally", or "over t'brush", as the sayings went – came in for little criticism [among their neighbours] though naturally everybody knew who was or who was not legitimate.'[14]

It has been suggested that the successive combinations of one man's name with wives with different christian names in the baptism registers may indicate common law marriage and divorce.[15] Of course it may also indicate that the lady concerned had more than one christian name, or even that the priest had misrecorded the name. This may be so if the odd christian name for a wife occurs in an otherwise unexceptionable run of baptisms. With a surname common in the area, sheer mobility may be the explanation for the succession of names. Take, however, the unusual surname of Gath. William and Mary baptized a child in 1740, William and Ann baptized four children in 1743–51, William and Sarah baptized a child in 1753. This family is, moreover, connected with a number of bastards (see figure 4.1, p. 147). There are no marriages in Ash for William Gath; nor are there any burials for the three (presumed) Gath wives.

If there were a sub-society of the bastard prone, it would most likely consist of this type of family, where the distinction between legal and illegal marriage, at any rate until the passing of Hardwicke's Marriage Act, was not clearly drawn. There is certainly some evidence which suggests that there was such a sub-society. In the first place, half of all those mothers of bastards whose own baptisms can be traced had parents for whom no recorded marriage in the parish is in existence. As suggested above, some proportion of these couples could be presumed not to be formally married. Secondly, there is the frequency with which certain surnames recur. Four times a man with the surname Andrews is the father of a bastard, and two girls with this name also bear bastards; six girls with the name Lawrence bear bastards, one Lawrence is named as the father of a bastard and two Lawrences marry girls who had borne bastards. Much of the largest group of bastards sharing a common surname is attributable to the Solly name set: at least ten girls and two men are involved. In some cases the long time intervals between the illegitimate baptisms may indicate even more mothers of bastards, instead of the assumed 'repeaters', but providing the births are within the range of the mother's childbearing years they have been combined into one name set.

Yet this does not necessarily mean that persons bearing the family name Solly were more given to fornication than most. It was also the name of a very large local lineage: in the 1841 census no fewer than ten separate households were headed by a Solly in Ash. They ranged from the rich yeoman to the poor widow. 'Of the family of Solly, the entries of baptisms at Ash alone amount to 292, of marriages to 104, and of burials to 176, exceeding those of any other in the register, except, perhaps, that of Lacy.'[16] Planché, writing in the mid nineteenth century, comments on 'this ancient family, of which so many descendents are resident in the

13. E. P. Thompson, *The making of the English working class* (1963), p. 56, in quoting Colquhoun sees this comment as an indication of the disruption of marriage bonds at a time when divorce for the poor 'was an absolute impossibility'.
14. R. Roberts, *The classic slum* (1971), p. 30.
15. L. Bradley, 'Common law marriage: a possible cause of under-registration' (1973), p. 43.
16. J. R. Planché, *A corner of Kent* (1864), p. 401.

parish at the present day . . . Some branches of the family had fallen into poverty early in the sixteenth century . . . and the name like those of Paramore and Hougham is still found amongst the labouring classes and in the humbler ranks of the community' (Planché, pp. 404, 406).

Surname evidence alone does not justify the assertion that there was a sub-society of the bastard prone. In one generation, perhaps, there are several members of a family in the same situation: the weaver's family of Rye, for instance, where three sisters, Ann (1816), Mary (1812) and Susan (1831) all bear bastards. (Three sisters all from the same family bearing bastards might suggest incest.) To trace such a community over several generations requires all collateral lines to be investigated, and particularly the children of marriages where the mother had herself borne a bastard. Because of the probability that some unions originated without a marriage, it is clearly impossible to trace many of the relationships through the female lines: the maiden names are impossible to recover. Links tend, therefore, to be established through the men. Indeed, of the 101 mothers of bastards who then married, only 6 had daughters who in turn produced illegitimate children. Five per cent of the mothers of bastards were themselves bastards. This in itself may be interesting confirmation of the cultural attitude to marriage, since it may be supposed that girls would tend to conform to their partners' wishes in the matter of formal ceremonies, so that the links of the sub-society would indeed exist through the men.

Two remarkable networks of families in Ash may be used to illustrate the male linkages. The first network starts with the Brown family. Henry Brown was married in church in 1709, but widowed almost immediately. His name is then linked in the baptism register with Catherine by whom he had four children. (There is no record in Ash of his second marriage.) Catherine Brown died, and Henry's name is then coupled, again with no record of a marriage, with Sarah. Two children were born of this union. From Henry's second marriage one son had a daughter who bore a bastard. From Henry's third marriage, the youngest daughter bore two bastards, and one of those bastards, Sarah, born in 1756, in her turn also had a bastard. This Sarah Brown initiated a complicated series of linkages between members of the Burville and of the Brittenden family, both of whom are remarkable for numbers of bastards. Sarah Brown formed a union, first illegitmate but then regularized, with Peter Burville. One of her legitimate children, Anne, extended the network by bearing a bastard and then marrying a bastard, James Brittenden. Her husband was one of two illegitimate children of Mary All Brittenden, who in her turn was one of two illegitimate children of Mary Brittenden. After James Brittenden's death, Ann remarried into the same family that her mother had married, to one of her Burville cousins. Her father and her two uncles all had links with bastards. Through Ann's first marriage to a Brittenden, she had also linked herself to another chain of illegitimacy through her mother-in-law, Mary All Brittenden. Mary All, herself a bastard and mother of two bastards, married Benjamin Burrows, whose sister also had had a bastard. After Mary All's death, Benjamin Burrows wedded as his second wife a girl with two confinements on the wrong side of the blanket, Ann Love, who after Benjamin's death went on to one more illegitimate child. Together this network spanned the period 1709 to 1823 and included 16 bastards. The network is displayed in figure 4.3(a).

The second network used to illustrate this bastard-bearing sub-society commences with Isaac Beerling and George Beerling. From their ages at death it seems probable that they were brothers, born respectively *c.* 1751 and *c.* 1757. No record of Beerlings exists in the parish prior to 1780, when George married Mary Williams. Stemming from Isaac Beerling is a network of ten bastards, from George a network of seven. Bastards fathered by married men occur and a link between Isaac Beerling and Ann Porter, followed by an illegitimate link with Phoebe Porter strongly suggests that these two girls were also related. Figure 4.3(b) illustrates this network.

Apart from the remarkable inter-linkages (and a number of other smaller examples of similar linkages could be exhibited), the striking features of these

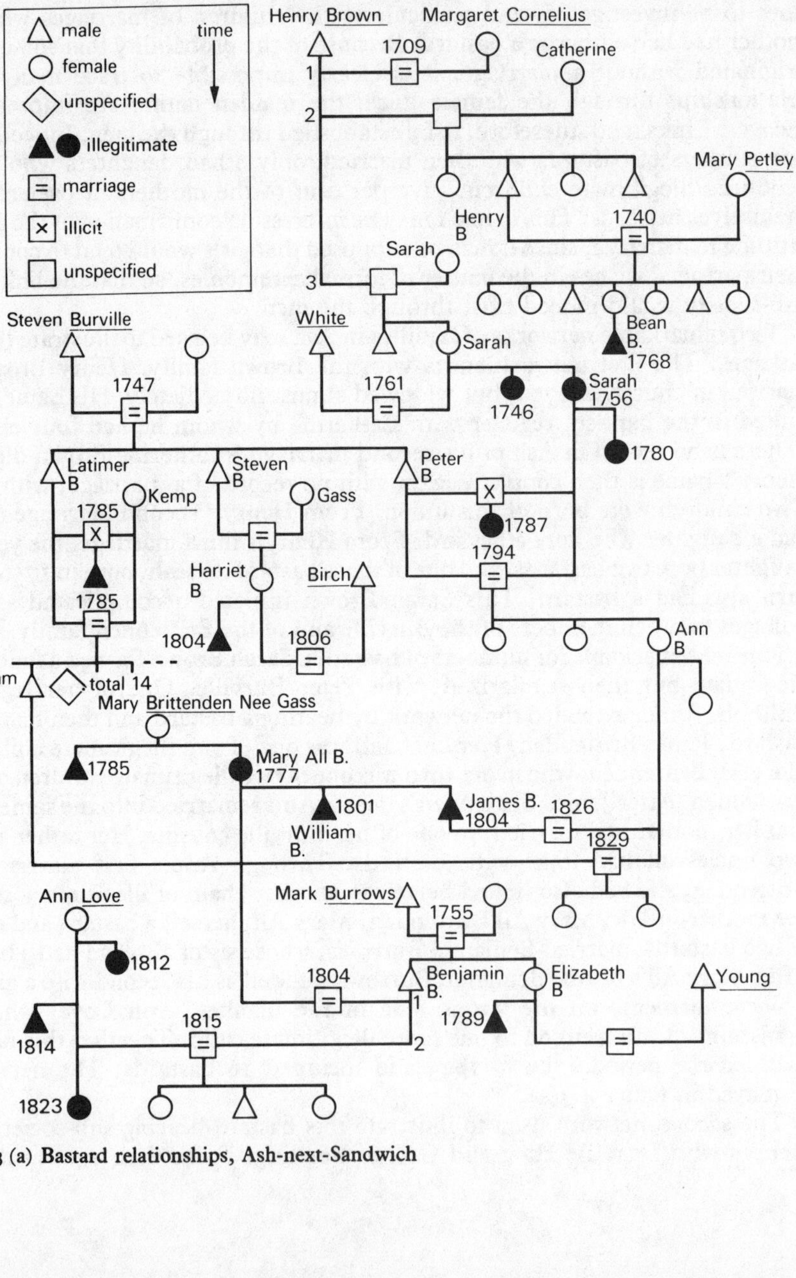

Fig. 4.3 (a) **Bastard relationships, Ash-next-Sandwich**

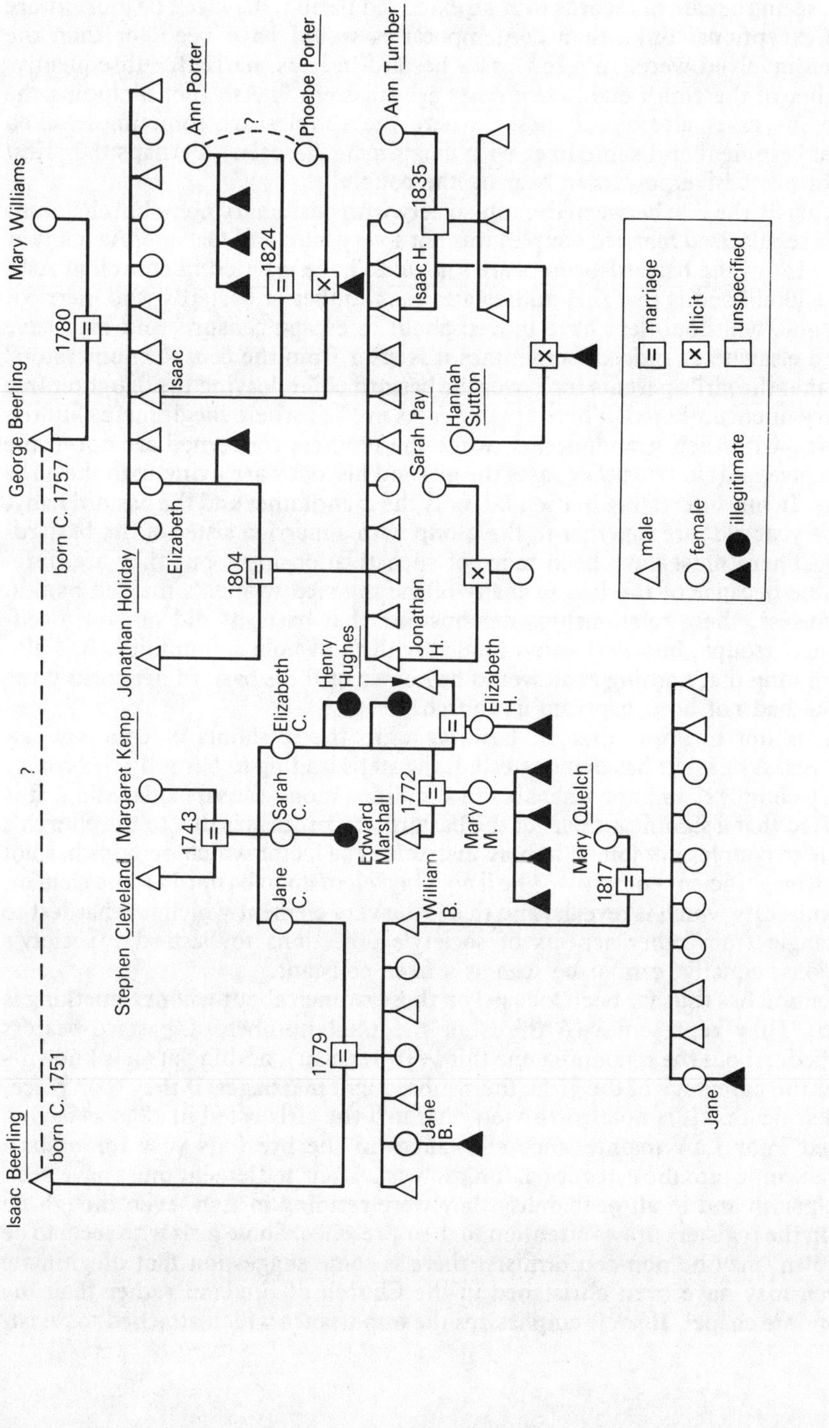

Fig. 4.3 (b) Bastard relationships, Ash-next-Sandwich

bastard networks is the frequency with which not only bastardy, but also church marriages, occurred in the families concerned. It would be wrong to lose sight of the many legitimate children in the networks, or of the numerous bastards and bastard-bearers who had legitimate partners and married in church. The historian, seeing a mass of records over an extended period, may well be more aware of the exceptional links than contemporaries would have been, or than the children involved were. In a few cases bastard-bearers married, subsequently, the father of the child; eight clear cases are apparent in Ash (not including the ambiguous cases already discussed where the couples are sometimes linked without comment and sometimes with illegitimate children). Perhaps the priest brought persuasive powers to bear on the couple.

Obviously the line between the sub-society with customary non-church unions and the regularized married couples was not a very hard and fast one. As many as 31 per cent of the bastard-bearers are known to have married in church in Ash, and the likelihood is that this understates the number of bastards who married, since some will doubtless have moved about to escape censure, and may have married elsewhere. Indeed, sometimes it is clear from the census enumerators' books that the girl's parents took over the bastard child, leaving the daughter free to marry unencumbered. There are five cases in 1841 where illegitimate children are living with their grandparents, while the mothers concerned are not in the same household; in two other cases the girl and her baby are living with the girl's parents. In one interesting household, only the grandfather and the bastard baby, under a year old, are together in the group with a married sister of the bastard-bearer. There must have been more of such relationships, but they are unrecoverable because of the loss of many of the married women's maiden names. Nonetheless, these relationships demonstrate that bastards did not form self-contained groups, but were intermingled with the whole community. It is also worth noting that nothing at all would be known of these bastard networks if the children had not been baptized in church.

This is not to argue that all bastards were the offshoots of common law marriages. As Laslett has demonstrated, the steps leading to bastardy recordings are very complex, and not amenable to simplified mono-causal explanation. It is suggested that a significant part of the bastardy recordings is due to the church's attitude to couples not joined in holy matrimony, a factor which perhaps has not been given sufficient emphasis. The 'shocking' element in bastardy is the element of promiscuity which it reveals, and this is the very element which it is hardest to disentangle from other aspects of society's objections to bastardy. Society's objections, equally, cannot be seen as a fixed constant.

Attention has thus far been focused on those women about whom something is known. They represent two thirds of the total number of bastard-bearers identified. About the remaining one third (31 per cent), nothing at all is known – neither the parentage of the girls, their subsequent marriages, if they took place, nor their deaths. It is noteworthy too, that half the girls listed in 1835 as having received Poor Law maintenance allowances in the previous year for bastard children come into the category of 'unknowns'. Their settlement must have been in the parish and in all probability they were residing in Ash, even though no event in the registers draws attention to their presence. Some girls who seem to be 'unknown' may be non-conformists; there is some suggestion that illegitimate children may have been christened in the Church of England rather than the appropriate chapel. If so, it emphasizes the importance which attached to registration, and also the stigma of illegitimacy. Excluded from the class of unknowns are those for whom several possible alternative links could be made.

These girls who only appear in the registers for the fleeting moment of a baptism have been likened to the sparrow flying through the lighted room – they come out of the dark and to the dark they return. 'Mary Hall, singlewoman, informed that John Castleden a fellow-servant with her at the house of Edward Rose of Chislett, Gent, meeting her abroad in her Master's orchard . . . did importune her, until he had the carnall knowledge of her body whereby shee conceived with child.'[17] It is not often we are allowed such a glimpse into past events. The entry illustrates vividly that isolated occurrences of bastardy must often have been the result of an 'unfortunate' incident.

17. Chislet parish records, Canterbury Cathedral Library.

5

The social context of illegitimacy in early modern England

David Levine and Keith Wrightson

Illegitimacy has recently been receiving a good deal of attention from social historians. Various hypotheses have been advanced to explain its remarkable rise in the later eighteenth and nineteenth centuries. There has, however, been less attention paid to earlier periods. Indeed, it is often assumed that there was a homogeneity of attitude and experience in the pre-industrial world. The eventual undermining of traditional social controls which had previously been effective regulators of premarital sexual activity is explained in terms of either a liberalization in attitudes towards sexuality or a change in the social environment resulting from the combined impact of industrialization and urbanization. Edward Shorter (1971, p. 237) has neatly condensed this argument in the following fashion:

> Sexuality in traditional society may be thought of as a great iceberg, frozen by the command of custom, by the need of the surrounding community for stability at the cost of individuality, and by the dismal grind of daily life. Its thawing in England and Western Europe occurred roughly between the middle of the eighteenth and the end of the nineteenth centuries, when a revolution in eroticism took place, specifically among the lower classes, in the direction of libertine sexual behavior.

Shorter's assertion that premarital sexuality in earlier times was 'frozen by the command of custom' must be revised in view of the evidence which Peter Laslett and Karla Oosterveen have derived from a sample of 24 English parish registers. Their illegitimacy ratios show that there was a sharp peak in the incidence of bastardy between 1591 and 1610 and then a marked decline to a new equilibrium level that obtained until the middle of the eighteenth century. Laslett and Oosterveen produce no explanation for this phenomenon, but they argue that there seems to have been an inverse relationship between the frequency of illegitimate births and the age at first marriage for women. They further note the possible existence of 'a sub-society of the illegitimacy prone' and speculate that the declining incidence of illegitimacy in the seventeenth century may have been due to the increasing regulation of these poor and dependent offenders by their social superiors (1973, pp. 256, 257, 269, 282–4).

In the present study we would like to examine both demographic and social aspects of the changing incidence of illegitimacy in pre-industrial England. First, we will analyse in some detail the demographic indices of illegitimacy, bridal pregnancy and age at marriage, by using evidence derived from nine family reconstitution studies. In the second section of this paper we will look very closely at the experience of one of these villages, Terling in Essex, and attempt to re-create the social context of illegitimacy in the late sixteenth and early seventeenth centuries. Finally we will propose an interpretation of how a disequilibrium between established attitudes and behaviour and sharply deteriorating objective circumstances may have produced the substantial rise in illegitimacy at the turn of the sixteenth and seventeenth centuries. We shall argue that the conflicts resulting from this situation were resolved by a complex readjustment of local social relationships, involving a conjunction of forces and resulting in the establishment of a new form of social equilibrium.

I

In their article 'Long-term trends in bastardy in England', Peter Laslett and Karla Oosterveen show that their sample of 24 villages experienced an illegitimacy ratio of 3.6 per cent before 1640 whereas the average for the sixty-year period after 1661 was 1.6 per cent, less than half its earlier level. They also noted that there appears to have been an inverse relationship between the age of women at first marriage and illegitimacy: 'When the parishioners of pre-industrial England married early, illegitimacy among them was high, and when they married late, the number of bastards went down.' The inverse relationship is thought to be important because it contradicts a necessarily positive connection between sexual deprivation and the procreation of children outside marriage. However, it is important to note that this inverse relationships is largely based on the changes reported for seventeenth-century Colyton and it is assumed that a rising age at marriage for women was commonly found in other villages (Laslett and Oosterveen, 1973, p. 269). We have sought to test this assumption by drawing upon the evidence of eight further reconstitution studies.[1] The results are presented in Table 5.1:

Table 5.1: Age at first marriage for women and illegitimacy ratios in nine English parishes, 1600–99

		No.	Mean	Median	Illegitimacy %
Alcester, Warwickshire	1600–1649	102	25.3	24.4	3.0
	1650–99	108	26.7	25.0	0.8
Aldenham, Hertfordshire	1600–1649	152	25.3	23.7	1.2
	1650–99	101	26.2	24.9	0.9
Banbury, Oxfordshire	1600–1649	149	25.3	24.7	1.0
	1650–99	101	26.0	24.8	1.2
Bottesford, Leicestershire	1600–1649	107	25.7	24.9	4.0
	1650–99	71	26.4	25.5	0.8
Colyton, Devonshire	1600–1649	236	27.1	25.9	2.8
	1650–99	99	29.4	27.8	3.0
Hartland, Devonshire	1600–1649	141	27.8	27.6	3.9
	1650–99	223	28.4	27.6	2.8
Hawkshead, Lancashire	1600–1649	282	24.6	23.9	2.0
	1650–99	216	26.3	25.9	1.0
Shepshed, Leicestershire	1600–1649	64	28.8	27.7	2.0
	1650–99	57	27.3	26.1	1.1
Terling, Essex	1600–1649	65	24.1	24.0	4.8
	1650–99	43	23.1	22.7	0.8

1. Information on Alcester, Aldenham, Banbury, Colyton, Hartland and Hawkshead is derived from family reconstitution studies carried out for the SSRC Cambridge Group for the History of Population and Social Structure by the late Mrs Peggy Ford, Miss Karla Oosterveen, Mrs Susan Stewart, Mr W. Newman Brown and Dr E. A. Wrigley. We wish to express our gratitude to the Cambridge Group for their characteristic generosity in allowing us to quote information from their files and to record particular thanks for their cooperation to Mrs Stewart and Miss Oosterveen.

If we refer to the evidence from these nine reconstitution studies it becomes clear that there was a wide range of experience. In the seven villages in which the age of women at first marriage rose over 1650 there was a substantial variation in the dimension of this movement. Moreover, in two of the nine villages (Shepshed and Terling), there was a falling age at marriage in the later seventeenth century. Another point which should be borne in mind is that if we concentrate on the median age at marriage – in contrast to the mean – the changes that occurred would be somewhat different. In Hartland there would have been no change at all whereas in Terling and Shepshed the decline would be somewhat greater. In Aldenham and Hawkshead the rise in the age at marriage would be more pronounced by using the median measure but for the four other villages it would be smaller.

To shift our attention from the individual experience of our nine parishes to an aggregated measurement yields interesting results. To a large degree these nine parishes are representative of the social and economic variety of seventeenth-century rural England. Geographically they are scattered across the length and breadth of the realm. Using this sample, the overall mean shows a rise of 1.3 years in the age at first marriage for women while the median rose by 0.8 years in the second half of the seventeenth century. However, this method of simple aggregation lends undue weight to the parishes like Hawkshead, which contribute a disproportionate number of observations, while undervaluing the experiences of Shepshed and Terling which are, in gross terms, under-represented. For this reason it would be preferable to aggregate the averages thereby allowing the individuality of the nine villages an equal role. A comparison of the mean-of-means for the two seventeenth-century cohorts yields a rising age at marriage of 0.6 years while the result of the mean-of-medians is 0.4 years. The results presented in table 5.2 suggest that the overall change in the age at first marriage for women in seventeenth-century England may have been considerably smaller than assumed when generalizing from the experience of Colyton.

Table 5.2: Age at first marriage for women, aggregated measurements for nine English parishes, 1600–99

		No.	Mean	Median
A) Simple aggregation	1600–1649	1298	26.0	25.2
	1650–99	1027	27.3	26.0
B) Aggregation of averages				
	1600–1649	9	26.0	25.2
	1650–99	9	26.6	25.6

While this simple aggregation does not seem to show any major overall change in the age at first marriage for women, the individual consideration of the nine parishes does highlight a series of quite distinct and often contradictory demographic adjustments that were occurring in response to local conditions. By studying each case in its local setting we can begin to make sense of this crazy-quilt of individuality. For instance, deindustrialization in Colyton and the shift away from labour-intensive corn farming in Bottesford may have produced rises in the age at marriage whereas, on the other hand, the coming of domestic industry to Shepshed and the commercialization of the agriculture of Terling in response to the London food market's growing demand may have led to a fall in the age at marriage.[2] Thus, the evidence derived from these nine family reconstitution studies shows no clear pattern in the age at marriage but rather a variety of demographic adjustments which reflected changing local conditions. Moreover, in the nine villages there was no clearly defined inverse relationship between the age at first marriage for women and the frequency of illegitimacy. In Alcester, Aldenham, Bottesford and Hawkshead the age at marriage went up in the later seventeenth century while the ratio of illegitimate births declined. In Banbury and Colyton the age at marriage rose but so did the proportion of illegitimate births. In Shepshed and Terling both the age at marriage and the incidence of illegitimacy fell. In the ninth village, Hartland, the existence of an inverse relationship depends on choosing the mean in preference to the median as a measurement of the average age at marriage.

Although there may not have been a clearly defined inverse relationship between the age at first marriage for women and the proportion of bastard births, there is suggestive evidence that the *age* at which women bore their first illegitimate child may have responded to the same factors which influenced the age at first marriage. Striking evidence supporting this assertion comes from a comparison of the age at marriage with the age of women at the birth of their first illegitimate child (see table 5.3). The evidence presented in table 5.3 shows that the bastard-bearers were neither markedly younger nor older than their contemporaries who married before the birth of their first child. As we have seen, shifts in the age at marriage were paralleled by a roughly commensurate rise in the age of bastard-bearers. The evidence presented in table 5.3 suggests that many illegitimate first births may have been conceived in the process of courtships which, for whatever reason, had not resulted in marriage. The fact that many 'honest women' had, in fact, been pregnant at marriage is illustrated by the results presented in table 5.4.

Table 5.3: Age at first marriage for women and age at first illegitimate birth in nine English parishes, 1600–99

	No.	Mean	Median
A 1600–49			
Age at marriage	1298	26.0	25.2
Age of mothers of bastards at birth of first bastard	146	26.5	26.4
B 1650–99			
Age at marriage	1027	27.3	26.0
Age of mothers of bastards at birth of first bastard	64	27.2	26.2

The rates of bridal pregnancy show a wide range of experience both between villages and, within each of the villages, across time. In aggregate terms the rate was roughly halved in the course of the seventeenth century: before 1600 almost one bride in three was pregnant but after 1650 the comparable figure was one in six. Only one of the villages, Aldenham, did not have a lower rate after 1650 although it should be noted that for eight other villages the timing and extent of the decline assumed no clear patterns. Reassembling the information describing

2. The interplay between economic and demographic behaviour in these four villages is discussed in David Levine, *Family formation in an age of nascent capitalism* (1977); for illegitimacy see especially chapter 9.

bridal pregnancy, taking the age at marriage as the critical variable, similarly produced no clear pattern. In contrast to women marrying after 25, younger brides were less likely to have been pregnant in the early seventeenth century but pregnancy was more frequent among these younger women both before 1600 and after 1650. Thus, the bride's age seems to have had little bearing on whether she was pregnant, which suggests that there was no necessary link between the enforced celibacy resulting from later marriage and premarital sexual activity. Moreover, there was no single pattern in the relationship between the proportion of pregnant brides and the incidence of illegitimacy. Alcester, Bottesford, Hartland, Hawkshead, Shepshed and Terling all had lower rates of prenuptial pregnancy and lower illegitimacy ratios after 1650 but Banbury and Colyton had rising proportions of bastard births and declining rates of bridal pregnancy.

The lower frequency of bridal pregnancy in the later seventeenth century suggests that premarital sexual activity became less common while the decline in the illegitimacy ratio may reflect changes determining the onset of sexual activity. The fact that bastard-bearers were almost exactly the same age as married women when they had their first child further suggests that women who had their first child out of wedlock were neither particularly gullible nor exceptionally promiscuous. They were, however, unfortunate. They, unlike the pregnant brides, were left to bear their children alone.

The demographic evidence, then, shows no clear relationship between the movement of the illegitimacy ratio and changes in the age at first marriage for women. A stronger relationship would appear to exist between the illegitimacy ratio and the proportion of women pregnant at marriage, though the experience of the sample parishes was not uniform. Finally, a striking similarity can be demonstrated between the age of women bearing their first illegitimate child and the age of women at first marriage. It is our contention that the impact of this demographic evidence can only be fully appreciated when it is placed in its full historical context. The incidence of bastardy was related to changes in the socio-economic complexion of English rural society in the course of the sixteenth and seventeenth centuries; to the growth of an impoverished labouring population which resulted from the combined influence of demographic expansion and inflation, to the exacerbation of the insecurity of the poor by grinding economic crisis and, finally, to the reaction of increasingly self-conscious parish élites to the problems produced by the emergence of the poor as a class. In order to explore these changes we have chosen to look closely at the experience of Terling, Essex.

The choice of Terling as the focus of our detailed examination has several provenances, the most important of which was the survival of a wide variety of civil and ecclesiastical records.[3] The changes which were taking place in Terling were also occurring in many other English villages, but it should be made clear at

3. The study of Terling is based upon every reference to the parish in the following sources. Essex Record Office (subsequently ERO): *The parish registers of Terling, 1538–1840*, T/R 60; *Essex quarter sessions records*, 1590–1650, Q/SR 111–343, Q/S Ba 1/24–39, Q/S Ba 2 1/171, Q/S Ba 4/3/3, Q/S Ba 5, Q/S Ba 6/8; Archdeaconry of Colchester, Acts and Visitations, D/ACA 18–855, D/ACV 1–5; Bishop of London's commissary in Essex and Hertfordshire, Acts, D/ABA 1–9; Bishop of London's consistory court, Visitations, D/ALV 1–2; Records of the manor of Terling Place, D/M 169–170, D/DQS 64; Terling wills as listed in F. G. Emmison (ed.), *Wills at Chelmsford* I & II (1958–9); N. McNeil O'Farrell (ed.), Calendar of Essex assize files in the Public Record Office (ERO typescript). Greater London Record Office (subsequently GLRO): Bishop of London's consistory court, Office Act Books, DL/C 305, 308, 322–5, 624. Public Record Office (subsequently PRO) Exchequer lay subsidies, E/179, 110/419, 111/509, 111/523, 112/588, 112/607, 112/638. C. A. Barton, *Historical notes and records of the parish of Terling, Essex* (1953), appendices I and III. The more extensive statistics set out in table 1.2 above were not available to the authors when this chapter was written.

the outset that Terling was not selected because it was 'normal', 'average', or 'representative'. Indeed, it might be said that the speed and completeness of the transformation of social relationships which we shall trace, as well as the precocious modernity of the village's agrarian economy, made it somewhat atypical. The value of studying a village like Terling is that it will enable us to show in some detail the conjunction of forces which produced a startling rise in the incidence of illegitimacy and the factors involved in the subsequent establishment of a stricter regime of sexual behaviour.

2

Between 1590 and 1640 there were 61 recorded cases of bastardy in Terling.[4] These cases were not, however, evenly distributed over time, 35 occurring within the first two decades, 22 being clustered in the years 1598 to 1605. The movement of the illegitimacy ratio in Terling by decade is illustrated in figure 5.1. In order to probe more deeply the causes of this phenomenon we have assembled all the evidence relating to Terling in the principal local sources and have employed it both independently and as part of a social network analysis to explore the place of the 'bastardy principals' (i.e. those persons bearing or begetting a base child) within the village community. In presenting the results of this analysis we shall be particularly concerned with the relative social standing of the persons involved, with the extent to which they were natives of the parish or immigrants, with the extent to which the circumstances of their offences can be reconstructed so as to cast light upon their sexual attitudes and behaviour, with their relationships both to one another and to their neighbours, and with the extent to which they may be said to have formed a 'sub-society' within the community.

Over the whole period of this study 50 women bore illegitimate children in Terling.[5] Nine of these women can be identified as being of middling social status, that is to say belonging to yeoman, husbandman and substantial craftsman families. Twenty-two were of low social status, being servants or coming from families of the poorer craftsmen and the labouring and cottaging poor. The 19 other women cannot be confidently placed in any social category, though their very obscurity in the records would suggest that they were of low social status and only briefly inhabitants of the village. Many may have been servants.[6] Of the 50 fathers of illegitimate children who can be identified, one was of gentle status, while 13 were of middling and 15 of low social standing. Twenty-one remain

4. In establishing the incidence of bastardy, we have used the parish registers, ecclesiastical court records and quarter sessions records. While parish registers remain the best single source, it is clear from our experience that a full picture of the incidence of bastardy requires the use of all three sources. Taking the sources individually, the parish registers reveal 54, the church courts 50, and the quarter sessions 5 cases of bastardy. Forty-four cases occur in both parish registers and church court records, two in both parish registers and quarter sessions, one in church courts and quarter sessions, and one in all three sources. Seven cases are revealed in the registers only, four in the church courts only and one in quarter sessions only. Comparison of the three sources proved valuable in excluding cases which might have been inferred from ambiguous parish register entries and in dating a number of cases. In addition church court and quarter sessions records provide invaluable detail on particular cases. In all cases the children concerned are unambiguously referred to as base in at least one source. The total of 61 cases excludes two further cases of base children mentioned in the register – one the child of a vagrant, the other a nurse child from another parish. It also excludes cases, revealed by the church court records, of bastards fathered by Terling men in other parishes.

5. Forty-one of the mothers were single women, three were married and six were widows at the time of their offences. Seven of them bore more than one base child, an issue to be discussed more fully below.

6. The more substantial villagers, who were most prominent in parochial and manorial affairs and who commonly left wills are, of course, by far the best documented section of the community. Extremely obscure individuals are most unlikely to have belonged to this section of the community.

Table 5.4: Bridal pregnancy in nine English parishes, 1550–1699

		%	No.	Illegitimacy ratio
Alcester	1550–99	23.1	6 of 26	–
	1600–1649	24.6	18 of 73	3.0
	1650–99	8.6	7 of 81	0.8
Aldenham	1550–99	16.7	1 of 6	–
	1600–1649	16.7	12 of 72	1.2
	1650–99	16.7	8 of 48	0.8
Banbury	1550–99	30.3	10 of 33	4.1
	1600–1649	16.0	23 of 144	1.0
	1650–99	10.0	8 of 80	1.2
Bottesford	1550–99	–	–	–
	1600–1649	36.0	23 of 64	4.0
	1650–99	25.0	13 of 52	0.8
Colyton	1550–99	39.7	31 of 78	4.6
	1600–1649	25.6	41 of 160	2.8
	1650–99	22.2	14 of 63	3.0
Hartland	1550–99	28.3	13 of 46	3.3
	1600–1649	24.0	32 of 133	3.9
	1650–99	23.6	33 of 140	2.8
Hawkshead	1550–99	–	–	1.6 [1571–99]
	1600–1649	19.8	38 of 192	2.0
	1650–99	18.7	26 of 139	1.0
Shepshed	1550–99	20.0	3 of 15	–
	1600–1649	12.8	5 of 39	2.0
	1650–99	6.3	3 of 48	1.1
Terling	1550–99	32.4	11 of 34	–
	1600–1649	20.5	8 of 39	4.0
	1650–99	7.4	2 of 27	0.8

Note: Bottesford and Hawkshead do not have data relating to the later sixteenth century because their parish registers started so late (Hawkshead in 1568 and Bottesford in 1581) that it was not possible to produce an adequate sample. This factor is also relevant in explaining the small number of observations for later sixteenth-century Aldenham as its register only started in 1560. Similarly, Alcester (1561), Banbury (1558) and Hartland (1558) were also late starters. The three other parish registers (Colyton, Shepshed and Terling) all began in 1538.

obscure.[7] Of these, 12 were in fact inhabitants of parishes other than Terling, as were 5 of the men whose social status is known.

Involvement in bastardy, then, was spread across the social scale. It was not, however, evenly spread. Taxation listings of the early and mid seventeenth century indicate that the poor made up roughly half the population of the parish. Yet even if we exclude the men who were not inhabitants of Terling, the poor and the obscure contributed a disproportionate number, almost three quarters, of the persons involved in bastardy. Moreover, this disproportionate involvement was increasing over time. Whereas in the two decades when the incidence of bastardy was highest, 1590–1609, 66 per cent of the Terling parishioners involved were poor or obscure, in the following two decades of declining incidence, the proportion had risen to almost 86 per cent. Examination of the social status of the parents of bastards, then suggests that we are dealing with not one, but two

7. Six of the fathers were married men and three widowers at the time of their offences. Twenty-two were definitely single and the remainder probably single though one cannot be certain in the cases of men from other parishes who were not stated to be servants.

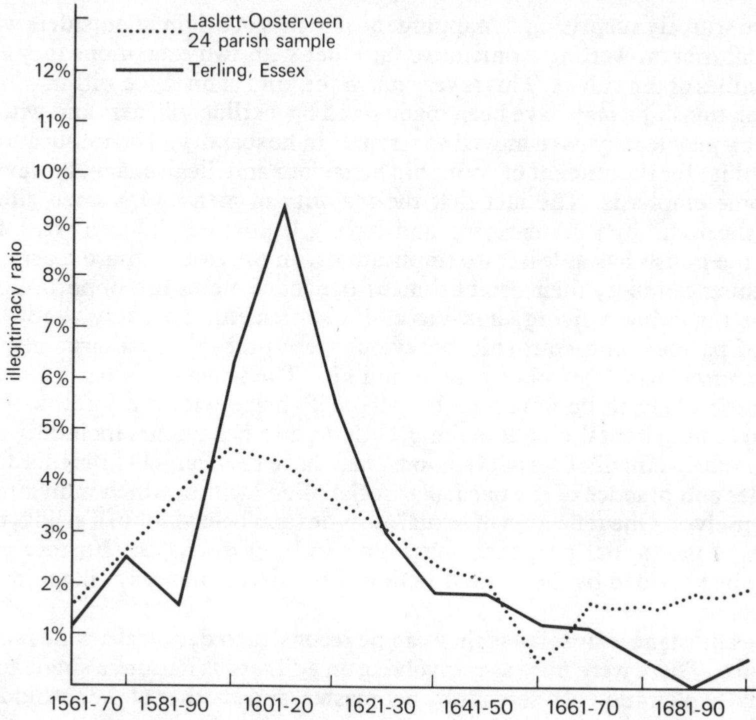

Fig. 5.1 Illegitimacy ratios, Terling, 1561–1700, by decade

phenomena. As the incidence of illegitimacy declined, bastardy was becoming more exclusively the province of the poor and the obscure.

The prominence of persons of obscure origins and of outsiders among the parents of illegitimate children in Terling prompts the question of whether the bastardy principals were natives of the parish or immigrants. In fact, only 38 per cent of the women and 12 per cent of the men were baptized in Terling. Failure to have been baptized in the parish is, of course, not certain proof that individuals were not born there. Some may have been born in Terling families but, for whatever reason, baptized elsewhere. Nevertheless, careful consideration of other evidence such as wills and incidental references to kin indicates that, while there are certainly exceptions, evidence of baptism provides at least a reasonable indication of origins. Moreover, it allows comparison with the population at large. An examination of the origins of all couples marrying in Terling who subsequently baptized children there over the period 1590–1629, reveals that only 34 per cent of the women and 19 per cent of the men were baptized in Terling.[8] The experience of bastardy principals in this respect, then, was not dissimilar from that of the population generally. Moreover, this similarity holds good if we compare the periods 1590 to 1609 and 1610 to 1629 separately.

Given what is generally known of population mobility in pre-industrial England, and of the mobility of servants and the young in particular, these

8. A number of these marriages were second marriages for one of the partners. Care was taken to avoid the inclusion of any individual twice.

findings are scarcely surprising.[9] Mapping the parishes of origin of outsiders who fathered children on Terling women, we find that with two exceptions they fell within six miles of the village. This is very much the kind of distance within which personal relationships may have been maintained by Terling villagers and within which young people may have moved as servants in husbandry. The implications of this mobility for the student of courtship behaviour and illegitimacy, however, deserve some emphasis. The fact that the majority of men and women either having bastard children or marrying and having legitimate children were not natives of the parish has at least two implications. In the case of those marrying and beginning families, their establishment depended upon the opportunities present for obtaining a living, housing and a settlement. Secondly, both the selection of partners and courtship behaviour were probably to a large degree outside the immediate control of parents and kin. The selection of partners was perhaps more likely to be governed by personal choice within a local pool of eligibles than by parental match-making.[10] Courtship behaviour, including the point of commencement of sexual relations, may have been largely influenced by the attitudes and practice of the particular social milieu within which individuals found themselves. One reflection of sexual attitudes and behaviour in Terling, the prevalence of prenuptial pregnancy, has already been discussed. Further evidence may be provided by the reconstruction of the circumstances of illegitimate conceptions.

These circumstances, insofar as they can be reconstructed, reveal a wide range of experience. There were five cases involving an adulterous liaison, a single case of the sexual exploitation of a servant by her master, and another of the forbidden relationship between a man and his former wife's sister. Three cases relate to a stable, though irregular liaison between a man and a woman who had three bastards together over a period of six years. Ten cases related to delays in marriage, since the partners declared in court that they were contracted and/or did eventually marry one another. A further eleven cases probably involved less secure activity on the 'marriage market', since one or both partners did marry quite soon after their offence, though not to one another. Twelve cases can be grouped as involving particularly sexually delinquent persons, since in the absence of other evidence relating to the particular case, one or both partners committed or was accused of a sexual misdemeanour on another occasion.[11] In eighteen cases, however, the circumstances remain unknown and cannot be inferred, though in three of these cases it can be said that one of the partners numbered sexual delinquents among their kin.

Analysing the types of case according to the social status of the persons involved, we find that persons of middling status were particularly prominent in

9. See e.g. P. Laslett and J. Harrison, 'Clayworth and Cogenhoe' (1963); J. Cornwall, 'Evidence of population mobility in the seventeenth century' (1967). R. S. Schofield, 'Age-specific mobility in an eighteenth century English parish' (1970).

10. One immigrant to Terling, a girl of yeoman status, twice ignored her father's wishes in choosing a husband and marrying 'beneath herself'. Her father later recalled that though he regarded her as violating 'one of the principal duties of a child', he had resolved, since 'the matter was now past remedie . . . to leave her to her self and to such choise as she had made'. Her suitor told him 'that he had already obtayned the good will of [his] daughter and if he might not have [his] good will he must bee contented with hers'. PRO Court of Requests, Elizabeth I, Bundle 245, no. 44. Lower in the social scale, one Terling immigrant labourer left an account of meeting and proposing to his wife in the market place at Aveley. She had been a former inhabitant of another village where he had been a servant. They went to London to be married and only later moved into Terling, ERO Q/SR 181/97. Such situations may have been not untypical of courtships among the poor.

11. This is a somewhat harsh category in that it includes offences occurring *after* an initial bastard birth as well as before, and also includes such a widely tolerated practice as prenuptial fornication.

the cases relating to marriage and in adulterous unions, persons of low status were primarily involved in marital cases, in adultery and in cases involving repetitive delinquents. As might be expected, persons of obscure status were concentrated in cases in which the circumstances remain impenetrable. It seems very possible that many of these cases resulted from unstable servant love affairs.[12] Examining the spread of cases over time, we find that the cases actually or probably relating to the processes of marriage entry make up a greater proportion of cases in the first two decades of our period (37 per cent) than in the two decades from 1610 (27 per cent), while the reverse is true of the various groups involving less ambiguous delinquency. The proportion of cases of unknown circumstances remains fairly constant. Nevertheless, cases of all types are found spread across the entire period and it is safest to conclude that patterns of behaviour, insofar as they can be discovered, seem to have persisted over time. On the other hand, however, both the incidence of cases and the social status of the persons involved were declining.

Ultimately, an attempted typology of behaviour of this kind is of limited usefulness. While it has the value of showing the very varied forms of experience involved in illegitimate conceptions, its mutually exclusive categories also tend to obscure the complexity of the situation with which we are dealing. Some individuals recur in different categories. For example, one girl was initially involved in a case of unambiguous anticipation of marriage but in a later case she was marked down as a repetitive delinquent. Again, known interpersonal relationships between individuals blur the edges between different categories. Such inconvienient facts combine to strengthen the impression that ultimately the connections between individuals, the dynamic world of interaction within their social milieu, was of greater significance in moulding their behaviour than would be indicated by the artificially abstracted circumstances of individual cases, be they contained in bastardy examinations or reconstructed. In short we must move beyond individuals to their social world.

Disciplined reconstruction from the surviving evidence of each individual bastardy principal's direct personal contacts reveals that the persons involved in bastardy were, to a remarkable degree, interconnected either directly or through mutual personal contacts.[13] Fifty-seven per cent of bastardy principals were connected to two or more, 46 per cent to three or more other bastardy principals, the precise number of such contacts ranging up to 22. Using linkages of this kind, it proved possible to construct a master network of bastardy principals involved in 32 or our 61 cases, all linked directly or at one remove to one or both of the two most central individuals. These two men were themselves interlinked. Were we to extend the degree of linkage considered, yet more cases would certainly be included. Interlinkage of this kind serves to indicate the degree to which these persons can be shown, even from surviving historical evidence, to have shared a common world of interaction. Its implications in interpreting their behaviour, however, can be fully brought out only when we turn to the nature of the links and to the characteristics of the social world in which the parents of base children moved.

12. There were cases, however, where marriage was intended. When Grace Burles appeared before the court in 1602 it was pointed out that 'Edward Shipman was the father therof who myndeth shortlye to marye her' but that 'he prest for a soldier in the last presse.' See ERO D/ACA 25, fos. 32v, 171, 198v.

13. The method employed is an adaptation to our historical material of the social network analysis proposed by J. A. Barnes in 'Class and committees in a Norwegian island parish' (1954) and most recently developed in such works as J. Clyde Mitchell (ed.), *Social networks in urban situations: analyses of personal relationships in Central African towns* (1969); J. Boissevain, *Friends of friends: networks, manipulators and coalitions* (1974), chapter 2; P. H. Gulliver, *Neighbours and networks: the idiom of kinship in social action among the Ndendeuli of Tanzania* (1971), chapter 1.

The content of the links, the types of relationship which they represent, are in fact extremely varied. They include kinship links, witnessing or benefiting from one another's wills, standing surety to one another's recognizances, regular joint participation in manorial or parochial affairs, relationships of service or tenancy, drinking companionship and sexual contacts. It might be objected, of course, that historical records provide evidence of only a small proportion of the inter-personal relationships which must have existed in the village and that the existence of evidence of interconnection in a community of this size is scarcely a finding of significance. While recognizing the force of such arguments we would nevertheless maintain that these *recorded* relationships do provide evidence of inter-personal connections of some significance, as opposed to the wink and nod of passing acquaintances. We have not felt justified, however, in proceeding to rank or weight the intensity of relationships of different types. For present purposes the range of individuals' recorded networks and their degree of interconnection provide sufficient evidence of the social context of illegitimacy.

Using network analysis to organize the scattered and disparate references to individuals in the full range of local sources at our disposal, a number of significant factors emerged. Persons most linked to other bastardy principals were clearly concentrated in the first two decades of our period. Offenders in this period were more closely involved both with one another and with the members of the surrounding community who linked them. Moreover, while the recorded contacts of bastardy principals were never wholly confined to any single socio-economic stratum, they were becoming more so over time. The world within which they moved, from which they emerged, increasingly became that of the poor.[14] Again, over the whole period, the parents of illegitimate children and their contacts were involved to a striking degree in the myriad petty 'disorders' of village life.

Excluding outsiders who fathered bastards, the bastardy principals and their direct contacts included 63 per cent of all persons who committed or were accused of sexual misdemeanours in Terling (including prenuptial offences). In addition, they made up 40 per cent of persons prosecuted for theft, 41 per cent of persons prosecuted for failure to attend church, 66 per cent of persons prosecuted for drunkenness, alehouse-haunting and drinking in times of divine service, 75 per cent of those prosecuted for unlicensed ale-selling and 75 per cent of those prosecuted for keeping disorderly alehouses. Indeed the village alehouses were, much as was claimed by contemporary moralists, central to the social world of the bastardy principals.[15] They themselves included one alehouse-keeper, four wives or daughters of alehouse-keepers and seven 'common alehouse-haunters'. Alehouse-keepers were particularly prominent among contacts linked to several bastardy principals.

To what extent do these findings represent the broader dimensions of a 'sub-society of the illegitimacy prone'? There is certainly evidence of the exist-

14. Independent confirmation of this situation can be provided from an examination of the involvement of the parish notables who served as jurymen at quarter sessions. Of the 33 men who served 1590–1604, 5 had fathered base children, 7 numbered bastardy principals among their wives, sisters or children and a further 12 left evidence of direct links with one or more bastardy principals. Of the 26 men serving 1610–24, only one had fathered a bastard, none had bastardy principals among their kin and only 10 had links to bastardy principals. Five men served in both periods. *They* provided the father of a bastard and 5 of the 10 men directly linked to bastardy principals in the second period.

15. See, e.g. the association of bastardy with the alehouses by Lambarde, quoted in J. H. Gleason, *The justices of the peace in England, 1558–1640* (1969), p. 13. Cf. Lancashire Record Office, Manuscript sermons of Christopher Hudson, D.P. 353, f. 53.

ence of a core of bastardy prone individuals, comprising both repetitive offenders and the members of families prone to bastardy over two generations.[16] Striking as the activities of these individuals and families are, however, we would hesitate to describe them as a 'sub-society'. With the exception of those involving Anne Rond, who was clearly regarded as a whore, and the daughters of the Lilly and Allen families who may have been in that position, the cases in which they were concerned were very varied in type, representing the full range of circumstances which could produce illegitimacy rather than a pattern of peculiar delinquency. The principal distinguishing characteristics of the bastardy prone were that they were very much more likely than other bastardy principals to have been natives and thereafter stable inhabitants of the village and that they enjoyed large numbers of contacts with other bastardy principals. These two facts are not just coincidentally related.

It is worth considering that the apparent peculiarities of their position may owe much to their relative immobility and consequently high degree of historical visibility. While they undoubtedly provided a core of offenders in Terling within our period, they should not be too readily divorced from the very much broader shifting group of persons to whom they were closely connected, whose problems and patterns of behaviour they shared, yet who are less visible in the records of a single locality.[17] For the most part, we would interpret their position as being less that of a sub-cultural group than that of a peculiarly vulnerable element within the popular culture itself. Moreover, their activities do not explain major changes in the incidence of illegitimacy in Terling. Their base children were fairly evenly spread over our period, while even if we exclude every case in which the bastardy prone were involved, the great peak of illegitimacy in the first years of the seventeenth century remains equally prominent. The bastardy prone were clearly an important element in the overall incidence of bastardy in Terling in the late sixteenth and early seventeenth centuries, but we must look beyond them if we are to explain why the high incidence of bastardy occurred and why it then steadily declined.

Detailed investigation of the case of Terling, then, shows illegitimacy to have been a compound phenomenon. It subsumed the activities of a core of repetitive delinquents, adultery, prostitution, the exploitation of servant by master, cases related to delays in the solemnization of contracted marriages, to less stable relationships among individuals seeking marriage partners and, finally, the obscure liaisons of transient couples. Yet all these forms of behaviour were contained in the essential context of a vigorous popular culture exhibiting a number of significant characteristics: the high mobility of adolescents and young adults; their assimilation to a popular culture centred on the alehouses rather than the church, which permitted a considerably larger area of flexibility in social and sexual behaviour than was strictly allowed by either church or magistrate: and their ultimate selection of marriage partners in a situation relatively free of either the constraints or safeguards of parental control. These conditions were fraught

16. Seven women, all of them poor, four of them widows, had more than one base child, as did two men, both of middling status. Four families, two of low and two of middling status had bastards over two generations. In addition, at the turn of the sixteenth and seventeenth centuries, two families of middling status had both a son and daughter involved in bastardy, while in one poor family, two sisters had base children.

17. For example, only a fortunate survival tells us that the Terling labourer Robert Johnson had formerly lived in the parish of Upminster where he had cohabited for a year with Elizabeth Whitland and had a child by her 'but was not maryed unto her . . . but would have married her if the inhabitants would have suffered him and therefore he left her there.' ERO Q/SR 181/97.

by the multiple insecurities attending the obtaining of economic independence, housing and settlement. Failure in any of these particulars could result in renewed mobility, dislocated expectations, even separation. This was the essential context from which bastardy emerged. Its characteristics are not those of a sub-culture, but of the popular culture itself. An explanation of the overall movement of illegitimacy in this period must take account of this broad social context, of both its stable characteristics and its element of change.

3

Why, then, was there such an explosion of illegitimacy in Terling at the turn of the sixteenth and seventeenth centuries? The following explanation can be offered. Population rise and the progress of commercial farming[18] in sixteenth-century Terling had led to a proliferation of the labouring and cottaging poor. The parish registers reveal, from 1538, a rapid rate of population growth to the end of the sixteenth century, then in the first quarter of the seventeenth century there was a noticeable slackening and in the period 1621 to 1680 there was little growth.[19] This demographic expansion had predictable results: while the population almost doubled, the number of labourers rose even more rapidly. Comparison of the 1524 subsidy assessment with the hearth tax assessment of 1671 indicates that while the lowest economic group represented in the subsidy assessment (those assessed on wages or lands to an annual value of less than two pounds) comprised a third of the villagers assessed, and doubtless included some temporarily resident servants as well as permanent labourers, the lowest group in 1671 (assessed on one hearth or excused payment on the grounds of poverty) comprised more than half the households in the village. While its numbers of yeomen, husbandmen and substantial craftsmen had remained stable, the parish had filled up at the bottom.[20]

Against this general trend towards an accentuated economic polarization, may be placed the severe difficulties experienced at the turn of the sixteenth and seventeenth centuries. From 1594, a series of disastrous harvests produced acute economic problems.[21] By Michaelmas 1595, a group of husbandmen were unable to pay their rents and suffered a distraint at the hands of their landlord, while wills of 1598 and 1599 reveal severe indebtedness among men of middling standing (ERO, Q/SR/131/25, D/ACw 4/79, 4/111). The starker realities at the bottom of the social scale are indicated by references in the burial registers to strangers found dead in the barns of the yeomen of the parish.[22] The crisis situation of these

18. Most of the land in Terling was, by 1598, farmed in large units and the yeomen farmers were much involved in the bulk supply of both local and distant markets. ERO Assize Calendar, Asz 35/17/2/55; Q/SR 304/57, 322/106. For the agrarian development of Essex in this period and the influence of the London food market, see F. Hull, 'Agriculture and rural society in Essex, 1540–1640' (1950), *passim*.

19. In terms of the excess of baptisms over burials, the three periods had the following annual average surpluses: 1541–1600, five per year; 1601–20, two and three quarters per year; 1621–80, just over one per year.

20. PRO E 179 108/154; ERO Q/R Th 5. In comparing the 1524 Subsidy assessment with the Hearth Tax assessment of 1671, we have followed the methods of M. Spufford, *Contrasting communities: English villagers in the sixteenth and seventeenth centuries* (1974), pp. 28–45. Such a comparison is, of course, adequate only for the making of broad generalizations. That the situation of 1671 was essentially in being by 1636 is suggested by analysis of the Ship Money assessment of that year, printed in Barton, appendix III.

21. For grain prices, see E. H. Phelps-Brown and S. V. Hopkins, 'Seven centuries of the prices of consumables compared with builders' wages' (1956); W. G. Hoskins, 'Harvest fluctuations and English economic history, 1480–1619' (1964); P. Bowden, 'Statistical appendix' (1967); C. J. Harrison, 'Grain price analysis and harvest qualities, 1464–1634' (1971).

22. Such references occur on 18 December 1596, 3 March 1596–7, 23 March 1596–7, 4 April 1596–7, 9 March 1597–8.

years is familiar enough to students of the period, Margaret Spufford (1974, pp. 82–4, 118) having recently argued that among small landholders, the effects of the disastrous 1590s continued to be felt into the first decade of the seventeenth century as they recovered from, or succumbed to their indebtedness. Lower in the social scale, conditions remained difficult. The labouring poor of the corn-exporting parishes of Essex, of which Terling was one, were described in 1605 as living in 'great want and penury' (ERO, Q/SR 171/57).[23]

The impact of the years of crisis, 1594–8, and of the slow recovery thereafter may have exercised considerable influence on the opportunities for establishing a family in Terling. To the extent that marriage was largely dependent upon the achievement of some form of economic independence, a sharp deterioration in the living standards of a considerable section of the population might well dislocate conventional marriage strategies, frustrating customary expectations. Moreover, these effects would be spread further than was usual up the social scale. Among the poor, the opportunities of obtaining settlement and a living as a smallholder, labourer or craftsman were limited at the best of times. Admission to a five acre plot of customary land cost a fine of £3 and upwards, while even a landless customary cottage cost a fine of 20 shillings or more (ERO, D/DM 170 *passim*).[24] In times of economic stringency real income was eroded, less work may have been available for the labourer, masters may have reduced their complement of servants, servants may have diverted their savings to meet immediate needs. Again, the parish authorities may have been peculiarly loath to permit the establishment of a potentially chargeable family in times of economic gloom. Higher in the social scale, husbandmen may have been neither willing nor able to assist financially in the establishment of their sons, or to lay out the £5 to £15 customary as a dowry for their daughters.[25] Finally, expenses at the solemnization of a marriage could be very substantial, even among the poor, for custom demanded some show.[26]

In the years of deep crisis, 1594–8, only half as many marriages were celebrated in Terling as in the comparable periods before and after. During these years of severely restricted marital opportunities, traditional forms of sexual behaviour at the point either of betrothal or of a less formalized anticipation of imminent marriage may have been temporarily suspended. In the initial years of recovery, however, as the yearly average of marriages regained its former level, couples may have practised once again a socially acceptable sexual anticipation of marriage. The essential difference may have been that in the post-crisis situation the chances of the dislocation of the planned or perhaps only vaguely anticipated end of their courtships had become greater. While sexual activity commenced among couples whose age and circumstances placed them among the pool of eligibles within the parish, resultant pregnancies were no longer so likely to lead to marriage. Sometimes this meant only delay. Katherine Jackson was contracted to Richard Chapman with her father's blessing when she bore his child in 1599. Her husbandman father declared in court that 'God willing she and the sayd Richard

23. It is clear from the data presented by Phelps-Brown and Hopkins (1956), pp. 312–13, that the peculiarly sharp depression of real wages in the later 1590s was never fully recovered from within our period.

24. There was little enough land to be had by the would-be smallholders at the best of times. The later sixteenth century had seen the taking in of the last tiny scraps of waste which remained, and even these found takers.

25. The size of dowries is estimated from sums left in wills to be paid to unmarried daughters on their wedding days. These ranged from 26 shillings and 8 pence among the smaller husbandmen upwards to between £20 and £40 for the substantial yeomen.

26. In 1644 Ralph Josselin, minister of another Essex parish attended 'a strange vaine wedding, a poore man gave a curious ribbands to all, gloves to the women and to the ringers; yett there was very good company.' Alan Macfarlane, ed., *The diary of Ralph Josselin, 1618–1683* (1976), p. 29.

Chapman intended to solemnize matrimony and lyve lyke man and wyf together', but it was a further three years before they attained that desired independence (ERO, D/ACA 25, f. 32v).

Poorer and less established villagers may simply have moved on, leaving a bastardy case of which almost nothing can be discovered by the historian. Such delays and frustrations need not have combined to produce a general rise in the age of marriage. It would be enough that they affected rather more couples over a period of time to push up the bastardy ratio dramatically by superimposing a peculiar concentration of such cases on to the more sporadic cases resulting from the activities of less ambiguously delinquent individuals.

Such an explanation may account for the peak of illegitimacy in Terling between 1598 and 1605. But we must also face the question of why the bastardy ratio declined. It might be argued that, as the legacy of indebtedness and impoverishment left by the 1590s receded, the courtships of the middling ranks of villagers regained their accustomed security, while the perennial insecurity attending those of the poor was reduced to more normal proportions. While this argument has its virtues, however, it fails to account for the fact that subsequent economic crises, the sufferings of the 1620s and of the dearths of 1630–31 and 1646–50 in particular, did not leave a scattering of bastardy in their wake.[27] This discrepancy may be accounted for by the argument that the early seventeenth century saw a stabilization which involved less economic change than a complex and many-stranded adjustment of social relationships in Terling. We have argued that the prolonged economic crisis at the turn of the sixteenth and seventeenth centuries could have effects on the bastardy ratio in Terling only because of the prevailing social and sexual norms of the mass of the villagers. From 1607, both these customary norms and the popular culture which transmitted and maintained them were under sustained attack.

Two elements were involved in this development. First came a gradual shift in the attitudes and behaviour of the 'better sort' of the parish, the yeomen, substantial husbandmen and tradesmen who monopolized the prestigious parish offices, administered the poor laws and sat on the presentment juries at quarter sessions. Secondly, their withdrawal from the world of popular custom was both reflected in and furthered by their promotion of a disciplinary initiative against a popular culture which was increasingly that of the poor.

Changes in the attitudes of more substantial villagers may have owed much generally to their position as mediators between the demands of a more aggressive secular and ecclesiastical magistracy and the village community. They certainly owed much to a sharper perception of the problem presented by the poor, which was reinforced as the establishment and consolidation of the Tudor Poor Laws bred a greater insistence that the labouring and cottager population conform to the statutory stereotype of the deserving poor. Such attitudes are strikingly evidenced in the terms of a charity established in the village in 1626 to provide occasional relief for the able-bodied poor. These forbade the granting of relief to any poor person who had not been a settled inhabitant for five years, who took alms of the parish, or 'those that are guilty of excessive drinking, profane swearing, pilfering and other scandalous crimes or are Vagrants or are Idle Persons or have been incorrigible when Servants or do entertain Inmates'. Those

27. The two latter dearths were very severely felt in Essex. That of 1630–31 is discussed in K. Wrightson and J. Walter, 'Dearth and the social order in early modern England' (1976), that of 1646–50 is vividly documented in Josselin's diary, pp. 54–220 *passim*.

relieved in clothing were to be badged by being given upper garments marked with the initials of the benefactor (ERO, D/P 299/5/1B).

The very practical reasons for disciplining the behaviour of the poor provided by the potential expensiveness of their misdemeanours were reinforced and complemented by a developing religious hostility to the customary disorders of rustic sociability. The Mildmay family, lords of the manor of Terling Place and patrons of the living, were notable puritans, who from the 1620s appointed markedly Puritan ministers (Barton, 1953, pp. 88–92). Even before this, however, radical Protestantism of a Puritan stamp was building up in the parish possibly under the influence of the Mildmays and the smaller resident gentry, the Shaas and the Rochesters, who shared the Calvinist piety. By the 1620s a group of yeomen had emerged whose wills not only bear the mark of deep piety but also indicate their interconnection both to one another and to the Puritan ministers, Mr Rust and Mr Weld.

Under Weld, a weekday lectureship was established in the parish and after his deprivation and emigration to New England, a secret conventicle met. The principal inhabitants, described as 'a praying and a fasting people', put up sustained resistance to Laud's liturgical requirements.[28] The attitudes current among this godly group may be indicated by the tone of one of Weld's letters to them from New England. He dwelt on the fact that justice was 'religiously carried' in New England, that 'the greater part are the better part here'. 'Here, blessed be the Lord', he continued, 'our ears are not beaten nor the air filled with oaths, swearers nor railers, nor our eyes and ears vexed with the unclean conversation of the wicked' (Barton, 1953, pp. 90–1). Presumably such sentiments found an echo among the 'better sort' of Terling.

We have, then, a superimposition of harsher attitudes towards the poor and a greater religious hostility to moral disorders upon an existing situation of increasing social and economic polarization. The polarization, which was in itself no novelty, became many stranded. This resulted on the one hand in the rejection of customary social and sexual norms by many of the more substantial villagers, and on the other hand in a greater willingness on their part to establish conformity to more disciplined canons of behaviour and to use both the Poor Laws and the secular and ecclesiastical courts to that end. Village officers, who in the period before 1607 had been themselves deeply involved in the popular culture which produced bastardy and who had turned a blind eye to minor misdemeanours, were replaced by men of a different stamp. Whereas the villagers' use of the royal courts had been characterized by their bringing to them of interpersonal disputes of various kinds, usually disputes between parties of middling standing, the years from 1607 saw an unprecedented upsurge of regulative prosecution directed at the poorer inhabitants and at those of the middling sort who countenanced or shared their disorders.

Unlicensed ale-selling, a common offence among the poor, was repeatedly attacked after 1609 and had largely been brought under control by the later 1620s. Licensed alehouse-keepers tolerating disorderly meetings of any kind, ranging from Sunday dancings to the harbouring of persons suspected of incontinency, were attacked in 1607–8 and then with great regularity from 1616 into the 1630s in quarter sessions, assizes and the church courts. In this initiative the parish authorities were deliberately rooting out the meeting places of the poor, the sites

28. Barton (1953), p. 92; ERO, D/ACA 47, f. 94v, 48, f. 29v, 51, f. 157, 52, ff. 226v, 227, 53, f. 195v, 54, f. 88v.

of unsupervised gatherings and courtships.[29] Other objects of regulative prosecutions on a novel scale were such offences as drunkenness, alehouse-haunting, tippling in service time and failure to attend church. In all these categories of prosecution, the records indicate an attack directed initially against widespread and customarily tolerated offences, many individuals being prosecuted, followed by the regular disciplining of repetitive offenders.

Concern with the disorders of the poor also involved the closer regulation of sexual and marital behaviour. Sexual incontinency unrelated to an actual pregnancy and therefore to a potentially chargeable bastard child, was infrequently prosecuted in the church courts before 1607. Thereafter prosecutions of sexual irregularities of this kind were a more regular feature of Terling presentments. In particular prenuptial fornication which had become evident only *after* marriage, was never presented before 1609. In subsequent years it was quite frequently presented, especially in the later 1620s. In addition there was a new concern with the marriages of the poor. In 1607 the marital status of three cohabiting couples recently arrived in the village was investigated by the parish officers, while later we have ominous evidence of the exercise of informal pressure to inhibit the marriages of the very poor. In 1615, Richard Sizer and Widow Patrick had a base child. When prosecuted, he admitted that they had cohabited for a year but complained that 'the parish would not suffer them to marry else they had bin married ere now.' They did marry, and were chronically poor when they died, their two children, as the churchwardens had presumably feared, falling on the parish poor rates.[30]

The initiative on the part of the parish officers bit perhaps most forcibly through the sanctions of the Poor Laws, and by the 1630s a new norm had been established in the relationships between the 'better sort' and the poor, which was inherited, consolidated and maintained by the officers and vestrymen of the later seventeenth and eighteenth centuries. We have already indicated the extent to which this process directly affected both bastardy principals and their direct personal contacts. It seems more than coincidental that as the seventeenth century advanced there was a steady decline in the incidence of both bastardy and bridal pregnancy, while such bastardy as occurred was the result of the offences of a harassed and steadily diminishing core of delinquent individuals and families, supplemented by occasional cases involving obscure and transient inhabitants.

4

Illegitimacy in Terling, then, was a complex phenomenon. It involved a stable element of 'bastardy prone' individuals and families. To their occasional bastards may be added the bastard children born to less regular sexual offenders, adulterers or an exploitative master. To both can be added the children base born as the result of delayed or dislocated marriages or the highly unstable courtships of the mobile young. All were contained within the context of the vigorous and, in the eyes of contemporary magistrates and moralists, disorderly popular culture of the late sixteenth century. The explosion of bastardy at the turn of the sixteenth and seventeenth centuries is to be explained neither in terms of the activities of the

29. John Aldridge, for example, was presented to the quarter sessions for allowing gaming and drinking among men 'soe poore that many of them have almes of the parishe and their wifs and children beg in the parishe', and on another occasion 'for suffering of pore men of the parishe to sit tiplinge and drinkinge'. ERO Q/SR 279/17, 284/10.

30. ERO, D/ACA 30, ff. 167, 179; Q/SR 181/97; D/ACw 9/62, 10/115; LCRO, DL/C/324, f. 51v.

'bastardy prone' core, nor in terms of a revolution in sexual attitudes. It related rather to a point of crisis in a growing disequilibrium between customary attitudes, expectations and sexual behaviour and deteriorating social and economic circumstances. This crisis affected not only the poor but also, briefly, a number of the children of their immediate social superiors. In the early seventeenth century that disequilibrium was resolved, partly by demographic and economic stabilization, partly by adjustments of attitudes and behaviour which were initially developed among the village's yeomen élite and then instilled in or imposed upon their social inferiors.

Terling is a single parish and, even within the county of Essex, perhaps not a typical one. Some of the factors which we have argued shaped its development, however, may have been operative elsewhere, though their chronology may have varied. The relative and absolute expansion of the labouring population; the harrowing experience of economic crises; the changing consciousness of a yeomanry involved in the currents of ideological change, in the administration of the Poor Laws and in the execution of regulative statutes – these are matters which belong to national history. What the case of Terling perhaps reveals is the extent to which the comparatively ordered social world of the 'closed' rural parishes of the later seventeenth and eighteenth centuries was the product of interconnected demographic, economic, social, administrative and ideological changes. The changing incidence of bastardy in early modern England cannot be understood independently of those changes.

6

The nadir of English illegitimacy in the seventeenth century

Keith Wrightson

Peter Laslett's and Karla Oosterveen's pioneering studies of the movement of English illegitimacy ratios over four centuries have resulted in the discovery of several phenomena of major importance to historians of pre-industrial English society.[1] An attempt has now been made to explain the most striking of these – the extraordinarily high illegitimacy ratios discovered in parish after parish at the turn of the sixteenth and seventeenth centuries – in terms of the complex after-effects of the economic crisis of the 1590s (see above, chapter 5). The equally marked decline in the illegitimacy ratio in the central decades of the seventeenth century, however, still awaits closer investigation. The coincidence of the lowest recorded illegitimacy ratios with the decades of 'Puritan' rule raises a number of issues of major concern. How effective was the social regulation of illegitimacy in early seventeenth-century England and was that regulation intensified by the Puritan governors of the Interregnum? Is it conceivable that such an intensification could have significantly affected the incidence of illegitimacy in England? How adequate was the recording of illegitimacy during the Interregnum, both in itself and as compared with earlier decades?

In discussing these questions, I shall attempt to demonstrate that the formal regulation of sexual behaviour in the period was dependent upon local support for its efficacy, to a degree which made it unlikely that it would be affected by political changes at the centre unless independent local support existed for the programmes of a reforming government. I shall argue that the Puritans brought little that was new to the regulation of sexual life and that such initiatives as were made during their period of major influence contributed more to undermining the recording of sexual lapses than to their reformation. Finally, I shall suggest a number of alternative hypotheses more appropriate to the explanation of fluctuations in the illegitimacy ratio than models centred upon the influence of political or ideological change.

The social control of the sexuality of the unmarried in the early modern English society must be considered in its relationship to the principal marital and social institutions of the period. The nature of the Western European marriage pattern, the preponderance of the nuclear family, the vitality of the institution of service are by now familiar features of the broad structure within which sexual and marital behaviour was contained.[2] Of the emotional pressures engendered by this institutional complex, of attitudes to sexuality, courtship, marital strategy and relationships within marriage, we know considerably less. It has been suggested

1. P. Laslett, *The world we have lost* (1971), pp. 141–5; P. Laslett and K. Oosterveen, 'Long-term trends in bastardy in England: a study of the illegitimacy figures in the parish registers and in the reports of the Registrar General, 1561–1960, (1973).
2. For a recent discussion of these characteristics, see P. Laslett, *Family life and illicit love in earlier generations* (1977), chapter 1.

that the maintenance of this structure depended upon the careful restraint of reproductive resources.[3] Such a viewpoint gains support from the consideration of its ideological and legal underpinning.

The church, the official agency of moral prescription, was unequivocal in its condemnation of sexual activity outside marriage. The Books of Homilies stated plainly that all forms of adultery and 'uncleanness' were repugnant to God's law and that abstinence from 'whoredom' in any form was necessary to salvation.[4] The degree to which such teachings influenced popular attitudes remains problematic. While there are examples of popular subscription to such values, such as the Essex youth who replied that 'God would never give a blessinge to such actions when solicited by a village whore',[5] counter-examples may be cited of the open boasting of sexual exploits. One Essex villager, for example, bragged 'that he had lain with John Colmans wife . . . as often as the said Colman her husband had' (ERO, Q/S Ba 2/71). Again, William Stout the Lancaster Quaker wrote with distaste of

> what's too common with not only youth but also married men and women with each other, to entertain each in a bantering way in such terms as could only tend to beget evil thought and excite to lewdness. And many who take that liberty are reputed chaste and good Christians, although inconsistent with true Christianity.[6]

Ambivalent as popular attitudes may have been, the ecclesiastical and secular magistrates stood ready to support the pronouncements of the church. Canon law required that both proven and suspected cases of adultery, fornication, incest and illicit cohabitation be presented by churchwardens to the ecclesiastical court, and surviving archidiaconal act books provide abundant evidence of their response.[7] In the year 1627, for example, the archdeacon of Essex dealt with 63 cases of sexual immorality, involving 104 individuals from 41 of the parishes within his jurisdiction (ERO, D/AE A 36, ff. 69–240).[8] In addition to the ecclesiastical courts, justices of the peace might, at their own discretion, bind over adulterers, whores, whoremongers and fornicators to be of good behaviour. In bastardy cases in which the child was, or might prove to be chargeable to the parish poor rate, they could bind parents to answer for their offence, make an order for the maintenance of the child by its parents and order their corporal punishment or the committal of the mother to the house of correction.[9] In 1630, the justices for the southern divisions of Lancashire dealt with at least 36 such cases from 15 parishes, while 1636 brought 54 cases from 17 parishes.[10]

3. E. A. Wrigley, 'Family limitation in pre-industrial England' (1966), pp. 108–9. Cf. Laslett (1971), pp. 136–7.
4. Homily 'Against Whoredom and uncleanness', in E. Griffiths (ed.), *The two books of homilies* (1859), pp. 118–19, 121.
5. Essex Record Office (hereafter ERO), Q/S Ba 2/61.
6. J. D. Marshall (ed.), *The autobiography of William Stout of Lancaster, 1665–1752* (1967), p. 104. Conventional verbal licence and ribaldry, of course, are not incompatible with strict morality and may indeed reinforce it. See C. M. Arensberg and S. T. Kimball, *Family and community in Ireland* (1968), pp. 198–9.
7. See e.g. *Articles to be enquired of within the diocese of London* (1631), Articles 21, 22; *Articles to be enquired of within the archdeaconrie of Essex* (1635), Articles 28, 29. For the jurisdiction, procedure and business of the ecclesiastical courts, see R. A. Marchant, *The church under the law: justice, administration and discipline in the diocese of York, 1560–1640* (1969); E. R. Brinkworth (ed.), *The archdeacon's court: Liber Actorum 1584* (1942, 1946); Brinkworth, 'The study and use of archdeacon's court records, illustrated from Oxford's records, 1566–1759' (1943).
8. These cases involved 33 children conceived in fornication, incest or adultery.
9. 18 Eliz. I c. 3 (1575); 7 Jac. I c. 4; M. Dalton, *The Countrey Justice* (1622).
10. Lancashire Record Office (hereafter LRO), QSR/26–7, 32–3; QSO/2/4–5, 9–10; QSB/1/66–7, 70–1, 73, 75, 78–9, 162–3, 166–7, 170–1, 174–5.

The weight of both ecclesiastical and secular sanctions, then, might fall upon the parents of bastards, as Alan Macfarlane shows in some detail in chapter 2. The essential concern of the church courts was to maintain the boundaries of permitted behaviour and to enforce, by the imposition of public penance, the public reaffirmation of the norms which had been breached. The justices on the other hand were primarily concerned with the more tangible challenge of a bastard birth; to see to the maintenance of the child without, if possible, burdening the parish; to clarify responsibility when necessary; to adjudicate conflicts aroused by a bastard birth between neighbours or parishes. Though the magistrates of church and state were capable of mounting vigorous regulative campaigns on occasion, they preferred in the main to adopt a more passive role, issuing their articles of enquiry and presentment, but dealing primarily with cases freely brought in for adjudication or punishment by local officials or private individuals. This simple procedural fact introduced into the regulation of social behaviour, including bastardy, a strong element of dependence upon neighbourhood opinion. Such dependence was felt at two levels: in the definition of delinquency and in the delinquents to be presented to the courts. The problem of bastardy amply illustrates this point.

So complex was the issue of what constituted valid matrimony that the greatest contemporary authority upon the subject ultimately referred the matter to local custom. Swinburne contended that 'the Simplicity of the Vulgar sort' and in particular their employment of forms of words sanctioned by local usage, rather than strict adherence to the forms recognized by law, led to the making of espousals which were of no binding force. Ultimately he allowed that in such cases

> if by the Common use of Speech or Custom of the place where the Parties do dwell, and were Contracted, they infer Matrimony; This being proved, the Contract is of that force That, if either party should afterwards Solemnize Matrimony with some other person, yet that Second Matrimony is unlawful although it were confirmed by carnal knowledge and procreation of children.[11]

Marriage and legitimacy, then, were to a significant degree defined by the neighbourhood, the same body which controlled, through presentment, those cases of moral laxity to be brought to the attention of the authorities, both civil and ecclesiastical.

What little is known of popular handling of this responsibility derives largely from the evidence of presentment by the churchwardens to the ecclesiastical courts and by the village constables to the justices of the peace. Attention to sexual regulation varied widely, both geographically and over time, and may have depended on such influences as the local pattern of settlement, population density and social structure; or upon the conscientiousness of the clergyman, the squire or the parish officers of a locality. However, there was generally a high degree of tolerance of certain kinds of offence, most notably of premarital fornication and bridal pregnancy, as Alan Macfarlane has pointed out in chapter 2.

But it is clear that neighbourhood opinion which was so complacent in such cases could harden in the face of bastardy: informal and formal sanctions merged. While the evidence of recognizances indicates that kin or neighbours might stand by a bastard-bearer in the important matter of giving surety to keep the child or to

11. H. Swinburne, *A treatise of spousals or matrimonial contracts* (1686).

be of good behaviour, there are examples of girls turned out by master or kin or driven away by local hostility. One Essex servant carried and bore her child in secret because 'it would have bine agreife unto her friends if she should have discovered it.' On top of that 'she feared she should not have bine relieved if she had made it known' (ERO, Q/S Ba 2/18; 'friends' in such a context includes relations). Joany Winter begged her landlord on her knees 'to forgive her base fact beinge afraid that [he] would turne her out' (LRO, QSB/1/1655, unsorted). The manorial jury of Broughton, Lancashire, systematically fined Margaret Ashton's father for keeping an 'inmate' until he turned out both her and her child (LRO, QSR/33). The records of quarter sessions abound with inter-parochial disputes sparked off by attempts of particular parishes to rid themselves of the responsibility of keeping a base child.[12] Ralph Josselin, a notably compassionate man, recorded with evident relief: 'Our town escaped, but one quarter of an houre a travelling woman's liing in with us.'[13]

The system of social regulation, then, was less imposed from above than initiated and energized from below. It functioned both to define the limits of tolerable behaviour and to resolve the conflicts produced by delinquency. Parish officers made their decisions as to what constituted a threat to the community and appealed to the courts for legitimation, security and the application of appropriate sanctions. Their decisions might be influenced by a variety of local circumstances, but in general it may be said that their principal concerns were with the avoidance of expense and the maintenance of local harmony. This was a period of demographic expansion and inflation. Parishes were witnessing a marked growth in the labouring and cottaging population and a widening gap between the poor and the prosperous rate-paying yeomanry. We can understand a growing willingness to discipline the misdemeanours of the poor in general and of bastard-bearers in particular (see above, chapter 5). Sanctions against bastardy were harsh and were applied with a regularity absent from the regulation of many other offences. What, if anything, did the Puritans add to this situation?

In questions of sexual behaviour, the Puritans added nothing to the official homilies of the church.[14] Their contribution lay more in the vigour with which they broadcast their views from press and pulpit and in their tactical sense as reformers. In tracts and sermons which reinvigorated the medieval tradition of moral criticism, they identified and denounced the institutions and attitudes which they believed to encourage or countenance sexual lapses. They pointed to the excitement of lascivious desire in dancing, drinking and May games and to lusting in the numerous alehouses of rural England and the brothels of the towns. More fundamental criticism was directed against popular attitudes, which were characterized as supporting the view that fornication was merely 'the tricke of youth'.[15] Such attitudes were believed to be reinforced by the laxity of the church courts, the inadequacy of such 'toyish censures' as 'pinning in a sheete'[16] The

12. See e.g., S. C. Ratcliff and H. C. Johnson (eds), *Warwick county records: quarter sessions order books* (1935–53), III, pp. 96, 153–4.
13. A. Macfarlane (ed.), *The diary of Ralph Josselin, 1616–1683* (1976), p. 391.
14. A good statement of Puritan views may be found in John Downame, *Foure Treatises tending to diswade all christians from Swearing, Drunkenness, Whoredom and Bribery* (1613), pp. 128 ff., which may be compared with the homily cited above. Examples of these often repeated accusations can be found in many Puritan works; for references see my doctoral dissertation (1974) cited below, note 18.
15. This phrase, which occurs in one of its variants in the homily 'Against Whoredom and Uncleanness' (p. 118) was much repeated as a description of popular attitudes.
16. W. H. Frere and C. E. Douglas ed. *Puritan manifestoes* (1907), pp. 17, 34; R. Cooke, *A white sheete* (1629), p. 13.

recommended remedy was more severe punishment and more preaching, godly reformation by sword and word, the sword to 'conforme the outside', the word to 'reform the inside of the people'.[17]

This energetic moralistic campaign undoubtedly bore effect in the half century before 1640. At the individual level it encouraged stricter conformity to the letter of Christian teaching on sexual behaviour. In the Essex village of Terling, the declining involvement of the village's yeomen families in sexual offences in the early seventeenth century may be partly explained by the success among them of a series of Puritan ministers. What is clearest is that religious hostility, superimposed upon the more general concern with the misdemeanours of the poor, could add an edge to the efforts of local notables seeking their suppression (see above, chapter 5).

The significance of the Interregnum was that the political victory of men who legitimized their actions partly in terms of Puritan ideology provided the opportunity for attempts to generalize such processes. Some progress was indeed made towards the application of the strategy of sword and word. Certain offences were more vigorously prosecuted by the justices. The church was extensively restaffed with well paid preaching ministers.[18] These efforts, however, were less than successful in transforming the texture of popular life. The apparent decline in the illegitimacy ratio during the period of Puritan ascendancy would appear to offer one of the few indicators of reforming success. Yet does it reflect a real shift in behaviour as a result of intensified social regulation? Looking more closely at events in two contrasting areas may supply the answer.

In south Lancashire, an area of high bastardy ratios, ecclesiastical discipline before 1640 may have been peculiarly weak.[19] Ironically, the ministers who served the area after 1645 succeeded in setting up a system of Presbyterian discipline in a substantial number of parishes. A rigorous moral discipline might also have been achieved had not the system been weakened both by political events and by the unwillingness of parochial lay elders to participate fully in its administration. In the years 1647–9, the Presbyterian classes of Bury, Manchester and Walton dealt with a number of sexual offenders, indicating that in some parishes 'the discipline' was successful.[20] But from 1649 onwards, church discipline was ineffective and although particular congregations attempted its continuance, recalcitrant offenders were able to defy ecclesiastical censures with impunity.

The justices of the area had long pursued a strict policy against bastard-bearers. In 1618 they firmly endorsed the legislation of 1609 by ordering that all mothers of chargeable bastards be committed to the house of correction, while in 1630 they went further by requiring the whipping of the fathers and mothers of *all* bas-

17. T. Ford, *Reformation sure and steadfast* (1641), p. 13. For unsuccessful attempts at more severe legislation frequently involving Puritan members of parliament, see J. B. H. Jones, 'Puritanism and moral legislation before the Civil War' (1954), p. 96 and J. R. Kent, 'Attitudes of members of the House of Commons to the regulation of "personal conduct" in late Elizabethan and early Stuart England' (1973), pp. 41–2, 44, 46 and *passim*.

18. An account of attempts at reformation by 'sword and word' in Lancashire and Essex can be found in K. E. Wrightson, 'The Puritan reformation of manners, with special reference to the counties of Lancashire and Essex, 1640–1660' (1974), parts 2 and 3. For similar events in other counties, see J. S. Morrill, *Cheshire 1630–1660: county politics and society during the 'English Revolution'* (1974), pp. 226, 229, 239, 244; A. H. A. Hamilton, *Quarter sessions from Queen Elizabeth to Queen Anne* (1878), pp. 138–61.

19. Marchant (1969), pp. 210–11, tables 28–9, deaneries of Leyland, Manchester and Warrington. See also D. Lambert, 'The lower clergy of Lancashire, 1558–1642' (1964), pp. v–vi.

20. W. A. Shaw (ed.), *Minutes of the Manchester Presbyterian classis*, (1890–1), pp. 25, 31, 49, 50, 80, 189, 206; Shaw (ed.), *Minutes of the Bury Presbyterian classis* (1896–8), pp. 19–23, 29; LRO QSB/1/296/35.

tards.[21] Despite these decisions, an examination of particular bastardy orders indicates that throughout the 1620s and 1630s real severity was reserved for repetitive bastard-bearers, who were almost invariably committed to the house of correction, while first offenders were only occasionally so treated.[22] The core of the 'bastardy prone sub-society' was therefore under vigorous attack.

From 1646, this policy was continued unaltered, though after 1649 an increasing rigour becomes evident, mothers of bastards being much more frequently committed for correction. From 1652, a minority of the parents of bastards also found themselves indicted under the 1650 Act against adultery, incest and fornication and were sentenced to three months in the county gaol.[23] Despite these signs of increasing severity, all bastardy cases continued to be presented on local initiative and no more aggressive policy of seeking out offenders was attempted until January 1657. In that month the justices at Manchester 'perceiving the wicked sin of furnication much to abound and encrease' because of their laxity in punishing 'divers wicked women', ordered petty constables to

> apprehend as well all such women within the severall divisions who have already had any bastard children and have not had punishment for the same . . . as all others who hereafter shall have any bastard children begotten upon their bodies within six months after the said bastard children are borne and them bringe to the house of correction there to remain for the space of one whole yeare [LRO, QSR/50].

This attempt at aggressive regulation crowned a policy of slowly mounting severity in the execution of the bastardy laws, a policy which had its parallels in Cheshire and in Devon.[24]

In Essex, a county with generally low bastardy ratios, the ecclesiastical courts which we have seen operating with some efficiency had no successors after 1640. The lack of a sessions order book before 1651 makes firm statements about the pre-1640 punishment of bastardy by the justices difficult, though it is evident that from 1651 onwards bastard-bearers were being regularly committed to the house of correction (ERO, Q/S Ba 2/75; QSO 1, *passim*). However, survival of both sessions and assize records for Essex allows some examination of the effects of the notorious 1650 Act in that county.

'Unclean persons' were among those on whom constables were ordered to report to the petty sessions of the justices in at least part of the county during this period, but we lack evidence of the response (ERO, Q/SR 346/22); probably it was minimal. Only a handful of sexual offenders were presented by constables to quarter sessions, the presentments echoing both the form and content of the once

21. E. Axon (ed.) *Manchester sessions* (1901), p. 53; LRO QSR/27. For earlier examples of the parents of bastards being whipped under the Elizabethan act, see J. Tait (ed.), *Lancashire quarter sessions records, vol. I, quarter sessions rolls 1590–1606* (1917), p. 141.

22. LRO, QSR/16–37 *passim*. For particular examples, see QSR/17 Alice Pendleton sentenced for 5 bastards, QSR/19 Thomas Greenhalgh for 7 bastards, QSR/21 Alice Mercer for 2 bastards, QSB/1/191/59 Margery Bromly for 'severall' bastards, QSR/38 John Worthington and Alice Scarisbrick for 2 bastards.

23. LRO, QSR/40–53 *passim*. The act of 1650 made incest and adultery capital offences, while convicted fornicators were liable to imprisonment for a first offence, death for subsequent offences. C. H. Firth and R. S. Rait (eds), *Acts and ordinances of the Interregnum, 1642–1660* (1911), II, p. 387.

24. In Cheshire there was a similar shift from committing only repetitive bastard-bearers to the house of correction to committing all bastard-bearers. Morrill (1974), p. 246. In Devon all women who had borne a bastard and had evaded punishment were to be committed for punishment. In addition some married women were indicted for premarital fornication. Hamilton, *Quarter Sessions*, p. 159.

plentiful presentments to the church courts, rather than invoking the 1650 Act.[25] Only 19 cases are known to have been privately brought under the new law, 13 of fornication, 5 of adultery and one of incest. Of the 35 individuals involved, 8 were sentenced to imprisonment, 8 were acquitted, 2 were discharged on the grand jury's rejection of the indictment and of the others nothing is known. No person is known to have been hanged under the act.[26]

Who brought these cases? The few constabular presentments may have reflected local opinion and may have been influenced by ministers. Only one clear case of a minister initiating prosecution has survived, that of Samuel Smith, the strongly Presbyterian minister of Sandon, who presented one of his parishioners in 1656 for having had a bastard and having received no punishment.[27] In privately brought cases, the tracing of known prosecuting witnesses in the judicial records reveals a complex picture. In some cases it would appear that common informers had been at work;[28] other cases appear to be malicious prosecutions inspired by local feuds;[29] one case may have emerged over a promise to marry dispute.[30] It is clear that there is no simple pattern of moral regulation here: an indictment cost time and money and the motives which led men to bring them were complex and not always pure. It has been argued that the passage of the 1650 Act owed less to religious zeal than to the desire of the Rump Parliament to attain respectability in the eyes of its 'Presbyterian opponents, combined with a fear of the spread of such radical sects as the Ranters, who tolerated sexual licence'.[31] The evidence of local prosecution would certainly suggest that its significance was symbolic rather than effective.

The punishment of bastard-bearers by the justices, then, may have intensified in certain counties during the Interregnum. In terms of the total volume of regulative activity directed against sexual offenders, however, their efforts can have done little to make up for the absence of the church courts. In this respect, the Interregnum may have been a period of relative tranquillity. Again, despite magisterial efforts at stricter control, the system still rested upon presentment or private action and the filtering of local opinion remained crucial. There seems to have been little enthusiasm for presentment.

Coercion aside, there were other, subtler consequences of the Puritan ascendancy which had their influence on the recorded incidence of bastardy. Most notable among these were the innovations of the Puritans in the matters of

25. ERO, Q/SR 342/28, 345/40, 346/24, 350/20, 353/26, 355/30, 359/25, 362/36, 367/28, 370A/53.
26. ERO, Q/SR 353/37, 358/20, 362/19, 364/13, 375/7, 375/12, 377/11; ERO Assize calendar 35/91/H/5, 35/93/H/27, 35/93/T/5, 35/94/H/13, 35/96/1 Sess/5, 35/96/1 Sess/7, 35/97/H/6, 35/97/H/7, 35/98/2 Sess/14, 35/98/2 Sess/15, 35/99/Easter/13.
27. ERO, Q/SR 367/28; H. Smith, 'The sequence of Essex clergy, 1640–1660', I, p. 57. Josselin's diary, pp. 51–2, provides a further instance of a minister appealing to a justice to bind over a parishioner for a sexual offence.
28. E.g. in 1656 George Burles was a witness against Thomas Gray and Sara Reed, ERO Assize calendar 35/97/H/7. Burles was a tailor and occasional alehouse-keeper who had acted as a prosecuting witness in a number of sessions cases. Q/SR 257/88, 235/37, 311/20, 21, 100; D/DU 472/13. Another witness, John Scull, who prosecuted Mary Martin and John Carter in 1654, was an Ingatestone mealman who had acted as prosecuting witness against a number of local people in other types of offence. Q/SR 362/19, 358/58, 360/65.
29. John Hart and William Raderam of Epping had assaulted John Sedcole in July 1653 before indicting him for fornication the next October. ERO Assize calendar 35/94/T/10, Q/SR 358/20, 356/74. Again, Thomas Hatch and his wife 'Ezra' were scarcely moral bulwarks of the community, though they acted against two neighbours for fornication in 1655. They kept a disorderly alehouse and appeared in court on several occasions as a result of local quarrels. Assize calendar 35/96/1 Sess/5, Q/SR 368/92, 369/23, 369/53, 376/37. Details of a clear malicious accusation, which was forestalled by a petition to the justices are revealed in Q/S Ba 364/12.
30. Anthony Charles, a yeoman, gave evidence against John Bush for fornication with Elizabeth Charles, Anthony's daughter. Elizabeth herself and another member of the Charles family acted as witnesses. ERO, Q/SR 273/57, 275/37, 361/15, 361/101, 275/7.
31. B. Worden, *The Rump Parliament, 1648–1653* (1974), p. 233.

baptism and marriage. The Directory of Worship, introduced in 1644, deprived baptism of both its sacramental status and the more significant elements of its ritual. Ministers were required to explain to their people that baptism was inessential to salvation; private baptism, the dipping of the child and the sign of the cross were forbidden; godparents were abolished and fathers were required to bring their own children to the font for baptism (Firth and Rait, I, p. 594). Nor was this all. Doubts long expressed among radical Protestants about the propriety of baptizing the children of doctrinally ignorant or morally scandalous parents were revived, as was the particular issue of the lawfulness of baptizing bastards.

As far back as the 1580s the Puritan classis of Dedham had discussed both these questions. They had resolved that the child of an 'offensive person' might be baptized if some godly person was prepared to answer for it, while bastards could be baptized with 'some approved Christians of the congregation undertakinge for their religyous education'.[32] On the former issue, the classes, synods, associations of ministers or gathered congregations of the Interregnum tended to agree that the children of the ignorant and scandalous should be baptized only after the examination of the faith of the parents, while some required signs of repentance, or the undertaking of responsibility for the child's religious education by a church member.[33] The issue of baptizing bastards was raised by Lancashire Presbyterians in 1647, but no conclusion was recorded: the matter was probably left to the discretion of ministers (*Bury classis*, pp. 31, 36).

Baptism was perhaps the most highly regarded of ecclesiastical services among the people and ministers who chose to withhold it or alter the ritual had long met with popular resentment.[34] Such resentment was also expressed in the Interregnum, both openly – as when one Lancashire father carried away his child in his own arms rather than present it for baptism (*Manchester classis*, p. 60) – and clandestinely among parishioners who sought the old ritual elsewhere. Clandestine baptisms were often available; the Lancashire Presbyterians struggled in vain against them.[35] Again, the Interregnum shift to the registration of births rather than baptisms may have made matters worse. However much baptism was valued, there is little evidence that mere registration was so highly regarded and where it was not incidental to baptism it may have been neglected. In 1654 and 1655, the Lancashire justices condemned such neglect of registration, prophetically commenting that it was likely to 'prove prejudiciall unto many in future tymes' (LRO, QSR/48, 49). At Preston, it was complained that parents both baptized their children clandestinely and failed to register their births (LRO, QSP/94/2). At Great Waltham in Essex, the registers appear well kept, yet we

32. R. G. Usher (ed.), *The Presbyterian movement in the reign of Queen Elizabeth as illustrated by the minute book of the Dedham classis 1582–1589* (1903), pp. 30, 39.

33. W. A. Shaw (ed.) *Materials for an account of the provincial synod of the county of Lancaster, 1646–1660* (1890), pp. 35, 48, 51, 84; 'Minutes of the Cambridge Classis', in *Bury classis*, appendix III, pp. 198–9; H. Fishwick (ed.), *The note book of the Rev. Thomas Jolly, 1671–1693: extracts from the church book of Altham and Wymondhouses, AD 1649–1725* (1895), p. 121; *The agreement of the associated ministers of the county of Essex proposed to their particular congregations* (1658), p. 5. The Essex decision was a compromise, some ministers being determined to withhold baptism until scandalous parents had evidenced reformation in their lives.

34. Some early separatists returned to the Anglican church out of fear that their children might die unbaptized. K. Thomas, *Religion and the decline of magic: studies in popular beliefs in sixteenth- and seventeenth-century England* (1971), p. 56. Examples of the disputes aroused by the attempts of Puritan ministers to impose their baptismal views can be found in R. C. Richardson, *Puritanism in northwest England: a regional study of the diocese of Chester to 1642* (1972), pp. 26–9.

35. *Manchester classis*, pp. 51, 98, 99, 101, 107–8, 109, 162; *Bury classis*, pp. 9, 121–2, 127, 128; *Lancashire synod*, pp. 31, 35, 62. The sessions records reveal yet more cases. Thomas Bispham, for example, ex-minister of Holland, was one who 'useth to goe about to christen children . . . according to the forme of the common prayer booke'. LRO, QSB/1/1656.

have the warning of the minister that 'I have endeavoured to perfect the register, but doe acquit myself from the blame of omissions which are many.'[36]

Problems of this kind were compounded by the effects of the Commonwealth legislation on marriage which further confused the issues of marriage and legitimacy.[37] The 1653 Act would seem to have resolved all ambiguities by outlining the new civil procedure and then declaring in a notorious clause that no other form of marriage was valid (Firth and Rait, II, p. 716). The problem was that too many circumstances were required for the validating of a marriage and that too few marriages, 'not one in a hundred' according to one member of parliament, were performed in strict accordance with the complex provisions of the act.[38]

Some couples were secretly married by the Prayer Book ritual (e.g. ERO, Q/S Ba 2/76). Some ministers ignored the act on a scale which brought a rebuke from the Lancashire justices in 1654.[39] The new civil 'registers' (registrars in our usage) sometimes so manhandled the provisions of the act as to invalidate marriages made in good faith, a practice sufficiently widespread to be presented by the Essex grand jury as a major grievance in 1656.[40] National resentment was expressed in the parliament of 1654 and more fully in that of 1656–7 when, after a fierce debate in which it was argued that families were being technically bastardized and inheritances jeopardized on a massive scale, the act was continued only after the repeal of the offending clause.[41] This left at least four forms of marriage valid.

Magisterial harshness, clandestine baptism, neglect of registration and confusion as to who was lawfully married may all have had their effects upon the recording of bastardy. Many continuously kept registers of the period show a decline in registered births or baptisms which may reflect either a declining population, or the withdrawal of certain individuals from the Commonwealth church. If the latter interpretation is valid, then one might suggest that bastard-bearers would be among the first to join such a withdrawal. This obviously happened in some parishes, as was shown in chapter 2 for Earls Colne. A number of bastard-bearers, then, escaped parish registration, though the omissions were small in these nucleated Essex villages with populations of 500 and 1,100 respectively.[42]

Far more worrying is the evidence from the vast parishes of the northwest. The parish of Bolton contained a large weaving town, five chapelries and 16 townships. A degree of general under-registration is discernible in the parish register after 1650. The registration of bastardy, however, had shown a sharp decline even before general under-registration becomes apparent. In the decade 1633–42, an average of some nine bastards per annum were registered in Bolton. From 1643 to 1649, well registered years in general, only six bastards were recorded in all. This selective under-registration, swiftly following the outbreak of local fighting, might indicate that bastard-bearers quickly seized an opportunity to pass registering their bastards. Thereafter there is clear evidence of the evasion of registration

36. ERO, D/P 121/1/0 Great Waltham, cf. ERO, T/R 106, Cold Norton, p. 65.
37. The Directory of 1644 had done nothing to clear up the confusion of the pre-war situation, contenting itself with the statement that it was 'expedient' that marriages be performed by a lawful minister, and that they should not be long delayed after contract. Firth and Rait, I, pp. 599–600. The Manchester classis went further on its own initiative by declaring all persons not publicly married to be automatically suspected of whoredom. *Manchester classis*, p. 48.
38. J. T. Rutt (ed.), *The diary of Thomas Burton* (1828) II, p. 44.
39. LRO, QSR/48 cf. for specific examples QSR/49, QSB/1/1655.
40. ERO, Q/SR 367/28. For similar grievances in Lancashire see LRO, QSR/50, QSB/1/1656.
41. *Burton's Diary* I, pp. xxxix–xl, clxxxiv, II, pp. 38, 44, 67–74; Firth and Rait, II, p. 1139.
42. Estimated from ERO Q/R Th/5 Hearth Tax 1671.

by bastard-bearers. In 1652 and 1658, the Bolton constables presented a total of ten cases of bastardy to the justices, all drawn from the principal township of Bolton. None of them appear in the parish register (of Bolton; LRO, QSR/45, 46, 51).

Rochdale was another huge parish, containing a market town and seven townships. The recorded incidence of bastardy in the registers was very high and a large group of repetitive offenders can be discerned among both fathers and mothers of bastards, some having several base children with the same partner, others offending more promiscuously.[43] The registration of bastards in the parish first falters in 1642–4, recovers its former levels briefly in the later 1640s and then plummets from 1650, only to recover in 1662. The dating is suspiciously neat.

What may have affected bastardy and its registration in Rochdale? First, the parish was within the division of Edmund Hopwood, fiercest of Lancashire justices in the struggle against ungodliness.[44] Hopwood regularly sent bastard-bearers to the house of correction and they might have been well advised to attempt to escape his notice. Secondly, the parish contained a parish church and four chapels, none of which kept separate registers. Mr Bath, the vicar was an active Presbyterian, a regular attender at the Bury classis and one of the nonconformists ultimately ejected in 1662.[45] Bath may have done his best to set the tone of the religious life of the parish, but he was inhibited from attaining a hegemony by a number of factors. The four chapels, spasmodically served by ill-paid curates prior to 1642, were given financial independence in the late 1640s by grants of their tithes under the parliamentary augmentation system. They were further considered worthy of independent parochial status and though this was not actually achieved, their ministers acted as if it were so.[46]

The various ministers known to have served the chapelries during the period 1647–58 seem to have been consistently at loggerheads with the Bury classis and by implication, with Mr Bath. Mr Stott, of Whitworth chapelry, was an Antinomian who defied the classis to its face. Mr Allen of Littleborough was an Episcopalian who had been sequestered from the parish of Prestwich. Mr Pollit of Milnrow was another Episcopalian who rejected the Presbyterian system, while Mr Core of Todmorden was objectionable to the classis less for his principles than for his scandalous life.[47] Clear evidence exists in the Rochdale registers that children were being baptized by these ministers in the chapels throughout the 1650s and subsequently registered in Rochdale, a practice of which there is little trace either before 1645 or after 1662.[48] In 1657, the Bury classis was obliged to

43. Parish registers of Rochdale. Of 272 known mothers of bastards, 1601–40, 67 had more than one base child. Of 332 recorded fathers, 68 fathered more than one base child. For references to the Rochdale register in relation to the national record of illegitimacy, see Laslett (1977), chapter 3.

44. For Hopwood's activities see Wrightson (1974), pp. 165–6.

45. A. G. Matthews, *Calamy revised* (1959), p. 36; Firth and Rait, I, p. 579; H. Fishwick (ed.), *Lancashire and Cheshire church surveys*, I (1878), p. xxiv; *Bury classis*, *passim*; H. H. Howarth (ed.), *The vicars of Rochdale, part I* (1883), pp. 92–108.

46. For augmentations and proposed parochial divisions, see W. A. Shaw (ed.), *The minutes of the committee for the relief of plundered ministers and of the trustees for the maintenance of ministers* (1893, 1897) I, pp. 38, 60, 85, II, pp. 291, 294–5, 302–3; *Church surveys*, pp. 19–21.

47. Stott: *Bury classis*, pp. 48–9, 68, 105, 108–10, 257. He had removed by 1652. Allen: *Bury classis*, pp. 32, 48, 105, 119; *Manchester minutes*, pp. 402–5; *The censures of the church revived* (1659), p. 11. For Thomas Bradshaw, who succeeded him see *Bury classis*, p. 215. Pollit: *Bury classis*, pp. 32, 48–9, 119, 251; *Censure of the church*, p. 11. Core: *Bury classis*, pp. 48–9, 105, 119, 223.

48. The Rochdale registers recorded *baptisms* throughout the period and never births as the Commonwealth legislation required. Explicit statements in registration that a child had been baptized at one of the chapels were very rare before 1645 and after 1662. Only 11 children were registered as baptized in the chapels 1645–9. From 1650 to 1660 the registers make it clear that 91 children were baptized at Milnrow, though registered in Rochdale, 34 at Littleborough, 11 at Todmorden and 6 at Whitworth. It is impossible to say how many were baptized in the chapels and not subsequently registered.

declare irregular the baptisms performed by an unordained Bolton husbandman who had installed himself in Whitworth and was enjoying some popularity there (*Bury classis*, pp, 149, 151). To complicate matters further, Rochdale couples were travelling outside the parish in 1656 to be unlawfully married by a former minister resident in Haslingden (LRO, QSR/50).

How many children, then, were baptized but never registered in a parish where clandestine or irregular sacraments were so abundantly available and how many of them were bastards? A sample of the extensive unsorted sessions files for 1650 and four alternate years to 1658 reveals 13 cases of bastardy from Rochdale.[49] Discounting two cases where it is unclear whether the girl involved was settled in Rochdale, this leaves 11 cases, of which only two appear in the parish register. Even allowing for the possibility that some of these children may have been born in other parishes or put out to nurse elsewhere, one still has strong cause to doubt the reliability of the registers as a source for the incidence of bastardy in this decade. Under-registration or a *selective* under-registration of bastards, then, was evident though marginal in Essex; in Lancashire it may have been chronic.

In the light of such evidence, it is impossible to argue with any confidence that the Interregnum period saw the nadir of English illegitimacy or that the low illegitimacy ratios calculated from parish register evidence for these decades reflect a real decline in the incidence of bastardy attributable to the Puritan triumph. Indeed it is difficult to see how even the most dedicated authorities could have achieved such a result with the instruments at their disposal. The Interregnum saw efforts to toughen and to apply more rigorously the already severe judicial sanctions available for the punishment of bastardy, but the system of social regulation remained too dependent upon local support to be readily usable for the imposition of reform from above. It was more suited to reflect and respond to local needs. Where support for regulatory initiatives existed among the parish officers who mediated between their local communities and the institutions of church and state, then both formal and informal sanctions could indeed be effectively applied, particularly against the poor and the powerless. Such had long been the case. But where such support was absent or had been alienated, the institutions of social regulation were ill-fitted to serve as instruments of repression, at least for more than a very brief period.

The innovations of the Interregnum served largely to alienate and to confuse. Though the parents of bastards liable to be chargeable to the parish continued to be prosecuted, the milder sanctions of the church courts against sexual offenders in general were replaced by a law too savage to be invoked save by the fanatical or the malicious. The Commonwealth marriage legislation added to the confusion surrounding the whole issue of marriage and legitimacy. The baptismal novelties of the Commonwealth church alienated large sections of the populace and resulted in the undermining of the system of registration. However significant may be the decline of English illegitimacy ratios in the seventeenth century as a whole, the apparent nadir of the Interregnum is an illusion.

If we are to achieve a more satisfactory understanding of illegitmacy in early modern England we must move beyond explanations centred upon political or ideological change and shift our attention from the single issue of coercive social control to the broader complex of circumstances surrounding illegitimate conceptions in the period. These circumstances can be studied in some detail from the

49. LRO, QSR/43–52; QSO/2/22–31; QSB/1/336–7, 340–1, 344–5; QSB/1/1652–8.

'examinations' of bastard-bearers made by justices in the course of bastardy proceedings. These documents are the nearest English equivalent, for the early seventeenth century, to French *déclarations de grossesse*. It must be said immediately that they are in some respects inferior to the French records. They survive for a minority of cases, though there is no compelling reason to suppose that they represent untypical cases. More seriously, they lack consistency of form and vary so greatly in the amount of information given that most figures based upon their analysis must be clearly understood to be *minimum* figures. What follows is based upon 64 such examinations from the Essex sessions files 1627–55 and 66 from the Lancashire files 1626–40.[50]

As might be expected, the women examined were on the whole single women, married women or widows being only occasionally involved. No mother examined was of higher social status than that of yeoman's daughter, while in Lancashire 24 per cent and in Essex 61 per cent of the mothers were in fact servants. The fathers of their base children were distributed over every social level, Lancashire fathers were predominantly husbandmen, artisans and craftsmen, Essex fathers, artisans, craftsmen and servants.

In Essex at least 23 per cent of fathers and in Lancashire at least 14 per cent were in a magisterial position vis-à-vis the mothers; that is, they were the masters of the girls, members of the master's kin, or gentlemen. Equally significantly, at least 28 per cent of the Essex and 8 per cent of the Lancashire fathers were fellow servants.

Seventy-five per cent of Essex and 65 per cent of Lancashire cases involved couples living in the same township. Indeed, 48 per cent of the Essex and 23 per cent of the Lancashire conceptions are known to have involved members of the same *household*; that is they were between master and servant, the master's immediate kin and servant, servant and servant or, very rarely, they were incestuous.

Some evidence of sexual promiscuity comes to light. Eleven per cent of the Essex mothers and 18 per cent of those in Lancashire were promiscuous in the limited sense that they confessed to having had sexual relations with more than one man, while 3 per cent of the Essex and 18 per cent of the Lancashire women had had more than one bastard. Of the 12 Lancashire 'repeaters', however, 8 can be distinguished as 'stable' in the sense that their offence was repeated with the same man. Whether such cases represent extra-marital cohabitation is unknown. Lastly, it can be shown, usually from the more detailed examinations, that in at least 28 per cent of the Essex cases the father had promised marriage to the mother, while in Lancashire, marriage was said to have been promised in 17 per cent of the cases and had actually been solemnized after the bastard child's birth in an additional 3 per cent of cases.

On the basis of this evidence, a number of tentative hypotheses may be formed. In cases of first or single bastard conceptions, servant women would appear to have been in a peculiarly vulnerable position. A good deal of master/servant exploitation is discernible. Most pregnancies, however, appear to have been the outcome of love affairs between neighbours or young people living or serving within particular households. Promiscuous behaviour, however broadly defined,

50. ERO, Q/S Ba 2/10–93; LRO, QSB/1/6–239. On occasion, deficiencies in the evidence of the examinations can be supplemented from information given in accompanying recognisances e.g. on social status and residence. The French *déclarations* are described in J. Depauw 'Amour illégitime et société à Nantes au XVIIIe siècle' (1972), p. 1155 ff.

is little in evidence. Some of the girls and men involved were plainly promiscuous, yet the cases in which they were involved are more than balanced by those which reveal that the bastard birth had resulted from a dislocated marital strategy which had misfired. Promises of marriage may have been alleged in defence, and in the majority of such cases there is clear evidence that a 'motion of marriage' was genuinely under way: friends had been consulted, promises made publicly, even banns called. It seems plausible that three types of behaviour may be distinguished in this period. The first is the sexual conduct of clearly delinquent individuals, the second the exploiting of girls by men in a magisterial position and the third the large number of cases which arose from the uncertainties and insecurities which surrounded contemporary courtship and marital customs (cf. the typology of cases attempted in chapter 5, p. 166).

What then of the moralists' 'tricke of youth'? There is little evidence of the existence of widespread sexual promiscuity. May not the fornication denounced by the moralists be largely accounted for by, on the one hand, the exploitation of parish whores and on the other by the well attested commencement of sexual relations between persons engaged in courtship?[51] On the latter issue, Peter Laslett (1971, p. 153) has argued that even rigorous moralists hesitated to denounce sexual relations *after betrothal* as sinful. On the subject of courtship fornications in general John Downame (*Four treatises*, p. 177) argued that many offenders excused themselves, saying that 'they are purposed before they commit this folly, to marry the party whom they have defiled and so make amends.' Such evidence may be supported by the frequency with which persons accused of fornication or incontinence in the church courts pleaded in their defence either a formal contract of marriage or a private determination to marry.[52] While the church courts left them in no doubt as to the illicit nature of their actions, the sanctions imposed were light and varied considerably between archdeaconries (Marchant, 1969, p. 137). Bridal pregnancy, of course, might subsume both the commencement of sexual relations after either formal or informal determinations to marry and cases in which the discovery of pregnancy governed the actual choice of partner and decision to marry.[53] Whichever the case in particular instances and little as we yet know of contemporary courtship practices, it is clear that they permitted a degree of sexual contact which was ill-defined at the level of normative prescription and which often extended to full sexual intercourse. It is perhaps upon this penumbral area that we must focus attention if we are to achieve a fuller understanding of the factors which could erode general restrictions upon sexual behaviour.

Further evidence can be provided by the closer examination of both bastardy and other sexual offences within a single village.[54] In the parish of Burnham-on-Crouch in Essex, 15 illegitimate children are known to have been conceived in the years 1626–46. These conceptions were not evenly distributed over the period, seven of them being concentrated in the two years 1633 and 1634. All 15 cases are

51. P. E. H. Hair, 'Bridal pregnancy in rural England in earlier centuries' (1966); Hair, 'Bridal pregnancy in earlier rural England further examined' (1970).
52. For frequent examples in a single year of court business, see *Archdeacon's court*, pp. 15, 33, 34, 52, 75, 91, 160, 165, 183, 205–15, 211, 220.
53. See the interesting discussion of this issue in J.-L. Flandrin, 'Marriage tardif et vie sexuelle: discussions et hypothèses de recherche' (1972), pp. 1373–4.
54. The discussion of Burnham is based on the records cited in note 50 above, supplemented by the court book of the manor of Burnham with Mangapp, ERO, D/DGe M 170, and the justices' reports on the dearth of 1630–31, PRO, S.P. 16 182/67, 188/93.

revealed in the parish register, 5 also appearing in the records of the church courts and two in the sessions files.

These illegitimate conceptions may be set in the context of other known sexual offences. In the same period, 25 prenuptial conceptions are revealed by the register and act books, to which may be added 6 cases of prenuptial fornication brought to the church courts which are not known to have resulted in a conception. A further 9 cases of adultery or fornication, 4 of 'living incontinently together' and one of incest appear in the church court records which are distinct from the cases of bridal pregnancy or bastardy. These offences were more evenly spread over the period than the cases of bastardy, but again show a tendency to be concentrated in 1633–4. Of the total of 60 known sexual offences, 23 are crowded into these two years. How can this extraordinary concentration be explained?

The evidence does not appear to have been biased by either uneven record survival or related institutional factors. The bulk of the evidence comes from the register and from the ecclesiastical court records, both of which are good over the whole period to 1640. Even if we restrict attention to the years for which all sources are available, 1626–40, 23 out of 41 cases belong to 1633–4. There was an episcopal visitation in 1634, but so there were in 1627 and 1637. Can the misdemeanours be attributed to the repetitive offences of a group of delinquent individuals? No repetitive bastard-bearers appear in this period. A handful of sexual offenders do occur in more than one of the other categories of offence, but their activities were not concentrated in the years of major interest. Other influences may be more important.

The years 1632–5 saw a flurry of marital activity in Burnham, 40 marriages being registered in those years as against 28 in 1628–31 and 27 in 1636–9. The year 1633, the first year for which the register supplies the previous marital status of all marriage partners, would appear to have been a year of particular opportunity for single men and single women making first marriages. Various factors may have affected this increasing activity on the marriage market. We may be witnessing the arrival at marriageable age of an early seventeenth-century baby boom, though a gap in registration in the early years of the century makes it impossible to test this hypothesis. Again, 1631 had seen heavy mortality among adult women and though direct links between deaths in that year and later marriages are not apparent, the marriage market may have been subtly affected. Marriage decisions do not seem to have been influenced by particular activity on the manorial land market, but a possible influence may have been the economic hardship of the harvest crisis of 1630–31, which did affect the area badly and may have led to the delaying of marriages and a subsequent flurry of activity. It may be noted here that in the parish of Terling the peak of bastard births at the turn of the sixteenth and seventeenth centuries was similarly associated with a burst of marital activity after a lull during the economic crisis of the late 1590s (see above, chapter 5).

To what extent might activity on the marriage market have stimulated extra-marital sexual activity in Burnham? Statements in church court cases, together with the record of bridal pregnancy make it plain that sexual intercourse or 'living together incontinently' after betrothal or in the course of marriage entry were common enough in Burnham. Moreover, many offences may be linked to the influence of the marriage market. Over the whole period, we have 60 distinct sexual offences which may be examined using register and church court records. Of these cases, 35, 58 per cent, may be definitely linked to marital activity: the 31 instances of prenuptial pregnancy or fornication, an incestuous marriage and three cases of bastardy, one in which marriage was alleged to have been promised and two in which girls appear to have 'shopped around' before marrying, their first children being subsequently stigmatized as base. In a further 5 cases, 8 per cent, circumstantial evidence would suggest that the offenders were probably involved in the marriage market, since one or other of the partners married within a year after the offence. A further two cases, linked by a single man (the recent death of his wife may have added to his attractions): one girl committed fornication with him, another lived incontinently with him and bore his child. Of the remaining 18 cases, 9 were cases of adultery, one of fornication between master and servant, while of 8 bastardy cases no further information is forthcoming. We have, however, a definite 58 per cent and a probable 67 per cent of sexual offences in the village over two decades linked to the stimulation of local marital opportunities.

In the light of this evidence and of that presented in the foregoing discussion, one may formulate a number of hypotheses about illegitimacy in early modern England. It may be reasserted first of all that the marital and domestic institutions of the society imposed a high degree of restraint upon the reproductive capacity of the population, a restraint which was underpinned by the teachings of the church and by the harshness of the informal and formal sanctions which might be invoked against sexual delinquents. Secondly, it seems possible that an easing of the internal social controls upon sexual activity may, except in the case of a minority of repetitive sexual delinquents, have been associated with improvements in the climate of marital opportunities in particular localities. Given the expense and shame involved in a bastard birth, the harshness with which chargeable bastardy might be treated by neighbourhood or justice, one would expect caution and the avoidance of the risk of pregnancy to have been paramount.

Yet in the shadow area surrounding marriage entry, where norms became blurred and risks were reduced, might not sexual restrictions have been loosened among those sections of the population perhaps influenced less by property transactions and parental wishes than by personal compatibility in their choice of partners and enjoying courtship customs which allowed a considerable degree of physical contact? Some of those whose age and circumstances placed them within a local pool of eligibles may have commenced sexual relations with a chosen partner, others may have 'shopped around' less cautiously. Most would eventually have married, some of the brides being pregnant, others may have been swept dangerously far on a tide of expectation, only to find themselves stranded by ill-judgement or ill-fortune. In years of good, or improving marriage opportunities, might there not have been significantly more sexual activity among the eligibles within a parish and significantly more risk of resultant bastardy where anticipated marriages failed to take place?

If this was indeed the case, then the illegitimacy ratio may be interpreted as an index of the degree of disjunction between socially acceptable premarital sexual activity and particular marital opportunities. It might be expected to be at its highest when marital opportunities existed and were perhaps improving, but where marked insecurities dogged the marital strategies of particular individuals or of particular sections of the population. Examples of the delays which could interrupt or the hard realities which could pre-empt desired matches lie readily to hand. Marriage might be delayed until a term of service was completed, till 'friends' agreed, it might be pre-empted by death, impressment, removal or the hostility of the neighbourhood, interrupted by the necessity of securing housing, a settlement, employment or land.[55] For a large proportion of the population, for the servants, smallholders and craftsmen who figure so largely in bastardy cases, such insecurities must have loomed large even at the best of times. It may be worth considering how far persistent regional variations in illegitimacy ratios can be attributed to the effects of local economic or social structural peculiarities upon the proportion of the population able to marry and upon the security of courtship and marital strategies.

A number of supplementary points may be introduced. First, if the above hypotheses are correct, then bastard-bearers may be expected to have their first base child at approximately the average age of first marriage for women in a given parish, whatever that age may happen to be. There is, in fact, some evidence that this was the case. Secondly, while a degree of individual sexual delinquency may be regarded as normal in any given community, those women whose marital bargaining position was peculiarly weak, perhaps for reasons of poverty or low family prestige, may have been peculiarly vulnerable to sexual exploitation, to being identified by the neighbourhood as whores and subsequently conforming to that role. Such processes may well have been facilitated by membership of particular families and may help to account for the persistent sexual delinquency observed in certain families over several generations (see above, chapters 3 and 5). Thirdly, while occasional bastards attributable to individual delinquency, magisterial exploitation or marital misfortune may be fairly constant elements in English illegitimacy in this period, the major national peak in illegitimacy ratios at the turn of the sixteenth and seventeenth centuries and smaller local peaks in other years have more complex causes.

The explanation suggested here is that they resulted from the superimposition on the pattern of occasional bastardy of larger numbers of cases resulting from the dislocation of courtships during the marriage booms which followed upon the restricted marital opportunities of years of economic crisis. Finally, it seems possible that the social control of bastardy was most effective not so much in the direct punishment of offenders as in influencing bastardy indirectly by placing firmer restrictions on local marital opportunities. Where marital opportunities were closely controlled, the courtship sexuality released by marital opportunity may have been subtly restrained. Such control may have been exercised by parish notables either informally, by virtue of their economic power, or more formally through manipulation of the newly established Poor Laws and settlement laws. In so far as the declining bastardy ratios of the seventeenth century were affected by the exercise of power in society, it seems likely to have been at the level of the village community and at the hands of local notables whose power and willingness to influence the behaviour of their neighbours were enhanced by the related social and institutional changes of the period.

These hypotheses remain unproven but are introduced in order to shift attention from fluctuations in the perennial hostility of moralists and magistrates, towards influencing individual decisions in extra-marital sexual behaviour. In his original discussion of illegitimacy over time, Peter Laslett suggested that the illegitimacy ratio did not appear to be an indicator of social demoralization. It is the argument of this chapter that illegitimacy was indeed the product not of demoralization but of the very vigour of the system. It was part of the price that was paid, by the poor and the vulnerable, for maintaining the vitality of the marital and domestic institutions which characterized English society in the past.

55. *Archdeacon's court*, pp. 52, 53, 160, 165; LRO, QSB/1/66/49, QSB/1/126/92; ERO, Q/SR 181/97, D/AC A 25, f. 198v.

7

Aspects of sexual behaviour in nineteenth-century Scotland

Christopher Smout

The main purpose of this chapter is to establish what differences there appear to have been between social groups in patterns of sexual behaviour outside marriage in nineteenth-century Scotland. It is not, quite honestly, a task which a historian can expect to do well without a great deal more work on detailed primary sources than I have undertaken: careful study of such demographic sources as the census enumeration returns and the original registrar's books of births and marriages could, for instance, greatly extend our understanding of the social context of illegitimacy and bridal pregnancy. In other directions – for instance for work on the details of courtship – sufficiently detailed information for the nineteenth century can probably never be found to carry the description much beyond the unsatisfactory outline presented here. But even a partial investigation can make us aware of the complexities of the patterns of human behaviour involved, and perhaps form a starting point for discussion and future research. It is sad (but currently inevitable) that research into sexual history should generally appear to be either prurient or trivial: if social history aims to reflect what is important in people's lives, sexual history deserves much more serious and central attention from social historians than it has had so far.[1]

The sexual ideal to which the acknowledged spokesman of Victorian Scotland paid lip-service was the traditional teaching of the Christian churches: all sexual intercourse before marriage was wrong, and all sexual intercourse after marriage except with the spouse was worse. Everyone knew that contemporary practice fell short of this ideal: the towns were full of prostitutes and illegitimacy, from 1855 when the figures were first collected, did not fall below 8 or 9 per cent of live births until the 1890s. The Church of Scotland had in the pre-industrial past made considerable efforts to compel society to conform to its teaching: in the seventeenth century, the local kirk sessions had regularly punished fornicators and adulterers by public appearances on the cutty-stool, culprits being made to stand

1. This paper first appeared in A. MacLaren (ed.), *Social class in Scotland, past and present* (Edinburgh, 1976); I am grateful to the publisher John Donald for permission to reprint it here. In the course of the research I incurred many debts. I am grateful for help from various friends and colleagues, but especially to Berrick Saul; to Ailsa Maxwell and Judith Gillespie of the Scottish Historical Demography Unit (Department of Economic History); to Emily Lyle, Alan Bruford, Donald Macdonald and John Macinnes of the School of Scottish Studies, Edinburgh University; and to Paul Thompson and Thea Vigne of the Oral History Unit, Essex University. They are not of course responsible for any errors of fact or interpretation here. I am also grateful to Kenneth Boyd, whose admirable Edinburgh (1973) doctoral thesis, 'The theological presuppositions of Scottish church pronouncements on sex, marriage and the family, 1850–1914', was finished at the same time as this paper, but of which I have made little direct use. His work is certainly exempt from the strictures of this paragraph. Since the completion of the paper there has appeared James Bulloch and A. C. Drummond, *The church in Victorian Scotland, 1843–1874* (1975), which has a section on these matters. I should perhaps add that a further consideration of the Scottish illegitimacy statistics by myself (embodying work on age-specific illegitimacy rates) appeared in M. W. Flinn *et al.*, *Scottish population history from the seventeenth century to the nineteen-thirties* (1977). The paper reprinted here was subject to critical comment and reply in the *Scottish Journal of Sociology* (1977): see Ian Carter, 'Illegitimate births and illegitimate inferences', and T. C. Smout, 'Illegitimacy – a reply'.

Sabbath after Sabbath in the face of the congregation until their sin was purged. If kirk discipline usually fell upon the weak, it did not altogether spare the powerful: there were several cases of landowners obliged to submit along with the peasant. In the eighteenth century, despite the experience of Robert Burns and his friends, the efforts of the church to secure public humiliation increasingly gave way to commutation, and sinners paid according to a more-or-less fixed tariff for their misdemeanours.[2] By the nineteenth century public punishment was rare but not unknown: it survived, for instance, in Lewis at mid century.[3] Private rebuke by the session, however, was still common enough in cases where a couple asked for marriage or baptism and subsequent inquiry revealed 'ante-nuptial fornication'.[4] We do not know if the church in the past had been more successful in imposing its standards than it was in Victorian times. But by then there were several different norms tacitly accepted in different social strata, all at variance with the church's ideal, though probably not totally uninfluenced by it. It is these we must examine.

1 The middle and upper classes: chastity and prostitution

It was the middle and upper classes who in some ways showed the greatest degree of ambivalence towards Christian teaching, owing to their frank espousal of the double standard. It does not, however, seem possible to make any very clear distinction between the moral norms of the upper classes (i.e. the landed families) and the bourgeois (i.e. professional, commercial and business families) in their expectations of the sexual behaviour of women of their own rank. For women, the Christian model appears to have been fully and elaborately followed. Cases of illegitimacy among upper-class and middle-class women were extremely rare. Of course, they had better opportunities for concealment, though until the coming of the great orphanage societies at the end of the century these were limited by the problem of disposing of the bastard: the evidence of the medical profession is, however, unequivocal that middle-class women were almost never the mothers of illegitimate children, and, equally, were almost never pregnant before their marriages (see below, p. 204). Indeed, the whole institution of Victorian bourgeois courtship, with its elaborate rules of chaperone and its romantic image of the undefiled and innocent maid, must have made it extremely difficult even for engaged couples to get to bed before they got to church. Once married, the bourgeois girl was expected to be unquestionably faithful: the sanctions against the adulteress, the difficulty of divorce and the gross unfairness of the law in respect of divorced women are well known.

For the male, however, lip-service paid to the Christian ideal was certainly not matched universally by the same real expectations of perpetual ante-nuptial chastity, and possibly not of post-marital faithfulness either. As one moralist put it: 'It appears to be almost taken for granted, as a matter of course, that young men should be found in a greater or lesser degree, giving way.'[5] For all that the teaching of religion demanded equal standards, the disapproval of the male peer group was evidently lacking. Doctors in Victorian times still occasionally

2. See G. D. Henderson, *The Scottish ruling elder* (1935).
3. Joseph Mitchell, *Reminiscences of my life in the Highlands* (1883), I (1971), p. 237
4. A. A. MacLaren, 'Presbyterianism and the working class in a mid nineteenth-century city' (1967).
5. Ralph Wardlaw, *Lectures on female prostitution* (1842), pp. 57–8.

recommended fornication on medicinal grounds for those of their own sex: to do so for women would have been unthinkable.[6]

Since the unmarried bourgeois male was thus disbarred from any sexual contact with girls of his own class, he had to seek it from girls in the class below him. Again, there was nothing new or specifically Victorian in this. Edinburgh, not without prostitutes even in the seventeenth century, took a turn for the worse between the 1760s and the 1780s: William Creech reported that whereas in 1763 there had been only five or six brothels and few whores, twenty years later there were 'twenty times' more brothels and 'every quarter of the city and suburbs was infested' with whores.[7] In the countryside the landowners or tacksmen might take mistresses from the daughters of their tenantry. In eighteenth-century Lewis it was even said that the peasant girls reckoned it was an honour to have a daughter by a gentleman as it made them more sought in marriage by their own class afterwards. In the Lowlands comfortable arrangements could also be made:

> Lord Crawfurd had a highland lass or mistress, a bonnie nymph, from Arran. Auld Auchinhane reported my Lord bairned her and [being tired of her] he garred Willie Orr, his servant to kipple with her, and take the wyte of his lordship's wane. Therefore Lord Crawford set Willie up as a farmer . . . and tochered Jean, the issue of his amour.[8]

What was perhaps new in the nineteenth century was not the fact of inter-class sexual contact, but the degree of anxiety, guilt and furtiveness that now accompanied it.[9] It would be interesting to know exactly why. Perhaps it was a reflection of the separation of classes themselves: if society moved to a polarity in which there was less and less day-to-day contact between the classes, the crossing of class barriers for sexual purposes might itself set up neuroses which would perhaps not have troubled Lord Crawfurd and his nymph. Again, the cult of respectability and the attendant spread of evangelical religious sentiments in Scotland, with their concomitant insistence on the importance of a 'lively sense of sin' in an individual's relationship with God, might have created extreme personal tensions in young men; they might be ground between religious prohibitions and the kind of peer group tolerance which amounted to equally lively expectations of extra-marital sexual behaviour.

There certainly appears to have been a greater fear of venereal disease, signified partly by the opening of Magdalene hospitals, in Edinburgh in 1797, in Glasgow about 1815 (Wardlaw, p. 138), partly by the amount of medical literature on the

6. William Logan, *The great social evil* (1871), p. 230. No doubt the usual view of the medical profession was for a long period the same as that of the former director of the student health centre in Edinburgh in the 1960s, encapsulated in the following report in the Edinburgh University medical students' journal *Synapse* 17, no. 2, p. 11: 'Dr Verney replied that to prescribe the pill for unmarried girls would be contrary to the dictates of his conscience and to the welfare of the community. . . . He felt that it was the duty of women to maintain moral standards in sexual matters and deplored the current *mores* of the university. It is necessary to the male students to prove their manhood by the experience of sex. Earlier they had found this sexual outlet outside the university but now found it within the university, with an associated rise in illegitimacy and venereal disease in the student population. This Dr Verney attributed to a decline of moral principles among the young women – in his day young women came to the university for education, not for fornication. In the tense and claustrophobic silence which followed Dr Verney's last comment the sense of most of what he had said previously was forgotten.'

7. *Statistical account of Scotland* VI (1793), p. 612.

8. Paisley Central Library: Andrew Crawfurd, 'Cairn of Lochwinnoch Matters', 21, p. 305. I am grateful to Dr Emily Lyle for this reference.

9. See Alex Comfort, *The anxiety makers* (1967).

subject, and partly by the debate on the Contagious Diseases Act. This anxiety might have been based on a real increase in the danger to public health: prostitutes who formed the pool of infection were almost exclusively urban, and as urbanization developed, prostitution and VD could be expected to grow in proportion. On the other hand the exacerbated fear of sexually transmitted disease might not have been so rationally grounded, but may have derived only from the growing psychological anxiety about extra-marital sex. Moralists liked to observe that syphilis was God's judgement on the fornicator and the adulterer (for example, Wardlaw, p. 71).

There is some indication that even in the nineteenth century the aristocracy and landed classes were less smitten by shame than the middle classes. The whores who flocked to Musselburgh races were openly welcomed by the young blades of the turf, and Dr Tait of Edinburgh reported:

> As an encouragement to brothel-keepers, some noblemen of the highest rank and title prefer taking up their quarters in a house of ill-fame rather than in a respectable hotel, and unblushingly visit all the 'lions' in company with the keeper and one or more of her ladies. Only last year, it was currently reported that a minister in the west of Scotland let his manse, during the entertainments at Eglington Castle, to a certain nobleman for the purpose of lodging his concubines.[10]

In economic terms at least such men had nothing to lose if they chose not to behave in a 'respectable' way; and their peer group did not condemn them as it would have done if (for example) they had been caught cheating at cards. On the other hand a young or insecure professional man might have to behave much more circumspectly, not necessarily because his peer group would disapprove of the action in itself but because to flaunt his fornication openly would be to challenge the canons of religion, and that challenge would not be approved by the peer group. A man discovered to be living with a mistress could not be thought respectable, and would be vulnerable to economic sanctions in his trade or profession. Thus a middle-class man might suffer from the social anxiety of being found out by his seniors, or betters, as well as the personal anxiety created by any private moral tensions. 'Victorian hypocrisy' was created by all these contradictions; it must have been a miserable thing for the unfortunate hypocrite to live with.

Middle-class men could only get their extra-marital sex from a working-class girl by persuasion or payment: in moral terms, the former was seduction, the latter prostitution. By the middle of the nineteenth century, they were unlikely to come into contact with many working-class girls on whom they could exercise their powers of persuasion except domestic servants living in the household. Servants, indeed, were vulnerable to sexual exploitation. On the one hand, they were regarded by their middle-class mistresses as frail beings, in great danger of being seduced from outside by working-class males from pimps to postmen. In many Edinburgh villas in the suburbs of Morningside and Newington the only barred window is on the maid's room. Furthermore, it was held that if they were kept from men their minds would be more concentrated upon their work. One critical observer of these views put it like this:

10. William Tait, *Magdalenism, an inquiry into the extent, causes and consequences of prostitution in Edinburgh* (1842), p. 199.

> The cry everywhere is 'No followers!' as if the young serving girl had no title to love or to be loved, as if all her cares were to be concentrated in sweeping carpets, making beds, cleaning, ironing and responding to a thousand daily tugs at the bell, as if it were her sole duty to waste existence in ministering to the wants and comfort of others, and be but a bank herself.

But even he could go on:

> Before you retire to rest lock the doors with your own hand, and deposit the keys upon your toilet table, otherwise, while enjoying the blessings of repose above you may not know what junketings are going on below. Precaution is all the more necessary when the maid's sleeping-room is remote from yours. Satan is never busier than at night; under its dark shadow he leads thousands to destruction.[11]

Young girls thus systematically deprived as far as possible of all contact with men of their own age and class were in a situation of misery in which they might easily fall for the blandishments of any male in the house. On the other hand if a servant became pregnant, or even if she made allegations about any man in the family, she was virtually certain to be dismissed without a reference and become unemployable. This was why so many prostitutes were former domestic servants: for example four fifths of the applications to the Edinburgh Magdalene Institute between 1855 and 1860 had once been domestic servants (List).

Prostitutes, however, were an extremely small percentage of the total number of domestic servants, and servants were a very large percentage of total females in employment. It is easy to be misled. We cannot tell how large a proportion of servants were seduced by their employers' families, or how many middle-class men got their extra-marital experience in this way. An investigation by the Registrar General in 1883 showed that almost half Scottish illegitimate births were to 'domestic servants' – but this includes very large numbers in rural areas sleeping in farm kitchens and elsewhere under no supervision at all (see p. 201), so one certainly cannot assume the majority of fathers were middle class.

Recent research on domestic servants in Edinburgh around 1870 suggests that while the 'general' servants of Newington in artisan or petty bourgeois households had at least as many bastards as women in other occupational groups, the 'higher' servants of the commercial or professional middle-class families living in St Andrew's Parish in the New Town had appreciably fewer. The case is not quite conclusive, because in the middle-class parish there might have been more pressure on the respectable servant to leave the area and have her illegitimate child elsewhere. Perhaps, in any case, conditions changed over time. The oral history evidence available at Essex University from interviews with Scots brought up before 1918 suggests that by the early twentieth century domestic servants were no longer cooped up in the way they had been, that they then had plenty of opportunities to meet young men of their own class, and that risk of seduction by the middle-class males of the household was not a prominent feature of their lives.[12] There was also, we must remember, an element of danger to the middle-class man if his adventure was discovered, in the sense that familial relations

11. See Alfred C. C. List, *The two phases of the social evil* (1861).
12. Elaine A. Corsie, 'Domestic servants in selected parishes of Edinburgh, 1871–91'. Also Essex Oral History Unit (OHU).

between the sexes in a respectable household would be unbearably strained if a brother or a son (let alone a husband) was known to be a fornicator. The evidence is inconclusive, but on the principle that it is a foolish bird that fouls its own nest, we may perhaps assume that the majority of middle-class sexual adventures were paid for, and took place outside the home.

Prostitutes were of many kinds, and commentators ranged them on a scale that varied roughly with the health, youth and beauty of the girls. At the one extreme was the kept mistress of the rich man maintained on private premises: at the other was the poor creature raddled with disease in a low-class brothel visited by soldiers. Virgins were the monopoly of the rich, a fact probably better explained by fetishism than by the much higher probability of their freedom from disease (Wardlaw, p. 94; Logan, p. 110). Child prostitution existed: Dr Tait knew of patients admitted to the Lock Hospital suffering from venereal disease at the age of nine and ten. The majority of prostitutes were in the later teens. Tait examined the records of 1,000 cases admitted to the Lock Hospital from 1835 to about 1840. The age breakdown of the prostitutes was as follows:

	%
under 15	4.2
15 – 20	66.2
20 – 25	19.9
25 – 30	6.9
30 – 35	1.6
35 – 40	0.6
over 40	0.6

But he qualified these figures with the comment that 'the above gives a very inadequate representation of the extent to which juvenile prostitution prevails, as the venereal disease amongst girls from ten to fifteen is much more common than the records of the Lock Hospital would indicate' (Tait, pp. 32–3; also Logan, pp. 96–7, 118).

The background from which the girls came was mixed. Former domestic servants were a very large category: so, too, were ill-paid or sweated female workers (seamstresses, milliners, tambourers, Dundee millworkers and the like). Shetland and Highland servants were said by Tait to be more prone to take to prostitution than others: perhaps they were vulnerable to seduction because they had least experience of the irresponsible urban male who could not be held accountable for his actions by social pressure, as a man would have been in the communities from which they came (see below, p. 213). The squalor in which prostitutes lived was often terrible, and Tait believed that 'perhaps not less than a fifth or a sixth part of all who had embraced a life of prostitution die annually' (Tait, pp. 277–8).

One fundamental distinction which commentators made was between the 'sly prostitute', or part-timer, and the professional. It was the latter whose numbers were more susceptible to economic pressure, and increased whenever the trade cycle threw numbers of millhands out of work or when the price for sweated labour sank desperately below subsistence. The numbers of prostitutes were in any case extremely hard to calculate. Tait in 1842 believed that in Edinburgh there were about 800 whole-time prostitutes, of whom a quarter were living privately and the remainder in about 200 public brothels (mainly in the Old

Town): in addition, he thought there were almost 1,200 sly prostitutes many of whom operated from 'houses of assignation' where a room could be hired and no questions asked. When surveying the cities of Edinburgh and Glasgow in 1870, William Logan thought that changes in the law had reduced the number of known brothels in the former to about 85, with a similar fall in the latter: 'The business is conducted with less ostentation and attractiveness to the outside world.'

Who were the customers of the prostitutes? Certainly they were all sorts and conditions of men, not just the middle class. The comparatively shameless behaviour of the aristocracy at one end of the social spectrum and the association of soldiers and seamen with harlots at the other we have already noted. Some observers classified brothels into first, second and third class, like railway carriages. William Logan, whose experience of the problem lay mainly in Glasgow, was one of these. First-class brothels, he said, were supported by 'noblemen, wealthy merchants, military officers, sea captains and *gentlemen* who move in the higher circles of society'. Second-class brothels 'are chiefly supported by men in business, clerks, warehousemen, shopmen, etc.', and by many medical students and some theological students. Third-class houses 'are chiefly frequented by persons from the country, mechanics, apprentices, soldiers and sailors' (Logan, pp. 107–10).

Dr Tait (p. 3) in Edinburgh gave a rather similar picture; on the one hand he stressed the upper and middle class importance in the market:

> In summer, for example, there are a third part fewer [prostitutes] than in winter; and in autumn the number is still further diminished. During these seasons, the decrease may be proportioned to the decrease of the wealthier portion of the community who then seek a residence in the country, and to the diminished number of students at the University.

On the other hand he drew attention to dancing schools and dancing parties 'of a particularly base description' which ended in the couples going to a house of assignation: 'the individuals who frequent them . . . consist of sewing-girls, sly prostitutes, and shop and trades' lads' (p. 185). John Dunlop, too, drew attention to the working-class brothel goers, and described the High Street prostitutes as 'the chief relievers of the pockets of the operatives on pay night'.[13] In Stranraer, one of the few country towns with a problem of prostitution, the customers were Irish navvies (List, p. 4).

Nevertheless, it is evident that middle-class observers were worried by the numbers of their own kind who were tempted inside. No one, of course, knows how many. There is a modern Edinburgh tradition that the brothels of Rose Street were never so busy as in the week of the General Assembly of the Church of Scotland. It was doubtless a calumny in recent times, but it can be traced back in documentary form at least to 1814 when a magistrate in the capital wrote to his business partners that 'I have the Police Court at present, and I will be needed very much to keep the whores and Ministers in order during the sitting of the Assemblies.'[14]

It was only too likely that the clergy were not immune from the frailties of the flesh which afflicted their other middle-class colleagues. The habit of depending

13. *The autobiography of John Dunlop* (1932), p. 99. This refers to the 1830s.

14. Scottish Record Office, RH, 15, 1856 at 20 May 1814: letter from Neil Ryrie, Edinburgh agent of Stein, Dewar and Co. distillers (Alloa) to the partners. I am indebted to Mr R. B. Weir for this reference.

on prostitution was formed among students living without parental control who were obliged both to delay marriage until their training was complete and to eschew all overtly sexual contacts (however partial) with girls of their own class. It put them in a situation from which not all would have the strength of character to escape unscathed.

2 The working class: the pattern of bastardy

The possibility that at least some sections of the working class might in important respects have different habits of sexual behaviour from those of the middle class which we have attempted to describe first became a matter of public debate following the coming of civil registration in 1855, and the subsequent publication of the illegitimacy ratio (i.e. the proportion of illegitimate births to total births; the illegitimacy fertility *rate*, the number of illegitimate births per thousand unmarried women of childbearing age, was not calculated by the early Scottish Registrars General). Most commentators before then, while being aware of 'improvement marriages' and even 'illicit unions' among the working class, seemed to associate them with industrialization, and contrasted them with older peasant virtues of 'virtuous attachment' and long and thrifty patience before the wedding.[15]

To understand the evidence of the sexual *mores* of the working class it is first necessary to follow the debate on illegitimacy. The first publication of the Registrar General to deal with illegitimacy appeared in 1858 and contradicted such early and complacent preconceptions: not only did Scotland appear to have an exceptionally high percentage of her children born before marriage, but the worst areas were the counties of the northeast and the southwest Lowlands where rural virtues might be expected to be deeply ingrained.

Scottish illegitimacy statistics did show two striking features. One was that the proportion of illegitimate births to total births was higher in the countryside than in the towns, instead of being very much lower as it was in many European countries. The other was the wide variety of regional experience, especially of rural areas. In the 1860s and 1870s, with the national average running at 9.3 per cent of total births illegitimate, it was rare for Ross and Cromarty, for example, to touch 5 per cent, and for Orkney and Shetland to reach 6 per cent: but Banff, Aberdeenshire, Moray and Kincardine in one corner of Scotland, and Wigtown, Kirkudbright and Dumfriesshire in the other, seldom had less than 14–18 per cent of their total births illegitimate.

Table 7.1 demonstrates some of these points, and also the convergence of most areas towards the Scottish national average in the years after the First World War.[16] Wigtownshire is the exception to this rule. It was these self-evident contrasts, combined with the feeling of national disgrace which was not easily dissipated, that gave rise to a lengthy discussion of the causes of illegitimacy, and ultimately, of the sexual *mores* of the Scottish working class – or, rather, mainly of its rural component. It began as an early example of a fruitful dialogue between moralists, mainly represented by the churches, and statistical experts in the Registrar General's Office.

15. e.g. Thomas Chalmers, *Christian and civic economy of large towns (1838–42)*, XVI, pp. 107–8.

16. These and similar statistics have been compiled by the Scottish Historical Demography Unit, operating with SSRC funds at the University of Edinburgh.

Table 7.1: Illegitimacy ratios in Scotland, 1861–1925

	1861/5	1871/5	1881/5	1891/5	1901/5	1911/15	1921/5
Banff	16.62	16.53	13.62	13.70	12.61	13.44	12.55
Berwick	10.75	10.60	10.57	10.33	9.89	10.28	8.39
E. Lothian	9.60	8.71	7.76	6.99	6.00	7.08	6.30
Inverness	7.96	8.40	7.59	7.42	7.26	8.74	7.89
Orkney	5.56	5.90	6.50	6.85	5.24	6.82	6.79
Perth	10.87	10.18	9.65	9.12	6.67	9.61	8.85
Ross & Cromarty	4.24	4.57	4.78	4.79	4.30	7.10	5.79
Wigtown	15.65	15.79	16.25	15.49	13.18	15.71	15.62
Zetland	4.63	4.57	5.16	4.33	4.02	5.78	6.48
Scotland (total)	9.79	9.09	8.27	7.41	6.50	7.21	6.78

Some of the alleged causes were easy to refute. Those who believed bastardy was correlated with illiteracy and could be cured by education were confounded by the Registrar General's demonstration that the least literate Highland counties (like Ross and Cromarty) had the lowest proportion of illegitimate births, while in Banff, Aberdeenshire and Dumfriesshire over 95 per cent of the men and between 85 and 95 per cent of the women were able to sign their names.[17] Those who attributed it all to drink were confounded to be told that in Banffshire almost all the illegitimacy occurred in the agricultural community and virtually none among the fishermen, although 'our country labourers and small farmers are as free from intemperance as our fishermen are from abstinence or even moderation.'[18] The justice of this observation is suggested by a glance at the illegitimacy statistics of Banffshire, 1861–5: in the deeply rural inland parishes of Inveravon with Auchbrek, Tomintoul and Kirkmichael, out of 553 births, 107 were illegitimate (19 per cent), while in the fishing and rural parishes of Cullen and Seafield, out of 639 births only 69 were illegitimate (11 per cent).[19]

Other observers attributed the black record of the northeast to orgies between farm servants at the annual hiring markets, and with some reason as it was possible to prove that the peaks of illegitimate births in Banffshire came nine months after the fairs: but hiring markets no less demonstrably Bacchanalian occurred throughout the rural Lowlands, even in counties with half the bastardy rate of Banff.[20] In the southeast of Scotland some attributed it to the bondager system, whereby a hind, or ploughman, was obliged to provide an able-bodied female to work alongside him at his job, and if he did not have a wife or daughter might hire any strong girl and share his working life, at least, with her: but the bondager system did not exist in the northeast (*4th report RC Agric. 1867*, pp. 53, 55–9; Seton, pp. 38–9). Some attributed it just to a local excess of females in the population, but in ostensibly virtuous Orkney and Sutherland the surplus was far greater than it was in Banff, Kincardine and Aberdeenshire.[21] Some again

17. *First detailed report . . . of the Registrar General for Scotland* [*1855*]. See also J. M. Strachan, 'Immorality of Scotland', *Scotsman*, 7 June 1870.
18. See *Report of committee on houses for the working class*. Free Church General Assembly Proceedings (henceforth cited as FCGA) 1863.
19. This was calculated by the Scottish Historical Demography Unit at Edinburgh University from civil registration material. See also W. Cramond, *Illegitimacy in Banffshire* (1888), pp. 17–21.
20. Cramond, pp. 25–6; Seton, pp. 12–13, 31, 33. *Fourth report of the Royal Commission on the employment of children, young persons and women in agriculture (1867)*, (henceforth *RC Agric. 1867*), pp. 25–6, 81.
21. *Fifth detailed report . . . of the Registrar General for Scotland* [*1859*]. Seton, pp. 17–18.

attributed it to the evident absence of prostitution in rural areas, but the Registrar General was able to show that in the rural parts of Midlothian and Lanarkshire, with no prostitutes, the illegitimacy rate was for once actually lower than in Edinburgh and Glasgow where they swarmed. And one county that did seem to have a great deal of prostitution for a rural area, Wigtownshire, shared a record in high illegitimacy with Banffshire, where prostitution was almost unknown.[22]

Others invoked race, past religious traditions and even climate, but these were even harder to sustain. How could rainfall be a factor, when Wigtown and Ross shared two of the wettest climates in Scotland and Banff had one of the driest?[23] It was argued that perhaps the northeast had not experienced the Reformation in a sufficiently Presbyterian form and so was lacking in moral fibre: but the south-west was just as bad for bastardy, and had held the very hearth-stones of the Covenanters (Cramond, pp. 48, 52). Some, believing that the Irish and the Highlanders shared a justifiable reputation for chastity, attributed this to a lack of natural force among the Celts. But others objected on the grounds of the Welsh: 'The laxity of morals among the female peasantry of Wales is unhappily notorious.'[24] And what about the Irish navvies, never distinguished in the local traditions of the railway age for their continence or lack of natural force in the parishes through which they passed? And how could this theory account for the Vikings of Orkney and Shetland, with almost as few bastards as the Celts of Ross and Cromarty? It was not easy for Victorians to account for such anomalies: it is not very easy for us.

More sophisticated and interesting were the arguments that hinged on the character of rural housing and the traditions of agricultural work. The simplest of these was the notion that the one-roomed house, so common in Scotland, made it impossible to observe the decencies: a family sleeping in the same room, with or without lodgers from other people's families, could not stay in ignorance for long of the facts of one another's lives. This, as the Society for the Promotion of Social Morality said, was 'a state of things very fitted to destroy delicacy of feeling' (*Report on houses for the working classes*, 1862). Unfortunately for the argument that this led to moral depravity, the Registrar General and others were able to show that the counties with the greatest proportion of one-roomed houses were by no means those with the highest rates of illegitimacy. Industrial areas with much the worst record of bad and overcrowded housing were not worst in respect of illegitimacy rates.[25]

An object of still stronger attack from the churches was the bothy system. Bothies were communal sleeping quarters for unmarried farm servants, often (though certainly not invariably) mere comfortless sheds rigged out with a row of beds, some straw, and the most meagre cooking and sanitary facilities. Most bothies were for males only; some (especially in the Lothians) were for females only; a few (notably in Caithness) were mixed. The objections to the last class were voiced by the Reverend Charles Thomson of Wick:

> Deeds of shame are shamelessly committed in those dens of darkness. . . . He could not tell the Presbytery certain facts he knew regarding these barns,

22. *Second detailed report . . . of the Registrar General for Scotland* [*1856*].
23. *Royal Commission on labour, 1893*, Agricultural Labourer III, Scotland, pp. 104, 113.
24. *Third report RC Agric. 1867*, p. 52. See also Thomas Rees, *Miscellaneous papers on subjects relating to Wales* (1867), pp. 29–36, and Leffingwell, pp. 56–63.
25. *Fourth detailed report . . . of the Registrar General for Scotland* [*1858*]; Cramond, pp. 31–2.

> but he might indicate by stating that it was not only women that congregated there, and that it was a 'shame even to speak of those things that are done of them in secret' [*Report on houses for the working classes*, 1862].

But even in more ordinary circumstances the church found much to object to on bothies. There was the total absence of family life: 'This divine basis of social morality has been swept away' (*Report on houses for the working classes*, 1861). There was the presence of quite young boys of thirteen, fourteen and fifteen under no supervision except from older farm hands. There was the almost complete absence of paternal interest in the life of the bothymen by the farmer, in contrast to the good old days when the gudeman had them all under his eye as they ate together round the farm table. In short, the bothy system let young men loose 'at the very age when the impetuosity of youth abounds', and the consequences were both morally and economically disastrous.[26]

Unfortunately the Registrar General once again expressed scepticism about cause and effect. Though the bothy system might well help to explain why Caithness had a higher illegitimacy rate than Sutherland to the south and Orkney to the north (where the system did not exist), it could not account for the situation in the main bulk of the eastern Lowlands. Bothies went with large farms that had a big labour force, and were especially characteristic of Perth, Angus and Fife, in all of which the illegitimacy rates tended below the national average, although above the level of the Highland zone. Banff, on the other hand, was a county of small farms (an average of 64 acres, compared to 110 acres in Fife and 219 acres in East Lothian): therefore it had comparatively few bothies.[27] How could the bothy system be to blame?

Those who knew Banffshire and the other northeastern counties most intimately began to claim that the root of its peculiarly high illegitimacy rate lay here in the scarcity of accommodation for married farm servants (Cramond, pp. 61–5). There were hardly any cottages attached to the farms. Even married horsemen often had to lodge in a room in the farm or in an outhouse, while their wives and children lived in the nearest town or village some miles away: bachelors and unmarried farm girls almost always did so, and there was abundant employment for the latter in and around the farm. This was the 'chaumer' system: the main difference in social terms between it and the bothy was that the farmhand ate and relaxed in the kitchen with the women instead of with other men in the bothy: there was no more social control in other directions but there was more occasion for social intercourse between the sexes. According to the commentators a tradition of incontinence and illegitimacy grew up because marriages were delayed in this environment. Dr Gerrard of Banff reported how he had discussed the matter with many fathers of illegitimate children in the rural community:

> The great regret of these men had been that, when the first offence occurred they had not the means of making the proper amends by marrying and sheltering the mother and child in a dwelling of their own: nay more they needed no hint to assure me that, if houses could have been readily had, they would in every probability have married early and their children would have been 'born in wedlock' [*Report on houses for the working classes*, 1863].

26. 'Digest of essays on the bothy system' (1843), pp. 133–44.
27. *First detailed report of the Registrar General for Scotland* [*1855*].

Such housing shortages, they said, did not occur among the rural workers in other Lowland east-coast counties to anything like the same degree. An area like the Merse of Berwickshire employed more farm servants per farm, but there were plenty of cottages to which a worker could move when he got married, and, indeed, the bondager system of the Borders might positively encourage marriage by the necessity for a ploughman to find a helpmeet at work. (*4th report RC Agric. 1867*, appendix, part 2, pp. 120–21).

It was an attractive theory, and it was evidently not directly contradicted by the Registrar General. Nevertheless, it was quite wrong to assume that the social conditions of the 'chaumer' system led to late marriage. Table 7.2 shows how, in the late nineteenth century, some of the rural counties married. In the first three, Orkney, Shetland, Ross and Cromarty, marriage for both sexes was distinctly later than for the remainder – but these had very low illegitimacy ratios. In Banff, men married just a little later than in East Lothian or Berwickshire – but women tended to marry just a little earlier. In Wigtownshire, with illegitimacy rates like those of Banff, the mean age of marriage for men was much like Banff, for women much like Berwickshire. It was probably perfectly correct to associate the high illegitimacy figures of the northeast with the absence of familial control, the 'chaumer' system, and the availability of jobs for unmarried female labour whether with children or not – but the association with late marriage was not borne out by the facts.

Table 7.2: Mean age of marriage in selected Scottish Counties, 1861–1901

		1861	1871	1881	1891	1901
Orkney	M	30.17	30.27	30.59	31.28	30.91
	F	27.08	26.68	26.94	26.98	27.96
Shetland	M	29.30	30.18	29.76	31.29	31.51
	F	27.05	27.64	27.30	27.97	29.00
Ross & Cromarty	M	30.85	31.38	31.44	31.46	32.11
	F	26.21	27.00	26.58	27.31	27.71
Banff	M	29.08	29.44	29.05	29.41	29.48
	F	25.89	25.77	25.99	26.30	26.53
E. Lothian	M	28.55	27.97	28.22	28.26	28.33
	F	26.26	26.09	25.76	26.07	26.42
Berwickshire	M	28.79	28.58	28.99	28.24	29.06
	F	26.21	26.18	26.40	26.25	26.90
Wigtownshire	M	29.08	29.51	28.62	29.38	29.25
	F	25.85	26.42	26.06	26.51	26.03

Data: compiled by Scottish Historical Demography Unit at Edinburgh from Registrar General's material.

3 The working class: Dr Strachan and the pattern of courtship

Up to a point, then, the foregoing was accepted at the time as a satisfactory explanation of the pattern of bastardy in different regions, yet even without raising the reality of the late age of marriage, it begged one very large question. It seemed to explain why there were more illegitimate children in Banff than in Berwickshire, but why could not the men and women of Banff contain their lusts until they had a house? The middle classes, too, often had to delay marriage until they could buy a house and keep their wives 'in the manner to which they had been accustomed', and condemnation of the early 'improvident' marriage was a cliché of popular moralists. But in the middle-class society, although many men were unchaste, delayed marriages manifestly did not issue in a great crop of bastards borne by their girlfriends. Was it possible that the working class as a whole had completely different sexual conventions with respect to their women? The matter was hinted at more than once in the debate on illegitimacy, but the most careful investigations and the most explicit statements were made by Dr J. M. Strachan of Dollar in a series of articles in the *Scotsman* for 1870.[28] He based his investigation on a search of the marriage and birth registers, on his own experience as a general practitioner and on consultation with his medical friends. Within limits, his findings are confirmed by what other commentators wrote, before and afterwards, in less systematic terms.

Strachan began from a suspicion that ante-nuptial pregnancies were the rule rather than the exception in certain sectors of society. He examined 1,569 marriages in 13 rural parishes in different parts of Scotland over the years 1855–69. Of these 1,310 could be traced by the continuing residence of the parties, and in 493 cases, 'or rather more than a third', a child was born and registered within six months of the wedding. In all but seven cases the parents were working class. He also looked at 1,206 illegitimate births in the 13 parishes: again, in all but 19 cases, the mother was working class. Most of the exceptions were daughters of small farmers, 'who in their manners and customs resemble the working class'.

Perhaps the immorality of working-class women was caused by upper-class men? The evidence did not bear it out. In the statistics of the Edinburgh maternity hospital, out of 337 cases of illegitimacy, only in seven were the fathers middle class: in his own 13 rural parishes out of 813 cases of illegitimacy (where the father was known), in 780 the fathers were working men, in 28 they were farmers, and only in five did they belong to any other class.

Evidence from other sources bears out the contention that illegitimacy was overwhelmingly restricted to working-class girls. James Valentine, in a paper on illegitimacy in Aberdeen covering the years 1855 to 1859, found that well over half the mothers were domestic servants or factory operatives and that almost all the rest were also working class: 'Scarcely a case occurs where the mother moves in the middle or upper ranks of society.'[29] In 1883 the Registrar General for Scotland tabulated the occupations of 10,000 mothers of illegitimate children known from the records of civil registration and drawn from all parts of the country. Forty-seven per cent were domestic servants, 24 per cent were factory girls, 10 per cent were farm girls (the line between them and domestic servants in rural areas must be very arbitrary), 6 per cent were seamstresses, 8 per cent were described as 'no occupation, chiefly daughters of working men', 4 per cent were described as 'no information, chiefly widows', and 0.5 per cent were the daughters of professional men (quoted in Leffingwell, pp. 67–8).

It is always more difficult to get evidence on paternity, but the Historical Demography Unit at Edinburgh looked at 679 illegitimate births in selected areas of Scotland for 1861: in nearly a quarter the father was known and his occupation given – the proportion of known fathers varied from 38 per cent in Orkney, 36 per cent in Lewis and Harris, and 34 per cent in Banff, to 22 per cent in Shetland, 15

28. 'Immorality of Scotland', *Scotsman*, 20 May, 2 June, 7 June 1870. All quotations are from this source without further reference.

29. J. Valentine, 'Illegitimacy in Aberdeen and the other large towns of Scotland' (1859), pp. 224–6.

per cent in East Lothian and only 10 per cent in Wigtown. The occupation of these fathers was overwhelmingly working class. One landed proprietor was mentioned, two farm managers and a few farmers and their sons. Six out of nine known fathers in Shetland were fisherman, but in Orkney the fathers were more diverse. In Wigtownshire, Banff and East Lothian farm servants accounted for between half and three quarters of known fathers (calculated from civil registration material). No doubt middle-class men had an advantage when it came to concealing paternity, and they may be better represented in the three quarters of the cases where the father was not disclosed.

Dr Strachan then proceeded in his articles to ask why there was more illegitimacy in the country than in the towns. He suggested it was because there was a higher proportion of middle class in urban than in rural areas, and also because 'in towns and manufacturing districts a large proportion of the working men consists of skilled artisans whose position and whose feelings and manners approximate to the class above them.' This observation, if true, is of interest in relation to the concept of a labour aristocracy – i.e. that there existed a distinct stratum of respectable and highly paid workers who accepted the values and aped the outlook of those above them in society. In this case they would be motivated to keep their daughters more closely than other working men, but not necessarily to impose the same sanctions on their sons if they visited brothels.

Plainly there were many working-class visitors in the 'third-class brothels'. From the frequency with which Tait, for example, refers to apprentices or shop workers, these customers included many in the categories of artisan and white-collar workers which are associated with middle-class aspirations. Whether such groups were dominant it is impossible to say. There may also be some confusion between the kind of brothel where you purchased a prostitute's services and one which was a 'house of assignation' where you simply paid for a room and, perhaps, brought your own girl. In an urban environment without barns and haystacks the latter may have had a function that had nothing to do with prostitution. Much courtship in town and country alike took place out of doors in any case – on the traditional walk where men and girls became better acquainted – but if you wanted to carry things further town life must have presented some problems.

There are, however, various other considerations in the urban situation. Firstly, there were apparently wide differences between one town and another. James Valentine illustrated this for the eight principal towns in 1858, showing that the percentage of illegitimate births in total births in Aberdeen was three times as high as it was in Greenock, with Dundee, Perth, Paisley, Edinburgh, Glasgow and Leith (in that order) coming between. He was inclined to link high urban illegitimacy with a low rate of marriage and a large excess of females together with the influence of the morals of the surrounding countryside (pp. 224–6). The substance of his argument largely disappears, however, if one corrects the figures to take account of the number of women at risk: cities with a large proportion of unmarried female workers aged 15–49 had more bastards mainly because there were more girls to have them, not because the girls were more 'immoral'.

More real were the differences between towns (as a group), and the countryside, demonstrating appreciably lower illegitimacy rates in the urban population. There were no doubt many reasons for this. Towns often had large Irish communities, whose morals (at least those of the girls) were often very different from those of the Scots (see below p. 209). Again, in addition to the higher proportion of middle-class people, and of workers voluntarily imitating the middle class, there was a higher proportion of girls controlled by the middle classes as domestic servants in their households than would be the case in rural areas. Thus in towns the sexual *mores* of working-class groups were probably very various, and it would be impossible to talk of one code of proletarian morality for the urban population as a whole.

Dr Strachan, having disposed of the towns to his satisfaction, then asked why there were substantial differences between the Highlands and the Lowlands. He examined in depth the records of four Ross-shire parishes and four parishes in Aberdeenshire and Banff and found that in the Highland ones only 5 per cent of working-class births were illegitimate, and in only 15 per cent of working-class marriages did a child come within six months, whereas in the Lowland ones 24 per cent of working-class births were illegitimate and in 65 per cent of working-class marriages a child came within six months.

Strachan's argument that ante-nuptial pregnancies were normal in at least the rural Lowland working class receives a good deal of supporting evidence from others who knew the south of Scotland. Thus one minister asked two colleagues with parishes in rural Lanarkshire if they ever performed the marriage service for women who were also pregnant:

> One replied, Oh Yes, frequently. Well, I said, think and tell me when you did it last. On reflecting he answered, I really do not remember when I last married a young woman who was not in the family way. The other minister at once replied. No, I seldom, if indeed ever, perform the service where it should not have been performed long before (Seton, p. 38).

Another said it was so important for Border hinds to have a family to work alongside them that 'it is very usual for a couple to cohabit in order to ascertain whether the woman is likely to prove fruitful' (Seton, p. 39).

The evidence from the southwest in particular, however, suggests something different from (or rather, perhaps, additional to) norms of cohabitation with a 'steady' girl and pregnancy followed by marriage. Several observers noted that illegitimacy there seemed often to be hereditary:

> Illegitimacy [is not] a true gauge of general impurity. My observations lead me to the conclusion that this is to a very large extent a hereditary sin. It can be traced through certain families. Very often a woman may have three or four illegitimate children, and the average is consequently raised. A frequent custom prevails of letting cottages to unattached women to procure field labour. These are mostly women who have been obliged to leave domestic service with illegitimate children and, I observe, they have an abandoned attitude and are, I fear, too often a temptation to young men in the district.[30]

Another commentator had analysed the parish of Monigaff in Wigtownshire, where between 1880 and 1893, out of 488 births 42 had been illegitimate, and two thirds of those came from nine families.[31]

30. *Report on the religious and moral conditions of farm servants* (FCGA, 1897). See also *Report of the commission on the religious condition of the people*, Church of Scotland General Assembly Proceedings (henceforth C of SGA), 1895, pp. 747, 749. See also Cramond, pp. 49, 67–8 for traces of the same thing in Banff.

31. *Reports of the schemes of the Church of Scotland* (C of SGA, 1895), p. 750. On 'repeaters' see chapter 8 below.

Among the social causes of a high ratio of illegitimacy Dr Strachan considered was the absence of any stigma on a girl who had slept with a man before marriage: 'Previous unchasteness even with another individual, does not form a very serious bar to marriage.' Here again Strachan was supported in this suggestion by a number of other observers. In remarks intended to apply to the whole of the eastern Lowlands one reporter to the Royal Commission on the Employment of Women and Children in Agriculture stressed that the crimes of abortion and infanticide were unknown in the countryside, for 'there is indeed no pressure on the women to commit any crime in order to conceal her lapse from virtue, as amongst her own class there is no feeling of indignation aroused in consequence of what they would call her "misfortune" ' (*4th report RC Agric. 1867*, p. 80). Another said, speaking of Roxburghshire: 'The stain of bastardy is little felt and forms no serious impediment to success in life' (appendix, part 2, p. 196). The Committee on Religion and Morals of the Free Church said: 'The people hardly regard it as a sin. They seem to think that marriage covers all.'[32]

In 1886 William Cramond wrote a remarkable pamphlet, *Illegitimacy in Banffshire*. He was able to illustrate popular attitudes in the northeast by numerous quotations from replies he had received to a circular asking for views on the causes of local immorality.

> Notwithstanding all our preaching and teaching this sin is not at all seen in its true light, in fact it is thought very little of – scarcely thought a sin at all, just a mistake, rather annoying and hard when the father does not take with the child and pay for it, but when he does it is not much better. There is no just sense of the soul-polluting, unmanly, unwomanly nature of the sin. – Parish Minister.
>
> A woman once said to me with reference to her erring daughter, 'It was not so bad as if she had taken twopence that was not her own.' That woman was a fair type of the average church member in this district, neither better nor worse. – Free Church Minister.
>
> In one instance it was put down to the 'will of the Almighty', a fatalistic idea which I fear is not so uncommon as one might think. – Parish Minister.
>
> I have heard many a mother of this kind say, 'It's nae sae bad as steeling, or deein' awa' wi' the puir craters'. – A Bank Official.
>
> A mother excuses her fallen daughter by saying, 'Puir thing, it's a misfortune, but she'll get ower it', and the neighbours chime in and add 'It wad hae been waur if she had ta'en anything'. – Clergyman.
>
> The only thing they seem to feel is if the father does not acknowledge the child. A woman who had five illegitimate children said to me that her mother said she was just the one to have them, as she always got a father [Cramond, pp. 44–50].

That these attitudes were not restricted to the northeast is made abundantly clear by the previous evidence, yet they remained very prevalent in that region.

Next, and most importantly, Strachan attributed working-class unchastity to distinctive habits of courtship which he plainly regarded as extraordinary,

32. *Report of the committee . . . on religion and morals* (FCGA, 1863).

uncouth and detestable. He explained to his middle-class readers how it was unusual for working-class lovers to meet in public: the ordinary thing was to meet after bedtime, at the back of a haystack or in a barn or an outhouse, or 'especially in the case of servant maids', in the girl's bedroom. Each meeting lasts for two or three hours, and is repeated weekly. A girl may 'pride herself on the number of such lovers she may have', and a boy 'not think it wrong to visit different girls after this fashion': as for the parents, 'not even the most particular thinks there is anything wrong in this manner of courtship.' There was not, he was careful to stress, necessarily any immorality arising immediately from this: 'The upper classes would be astonished if they knew how long such visits were continued without a fall from virtue. In many cases they are so continued for years. In some . . . no fall from virtue takes place.' In other words there was often heavy petting but not intercourse. But in too many cases, by this activity the 'outworks are dismantled, the citadel [left] defenceless', and 'they learn, when it was too late, what women can never learn too early or impress too strongly on their minds – that a lover's encroachments, to be repelled successfully, must be repelled and negatived at the very outset.' Hence the high rates of illegitimacy and ante-nuptial pregnancy.

This description of working-class courtship fitted in exactly with what other writers had written in a more sensationalized way about the midnight prowling of the bothymen and other undisciplined rural labourers, and, as Strachan himself pointed out, it fitted in with the traditional picture of peasant love 'among the rigs o' barley' that came down from Burns. The traditional so-called 'Bothy Ballads' of the Lowland farm servant are full of descriptions of midnight visiting by bands of men or individuals. It was not really anything new and decadent: as an old peasant told William Cramond (p. 51) almost two decades later, it was 'bred i' the bane'.

Despite this corroboration, however, it is difficult to believe that Strachan's account told the complete story of Scottish courtship. The evidence of oral history from the early twentieth century stresses rather that young people first met at dances or social gatherings of the family or community, and became closer acquainted first on walks or visits to the theatre and music hall (in late Edwardian times, the cinema). But once this stage was past, Strachan was probably accurate enough. One Free Church moralist put it in a nutshell in 1897:

> They do not mean to do anything wrong, but simply to take what amusement they can, and courting is an amusement, and they go into it as into a dream, from which many awake too late, to find their lives for ever overshadowed with a dark remembrance [Report on farm servants].

The only problem from the moralist's point of view was that the memory was not as dark as it should have been.

Strachan's picture, in summary, is of working-class girls distinguished from middle-class girls in the degree of their premarital sexual adventures, which often included intercourse and pregnancy, while the working-class man was distinguished by the fact that he was more likely to take sex *gratis* from willing girls of his own class than to buy it from a prostitute. It carries conviction only where it is most often corroborated by other observers – in respect of the Lowland countryside. It can be extended to the towns only with the qualifications we have discussed already. There were, however, certain other groups within the Scottish working class – the Irish immigrants, the Highlanders and the inhabitants of the northern islands – which he either does not consider at all or considers only in an adequate way. To these we must now turn.

4 The Irish, the Highlanders and the Islanders

A case for believing that the Irish had, in their native land at least, an exceptional respect for premarital chastity has been strongly argued, with a wealth of convincing statistical and non-statistical detail, in Connell's brilliant essays.[33] It is abundantly confirmed by nineteenth-century observations of Irish immigrant habits in Britain, though not of those of the unaccompanied males. As one commentator put it, considering the behaviour of Irish labourers in Stranraer: 'We very much fear that our brethren of the Green Isle can lay no claim to the possession of that jewel [chastity] which is the brightest ornament of their women' (List, p. 4). The men, uprooted from their families, priests, and culture and herded into navvying teams under brutalized conditions, behaved notoriously badly.

But where immigrant Irish families were thick on the ground – as in Dunbartonshire and Renfrewshire or in the burgh of Greenock – illegitimacy rates were usually exceptionally low, and in mixed communities the Irish were seen to behave totally differently from the Scots. A Scottish tailor who acted as voluntary baillie in the village of Raploch in Stirlingshire had this to say of his Irish neighbours:

> About the beginning of May they go with their families to the bark peeling. . . . They stay out about two months and sleep in wooden sheds, lying together as thick as bees, but there's no immorality among them; indeed they just behave to each other like a wheen children, you would think they had not the same notions as other folk. I have only known two or at the most three Irish girls go wrong, and it was always with Scotchmen. [*4th report RC Agric. 1867*, p. 66].

Macgill's novels make the same point about the childlike relationships of young Irish immigrants towards each other, and in other contexts Mayhew speaks of the chaste nature of the Irish coster girls in London (surely a most unexpected tribute) and Keating of the same thing among Irish girls in the South Wales coalfield.[34]

It is difficult not to associate this with the nature of nineteenth-century Catholicism in Ireland, with the great strength of the priests and the emphasis on the worship of Mary and the holiness of the virgin state. It would probably also be naive not to imagine that there is a relationship with the scarcity of land in Ireland. After the famine with late marriage for the males and few holdings to go round, the teaching of the priests was reinforced by a quite separate economic sanction. For immigrant industrial workers into Scotland the economic situation was obviously of another kind, but the cultural and moral habit formed in Ireland would not immediately collapse.

The Highlands and Islands present a much more difficult picture to interpret. Taking the overall illegitimacy statistics for the Highland counties – Argyll,

33. K. H. Connell, *Irish Peasant Society* (1968).
34. *London labour and the London poor* (1861), I, pp. 104–5; *My struggle for life* (1916), p. 14.

Inverness-shire, Ross and Cromarty, and Sutherland – together with Orkney and Shetland, one has the impression of an area intermediate in character between the Scottish Lowlands and Ireland: the illegitimacy ratio in Ross and Cromarty and Shetland, for instance, was generally about one third of what it was in Banff and Wigtown. Middle-class observers, too, sometimes gave the impression that the sexual *mores* of Highland girls were not unlike those of Irish girls. For instance, one who had been inspecting the female bothies of the Lothians remarked:

> Those I saw were inhabited by Highland girls, whose modest character is well known, and I heard no complaint of the misconduct of farm bothy women. That it would be far otherwise if the bothy women were natives of the South of Scotland I can well conceive [*4th report RC Agric. 1867*, p. 80].

Free Church and Church of Scotland reports from the 1870s and the 1890s, covering parishes in the west – for instance the Presbyteries of Mull and Skye on the islands, and Lochcarron, Tongue and Glenelg on the mainland – gave the impression that 'immorality' was rare or very rare: when there was an illegitimate birth, it was generally blamed on outsiders, or was said to have been the result of a girl going to the south to farms, to domestic service.[35] Oral tradition sometimes points in the same direction. For instance, in the Catholic parish of Barra the Essex University team were told that bastardy cursed a family 'from generation to generation'. It was so rare that the informant could only recollect two instances, one concerning a girl who had emigrated south. Courtship was fairly strictly controlled, both by teenagers being called early back home in the evenings by their parents, and by moral precepts like 'if you go with anybody to any lonely or out of the way place the devil is the third person' (Essex OHU). This appears to have strong overtones of the Irish situation.

On the other hand the Highlands cover a large area, and some parishes had very different reputations. Church reports were not so complacent about, for instance, Islay and Coll.[36] Tomintoul, like Barra, was a Catholic locality but here illegitimacy was as high as it was in the Lowlands of Banff to which it lay adjacent: 29 births out of 114 between 1861 and 1865 were bastards (Cramond, p. 59; calculations 1861–5 by Edinburgh University Historical Demography Unit). Again, there were remarks about certain parishes in the west considerably more adverse than the general run of outsiders' opinion:

> The Dumfriesshire shepherds, I believe, have had laid upon them the *onus* of introducing illegitimacy into the Highlands, and I must say that, if so, it has not suffered by the transplantation, seeming, as it does at the present day, to be indigenous to the soil. In Alvie, Glenshiel, Lairg, Croy and Edderton, the parishes wherein it attained unenviable superiority, the reputed fathers were thorough-bred Highlanders. Is there any part of Scotland in which illegitimacy exceeds the proportion of 18.18 per cent found in the thinly populated parishes of Alvie and Glenshiel? I rather think not [Seton, p. 32].

Nor can we disregard the very large body of traditional Gaelic songs which are on tape at the School of Scottish Studies, and which are not really specific to any one

35. *Reports of the schemes of the Church of Scotland* (1897), pp. 942, 946, 951. *Report of the committee . . . on religion and morals* (1870), pp. 19–21; and (1873), pp. 45–8.
36. *Reports of the schemes of the Church of Scotland* (1898), pp. 887, 893.

locality. One common and repeated feature concerns courtship at the shielings – the isolated upland pastures where the women and girls lived in summer making butter and cheese, and looking after the animals. Tales of visits to the shielings by bands of men, and of romps in the heather that followed, are as common a feature of these songs as tales of midnight prowling are of the Bothy Ballads in the Lowlands. It is certainly difficult to make this sort of evidence dovetail in with the remarks of Free Church commentators, for instance, the rarity of immorality in the Presbytery of Glenelg, especially if one recalls that the Free Church regarded even dancing and loafing as tending to dangerous temptations.

In the face of all this conflicting but thinly spread evidence it may help to turn to two areas about which just a little more is known – the northern isles, and Lewis. Orkney and Shetland were particularly interesting in view of their low illegitimacy ratio (less than 5 per cent usually), combined with assertions by the church that local courtship practices were indecent and that ante-nuptial pregnancy was common:

> The absence of illegitimate births . . . can hardly be regarded as a fair index of the real state of things. . . . While cases of illegitimacy are comparatively rare, cases of ante-nuptial fornication are not infrequent, and are little thought of, marriage being supposed to set all right. The system of courtship in many cases is conducted in a way which is very questionable. It is not easy to say at whose door the blame lies here. Young men and women and parents seem to be equally culpable.[37]

Nineteenth-century church sourcess do not explain what the courtship customs were, beyond saying they were long engrained and hard to eradicate. Oral tradition, however, tells more. Some were of the shieling type: one informant described a 'flatchie carding' in Shetland. After six or so girls had been carding wool out of doors, they would spread pallets on the floor about midnight; 'This was a signal for the boys to come in, and they would come bounding in and spend the night rolling around with the girls, jumping and rolling over them' (Essex OHU). This does not imply sexual intercourse. Others were associated with marriage celebrations: there are stories of a 'lang bed' in which the unmarried couples would all get together after the wedding party. A nineteenth-century account spoke of the 'members of each sex being alternately ranged along the floor on a huge couch of straw', but went on, 'the people enter quite innocently into these "barn bundlings" as they are termed, and . . . the testimony of respectable persons who have taken part in them prove that nothing immoral occurs.'[38]

There was also the custom of individual bundling, the couple remaining fully clothed, and often lying in bed with a bolster or deal between them: 'You know in other parts of the country except for Shetland, if a girl and a boy go to bed together it's for one purpose and one purpose only. But here in Shetland a girl and a boy would go to bed together as they might go for a walk' (Essex OHU). The implication once again, of course, is that they got into bed to pet: intercourse would not by any means necessarily follow. The church was certainly not quite fair in suggesting that bundling normally led to unchastity, still less to promiscuity.

37. *Appendix to the report on the state of religion and morals* (FCGA, 1884).
38. R. Cowie, *Shetland and its inhabitants* (1874), p. 100.

What seems characteristic of Orkney and Shetland, however, is that parents (or employers) make little attempt to supervise the courtship of their teenagers and often did not know of it. This is illustrated by a story collected by the School of Scottish Studies concerning the wife of an Orkney farmer who accidentally disturbed a young man in bed with the maid early one Sunday morning. She found herself obliged to go to great lengths to explain obliquely to the young man and the community at large that she was not a peeping tom and that it had been the merest accident she had disturbed the two of them. Evidently the community would attach blame to her, for interfering, not to the couple, for being in bed together.[39]

We shall never know how often couples went beyond petting, but Orkney and Shetland illustrate a situation where you could have plenty of 'midnight visiting' and still get low illegitimacy rates. It may well be relevant that the islands were still essentially a society where everyone knew everyone else, and young men could not readily escape identification or their responsibilities to a pregnant girl. Correlation with the age of marriage is not very conclusive. While it is true that, in 1871 for example, men got married in Orkney and Shetland about eighteen months later than the national average, and women one year or two years later, in the Highlands (where illegitimacy overall was above what it was in the northern isles but below what it was in the Lowlands), men were on average over three years older than the national average, and women much as in the northern isles. These figures certainly do not support the contemporary view that delayed marriage led to a growth of bastardy.

The case of Lewis makes another interesting study: it presents a combination of enthusiastic membership of the strictest Presbyterian churches (there was much more adherence to the Free Church than in the northern isles), very low illegitimacy rates, and 'bundling' courtship customs.

Certainly, by the middle of the nineteenth century Lewis had taken on its reputation for godliness and good behaviour. Adherence to the Free Church was overwhelming: and by the end of the century many also adhered to the more extreme sects emanating from the Free Church. The island was famous for its Sabbath observance. It was equally famous for its very low illegitimacy ratio. Ross and Cromarty, indeed, vied with Orkney and Shetland for the distinction of the lowest county illegitimacy ratio in Scotland, but when Lewis is separated out from the mainland the record is even more remarkable.[40]

At the same time Lewis had a high birth rate: in the 1890s it varied between 32 per thousand and 25 per thousand, compared to a variation between 22 per thousand and 19 per thousand on the mainland of the county. There was no word in the various church reports of the period hinting at high levels of prenuptial pregnancies or of undesirable courtship customs. Could it be that nineteenth-century Lewis was a place where Dr Strachan's beliefs in the 'modesty' of the Highlands were justified, and where the church ethic was for once properly followed by both sexes?

This may well be the correct conclusion, but when in the last quarter of the nineteenth century others began to comment on such things it became clear that rural Lewis, no less than Orkney and Shetland, also had a long-engrained tradition of 'bundling' and courting at the shielings. For instance, an outsider who had stayed for a long period in Lewis wrote in 1874:

39. I am grateful to Dr Alan Bruford of the School of Scottish Studies for this story from his collection.
40. *Report to the Secretary for Scotland . . . on the social condition of the people of Lewis in 1901 . . .*, pp. xcix–ci.

Table 7.3: Illegitimacy ratios in Lewis and Ross & Cromarty, 1880–99

	Island of Lewis	Mainland of Ross & Cromarty
1880	2.1	6.3
1885	2.2	6.6
1890	1.9	6.4
1895	3.2	6.3
1899	1.9	7.0

Closer analysis showed, that, as in Shetland, the more rural the area the lower the ratio:

	Rural registration districts	Stornoway RD
1880	1.8	2.4
1885	1.5	3.2
1890	1.7	2.1
1895	2.8	3.7
1899	1.2	2.8

> Most of the unmarried young men pass the winter nights with their sweethearts. The want of light in most dwellings, the numbers of dark corners even in daylight, and the general habit among the people of throwing themselves down on the straw simply divested of their outer garment, gives every facility for courtship in the Hebridean fashion. As the girls are, at the same time, 'very kind', courting assiduously, and are possessed of far greater energy then the men, they acquire a great hold on their affections.[41]

Bundling, indeed, lasted until well into the twentieth century in Lewis, but oral accounts of what actually happened explain it as carefully controlled.[42] Hebridean houses had only one room; with the whole family present, it was impossible for the parents not to know who was with the girl, and impossible for intercourse to take place. Similarly on the shielings the girls were accompanied by a few older women who exercised by their presence a restraining influence. On Lewis 'bundling' seems to have been a more acceptable courtship custom than walking out, for walking removed the control of other people over the lovers. The island, of course, was an extremely tightly knit, traditional society with a highly developed awareness of kinship, and the ethos that made social responsibilities very difficult to avoid: if a lad had made a girl pregnant and deserted her, his family would never have been allowed to live down the shame. At any rate the correlation in the rural districts between the normal practice of courting by 'bundling' and the very low rates of illegitimacy and (apparently) of ante-nuptial pregnancies, indicates that under some circumstances 'bundling' was perfectly compatible with chastity.

5 Conclusions

Some conclusions are easy, others must be speculative. First of all, the middle and upper classes had a distinctive code of sexual morality which involved the women

41. W. A. Smith, *Lewisana* (1874), p. 79.
42. For this I am especially indebted to conversations at the School of Scottish Studies with Mr Donald Macdonald of Lewis and Edinburgh.

in an extraordinary degree of premarital chastity, and in lack of physical contact even of a minimal kind until very late in courtship – even then it did not go far: the men, if they were not themselves chaste, pursued girls of lower social status for casual intercourse, which gave rise to a great deal of prostitution. It is not unreasonable to attribute the almost superstitious protection of women at least partly to the fact that marriage was, as well as a sexual contract, also a contract by which property was transferred. Dr Johnson expressed it well in a conversation at Dunvegan: 'Consider of what importance to society the chastity of women is. Upon that all the property in the world depends. We hang a thief for stealing a sheep, but the unchastity of a woman transfers sheep, and farm, and all from the right owner.'[43] Engels had essentially the same interpretation.[44] It is not, of course, necessary for everyone in bourgeois society to be aware of this foundation for the prevailing morality for it to be a valid explanation, especially as it was a morality backed (as far as the women were concerned) by the church. But when one considers the degree to which the unchasteness of middle-class men was tolerated, and the extent of the ensuing prostitution, it becomes obvious that we can hardly speak of the middle classes as a whole following the church ethic.

Secondly, in the town, working-class morality was probably more heterogeneous than anywhere else. Some were heavily influenced by 'middle-class morality' – either those who were most firmly controlled by the middle classes, like domestic servants, or who aspired in this and other respects to resemble the middle classes, like shopworkers and craftsmen. Some took the tone of their behaviour from the rural areas from which they had emigrated – and in the case of the northeastern Lowlanders, rather a low one. Others lived, or partly lived, on the receiving end of prostitution. It seems impossible to discover any proletarian norm of urban society: this is probably because there was not one, but many.

In the countryside, morality varied according to region. In the Lowlands it would seem that sexual intercourse before marriage was common, and in some parts – the southwest and the northeast – for peculiar local reasons gave rise to exceptionally high rates of illegitimacy. In the Highlands and Islands the situation is obscure and varied, but low illegitimacy ratios in the northern isles were associated with what the church, perhaps unjustly, considered to be 'licentious' morals, while even lower illegitimacy ratios in Lewis were associated with as high a regard for female chastity as in rural Ireland.

The one feature common to all these places, however, was that it was general to court after dark, indoors, and often in bed. Where parental surveillance was close, as in Lewis, a very high degree of chastity was nevertheless preserved. In other areas where peasant society was homogeneous and relatively stable, even if parental surveillance was not close, as in the northern isles, there were few illegitimacies because pressure could be brought to bear on fathers in order to prevent the desertion of pregnant girls whose children would then become a burden on the grandparents. But in the Lowlands, society was not of this kind – it was a world of farm labourers, not of peasants. In one area, the Borders and the Lothians where the bondager system prevailed, one might explain the frequency of sexual intercourse before marriage by the fact that couples wished to prove their partners' fertility, which was important for their job prospects where the work unit was the family, not the single employee. This is perhaps premarital intercourse condoned by parents for economic reasons.

43. James Boswell, *The life of Samuel Johnson . . . to which is added the journal of a tour to the Hebrides* (1897), p. 593.
44. *The origin of the family, private property and the state* (1942).

Nevertheless, this might not do as a general explanation of the frequency of prenuptial pregnancy in other parts of the Lowlands, and it is no explanation of higher illegitimacy anywhere – as the point of Border practice presumably was that the couple should marry if the girl was fertile. One cannot ignore, in an explanation of the frequency of prenuptial pregnancy in other parts of the Lowlands, the relative weakness of parental authority where the children of one sex or both lived away from home: the family cottage system of the south was replaced elsewhere by the bachelor bothy or the chaumer, where the young could do as they wished without danger of interruption, or the need to face mother and father in the morning. The chaumer system of the northeast, with the girls living away from home yet having constant occasion to mix with the young men who came into the house kitchens to eat, was the most unrestricted environment of all. Certainly farmers were not going to step in to exercise quasi-parental discipline in these matters. The collapse of paternal relations was a constant theme of church comment here and elsewhere in the Scottish Lowlands in the nineteenth century.[45]

It is reasonable to assume that levels of illegitimacy will be related to the frequency of premarital intercourse in society, but that they will also depend on other circumstances. One must be the perceived need of society to enforce marriage for the sake of the girl and her child; another, the ability of society to do so.

The perceived need for marriage was obviously less if the unmarried mother could support herself without recourse to her parents: the burden of her child would then not fall on her kin, or on anyone else. This was certainly possible where, as over the Lowlands as a whole, the agricultural system provided some constant employment for single women in milking, hoeing and similar work. It was nowhere more possible than in Banff and Wigtownshire, where the chaumer system and the cottage let to an 'unattached woman' prevailed respectively, where there was much dairying, and a good deal of turnip husbandry. One commentator in the southwest noted that high levels of illegitimacy followed the line of turnip cultivation.[46] The girls were able to keep their jobs if they became pregnant or not: they were not an economic burden on their parents before, and they did not become one subsequently.

In any case, the ability of society to enforce marriage on the father of a pregnant girl was weaker in the Lowlands than in the Highlands. Both married and single labourers were notoriously mobile, moving restlessly from farm to farm and district to district, and relatively seldom settling down to a sojourn in one place over decades. This made it easy for an unmarried father to evade his responsibilities. Not only was there nothing abnormal in his leaving the district, but if rural society did not consist of a fixed cohort of families resident over generations it lacked a corporate memory which could rebuke the irresponsibility of neighbours. In the Highlands even the flight of a young man would not have saved his family from disrepute. In the Lowlands it was not likely the man or his family would stay in the locality to be remembered.

For these reasons, it seems, Lowland lovers in rural areas could get into bed together without the context of most of the social restraints that operated in, for

45. See for example, *Report . . . on Houses for the working class* (1863); *Report on . . . farm servants* (1897); *Reports of the schemes of the Church of Scotland* (1895), Commission on the religious condition of the people, pp. 745–6. There is a full discussion in Kenneth Boyd's thesis (1973) cited in 1 above.

46. *Royal Commission on Labour, 1893* Agricultural Labourer, III, Scotland.

example, the northern or western isles. In the Lowlands, therefore, and particularly (for local reasons) in the extreme southwest and the extreme northeast, a very 'unbourgeois' and even 'unpeasant' morality could grow up which not only accepted ante-nuptial pregnancy as normal, but which also accepted illegitimacy as conferring no stigma on mother or child, and did not regard refusal to accept responsibility by the man as a very grave sin.

Sexual morality in Victorian Scotland, then, was in practice largely a function of the authority relationship between parents and children, and the economic situation of both. Where parents were in a position to exercise control they often enforced sexual restraint and responsibility on their sons and daughters, or at least other people's sons were obliged to accept responsibility for what they did to daughters. This was especially true where illegitimate additions to the family imposed new burdens on an existing household. Conversely, where parents did not have this power (as over young theological students at college, or farm servants in a bothy), or where there was independent employment even for unmarried mothers (as in Banff), young people tended to experiment in a way that increased prostitution and illegitimacy. But in those areas where these things became common, working-class society tended to accept them as normal. Even from the middle class, there was no crusade for 'Victorian morality.' Breaches in the church's code were visible everywhere, and if commentators from time to time raised their eyes to deplore them, no one was prepared to unleash a campaign against fornicators, as they might possibly have done in the Reformation centuries. At root the Victorian moralist, like the Victorian businessman, was an individualist with a privatized vision: it was enough for him if he was pure, even if Sodom and Gomorrah were to be destroyed down the road.

8

The bastardy prone sub-society

Peter Laslett

Since it was first put forward in 1973, the notion of a bastardy prone sub-society existing in local communities over time has gained some currency. Each of the contributors to the English section of our volume refers to the concept, and it is used by one or two of them in a explanatory way. Those dealing with some of the other countries mention it too. Christopher Smout's chapter (above, number 7) is illustrative in several ways of the themes of the present one. This is especially interesting in that Scotland was our chosen example of localism and micro-localism.[1]

Some of the statements made by our contributors raise doubts about the bastardy prone sub-society, and about the usefulness of the hypothesis for the study of the history of sexual nonconformism. In the final chapter relating to the British Isles our object is to try to define such a hypothetical society as closely as we can, and to examine the evidence for its presence, its construction and its workings. This turns out to be no easy task. Simple at first sight, the concept of a bastardy prone sub-society becomes complicated when pursued, especially when the source is confined to parochial recordings as it is in the present case. If we had been able to investigate the relevant evidence in the published records of national registration offices, as was possible for locality persistence values, we should perhaps have come closer to a full understanding.

In order to discuss the sub-society, however, nominal information is essential, records that is of births of named children to named parents. But civil registration offices do not release such details in Britain, which is why we have had to be content with what can be learned from the parish registers. And the evidence which might bear upon a bastardy prone sub-society in literary and other sources has not yet been surveyed, though it is occasionally cited by our contributors.[2]

1 Definition and membership of the sub-society

As originally conceived, the bastardy prone sub-society, or sub-community, was fairly simple in its supposed composition. It consisted in a series of bastard-producing women, living in the same locality, whose activities persisted over several generations, and who tended to be related by kinship or marriage. Many of these women were credited not with one illegitimate birth only, but with several. At times when all births were on the increase and illegitimacy was also

1. See section 8 of chapter 1 above. In M. W. Flinn, *Scottish Population History* (1977), part 5, chapter 4, pp. 363 ff. Smout cites the sub-society. Note 19 to that chapter implies that in our original study the bastardy prone sub-society was reported from northwest England only, which was certainly not the impression intended.
2. It must be obvious that researchers in countries where nominal information is made public about bastard-bearers might be able to clear up the problems described here and decide once and for all about the sub-society. Chapter 3 above presents the outcomes of examining the reconstitution files of some English parishes, with the features of the sub-society in mind, especially what is there called 'repeaterdom'.

high, the repetitive bastard-bearing of such persons accounted for a noticeable proportion of the numbers of spurious children born, though never for a majority of them. 'As general fertility rose', the hypothesis stated, 'the fertility of these women rose too, but faster still. It is possible that at such times, the shadowy society of the bastard-bearers itself grew larger.'

'Some of the bastard-bearers of this type were sisters, some got married, mostly to men who were themselves illegitimate or who had fathered bastards.' Since they were the same to some extent a kin-connected nexus of women, it was inferred that repetitive tendency might be inherited. A sharp distinction was drawn between such repeaters and singletons, girls who had one bastard only.

Many mothers of single bastards only appeared in the parish register at the baptism of their child, and a literary metaphor was adopted to describe and distinguish them. In a famous passage in Bede's *Ecclesiastical History*, a sparrow was invoked as flying in from the winter darkness through one door of the banqueting hall, spending a moment in the light of the fire, and flying out of the other door. Sparrows were quite independent, individual girls whose once-and-for-all offence did not necessarily associate them with the sub-society of which the repeaters formed the nucleus.

Most of the sparrows, probably because they were so often servants, were not permanent members of the population of the parish. Their illegitimate children could be looked upon as constituting part of the price of marriage in terms of sexual nonconformism. These spurious births, we must insist, made up by far the larger part of the total of illegitimacies at all times, even those of booming bastardy. The offences of the sparrows were punishable, and sometimes punished, especially if they threatened to be a burden on the neighbourhood. But the women to whom we have given that name were engaged, we believe, primarily in courtship and were not looked upon by their contemporaries as necessarily deviant. It was, and is, otherwise with the repeaters.

In respect of this small minority of bastard-bearers we have been more ambitious. We have sought to discover, for example, how much more likely it would have been for a woman to 'bear a bastard if she herself was a bastard, of if either of her parents or any of her grandparents had been bastards, and how much more probable . . . that she would marry a bastard, or the descendant of a bastard, or a bastard begetter.' We should particularly like to know such things in respect of repetitive bastard-bearing. If they could be determined, the bastardy prone sub-society would begin to define itself in terms of the probabilities of bastard-begetting and -bearing, given specified conditions.[3]

Exploration and analysis of the evidence since these objects were formulated have shown that some of them, certainly those to do with probabilities, may be unrealistic. The difficulties reported in chapter 4 in tracing the lineal relationships of bastard-bearers and begetters, and the paucity of cases of 'inheritance' found there and by other researchers into the question warn us that these probabilities may have been lower than we had anticipated. Contemporary American evidence on the inheritance of illegitimacy points this way too. We may never be able to estimate how much more likely it would have been for a man or a woman with illegitimacy among the ancestors to become involved in illegitimacy than one with entirely 'innocent' forebears. This means that there is little prospect, at least at present, of the sub-society defining itself.

3. Peter Laslett, *Family life and illicit love* (1977), pp. 149–50.

The phrase 'innocent forebears' allows, of course, for the presence of a sparrow or sparrows in the family line. To have one bastard only, and to display no other connection whatever with nonconformism, does not qualify for membership of the sub-society. In practice we have found the concept of *sparrow* somewhat less helpful than we had hoped.

This is because our study, as we have made plain, is usually confined to the baptismal recordings of one community only, one ecclesiastical parish. But we know that young unmarried persons were highly mobile in traditional English society. An unmarried mother clearly had a strong motive to have her baby baptized in a church where she was unknown. In chapter 3 Richard Smith makes it clear that bastard-bearers are not all, or always, as footloose as other girls of their age. If they moved when pregnant they may mostly have done so in order to return to their home parishes, which would make them appear static from our point of view. In any case it is no simple matter, as we shall see, to arrange a christening in a strange village within a day or two or even a week or two. Nevertheless, we cannot exclude the possibility that a person appearing to be a sparrow in one register would turn out to have been a repeater, if the evidence of two or more registers became available.

We now proceed to a definition of the sub-society of the illegitimacy prone as we have sought it in the ecclesiastical registration of England. In view of our limited knowledge of the life histories of the vanished individuals with whose conduct we are concerned, the definition will have to be general and loose rather than detailed and precise, negative rather than positive. It will also have to be exclusively in terms of bastard-bearing or of prenuptial pregnancy, with the one exception of prostitutes, who are sometimes so described in parish registers.

> No individual is to be regarded as having belonged to the sub-society unless he or she is known to have engendered more than one illegitimate child, or, if the parent of a single bastard, is known to have been connected with persons obviously nonconforming in their behaviour, either by bearing or begetting bastards or exhibiting other forms of sexual irregularity, or both.

Even this negative and lax definition has its difficulties. For example, a person who has one illegitimate child is absolved from membership in the sub-society, but is inculpated if connected with another person in the identical position. The bastardy prone sub-society turns out to be somewhat complex as a concept, disconcertingly blurred at its edges. It may be useful, therefore, to set out a scheme of membership, with the persons affected distinguished into sets. The membership of each set consists in likelihoods as well as certainties. The obstacle to the acceptance of these distinctions as always reliable is that they rest on disconnections. To be confident of disconnections it is necessary to be aware of all connections, and this is certainly not the case for our knowledge of illegitimacy in the past.[4] The scheme attempts to proceed from clear non-membership to certain membership of the sub-society. Though the graduation seems to be correct in general, greater or more accurate knowledge might be expected to displace some

4. Family reconstitution decidedly does not yield knowledge of all kin connections within a parish, and is a very imperfect guide to kin relations beyond parents and siblings even for those families which can be reconstituted. We have had to leave 'connection' undefined in discussing the sub-society, but it is our hope that network analysis, as described in a preliminary way by Richard Smith in the appendix to this chapter may finally enable us to be definite about it. Although kin relationship is its most significant element from our point of view, other personal, economic or legal relationship could constitute a connection.

individuals from one side of the barrier to the other. In most cases, no doubt, it would move them downwards, that is towards or definitely into the sub-society.

Table 8.1: Scheme of non-membership and membership of the bastardy prone sub-society

Sets 1–4,	*those certainly not members and those not likely to be members*
Set 1,	persons with no known connection whatever with bastardy or with any other form of sexual nonconformism.
Set 2,	persons connected with begetters or bearers of bastards but not themselves begetters or bearers.
Set 3,	persons involved in sexual nonconformism short of illegitimacy, whether or not connected with begetters or bearers.
Set 4,	sparrows, singletons known exclusively from the fact of a solitary bastard birth.
Sets 5–7,	*those likely or certain to be members*
Set 5,	singletons, especially those showing other forms of sexual nonconformism, having connections with other nonconforming persons, even if those are not themselves known to have produced a bastard.
Set 6,	connected singletons, that is begetters or bearers of a bastard, connected with each other or with repeaters.
Set 7,	repeaters, that is, begetters or bearers of more than one bastard, whether or not connected with each other or with those in set 6; prostitutes, even if they are not known to have borne bastards.

Now that we have ventured to allot everyone who lived in an English parish to one or other of these seven sets of persons, let us ask ourselves whether, if we posit the existence of a sub-society, we have to think of it as always to be found in every settlement. A survey of the evidence in the preceding studies makes it plain that the first set, the entirely 'innocent', existed nearly everywhere, and probably made up the largest part of the population everywhere and at almost all times. But the bastardy free were never the whole people, in any community or at any time. Decades could go by with no illegitimacy being recorded in a well kept English register, especially in small places in eastern England and during the century between the 1650s and 1750s. Still, prenuptial pregnancies were always occurring, as we have seen in chapter 1, and it has to be remembered that an affianced man had only to be thrown from a horse and killed before the wedding for a prenuptially conceived child to become a bastard.

In view of the evidence about the variation in bastardy levels by locality and micro-locality which we have surveyed in chapter 1, we must expect the willingness to accept the innocence of sparrows would vary between communities. The probability is that the extent of incorrigible bastardy proneness would also differ from region to region, and even place to place. The evidence strongly suggests, moreover, that numbers of persons in the sub-society likewise fluctuated over time in individual areas and over the whole country. There were decades when sexual nonconformism must have been very restricted and others when it must have been very widespread. In spite of these complications it would seem best to assume that a sub-society always potentially existed everywhere, the variations in its strength, or potential strength, being an important element in the locality persistence of illegitimacy levels. It would certainly be difficult to demonstrate the entire absence of the sub-society at any one place at any one time using the evidence available to us.

2 Coherence and continuity in the sub-society

It would certainly be proper to suppose to begin with that tendencies towards illegitimacy and sexual nonconformism would be randomly distributed amongst individuals throughout the population. But a little reflection should convince us that this is really rather unlikely ever to have been so. For such a proposition would imply that for a person to have been born within a particular family with a particular history and situated at a given level in the social structure had no effect on his behaviour in this direction. Only where precedent, example and personal influence were negligible in sexual matters would this be possible, and this could surely only happen when society was so lacking in coherence and was changing so rapidly that permanent and stable relationships were at a minimum. Traditional European villages were decidedly not like this, although the effectiveness of the family units in them has sometimes been called into question and although the extent of solidarity within them can be seriously doubted, if only because the turnover of their populations could be astonishingly high.[5]

For the process of primary socialization which goes on in the very earliest years between parents and their children must have been universal then as it is now in spite of the shifting of population and the comparative brevity of married life. In this process matters of sex, marriage and reproduction must have been peculiarly important. When reference was made earlier to inheriting a disposition towards sexual nonconformism, nothing biological was intended: only that children brought up in families where such a disposition existed would be more likely than other children to display the same traits, and so perhaps to transmit them to their own offspring.[6] The child of a mother who had lovers as well as a husband; a bastard or a child of a bastard; a girl whose aunt was a prostitute, or a boy whose brother was living with his mistress or whose grandfather had been a notorious womanizer: all these would be candidates for sexual irregularity themselves.

It would seem, therefore, to be a commonsense observation that bastardy 'runs in families', in any locality, a village, or more likely, a group of villages where different branches of the same 'families' are to be found. The 'locality' could no doubt include a town, or particular areas of a town or a city. No one is surprised when a drunken father has a drunken son, though drunkenness is not a genetic matter and seems less likely than sexual peculiarity to be salient in the socialization process.

But a predisposition to sexual nonconformism does not necessarily result in bastard-bearing or -begetting. No one would expect all children to behave like their parents; on some indeed the effect would be in reverse, for they would strive to be as different as possible in their conduct. Nevertheless, it might still be said that the characteristics they had reacted against were latent in their own succeeding families. At least it is another commonsense observation that grandchildren or

5. Ariès, Bouchard, Stone and others have doubted whether the nuclear family unit was always permanent and stable enough to perform the socialization functions usually attributed to it: see P. Laslett, 'Philippe Ariès and la famille' (1976), for a critique of this. For turnover see below, p. 234.

6. Venereal disease could have been handed down by contagion between parent and child, with consequent low fertility, high mortality, and even a tendency towards insanity. Keith Snell has read many medical accounts relating to bastard-bearers after the year 1795, and has found neither syphilis nor gonorrhoea mentioned; it was usually child bed complications, flu, or tuberculosis. But we may recall what was said of Mary Grant of Earls Colne at an earlier period, and her 'rotting flesh' in chapter 2. We may also surmise that the bad health of bastard-bearers would be likely to cause the descent lines concerned to die out more frequently than others. Venereal disease, if it was prevalent, might have contributed dramatically to the 'marker' effect discussed below. What is becoming known of the low life expectancy of whores, and their inefficiency in reproduction, is certainly relevant here.

even more remote descendants may revert to practices rejected by the immediate predecessors. Once a breach of the norms had occurred, therefore, the expectation might be that a further breach would come sooner or later among the progeny of the first defaulter.

These are the theoretical grounds on which we should try to understand the evidence of genealogical connection between illegitimacy prone individuals reported in our English studies. We must emphasize that the effect of such connection might have been weak and it is important to notice that these relationships mostly go through the males, although they cannot, in fact, be referred to an original defaulter, a bastardy prone patriarch, so to speak, who has had to be invoked here for expositionary purposes only. The reason why reckoning connections through males predominates is that we have to rely so much on surnames in tracing them from generation to generation. But the transmission of traits by successive socialization must in fact have gone through the females more than through the males. Under these conditions we can only hope to gather from our main source, the individual parish register, some threads of the whole network existing at any time, with information from other sources to fill at least some of the gaps in that network.

In so far as it was kin-connected the bastardy prone sub-society must have been interlocal, which means, among other things, that when its members moved or were forcibly removed from parish to parish, they may often have found relatives awaiting them. But though kin connection would account for the continuity of the sub-society over time and between places, it does little to suggest that it had much coherence in any one parish or locality. We have found that kinship was of problematic importance in English history in integrating individuals into associations, however important it was on particular occasions, such as getting a job or migrating. When we ask ourselves whether it was likely that the members of the sub-society felt any sort of solidarity with each other, we find ourselves invoking the character of sexual nonconformism itself.

At a time when marriage was officially and peremptorily demanded of procreating couples, and chastity was required of all others, when shame was the sanction for sexual compliance, it might be thought inevitable that a nonconforming minority should have been set aside from the conforming majority. We have invoked the principle of the conspicuousness, the unacceptability of such behaviour in arguing for the overall reliability of illegitimacy registration, and when commenting upon the frequent claim that in such a place at such a time bastardy mattered little or not at all. In Sweden, as we are told, loose women were indeed given social salience in folk practices during the nineteenth century. They had to wear a particular headdress to mark their avocation, as we shall see in due course.

A similar custom seems to have existed in medieval France, but in neither instance does it seem that the girls we should class as sparrows were affected, probably the repeaters only. We know of nothing like this in England at any time, and Alan Macfarlane fails to confirm such practices from the ultimately meticulous examination he has made of villages in Essex and Lancashire. There need be no surprise, however, if the knot of interrelated families associated with actions so notorious did have an identity in an English locality nevertheless, and that some of the individuals so marked out should end by acting as expectation demanded.

It is certainly not excluded, therefore, that the bastard-begetters and -bearers appearing in a parish register in a later century should have had genealogical connections with those living there in a former century, even sharing the same surname. The Hoares of Colyton are an example.[7] But such direct lines of descent in the same parish are likely to be rare: first because patrilines did not stay put in the same place; they disappeared by dying out, or moving away, or both. The bastardy prone were likely to have been more liable to die childless than others. Second, because those who moved out were succeeded by others who moved in, and though some of these newcomers might conceivably have had sexual nonconformists in their ancestry who had lived in the village they were entering, this would obviously not be common. Third, because as has been said, a disposition to act in imitation of forebears affects a few persons only: most will not act like this, and some will quickly lose all association with such ancestral characteristics. Fourth, because some bastardy prone descent lines will have developed the association in the meantime, because of the experiences of certain individuals.

Of course, we cannot be sure that these experiences were the sole reasons for a particular family joining a bastardy prone sub-society, since the tendency might have been latent in the way described. The principle of latency, in fact, is rather too effective in suggesting apparently unlikely associations, and, along with successive socialization, requires us to assume that a new offender against the sexual code is more likely than other persons to have sexual nonconformism in the ancestry. Such developments need not be confined to sexual matters, of course. Class awareness can be, must be, transmitted by socialization as well as by all the other instruments of collective continuity.

What we have found about sexual nonconformism might help us to understand, for example, how the levelling notions held by some of the humbler people of the mid-seventeenth century reappeared among their distant successors, the Chartists, in the early nineteenth century, although there was little in the way of published literary continuity. We should not expect a group of radical-minded villagers to have the same definiteness as our bastardy prone sub-society, nor that the handing down would have gone on quite as literally from parent to child within the elementary family in the earliest years of life. If such a mechanism existed, it would have existed, we may believe, quite independently of the transmission of sexual nonconformism. Perhaps it may be thought that if the circumstances which gave rise to our sub-society were as we have described them, more complete evidence should have come to light to convince us of its existence and its continuity. We must therefore consider the difficulties inherent in the hypothesis.

3 The bastardy prone sub-society: paradox and uncertainty

Let us return for a moment to questions of membership and definition. The sparrows were exempted because we believe that courtship, at least below the level of the élite, might sometimes end in an illegitimate birth, but without giving

7. For family links between the Hoares (75 name sets, 6 mothers and/or fathers of bastards) with other bastard-producing families in Colyton in particular the Halletts (6 name sets, 3 mothers and/or fathers of bastards) and through them with the Dometts and the Greens, see chapter 3, and table 3.10. Keith Snell of King's College Cambridge, supplies from the appendix to the famous Poor Law Report of 1834 a reference to 'a parish near Devonport' where 'there is a family of hereditary paupers which contains a regular descent of bastards. The fourth generation of illegitimate children . . . appeared some years ago.' 'Hereditary' illegitimacy in Scotland is illustrated in the evidence surveyed in chapter 7, and it is overtly named in one of the sources used by George Seton, (1860) (see notes to figure 1.6). The examiner of the Southern District registers of 1856, reported a woman with 7 or 8 bastards by different fathers, and of her daughters 3 had bastards too; in Hawick a bearer of 11 bastards had a mother and a grandmother said to have borne exactly the same number each.

rise to the notoriety attached to persons assigned to the sub-society. It has to be admitted, however, that to distinguish as sharply as this between the sparrows and the repeaters may be quite unrealistic about local opinion, which is very unlikely to have been as consistent as we must be, or to have weighed differences as carefully.

Perhaps there were areas and periods in which every person ever involved in irregular procreation was proscribed for life, and the family too. This at one extreme, and at the other a position in which for a bastard-bearer to be the sister of another, or to repeat a misdemeanour, made no difference: only the really brazen, particularly those who lived off the proceeds, were to be ostracized. There may even have been places where nobody was classed in this way, or where it was felt that no line could be drawn between those who should and those who should not be separately classified. We must never forget that attitudes to bastard-bearing, repetitive or otherwise, would have differed from class to class. Officialdom, and the local notables, would no doubt have seen distinctions, and assigned disgrace, where ordinary people might be much less concerned.

Nevertheless, the opinion of the neighbourhood generally might be decisive. We have repeatedly stressed the part which such opinion played in insisting that illegitimates, if they were so regarded must be marked as such in the church register. Both Alan Macfarlane and, especially, Keith Wrightson (above, chapter 2, p. 78, and chapter 6, p. 178) have also dwelt on the importance of neighbourhood opinion in deciding what was and what was not, a marriage. This meant that the parish priest must have hesitated before he set down as illegitimate the children of a union which he was confident had had no blessing from the church, because his parishioners might well have accepted the couple as married for all social purposes. Sometimes he might go one way for the baby born to a particular pair, sometimes the other way. Many of the studies in this book, British and foreign, report that a settled, decent relationship accepted locally might pass for marriage.[8]

But the resident cleric was after all the representative of the established conventions, which were also the values of the Christian church and of the ruling élite. The more he fulminated against sexual misconduct, the more conspicuous would the offenders become, and so, presumably, the more clearly defined the sub-society. In chapter 4 we have read of the parson at Ash, referring to 'two unhappy violators of God's holy law', and we may add a baptismal entry from Lesbury in Northumberland in 1806: 'Richard, third son of Robert Elliot, labourer, by Margaret Fish and of course illegitimate'. Margaret had had four previous bastards, all by different men, and the 'of course' consigns her for ever to the sub-society as we define it.

But there is paradox here as well, similar to that which was pointed out when the registration of bastards was under review (chapter 1, section 9, p. 48). Hostility to these practices could perhaps reduce their prevalence, but it would certainly increase evasion. While the zealous priest was congratulating himself on his success, he might have been becoming less aware of what was going on. If the

8. See chapter 4 for inconsistent decisions about those to be marked illegitimate in the register, and the studies of North America (chapter 14 and 15 below) for socially accepted yet not obviously regular unions. Parsons, especially in the eighteenth century could be remarkably matter of fact about bastardy, like Woodforde, the famous diarist, whose equanimity as to the pregnancy of his own maidservants surprises the modern reader. He records without adverse comment the case of a fine lady who had a base child with a manservant, which is perhaps the most outrageous of all violations of élite sexual orthodoxy, in spite of the impression which Rousseau's *Confessions* might have given.

example of the boarding school master is anything to go by, he would probably have been largely ignorant of the sexual practices of his charges, full of suspicion but with no real information until something scandalous happened. He would often, no doubt, have been disposed to believe for the sake of his own self-esteem that the Christian code was being represented much more than it really was. The effect of this on the activities of our hypothetical sub-society and on the recordings in the parish register may have been appreciable, but difficult to estimate.[9]

Uncertainty of this kind was particularly likely where the official values were accepted for the most part by the mass of the society, but with a reservation or so and a considerable amount of tolerance. The tolerance was for those whose anomalous conduct did not go so far as to make people uneasy. The outstanding reservation on the part of ordinary people as to the content of the code was about sexual relations during courtship. If it is correct to look upon bastardy as the correlate of courtship among the people at large, then it cannot be true that they wholly accepted the rule of respectability on this point. The priesthood was preaching élite values, but their lieutenants, the substantial villagers who held office in the parish, were in a much more equivocal position, like the prefects in an English public school.

We know of one churchwarden who had cohabited with his wife before their marriage, Ralph Meers, a labourer of Clayworth in Nottinghamshire in the 1680s. They had been refused Communion only a few years before for this flagrant offence, at the very rails of the altar, when the wife to be was already pregnant.[10] Here a representative of the ordinary people found himself acting as spokesman for a sexual prohibition which ordinary people did not consistently observe and which he had conspicuously violated. With prenuptial pregnancy as common as it was in England, there must have been many churchwardens expected to present their neighbours to the ecclesiastical court for actions they themselves had committed.

These paradoxes, evasions and uncertainties, added to the fragmentary character of the evidence, make it impossible for us to be more definite about the lineaments of the bastardy prone sub-society. We might perhaps convince ourselves that the indications which have been found are about all that we can expect in the way of support for the hypothesis. However, we have yet to consider a challenge to that hypothesis in the form in which we have expounded it, a challenge not so much to the identity of the sub-society as to its informing principle.

The questions we still have to answer go like this. How do we know that the relationship between the people whose behaviour interests us did have much to do with their common connection with bastardy and with their descent? Could it not have been rather their poverty which bound them together, their common situation at the bottom of the hierarchy which dominated the places where they lived and the society at large? Should we not suppose that their proletarian status was in fact what set them apart from the rest of the population, the reason why

9. On the Victorian public schoolmaster and desperate ignorance of the extent to 'sin' among his boys, going with a conviction that Christian standards were being maintained, see J. R. de S. Honey, *Tom Brown's Universe* (1977), p. 167 ff. Unlike Woodforde, the parish priests of the late eighteenth and early nineteenth centuries, when our sub-society was so much in evidence, seem to have had a similar attitude, especially the Evangelicals.

10. Laslett (1977), p. 52. In their book on the village of Terling entitled *Poverty and Piety in an English village, Terling, 1525–1700* (1979), a village which figures so largely in their chapter in this volume, Levine and Wrightson describe a whole group of the late sixteenth-century village notables, substantial men in office, but all to some degree sexually nonconformist.

they intermarried and perpetuated themselves, rather than their sexual singularities? Being poor, we have been told in chapter 5, might be grounds for a parish preventing a couple from marrying, so ensuring that any children they had were bastards. If they had more than one child in this way, they would fall into our sub-society.

In considering change over time we might further be asked the following. Were not the fluctuations in the activity of the sub-society from time to time simply variations either in the size of the proletariat or in the opportunity of its members to reproduce themselves, or both? For it is a salient fact of English social history that the two known periods when the bastardy prone sub-society was most evident, the turn of the sixteenth century and the late eighteenth century, seem also to have been times when proletarianization was increasing and when obstacles may have been placed in the way of proletarian marriage. They were certainly the periods during which, as we have surmised, courtship was at its most intense, and when poor people were most caught up in that process.

4 Proletarianization, prostitution and the bastardy prone sub-society

An effective set of replies would require information not yet available and perhaps never to be available. Though we already know that not all the bastardy prone were of the poorest, the queries we have set down certainly go to the heart of our present topic. In order to deal with them adequately, we should have to take into consideration how far sexual convention can have been a cause of conduct independent of other features of the social structure. We should also have to estimate how widespread proletarian status was in pre-industrial communities and how variable over time. Furthermore, we would be required to decide how far poverty, powerlessness, marginality may have been 'inherited' in the past, indeed down to the present, and above all to what extent these circumstances led to low fertility. Finally, it would be necessary to gauge the degree to which the mode of transmission has been successive socialization, and whether sexual nonconformism can be thought to have functioned to any extent as a marker of social salience, like the blackness of the North American blacks.

We certainly cannot hope to settle all these wide-ranging issues here. The very fact that they arise in such an urgent way demonstrates once more how the study of the history of bastardy compels a searching analysis of the social structure, past and present. A study of the history of the English proletariat, its size and its vicissitudes, over long stretches of time belongs to an entirely different enterprise. But we can make a little progress with the overlap between a bastardy prone sub-society and the *Lumpenproletariat* by citing an accepted proposition in the study of social structure in relation to social norms.

Normative regulations are always less respected in the lower classes than they are in the higher. The person who gets little or nothing out of the established order is likely to be less inclined to accept its constraints than one who gets much more. This might be particularly true of the irksome discipline going with codes of sexual comportment. Moreover, the poor have been and still are the worst instructed, not only in the content of sexual regulation but in the likely consequences of their own actions. We need not accept the claims made so often in the past by the socially superior about poor people being poor, and even disposed to be criminal as well, because they were stupid, even half-witted, to recognize that the least informed are likely to act irresponsibly in matters of intercourse and procreation.

We must be careful, nevertheless, not to treat normlessness as if it were transparent, self-evident in a way in which it has appeared at all times to the respectable and law abiding, and to many of the social scientists among them. Paul Rock, quoting one of his predecessors, says:

> The deviant is one to whom that label has been successfully applied; deviant behaviour is behaviour that people so label. And it is nothing more. This is a definition which regards as problematic what many criminologists have taken for granted. It does not assume in advance that crimes are alone the proper study of the sociology of deviancy; that deviancy can be construed as 'antisocial' behaviour; that it is statistically infrequent activity; or that it is behaviour which flouts widely held norms. Moreover it does not prejudge the character of the causal processes that can generate deviancy. Whilst it treats social rules as an identifying system, it presupposes nothing else about the characteristics of those who may become deviant or the experiences which they may share as a result of their having become deviant. It is thus a definition of great potential fruitfulness.[11]

Bearing this in mind, we should be cautious about an account of the sub-society which treats bastardy and prenuptial pregnancy simply as the accepted manifestations of the normlessness and ignorance which go with poverty. Proletarian status may have done most to give the members of the sub-society, or most of them, a common identity, but it did not necessarily drive them into deviance. The poorest part of the population showed forth this behaviour more consistently than any other, nevertheless. So acute was their penury that they might sometimes be tempted or even compelled to barter their bodies for extra food, like the fifteen-year-old Victorian girl who 'let men fuck her for sausage rolls, yes, meat pies and pastry too'.[12]

This is what we are told by a Victorian middle-class fancier of whores and of sexual experience. But although what he says may ring true, the work which has now begun on the routine, official records, mostly police court records, of prostitution in the past, the Victorian past anyway, scarcely confirms the general reliability of such sources. Poverty, if an almost entirely necessary reason, was certainly not a sufficient reason why working class girls took to the streets.

Selling yourself on the streets in a literal sense, that is on the pavement of the alleyways which went to make up the Victorian slum, was the lowest form of prostitution. It was usually the last resort of the desperate among the young women in the trade. In her study of the whores of York now in the course of publication, Frances Finnegan argues with considerable conviction that most of their clients must have come from the working class as they did in Scotland. In her

11. See Paul Rock, *Deviant behaviour* (1973), pp. 19–22. The definition he quotes from H. S. Becker, *Outsiders* (1963), p. 9. We may notice that the ignorance of the bastard-bearer of earlier times never went as far as ignorance of what the Victorian parent called 'the facts of life'. No one pleaded such ignorance as a defence in any of the ecclesiastical court records I have seen.

12. See Steven Marcus, *The other Victorians* (1966), p. 107, quoting *My secret life*, introd. G. Leman (1962) etc. 'Her widowed and impoverished mother', the text continues, 'did not know of her doings, and would have deeply disapproved, which is why the girl indignantly refused the title "gay".' This anonymous scatological diary certainly shows extraordinary insight into the conditions and attitudes of working class and proletarian people who must have belonged to the sub-society. It is a work of surprising literary quality, which hinders rather than helps us to decide how much of its content is genuine observation, and how much fantasy.

view the title 'the oldest profession' is a caricature of a cruel and deceptive kind, and the use of middle-class reminiscence, middle-class sexual fantasy as a source, must lead to distortion. The swarms of these destitute and near-destitute girls who thronged the central areas of a cathedral city and county capital in Victorian England must all have come from poverty-stricken families, some of them broken families which had inflicted suffering on them in early life. Their own persistent drunkenness and appalling liability to disease are themselves adequate to explain why they had so few bastard children, although they did have some.

Prostitution is considered here as an activity wholly contained within the bastary prone sub-society, as indicated in table 8.1. We suppose that recruits to this activity, male as well as female, although we know nothing about male prostitutes historically, came predominantly or almost exclusively from the sub-society. But though it might be proper to claim that wherever there were prostitutes, there was a body of the sexually deviant and hence our sub-society, we must make careful distinctions. It would be an error, at least in the English case, to think that all members of the sub-society had its extreme characteristics. Just as it is true to say that not all proletarians were members of the sub-society, it is also true to say that not all the girls in the sub-society were whores.

The difficulty we have found in keeping this last distinction can be illustrated in Sweden. A recent study in that country portrayed as whores of the countryside (*Horan i bonde samhallet*) girls of suspect reputation, usually apparently bearers of bastards who went further than the 'sparrows' of our own terminology. The author of this study has been sharply criticized for using the term 'whore' since that word implies that all the women were true prostitutes. However this may be, it would seem that there must have existed in Sweden a body of the sexually and maritally deviant much better marked off than any deviant group we have identified so far in England. A *Löndahora* had to wear a special headdress; she was under church sanction, and lay sanction as well; an evil eye, an evil tongue and an evil touch were all ascribed to her; no doubt witchcraft too, if it seemed appropriate. Meeting one, oddly enough, was lucky for a man, though not for a woman, and they were auspicious on some agricultural occasions.

In Sweden, therefore, whatever the relationship of sparrows to repeaters, there was a recognized group of the bastardy prone who had characteristics other than poverty, and these were cultural characteristics. That extreme poverty did not always lead to prostitution can be vividly illustrated from the city of York in Victorian times. The poorest people of all in the slums there were the immigrant Irish, who actually lived in the red light district. But it was rare for an Irish girl to be convicted of prostitution. Something in being Irish seems to have prevented your becoming a harlot.

The whores of York tended to persist in their trade in spite of attempts at rehabilitation. They were certainly recidivist, as those who ran the home for fallen women in that city found to their disappointment and chagrin.[13] But they seem peculiarly difficult to class with the women in France who worked in those established, church-recognized public brothels which were a regular feature of

13. I owe all the information about the whores of York to Frances Finnegan; it is to be found in her book entitled *Poverty and prostitution* (1979). Compare also chapter 10 of her PhD dissertation, written as F. E. Beechey, on the 'Irish in York 1845–1875'. For whores in the countryside in Sweden see the title given in the text by Jonas Frykman (1978), English summary pp. 220–9. I have benefited from correspondence with him, with Birgitte Frykman of Gothenburg (not related) about this study, and with Ann-Sofie Kälvemark, whose review of Jonas Frykman's work will appear in *Social History*.

the cities in the valley of the Rhône in the fifteenth century, or with those in the 'public stews' in the Continental cities so frequently referred to by English travellers at all periods. In England in the nineteenth century, however, a market town could have its notorious areas resembling that around York cathedral. A survey of Banbury in 1859 revealed five out of a row of eight houses inhabited by cohabiting couples. Nearby a labourer, 'Badger Willson', lived with Susan Owen his 'housekeeper', a prostitute whom he finally murdered.[14]

The economic theory of prostitution presumably goes like this. Where an effective demand exists for sexual services outside marriage and a potential supply, a market will come into being. Connections between the suppliers, such as we have identified in our sub-society, genealogical connections or otherwise, would be important only in so far as they facilitated the flow. Demand would ensure that some individuals would offer the commodity whatever their ancestry and upbringing. Signs of such a market can be found in the essays contributed by English scholars on England and such signs are to be found, according to the appendix to this chapter, right back to the thirteenth century.

These writers seem to shrink from supposing that these errant individuals whom they have identified offered themselves in any organized way, or were in it full time. But it could still be argued that such economically interested persons played a significant part in the sub-society in England and gave it something of its structure, even if they were not common there, and even if only some of them were publicly recognized strumpets like those of Sweden or of France. We can think of them as that portion of the poor, mostly of the very poor, showing a disposition which allowed or inclined them to traffic in sexual services. It does not follow from this that all proletarian women were likely to take part in the business, even if they were members of the sub-society. Nor does it follow that all sexual irregularity took place in this particular social area.

Not all of our contributors, as we have said, seem prepared to accept such statements without modification or to credit the distinctions here laid down. In their studies of the social context of illegitimacy and the decline of its incidence in the early seventeenth century, for example, David Levine and Keith Wrightson are evidently unwilling to pronounce on the distinctiveness of the bastardy prone let alone the traffickers among them. At one point they hesitate to allow of the existence of a sub-society at all. They take up one of the positions which we touched upon earlier: there were no divisions, but a continuum.[15] It is important for the exact examination of such issues as that of the bastardy prone sub-society that they should proceed by making use of network analysis to sanction this judgement. But in his appendix to this chapter (p. 240), Richard Smith goes into their argument from the use of this technique and decides that it lacks conclusiveness. If it cannot be said that a clear line drawn round the sub-society is discernible in the historical evidence so far available from any past community, neither can it be shown that such a line did not exist.

14. For the official bawdy houses of the Rhône and southeastern France, see J. Rossiaud, 'Prostitution, youth and society in the towns of southeastern France in the fifteenth century' (1978). Public prostitution is a vast subject in itself, and can only be touched on here in relation to the sub-society. For Banbury, see B. S. Trinder, 'The Banbury poor in 1850', *Cake and Cockhorse*, Journal of the Banbury Historical Society (1966). Our English studies fail to reveal a marked tendency for the bastardy prone to live close to each other in places like Colyton. But little seems to have been done for England on any form of prostitution before the nineteenth century, though Stone (1977), p. 618 and refs., has an interesting passage on the 1750s (see note 17 below).

15. Compare also the statements in chapter 3 above and those in David Levine's, *Family formation in an age of nascent capitalism* (1977).

Like the remarkable series of facts reported by Alan Macfarlane from Earls Colne in chapter 2, the researches presented in chapter 5 by David Levine and Keith Wrightson tend to echo and confirm the findings made in so many parish registers by others. But in my view it seems fair to say that they do little to revise or to contradict them. When Levine and Wrightson describe the amorous escapades of poorer people as part and parcel of a vigorous popular culture, they themselves suggest that a somewhat different attitude to sex and marriage was a feature of life below the level of the élite. We need not wonder, then, that courtship sometimes ended in pregnancy among quite self-respecting if usually lowly people, nor need we suppose that it was only simple normlessness which informed the practice of those who could be called disreputable, the members of the bastardy prone sub-society. Persons placed as they were placed must have been even more disposed to heterodoxy in sexual matters than the poor at large, heterodoxy from the point of view of the dominant majority, that is to say. It evidently disposed some of them to live as prostitutes, or from prostitution.

Of course, it could be maintained that the behaviour of these last named persons made economic sense, for they did provide a service on the market. We might call the outlook which all this implied the outlook not of the deserving, but of the undeserving poor. This is a phrase which has been consecrated by generations of social ameliorators and administrators of the Poor Law, although they must have meant rather different things by it at different periods. We have only to remember such things as the changing legal definition of 'vagrancy' to recognize this, or the changing degrees of stigma attached to poor relief. The officials, however, were not the only superior people who came into contact with disreputable proletarians. The sexually incontinent among the upper class often did so too. Christopher Smout has shown us in chapter 7 what these individuals were like in nineteenth-century Scotland. We shall call such persons libertines.

5 The undeserving poor and the libertines: a somewhat different sexual code?

In insisting that poverty alone cannot explain the existence of a bastardy prone sub-society, we have admitted that predisposition and psychic history have a part to play as well. Moreover it might be said that the notion of a sub-society implies the holding of a positive outlook, however vague and intermittent; it should not be assumed to have been informed simply by belieflessness. In this way the undeserving poor must be supposed to have had a differing sexual and marital code, even if we find it impossible to specify what that code can have been, except in rather general terms. This unorthodox outlook, whatever it consisted of, must have been shared with the sexually nonconforming among those who were not poverty stricken, the libertines in fact.

To recognize the presence of substantial persons among the bastardy prone, we have only to look back over our earlier chapters. There are the statements in chapter 2 and chapter 7 about the status of sexual offenders, for example, and the astonishing story of Michael Becker's twelve bastards begotten at Ash on Hannah Solley, set out in chapter 4. As an overseer of the poor, Becker was responsible for maintaining bastards and their mothers, and he was expected to keep expenses down. Nevertheless, by our definition he was a member of the sub-society himself, along with all masters who got their housekeepers or their maidservants with child, if they did it more than once or were nonconforming in other ways.

If another example is needed, we could cite that of William Tyler of Myddle in Shropshire in the late seventeenth century. He is recorded to have 'debauched Hussey's wife and caused them to part. She went to Little Drayton and there this Tyler visited her sometimes, and at last he had a child by her which was commonly called Nell Hussey. When she was grown up and able to do service, Tyler took her to be his housekeeper, and had a bastard by her. Illegitimacy and incest on the part of a man who seems to have had a little estate.[16] Taking advantage of superiority over the undeserving poor to enjoy promiscuity, defying the conforming pressure which came from higher status, placed a yeoman, a farmer or a gentleman in the sub-society along with many or even most of the undeserving poor themselves. So did taking a concubine and having two daughters by her, as Erasmus Darwin did, or having a succession of by-blows by a series of mistresses, like Robert Burns, or being guilty of both these activities and of incessant whoremongering as well, like James Boswell.[17] Even the eminently respectable William Wordsworth can be classed as belonging to the bastardy prone sub-society as we define it, for he had an illegitimate daughter in France before his marriage, and a first cousin who was also a bastard-begetter.[18]

Although most of the clients of most of the proletarian girls who took to the streets were themselves workers, it does not follow that going with prostitutes was uncommon with gentlemen, gentlemen libertines. It was, and perhaps still is, a peculiarly interesting form of intercourse between the classes. The libertine did not confine his activities to harlots, of course, and it was the ruination of 'women of character' which incurred the harshest condemnation from contemporaries.

The provision of sexual satisfaction and companionship to these people can logically be called a service on the market. The same could be said for the working men who resorted to prostitutes, and it is possible to suggest a wider social role for women of easy virtue among the people at large. Although we have no ground for supposing that the popular culture of the alehouses and village greens depended to any considerable degree on the existence of prostitution, the local whores seem to have been figures on that social scene which puzzled no one. These representatives of the undeserving poor were also part of holiday.

Bastardy proneness certainly cannot have been as efficient a marker of proletarian status in traditional England as blackness has been for a portion of the population of North America. But their distinctive traits may have had somewhat

16. Gough, *Antiquityes*, p. 110: see note 22 below.
17. For a splendid description of James Boswell's sexual life, for Erasmus Darwin and for other illustrative careers of the sexually nonconforming in England like Samuel Pepys, see Lawrence Stone, *The family, sex and marriage in England, 1500–1800* (1977): on Burns's bastard begetting see DNB. As Stone recognized, the motives of the women who became the kept mistresses or the occasional companions of such men have also to be understood. He seems to believe that they can be explained by family misfortune taking place in the lower level of the élite, where young women had little prospect of marriage and no other expedient but sexual dependency of this kind. This is a persuasive argument. Yet only some of the women in this position took to adultery or fornication, and he describes numbers of those who did so without obvious economic motives. These women might have been classed in the sub-society, along with the men, but it seems to have been rare (though see above, p. 224) for them to have been partnered by the proletarian members of the sub-society as was the case with so many of the males.
18. William Wordsworth's aunt, Anne, married Reverend Thomas Myers, and their son, Thomas Myers, had an illegitimate daughter, alive in 1795. Erasmus Darwin's second wife's first husband had a bastard too. The list of English men of letters who had bastards is a long and interesting one. To those cited already must be added for example Byron, Shelley, Thomas de Quincey (begotten of a local Grasmere girl whom Wordsworth advised him not to marry, advice which he ignored) and Thomas Hobbes (information from Professor Samuel Mintz of City College, New York). Some at least of these must have conformed to our definition for membership of the sub-society. See Emile Legouis, *William Wordsworth and Annette Villon* (1922), especially pp. 5 and 55. This author's attempts to assuage the outraged respectability of his readership seem a little strange half a century later. He accounts for the unfortunate happenings by referring to the licentiousness generally prevalent among the intelligentsia of the late eighteenth century.

similar functions, and there is the same paradox that these traits were in each case shared by individuals decidedly not in a proletarian position. There have always been some middle-class American blacks, as well as substantial Englishmen who were libertines. In southern France, as is well known in that country, the descendants of lepers are still proscribed persons in some communities, even though leprosy itself died out many generations ago. The inherited taint is enough to mark such unfortunates as outcasts, and if this can be so why should not bastardy proneness be perpetuated by the same sort of ascribed apartness?

The value of even so qualified a conclusion to the historian of the proletariat should be obvious, and perhaps the much needed sociological history of the lowest classes should begin with the study of the bastardy prone. This is as far as we should try to go in resolving the questions about proletarianization and the sub-society. We can see that to translate that title into the 'undeserving poor' is not quite right, interesting as are the suggestions conveyed by that phrase. Perhaps we ought to leave the issue about the libertines an open one, and contemplate a separate sub-society amongst the élite, which would have to include the aberrant intellectuals as well, separate but connected by innumerable if mostly evanescent contacts with the deviant amongst the proletariat.

We shall also have to leave undecided the question of how often the bastardy prone were also criminals or idiots or psychotics. It is known that prostitutes are often thieves as well, and they must steal from members of their own class, their own sub-society, more often and more in total than they do from others (Finnegan, see note 13). There are innumerable references in our English sources to madness among the bastardy prone, and not all of them can be the rationalizations of the conventional official.

As for the relationships between the sub-society and all other sets of persons, meaning by this the sets distinguished in our table of memberships (table 8.1, p. 233), we may cautiously affirm that there seems to be no point in trying to revise that series of highly provisional social distinctions. We must guard against too rigid a view of the apartness of those who do not do as others do, since collaboration for most social purposes goes on with nearly all of them for nearly all the time, even with convicted criminals. Sexual nonconformism marked some people off for some purposes, but not for all purposes. We do not have to suppose that a sub-society had to have wholly separate principles of organization in order to exist at all.

6 The repeater effect, family relations and the sub-society

We should be prepared to expect from our argument so far that repetitive bastard-bearing and genealogical connection between bastard-bearers would mark the historical record of any community. But what we shall call the repeater effect, the circumstances that when illegitimacy is high more bastards are due to repetitive bastard-bearing than when it is low, may be more difficult to accept. For this will only be present if the bastardy prone sub-society did act in the way suggested, as a continuing source of illegitimate births, more prolific at times of high illegitimacy than at others. It is necessary, therefore, that we should be confident that the repeater effect was genuine.

Our English chapters make it plain that during the later eighteenth-century rise in illegitimacy, repeaters became much more common, and that they were rare in the later seventeenth century, when illegitimacy was low. This relationship is particularly well marked at Ash as will be seen in figure 8.1. Here, as well as at Colyton and elsewhere, the rise in illegitimacies during the late eighteenth-century high was not simply due to an increase in the numbers of girls having bastards, but to those having them having more. This we take to be the bastardy prone sub-society in action. Its booster effect on the total of illegitimacies is quite patent, together with the fact that the rise in illegitimacies was to a certain extent confined in its source.

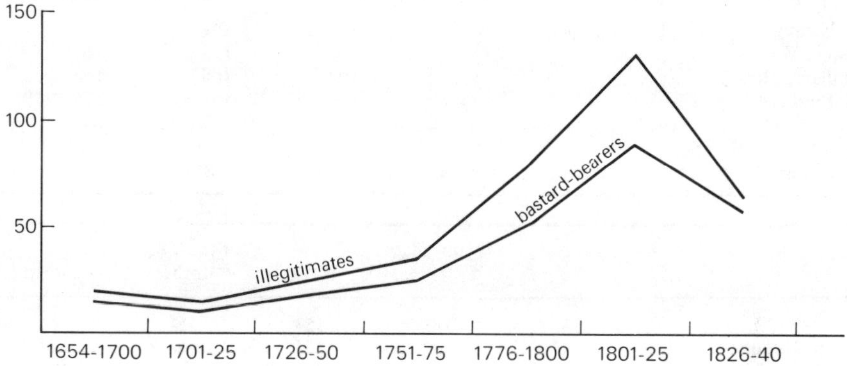

Fig. 8.1 Illegitimates and bastard-bearers at Ash, Kent (data supplied by Anthea Newman, from the Ash reconstitution)

To be a general feature of illegitimacy, however, the repeater effect would have to be demonstrated for the whole known numerical record. This means that the peak in the bastardy ratio in the sixteenth and early seventeenth centuries would have to be accompanied by a greater proportion of births out of wedlock due to repeaters. The statements about Earls Colne in chapter 2 and about Terling in Essex in chapter 5 suggests that this is what happened at that time in those places, but not all the other evidence points so clearly in this direction. In table 8.2 a repeater index is set out for seven parishes, the only ones for which we have relatively complete information over the whole stretch of years. The figures show that this index did go up and down in rough accordance with the bastardy ratio during the two centuries, beginning in 1640. It cannot be said to demonstrate with any conclusiveness, however, that repetitive bastard-bearing was a characteristic of the illegitimacy wave in the latest decades of the sixteenth century and the earlier decades of the seventeenth century. At Alcester, nevertheless, the index for 1540 to 1589 was very high indeed at 139, and it must have risen to about 125 at Earls Colne between 1600 and 1627.[19] In spite of the pronounced absence of repeaters at other parishes at that time and in spite of the difficulties with small numbers before 1600, we need not give up hope that further research may confirm a point of importance, that the earlier, lower wave of illegitimacy in England did resemble the later, higher wave, in respect of repetitive bastard-bearers.

There may be obstacles to accepting the importance of the repeater effect even if this forecast should turn out to be justified. For it is conceivable that the increased number of repeaters found in baptismal records at the two peak periods

19. Compare chapter 3, table 3.2 and Levine (1977), p. 138, where 35 per cent of all bastards are shown to have been due to repeaters at Colyton during the period 1540–89. The figures for Alcester and Earls Colne show that Colyton was not quite as exceptional as Levine seems to suppose. Richard Smith also concludes that the repeater effect cannot be demonstrated from available evidence from the late sixteenth and early seventeenth centuries; see above, p. 86.

Table 8.2: Repeater indices and bastardy ratios for seven English parishes, 1540–1840

	1540–90	1590–1639	1640–89	1690–1739
Wem, Salop	(150)[a]	115	112	113
Colyton, Devon	118	111	100	126
Hawkshead, Lancs.	–	103	100	107
Campton-with-Shefford } Southill, Beds.	100	100	100	115
Gainsborough, Lincs.	106	100	102	116
Alcester, Warws.	139	100	115	107
Aldenham, Herts.	(117)[b]	100	108	108
Period indices (7 parishes)	119	106	105	116
Mean of bastardy ratios (6 parishes)	1.94%	2.51%	1.28%	2.85%

	1740–89	1790–1840	1540–1840 Births	1540–1840 Mothers	1540–1840 Index
Wem, Salop	127	127	552	451	122
Colyton, Devon	136	135	551	452	122
Hawkshead, Lancs.	128	119	435	377	115
Campton-with-Shefford } Southill, Beds.	136	112	304	260	117
Gainsborough, Lincs.	122	109	642	574	112
Alcester, Warws.	111	117	307	267	115
Aldenham, Herts.	137	116	207	173	120
Period indices (7 parishes)	127	118	2998	2554	117
Mean of bastardy ratios (6 parishes)	5.25%	4.10%			

(a) 3/2 (b) 7/6

Data: from family reconstitutions, Cambridge Group.

Note: The repeater index is the number of bastards borne by 100 women bearing bastards, where 100 means one bastard each (no repetitive bastard-bearing) and 200 would mean that nearly every mother had more than one bastard (practically all bastard bearing repetitive). It is the least unsatisfactory of the possible indices, though it is based on the children rather than the mothers, because it may compensate to some degree for the many bastards never baptized.

arose not so much because of greater numbers of bastards born to each bearer as because of the greater tendency of those women to baptize successive illegitimate children in the same church. The repeater effect may be due to differential migration, at least in part. This possibility may be seen as the most formidable in the way of acknowledging the existence of a bastardy prone sub-society. For this reason Richard Smith's discussion of the relationship between 'repeaterdom' and migration in the first section of chapter 3 above is of particular importance. His discussion, it will be remembered, went some way towards establishing the view that migration was high at the time of the peak in sexual nonconformism in the late sixteenth and early seventeenth centuries, and low at the time of the further and higher peak in the late eighteenth and early nineteenth centuries. From this it seems permissible to infer two possibilities. The first is that a reason why our repeater index is so often lower than we might expect during the earlier high is that repetitive bastard-bearers were more mobile at that time. The second is that the nature of the sub-society may have differed between the two periods. It may have consisted under Elizabeth of vagrant persons, in that classic age of vagrancy, but under the later Georges of settlement-bound paupers.

These inferences, like so much else about the hypothetical sub-society, have to remain provisional. This is so if only because the general impression of the poorer people of earlier times is of perpetual footlooseness. The facts about the astonishing rates of turnover of population, especially among servants, have been fairly well established, and they are enough to explain all that has been said about the sparrow.[20] Nevertheless we have abundant evidence that the entry of a girl liable to bear a bastard into a parish was likely to be strongly resisted at all times by the parish officials. We can see these things happening in Essex in the early seventeenth century in chapter 6; and there was an established offence in the church courts called harbouring, that is giving houseroom to such undesirables as bastards. This offence had existed since the middle ages and was certainly the subject of prosecutions for as long as these courts were effective, that is to the late seventeenth century.[21]

The overseers of the poor remained very active against the threat of being saddled with bastard children, as can be seen from the settlement papers: in the early eighteenth century, for example, the authorities of Harefield in Middlesex 'gave to a woman that was ready to cry out and to two women to have her away to another parish, three shillings'.[22] 'Ready to cry out' was a common expression for about to give birth. Richard Gough, the chronicler of Myddle in Cheshire, tells us a complementary tale of three daughters of a 'light housewife' who lived in his village, 'two of which are as impudent whores as any in this country; one of them has two bastards, and she being run out of the country, they are both maintained by the parish. The other is now [20 January 1701] great with a bastard, and at Christmas last was sent by order into Wem parish, where her last service and settlement was.'

Gough's story reminds us that a servant had a settlement in a village where she had served for a year. She could not be forced out of that village if she threatened to produce a bastard, though she might be returned to it under these circumstances if she had gone elsewhere. This may help to explain the sparrows. Moreover, she would presumably be well enough known in the village where she was in service or had served to be able to secure godparents for her baby, which were necessary for it to be baptized. We know that godparents were always a difficulty at the christening of illegitimates, and a case from Wilburton in Cambridgeshire in the year 1665 shows how unwilling people were to stand up in front of the congregation and answer for such a child.[23] This obstacle must always have been greater in an entirely strange parish.

20. For migration generally, see for example, P. Clark, *Poverty and social policy 1750–1870* (1974), and for turnover, Laslett (1977), chapter 2.

21. See e.g. P. Hair, *Before the bawdy court, selections from church court records . . . 1300–1800* (1972), p. 246; and reports of cases of harbouring in 1458, 1530, 1595, 1623 and 1640. For the overseers of the poor acting in this way in the mid-eighteenth century, see Dorothy Marshall, *The English poor in the eighteenth century* (1926), pp. 213 ff.

22. Mary Hopkirk, *Nobody wanted Sam* (1949), p. 18. This is a popular history of illegitimacy in England with valuable illustrative material not adequately referenced. Gough's *Antiquityes and Memoyres of the Parish of Myddle* (see p. 148) was printed in 1875 and recently republished in facsimile by the Shropshire Record Office. I owe reference to this work, which aptly illustrates many of the points made in the present chapter, to Alan Macfarlane.

23. Ely Diocesan Records, Cambridge University Library, B2/56. The difficulty about godparents perhaps explains why bastards always seem to have been baptized later than legitimate children. That godfathers were required for bastard babies at baptisms, and even sometimes named in the parish registers, is confirmed for the years 1580, 1607–14 and 1609–12 in J. C. Cox, *The parish registers of England* (1910), pp. 54–5. In chapter 2 above, Macfarlane records the doubts of some Puritans as to whether bastards should be baptized at all.

The conclusion, though necessarily still provisional, has to be that there is no persuasive case for supposing that the repeater effect is an artefact of differential short distance migration. Such migration and its fluctuations must have affected the bastardy prone sub-society and the records it has left behind, because, as has been insisted, its members were likely to be migratory. But it is difficult to assess how these circumstances influenced the recording of their illegitimate baptisms in the parish records.

Familial interrelationship is as important to the concept of the bastardy prone sub-society as the repeater effect. If it is to be accepted we must be confident that its members were genealogically interconnected more often than others living at the same time and in the same place. There are two ways in which this extra interrelatedness could in theory be demonstrated – from the evidence of family reconstitution studies and from network analysis. But it cannot be said as yet that either fund of evidence yields a straightforward answer to the question. We know that such persons were often related; we have many indications that they were more so than other people in the communities where they dwelt, but we cannot offer strict proof.

Network analysis may finally make demonstration of this kind a possibility. It is, however, a technique not yet proven for data of this kind and on problems of this description. It requires intricate argumentation and we have thought it best to present such preliminary results from network analysis as are already of significance as an appendix to this chapter.

The notable feature of Richard Smith's discussion is that he uses two sets of data about bastard-bearing. The first is that from Terling in Essex recovered from the original documents by Levine and Wrightson and also used by them in chapter 5 for network analysis purposes. The second comes from an entirely different source and a very different period, the manor rolls of Rickinghall in Suffolk in the later thirteenth century.

It seems that Rickinghall in high medieval times may have had a body of familially connected bastardy prone individuals forming a sub-society of the kind we have been discussing here. This is as we should expect, perhaps, in view of our earlier arguments. It is particularly interesting in that the period concerned is always supposed to have been one of high fertility and rapid population growth.

The evidence of reconstitution as to the familial interconnection of bastard-bearers has been extensively cited in our earlier chapters, and the attempt has been made to use that evidence in a formal demonstration. The data consist in what may be called *name sets*, that is, collections of surnames which appear in the registers of baptisms, marriages and burials in the parishes where reconstitution has been carried out: all the Hills occurring in the Aldenham register, for example, or all the Heards of Hartland. If the bastardy prone sub-society were a reality, it should appear that only some of these name sets were genuinely bastardy prone, though we can expect that a good proportion of them could contain sparrows and singletons. Repeaters in a name set would be a very clear indication of its being associated with the bastardy prone sub-society.

Experience has shown, as has been said already, that English villages did not consist of a given collection of family lines each persisting over the generations, handing down the same surnames from father to son, grandson and great-grandson. In fact, only a tiny proportion of patrilines existed in the same place for the whole three hundred years during which the parish registers allow family reconstitution to be carried out. Most surnames appear, last a generation or two and then disappear; some only remain for one generation. The importance of this to our earlier discussion on 'inherited' bastard-bearing, and on the residual character of familial connections over time will be clearly apparent. Some surname sets in a reconstitution will be large, because lots of members of a number of related families lived in the place over a long period, and some will be small, because a few members of a few families, or of only one family, lived there for a short period.

With these reservations in mind we turn to the surname sets of the reconstitution of Hawkshead. In figure 8.2 is illustrated the relationship between the numbers of children baptized within a set and the numbers of bastards. In general the figure shows just what we should expect, that the larger the number of baptisms, the larger the number of illegitimacies. But there are interesting exceptions: some surname sets have markedly more bastards than we should expect from their numbers of baptisms, and some markedly fewer. The case for an uneven distribution of the tendency towards illegitimacy among families and descent lines in Hawkshead, and with it the bastardy prone sub-society, rests on such instances. A few surname sets are very marked in this way, such as the Martins of whose 49 baptized children 9 were base, and were borne by women who, in some instances, were repeaters. Assuming the Martins to be interrelated we can place them firmly in the sub-society, and it is clear that there were other name sets like theirs.

It will also be noticed that in figure 8.2 there is a tendency for some name sets with fewer baptisms to have higher proportions of illegitimacies, and that the reverse is also true. Some of the name sets with very large numbers of baptisms have very few indeed marked as bastards. These last represent that majority of the completely innocent to which we have referred several times. We have prepared

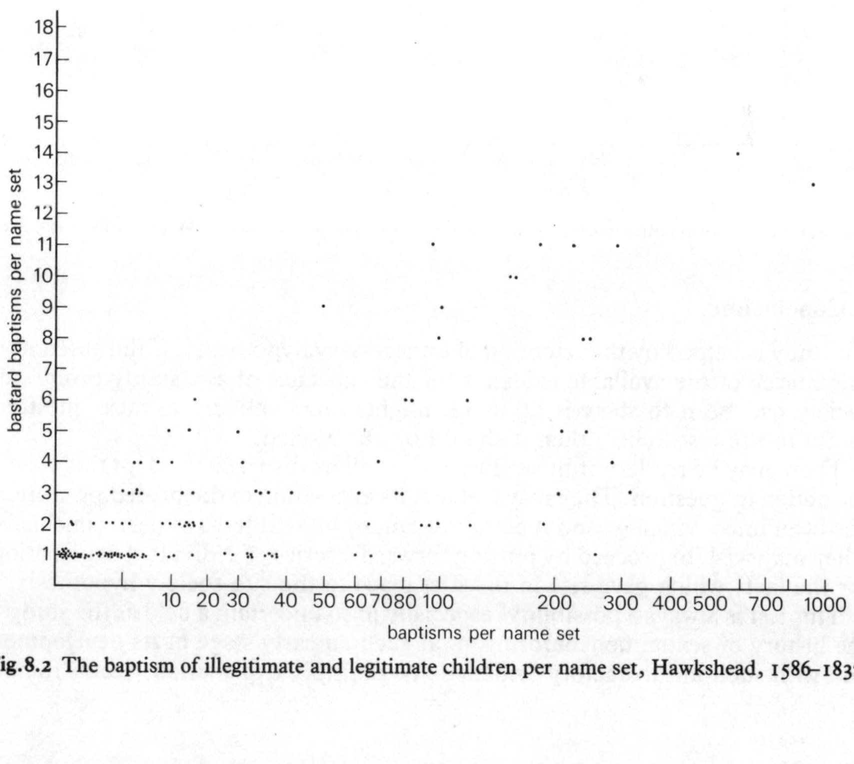

Fig.8.2 The baptism of illegitimate and legitimate children per name set, Hawkshead, 1586–1837

another figure, 8.3, to illustrate the finding, and in this figure baptisms are replaced by the family reconstitution forms themselves, each representing a marriage which ordinarily established a family group in the parish.

Here once again some name sets with smaller numbers of family reconstitution forms (FRFs) produced disproportionately more bastards, and we can give this a further interpretation in terms of a geographical mobility. It seems as though collections of persons bearing the same name, related persons for the most part, of course, who arrived in a parish, did not stay there very long if they were bastardy prone. These 'families', descent groups or patrilines, associated with our sub-society in this parish, seem to betray in these reconstitution records that circulatory tendency which we have commented upon, a footlooseness which was also, perhaps, marginality. They may have been relatively static in the later eighteenth century, but it is difficult ever to regard them as a settled and accepted part of the community.

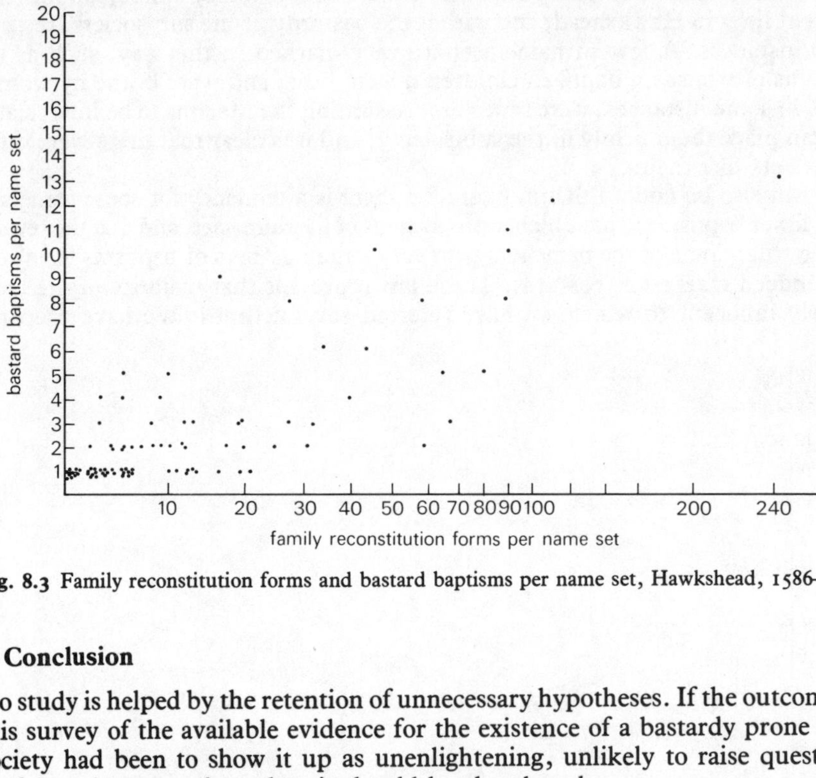

Fig. 8.3 Family reconstitution forms and bastard baptisms per name set, Hawkshead, 1586–1837

7 Conclusion

No study is helped by the retention of unnecessary hypotheses. If the outcome of this survey of the available evidence for the existence of a bastardy prone sub-society had been to show it up as unenlightening, unlikely to raise questions useful to the researcher, then it should be abandoned.

There may be readers of this volume who will be disposed to adopt this view of the notion in question. They may feel that its exposition in the preceding sections has been unconvincing, and it certainly cannot be said to have been conclusive. They may wish to proceed by putting forward a series of individual explanations for the facts which gave rise in the first place to the sub-society hypothesis.

This last is always a possibility, especially in so uncertain a field as the study of the history of sexual nonconformism, at such an early stage of its development and with such unsatisfactory evidence. To multiply explanations seems to have been the tendency of critics of the hypothesis, though it offends in its turn against that which social scientists so often and so rightly refer to – the principle of Ockham's razor. If such critics were to suggest a different simplifying assumption, more satisfactory and efficient than that of the bastardy prone sub-society, then a stage would be passed in the pursuit of the analysis.

We have no desire whatever, as was pointed out in the preface to this volume, to impose a particular explanation, or set of explanations, on the comparative history of bastardy. We have, however, felt it to be important that as many fruitful and interesting hypotheses as possible should be present in our survey, whether or not they are consistent with each other, and however much they may differ in the amount of evidence which can be brought forward to support them. It is in this sense, and in this sense only, that the notion of a bastardy prone sub-society has been retained in the discussions of the British data, and expounded in the present chapter.

Four points may be brought forward, so it seems to us, in favour of retaining the notion of a sub-society of the illegitimacy prone, at least for the present. The first is its efficacy in explaining what has been called the booster effect which seems to come into operation when illegitimacy rises to a peak, at least in England.

It is surely of great interest and importance that a rise in illegitimacy beyond a certain point is no longer also a rise in the numbers of women who have bastards, but rather in the numbers of bastards borne by a minority of them. Such an effect may tell us a great deal about the character of sexual nonconformism and of the attitudes of most persons towards it, and so by analogy of other forms of nonconformism too. It can only be explained, so it seems to us, by appeal to a bastardy prone sub-society in some form or another. It is a pity that the phenomenon has not been observed numerically in files other than the English. But there are plenty of references to its probable presence outside the British Isles, especially in the outstandingly interesting work on Austrian sexual nonconformism carried out by Michael Mitterauer (1979).

The notion of a bastardy prone sub-society explains in the second place the frequently observed kin connectedness of those engaged in sexual nonconformism, and especially of bastard-bearers. We have surveyed this phenomenon at some length here, and explained why such observations have to be so fragmentary. We have made it plain that no one could expect to be able to recover anything more than a small portion of kin connections, or hope to trace them over more than two or three generations. There could be several reasons why repetitive bastard-bearers should be kin connected, but a bastardy prone sub-society is certainly as persuasive a reason as the others.

The bastardy prone sub-society may help us to understand in the third place the disposition of some couples in some places to live in consensual unions. There are many ways of looking at such unions, and the reasons for them, of course. But one of them is to suppose that any man or woman willing to join with another and procreate children, whether on a visiting basis or as a united household, was different in some way from the rest of society, consisting as it did of persons unwilling to take such a step or series of steps. Since only some persons had this trait it may be legitimate to look on them as associated by it.

The fourth point is rather less specific and has to do with attitudes, attitudes regularly commented upon by our contributors but so far not given any systematic ordering, if they are in fact capable of it. There does seem to have been a deviant outlook at large in European society in the past as to sexual nonconformism, however, and if there was such, a bastardy prone sub-society would explain it. Little follows, of course, as we have found, about the composition and structure of such a society from such considerations. But this counter attitude must have resided somewhere, and must have had some continuity. We have already drawn attention to the implications of its existence for social structure generally, for what might be boldly called its federal characteristics.

Here we must leave the bastardy prone sub-society. We do so in the hope that this collection may help to further the investigations which will decisively establish it as a reality, or dispose of it conclusively.

Appendix: A note on network analysis in relation to the bastardy prone sub-society

Richard M. Smith

In what follows we are searching for a technique or a bundle of techniques which on the one hand allow us to define groups and on the other permit us to observe links which cut across groups or socio-economic strata in our analysis of behaviour. Not the least important of the qualities of this technique should be its logical coherence and, particularly, a capacity for exact replication by other researchers to facilitate comparative testing.

Our concern, therefore, is with the social networks within which the fathers and mothers of bastards operated. For a variety of reasons, however, historical networks have generally been described only metaphorically. Networks of this kind have their uses as rather clumsy conceptual tools, but because they lack precise definition, they are limited in their empirical utility. An extended discussion of social network analysis as a really effective method of investigation is scarcely in order here but we can be confident that when properly carried out it can be used to combine the qualitative and quantitative dimensions of historical research. The aim is to provide measures of the structural properties of real world networks by abstracting the system as a set of points, or nodes, and routes or lengths.

It has recently been suggested that social networks should preferably be set in the context of whether they are bounded or unbounded, finite or infinite, partial or total.[24] At one extreme we have the following kind of set, involving certain kinds of link only (partial) connecting a limited number of people (finite) and within a universe in which some persons exist who are not included in the network (bounded). At the other extreme we have a set composed of all kinds of links (total) connecting an unlimited number of persons (infinite) in a universe in which no persons are excluded (unbounded). Figure 8.4 depicts the variety of possible permutations of these characteristics. Historians invariably find themselves in the left-hand arm of figure 8.4 because of the specific nature of their documentary evidence although, partiality, finiteness and boundedness are interdependent characteristics.

Let us look at the example of a will. Its partiality is determined by the nature of the evidence assumed to be inferable from the bond between executor and/or witness and will-maker and beneficiaries in the will, plus incidental detail on such matters as debt owed to or by the will-maker and so on. Its *finiteness* is predetermined, although this may be minimized when all will-maker networks are analysed, aggregated or conflated with those derived from other coexisting contemporary sources. It is bounded by the extent to which

24. N. E. Whitten Jr and A. W. Wolfe, 'Network analysis' (1974), p. 727.

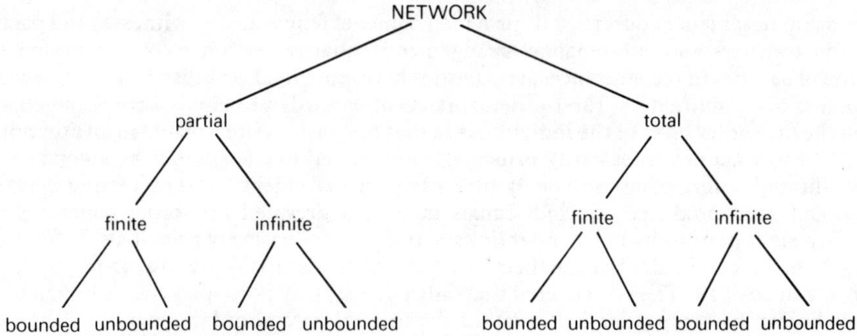

Fig. 8.4 Some categories of social networks

the proportion that the will-making population constitutes of the total population and variation in this phenomenon over space and time. *Boundedness* will always be a function of the spatial and social specificity of the data source and finiteness will be determined by the degree of documentary interlinkage undertaken or possible.

All these points are pertinent to varying degrees in a consideration of the major documents which could be mobilized for the network study of bastard-bearers and begetters (or 'principals'). From the sixteenth to eighteenth centuries those would be parish registers, manorial court rolls, wills, Poor Law records, quarter sessions and ecclesiastical court proceedings. As the data sets are reworked and amalgamated the networks may be conceived as spreading further and further to the right hand side of figure 8.4, although swinging like a pendulum from a suspension point which is indisputably anchored in the partial sector. This unfortunate attribute of such evidence is made worse by the partiality arising from its time-specific character, and by variability in documentary losses through time.

It would be extremely difficult, in explaining any one person's behaviour, to take account of all the indirect influences on him that may be mediated by or through interpersonal and inter-group bonds from the far ends of the earth. Generally in this sort of analysis, with moderately sized communities, we narrow our range of interest to a manageable number of individuals. However, with groups of ten or more analysis usually begins by selecting an individual and identifying the other members with whom he is linked directly. These are his *first-order* contacts. The portion of the network observed at this simple level is known as the individual's first order *star*. From this point it is possible to proceed towards a full network analysis via two routes. Either we look at the relations between any given individual's first-order contacts, or else we can move on from first-order to higher-order contacts and examine the indirect relations between a given individual and those people he can reach only through intermediaries.

We will discuss this second approach with reference to examples from late Tudor and early Stuart and also from late thirteenth-century England. The discussion as it relates to early modern England is entirely derived from the data presented and analysed in chapter 5 by David Levine and Keith Wrightson. Levine and Wrightson used this particular species of social network analysis to investigate the social environment of what they termed 'bastardy principals' in the Essex village of Terling. 'Bastardy principals' were defined as persons either bearing or begetting a bastard. The recorded relationships, in terms of kinship and reflected in neighbourliness patterns as they exist in the surviving village and regional legal institutions, were used to construct these networks. First-order networks were constructed for every 'bastard principal' which included fathers, mothers, siblings, stepfathers or mothers and half-brothers or sisters, husbands, wives, children or step-children where such linkages were known.

All persons with whom a principal was connected in recorded interactions were included in this first order star. For example, witnesses and executors in wills gave indications of friendship ties; manor court records provided names of fellow jurors, witnesses and parties to land transfers and sub-tenancy arrangements; quarter session records revealed the names of sureties in recognizances, and parties in disputes and ecclesiastical court records gave lists of compurgators. First-order contacts of bastardy principals were obtained and then the first order links of the individuals in that first order were isolated in an attempt to establish to what extent bastardy principals were linked to one another by second-order links through intermediaries. The 63 bastardy principals identifiable in Terling between 1590 and 1640 produced 445 individuals in their aggregated first-order contact zone. Twenty-eight persons had first-order links to two or more bastardy principals. Fifty-eight persons had second order links to their bastardy principals: 16 to1, 12 to 2, 22 to 3 to 5, 4 to 7 to 8, 4 to 10 to 18. They discovered that only two bastardy principals can be linked to no other known bastardy principal in either the first- or second-order zones.

The logical simplicity of this analysis is attractive, particularly as it is capable of relatively easy replication with comparable amalgamations of source materials. The same procedure can be undertaken in a much earlier context with evidence from thirteenth-century manorial court rolls which, with the notable exception of church court matters, include a great deal of information on links stemming from witnessing, acting as a guarantor or surety (that is, pledging), to information on kin links. A comparable analysis to that of Levine and Wrightson is attempted here with data from the manorial court rolls of Rickinghall in Suffolk in the period 1260–93.[25] However, certain characteristics of the bastardy principals in Rickinghall differ from those of Terling. The bastard-bearers represent only a sub-set of the community in that they are the daughters of customary tenants who were fined for *childwyte*.[26] We know very little, if anything, concerning the fathers of these bastards and for this reason the field of principals for linkage analysis is more restricted than with the Terling data.

An example can perhaps best depict these differences and similarities: Agnes Alwyne of Rickinghall was fined for *childwyte* first in 1273 and again in 1281, but married very soon after 1283, perhaps the father of the second bastard, Adam son of Walter Adam.[27] If we include William Alwyne and Alice Alwyne, father and mother of Agnes, Margaret, Gilbert and Nicholas her siblings in her first-order kin network plus the contacts she had with eight others, including her husband, we can define a first-order network. Five of these eight individuals can be linked to other female bastardy principals: John Dolitil, father of Lucy and Margaret Dolitil who gave birth to bastards in 1271 and 1281, Wydo Goding brother of Alice Goding who was fined for *childwyte* in 1289, John Bunting, cousin of Lucy and Margaret Dolitil, Galfridus Sparke, brother of Agatha Sparke fined in 1289 and Adam Walter her husband and possible father of her second bastard whose sister Beatrix had also given birth out of wedlock in 1262.[28]

The first-order network had contacts, even if we exclude immediate kin, with 218 others between 1260 and 1293. These second-order individuals had within their own first-order networks the direct kin (fathers and brothers) of another 12 *childwyte* fine payers and of

25. Rickinghall Manorial Court Rolls in the British Museum. Additional Manuscripts 63378–407 (Henceforth referred to as BM Add. Ms.)

26. *Childwyte* or *childwite* variant spellings of the Old English *cildwit*; *cild* (child) plus *wite* (penalty). A fine paid to the lord, in this case, by women giving birth out of wedlock (*quia peperit extra matermonium*). See G. C. Homans, *English villagers of the thirteenth century* (1940), p. 169. On these Suffolk manors within the estates of the abbots of Bury St Edmunds, *childwyte* was clearly a payment made for a bastard birth as distinct from fornication for which on certain manors *leyrwyte* was paid. For the latter penalty see Homans (1940); H. S. Bennett, *Life on the English manor* (1969), pp. 245–7; A. E. Levett, *Studies in manorial history* (1962), p. 235; and J. Scammell, 'Freedom and marriage in medieval England' (1974), pp. 526–7.

27. BM Add. Ms. 63393 court held Thursday 27 April 1273;
BM Add. Ms. 63398 Saturday 22 February 1281;
BM Add. Ms. 63399 Wednesday 9 June 1283.

28. BM Add. Ms. 63391 court held Wednesday 18 February 1271;
BM Add. Ms. 63398 Thursday 17 July 1281;
BM Add. Ms. 63403 Tuesday 8 March 1289;
BM Add. Ms. 63403 Saturday 23 July 1289;
BM Add. Ms. 63383 Thursday 21 October 1262.

these 218 individuals 17 had links either directly or indirectly to 6 other female 'bastardy principals' in their individual first-order networks. In other words, by entering the bastard-bearer group through Agnes Alwyne it is possible within her first- and second-order zones to encompass 82.2 per cent of the immediate kin of the female bastardy principals whose misdemeanors are recorded between 1260 and 1295.

If the first-order stars of all the female bastardy principals are aggregated in the manner of Levine and Wrightson, the bastard-bearers can be shown to be an inter-linked group that spreads its mantle completely over local society. The immediate reaction to this finding is to suggest, as have Levine and Wrightson, that no part of the bastard-bearing belongs to a bastardy prone sub-group in local society, but that it must be seen against the background of the complex transactions and flows of social intercourse in a common or popular sexual morality that cuts through lines drawn upon a socio-economic basis. While these are important points and eloquently made in their work, a good deal of caution must be exercised with that interpretation, particularly as these results are based upon such a 'low-level' network analysis.

Indeed, the rudimentary nature of this form of linkage investigation is acknowledged by Levine and Wrightson, although they mistakenly consider that existing inter-connections are alone sufficient to establish the social context of illegitimacy. This assumption has to be qualified considerably.

What are these qualifications? Let us observe first of all the inter-linkage of these networks based upon the extended first-order zones to second-order zones. What significance should be given to the fact that almost all bastardy principals appear to be interlinked to at least one or other bastardy principal? If we considered individuals in terms of certain other characteristics or criteria, for example being premarital conceivers, or creditors in debt cases, or net-sellers in land transactions, or receiving more pledging support than given, would not the same pattern of interconnection emerge? What inferences can be drawn from such a pattern?

For we have always to bear in mind that we are dealing with *partial* networks, determined by the types of links encountered in the documents. We are also looking at finite networks which are limited to the second-order zone and as such are bounded by the associated probability of villager and non-villager inclusion. This latter point is of considerable importance for the occurrence in the first-order zone of individuals possessing very wide-ranging networks or, technically defined, as having a large network *span*, can greatly increase the extent of the second-order zone's spread through local society. This would be particularly so if active, litigious and office-holding individuals are caught in the first-order zone. Such individuals tended to be among the most immobile village inhabitants of the early modern period in England and are therefore seen to be active in the records over long time periods – time periods that may have no relevance to the years during which the bastardy principal may be begetting or bearing a bastard. Obviously, the extent to which this becomes a major problem in this form of analysis will depend on the village population size and the selectiveness of the local documentation. It would be interesting to know for a range of village population sizes to what order of network zone one would have to proceed and over what length of time period it should be extended to encompass the whole society, using as one's starting point a set of individuals with shared characteristics, that is 'bastardy principals'. When such an issue is raised it becomes clear that network analysis of the Levine/Wrightson kind can only be called open ended.

Findings for their sort of network analysis are thus somewhat inconclusive without some attempt to test for frequency, durability and content of the interactions between the network members. The record of contact between A and B tells us nothing of the motivations of either party. This is an infuriating and partially insoluble issue in network analysis based upon documentary references to social links, since one contact of a specific type between A and B may have much more significance to the two parties involved than may scores of very different contacts between A and C.

Some of these difficulties can be illustrated with reference to the network of Richard Gaymer of Terling. Levine and Wrightson have shown this individual to be a central figure both as a direct contact with 'bastardy principals' in his own first-order zone, but much more importantly as an intermediary in the second-order zone linking many other bastard-bearers and -begetters. We know, for example, that he had three direct links with 'bastardy principals' in his first-order zone. However, these contacts constitute only three of some 36 first-order contacts. We might ask whether there is any connection between the span of this first-order zone and the number of bastardy principals which are included. That is to say, would the operative hypothesis be that the larger the span, the larger the number of 'bastardy principals' the network is likely to include? Or vice versa? If for the data set as a whole it could be shown that there was no significant statistical relationship between the number of bastardy principals and the number of individuals upon which the network has been anchored, one would feel with greater certainty that one was not dealing with the artefacts of data collection and survival, but rather with the result of 'real' socially distinctive and selective processes. Some 16 of Richard Gaymer's first-order linkages lead on directly to bastardy principals in the second-order zone and similar tests to those referred to above should have been employed in this stage of Levine and Wrightson's analysis.

The detection of links *per se*, even controlling for such issues as overall span and personal degree numbers is analytically somewhat limited and still displays many of the 'metaphorical' characteristics for which network analysis has been persistently criticized. One of the hypotheses underlying its use in the study of behaviour is that which states where a many-stranded or multiplex relationship exists between two persons, there is great accessibility and responsiveness to pressure. Also the relations will be likely to be more intimate. The standard measure for multiplexity or many-strandedness is to divide the total number of multiplex relations by the total number of all relations.

Unfortunately, in the Terling material on Richard Gaymer, it is rather difficult to establish whether the links between 'bastardy principals' are associated most frequently with uniplex or multiplex relationships, or whether they seem to display no tendency to associate at either extreme of the spectrum of relationships. We would need to know whether relationships of the first-order zone were more multiplex with 'bastardy principals' than 'non-bastardy principals'. Similar tests would necessarily have to be made on the other zone or zones. From the evidence we have seen it appears that at least one of the three links direct to 'bastardy principals' in Gaymer's first-order zone could be seen as multiplex, 7 of the 16 which members of his first-order zone had directly with 'bastardy principals' and 5 of the 34 which 'bastardy principal' members of the second-order zone had directly with other 'bastardy principals'. Whether this is high, low or modal for an individual ego known to have been a 'bastardy principal', we simply do not know.

In our thirteenth-century materials the first-order links of a woman called Agnes Alwyne, with the exception of her activities with Nicholas Alwyne, her brother, would superficially appear to be of a uniplex nature if based on the contact information found in the court proceedings. But the bias of manor court rolls with their rather limited information on the activities of women is an obstacle here. If we persist in looking at the character of the links between members of Agnes's first-order zone we observe some very interesting patterns. Indeed, those most connected in the network defined by its anchorage on Agnes Alwyne, Nicholas Alwyne her brother, John Bunting, John Dolitil and Adam Walter, her husband, are complexly interlinked in quite dense social and economic relations. These individuals were all immediate kin to females known to be 'bastardy principals'.

John Dolitil had two daughters both bastard-bearers who were also the cousins of John Bunting. Adam Walter had a sister who paid *childwyte* and finally married a 'bastardy principal' himself. Furthermore, if we look at these individuals in the first-order network in terms of the number of multiplex relationships they had both in Agnes Alwyne's first- and second-order zone, additional interesting patterns emerge. There is a clear tendency for those above-mentioned individuals to have identifiable relationships with the kin of 'bastardy principals'. Moreover, if we consider the number of transactions in multiplex encounters between 'non-bastardy principals' or their kin in the first- and second-order zones, the mean number per person or per link is 3.0, but between individual 'bastardy principals' or their kin the figure is 5.7. In fact contacts reported in manorial court proceedings show up a group of individuals who are the immediate kin of 'bastardy principals' and who have very close social and economic relations among themselves.

It would, however, be dangerous to proceed to argue that we have isolated individuals or families that constitute part, or a sub-set of a bastardy prone group in local society. Without evidence or durability in this behaviour trait over time and persistence in their intra-familial contacts over time, it would be hazardous to define this group as an enduring cluster or clique. To isolate them as a sexually deviant component of local society might also be unjustified in view of the fact that many of the sisters of girls paying *childwyte* are seen to have married in a normal fashion, as indeed did some of the *childwyte* payers themselves, subsequent to their misdemeanours. The *childwyte* fine payers of Rickinghall in general appeared to be landless or land deficient individuals, for only two of the individuals are known to have been property holders. It may well have been that daughters in these deficit families were left unprovided for because of their family's short-term economic privations, but anticipated marriage nevertheless.[29] They could have been *sparrows* or singletons rather than repeaters. But this economically deterministic argument has its limits as an explanation of the possible behaviour patterns. Agnes Alwyne is known to have produced two bastards and then to have married, after the second bastard was born, Adam Walter, brother of the bastard-bearing daughter of Walter Adam. Furthermore, we find Adam Walter in court in a slander case with Robert de Herst subsequent to his marriage.[30] Robert claimed in the course of the proceedings that he had known Agnes Alwyne carnally, which does indeed suggest that Agnes Alwyne may have been promiscuous in her sexual behaviour and classable in our sub-society. We should also take note of the fact that repeaters certainly existed in this community, women who produce three and sometimes four bastard births over a number of years. Some examples should perhaps be given here.

There was Walter son of Edrich the Parmenter, whose twin sisters Tissanya and Matilda both paid *childwyte*, and who eventually married Alice Rowe.[31] Alice had herself paid *childwyte* some years earlier.[32] There were others like Nutkyne from the neighbouring manor of Redgrave, whose known kin connections with other customary tenants are very hazy, but who certainly produced four bastards between 1267 and 1273;[33] or the Hose sisters who gave birth to four bastards between 1269 and 1289;[34] or Margaret Pecke who had three bastards between 1262 and 1270.[35] Moreover, each of these families seems to have been peripheral to the mainstream of local manorial or village society, not holding manorial office or performing jury duty, not active in pledging tasks, but seemingly committed to the brewing and retailing of ale (Smith, 1974, pp. 150–78 and 454–61). It could be suggested of these people that they did belong to a bastardy prone sub-society, and that this may have acted as a marker in their case, a marker of something like proletarian status.

29. R. M. Smith, 'English peasant life-cycles and socio-economic networks' (1974), pp. 460–61.
30. BM Add. Ms. 63404 court held Thursday 27 April 1290.
31. BM Add. Ms. 63388 court held Wednesday 12 October 1267;
BM Add. Ms. 63383 Thursday 21 October 1262. And BM Add. Ms. 63385 Friday 27 March 1265.
32. BM Add. Ms. 63382 court held Thursday 29 November 1261.
33. Redgrave manorial court rolls in the Bacon Collection of the University of Chicago Library. Bacon Manuscripts 1–7 (henceforth Bacon Ms.). And Bacon Ms. 2 court held on Sunday 8 March 1267;
Bacon Ms. 2 Saturday 20 September 1270;
Bacon Ms. 3 Wednesday 4 November 1271;
Bacon Ms. 2 Thursday 14 September 1273.
34. Bacon Ms. 2 court held Friday 27 September 1269;
Bacon Ms. 2 Thursday 11 May 1273;
Bacon Ms. 4 Friday 27 September 1280;
Bacon Ms. 5 Wednesday 28 September 1289;
Bacon Ms. 5 Friday 18 November 1289.
35. Bacon Ms. 1 court held Friday 2 December 1262;
Bacon Ms. 2 Tuesday 2 November 1266;
Bacon Ms. 2 Tuesday 1 July 1270.

It may be appropriate to end by suggesting some simple measures that network analysis can provide for the systematic study of bastard-bearers in as broad a social and economic context as possible in village society.

1 The derivation of social network characteristics of all, or a systematically derived sample of individuals in the community grouped according to certain economic and social criteria. The network span, density and multiplexity of these groups would then be available and could be used as a background against which to consider the ego-centred network characteristics of bastard-bearers or their families. This would allow us to detect whether bastard-bearers exhibited an unstructured range of patterns, or patterns that were specific to any particular sub-section of society.
2 We would also be able to see if, for example, the network densities of repeaters were distinct or whether families who did not actually have repeaters but did have more than one female sibling giving birth to one bastard were also distinct. Indeed any of the sets defined in this chapter could be so treated.
3 In general it would be prudent to concentrate on ego-centred first-order zones for this would diminish the complications associated with the inclusion of an intermediary with a very broad span of contacts who could artificially inflate the original ego's second-order zone. In other words, we could control for first-order network size, the proportion of first-order links direct to 'bastardy principals' or their immediate kin and the span of the second-order zone.

Using such relatively simple measures we should be able to see if the bastardy prone sub-society defined as repeaters in fact had relatively small or large first-order networks; whether their contacts were multiplex or uniplex in general or whether solely multiplex with other repeaters or their kin, and whether these patterns changed in time as the overall incidence of bastardy waxed and waned. The work of Levine and Wrightson must be seen as a pioneering venture into this field but their use of network analysis is inconclusive with regard to their argument. With the development of more precise techniques the questions can be made more specific and, it is hoped, the answers more meaningful, since the bastardy prone will be disaggregated into a number of distinct and, in certain contexts, overlapping groups.

II Western Europe

9

Illegitimates and foundlings in pre-industrial France

Jean Meyer

In France, as in all Western European countries, a basic tenet of the Catholic church has always been the indissolubility and absolute sanctity of marriage, insisting on the prohibition of premarital sexual relations, of adultery and of divorce. But the law of monogamous marriage could never be strictly enforced by either civil or ecclesiastical courts, while in the middle ages the Merovingian and Carolingian ruling classes still practised polygamy. No stigma attached to the word 'bastard' which was, on the contrary, a title to be proudly emblazoned on one's crest. In the mid sixteenth century the lord of Gouberville, a country gentleman of Cotentin, thought it quite natural to bring up his bastards at home together with his legitimate children.[1] Sexual licence outside marriage was by no means confined to the nobility but was present in all sections of society, though it varied between classes, between regions and over the centuries. The religious laxity of the late middle ages was reflected in general moral laxity, but with the Reformation and the Catholic renaissance came a reaffirmation of the sanctity of marriage culminating in the austerity of the Jansenists and of the *Catéchisme de Nantes* (1689), in which Mesnard, its author, laid down that 'conjugal chastity must keep lust and passion within bounds.'[2] Inevitably this period was followed by a reaction in the eighteenth century, reaching its culmination in Diderot's dictum: 'What is marriage? To consent to live in the same hut and to sleep in the same bed as long as it suits us. And when it is no longer agreeable? Then we separate.'[3]

Before considering the sporadic numerical evidence of bastardy previous to the seventeenth century, the more plentiful quantitative material for later periods and the research which has been done on it, we must say something of the practice of abandoning children. This practice, so prevalent in seventeenth- and eighteenth-century France, would appear to go back to the middle ages and to have arisen from the habit of putting children out to nurse. The problem of illegitimacy and of abandonment are intimately linked: the figures we have from foundling hospitals do not always clearly distinguish between legitimate and illegitimate among abandoned children.

We begin by examining the available quantitative material for the *ancien régime* which is not, unfortunately, very detailed for the sixteenth century. For the *comté* of Nantes only has a comparative study of town and countryside been carried out, from which certain generalizations may be made. Looking at individual parishes within the *comté* we find that St Similien in the city, had a bastardy ratio of 7.3 per cent in the crisis period 1593–1600, while rural Abbaretz showed a ratio of 4.6 per

1. E. Le Roy-Ladurie, *Une sire de Gouberville, gentilhomme campagnard du Cotentin, de 1553 à 1562* (1972), pp. 691–798, 30–3.
2. *Catéchisme du diocèse de Nantes* (1689), pp. 344–5.
3. *Supplément au voyage de Bougainville* (1966).

cent for the century as a whole; the difference between urban and rural ratios was quite small.[4] The ratios varied between 0.3 per cent and 3.9 per cent for city parishes, and between 0.3 per cent and 4.6 per cent for the villages, and the higher among them were clearly above those found a century later. There were very few abandoned children, and it is interesting that some of the bastards were the offspring of unmarried couples who had several children together but refused to go to the altar.

One fact that stands out from the large body of data in the seventeenth-century registers is the very small number of illegitimates anywhere in the countryside and the insignificant role they played in most of the towns where they have been studied. Ratios of 2 per cent and 4 per cent respectively would be considered high, and in the country areas three levels may be distinguished. The first is from 0.1 per cent to 1 per cent, the second around 1 per cent and the third a good deal higher at over 2 per cent, rising to 4 per cent in some instances. Different levels could occur in places close to one another: in the agrarian area of Léon in Brittany Milizac had a bastardy ratio of only 0.7 per cent for the period 1605–1715, while at Ploudalmezeau the ratio was 1.6 per cent with a maximum of 4.5 per cent between 1646 and 1655.[5] While a ratio of around 1 per cent found in Beauvais seems to be typical of seventeenth-century France, a number of regions showed considerably lower bastardy levels. At Jargeau in the Loiret and at St Lambert des Levées in Maine-et-Loire the ratio fluctuated between 0.3 per cent and 0.4 per cent.[6] At Tourouvre-au-Perche in Lower Normandy the ratio was 0.8 per cent from 1640 to 1769; some country districts showed little change from the seventeenth to the eighteenth century.[7]

This impression is broadly confirmed by the better data on the eighteenth century. The ratio at Azereix in Burgundy was 3 per cent in the period 1736–98, making quite a high level of bastardy, but one to which A. Zink (1969, p. 73, n. 1) devotes only three lines. The ratio was around 1 per cent at both Châteauneuf d'Ille-et-Vilaine near St Malo and Chalons-sur-Marne.[8] In 1700–90 similar ratios were to be found at Thezels and Saint-Sernin in Bas-Quercy in Aquitaine (19 bastards out of 1,720 live births);[9] and if one may generalize from these few figures the 1 per cent ratio would seem to have been more general than in the previous century. Islands of high illegitimacy also seem to have been more common: one such was the Normandy coastal region where ratios rose from 0.7 per cent at Crulai to 3.7 per cent at Isigny, 4.5 per cent at Trevières, 4.7 per cent at Saint-Viger and 5.8 per cent at Troumeauville.[10] Despite a rural ratio of around 1 per cent and a ratio of 2.2 per cent at Sérignan, the record of other urban districts brought the ratio for Languedoc as a whole up to 4 per cent, making this another island of high illegitimacy.[11] Anjou, on the other hand, with a low and

4. A. Croix, *Nantes et le pays nantais au XVIe siècle* (1974), pp. 94–5.
5. R. Leprohon, 'La démographie de pays de Léon au XVIIe siècle', (1972).
6. P. Goubert, *100 Français au XVIIe siècle* (1968), p. 54.
7. *Cahier INED*, No. 55.
8. J. P. Grain, 'Démographie de Châteauneuf d'Ille-et-Vilaine au XVIIIe siècle, (1693–1792)' (1970), pp. 58–60; P. Housseau, 'Chalons-sur-Marne, étude démographique (1660–1789)' (1970), (40 illegitimates out of 3,531 live births).
9. P. Valmary, 'Familles paysannes en Bas-Quercy au XVIIIe siècle' (1965).
10. E. Gautier and L. Henry, *La population de Crulai, paroisse normande* (1958), p. 67. P. Chaunu *et al.*, (1970), pp. 370 ff. Mohammed El Kordi, 'Bayeux au XVIIe et XVIIIe siècles' (1970), pp. 132–3.
11. A. Molinier, 'Enfants trouvés, enfants abandonnés et enfants illégitimes en Languedoc au XVIIe et XVIIIe siècles' (1973), ppp. 445–76.

constant ratio may have been more typical of much of the countryside.[12] Finally, we know that three villages in the Ile-de-France had low ratios of around 0.7 per cent throughout the eighteenth century, a remarkable record of stability in an area so close to Paris itself.[13]

These results are confirmed by a comparative study of Brittany and Anjou where from 1740 to 1820 illegitimates formed 1.1 per cent of all births. The ratio rose gradually from 0.7 per cent in 1740–50 to 2.0 per cent in 1820–30, and one may contrast the four Breton *départements* on the one hand with Maine-et-Loire and Loire-Atlantique on the other. In the former the ratio was below 3 per cent, in the latter it rose to 6.7 per cent and 5.2 per cent respectively.[14]

A. d'Angeville in his *Essai sur la statistique de la population française* gives us an idea of the geographical distribution of illegitimacy in France at the beginning of the nineteenth century.[15] The data he presents shows centres of high illegitimacy in the industrial north (Nord and Pas-de-Calais), in the agricultural region south of the Paris basin (Loire, Loire-et-Cher, Nièvre), to the west of the basin of Aquitaine (Landes, Basses Pyrénées, Gers) and in some isolated *départements* (Seine Maritime, Calvados, Bas-Rhin, Haut Sâone, Isère, Bouches-du-Rhône). Some of these districts were predominantly rural, so that high illegitimacy ratios were, at that time, not an exclusively urban phenomenon. Small numbers of bastards are recorded in some large towns, not adding appreciably to the total for the *départements* concerned (Ille-et-Vilaine and Loire-inférieure).

A further surprising fact is that figures for illegitimate and abandoned children to some extent complement each other. Broadly speaking, there were few abandoned children in the northeast corner of France except at Le Havre, on the Marne and in Paris itself, while *la France traditionelle*, with the exception of Brittany, Ardèche and Lot had fewer bastards but abandoned its newborn more readily. Again, the Mediterranean south was an area of high bastardy ratios; low illegitimacy was confined to an area running from Brittany in the northwest to the Alps in the southeast.

These comparisons suggest that while urban agglomeration may be one of the factors associated with bastardy, it can only be one of many. Despite the sudden rise in illegitimacy ratios in urban districts which is an outstanding feature of the eighteenth century, there are such cases as Nantes, a port town *par excellence* which, together with its surrounding districts seems to have been more 'moral' than Maine-et-Loire or Anger. The urban rise was particularly marked in Paris itself and E. Charlot and J. Dupâquier (1966, pp. 311–519) have published figures on foundlings during the *ancien régime*. But as these are incomplete, they are open to criticism.

From 1640 to 1700 the number of foundlings registered in Paris seems to have been very small (about 700 out of at least 17,000 baptisms each year around 1670, perhaps 4.6 per cent of all baptisms). In the mid seventeenth century they were between 300 and 400 a year, less than 3 per cent of all baptisms. But the

12. F. Lebrun, 'Les enfants trouvés en Anjou au XVIIIe siècle' (1972), p. 1184.

13. J. Ganiage, *Trois villages de l'Ille-de-France* (1963). See also H. Charbonneau, *Tourouvre au Perche au XVIIe et XVIIIe siècles* (1970), p. 65 (0.8 per cent). A. Poitrineau, *La vie rurale en Basse-Auvergne au XVIIIe siècle (1726–1789)* (1965), pp. 59–60 (barely 50 illegitimates of 48,825 baptisms). P. Gouhier, 'Port-en-Bessin (1597–1792), étude démographique historique' (1962), p. 43 (2.5 per cent).

14. Y. Blayo and L. Henry, 'Données démographiques sur la Bretagne et l'Anjou de 1740 à 1829' (1967), pp. 91–171; Résultats à confronter avec d'Angeville, pp. 106–7, 318–19.

15. *Essai sur la statistique de la population française, considérée sous quelques-uns de ses rapports physiques et moraux* (1969), pp. 318–19 and 28–9. Compare the figures established by Yves Blayo for the late eighteenth and early nineteenth centuries (below, chapter 11).

eighteenth century saw a spectacular rise in the number of foundlings as is shown in table 9.1.[16]

Table 9.1: Foundlings recorded in Paris in the eighteenth century

Date	Foundlings	Births	Foundlings as a % of births
1721	1730	19917	9.0
1730	2401	18966	13.0
1740	3150	18632	17.0
1750	3783	19035	20.0
1760	5131	17991	29.0
1770	6918	19549	35.0
1780	5296	19617	27.0
1790	5842	20,005	29.0
1800 (an VII)	3510	22,953	15.0
1810	4502	19037	24.0
1820	5108	24858	21.0

The figures in table 9.1 can be checked to some extent by comparing them with d'Angeville's, though the information he gives us starts slightly later than Charlot and Dupâquier's figures on bastardy, which begin in 1800. Their figures for 1810 show bastards as 38 per cent and foundlings as 24 per cent of births and for 1820 as 36 per cent and 21 per cent (8,870 and 5,108 cases respectively). This figure for foundlings differs little from that given by d'Angeville (5,432, or 324 more cases), but the figures for bastards are much further apart, d'Angeville giving 10,721 cases, 1,851 more than Charlot and Dupâquier. Nor has the position been clarified by the article by A. Chamoux (1973b, pp. 418–25), whose figures also conflict with those of Charlot and Dupâquier, nor by the work of Delaselle (1975, pp. 187–218).

Using a manuscript by J. R. Tenon (1724–1816) Antoinette Chamoux demonstrates that illegitimacy ratios were lower in eighteenth-century Paris than might have been deduced from the other figures presented. The bastardy ratio seems to have risen as follows:

Date	Bastardy ratio (%)
1713–22	8.6
1723–32	11.4
1733–42	13.3
1744–54	16.3
1755–64	21.2
1765–74	24.9
1775–84	23.2
1785–94	19.8
1795–1804	15.3
1805–8	18.2

16. We have calculated the percentages on the assumption that foundlings were included in baptisms, contrary to what has been stated on p. 512 of Charlot and Dupâquier (1966). This is proved indirectly by a comparison of these tables with those of d'Angeville, since d'Angeville's totals give 24,858 births as against 23,506 births in the tables by Charlot and Dupâquier; together with the foundlings this would therefore add up to 28,614.

Chamoux also gives the number of foundlings for the five-year period 1773–7 as 31,951, a figure which tallies with what was already known. This source is also valuable because it gives an idea of the numbers of foundlings registered in Paris though born in the provinces. For the same five-year period about one third of the total number, 10,414 children, answer to this description.[17]

Comparing the data from all three sources, we see that there is a good deal of inconsistency: for the period around 1810 we have estimates of the bastardy ratio of 18 per cent from Chamoux and of 38 per cent from Charlot and Dupâquier, for that around 1820 the latter give us 36 per cent to d'Angeville's 31 per cent. In the present state of the evidence it is impossible to know which are the most reliable figures. Probably the accuracy of the figures is less important than the trends they show, and in this respect all the material agrees in confirming the great rise in both illegitimacy and abandonment ratios in eighteenth-century Paris, with some tailing off after the 1770s. It would appear that at the end of the century over a third of the children registered in Paris were born outside the traditional family and that, if Charlot and Dupâquier's figures may be relied upon, this proportion could rise to over one half. And, to extrapolate from Tenon's figures, one might assume that the provinces produced one third of these irregular births.

There are two major problems with the interpretation of these figures: firstly, that of the relationship between illegitimate and foundling births and secondly, that of the extent of the migratory movement of foundlings between town and country, and the movement to Paris in particular. One might be tempted to assume that all abandoned children were illegitimate, and that a figure for the actual bastardy ratio might be arrived at by simply adding the two series together. But the testimony of d'Angeville and a number of his contemporaries indicates that the position was not quite as simple as this. He suggests that the number of foundlings increased with increasing provision for their maintenance, and cites the instance of Mayence (p. 33). Here the number of foundlings increased from 30 in 1799–1810 to 516 in 1811–15, the period for which a foundling hospital existed in the town. After its closure there was a drop in the number of foundlings to 63 in 1815–24. The July monarchy (1830–48), frightened at the growing cost of such hospitals, decided to transfer the children to neighbouring *départements*, and 'many mothers rushed to reclaim their children' (d'Angeville, *supplément*, pp. xii–xiii).

Many local authorities, however, did count all abandoned children as bastards, which prevents any further analysis, but we know that in Paris 83 per cent of foundlings were illegitimate, while in Morbihan (a *département* of southern Brittany) the proportion varied between 20 per cent and 60 per cent, though some of this variation is due to the small numbers in question. It seems likely that the proportion in most large towns was over 60 per cent.

The second issue is even more important, casting doubt, as it does, upon the usual assumptions we make about differences between town and country. We have already seen that in Paris the figures for foundlings included a substantial number brought in from the country, and d'Angeville states that of the 13,000 to 14,000 foundlings registered each year in Lyons over 6,000 came not from the Département du Rhône in which the city lies but from the Département de l'Ain.

17. Jacques René Tenon (1724–1816) was one of the great French surgeons of the eighteenth century. After entering the Academy of Science in 1773 he reorganized the administration of the Paris hospitals from 1788 onwards. He assembled an enormous amount of material at the end of the *ancien régime*, particularly about the Paris hospitals, and did much to promote the early science of statistics.

He also noted that a change in the basis of the census between 1831 and 1836 caused them to be counted on the former occasion as resident in the homes of their nursing mothers, and on the latter occasion in the hospital, thus preventing a direct comparison between the two (d'Angeville, *supplément*, pp. iv–v; he cites the particularly convincing example of Lyons where the 13,700 foundlings came to 10 per cent of the total population).

Similar statements can be made for the north, and in Nantes, according to Tenon's inquiry in 1790 for the National Assembly, 19.5 per cent of foundlings came from outside the city. At Bourg in the Ain this proportion was 32 per cent, while among the smaller foundling hospitals the figures varied widely. Finally, for Paris again, Flandrin notes that in the eighteenth century '2000 children born in the distant provinces came to the city every year.'[18] Thus the steep rise in urban illegitimacy ratios may have included the greater part of the increased illegitimacy occurring in rural districts. Further research must not, therefore, be confined to parish registers, but should be extended to cover records more directly concerned with illegitimacy itself, both quantitative and qualitative.

There is no lack of these. Apart from the great inquiry of 1778–80 (now kept in the basements of many local government offices) which should provide the material for a fairly complete survey of France, there are dossiers of declarations of pregnancy in hospital archives. At Rennes in Brittany, for example, municipal legislation forbade the admission to hospital of children born outside the city except in special circumstances (article 24 of the statute of 1717). The records of the hospital of St Yves de Rennes show that less than 10 per cent of the children admitted came from outside Rennes.[19] Parents could entrust their children to the hospital simply by presenting a certificate of poverty issued by their parish priest, and admission could be decided on even before the birth of the child.

The existence of these certificates makes it possible to determine fairly accurately how many of the children were bastards. It appears that between 75 per cent and 80 per cent were illegitimate, and that of the foundlings from outside the city nine in ten were (Pottier, 1974, pp. 16 and 61–2). The hospital divided foundlings into three categories, and of the 4,845 children admitted in 1730–50, 67 (1.4 per cent) were given as anonymously abandoned, 1,096 (23 per cent) as legitimate children taken in in the normal manner, and the remaining 3,682 children as illegitimate (76 per cent). When in the middle of the eighteenth century St Yves was replaced by a general hospital the method of registration changed so that it is only possible to make a limited comparison. In the decade 1775–84, 517 of the 2,003 children admitted were those 'negotiated' by known parents. At St Malo, on the Brittany coast, the foundling hospital recorded 35 cases of abandonment (1 per cent), 109 were legitimate children of married couples (31 per cent) and 208 were bastards (59 per cent).[20]

These figures are of interest because of the light they cast on those put forward for Paris by L. Lallemand, who claimed that of the 5,032 foundlings registered in the city in 1760 only 735 (15 per cent) were legitimate.[21] These sources also allow

18. J. L. Flandrin, 'L'attitude à l'égard de l'enfant' (1973), p. 170.

19. Yves Pottier, 'La population de l'hôpital Saint-Yves de Rennes durant la première moitié du XVIIIe siècle' (1974), p. 14.

20. Archives départementales d'Ille-et-Vilaine (ADIV) C.1286 and C.1287, Données sur l'hôpital général de Rennes.

21. *Histoire des enfants abandonnés et délaissés. Etudes sur la protection de l'enfance aux diverses époques de la civilisation* (1885), p. 163 (735 legitimate children of 5,032 admitted in 1760).

us to trace the movement of foundlings. The general hospital at Rennes complained that the royal decree of 1779 preventing the transportation of foundlings[22] caused a considerable increase in numbers and upset its entire budget. From between 142 and 165 a year they rose to 174 in 1779, 203 in 1780 and over 224 in the following years.

This would indicate that before the decree perhaps one quarter of the children abandoned in Rennes failed to appear in the town's statistics and one might assume that they had been transported to Paris. This was thought to have been the case at Fougères, which is also in Brittany; in 1777 the delegate of that town replied to the *intendant* that there were 30 to 36 foundlings there every year, but he added that 'three times more go to Paris' (ADIV, C.1287; see also the map in Delaselle, 1975). We may discern the character of what one is forced to call the 'traffic in children'.

The register of declarations of pregnancy at Nantes has been studied by J. Depauw (1972b, pp. 37–60). Since these concern the unborn they tell us nothing about foundlings, but they do provide information on bastardy. Of 8,000 pregnancy declarations for Nantes between 1725 and the Revolution the proportion of bastards rose from 3 per cent to 10 per cent, with the regions around accounting for 807 of the declarations. This corresponds with the figures for St Yves de Rennes, but we cannot be sure that they are typical of the country as a whole. In Toulouse, surrounded by a countryside with bastardy ratios of around 1 per cent, the control of admissions to the foundling hospital seems to have been as strict as at Rennes, implying that these low rural ratios were not produced by moving children to the town.[23] But the fact remains that Paris and Lyons had the highest illegitimacy ratios in France. Between 1750 and 1789 the Lyons hospitals took in 50,670 children, the rate of admission increasing by 72 per cent over the period. The number of abandoned children rose from 3,640 to 8,250 between the first and last decades, or by 134 per cent, and formed 43 per cent of admissions for the whole period, bastards and legitimate children each being about 30 per cent of the total.[24] Unfortunately it is not known what proportion came from the countryside.

Let us now consider those overall figures that are known. Mols tells us that bastardy was low everywhere at the beginning of the eighteenth century, but reached 17 per cent at Bordeaux and 25 per cent at Toulouse on the eve of the Revolution.[25] The proportion of children abandoned at Toulouse has recently been estimated at 10 per cent in the first half of the century and 17 per cent in the second (Wolff, 1974, pp. 338–40). This may be compared to a rate of 6 per cent at Le Puy, a much smaller town, for the whole century (Molinier, 1973), rising from 3.8 per cent in 1698–1702 to 12.4 per cent in 1783–7, though these figures take illegitimate and abandoned children together. The parish registers indicate that most such towns displayed greater 'morality', but the registers are not always to be trusted. At Vitré in Brittany, for instance, a town of only 8,000 inhabitants, they suggest a very low bastardy ratio of 0.6 per cent (research in progress). Yet the place was denounced as a depositary for foundlings, an entrepot for children on their way from Dinan to Paris (ADIV, C.1287).

22. Decree of the Council of 10 January 1779 (cited before).
23. Ph. Wolff (ed.), *Histoire de Toulouse* (1974), p. 340.
24. M. Garden, *Lyon et les Lyonnais au XVIIIe siècle* (1970), pp. 102, 116–40; and pp. 102–3.
25. R. Mols, *Introduction à la démographie historique des villes d'Europe du XIVe au XVIIIe siècle* (1955), II, pp. 300–3.

St Malo is another peculiar case: a port town with 15,000–18,000 inhabitants, one would have expected it to have high bastardy ratios but in the late seventeenth century it had 0.7 per cent of illegitimate births, scarcely more than the surrounding country. Abandoned children, at 1.2 per cent, were somewhat more common.[26] This figure increased to 4 per cent in the first half of the eighteenth century, while the number of bastards tripled,[27] a significant shift in view of the static and even declining population of the town after 1720. The second half of the century saw the usual rise from 3.0 per cent in 1751–60 to 4.5 per cent in 1780–89 and 6.5 per cent in the period of the Revolution. The ratios of abandoned children were 2.2 per cent, 5.8 per cent and 4.3 per cent respectively.[28] Finally, between 1775 and 1784 the town hospital admitted 352 children: 35 foundlings, 208 bastards and 109 legitimate children (ADIV, C.1287).

Table 9.2: Illegitimates and foundlings in St Malo, 1650–1799

Period	Illegitimates %	Foundlings %	Total %
1650–99	0.6	1.2	1.9
1700–1749	1.7	3.9	5.7
1750–99	5.9	6.0	11.9

The fact that St Malo shows more foundlings than bastards, the opposite of the position in Paris, may be the result of the foundation there of a foundling hospital in 1674. When during the Revolution disorganization limited the numbers of children that could be admitted, the number of bastards increased, that of foundlings decreased, leaving the total almost unchanged.[29]

Table 9.3: Illegitimates and foundlings in St Malo, 1780–1800

Period	Illegitimates	Foundlings	Total
1780–1789	173	222	295
1790–1800	226	151	377

Several features make St Malo untypical: it had a high literacy rate with 58 per cent of men and 43 per cent of women able to sign their names at the end of the seventeenth century. By the mid eighteenth century this had risen to 70 per cent for both sexes, and at the end of the period to 74 per cent and 66 per cent respectively (notes 26 and 27, and ADIV, C.1287). D'Angeville (p. 37) states that there was a definite connection between literacy and immorality.[30] Like Nantes, St Malo's position as a port seems to have had little effect on bastardy (Depauw, 1972b, confirms the estimates by Croix, 1974, for the sixteenth century), but it

26. D. Creff and C. Regent, *Saint Malo, étude démographique, 1701–50* (1967), p. 73.
27. C. Mancarte, D. Quillere and M. R. Rannou, *Saint Malo, étude démographique, 1701–50* (1968), pp. 58–60.
28. M. Brigardis, C. Durand, J. P. Gauvrit and J. C. Rouxel, *Saint Malo, étude démographique, 1751–89* (1969), pp. 71–4.
29. The slight decrease may be explained by the difficulties the hospital experienced, which limited the number of admissions. There remains the question to what extent the population of St Malo had decreased; it is probable that the real percentage in relation to the total population had increased somewhat.
30. His position is, in fact, very equivocal as may be seen from the following passage: 'Reason is always wanting in matters connected with foundlings; nevertheless there is one constant reason for the *increase* in numbers and that is ignorance. Departments where primary education is at a very low level have a greater number of abandoned children – with one reservation – this observation does not apply to some departments of Brittany.'

was also a town with a good deal of immigration and considerable population movement. In the mid seventeenth century 23 per cent of its men seem to have come from other dioceses, in 1700–50 56 per cent and in 1751–1800 75 per cent (see notes 26–8). And during the latter period some 30 per cent of the newly married were not Bretons. Perhaps these anomalies can help us to reconcile high illegitimacy ratios with the notably moral and intellectual tone of the episcopate of St Malo.[31] It must also be pointed out that the ratios were considerably below those of Rennes.

A comparison with other towns is illuminating. Foundlings in Grenoble formed 11 per cent of all births.[32] In the parish of St Laurent in Strasbourg the bastardy ratio, already quite high at 7.4 per cent in 1710–19, reached 30.5 per cent in 1785–6.[33] For the whole town the 256 bastard births were 30 per cent of the numbers born to Catholics, and 17 per cent of the total when both Catholics and Protestants are counted. That there was a religious differential in illegitimacy may be partly explained by the social strata occupied by the two groups, the Catholics being mainly immigrants and on the lower levels, the Protestants being the main part of the bourgeoisie. Total bastardy figures for a town may thus be too crude an indicator if the ratio varied considerably from one parish to another. The figures for abandoned children in Toulouse show this, the ratio rising from 10 per cent in the parish of la Daurade to 15 per cent in St Etienne and 31 per cent in the rather poor quarter of St Pierre de Cuisine (Wolff, 1974, p. 338). A similar pattern emerges at Reims though all the ratios were lower there.[34]

There were also pronounced differences in bastardy ratios between districts in Rennes. Paradoxically one of the central parishes, St Germain, admittedly of a rather mixed character, showed high ratios. They rose from between 5 per cent and 10 per cent to between 20 per cent and 25 per cent by the end of the century.[35] At St Etienne the increase was also marked, from 7 per cent at the beginning of the century to over 15 per cent in 1789. Both urban and suburban in character, St Aubin reached a local record at 30 per cent around 1774, but St Helier, straddling the suburbs and the countryside showed ratios of 0.8 per cent in the 1720s and 2.8 per cent in 1790, figures much more like those of rural areas. Rennes thus experienced a severe crisis of bastardy despite being in the low illegitimacy area of Brittany, and this continued into the early years of the nineteenth century as is shown in table 9.4.[36]

Table 9.4: Bastardy ratios in Rennes, 1809–14

Year	Bastards	Births	Bastardy ratio %
1809	325	1377	23.6
1810	350	1389	25.2
1811	377	1548	24.4
1812	397	1416	28.0
1814	213	1359	15.7

31. Ch. Berthelot du Chesnay, 'Le Clergé diocésain en Haute Bretagne au XVIIIe siècle'.
32. R. Bligny (ed.), *Histoire du Dauphiné* (1973), chapter by R. Bonnin and J. Sole, p. 281. The rate of illegitimate births was about 3 per cent. By comparison, at the beginning of the nineteenth century, d'Angeville gave 8.4 per cent of bastards and 3.1 per cent of foundlings for the whole *département* of Isère.
33. S. Dreyer-Roos. *La population Strasbourgeoise sous l'Ancien Régime, 1681–1789* (1969), pp. 186–9. Also his article with the same title (1967), pp. 267–73.
34. A. Chamoux, 'L'enfance abandonnée à Reims à la fin du XVIIIe siècle' (1973), p. 272.
35. J. Meyer (ed.), *Histoire de Rennes* (1972), pp. 282–4.
36. M. Vie, 'La ville de Rennes sous le premier Empire' (1971).

What were the causes of this urban crisis? It may have had its origin in such things as the *amours ancillaires*, which we have seen in the sixteenth-century example of the lord of Gouberville, and which continued throughout the seventeenth century, growing in some towns with the increase in the numbers of servants. But the lead was taken by other kinds of extra-marital relationships; in spite of the moral enthusiasm of the seventeenth century, prostitution flourished, as J. Solé has shown in his study of Grenoble,[37] which seems to have been a prosperous town in the eighteenth century where prostitution was highly organized. Kept women, almost unknown in the seventeenth century, increased in numbers throughout the eighteenth, and became widespread in the nineteenth century.[38] It might seem reasonable to link these developments with population growth in the towns, but this kind of argument must be handled with care. The population of Paris, for instance, increased only slightly from 1700 to 1789, by about 10 per cent, and its relative population actually fell. It also seems that there was only a trifling change in the social structure of the city, and that this change proceeded quite slowly. From this alone it would seem implausible to argue that it was only population change which gave the impetus to higher illegitimacy ratios in the eighteenth century.

The above description seems to indicate a growing indifference both to children and to the traditional family pattern in French towns in the eighteenth century. This may seem paradoxical, given such things as the growing cost of education in the period, which implies a greater willingness to spend money on the young. The development of education which represents a considerable investment in children, especially for a pre-industrial society, raises the question of whether such investment was profitable. But this consideration applies only to older children; we are more concerned with the very young. The age-old custom of putting children out to nurse, frequently resulting in abandonment and giving rise to such abuses as the transportation of children to Paris from the provinces, is one aspect of this. It caused such high mortality that we suspect it to be a form of family limitation, though bordering on the illegal and attacked by royal legislation in 1779. It was organized on a full business footing, with disastrous effects on the children subjected to it. If we return to the hospital of St Yves at Rennes, we find that of the 112 children admitted in 1747 only 2 survived for a year. And in 1784 only 674 still survived of the 2,000 children admitted to the general hospital there during the previous decade. In the period 1824–33, d'Angeville noted, 'for every 100 surviving children there are 159 who perish: on average more than 61 per cent of all children in France put out to nurse and abandoned by their parents', (ADIV, C.1287).

This represents a total of 198,000 deaths, of which 23 per cent were in hospitals and 77 per cent in the homes of private nurses. In Paris the proportion of deaths was about 77 per cent (d'Angeville, pp. 33–4). As we do not know the mortality among those put out to nurse but not abandoned by their parents, we can only assume a smaller but still considerable number of deaths. Can the parents of abandoned children have failed to realize that this was the state of affairs? There may have been some mitigation in the severity of the system when the children were given to foster mothers, many of whom were attached to foundling hospitals. The choice of nurse among those who put out their children privately was of

37. J. Solé, 'Passion charnelle et société urbaine d'ancien régime, amour vénal, amour libre et amour fou à Grenoble au milieu du règne de Louis XIV' (1969), pp. 211–32.
38. A thesis is being prepared on this subject under the editorship of P. Goubert.

great importance and the medical books of the period were full of advice on the matter. Finance must have been crucial in determining whether and to whom the child should be entrusted, but those who were transported all suffered the same risks.

Putting children out to nurse had been an organized business since the middle ages. There is a good deal of evidence on it and it is possible to reconstruct its mode of operation. Surgeons and midwives would advise expectant mothers on the means of putting children out to nurse. In Paris there was a network of *recommanderesses*, in Lyons they were called *messengers*. But they all had the function of handing the babies over to agents, often just carriers, who transported them in their swaddling clothes by the waggon load. From Rennes they might be taken up to 40 kilometres in all weathers and seasons. So common was the practice that in 1785 the general hospital harboured 175 children along with 106 sick and 353 poor, while 330 children had been sent to foster mothers in the countryside. Garden (1970, p. 116) cites a decree of 1350 for the Paris region showing that at the time of the Black Death the practice of putting out to nurse was already common in the Ile-de-France. By 1680–90 it had spread as far as Nivernais in Burgundy, where a number of families were exempted from the poll tax because the mother was a wet-nurse (information kindly given by P. Goubert). It was often difficult to discover what became of the children because the carriers were illiterate and no records were kept. Garden (1970, pp. 119–20) cites cases of children put out to nurse and forgotten by their parents.[39]

The behaviour of Jean Jacques Rousseau sheds some light on parental attitudes, for it is well known that he had several children by his mistress Thérèse and abandoned all of them. Nor did he attempt to deny this: 'Five children resulted from my liaison with the poor girl who lived with me, all of whom were put out as foundlings. I have not even kept a note of their dates of birth, so little did I expect to see them again.'[40] Rousseau's case is only one among many and indicates the moral climate of the period. This sort of thing seems to have gone on in all classes of society in Paris, making one doubt whether high officials and the aristocracy should be singled out for charges of corruption. It is easy enough to find examples of great families of more austere morals; one would like to know whether the accusations levelled by historians apply to a majority.[41]

Diderot and Grimm, though scarcely scrupulous in their attacks upon Rousseau, found nothing wrong in his behaviour towards his children, of which he explained: 'I make no mystery of my conduct because I see no wrong in it. All things considered I did what I thought was best for them.'[42] And elsewhere (p. 1089) 'the fear of an almost inevitable destiny that would be infinitely worse for them' was what decided him. He also accused Thérèse and her family: 'I shudder to think of handing them over to that badly brought up woman to be still worse brought up. Far better to risk having them raised as foundlings.' If these were the reasons that persuaded people to abandon their children one might well suspect a strain of insensitivity running right through the eighteenth century.

There are, of course, other explanations, such as that of poverty, put forward by Garden (1970, pp. 136–8). This is not wholly satisfactory, and to decide on its

39. Garden, pp. 119–20. One can measure the importance of the problem by adding the figures given by Garden on p. 86: 21,870 abandoned children against 50,670 baptized.
40. *Correspondence générale*, VI, p. 146 (lettre du 12 juin 1761 de J. J. Rousseau à la maréchale de Luxembourg).
41. Mme Prejean, 'Les Schoembergs, étude familiale d'une famille de noblesse de cour' (1975).
42. J. J. Rousseau, *Les confessions* (1969), pp. 358–9 and 415.

validity one would have to know something of the background of the abandoned, which is scarcely ever available. The occurrence of cases in noble families such as the d'Alembert family can certainly not be attributed to poverty. In general, it seems that the economic position of such cities as Paris or Lyons was no worse in the eighteenth century than in the seventeenth while at the same time the numbers put out to nurse greatly increased. In Lyons in 1710 nurse children were confined to the city itself, but in the course of the century they became familiar in all the neighbouring provinces. In 1716–17 the Hôtel-Dieu boarded out its children in the nearby mountain areas; by 1757–8 they went as far afield as the Jura and the Vivarais (Garden, 1970, pp. 663–4), because of the competition for wet-nurses from privately put-out children. Apart from the influence of economic conditions, certainly a necessary but not perhaps a sufficient reason for such a change, there was considerable dislocation of traditional family life in the towns. This was an eighteenth-century phenomenon, but one which had long been foreshadowed in the habit of putting children out to nurse, a form of temporary abandonment.

Was this behaviour motivated by a collective instinct, obscured by more conscious attitudes? It looks as though, unable to use birth control to balance population against available resources, people in the crowded towns of France put their children out to nurse and then abandoned them as a way of limiting their families. Though it has been fashionable since Molière to jeer at the medical science of the *ancien régime*, its practitioners were instrumental in calling attention to the phenomena we have been discussing. In the mid eighteenth century a series of medical treatises on children were published, among them Boerhaave's *Traité des maladies de l'enfant* (Avignon, 1759), Boudier de Villemert's *L'ami des femmes* (Paris, 1758), and above all, Désessartz's *Traité de l'education corporelle des enfants en bas age* (Paris, 1760). Rousseau's *Emile* dates from 1762. They carried on a debate that went back to antiquity, upon the advantages and disadvantages of suckling your own children (we recall the role of the nurse and confidant of the classical theatre).

Virgil, one of the principal sources of ancient tradition, thought that the mother's milk transmitted its qualities to the child. Thus to drink the 'tiger's milk' gives one courage while an immoral nurse would transmit her vices to the suckling child. (Romulus and Remus were suckled by a wolf, a legend not without ambiguity.) Learned discussions were held on this matter right up to modern times, and the harm done by substituting animal for human milk was a point of serious concern. One of the most serious charges levelled at the wet-nurses of the Lyons area was that they substituted goat's milk for their own (Garden, 1970, pp. 136–8). To Boerhaave this was all just prejudice, while Rousseau maintained that the mother should suckle her child as nature wished or else 'not content to stop suckling, women would no longer wish to have children.'[43] Indeed, suckling was one of the bases of the social reforms he dreamed of since 'women who suckle . . . must abstain from intercourse', for fear that their milk would not be warm, a precaution enjoined by the religious authorities.[44]

This dispute was very characteristic of France at the time, and although learned men theorized and were divided in their opinions, they could come to no conclu-

43. Rousseau, *Emile*, p. 256 and p. 258: 'If mothers were to nurse their children, then morals would reform themselves.'

44. Flandrin (1973), annexe II, 'women who suckle their children must abstain from Venus', pp. 207–8 and annexe III, pp. 208–10.

sion, given the state of science in the eighteenth century. While in England and Scandinavia increasing use was made of cow's milk on empirical grounds, Rousseau brought the debate to the attention of the general public and of the administration, which represented a large section of informed opinion, and the question of putting children out to nurse became a matter of concern to the government. Nursing offices had already been set up in Paris and several other towns to counter the abuses of the system. They were more or less responsible to the municipal authorities and, though remaining largely unknown, they played an important part in improving conditions. It is estimated that around 1770 there were some 15,000 nurses serving in the capital of whom 5,000 were in private practice and the rest registered with the boards. Scattered over Normandy, Champagne, Burgundy (especially in Autun) and Picardy they were to 'take care of the children of servants and artisans' (Chamoux, 1973b, pp. 418–22). Thus each town had wet-nurses available to it. The villagers of Plougastel near Brest took in children from all classes, from the nobility to carpenters, fishermen and even day labourers.[45]

Despite the controls, abuses continued to occur, particularly in the region of Liège, and starting in 1770 there was an enquiry into the network serving Paris.[46] In 1779 the Controle Général set another enquiry in motion, this time covering all the children's hospitals in France. The figures alarmed the authorities, for in 1770–6, 15,419 of a total of 21,002 children had died before the age of four. The enquiry also revealed the commerce in abandoned children in the north of the country. Since these children came mostly to Paris where they were sometimes resold or redirected to the country, the government decided to forbid transportation to Paris and the decree of the Council of 10 January 1779 denounced the commerce in children 'who came from far distant provinces, were sent without due care and taken by public carriers who have other business interests and who are obliged to take a long time on the journey'. The result was that 'nine tenths die in the course of the journey.'

An enquiry was made in Brittany in 1776–9, which enables us to trace the routes by which nurse children were taken to Paris. There seem to have been two principal routes from Brittany to the capital, a northern one via Dinan and Fougères and a southern through Rennes and Vitré; the trade did not penetrate far beyond these places. In the west the *recrutement infantil* went no further than Lannion and only rarely reached St Brieuc, while to the south it covered only the Rennes area; Nantes reported no such activity. Vitré seems to have been the main entrepot where children were collected from Rennes and Dinan to be sent on to Laval (ADIV, C.128 and C.1287).

For France as a whole a rough outline of the areas involved in the trade might be as follows: around all the towns, and particularly around Paris there were a number of villages whose wet-nurses were linked to the conurbations by networks of *recommanderesses*, doctors, barber-surgeons and carriers. The area from which the children came into Paris was much bigger, but the numbers involved smaller, and only abandoned children were involved. There was a third phenomenon, not an organized one, which was the influx of girls and single women in distress,

45. R. Bothuan, 'Etude sur l'économie, la vie sociale et démographique de la paroisse de Plougastel au XVIIIe siècle' (1967).
46. H. Helen, 'Une sollicitude ambigue: l'évacuation des enfants abandonnés' (1973), pp. 225–9. On all these problems see, R. Mercier, *L'enfant dans la société du XVIIIe siècle* (1961); and H. Berques, *La prévention des naissances dans la famille* (1960).

seeking in the cities a refuge from the shame and the social stigma that resulted from mothering a bastard in the countryside. With the disruption of family life in the towns the situation became explosive. The idea of a child as a precious object was one entertained only by a section of French society and it applied only to children over a year old.

A reaction set in after 1770 under the influence of medical opinion and of a literary campaign of which *Emile* was only a part. Symbolized by the shepherdess and dairy maid of Marie-Antoinette's Trianon, this 'back to nature' movement has helped to conceal, behind the sentimental picture of family life as portrayed in the paintings by Greuze, a huge rise in the numbers of bastard and abandoned children in Paris. To Desessartz's plea for an end to 'the criminal negligence of parents for their children' corresponds Rousseau's plan 'that if mothers would deign to nurse their children morals would improve automatically' (see n. 43).

As an afterthought, it has only recently been realized that prolonged lactation has the effect of limiting fertility.[47] So fashion brought children back into urban family life from which they had been increasingly excluded, particularly among the ruling classes. But the upper classes were not the only ones where children were brought up by nurses and later sent away to school, with parents scarcely knowing their children at all. One of Balzac's heroines recounts that 'sent to the country as a nurse child and ignored by my family for three years, I counted for so little on my return home that I aroused people's pity.'[48] Another recalls (pp. 773, 775) that 'at the age of five I was sent as a day pupil to a boarding school in the town, taken in the morning and brought back in the evening by a valet. As soon as I could read and write, my mother had me sent to Pont-le-Voy, a school which took children of my age.' But the most extreme form of this system was reserved to the Russian nobility whose children had no contact with their parents at all, their friends playing the part of a family.[49]

The phenomenon of rising illegitimacy, which seems to have been common to most of Europe at this period, was probably the result of a reduction of social and religious pressures against it, though economic circumstances also played a part. As Depauw (1972a, pp. 1155–82) has demonstrated in the case of Nantes migration to the towns was important, but we are probably not justified in attributing the rise to this single cause. Though in Nantes the servants came from the countryside there were other women involved in the nether-world of the bastard-bearer, and these were the workers in the textile industries which mostly came from the city itself. Nonetheless, the speed of the rise in illegitimacy was so variable that one is tempted to divide areas by their record of bastardy into the following tentative categories: firstly, the greater cities where there was rapid disruption (*déstructuration*) of family structure; secondly, the larger towns where a similar disruption was in evidence, though these towns differed in character; thirdly, the small towns which remained morally 'healthy'; and finally, the countryside which resisted the general trend though, because of the exodus of children to the towns, this may not have been as marked as the overall figures suggest.

47. The sexual act is supposed to heat the milk of the wet-nurse. Furthermore, all maternal love 'is sucked up with the milk'. The origin of this belief may perhaps be explained by the frequent cases of syphilis infection.

48. H. de Balzac, *Le Lys dans la vallée* (1955), p. 771.

49. J. Meyer, *Noblesse et pouvoirs dans l'Europe d'ancien régime* (1974), pp. 170–5. M. Raeff, 'Origins of the Russian intelligentsia', *The eighteenth century nobility* (1966).

Whatever the true position in the countryside, putting children out to nurse was clearly one of the main causes of disequilibrium in the towns, both in the movement of population and the excess of mortality. This must be the rejoinder to Shorter's recent remarks.[50] In any case we are a long way from the traditional picture of moral disintegration brought about entirely by an aristocracy indulging in every kind of vice and *liaison dangereuse*. The rising trend of bastardy did not stop with the Revolution, though it did come to a temporary halt in some places. Illegitimacy would seem to be one of the characteristics of industrial Europe, but industrialization was not the cause of rising illegitimacy: indeed, that rise long preceded the industrial revolution.

50. See the relevant passages in *The making of the modern family* (1975). The historian could pursue this enquiry in many other directions, such as the role of bastardy in political history. One could, for example, measure the importance of this phenomenon in politics and in literature. The Second Empire was the great epoch for bastards with Flahaut, Morny, Walewski, etc., not to mention George Sand and Delacroix.

10

Illegitimacy in France during the nineteenth century

Etienne van de Walle

1 The Civil Code and natural children

In France the nineteenth century started conveniently in 1803 with the promulgation of Title VII, 'Of Paternity and Filiation', of the *Civil Code*. Together with the provisions of the Code on inheritance this was to constitute the charter of illegitimacy in France for approximately one hundred years. Since the law also determined the meaning of the available statistics we must discuss it in some detail.

It must be stated at the outset that it would be wrong to use the term 'bastard' in this context. Bastardy was specifically abolished in France by the law of 12 Brumaire of the Year II (2 November 1793), and the term 'extra-marital children' (*enfants hors mariage*) was substituted. With true revolutionary generosity the law of 1793 gave those children the same inheritance rights as legitimate children; even adulterine children were given some claim to inherit. However, the system was short-lived and without lasting consequences. It was 'virtually nullified by the courts, the Minister of Justice and Cambacérès's committee as early as the autumn of 1795'.[1] The euphemism 'natural children' (*enfants naturels*) was henceforth adopted; the term 'nature' carried great weight at the time, though it must have been unclear even then why some children should be more natural than others.

The French law of the nineteenth century may be summarized as follows:

1 There were two categories of natural children, the acknowledged and the unacknowledged ones (*reconnus et non reconnus*). Acknowledgement was voluntary, even on the part of the mother. It was prohibited in the case of children born as a result of an incestuous or adulterous relationship.
2 Acknowledgement could sometimes be forced by legal action. Paternal filiation proceedings (*recherche de la paternité*), rendered by the American translator of 1841[2] as 'scrutiny as to paternity' were forbidden, with the exception of the abduction of the woman at the presumed time of conception. This is the famous Article 340 of the Napoleonic Code. 'Scrutiny as to maternity' was allowed. Filiation proceedings were never allowed in cases of adultery or incest.
3 Natural children could not inherit (Article 756), but if they were acknowledged, they had limited rights of inheritance, that is, one third of the portion a legitimate child would get if he were in competition with legitimate children.

1. Crane C. Brinton, *French Revolutionary legislation on illegitimacy* (1936).
2. *The Code Napoleon . . . literally translated from the original and official edition*, by a Barrister of the Inner Temple, New York, 1841.

4 A child born within marriage was presumed legitimate. Disavowal by the father was extremely difficult, even if the child had clearly been conceived before marriage or while the husband was absent. It had to be disavowed shortly after birth, or after the husband had been informed of the birth. In other words, it was considered that a natural child is not normally born to a married woman.
5 A natural, non-adulterine child could be legitimated by subsequent marriage and was from then on placed on the same footing as legitimate children.
6 Registering the birth was the normal way of establishing legitimacy. Acknowledgement of a natural child had to be done by an authentic act and the best time to do so was at the time of registering the birth.

The Civil Code marked the beginning of the nineteenth century, but the end of the century witnessed major changes in two of its essential provisions. In 1896 the inheritance rights of natural children were greatly strengthened; in 1912 Article 340 was modified to allow scrutiny as to paternity under specifically listed circumstances. The nineteenth century avowedly aimed at protecting the family and its patrimony against the claims of spurious issue. It was generous neither to the child nor to the mother. The First Consul intervened personally to proclaim that 'society has no interest in the recognition of bastards' (Brinton, 1936, p. 66), and reasons of state prevailed against the plight of individuals. This was a reaction to a maxim of the *ancien régime*, *creditur virgini*, according to which pregnant girls could implicate their seducers. It has been suggested that the lawmakers of 1804 were bourgeois lawyers who imagined illegitimacy under peculiar social circumstances. The cases most likely to come to court were those where poor girls had been seduced by rich boys.[3] It appeared essential that good families were not to be dishonoured by foolish marriages, and that the young men of these marriages were to be protected from the extravagant claims of lovely but upstart maidservants. Of course, boys would be boys, and the sowing of wild oats had to be tolerated. Even when the father generously recognized his responsibility towards the child, it was important to protect the family by restrictive inheritance laws, so that the legitimate children would not suffer because of the claims of an illegitimate stranger.

It is only fair to add that the concern to spare the family disruptive lawsuits operated sometimes to the benefit of mother and child. Children born to married women were practically always legitimate. There appear to have been few illegitimate children of married women in France, though there seem to have been a considerable number in England.[4] It is not known, of course, how many married women may have hidden the birth and abandoned the child who would then appear as illegitimate in the statistics. But these must have been small in number, just as there was only a small proportion of legitimate children among foundlings.

2 Acknowledgement and legitimation

The natural child was a pathetic figure and the symbol of persecuted innocence to the romantic mind, as the success of *La Dame aux Camélias* would indicate. Acknowledgement was a compromise solution allowing material compensation to

3. Jean Savatier, 'L'évolution de la condition juridique des enfants naturels en droit français' (1965).
4. S. F. Hartley, 'Illegitimacy among married women in England and Wales' (1969), pp. 873–924.

the child. It is not surprising that there was a tendency to be lenient in this respect. Both the law and the practice of the law were somewhat ambiguous about the form of recognition. Article 57 of the Code required that the names of both parents be mentioned on the birth certificate without directly stating that the child was legitimate. Article 334 specified, moreover:

> The acknowledgement of a natural child shall be made by an authentic act, whenever it shall not have been done in its act of birth [American translation, 1841].

The text left open the possibility of confusion between mere mention of the name of the father and formal recognition. Many men must have assumed that they acknowledged the child when they reported its birth; much probably depended on local administrative practice and the attitude of the registrars. The official statistics of births after 1858 distinguished acknowledged children from other natural children. There are large fluctuations in the proportions, as demonstrated by the following selected years of peaks and troughs:

Proportion of natural children reported as acknowledged

year	%
1861	30
1863	36
1865	31
1866	38
1880	34
1886	45
1891	41
1892	30
1897	18

Administrative practice was changing over time, and was probably not the same all over France. The unreliability of these statistics was recognized:

> In the beginning, those natural children whose parents were *declared* by the witnesses and thus included on the birth certificate, were considered as acknowledged, even though these declarations are not acknowledgements in the legal meaning of the word.
>
> Starting with 1892, the circulars relative to the yearly statistics of vital registration specified that mention was to be made only of the children acknowledged by the father. This rule does not appear to have been followed immediately in all departments.[5]

Thus the steep drop of the proportions after 1892 is the result of eliminating acknowledgements by the mother; and the 1848 yearly statistics clearly specify yet another restriction in the headings of the table, 'acknowledgements by father on the birth certificate'. This eliminates the later recognition by the father which may represent a considerable part of the total. (Only some of those, however, as we shall see, had been included previously in the statistics.)

5. France, 1901, *Statistique de la France. Statistique annuelle*, p. lxxx.

Only for Paris do we have some details about the various kinds of acknowledgements, and it turns out that only the father would recognize the child on the birth certificate, probably because registration occurred so soon after confinement that the mother could not yet walk to the city hall. Later acknowledgements were largely by mothers (as far as I am aware, the declarer of a vital event to the registrar is always a man during the nineteenth century). For example, in 1884 there were 17,613 illegitimate births in Paris; 3,538 were acknowledgements immediately by the father on the birth certificate, or 20 per cent. Later acknowledgements were as follows:

238 by the father only
3,650 by the mother only
297 by both father and mother.

It is not clear what proportion of the later acknowledgements referred to a birth of that year, but nothing prevented an individual from recognizing his child several years after its birth. This introduces a problem of interpretation of the French annual data on acknowledgements, at least before 1892. Since these data are part of the birth statistics and since the *non reconnus* plus the *reconnus* add up to the annual total of natural births, the recognitions of children born in a previous year cannot have been included, but the figures clearly do include more than the acknowledgements at the time of birth registration.[6] It would appear that the registrar counted illegitimate births at the end of each year, in time for the annual report. He would then take into account all acknowledgements mentioned in the register at that time. This would include on average only those acknowledgements made during the first six months of the life of the child (assuming that births are distributed equally during the year). This interpretation is only a hypothesis, but it casts further doubt on the meaning of the statistics.

The 1892 circulars were correct in their decision to delete acknowledgements by the mother from the statistics as meaningless. Of course, there were many women who made the effort to go to the city hall to acknowledge their child, but the meaning and purpose of this act could not always have been clear to others. The natural child would normally be raised by its mother, except in the case of foundlings and abandoned children. It would receive her name, unless recognized by the father, and could usually resort to filiation proceedings against its

6. Two different sources provide the number of births in the city of Paris, the *Annuaire statistique* . . ., and for the Seine *département* including Paris, the *Statistique de la France*. Only the Paris statistics give the date and author of the acknowledgement. The data for 1884 are as follows:

	Seine	*Paris*	
Total births	80270	63840	
Illegitimate births	20319	17613	
Acknowledged	7386		
Immediately		3538	
Later		4185	
(By the father			535)
Unacknowledged	12933		
Immediately		14075	
(By the father, incl. later			13540)

The two series are clearly incompatible. If we include only the immediate acknowledgements or all acknowledgements by the father only, Paris has more unacknowledged children than Seine; some acknowledgements by the mother (i.e. later than at birth) must therefore have been included. But not all. If they had been there would be more acknowledged children in Paris than in Seine.

mother. Conflicts of guardianship and inheritance, when the fact of acknowledgement by the mother would make a difference, were infrequent; illegitimacy was most widespread in those classes of society which settled their disputes outside the judicial system and legal definitions. There was a kind of *de facto* recognition which must have been frequent.

The Paris yearbook of 1893 tabulates for the first time the acknowledgement status of children legitimated by subsequent marriage. The data are as follows:

	no.	%
Acknowledged by father	719	20
Acknowledged by mother	887	24
Acknowledged by father & mother	463	13
Not acknowledged	1562	43
Total legitimated	3631	100

In almost half the cases the child had not been recognized at all; in almost two thirds he had not been acknowledged by this mother, although she showed enough devotion to the child to give him the status of a legitimate child at the time of marriage. Mother and child had often lived together for a long time before marriage: at the time of marriage only 13 per cent of the legitimated children were less than one year old, 35 per cent were more than five years old.

French statistics on legitimation are available from the mid 1850s onwards. They give both the number of marriages with legitimated natural children, *mariages réparateurs* or marriages of reparation, as they were called, and the number of children legitimated by those marriages. This appears to be useful information and to indicate real time trends and regional differences. Before we turn to these statistics, however, and to those on illegitimacy itself, there is yet another point of definition that must be cleared.

3 The children of stable consensual unions

Marriages which legitimate children of more than five years of age raise one of the recurrent problems in the study of illegitimacy. Is there a sub-culture of consensual unions or 'common law marriages' beside the mainstream of legally sanctioned marriages? Stable consensual unions are an important category in many countries of Latin America, where illegitimate births constitute the major part of all births. Similar situations have been found in parts of Europe.[7] The cost and formality of the marriage ceremony may deter substantial numbers of the population who do not see compensating advantages in the legal protection and the aura of respectability conferred by a civil wedding. For these people there would be no blame, no sin in having natural children. Eventually, at a later date, they might confirm a relationship that had withstood the test of time, with the children possibly attending the wedding, as in Brassens's *Cortège Nuptial*:

> Je garderai toujours le souvenir content
> Du jour de pauvre noce où mon père et ma mère
> S'allèrent marier devant Monsieur le Maire.

7. Edward Shorter, John Knodel and Etienne van de Walle, 'The decline of non-marital fertility in Europe, 1880–1940' (1971).

Is there any evidence that these enduring consensual unions were an important feature of French marital custom? Many writers refer to them in the context of urban populations, particularly for Paris. Levasseur himself goes to some trouble to point out that, 'before condemning [illegitimacy in Paris], one ought to divide extra-marital births into four parts': one fourth, born in hospitals and other institutions, many of them to outsiders, who come to hide their shame and conceal the delivery in Paris; one fifth, children acknowledged at birth or legitimated, who belong to stable irregular unions, and are usually benefiting from childcare similar to that received by legitimate children; one fourth, children acknowledged later, one seventh of them by their father (presumably the latter also being to consensual unions in Levasseur's reckoning); 'the balance . . . represents the true product of Parisian immorality.'[8]

More will be said later about the extent to which confinements in Paris institutions may be attributed to women of the countryside. A similar computation was made by Bertillon in the *Statistical Yearbook* of Paris, in an 'attempt to evaluate the minimum number of concubinary marriages in Paris'.[9] He concluded that, out of a total of 14,269 births in 1880, at least 4,000 originated in stable consensual unions (*concubinats réguliers*). Chevalier speaks of the concubinage of workers, 'this form of feral existence that the illegitimacy statistics permit us to measure'. Chevalier approves of Bertillon's computation and assumes that acknowledgements are a reliable indicator of stable concubinage during the second half of the nineteenth century. He goes even further, however, and points out that about half of the unacknowledged children during the first half of the century were born 'at the residence of their parents' and must therefore be the result of stable unions.[10]

Here Chevalier allows himself to be carried away by the romantic image of these dangerous social classes living their parallel lives on the margin of bourgeois society and perpetuating themselves by illegitimacy. Since the choice appears to have been between delivering the natural child in a hospital, an infamous and insanitary solution, or at home, there is not much to be concluded here on the subject of the stability of unions. Even acknowledgement is a doubtful indicator. Otherwise we would have to conclude that stable concubinage was a widespread phenomenon all over France, where a substantial proportion of natural births were acknowledged. More revealing, perhaps, are the legitimations of natural children by subsequent marriage. Stability of relationship is indicated by the fact that they involved fairly old children and often several of them: in 1893, 100 of these marriages on average legitimated 142 natural children. It must be granted, however, that it is only by virtue of a legal fiction that the groom automatically became the father of these children, who may actually have been sired by another man. To accept the children together with the bride would often seem to have been the only solution to those who had decided to make an honest woman out of a girl who had 'sinned'.

Clearly then, illegitimate births, in Paris or elsewhere, are not all the product of casual promiscuousness; but the mere act of acknowledgement and legitimation is not a valid indicator of lasting relationships. Both reflect seriousness of purpose on the part of the father, but it is difficult to say much more.

8. *La population française* (1891) II, Rousseau, pp. 399–400.
9. *Annuaire statistique de la Ville de Paris* (1880), pp. 155–6, préfecture de la Seine.
10. Louis Chevalier, *Classes laborieuses et classes dangereuses à Paris pendant la première moitié du XIXe siècle* (1958).

4 Trends in illegitimacy

Table 10.1 gives the illegitimacy ratio for the whole of France; it is the only index of illegitimacy available for the entire nineteenth century. It represents the percentage of illegitimate births of all live births. The defects of this index are well known. The ratio is a most misleading indicator of illegitimacy because it is influenced by whatever factor modifies the ratio of illegitimate births to all births: changes in the proportion of single women either by changes in the age distribution or in the proportion married, and changes in the fertility of married women who contribute most of the births, as well as changes in the propensity to illegitimacy. During the nineteenth century there was a steep decline in marital fertility in France, and the illegitimacy ratio rose because natural births were not controlled to the same extent as births within marriage. Note that the rise in the illegitimacy ratio at the beginning of the century has often been ascribed to improved statistics (for example, by Levasseur, II, p. 32). There appears to be little evidence on this point.

Table 10.1: Illegitimacy ratios in France, 1801–1900

	%		%
1801–5	4.75	1851–5	7.28
1806–10	5.43	1856–60	7.52
1811–15	6.04	1861–5[(a)]	7.56
1816–20	6.61	1866–9	7.58
1821–5	7.16	1871–5	7.24
1826–30	7.21	1876–80	7.18
1831–5	7.31	1881–5	7.82
1836–40	7.41	1886–90	8.34
1841–5	7.15	1891–5	8.77
1846–50	7.16	1896–1900	8.84

(a) Data for 1870 incomplete and omitted.
Source: Statistique de la France, passim.

Table 10.2 presents an indirectly standardized rate, I_h.[11] It expresses the illegitimate fertility of the population as a percentage of what it would have been if its unmarried women had been exposed, by age, to the highest known fertility, that of married Hutterite women. It is not influenced mechanically, as is the illegitimacy ratio, by the decline in marital fertility, nor by changes in age distribution, nor in the proportions of women married. Interestingly enough,

Table 10.2: I_h index of illegitimate fertility in France, 1831–1901

1831	44	1871	44
1836	44	1876	41
1841	43	1881	43
1846	41	1886	46
1851	41	1891	45
1856	43	1896	45
1861	45	1901	44
1866	45		

Source: van de Walle, 1974.

11. Ansley J. Coale, 'The decline of fertility in Europe from the French Revolution to World War II' (1969).

therefore, the rate shows no evidence of long-term trends in illegitimacy between 1831 and the end of the century, at least for France as a whole. We shall see below that there are regional trends which cancel out at the national level.

The trend of legitimations set out in table 10.3 is unambiguous. The proportion of 'marriages of reparation', those that involve the legitimation of at least one child, increased markedly during the second half of the century, that is, over the period covered by the statistics. The average number of legitimated children compared with the total of natural births during these five-year periods rose steadily. Since the marriages may occur in a different period from the births, this is an approximate computation, but the trend is quite clear. It implies either an increase of stable concubinage (see the discussion of the preceding section) or an increase in the ability of women to extract marriage vows from their seducers. It would be interesting to see whether this ability is also reflected by an increase in the proportion of premarital pregnancies which are resolved by marriage; unfortunately we have no statistics about bridal pregnancies for that period.

Thus the real impact of illegitimacy seems to be somewhat reduced as time passes by the tendency to integrate children born out of wedlock into the family of their parents. But it is noteworthy that the decline of marital fertility in France is not accompanied by a parallel decline in illegitimate fertility, in contrast to what happened in other European countries (Shorter, Knodel and van de Walle, 1971). The puzzle is that the data for the whole country reveal no tendency for the French to use the proficiency they are increasingly gaining in the use of contraceptive methods to avoid births out of wedlock. Some light on that issue, however, can perhaps be shed by a consideration of the regional data.

Table 10.3: Legitimations of illegitimate children in France, 1856–1900

	Proportions legitimating marriages	Legitimated children per legitimated marriage	Legitimate children in proportion to illegitimate
	%		
1850–60	4.40	1.224	18.9
1861–5[a]	4.85	1.233	21.5
1866–9	4.61	1.272	24.9
1871–5	4.93	1.245	26.4
1876–80	5.24	1.234	25.4
1881–5	5.85	1.231	25.1
1886–90	6.01	1.253	27.5
1891–5	6.62	1.292	29.7
1896–1900		1.256	32.4

[a] Data for 1870 incomplete and omitted.
Source: Statistique de la France, passim.

5 Illegitimacy by *départements*

Figure 10.1 provides an oversight of the distribution of illegitimacy as measured by the index I_h in 1866. Figure 10.2 gives the changes between 1831–6 and 1896–1901, in absolute values of I_h. It is clear from the first of these maps that illegitimacy is strongly concentrated in the upper corner of France, although the urban *départements* (Bouches-du-Rhône, Gironde and Rhône) also stand out. A second fact, evident from the second map, is also interesting: there are contrary

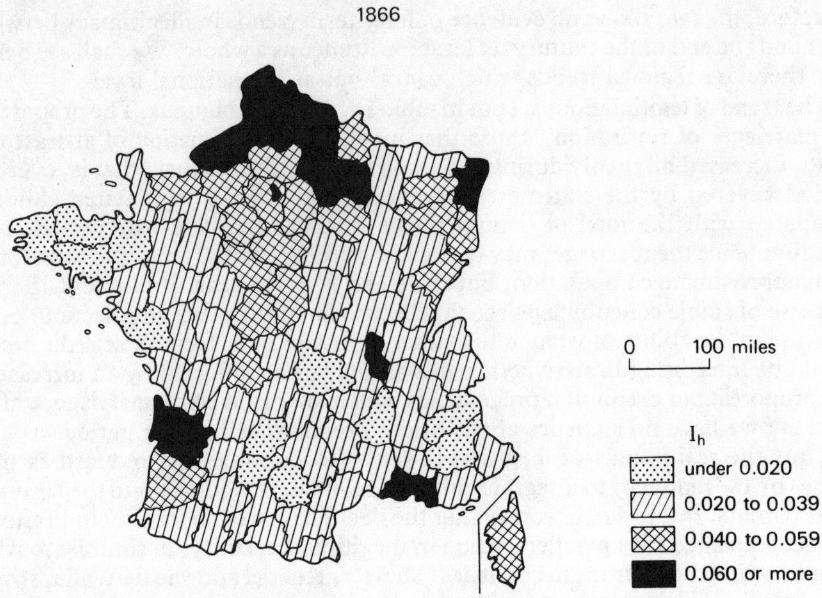

Fig. 10.1 Illegitimate fertility (I_h) by *département*, 1866

regional trends in illegitimacy. The increase is often quite considerable in several areas in the north of France and the decrease quite considerable in the south. Thus, although I_h remains very stable for the country as a whole, there are local movements in opposite directions which cancel out. I_h in Seine decreases from 0.161 to 0.090 over the period 1831–1901; in Somme it increases from 0.040 to 0.085. French writers have often remarked on the high illegitimacy of the northern departments, and they have given a specific explanation for it: the prevalence of 'trial marriages' (*mariages à l'essai*).[12] There is little doubt that bridal pregnancies were exceptionally high in parts of this area during the nineteenth century.[13] This is also the area where subsequent marriage legitimates the most natural births. Figure 10.3 gives an impression of the distribution of legitimations in the years 1861–5. Trial marriage is another term for consensual union. A large proportion of the illegitimate children will really be absorbed, together with their younger brothers and sisters, and without prejudice, within the family fold. We have therefore attempted to correct the illegitimacy index I_h so as to take the legitimations into account. The revised index I'_h is computed as follows:

$$I'_h = I_h \times (1 - \text{legitimations/illegitimate births}).$$

Its meaning is quite clear: it measures the extent of definitive illegitimacy, that is, the hard core not affected by the integration of the child into a nuclear family with full inheritance rights through marriages of reparation. As legitimations are

12. Chantal Blayo, 'Chapitre III – Natalité, fécondité' (1974).
13. Raymond Deniel and Louis Henry, 'La population d'un village du nord de la France, Sainghin-en-Mélantois, de 1665 à 1851' (1965). Louis Henry and Jacques Houdaille, 'Fécondité des mariages dans le quart nord-ouest de la France de 1670 à 1829' (1973).

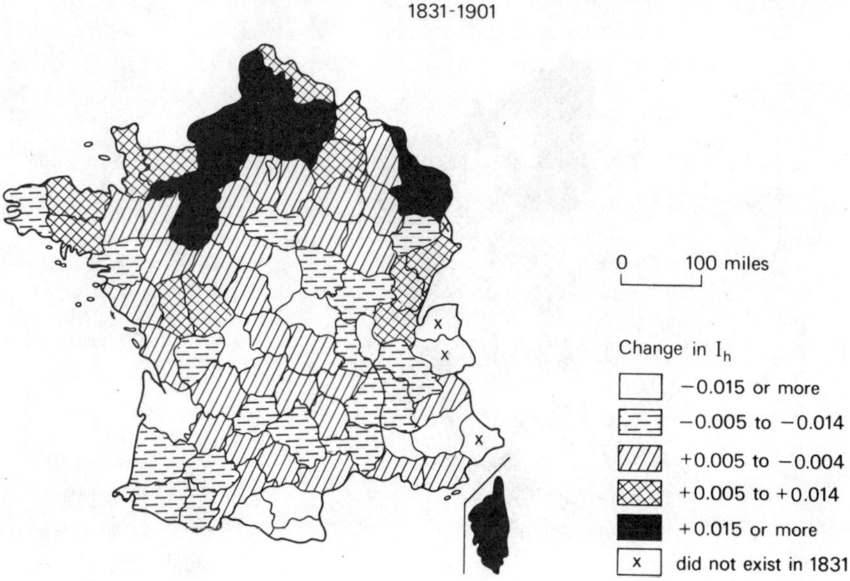

Fig. 10.2 Absolute changes in illegitimate fertility (I_h) by *département*, 1831–1901

closely correlated with illegitimacy, the dispersion of I'_h is much less than that of I_h.

Table 10.4 gives the matrix of correlation coefficients between the previously discussed measures related to illegitimacy (including legitimations and acknowledgements) and a series of demographic variables drawn from my earlier work (van de Walle, 1974). Marital fertility (I_g), proportion married (I_m) and age at marriage for 1866. I_h, I'_h and the illegitimacy ratio are closely intercorrelated (van de Walle, 1974). The major defects of the illegitimacy ratio appear when one studies time periods, but it would often be quite adequate as a measure of illegitimacy when used in a cross-section of areas at one point in time. As was argued earlier, the number of legitimated children per marriage involving at least one legitimation probably measures the incidence of consensual unions at least to some extent; this is positively correlated to all our measures of illegitimacy. As indicated, acknowledgements were poorly defined and measured; for what it is worth, they are in general negatively related to illegitimacy.

The most striking ecological relationships (or lack of relationships) are with the marital fertility and nuptiality indices. In France the continual decline in marital fertility is not accompanied by a decline in illegitimate fertility, and regionally there is no association between I_g and I_h, nor does there seem to have been any significant association at any time in the century. The latter finding duplicates in essentials the situation in Germany.[14]

There is no significant relationship between I_h and I_m but an interesting negative correlation appears between illegitimacy and age at marriage. Common sense leads us to expect that late age at marriage should provide plenty of opportunity for illegitimate births and that the correlation should be positive. Moreover, if late marriage were justifying informal unions and 'trial marriages',

14. John E. Knodel, *The decline of fertility in Germany, 1871–1939* (1974).

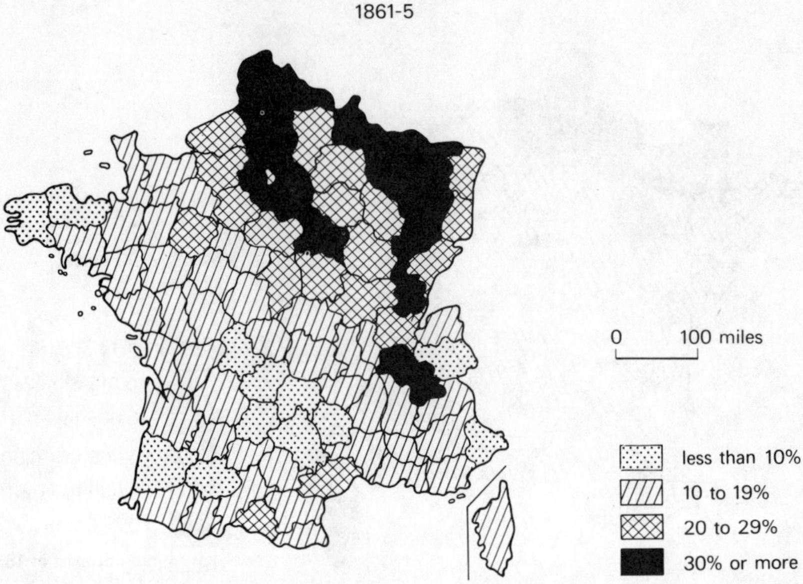

Fig. 10.3 Proportion of the illegitimate children legitimated by subsequent marriage, by *département*, 1861–5

there should be many children legitimated by marriage in those areas where age at first marriage is high. However, we have found the correlation to run in the opposite direction. There seems to be an association between late marriage and sexual restraint before marriage which must be explained by regional mating customs and attitudes.

Table 10.5 presents first order correlation coefficients between illegitimacy indices (I_h, I'_h, the change in I_h between 1831 and 1901, the proportion of illegitimate births that are legitimated by marriage, and the number of legitimated births by legitimating marriage) and some socio-economic indices that are known to be correlated with illegitimacy: urbanization and income measures.

The association of illegitimacy with urbanization in France has often been noted. One additional comment occurs in the nineteenth-century yearbooks and official compilations every time the urban-rural differentials are discussed:

> A certain number of illegitimate births registered in the cities do not belong to their resident population. Many unmarried mothers from the countryside come to the city to be delivered, and neighbouring towns provide the cities' foundling hospitals with a substantial portion of their annual quota of abandoned children: the latter children are always recorded as natural, although everyone knows that some of them were born in wedlock. (France, 1861, p. xxii)

Sometimes the comment refers specifically to Paris:

> One should not lose sight of the fact that a large number of unmarried mothers from the provinces have their child delivered in the capital, where they can more easily hide their sin. (France, 1872, p. xxxii)

Table 10.4: First order correlation matrix between fertility, illegitimacy and legitimation measures, *départements* of France (N=89), *c*. 1866

	I_h	I'_h	Illegitimacy ratio	% acknowledged	% legitimated	Legitimated per marriage	I_g	I_m	Age at first marriage
I_h, Illegitimate fertility		.972*	.941*	−.350*	.399*	.487*	−.166	.116	−.405*
I'_h, Illegitimate fertility adjusted for legitimations	.972*		.946*	−.323*	.190	.450*	−.162*	.087	−.406*
Illegitimacy ratio	.941*	.946*		−.405*	.272	.452*	−.137	−.070	−.412*
% Acknowledged among illegitimate	−.350*	−.323*	−.405*		−.249	−.274	−.033	−.175	.095
% Legitimated among illegitimate	.399*	.190	.272	−.249		.280	−.196	.227	−.124
Legitimated children per legitimating marriage	.487*	.450*	.452*	−.274	.280		.083	.013	−.248
I_g, marital fertility	−.166	−.162	−.137	−.033	−.196	.000		−.833*	−.125
I_m, proportion married	.116	.087	−.070	−.175	.227	.013	−.833*		.130
Age at first marriage	−.405*	−.406*	−.412*	.095	−.124	−.248	−.125	.130	

* Significant at .001 level.
Sources: Statistique de la France, passim; van de Walle, 1974.

Table 10.5: First-order correlation coefficients (r) between illegitimacy and legitimation measures as dependent variables, and indices of industrialization, urbanization and average income as independent variables, *départements* of France, *c*. 1866

	% in cities of 10000–20000	% in cities of 40000 +	% in industry	% in textiles	% in mining	% in metallurgy	Income per head	Average income from non-agricultural activities	Average salary
I_h	.020	.656*	.655*	.344*	.003	.056	.569*	.753*	.634*
I'_h	−.010	.714*	.569*	.254	−.077	−.042	.526*	.756*	.587*
% of illegitimate births that are legitimated	.095	.006	.540*	.390*	.305	.307	.404*	.273	.462*
Legitimated children per legitimating marriage	.036	.365*	.415*	.174	−.010	.126	.346*	.426*	.364*
Absolute change in I_h between 1831 and 1901	.104	−.320*	.234	.375*	.045	.006	.038	.370*	.135

* Significant at .001 level.
Note: N=89 except for changes in I_h between 1831 and 1901, when N=86.
Sources: 1866 French Census (1869); Déléfortrie and Morice, 1959; see also previous tables.

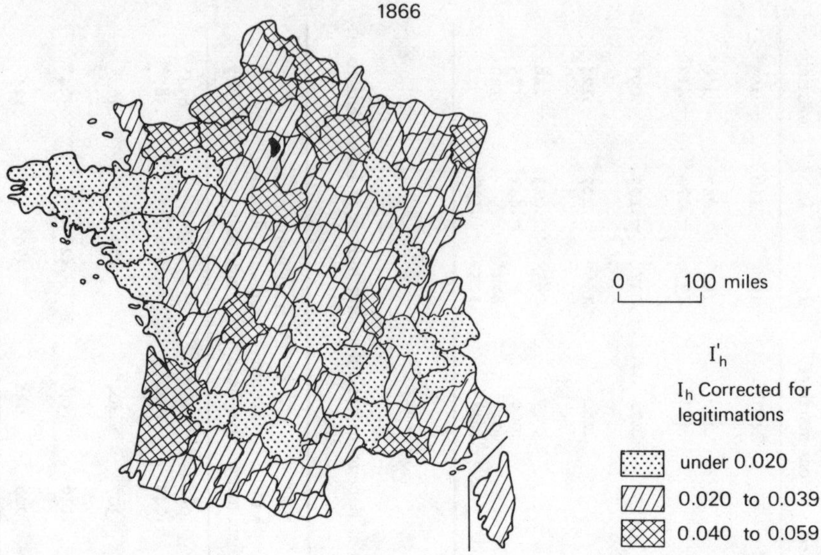

Fig. 10.4 Adjusted illegitimate fertility (I'_h), after correction for legitimation, by *département*, 1866

But in the instance of Paris at least, there exists abundant statistical evidence that mothers of illegitimate children were almost always domiciled in the city at the time of delivery. In 1880, for example, of a total of 2,733 acknowledged and 12,237 unacknowledged natural children only 28 and 673 respectively had been borne by women who were said to have their legal residences outside Paris (Paris, 1880, p. 185). Many of those had been born in maternity hospitals where they were accepted only because some outlying communes had formal arrangements with the city of Paris. The rules were strict: Parisian welfare institutions did not want to be overwhelmed by paupers from the countryside and restricted admission to the local population.

The argument really hinges on the meaning of the word 'domicile'. It would have been difficult, if not impossible for girls to make a brief trip to the capital at the time of delivery, to get rid of the children at a foundling agency, and to return unobserved to their villages. But it is likely that some pregnant girls settled in Paris long enough to acquire legal residence and that they tended to stay after the birth and become part of the city's permanent population as a result of illegitimacy. The high urban rate would then be in part the result of a selection process which led illegitimacy prone girls from a large hinterland to change their residences to a less rigidly controlled environment. It is true, in a sense, that these births were, as Levasseur says, a product of the immorality of the countryside, but in another sense, they were genuine urban births which belonged to the resident population.

Be that as it may, illegitimacy is closely and positively correlated with the urban population of certain departments. This seems to be the most significant and persistent ecological correlate of I_h throughout the century. But a refinement of the urbanization measure shows that illegitimacy is mostly related to a proportion of the population in large cities, those of 40,000 inhabitants and over. There is no significant correlation with the proportion living in cities of 10,000 to 40,000, perhaps because the atmosphere prevailing in small provincial capitals was no less straitlaced than in the villages. The number of children legitimated by marriage is also related to the percentage of the population in large cities, probably because of the prevalence of consensual unions in these cities. It is also in the large cities that the illegitimacy index appears to have declined most between 1831 and 1901.

Table 10.5 also presents some coefficients of correlation between our dependent variable and economic indicators drawn from the 1860 census or from the Déléfortrie and Morice study (1959) of the components of departmental incomes in 1864. There is a high degree of association between the proportion of the population making their living from industry, or between the average income from non-agricultural activities and the dependent variables. Since non-agricultural activities are heavily concentrated in the cities this relationship may not be different from that found previously in urbanization. It is to be noted that there is a more significant association with the textile industry than with other industries.

6 Conclusion

The official birth statistics reviewed here afford no more than a glimpse into illegitimacy and its ramifications. They constitute the essential starting point for the investigation into this complex phenomenon, but the user should be warned of their intrinsic limitations. Two basic errors must be avoided. The first one is to believe that a measure of illegitimacy provides an indirect picture of that dark side of human behaviour that is usually inaccessible to the social statistician. Many other factors are reflected, ranging from regional differences in mating customs to the efficacy of contraception. One must repeat the warning given by Laslett and Oosterveen (1973) that 'to look upon them as the record of fluctuation in the extent of fornication alone is a serious misunderstanding.' The registration of births reflects, and imperfectly at that, the interplay of public laws and private morals.

The second mistake would be to believe that the illegitimacy indices measure the impact of illegitimacy on the persons concerned (mother, child and relatives), and on society at large in a satisfactory way. The mention in a birth register that *la demoiselle* Marie Charlier had borne a child at the residence of the declarant, her father, Jean Charlier, and that the child received the name of Désiré Charlier, will either remain an inconspicuous accident or become the indelible brand of the 'fierce quality' that will distinguish it from 'a whole tribe of fops got 'tween asleep and wake' (the quotation is from Edmund's apology of bastardy, Shakespeare, *King Lear*, act I, scene ii).

The shame of birth may wear off and perhaps disappear. The study of illegitimacy through birth registration has nothing to contribute with regard to the assimilation of the child in society. The after-effects can be studied, however, from other historical documents: records of inheritance, marriage registers attesting legitimations, nominal lists of children who bear the name of the mother rather than that of the head of the household, unaccountable changes in family names that may foil attempts at record linkage.

11

Illegitimate births in France from 1740 to 1829 and in the 1960s

Yves Blayo

The variable legitimate or illegitimate was recorded for every birth contained in the sample (1 in 500), worked by the Institut national d'études démographiques for the whole of France between 1740 and 1829.[1] Hand manipulation of these data has made it possible to calculate the proportion of illegitimate births both by region and for the whole country. A difficulty arises from the presence of foundlings (*enfants trouvés*), since many of these children were certainly illegitimate, though it is far from clear whether they were registered as bastards at birth or baptism before their abandonment. It was decided to calculate an upper limit for the proportion of illegitimate births by adding to the number of recorded bastards the number of foundlings. The city of Paris poses a problem too, because no evidence about illegitimacy is available there until 1805.

1 Proportions of illegitimate births by regions

Percentages of all births (or baptisms) registered as illegitimate in the ten regions of France marked out on figures 11.1 and 11.2 were calculated for the periods 1740–89 and 1790–1829. These percentages are presented in table 11.1.

Table 11.1: French regional illegitimacy ratios, 1740–1829

	1740–89		1790–1829	
	Illegitimates only	Illegitimates & foundlings	Illegitimates only	Illegitimates & foundlings
	%	%	%	%
Region 1	0.8	0.8	1.5	1.5
Region 2	1.1	1.1	2.9	2.9
Region 3	1.0	1.0	5.1	5.1
Region 4	0.5	0.5	3.4	3.4
Region 5	1.4	1.5	3.6	3.6
Region 6	2.0	2.0	3.6	3.6
Region 7	0.6	0.6	1.4	1.4
Region 8	0.7	0.7	1.9	1.9
Region 9	1.7	1.7	2.6	2.6
Region 10	0.5	0.5	1.9	1.9
Small towns	2.7	4.6	5.8	16.2
Middle-sized towns	2.6	6.6	10.6	20.0
Large towns (excluding Paris)	7.9	13.0	14.7	22.5

1. See *Population* 25, numéro spécial, *Démographie historique*, November 1975. A joint article by Louis Henry and Yves Blayo appears in that number on the reconstruction of the population of France by age and sex between 1740 and 1860, and other articles by Blayo alone on population change, on mortality and on illegitimacy. It is this last study which is translated here, with a short addition specified in note 2.

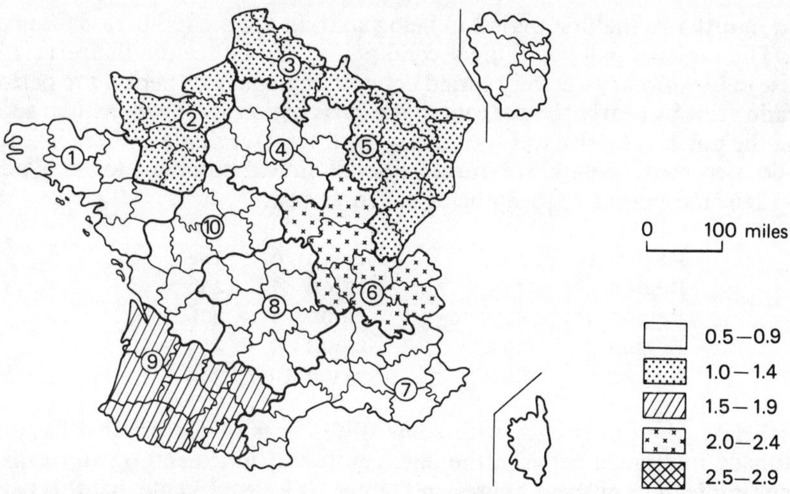

Fig. 11.1 French rural illegitimacy ratios by region, 1740–89

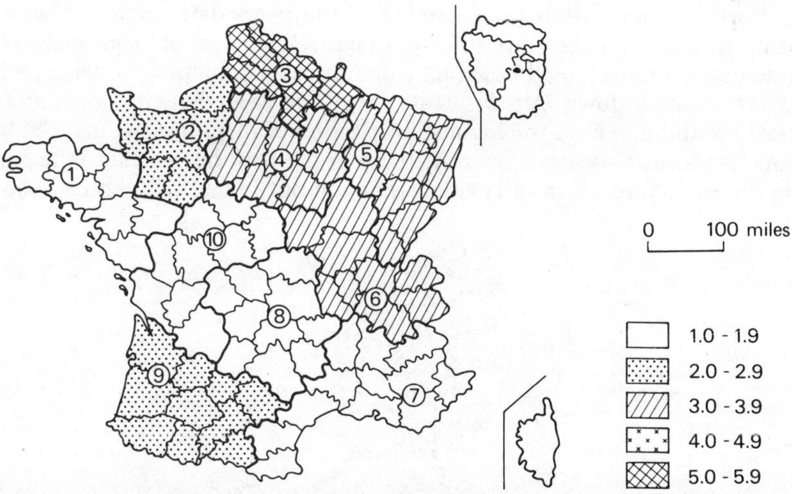

Fig. 11.2 French rural illegitimacy ratios by region, 1790–1829

2 Rural population

Foundlings were rare in the rural population and the proportion of illegitimates is not changed if it is assumed that foundlings should be classed with them. In the period 1740–89 the illegitimacy ratio only rose as high as 2 per cent in region 6 (west southwest including Savoy). It was lower than this in all the other regions. During the following period 1790–1829, it exceeded 2 per cent in six regions. Five of these were in the northeastern portion of France, and a distinction between this area and the rest of the country has often been observed. In the second period, then, illegitimacy was highest in region 3, the northernmost area, followed by region 5, the north northeast, then region 6, already referred to, then the Paris region, and finally region 2, Normandy. Region 9, the southwest, fell from being second in order in the first period to being sixth in the second period (see figure 11.1). The regional pattern in the second period can be seen in figure 11.2 The increase in illegitimacy was very varied between regions from period 1 to period 2. The ratio grew by nearly 700 per cent in the Paris region and by more than 500 per cent in the north. The rise was least in the southwest (region 9), where it reached only 60 per cent. Below are rural regional index numbers for the period 1790–1829, the period 1740–89 being taken as 100.

Region 1	183	Region 6	184
Region 2	255	Region 7	256
Region 3	517	Region 8	276
Region 4	692	Region 9	158
Region 5	260	Region 10	344

Nevertheless, the persistence with some differences of the original pattern of illegitimacy in France between the eighteenth and nineteenth centuries is the outstanding feature of these figures and tables. It is remarkable that this pattern should have survived to such an extent despite the changes in social structure which took place over this eventful period, but it is even more remarkable that it should have remained almost the same until the latest date for which we have information, that is for the years 1967–9. In figure 11.3 a set of illegitimacy ratios for these years is represented based on contemporary statistical evidence, which breaks the country down into 21 areas. It will be seen that the north and the northeast continue to have the highest proportion of illegitimates, that the band with low levels running south from Brittany in the west northwest to the Rhône Alps in the east southeast is still evident, though not so marked, with a region of

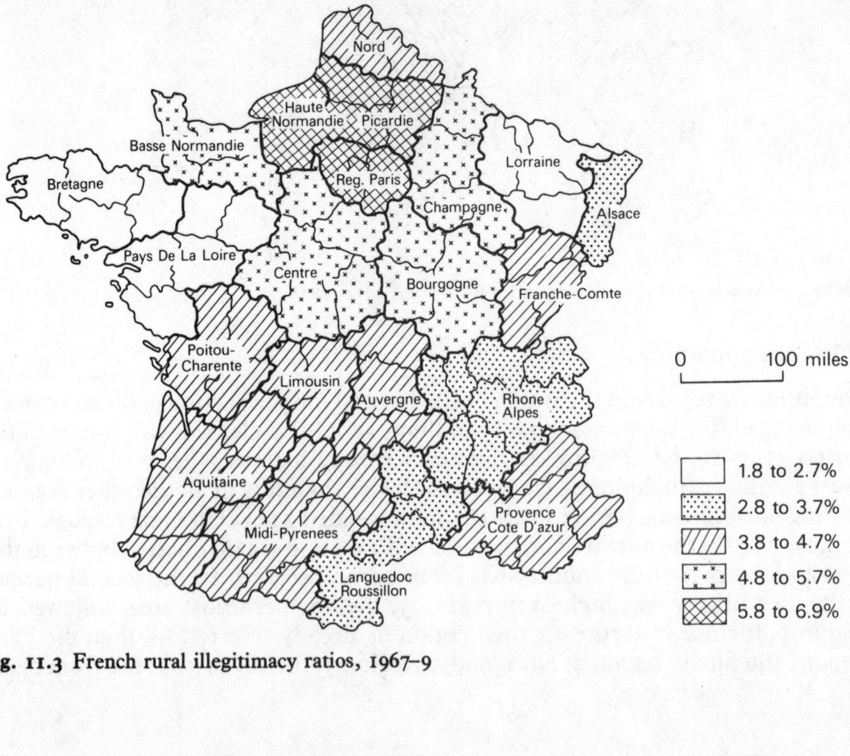

Fig. 11.3 French rural illegitimacy ratios, 1967–9

somewhat higher ratios in the southwest. There have been some interesting modifications, especially in the northernmost area and in Provence and these have been discussed in a study carried out after this chapter was prepared.[2] But it remains true to say that the geographical distribution of French illegitimacy ratios has been much the same for the last two hundred or two hundred and fifty years, that is for as long as the figures are obtainable.

3 Urban areas (Paris excluded)

The proportion of illegitimate births in urban areas is considerably different if one takes foundlings to be bastards where baptism or birth has not been registered from that if one leaves foundlings out of account. To adopt the former approach seems a little perverse and leads to a double counting, as was shown elsewhere.[3] The illegitimacy ratio, leaving foundlings out of account, was higher in urban areas than in villages, slightly higher from 1740 to 1789 in the smaller towns and very much higher in the large towns. During the second period the ratio in medium-sized towns was about as high as in the large ones; it increased fourfold compared with 1740–89, while it only doubled, approximately, in the small and large towns. With the definition of towns adopted in our survey, the small and middle-sized towns were still, in the period up to 1789, very much like villages; but after that date, the urban character of the medium-sized towns became quite pronounced in respect of bastardy. While the proportion of foundlings decreased with the size of towns in 1740–89, the situation was reversed in the following period.

4 The course of illegitimacy in France by decades

In order to proceed from results by region to results for the whole of France (without Paris), we have applied 'estimators' (*estimateurs*; defined and described in *Population*, 1975, pp. 26–7) to each of our regional results for each decade. The outcome of this procedure is given in table 11.2, and it will be seen that the illegitimacy ratio, low in 1740–9 (1 per cent), increases steadily up to 1820–9.

Table 11.2: Illegitimacy ratios in France (without Paris) by decade, 1740–1829

Period	Illegitimates only	Illegitimates and foundlings
	%	%
1740–49	1.0	1.3
1750–59	1.1	1.3
1760–69	1.4	1.8
1770–79	1.5	2.2
1780–89	1.9	2.6
1790–99	2.3	3.3
1800–09	3.6	4.4
1810–19	3.9	5.4
1820–29	4.8	6.6

2. See Chantal Blayo and Yves Blayo, 'L'illégitimité en France en 1800 et en 1968' in Ve *Colloque National de Demographie du Centre National de la Recherche Scientifique* 935 (1976), pp. 221–6. The figures for 1967–9 are taken from Jean-Claude Lasat and Jean Videau, *Données de démographie régionale*, 1968 (1969).
3. See Yves Blayo, 'Mouvement naturel de la population française de 1740 à 1829' (1975).

A statistical publication, *Recherches statistiques sur la ville de Paris et le département de la Seine*, issued in 1823, which records the annual number of births for Paris after 1670, only includes illegitimate births after 1806. In order to take Parisian illegitimacy into account, therefore, we have to estimate its incidence. We know the ratio for Paris for 1810–19, which is 36.8 per cent of all births. At the same time the bastardy ratio in two other large cities, Lyons and Rouen, was 21.7 per cent and 19.1 per cent respectively; in all the large towns it was 17.5 per cent, that is not much more than half of the Paris level. It can be assumed, therefore, that the illegitimacy ratio at Paris was either twice the one found in the other big cities, or the sum of the ratios worked out for Lyons and Rouen. As table 11.3 shows, the two series are somewhat different.

Table 11.3: Illegitimacy ratios for Lyons, Rouen, and all large cities, 1740–1829

Period	Lyons (a)	Rouen (b)	(a) + (b)	All large cities (c)	(c) × 2
	%	%	%	%	%
1740–49	4.2	4.3	8.5	7.3	14.6
1750–59	10.8	9.8	20.6	7.7	15.4
1760–69	6.9	8.9	15.8	7.9	15.8
1770–79	8.8	1.8	10.6	8.5	17.0
1780–89	8.2	5.1	13.3	7.9	15.8
1790–99	15.4	16.4	31.8	10.1	20.2
1800–09	22.1	16.0	38.1	15.9	31.8
1810–19	21.7	19.1	40.8	17.5	35.0
1820–29	14.3	10.6	24.9	15.3	30.6

When these proportions are applied to births in Paris,[4] a total of illegitimates is obtained for the city, and thus it is possible to calculate an illegitimacy ratio for France as a whole. The results set out in table 11.4 have been worked out on the two sets of assumptions mentioned above. The two series are very close together and it seems clear that we have a close approximation to the order of magnitude of

Table 11.4: Illegitimacy ratios in France by decade, 1740–1829

Period	1st hypothesis %	2nd hypothesis %
1740–49	1.2	1.1
1750–59	1.4	1.5
1760–69	1.6	1.6
1770–79	1.8	1.7
1780–89	2.2	2.1
1790–99	2.7	3.0
1800–09	4.2	4.4
1810–19	4.7	4.8
1820–29	5.5	5.4

Note: The first hypothesis applies to totals of births for Paris, twice the illegitimacy ratio obtained for the other big cities. The second hypothesis applies the sum of the ratios for Lyons and Rouen.

4. Births in Paris were adjusted to take account of the variations in the administrative boundaries of the city between 1740 and 1829.

the proportion of illegitimate births for the country. The rise in the proportion was greater in the period 1740–1829 than in the succeeding hundred and fifty years as is evident from figure 11.4. In 1972 the proportion of births registered as illegitimate in France was 7.2 per cent.

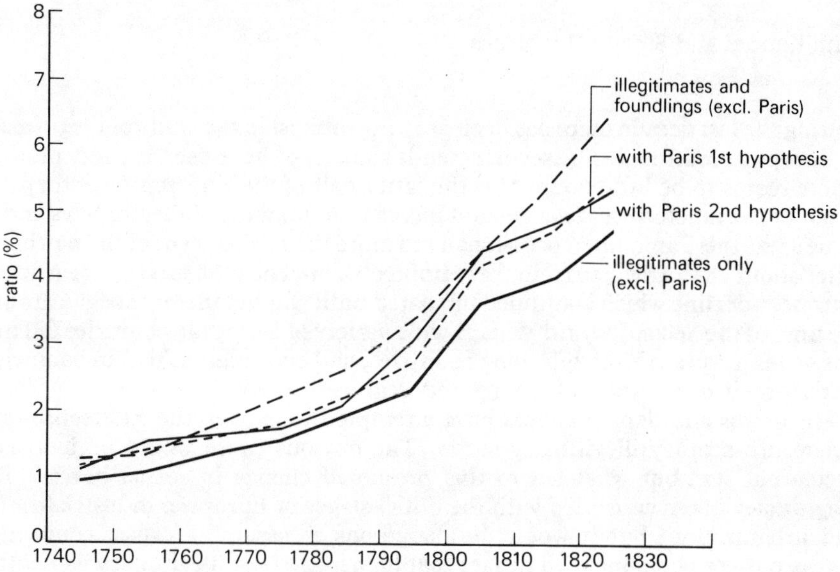

Fig. 11.4 Illegitimacy ratios in France by decade, 1740–1829

12

Urban and rural illegitimacy in Imperial Germany

John Knodel and Steven Hochstadt

During the last decade there has been growing interest in the study of illegitimacy in European countries. The secular trends since 1750 have been broadly plotted. There seems to be little doubt that the latter half of the eighteenth century and much of the nineteenth saw a general increase in numbers of illegitimates and in some areas these amounted occasionally to more than 25 per cent of the newborn. After about 1880 a decline from these unprecedented heights was apparent across Europe, a decline which continued unabated until another increase began around the time of the Second World War. A wide variety of European countries fall into this general pattern although some countries, and even regions within countries, display their own curves of timing and degree.[1]

Historians and demographers have attempted to explain the eighteenth- and nineteenth-century illegitimacy surge. The obvious cause would be increased premarital sex, but what led to this presumed change in sexual habits? The illegitimacy boom coincided with the initial stages of European industrialization and urbanization, but it would be dangerous to assume a causal connection between these phenomena. The fact that higher levels of illegitimacy were often reached in the less industrialized regions of Europe casts grave doubts on the assumption that illegitimacy was directly correlated with modernization (Shorter, Knodel and van de Walle, 1971, pp. 386–7). Much more statistical spadework needs to be done before grand hypotheses can be properly advanced. Theory-building may serve to direct research along untravelled paths and open up new lines of enquiry. But premature speculation may also divert attention from a more intensive study of the phenomenon, an essential preliminary to the building of valid theories.

The present study reviews in detail the empirical evidence from one European nation, Germany and more particularly, Prussia. The time is covered is the era of Imperial Germany between unification in 1871 and defeat at the end of the First World War, although the decades just before and after this period are sometimes included. Our intention is to discover the patterns of illegitimacy in rural and urban communities during this critical period of the emergence of Germany as a modern, industrial nation. German communities and regions were characterized by a wide range of demographic behaviour; they experienced levels of illegitimacy covering nearly the entire range found in the countries of Europe (Shorter *et al.*, 1971, map 1). A diversity of socio-economic conditions prevailed: rapid industrialization and urbanization in the Ruhr valley, manorial agriculture in East

1. Edward Shorter, 'Illegitimacy, sexual revolution and social change in modern Europe' (1971), pp. 237–72; 'Sexual change and illegitimacy: the European experience' (1972); and 'Female emancipation, birth control, and fertility in European history' (1973), pp. 605–40. Edward Shorter, John Knodel and Etienne van de Walle, 'The decline in non-marital fertility in Europe, 1880–1940' (1971), pp. 375–94. Peter Laslett and Karal Oosterveen, 'Long-term trends in bastardy in England' (1973).

Prussia and peasant farming in Bavaria. On the borders of the *Reich* Danes, Czechs and Poles mingled their cultural patterns with those of the Germans. All these factors combine to make Germany an ideal subject for a case study of illegitimacy.

There are several reasons for the choice of urban-rural comparison: first, the availability of information. Nineteenth-century scholars and statisticians considered the urban-rural division fundamental to the delineation of sub-populations differing in demographic and social behaviour. Demographic extremes were to be found, on the one hand, in the most rural areas and, on the other, in the largest cities.[2] Thus, in many German states and, in fact, throughout Europe, statistical bureaux drew up their tables in accordance with a scheme of urban-rural classification, and have, therefore, made possible the calculation of rural and urban illegitimacy indices. The second reason for our preoccupation with town and country is the conviction that understanding of the demographic changes which accompanied the transformation of European communities into modern industrial societies must take account of this contrast. Urbanization is almost a defining characteristic of modern society. It is therefore essential to assess the impact of urban life on illegitimacy if we are to understand the relationship between modernization and illegitimacy.

Many of the theories about the reasons for the increase in illegitimacy in the late eighteenth and early nineteenth centuries attribute a central role to the rise of cities and postulate, implicitly or explicitly, the existence of differences in illegitimacy levels between urban and rural communities. Models linking demographic change with economic and social modernization generally assume that growing urban agglomerations differed in their demographic patterns from traditional agrarian society. These models are easily extended to illegitimacy. Were the single migrants of both sexes who crowded into the expanding towns and cities of nineteenth-century Europe at the basis of the illegitimacy boom? Were the high levels of non-marital fertility found in various areas of Europe in the latter half of the century a consequence of the influence of the large city on its own population and that of the surrounding area? Did some mixture of social disorganization, anonymity and consequent anomie, the breakdown of traditions, the relaxation of social controls, increased individual freedom and the hedonism sometimes ascribed to city life contribute to looser sexual behaviour and higher rates of bastardy? Arguments can easily be put forward to support such views.

Finally, urban-rural patterns of illegitimacy in the last century are worthy of study because of their implications for our understanding of the urban life of the period. Conventional wisdom suggests a higher level of illegitimacy in towns and cities than in the countryside as a consequence of social disorganization and related urban characteristics. Would this view of city life be incorrect if urban illegitimacy rates should, in fact, turn out to be lower than has been assumed? We hope to deal with some of these questions at the conclusion of our main task: a straightforward description of illegitimacy in Imperial Germany.

1 Measuring illegitimacy

There are several ways of measuring illegitimacy. The simplest and most common measure is the ratio of illegitimate births to total births, usually termed the

2. E. A. Wrigley, *Industrial growth and population change* (1961).

illegitimacy ratio. Because this index depends on the number of legitimate births in the denominator, its value can be affected not only by the propensity of unmarried women in the reproductive ages to have illegitimate births but also by the proportion of women in the reproductive ages who married and by marital fertility. The major advantage of the illegitimacy ratio is that it requires only data on births by legitimacy status for its calculation and this can be computed merely with vital registration data when census data on unmarried women is lacking. The second measure, the general illegitimate fertility rate, or simply the illegitimacy rate, relates the number of illegitimate births to the total number of unmarried women in the reproductive ages, usually defined as 15 to 49. It requires both the number of illegitimate births from vital registration and a cross tabulation of the number of women by marital status and age which is normally provided by censuses. The advantage of the general illegitimate fertility rate is its freedom from any direct influence of nuptiality patterns or marital fertility, and its being an indicator of the propensity of unmarried women to bear illegitimate children.

Age-specific illegitimacy rates represent a further refinement in the measurement of illegitimacy by relating the number of illegitimate births to women in individual age groups to the number of non-married women in the same age groups. This has the advantage of eliminating any disturbing influence that differing age distributions of unmarried women may have, while revealing the considerable fluctuations in illegitimate fertility during the childbearing age. Data for this measure are less likely to be available than for the previous measures since in Germany, as in many other European countries in the nineteenth century, statistical bureaux published census data on the age distribution of women by marital status and births by legitimacy status, but not by age of mother.

A set of interrelated demographic indices including an index of illegitimacy has been developed by Ansley Coale (1969) to take full advantage of this typical combination of data. These indices attempt to control for effects of varying age distributions within populations by weighting age groups according to their presumed fecundity. The index of illegitimate fertility (I_h) is defined as follows:

$$I_h = B_I \; \Sigma \; u_i F_i$$

where B_I is the annual number of illegitimate births, u_i is the number of non-married women in each five-year age interval from 15 through 49, and F_i is the marital fertility in the corresponding age group of Hutterite women. (Hutterite women were members of a religious sect in North America who did not practise contraception and who had the highest marital fertility ever recorded.) The index I_h, therefore, is an illegitimacy rate which indirectly standardizes for the age structure of 'natural' fertility.[3] The present study utilizes data prepared in connection with a study of German fertility based on the Coale indices[4] and thus relies primarily on I_h as the measure of illegitimacy.

The index I_h differs relatively little from the general illegitimacy rate. As table 12.1 indicates, there is almost a perfect correlation between I_h and the general illegitimacy rate whether they are used to measure either the level of illegitimacy in the German administrative areas both in 1880 and 1925 or the change in illegitimacy between 1880 and 1925. This indicates that the effect of indirectly

3. Louis Henry, 'Some data on natural fertility' (1961), pp. 81–91.
4. John Knodel, *The decline of fertility in Germany, 1871–1939* (1974).

Table 12.1: Correlations between measures of illegitimacy in German administrative areas, 1880 and 1925

Measures	Levels 1880 (N=71)	1925 (N=66)	Change 1880–1925 (N=64)
I_h and general illegitimate fertility rate	·999	·999	·998
I_h and illegitimacy ratio	·954	.874	.141
Illegitimacy ratio and general illegitimate fertility rate	·957	.852	.131

standardizing for the age structure of unmarried women is minimal in the case of Germany and that the general illegitimacy rate and I_h are in effect equivalent measures of illegitimacy. The correlations between either of these two measures and the illegitimacy ratio, however, show a quite different story. Correlations between the levels of illegitimacy in either 1880 or 1925 as measured by the ratio and by the two other measures are high, although distinctly lower than those found between I_h and the general illegitimacy rates themselves. The correlations between changes in the illegitimacy ratio from 1880 to 1925 and changes in either of the other two measures are far lower.

The differences in the extent of change indicated by the ratio and the other measures stem largely from the influence of declining marital fetility on the former. In Germany marital fertility fell by more than 50 per cent between 1880 and 1925 according to almost all measures. The propensity of unmarried women to have illegitimate children, as measured by either I_h or the general illegitimate fertility rate also declined but only by 43 per cent. Since the decline in marital fertility was greater than the decline in non-marital fertility the ratio of illegitimate to total births actually *increased* by 29 per cent (Knodel, 1974, pp. 266–9). Thus, the inadequacies of the illegitimacy ratio obscure the decline in illegitimacy fertility that occurred in Germany during this time.

It is interesting to note that the problems of measuring illegitimacy by the use of the ratio were well recognized by a number of contemporary scholars in the German *Reich*, who were at pains to point out the advantages of the general illegitimacy rate.[5] However, the advantages were not appreciated by some present-day analysts of illegitimacy. William Goode, for example, completely overlooked the major shifts in illegitimate fertility in the Western nations during the last half century by relying on the illegitimacy ratio.[6]

The choice of illegitimacy measures is of critical importance for the study of urban-rural differentials in Imperial Germany. We have seen that it would make little difference whether the general illegitimate fertility rate or the index I_h is used, but quite a different picture of urban-rural differentials would emerge if we relied exclusively on the illegitimacy ratio. Table 12.2 which presents relevant data for the three largest German states in 1880, demonstrates this clearly.[7] The illegitimacy ratio in Prussia was 90 per cent higher for Berlin and 37 per cent

5. Hans Hindelang, 'Die eheliche und uneheliche Fruchtbarkeit mit besonderer Berücksichtigung Bayerns' (1909). Friederich Lindner, *Die Uneheliche Geburten als Sozialphänomen* (1900). C. Rauhe, *Die Unehelichen Geburten als Sozialphänomen* (1912).
6. William Goode, *The family* (1964).
7. For convenience, illegitimacy indices will be dated in the text and tables according to the date of the census used in their computation. For the exact period covered by the birth data, see Knodel (1974) appendix tables.

higher for other cities (with over 20,000 population) than it was for the rural areas. The index I_h, on the other hand, indicates a level of illegitimacy in Berlin only 27 per cent higher than in the rural areas and in the other cities a level identical with that of the rural areas. Saxony provides an even more striking example. Although the illegitimacy ratio for the three largest cities is 30 per cent *above* the rural level, the I_h index is 33 per cent *below* the rural level. In all three states the illegitimacy ratio clearly exaggerates the illegitimacy level of urban areas relative to the rural ones. Reliance on the illegitimacy ratio to measure urban-rural differentials in non-marital fertility would be entirely misleading.

Table 12.2: Comparison of illegitimacy measures and indices of marital fertility (I_g) and proportions married (I_m) by urban-rural categories in Prussia, Bavaria and Saxony, 1880

					Index value (rural = 100)			
	Illegitimacy ratio	I_h	I_g [a]	I_m [a]	Illegitimacy ratio	I_h	I_g [a]	I_m [a]
Prussia [b]								
Berlin	13.3	.079	.590	.467	190	127	78	90
Other cities	9.6	.062	.686	.459	137	100	91	88
Towns under 20,000	7.8	.058	.719	.487	111	94	95	94
Rural	7.0	.062	.758	.520	100	100	100	100
Bavaria								
Munich	27.7	.160	.589	.415	232	155	72	86
Other urban	15.9	.098	.647	.445	134	95	79	92
Rural	11.9	.103	.823	.483	100	100	100	100
Saxony								
Large cities [c]	16.3	.089	.577	.443	130	67	79	79
Other urban	11.1	.109	.713	.550	89	82	97	98
Rural	12.5	.133	.733	.559	100	100	100	100

[a] The marital fertility index labelled I_g by Ansley Coale, represents the ratio of births to married women compared to the number they would have had if they had experienced the Hutterite marital fertility schedule. I_g is calculated in a manner analogous to I_h with legitimate replacing illegitimate births and married replacing unmarried women. The proportions married index, labelled I_m by Coale, is a weighted index of the proportions married among women in the reproductive ages with the Hutterite marital fertility schedule used as weights. It thus gives the greatest weight to the proportions married in the most fertile ages and the least weight to those in the least fertile ages.

[b] Fertility indices for Prussia are based on births in 1880–1 and for Bavaria and Saxony on births in 1878–82.

[c] Dresden, Leipzig and Chemnitz.

Further light is shed on the patterns of illegitimacy depicted by these two measures by the additional statistics in table 12.2, an index of marital fertility and an index of the proportions married among women in the reproductive ages. In all three states the large cities experienced the lowest marital fertility and lower proportions married among urban women served to depress the number of legitimate births, thereby inflating the urban illegitimacy ratio relative to rural areas. These factors do not affect the level of I_h. Therefore, the urban-rural patterns of illegitimacy indicated by I_h are quite different from the patterns revealed by the illegitimacy ratio.

Although age-specific illegitimate fertility rates were not generally available for German states during the period under investigation, a few sets could be derived from scattered sources for the years around 1880 and these are presented in table 12.3. The results suggest that urban-rural differences in age patterns of illegitimacy are not likely to distort the differentials measured by either I_h or the general illegitimate fertility rate. Only for Oldenburg could age-specific rates be calculated separately for rural and urban areas. In this one case it is clear that the age patterns of illegitimacy were practically identical in rural and urban communities. A comparison of Berlin, the largest city in Germany, with the various states represented in table 12.3 also suggests the lack of major urban-rural differences in the age pattern of illegitimacy. For example, despite the fact that women in Berlin experienced noticeably higher illegitimacy rates at every age than women in Hesse, the index values show that the shape of these two illegitimate fertility schedules are quite similar. In general, all the illegitimate fertility schedules in table 12.3 follow a roughly similar course with respect to age. Illegitimacy is highest during the twenties and drops off steadily at older ages; the rates for women aged 15–19 are only a fraction of the rates experienced by women in their twenties and are also substantially lower than the rates experienced by women in their thirties. Although more direct evidence is required before a final judgement can be made, the limited data presented here suggests that differences in age patterns of illegitimacy between urban and rural areas are minimal.

Table 12.3: Age-specific illegitimate fertility rates for selected German areas, *c.* 1880

Age	Oldenburg (a) 1876–85 Rural (b)	Oldenburg (a) 1876–85 Urban (c)	Berlin 1878–80	Hesse 1879–82	Saxony 1876–80	Sachsen-Meiningen 1878–9	8 German states (d) 1876–80
			Rates per 1000 unmarried women				
15–19	5.1	6.1	15.6	8.2	23	13.7	12
20–24 }	26.6 }	27.4	50.1	40.3	90	68.7	58
25–9 }			54.5	44.6	83	78.9	55
30–34 }	14.9 }	18.2	45.0	33.0	55	51.8	38
35–9 }			28.6	20.3	35	42.1	27
40–44 }	3.2 }	3.2	10.1	8.5 }	6	18.7	9.5
45–9 }			1.2	0.8 }		0.7	0.9
			Index values (highest age group = 100)				
15–19	19	22	29	18	26	17	21
20–24 }	100 }	100	92	90	100	87	100
25–9 }			100	100	92	100	95
30–34 }	56 }	66	83	74	60	66	66
35–9 }			53	46	38	53	47
40–44 }	12 }	12	19	19 }	7	24	16
45–9 }			2	2 }		1	1

(a) Includes the principalities of Birkenfeld and Lübeck (Oldenburg).
(b) Communities with under 2000 inhabitants.
(c) Communities with 2000 or more inhabitants.
(d) The six united Thüringian states, Brunswick and Oldenburg.

Note: The rates for Berlin and Saxony include stillbirths. The rates for the 8 German states are based on confinements.

2 The data

The present study is based on the official statistics of the Imperial Statistical Bureau (Statistisches Reichsamt) and the various state statistical bureaux.[8] Since

8. For a fuller discussion of the sources and a bibliography of the official statistical series used, see Knodel, 1974, especially pp. 19–23 and 292–3.

the German *Reich* was subdivided for administrative purposes, official statistics for these units are also available. However, not all states were subdivided in the same way, nor were identical statistics for all administrative units published in any particular state. Most commonly the data needed for calculating I_h indices are available for the whole state, and in the larger states for subdivisions, mostly called *Regierungsbezirke*. For this study Germany is divided into a number of administrative areas which frequently, but not always, correspond to these units. In some cases they refer to entire small states, such as Anhalt, or to the Hanseatic city-states of Bremen, Hamburg and Lübeck.[9] (Figure 12.1 shows these areas according to their 1900 boundaries while figure 12.2 shows the division of Germany into the more familiar states or provinces.)

A series of I_h values for the administrative areas from just prior to unification to the beginning of the Third Reich can be calculated on the basis of censuses held in 1867, 1871, 1880, 1890, 1900, 1905, 1910, 1925, and 1933, and continuous official birth registrations, although certain areas have gaps in some years for various reasons, such as the loss of German territory in 1918 (the results of these calculations are presented in Knodel, 1974, appendix table 2.1). However, the data required for the calculation of separate rural and urban I_h indices are not available for all administrative areas. For example, for 1880 the rural and urban I_h could be calculated for only 48 of the total of 74 administrative areas and for one larger unit comprising three administrative areas (the 48 administrative areas include Berlin for which there is no rural component; the large unit is the Grand Duchy of Oldenburg). The loss of coverage is not serious, since the data fortunately include the three largest states, Prussia (34 of its 36 administrative areas), Bavaria (all 8 areas) and Saxony (all 4 areas) as well as Oldenburg (the whole of the Grand Duchy), Brunswick and the city-state Hamburg. Together these areas represent almost 80 per cent of the German population at this period. For each of these administrative areas limited time series of rural and urban I_h can be calculated. In addition urban-rural I_h indices can be computed for a number of the remaining administrative areas for at least one date during the latter nineteenth century.

The I_h series for rural and urban areas of administrative units are not uniformly comparable because the Imperial Statistical Bureau did not publish census age and marital status distributions or vital statistics according to an urban-rural cross-classification. The necessary data originate from independent publications of the individual state statistical offices, which enjoyed substantial autonomy, each with its own scheme of urban-rural classification. In essence two systems were used: one classified districts as rural or urban according to population size; the other was based on the legal status of a district.[10]

9. A more complete description of the method of defining the administrative areas used as units of analysis can be found in Knodel, 1974, pp. 9–14. The method used here is a slight modification, which keeps the *Regierungsbezirke* Allenstein, Gumbinnen, Königsberg, Stettin and Stralsund in Prussia and the *Kreishauptmannschaften* Bautzen and Dresden in Saxony as separate areas.

10. A special study done by the Oldenburg Statistical Bureau (1874, p. 20) compared the numerical scheme, where urban meant over 2,000 inhabitants, with the legal system for a number of German states and Prussian provinces in 1871. In 7 of the 23 areas listed the percentage of the total population designated as urban by the two systems differed by less than 1 per cent; in seven others the difference was 5 per cent or less. The biggest disparities were found in two Prussian provinces, Rhineland and Westphalia, where the percentage judged to be living in urban areas was approximately 20 percentage points higher when using the numerical definition in comparison to the legal definition. Some of the problems with each of these systems have been discussed in Knodel, 1974, pp. 89–93.

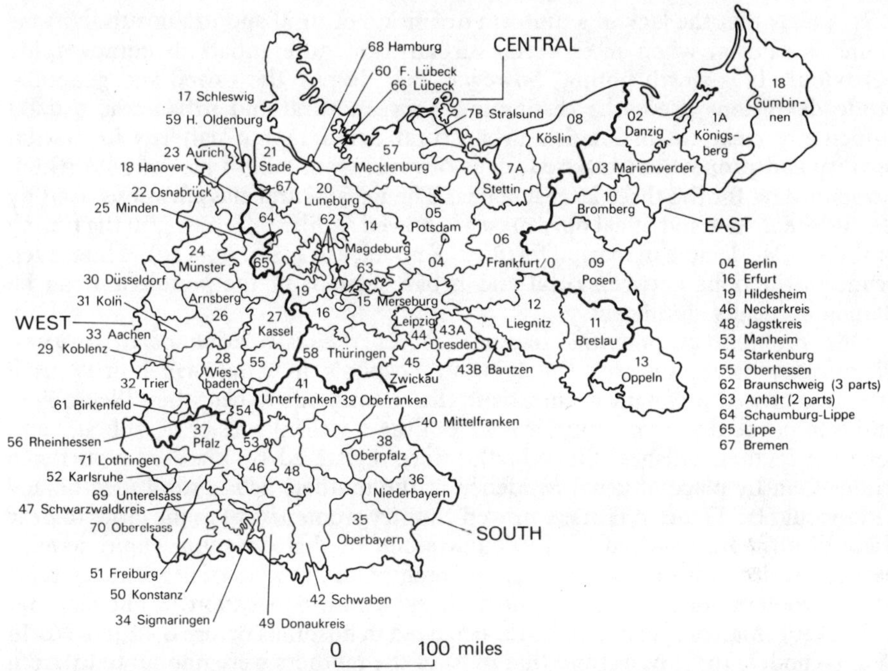

Fig. 12.1 Administrative areas of Germany, 1900

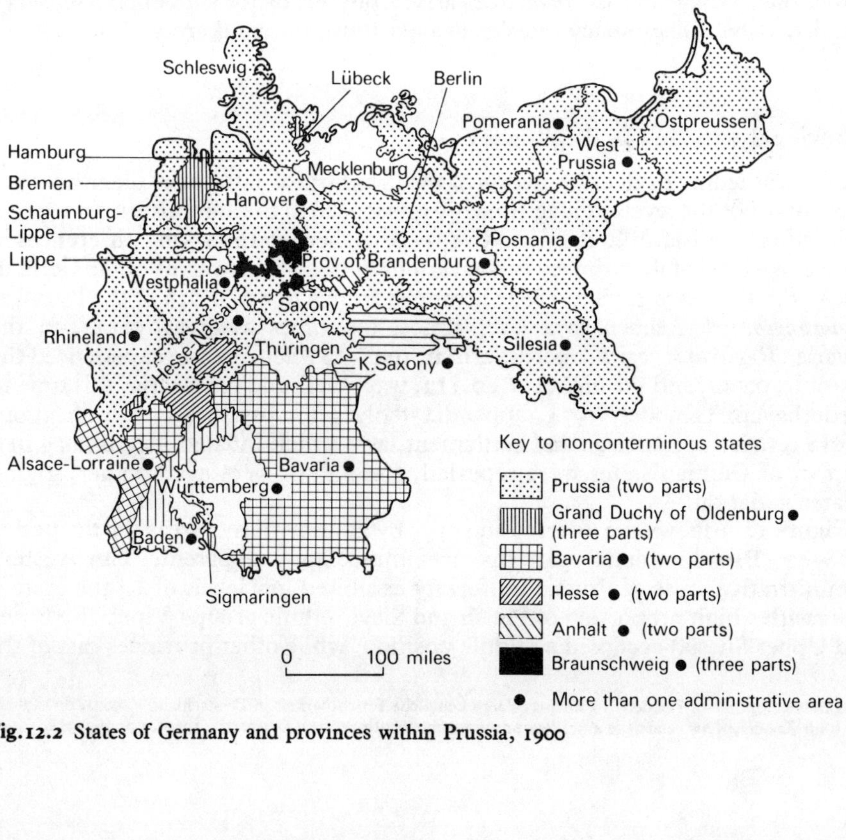

Fig. 12.2 States of Germany and provinces within Prussia, 1900

It is clear that the lack of a uniform definition of rural and urban subdivisions counsels caution when interpreting urban-rural differentials in demographic behaviour. It is worth noting, however, that despite the varied and generally crude definitions used, the distinction between rural and urban was usually sufficiently clear to distinguish urban-rural demographic patterns in marital fertility and proportions married, as is obvious from table 12.2 (p. 288) which presents data for the three largest states. The urban-rural classifications used by the different state statistical bureaux also showed similar differences in the timing of the secular decline in marital fertility (Knodel, 1974, pp. 93–110). Thus, even crude distinctions between rural and urban sections of the population can be demographically significant.

One problem of potential importance for the calculation of urban-rural illegitimacy rates concerns the lying-in hospitals in cities which may have attracted unwed pregnant women from the countryside to bear their illegitimate children in relative anonymity, away from the watchful eyes of neighbours and relatives in their villages. Since births were registered by place of occurrence rather than by place of usual residence of the mother, urban-rural illegitimacy rates would be distorted if many unwed country women went to the cities to bear their illegitimate children. A thorough study of this question would require extensive, time-consuming research. Contemporary studies of illegitimacy refer to the problem but provide no systematic evidence on its extent.[11] The fact that only a very small proportion of births occurred in hospitals before the First World War (Knodel, 1974, p. 92) and that most of the mothers were undoubtedly from the city or town where the hospital was located suggests that the problem is not a serious one. Whatever distortion does arise from this factor will, of course, serve to inflate urban illegitimacy rates as against those for rural areas.

3 Regional variation in illegitimacy

Before proceeding to an examination of the urban-rural patterns of illegitimacy, a brief survey of the levels of illegitimacy experienced in the administrative areas in their entirety is useful. In the period 1871–1914 there were striking differences in the average level of illegitimacy in the various administrative areas of the German *Reich*. For the years 1878 to 1882, I_h ranged from a low of 0.016 in the Prussian *Regierungsbezirk* Aachen to a level almost ten times as great, 0.144, in the Bavarian *Regierungsbezirk* Oberbayern; in 1908–12 Aachen again experienced the lowest I_h, 0.014, and the highest I_h, 0.112, was still found in Bavaria, this time in Niederbayern (Knodel, 1974, appendix table 2.1). Just prior to unification, before restrictive marriage and settlement laws which inflated illegitimacy in a number of German states were repealed, some rates were even higher, giving greater variation.[12]

Figure 12.3 shows the distribution of I_h by administrative areas for the period 1878–82. Broad regional patterns are immediately apparent. The western administrative areas of Prussia uniformly exhibited low levels of I_h, the eastern areas with a high proportion of Polish and Slavic ethnic groups (especially Posen and Upper Silesia) occupied a middle position, while other provinces east of the

11. Lindner, pp. 88–9. Friederich Prinzing, 'Die uneheliche Fruchtbarkeit in Deutschland' (1902), pp. 37–46.
12. John Knodel, 'Law, marriage and illegitimacy in nineteenth-century Germany' (1967), pp. 297–318.

Elbe experienced fairly high levels. Particularly high illegitimacy characterized southeastern Germany and Saxony, while somewhat more moderate levels prevailed in the southwestern areas.

Differences between administrative areas remained remarkably stable during the period of Imperial Germany and even until the 1930s, despite the fact that the national average of I_h declined from 0.079 in 1866–8 to 0.033 in 1931–5. Around 1880 the values of I_h in the various administrative areas correlated at 0.96 with the corresponding values around 1900 and at 0.83 with I_h values around 1933 (Knodel, 1974, p. 76). Thus, the changes in national governments, the vast economic transformation of Germany and the turmoil of the inter-war years did not greatly alter the regional pattern of illegitimacy. Indeed, the most challenging problem confronting scholars studying historical patterns of illegitimacy in Germany is undoubtedly the substantial and persistent regional differences so clearly evident in figure 12.3. Various hypotheses have been suggested, rejected and resurrected in the spate of studies published since the end of the nineteenth century. No really satisfactory explanation has emerged so far. Although our own study is not intended to deal exhaustively with this complex problem, since it is focused on the narrower question of urban-rural differentials in illegitimacy, we hope nevertheless it will make a contribution to the solution of the problem.

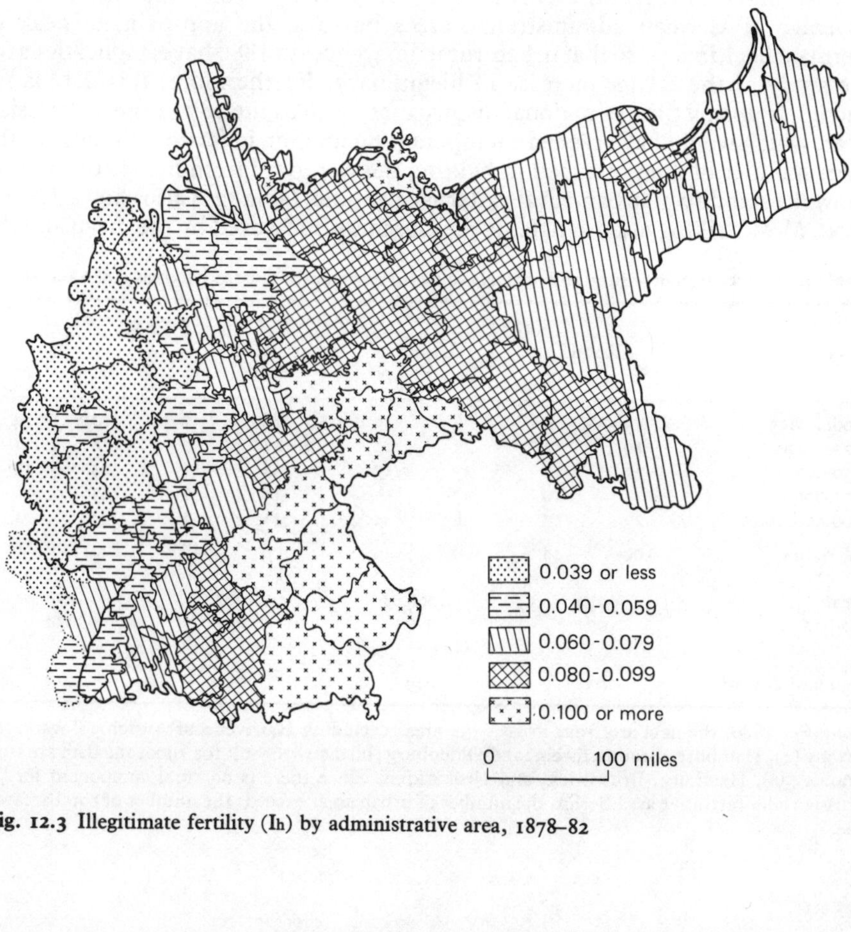

Fig. 12.3 Illegitimate fertility (I_h) by administrative area, 1878–82

4 Urban–rural levels, differentials and trends

Although our full set of urban and rural I_h indices for German administrative areas contains some gaps in the time series and a number of administrative areas are not represented at all, to the best of our knowledge we have included urban rural I_h values in all cases where the requisite data are available.

The first question to be asked of this mass of data is whether it displays any consistency over time. The remarkable persistence of the geographical patterns for entire administrative areas has already been demonstrated. Results are very similar for the rural and urban populations. The two periods for which most data on rural and urban I_h are available are the years around 1880 and 1890. The correlation between the rural I_h values for these periods is 0.98 (N=43) and for the urban 0.96 (N=44), a clear indication that the rural and urban values show considerable regularity. A longer time span can be tested by correlating the rural and urban I_h for the Prussian administrative areas between the periods 1880–1 and 1910–11. Again the coefficients are quite high. 0.93 for rural (N=33) and 0.90 (N=34) for urban. As the urban-rural population balance was changing rapidly in this thirty-year period and the average level of illegitimacy was falling, the close correspondence in the geographical patterning of rural and urban illegitimacy is striking.

For several reasons the data for 1880 are the most appropriate for an intensive analysis of urban-rural differences. This year gives us not only the most complex coverage of German administrative areas but also the approximate peak of German illegitimacy, so that urban-rural differences in 1880 have implications for the study of the earlier increase in illegitimacy. Furthermore, this date is far enough from any time of national disturbance, such as the 1870 Franco-Prussian War, which would have casued a temporary fluctuation in fertility because of the large number of men involved in fighting the war away from home. In order to show the stability of urban-rural patterns over time, table 12.4 also shows data for 1900. Most striking at both dates is the closeness (measured by the mean and the

Table 12.4: Distribution of rural and urban I_h values in German administrative areas, 1880 and 1900

I_h value	1880				1900			
	Rural		Urban		Rural		Urban	
	%	N	%	N	%	N	%	N
Under .025	13	6	6	3	18	7	10	4
.025–.049	19	9	22	11	21	8	28	11
.050–.074	21	10	27	13	32	12	44	17
.075–.099	21	10	37	18	18	7	15	6
.100 and above	27	13	8	4	11	4	3	1
All values	100	48	100	49	100	38	100	39
Mean I_h	.072		.068		.057		.056	
Median I_h	.071		.070		.054		.054	
Standard deviation	.038		.029		.030		.022	

Note: For 1880, the data are from Prussia (34 areas excluding Hanover and Aurich), Bavaria (8), Saxony (4), Hamburg, Braunschweig, and Oldenburg (births 1876–80); for 1900, the data are from Prussia (36), Hamburg, Brunswick, and Neckarkreis. Since there is no rural component for the Prussian administrative area Berlin, the number of urban areas exceeds the number of rural areas by one.

median values) of the average rural and urban levels. At the same time there is an interesting contrast in the distribution of values, with urban areas clustering more in the central categories as reflected in the higher standard deviation for rural values at both dates. The decline in illegitimate fertility between the two dates is also apparent but seems to affect both distributions alike.

National averages may mask important differences between urban and rural values in administrative areas within the country. Table 12.5 indicates the distribution of these differences for 1880 and 1900, using both relative and absolute criteria of differentiation. Both methods reveal two salient points: 1) German administrative areas are divided fairly evenly between those with higher urban and those with higher rural I_h at both dates; 2) in spite of the very wide range of absolute values as shown in table 12.4, the size of the urban-rural difference is quite small. In 1880, out of the 48 administrative areas for which data are available, 29 had less than a 25 per cent difference in urban and rural values. Overall there is a slight preponderance of districts with higher rural illegitimacy. This tendency is confirmed by the calculation of the average value of the differences in districts with higher rural I_h as opposed to those with higher urban I_h. The figures are 0.019 and 0.012 in 1880 and 0.017 and 0.014 in 1900. These differences are quite small considering the overall level of illegitimacy. In the last decades of the nineteenth century when German illegitimacy was close to its highest level, urban and rural I_h displayed a wide range of values, but on the whole high urban coexisted with high rural illegitimacy and low urban with low rural. The correlation coefficient between rural and urban I_h is 0.84 for 1880 and 0.73 for 1900. Geographic location had a greater influence on I_h values than size of community.

Table 12.5: Distribution of rural-urban differences in I_h values in German administrative areas, 1880 and 1900

	1880		1900	
	%	N	%	N
Absolute differences				
Rural higher by .010 or more	33	16	34	13
Rural higher by .005–.009	8	4	3	1
Difference less than .005	27	13	26	10
Urban higher by .005–.009	13	6	16	6
Urban higher by .010 or more	19	9	21	8
All districts	100	48	100	38
Relative differences				
Rural higher by 50% or more	13	6	8	3
Rural higher by 25–49%	6	3	18	7
Rural higher by 10–24%	21	10	13	5
Difference less than 10%	23	11	26	10
Urban higher by 10–24%	17	8	8	3
Urban higher by 25–49%	10	5	8	3
Urban higher by 50% or more	10	5	18	7
All districts	100	48	100	38

Note: For 1880 the data are from Prussia (33 areas excluding Hanover and Aurich), Bavaria (8), Saxony (4), Hamburg, Braunschweig, and Oldenburg (births 1876–80); for 1900, the data are from Prussia (35), Hamburg, Brunswick, and Neckarkreis. Berlin is excluded since it has no rural component.

Table 12.6 shows that differences between rural and urban levels of illegitimacy, although relatively small and not consistently in one direction, bear a definite relationship to the overall level of illegitimacy. The overall level is negatively correlated with both absolute differences (measured as urban minus rural) and relative differences (measured as the ratio of urban to rural). The negative correlations indicate that when the overall level is low, illegitimacy is higher in urban than rural areas, and hence the absolute difference is negative; but where the overall level is high the reverse is true. In order to remove the bias caused by the fact that in most administrative areas the rural population was greater than the urban, table 12.6 also shows the correlations between the urban-rural differences and the unweighted average for the area, that is, the simple average of the rural and urban I_h without considering the proportion of the population in each sector. Although this adjustment reduces the correlations, the negative association is still clearly evident.

Table 12.6: Correlations between urban-rural differences and overall levels of illegitimacy in German administrative areas, Prussian administrative areas, Bavarian districts, Saxony districts and Thüringian states

Administrative units and variables correlated	Absolute differences		Relative differences	
	r	N	r	N
German administrative areas				
Urban-rural difference 1880 and area I_h	−.540**	46	−.539**	46
Unweighted average of urban and rural I_h	−.436**	46	−.458**	46
Prussian administrative areas				
City[a]-rural differences 1880 and area I_h	−.545**	30	−.585**	30
Unweighted average of city and rural I_h	−.298	30	−.388*	30
City[a]-rural differences 1905 and area I_h	−.578**	31	−.539**	31
Unweighted average of city and rural I_h	−.417**	31	−.433**	31
Bavarian Districts (*Kreise*)[b]				
Urban-rural difference 1879–88 and unweighted average of rural and urban general illegitimate fertility rates	−.228	46	−.137	46
Saxony districts (*Kreise*)[c]				
Urban-rural differences 1890–9 and district illegitimacy ratio	−.624**	27	−.556**	27
Unweighted average of rural and urban illegitimacy ratios	−.455**	27	−.397*	27
Thüringian states				
Urban-rural differences 1872 and state illegitimacy ratio	−.630*	8	−.576	8
Unweighted average of rural and urban illegitimacy ratios	−.536	8	−.478	8

(a) City refers to all cities in the administrative area with more than 20,000 population in 1880.
(b) Since all cities in Bavaria constituted separate districts, each urban district was matched with the surrounding rural districts.
(c) Excluding the cities of Dresden, Leipzig and Bautzen.

Note: Absolute difference is defined as the urban minus the rural value; relative difference is defined as the ratio of the urban to the rural value. Significance levels (using one-tailed tests) are indicated as follows: * = significant at the .05 level; ** significant at the .01 level.

Sources: include Hindelang, 1909; Prenger, 1913; Thüringen Statistical Bureau, 1874.

In addition to the rural and urban I_h values for all the available German administrative areas, individual data sets were used to test the general relationship under different circumstances. For Prussia it is possible to compare the differences between I_h in the large cities (those with more than 20,000 population in 1880) with the rural level by excluding the smaller towns from the urban category, thereby testing the relationship of city-rural differences with overall I_h. A negative association between these differences, both in absolute and relative terms, and the overall area level is apparent in both 1880 and 1905. Again, using an unweighted average to measure the overall level reduces but does not eliminate the correlation.

To test if this same relationship between urban-rural differences and overall level characterized Imperial Germany on a more local level, data from three contemporary studies were used: Hindelang, 1909, Prenger, 1913, and the Thuringian Statistical Bureau, 1874. All three studies indicated considerable local variation in the overall level of illegitimacy. In Bavaria, during 1879–88, the difference in the general illegitimate fertility rate between local towns and their rural environs correlated weakly with their unweighted average. The results for Saxony in 1890–9 and the Thuringian states in 1872, based on the illegitimacy ratio since I_h values are not available, are more in line with those found for the larger German and Prussian administrative areas. There is thus some evidence that the negative association between urban and rural differences in illegitimacy and the overall level characterizes large and small administrative units alike.

We have seen that urban-rural differentials in the level of illegitimacy in 1880 and 1900 are not consistently in one direction. Is this also true with respect to the timing of the illegitimacy rise and fall? Since the rise of illegitimacy was generally complete before our series begin, that part of the question cannot be answered here. Illegitimate fertility, however, began to decline generally during the period of Imperial Germany and thus our data should provide some insight into urban-rural differences in the timing of this decline. While the determination of the onset of the decline is inexact and somewhat arbitrary due to the lack of a sufficiently long time series for each administrative area, the process should be sensitive enough to allow any strong patterns to emerge. The onset of decline is defined as the period immediately following the date at which the highest I_h value was reached, followed by a steady drop to substantially lower levels. In order to facilitate this dating, the rural and urban I_h values were supplemented with data on the overall I_h for each district from 1867 to 1933. The success of the exercise may be judged by the fact that dates could be assigned to more than four fifths of the rural and urban time series.

Table 12.7 shows that there is no striking difference in the timing of rural and urban decline in illegitimate fertility. Urban sections of administrative areas show a greater divergence in dates of decline, a few more by 1880 or after 1900 than the rural sections. For both rural and urban I_h, less than half the districts appear to be declining by 1880. A number of these areas, such as most of the Bavarian *Regierungsbezirke*, were affected by the repeal of restrictive marriage and settlement laws in the 1860s. Most, whether rural or urban, showed signs of declining illegitimacy by 1910. For 33 or the administrative areas it was possible to determine whether the urban decline in illegitimate fertility preceded or succeeded the rural decline. In six areas the onset of the decline began at the same time in town and country; in the remaining 27 areas the timing of urban and rural decline was divided almost equally. In most of these administrative areas there

Table 12.7: Date of onset of rural and urban declines in I_h, German administrative areas

Date	Rural %	Rural N	Urban %	Urban N
1880 or earlier	25	13	38	20
1881–90	20	10	4	2
1891–1900	22	11	25	13
1901–10	8	4	13	7
After 1910	8	4	8	4
Indeterminate	18	9	12	6
Total:	100	51	100	52

Note: The number of urban areas exceeds the number of rural areas by one since there is no rural component for the Prussian administrative area Berlin.

was at least a decade between the two dates, so that the results of this comparison cannot be the fortuitous outcome of arbitrary methods. Thus, no pronounced or consistent urban-rural differential is evident in the timing of the illegitimacy decline and the levels of illegitimacy.

5 Regional patterns of urban-rural illegitimacy

Figure 12.4 indicates that around 1880 urban-rural differentials in illegitimacy had a definite regional patterning. Despite lack of data for a number of administrative areas, it is clear that the differentials were not scattered randomly across the German *Reich*. The westernmost areas were characterized either by higher urban illegitimate fertility or a lack of substantial difference, the eastern and central areas more frequently by higher rural illegitimacy while Bavaria shows a very mixed pattern of differentials. Figures 12.3 and 12.4 suggest that a regional classification of administrative areas into East, Central, West and South[13] may help to reduce the complexity of the data by highlighting patterns which characterized particular parts of Germany and by maximizing the illegitimacy homogeneity of each region.

The East region contains seven Prussian *Regierungsbezirke*, which formed the Prussian provinces of East Prussia, West Prussia, Posen and Upper Silesia. All these areas contained substantial numbers of non-German ethnic groups, especially Polish and Masurian (Knodel, 1974, pp. 141–2). The South region includes the eight Bavarian administrative areas, as well as Neckarkreis and Sigmaringen. The West region consists of Oldenburg and the Prussian provinces of Rhineland, Westphalia, and Hesse-Nassau, as well as Aurich and Osnabrück. The Central region includes the rest of Hanover, the Prussian provinces of Pomerania, Brandenburg and Berlin, Lower Silesia, Schleswig-Holstein and Saxony, plus the Kingdom of Saxony, The Hanseatic Cities and Brunswick (areas lacking the requisite data are not included in either our analysis or our discussion of regional groupings). This Central region largely separates the overwhelmingly Protestant areas from the mixed Catholic, industrialized Rhine and Ruhr valleys in the West.

13. The regional groupings used in the present study are not identical with those used in Knodel (1974). Since the number of administrative areas with urban-rural illegitimacy data is substantially below the total number, a broader regional classification was more appropriate.

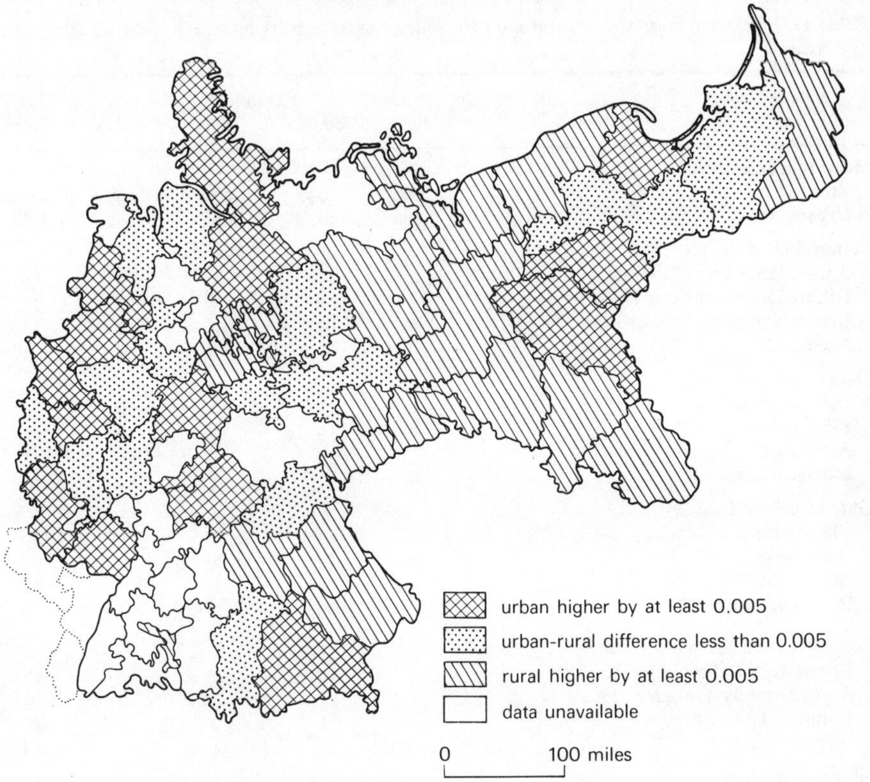

Fig. 12.4 Urban-rural differences in illegitimate fertility (I_h) by administrative area, 1880

Table 12.8 presents the regional division of rural and urban I_h values in 1880 as well as the onset of urban and rural illegitimacy decline. The differences in averages of both urban and rural values are striking, with each region having its own characteristic level of illegitimacy. In each of the regional groupings average urban and rural I_h were very close: the Central region generally had a greater rural I_g at high levels, while the West had predominantly higher urban I_h, but at low illegitimacy levels. The East with moderate levels and South with high levels both showed mixed urban-rural differentials. The low urban and even lower rural I_h in the West contrast with the Central and Southern regions. The West could not have participated to any great extent in the nineteenth-century illegitimacy boom which gave Germany one of the highest illegitimacy levels in Europe.

The four regions also showed differences in the onset of the illegitimate fertility decline. In both rural and urban parts of the South illegitimacy was well on its downward course by 1880, spurred by the earlier repeal of legislation restricting marriage and settlement. The decline continued in both parts during the decade 1880–9, suggesting that legal liberalization was not the only factor. By contrast, the early decline in illegitimacy did not take place everywhere in the other regions. Again, the patterns of rural and urban decline varied within each of the regions. In most Western administrative areas, with low overall rates, there was no definite sign of declining urban illegitimacy before the turn of the century although rural illegitimacy often declined before 1900. In both the Central and

Table 12.8: Selected measures of rural and urban illegitimate fertility by region, German administrative areas

	Region				
	East	Central	West	South	Total
Mean I_h levels, 1880					
Rural	.068	.090	.026	.099	.072
Urban	.066	.078	.033	.092	.068
Comparison of levels, 1880					
Rural higher by 10% or more	2	13	1	3	19
Difference less than 10%	3	4	1	3	11
Urban higher by 10% or more	2	3	10	3	18
No data	0	2[a]	1	1	4
Date of rural decline					
1880 or earlier	0	2	2	9	13
1881–1900	6	9	6	0	21
After 1900	1	4	3	0	8
Indeterminate	0	7[a]	2	1	10
Date of urban decline					
1880 or earlier	3	7	1	9	20
1881–1900	3	10	2	0	15
After 1900	1	2	8	0	11
Indeterminate	0	3	2	1	6
Comparison of dates of decline[b]					
Urban decline first	3	10	0	0	13
Approximately the same	1	5	0	0	6
Rural decline first	3	2	9	0	14
Indeterminate	0	5[a]	4	10	19
Number of areas	7	22	13	10	52

(a) Including Berlin which has no rural component.
(b) In certain cases for which approximate dates for rural or urban decline cannot be determined, it is possible to ascertain which type of community began to decline earlier. On the other hand, there are cases for which both rural and urban decline dates can be established, but no comparison can be made, e.g. when both rural and urban communities are declining by the date the I_h series begins, as for all the 8 districts of Bavaria.

East regions, the majority of areas experienced declining illegitimate fertility before 1900 in both urban and rural sectors

The contrast in regional levels and trends in illegitimacy are underlined in figure 12.5, which plots the rural and urban regional averages of I_h (unweighted by population) for Prussian regions with the longest consistent time series (since only one Prussian administrative area, Sigmaringen, was in the South region, it has been excluded from figure 12.5). The West region is clearly distinctive. Although the illegitimacy level was substantially lower in the West than in either the East or Central region, urban I_h was steadily rising until almost the end of the period of observation, long after illegitimacy showed a declining trend in rural communities in the West and in both rural and urban I_h in the other regions. The tardy decline in urban I_h in the West is particularly interesting when we consider that the most likely immediate factor to account for the general decline in illegitimate fertility in Europe during the period is the increasing use of birth control (Shorter *et al.*, 1971) and there is reason to expect birth control to spread sooner and more rapidly among city than country people. Marital fertility

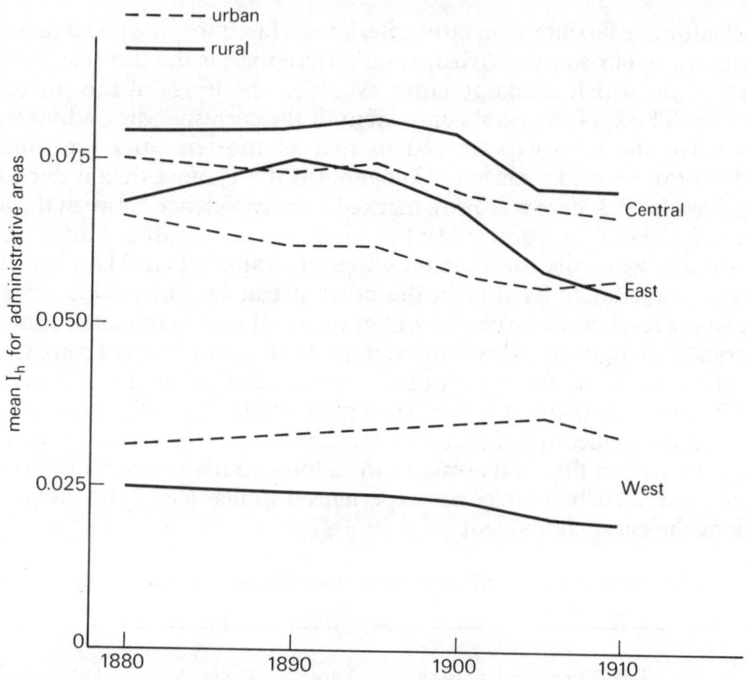

Fig. 12.5 Illegitimate fertility (I_h) by region (unweighted average) and urban-rural category, Prussia, 1880–1910

declined earlier in urban than in rural areas in the West as it did generally throughout Germany (Knodel, 1974, table 3.3). The inter-connection between regionality, level of illegitimacy and onset of decline raises the question as to whether illegitimacy can be explained on a national basis. The regional clustering of similar I_h levels suggests that common regional customs exerted a crucial influence on the overall level of illegitimacy. The general lack of substantial urban-rural differentials in levels for any region implies further that regional customs had a greater impact on illegitimacy than the rural or urban nature of communities.

6 City size, urbanization and illegitimacy

Urban communities as defined by the various German statistical bureaux included small towns with less than 2,000 inhabitants, as well as large cities, and therefore comprised quite a range of urban places. Thus the main difference in levels of illegitimacy may have been not between villages and small towns, but between villages and small towns, on the one hand, and very large cities on the other. Table 12.9 presents the I_h values in 1880 for German cities with at least 100,000 inhabitants; for the purpose of comparison the level of I_h in the rural and other urban sectors of the administrative area in which each city is located is included wherever available. In 1880 the largest cities of Germany varied greatly in levels of illegitimacy. Values of I_h ranged from 0.041 in Frankfurt am Main to almost four times this level in Munich. Berlin, by far the largest city in Germany at this time, fell between these extremes. Danzig, the smallest, experienced higher illegitimate fertility than either Berlin or Hamburg, the two largest. Even more relevant to our study of urban-rural differentials is the fact that there is no clear pattern in which the large cities exceeded the levels of the surrounding countryside. The I_h of the rural component of the corresponding administrative area exceeded the level experienced in four of the ten cities for which this comparison can be made. Only in Cologne was the I_h more than a third higher than the rural level. There was also a marked correspondence between the level of I_h in the cities and in the rural areas: the rural area surrounding Munich had the highest rural I_h while the rural surroundings of Frankfurt am Main had close to the lowest. Illegitimate fertility in the other urban categories also correspond roughly to the level of the large city and of the rural area in the same administrative district, although within each district the relationship was not consistently in one direction. In the administrative district of Cologne (Köln), for example, the I_h for cities between 20,000 and 100,000 was higher than that of the city of Cologne, but the I_h of the smaller urban areas was much less than either, closely resembling the I_h experienced in the rural areas. In the administrative district of Breslau, on the other hand, all urban categories experienced similar levels of I_h but at a level lower than the rural component.

Table 12.9: Urban-rural I_h values by size of urban population for areas with a city of 100,000 or more, 1880

City	Population in 1000s	Administrative area	Values of I_h index: Large city	Other cities 20000 +	Other urban	Rural
Berlin	1122	Potsdam[a]	.079	.071	.083	.087
Hamburg	410	Hamburg	.062	–	–	.050
Breslau	273	Breslau	.086	.082	.079	.103
Munich	230	Oberbayern	.160	–	.128[b]	.137
Dresden	221	Dresden	.100	–	.089[b]	.113
Leipzig	149	Leipzig	.073	–	.130[b]	.121
Köln (Cologne)	145	Köln	.064	.082	.028	.026
Königsberg	141	Königsberg	.089	–	.070	.078
Frankfurt a.M.	137	Wiesbaden	.041	.035	.024	.031
Hanover	123	Hanover	.077	.080	(c)	(c)
Danzig	109	Danzig	.096	.081	.062	.080

(a) Although Berlin was officially an administrative area in its own right it is surrounded by the *Regierungsbezirk* Potsdam.
(b) Including all cities other than the named city, regardless of size.
(c) Data unreliable for these categories.

Although the data for the largest cities suggest that there was little connection between city size and illegitimacy level, we may be obscuring a genuine relationship by excluding middle-sized cities. A correlational analysis using data for individual Prussian cities with more than 20,000 inhabitants in 1880 is presented in table 12.10. The lack of any substantial association between city size and the level of illegitimacy is confirmed by various means. City size was measured in two ways: by the actual population in 1880 and by its logarithm. The latter measure was intended to reduce any extreme influence the largest cities might exert on the correlations. Since Berlin is by far the largest city and could potentially distort the results, a set of correlations excluding Berlin was computed. Furthermore, since regional adjustments to the data were made to control for its influence. The adjustment consisted in calculating deviations from the regional mean for each variable. Thus regional influence was removed from both I_h and the two measures of city size. These deviations from the regional means were then correlated with each other to yield a separate set of correlations.[14]

We have shown that there is a close connection between rural and urban levels of illegitimacy in the same administrative area, which suggests that local customs affecting the behaviour of both rural and urban people had a strong influence on illegitimate fertility. In order to focus on the consequences of city size we attempted to control statistically for this effect in two ways: first, we computed the partial correlation between city size and I_h removing the effects of the rural level of I_h in the administrative area in which the city is located; secondly, we removed the influence of the rural level by computing the difference between city and rural and then correlating these differences with city size to yield a result 'adjusted for rural I_h'. In both situations additional control for regional location is no longer necessary, since rural I_h and regional location are closely associated with each other. Regardless of our controls, there is only a very weak positive correlation between city size and illegitimacy. In Prussia the largest cities had no monopoly of high illegitimacy, which they frequently shared with the middle-sized cities.

Table 12.10: Correlations between illegitimacy and city size, Prussian cities with at least 20,000 population, 1880

Correlation between city I_h and	Unadjusted for regional location	Adjusted for regional location[(a)]	Partial r holding rural I_h constant	Adjusted for rural I_h[(b)]	N
Absolute city size					
With Berlin	.141	.089	.071	−.011	69
Excluding Berlin	.165	.207*	.169	.114	68
Log of city size					
With Berlin	.178	.218*	.179	.118	69
Excluding Berlin	.152	.246*	.201	.173	68

(a) Correlations of deviations from regional means.
(b) City I_h values were adjusted by subtracting the I_h of the rural area in the corresponding administrative area. In the case of Berlin, Potsdam was used as the corresponding administrative area.

Note: None of the correlations were significant at the .01 level; those marked * were significant at the .05 level on a one-tailed test.

But what about the small towns? Data published by the Prussian Statistical Bureau allow I_h to be computed for three separate categories: cities with at least 20,000 population, towns with less than 20,000 and rural areas. Table 12.11 shows the relative differences in the level of illegitimate fertility in 1880 and 1905 in these three groupings. When all the Prussian areas are considered together no consistent pattern emerges at either date. Illegitimacy was sometimes higher in the cities than in the smaller towns and sometimes lower. Comparisons between rural and town and between city and rural illegitimacy are equally inconclusive.

14. The effect of this adjustment is identical to partial correlation in which regional location is used as a control variable. More exactly, if three new variables are created, one for presence or absence in each of the three regions, the partial correlation between the two main variables, controlling for any two of the three regional variables, yields the same results as adjustment for regional location. We are indebted to Colin Loftin for this explanation.

Nevertheless, it would appear that rural and town I_h are more often closely related than the other combinations, particularly in 1880. One regional difference is the distinct tendency in the West for the city I_h to exceed both that of the town and rural portions of each administrative area.

Table 12.11: Distribution of Prussian administrative areas according to the relative differences in I_h between rural and urban categories by region, 1880 and 1905

	1880				1905			
	East	Central	West	Total	East	Central	West	Total
Cities versus other urban								
Cities at least 10% above	5	4	9	18	4	4	7	15
Difference less than 10%	0	1	0	1	1	4	1	6
Other urban at least 10% above	2	7	2	11	2	5	3	10
Other urban versus rural								
Other urban at least 10% above	2	2	3	7	2	2	7	11
Difference less than 10%	1	6	5	12	1	4	3	8
Rural at least 10% above	4	4	3	11	4	7	1	12
Cities versus rural								
Cities at least 10% above	4	1	9	14	2	3	10	15
Difference less than 10%	1	3	1	5	4	2	1	7
Rural at least 10% above	2	8	1	11	1	8	0	9
Total N	7	12	11	30	7	13	11	31

Note: Cities defined as those with 20000 or more population in 1880. Sigmaringen, Aurich, Lüneburg, Stade have no cities with at least 20000 in 1880 and therefore are excluded. Berlin has neither a rural nor an other urban component and is thus also excluded. Hanover is excluded in 1880 due to unreliable data.

The question arises as to whether the towns were more closely associated with the rural areas than with the larger cities. Table 12.12 indicates the correlation coefficients between each possible pair of I_h values of the three Prussian rural and urban groupings in 1880 and 1905, the earliest and latest dates for which I_h indices could be calculated separately for the city, town and rural components of most areas. Because the level of I_h regardless of the category varied sharply with the regional location of the administrative areas, results are also presented both adjusted and unadjusted for this factor. As with table 12.10 (p. 303), the adjusted results represent correlations between deviations from the regional means. These sets of correlations indicate that rural communities and towns were more closely associated with each other than with the larger cities in the level of illegitimacy. Adjustment for regional locations reduces all the correlations but the association between rural area and town is still substantial at both dates while the correlation between town and city practically disappears. However, the fact that the level of illegitimacy in larger cities is relatively independent of the closely associated levels of town and village when regional location is controlled should not obscure the earlier finding that the levels of all three urban-rural groupings are closely associated with each other when compared across regions. Thus, within a region there appears to be one set of influences determining the illegitimacy levels of the large cities and another set common to towns and rural areas. But between regions there seems to be a more powerful set of factors, possibly regional customs, which operate in all three categories.

Table 12.12: Correlations between illegitimacy levels (I_h) in three urban-rural categories, Prussian administrative areas, 1880 and 1905

Date and variables correlated	Unadjusted for regional location	Adjusted for regional location[(a)]	N
1880			
Rural I_h and other urban I_h	.912**	.555**	30
Other urban I_h and city I_h	.611**	.127	30
Rural I_h and city I_h	.644**	.159	30
1905			
Rural I_h and other urban I_h	.814**	.553**	31
Other urban I_h and city I_h	.374*	−.031	31
Rural I_h and city I_h	.627**	.347*	31

(a) Correlations of deviations from regional means.

Note: Statistical significance levels (using a one-tailed test) are indicated as follows: * indicates significance at the .05 level; ** indicates significance at the .01 level. For exclusion see notes in table 13.11.

The absence of consistent urban-rural differentials in illegitimacy and an association between city size and illegitimacy do not preclude a connection between illegitimate fertility in an area and the growth and spread of towns. In the long run illegitimate fertility levels dropped with the progress of urbanization. At any given time, however, regions with high proportions of its inhabitants living in urban areas were affected by the spread of 'urbanism', which resulted in the surrounding rural populations acquiring an 'urban' character, with a consequent reduction in differences in styles of life. If the primary effect of the spread of urban ways was to reduce constraints in extra-marital sexual behaviour, we would expect illegitimacy to be higher in areas with a largely urban character than in areas with a predominantly rural population. If, on the other hand, the spread of knowledge and acceptance of birth control was the predominant effect of urbanism, the opposite relationship should hold. Thus the direction of the association of urbanization with illegitimacy is difficult to predict. For all administrative areas of Germany in 1880, I_h correlated only 0.11 with the percentage of the population living in towns with at least 2,000 inhabitants; in 1900 the equivalent correlation was only 0.07, and I_h correlated only 0.16 with the percentage living in cities of 20,000 or more (N=71 in all cases). Such results suggest little interaction between these variables.

A more interesting test of the effect of urbanization on illegitimacy is provided by the Prussian data which permit us to correlate the urban proportion in an administrative area with the rural I_h. The results for 1880 and 1900 are presented in table 12.13. Higher levels of urbanization and thus, presumably, more widespread urbanism in the rural areas are not associated to any extent with high levels of rural illegitimacy. Without adjusting for regional location, the correlation is virtually nil at both dates; after adjustment only a very weak association emerges for 1880 while results for 1900 remain almost unchanged. The lack of a strong association between the extent of urbanization and the absolute value of the difference between rural and urban illegitimacy in Prussia indicates that a highly urbanized area is not more likely to experience similar levels of illegitimacy in its rural and urban sectors than an area where the urban component is only a small part of the population.

Table 12.13: Correlations between illegitimate fertility and measures of urbanization and urban growth. Prussian administrative areas, 1880 and 1900

Variables correlated	1880 r	1880 N	1900 r	1900 N
Percent urban and rural I_h				
Unadjusted for regional location	.095	33	.130	34
Adjusted for regional location[(a)]	−.265	32	.150	34
Percent urban and absolute value[(b)] of difference between rural and urban I_h	−.264	33	−.042	34
Percent growth in urban population[(c)] and urban I_h				
Zero order	−.268	34	−.169	35
Partial controlling for rural I_h	.183	33	.153	34

(a) Correlations of deviations from regional means.
(b) The sign of the value is ignored.
(c) For 1880, growth refers to the period 1867–80; for 1900, growth refers to the period 1880–1900.

Note: None of the correlations are statistically significant at the .05 level. Berlin is excluded from correlations involving rural I_h in both 1880 and 1900. For 1880, all correlations exclude Hanover and Aurich and in addition Sigmaringen is excluded when adjustment is made for regional location; for 1900 all correlations exclude Sigmaringen due to changes in the definition of the urban population.

Finally, the Prussian data suggest that a rapid increase in the population of the towns and cities of an area does not lead to greater social disorganization and a higher level of illegitimacy. The rate of urban growth shows a weak *negative* association with the level of urban illegitimacy both in 1880 and 1900. In order to allow for the substantial differences in illegitimacy that are associated with the regional location of each area, and which might confound the relationship between urban growth and urban illegitimacy, we statistically controlled for the level of rural I_h through partial correlation. The resulting correlations, although now in a positive direction, are still negligible, indicating little association between urban growth and illegitimacy whatever the level of illegitimacy in the surrounding rural area.

7 Sex ratios, migration and urban-rural illegitimacy

One factor often mentioned by contemporary scholars as influencing illegitimacy levels in Imperial Germany was the numerical balance between unmarried men and women. In one of the earliest studies the Imperial Statistical Office advanced the hypothesis that 'where non-married men are particularly frequent in relation to non-married women, the frequency of illegitimate births is especially high due to the stronger temptation to which the latter are exposed.'[15] Others argued that the relationship would be in the opposite direction, namely that an excess of women rather than of men could lead to more frequent illegitimate births. Hindelang (p. 121), for example, states: 'According to the relation of supply and demand, in the case of a surplus of women and the consequent increase in competition for men, girls will be more compliant towards temptation than in a situation with a male surplus where most women are assured to come in line for marriage'. In other words, women yielded sexual favours, which could lead to illegitimate births, in order to catch husbands and were more likely to do so if

15. Statistisches Reichsamt, *Statistik des Deutschen Reichs* XLIV (1892).

competition for potential husbands was made harsher by a short supply of marriageable men. Prinzing agreed with Hindelang and believed that the excess of single women caused higher illegitimacy in eastern than in western Prussia.[16]

Whatever the validity of the assumptions underlying these opposing views, efforts to test them led to largely negative results. The Imperial Statistical Office, in an attempt to test its hypothesis, compared the ratio of unmarried men to unmarried women aged 15–50 with the general illegitimate fertility rate in various Prussian provinces and German states during the period 1872 to 1880 and concluded that the data did not support the assumed relationship. These data yielded a correlation of −0.25 (N=38) indicating, at best, a weak negative association. Using data for selected Bavarian districts, Lindner (pp. 122–4) also found no systematic association between imbalances in the sex ratio and illegitimacy.

It is useful to check the negative findings of these earlier studies and to test for a possible association between the sex ratio of the unmarried population and illegitimacy within the urban-rural context; and, in particular, to ascertain whether this relationship operated differently for rural and urban populations and whether it could help to account for urban-rural differences. Both data for the total rural and urban populations of administrative areas and for individual Prussian cities with at least 20,000 inhabitants were used for the period around 1880. The results are presented in table 12.14.

Table 12.14: Correlations between the sex ratio of the unmarried population aged 15–49 and illegitimate fertility, German administrative areas and Prussian cities with 20000 or more population, 1880

Variables correlated	Unadjusted for regional location	Adjusted for regional location[(a)]	N
Sex ratio and I_h			
Rural areas	−.430**	−.159	46
Urban areas	.090	−.084	47
Prussian cities	.076	−.022	69
Urban-rural differences in I_h and in sex ratio, German administrative areas			
Absolute differences	−.171	–	46
Relative differences	−.236	–	46
City-rural differences in I_h and in sex ratio, Prussian cities[(b)]			
Absolute differences	−.106	–	69
Relative differences	−.183	–	69

(a) Correlations of deviations from regional means. This adjustment was not made when correlations were based on differences between urban and rural levels.
(b) The rural population corresponding to each city refers to the rural population of the entire administrative area in which the city was located.

Note: The sex ratio is defined as the ratio of unmarried men 15–49 to unmarried women 15–49. The correlation marked by ** is significant at the .01 level using a one-tailed test. The data for the German administrative areas are from Prussia (34 areas excluding Hanover and Aurich), Bavaria (8), Saxony (4), and Hamburg. Berlin is excluded when correlations incorporate rural values since Berlin has no rural component.

16. Prinzing (1902) and Friederich Prinzing, 'Uneheliche Geburten' (1911).

Only for rural areas does an association of even moderate strength emerge. Higher ratios of unmarried men to unmarried women aged 15–49 are negatively correlated with rural I_h and this association practically disappears once regional location is taken into account. In the urban components of administrative areas and the individual Prussian cities the correlations are close to zero. There also seems to be little association between urban-rural differences in the sex ratio and in illegitimate fertility. This holds true whether we consider differences between the rural and urban components of administrative areas or between the individual Prussian city and the remainder of the administrative area in which it is located.

In some respects, the lack of an association for the individual Prussian cities is surprising, especially when compared to the rural areas: when only Prussian administrative areas are considered, the sex ratio is correlated −0.53 (N=33) with I_h in the rural sector, which is reduced to −0.36 (N=32) when adjustment for regional location was made. There are several reasons which might lead us to expect that the impact of imbalance in the sex ratio would be greater in cities than in the countryside. First, in comparison to rural areas, the range of sex ratios in cities is much greater, due undoubtedly to sharp sex differentials in the migration to some cities. For example, among the rural portion of the Prussian administrative areas the ratio of unmarried men to unmarried women aged 15–49 ranged from 0.90 in Breslau to 1.54 in Arnsberg; among the cities the sex ratio ranged from 0.67 in Wiesbaden to 3.01 in Spandau.

Secondly, it seems plausible that each city, as a unit, would be closer to a self-contained 'marriage market' than the rural component of the region, which undoubtedly contained many more locally defined marriage markets. On the other hand, the average sex ratio of the rural area may mask sharp local imbalances which exceeded those found even in the most extreme cases among the larger cities, and have sharp repercussions on the marriage prospects of local women. In addition, the source of an imbalance in the sex ratio in the cities might have an important bearing on illegitimacy. For example, a relative shortage of women caused by an influx of male migrants seeking a living in the city might have depressed illegitimacy levels. If, however, the excess of males in the city resulted from large numbers of soldiers stationed at the local garrison or from students at the local university, the situation might have been the opposite. Both soldiers and students were probably in a poor position to marry, and the students, coming from a higher social class than most of the local women, would be reluctant to marry the girls even in the event of pregnancy. Thus, before imbalances in the sex ratio can be finally dismissed as unrelated to the general level of illegitimacy, a more detailed study at a a more local level, taking into account the causes of the imbalance would be required.

Although one source of imbalance in the sex ratio was undoubtedly different migration patterns among men and women, migration could also have influenced illegitimacy in a more direct manner. The fact that illegitimacy ran in regional patterns and that regional differences in either rural or urban levels were greater than urban-rural differences within regions suggests that local customs were more important in determining the level of illegitimacy than were differences between rural and urban conditions of life. Inter-regional migration may have influenced illegitimacy if the migrants retained the customs of their place of origin after migration. In areas where illegitimacy was unusually low, inter-regional migrants, if they behaved according to the customs of their place of origin, would experience higher illegitimacy than the native population, and would raise the illegitimacy level. In areas where illegitimacy was unusually high the reverse would take place. The effect of migration would be to alter the level of illegitimacy in areas where it was either unusually high or low.

Such a process would have particular importance for urban levels of illegitimacy and for urban-rural differentials, since inter-regional migration was disproportionately urban-bound. For example, in 1880 16 per cent of the German-born population living in Prussian cities with over 20,000 inhabitants came from outside the Prussian province in which the city was located, whereas only 5 per cent of the non-city population of the province was born elsewhere. Thus, inter-regional migrants may have altered the urban illegitimacy level more than the rural. This hypothesis is consonant with our finding that urban illegitimacy tended to exceed rural illegitimacy where the average level was low, but tended to be lower than rural illegitimacy where the average level was high (see table 12.6, p. 296). A similar effect may also have been produced at a more local level if there were sufficient local variation in illegitimacy and if local migration were mainly to urban areas.

If migration did affect illegitimacy in this way, it would help to explain why in the West region, where illegitimacy was generally low, urban illegitimacy exceeded rural levels and usually declined later. As industrial expansion took place in the West, particularly in Rhineland and Westphalia, large numbers of migrants, especially from the economically stagnant East, flocked to the growing Western cities. This could account for the higher urban illegitimacy if their customs led to higher illegitimacy than was typical of the native population. The flow of migration intensified towards the end of the nineteenth century and would explain the relative delay in the decline of urban illegitimacy in the West region.[17]

Unfortunately data to test directly whether migrants and native born populations were characterized by different levels of illegitimacy are not available, precluding analysis at the individual level. The 1880 Prussian census does provide information on province of birth for the populations of each administrative area and each city with more than 20,000 population. We can therefore test through ecological correlations whether the I_h in the cities of the West was raised by migrants from the other regions, all of which had much higher illegitimacy. Because the data indicate only *province* of birth, for this test the West region will comprise only the provinces of Rhineland, Westphalia and Hesse-Nassau. The percentage of migrants is defined as all residents of the West region born in Germany but outside these three provinces.

In these three provinces the proportion born elsewhere in Germany was substantially higher in the city than in the non-city population. In 1880 among the 28 cities with more than 20,000 inhabitants only one had a smaller percentage of the total population born elsewhere in Germany than did the non-city population of the surrounding area; in most of the cities the proportion born outside the provinces was at least twice as much as in the corresponding non-city population. Among these cities the percentage of the total population born in other provinces or states ranged from less than 2 per cent to almost 33 per cent. In fact, these proportions understate the potential impact migrants could have on illegitimacy since, as indicated by tabulations from the 1900 German census, the proportion of the population born outside the province of residence is substantially higher in the reproductive ages than for the total population (Wrigley, 1961, table 47). It is

17. Wolfgang Köllmann, 'The population of Germany in the age of industrialism' (1964).

also likely that migrants were disproportionately concentrated among the unmarried adult population. If our hypothesis is correct, the amount of inter-regional migration was therefore probably sufficient to account for much of the urban-rural difference.

Results of a correlational analysis lend little support to the presumed impact of migration on illegitimacy in the West. According to our hypothesis, the level of illegitimate fertility in the cities of the three Western provinces should show a positive association with the percentage of the population that is not native to the West, while the differences between city and non-city illegitimacy should be positively related to differences in the percentage of extra-regional migrants. Little association exists between I_h and the percentage of extra-regional migrants in the 28 cities. Absolute differences between the city I_h and the non-city I_h of the corresponding administrative area are virtually uncorrelated with the absolute differences in the percentage of migrants; relative differences (expressed by the ratio of the city to the non-city) in I_h are only weakly correlated to relative differences in the percentage of migrants.

Our attempts to test the effects of the sex ratio and migration on urban-rural patterns of illegitimacy have met with very limited success. The failure to demonstrate stronger relationships may reflect as much the inadequacy of the tests as the validity of the arguments behind the hypotheses. Relationships between illegitimate fertility and either the sex ratio or migration may be too complex to be detected by the simple tests and crude data so far brought to bear on them. A more adequate testing of the sex ratio hypothesis, for example, would require that the source of imbalance between the numbers of unmarried males and females be taken into account. The role of migration in moderating urban levels of illegitimacy in comparison to rural levels requires data on an individual level so that the illegitimacy of natives and migrants can be directly compared. Comparisons of illegitimacy levels of ecological aggregates, such as entire cities, which differ in the proportion of the population that is non-native, are poor substitutes. Furthermore, if illegitimacy patterns are related to the socio-economic position of the individual, the selectivity of migrants also needs to be taken into account. Finally, and perhaps most important, an understanding of the factors underlying the sharp regional differences in illegitimacy would undoubtedly facilitate a more complete understanding of the impact of inter-regional and country to city migration on illegitimacy in the receiving populations.

8 Conclusions

Conclusions drawn from this survey of rural and urban patterns of illegitimacy in the German *Reich* are of importance to the study of the part illegitimacy played in the history of Europe. They suggest, in the first place, that models, old and new, which assign a central place to the city or to urbanization in explaining levels and trends of nineteenth-century illegitimate fertility need reformulation.[18] Emphasis on urban occupations, urban social disorganizations or other aspects of urban social structure in accounting for high levels of illegitimacy will have difficulty, at least in the case of Germany, in accommodating findings which indicate roughly equal rural and urban illegitimate fertility rates. Likewise

18. See, for example, Louise A. Tilly, Joan W. Scott and Miriam Cohen, 'Women's work and European fertility patterns' (1976); also Shorter (1972).

models which incorporate urbanization and associated changes in the social and occupational composition of the urban population as major factors in the eighteenth- and nineteenth-century rise in illegitimacy do not account for the fact that at the peak high illegitimacy was as likely to characterize the village as the metropolis and that the unmarried female population of many large and rapidly growing cities experienced only low or moderate rates of illegitimacy. We suspect that, rather than uniformly raising illegitimacy in receiving urban centres, the inter-regional and rural-to-urban migration which accompanied industrial expansion played a role in moderating levels of urban illegitimacy in either direction. This interpretation is consistent with our finding that the level of urban illegitimacy tended to be higher than the rural in areas where illegitimacy was generally low but to be below the rural level where illegitimacy was generally high.

The strong and persistent regionality of illegitimacy during a period of major socio-economic change, and the high correlation between rural and urban levels across Germany suggest that local and regional customs, shared by villagers and townspeople alike, were key determinants of an area's illegitimate fertility level. Indeed, the importance of cultural as well as social and economic differences had already impressed contemporary students of German illegitimacy. A major conclusion of Lindner's repeated *verbatim* by Hindelang (p. 138), was reached after exploring the connection between illegitimacy and a variety of structural variables: 'In the final analysis one must consider the differences in folk customs [*Volkssitte*] and folk attitudes [*Volksauffassung*] as the basic source of differing frequency of illegitimate births.' This interpretation of differing patterns of illegitimacy in Germany is, of course, no explanation as it leaves unanswered the crucial questions of the origin of differences in customs with regard to illegitimacy and the causes of their persistence in spite of major social and economic changes. Indeed, we believe the efforts of model-builders and theorizers would be better directed towards answering these questions instead of concentrating on possible links between socio-economic structure and illegitimacy and ignoring cultural differences.

Attempts to explain urban illegitimacy as a separate phenomenon may also be misleading, if the close empirical association with rural illegitimacy is ignored. Sharp urban-rural differences, at least in Imperial Germany, appear to be the exception rather than the rule. The search for explanatory variables might be better directed towards features common to city and countryside, within particular regional and local settings than towards factors entirely urban.

Our findings may also tell us something about urban life during the early periods of industrialization in Germany. Evidence has been accumulating recently which calls into question the conventional view of cities as characterized by severe social disorganization in comparison with the more stable, traditional forms of social life prevailing in the countryside.[19] In so far as illegitimacy is a symptom of such disorganization, our results concur with this revised view. Either disorganization has been exaggerated for the city or underestimated for the countryside. We hasten to add, however, that the right answers to such questions require a fuller understanding of illegitimacy in history.

Illegitimacy was, and is, an extremely complex phenomenon. We have employed the most refined aggregate measure of illegitimate fertility, using the data

19. Charles Tilly, *An urban world* (1974).

available in official statistical publications, but we recognize the inadequacy of this method to fathom the complex nature of the underlying behaviour. Official statistics and the measures based on them are severely limited in their revelation of social class differences, possibly crucial to illegitimacy. A hint of how striking such differences may have been is provided by Pinzing (1911, p. 37), who demonstrated that the illegitimacy ratio in different districts of Berlin showed a dramatic negative association with average rents of apartments. Much more data on social and occupational differentials in illegitimacy and their relation to rural and urban residence are prerequisites for any comprehensive explanation of illegitimacy, and are needed to test some of the models already developed.

An equally important limitation of the data on which we have based our survey is its inability to distinguish between different types of illegitimacy. Although unions resulting in illegitimate births are of many different kinds, they may be reduced to three basic types: casual unions of short duration in which even the name of the father may be unknown to the mother; consensual unions of varying lengths with some stability but not leading to marriage; and premarital unions for which later marriage legitimized previous offspring (Prinzing, 1911). These three categories constitute neither an exhaustive nor sufficient classification scheme, but they do serve to point out that very different circumstances can lead to births which eventually are aggregated as illegitimate in the official statistics. Some hint of substantial urban-rural differences in the distribution of illegitimate births according to the above classification can be found in legitimation statistics. In Saxony, for example, the ratio of legitimations to illegitimate births during the years 1904–10 was distinctly lower for each of the three largest cities, Dresden, Leipzig and Chemnitz, than for the remainder of the administrative areas in which they were located, which suggests that the third type of union was more common in rural areas.[20] We may then ask whether this implies differences in the intentions of couples when the unions were formed or in the social pressures that were brought to bear after the birth of an illegitimate child.

There remains the question as to whether Germany was different from other European countries. Although it is already evident that northern and central Europe showed a pattern of mixed urban-rural differentials at the turn of the century (Shorter *et al.*, 1971), much detailed research still needs to be directed towards this important aspect of demographic behaviour. In the final analysis a general model of illegitimacy will be successful only if it is consistent with the empirical findings that emerge from such research.[21]

20. Georg Prenger, *Die Unehelichkeit im Königreich Sachsen* (1913), table 17.

21. The full series of I_h values are included as an appendix table in an earlier draft of this chapter reproduced as a working paper (with the same title as the present chapter). It may be obtained by writing to the Center for Western European Studies, University of Michigan, Ann Arbor, Michigan, 48109, USA.

13

Illegitimacy in seventeenth- and eighteenth-century east Sweden

David Gaunt

This chapter is a short statistical investigation into illegitimacy in Sweden over a long period before the appearance of national statistics in the middle of the eighteenth century. It aims to discover the long-term trends in illegitimacy in the east Swedish demographic region and to examine cultural and social aspects of birth outside wedlock. Demographers and historians have not studied illegitimacy in the period up to 1750, although the subsequent period is relatively well documented.

The period 1610–1750 is marked by transition in both urban and rural Swedish society though agricultural and industrial methods remained unchanged. The country was economically prosperous until the middle of the seventeenth century, but then followed a general decline which lasted into the middle of the eighteenth century. Religious observance which was fairly lax until the middle of the seventeenth century became puritanically austere throughout the whole country in the 1680s. From this time on the absolute state effectively involved itself in supervision of religious unity and orthodoxy even down to parish level.

It is easier to justify the study of illegitimacy to demographers and sociologists than to historians. Illegitimacy is one of the few types of social deviation which can be measured over a period of centuries. Births outside wedlock took place in almost all pre-industrial societies, but they were universally condemned. At the same time there were considerable variations in propensity to illegitimacy in different cultures, countries and regions. By comparing patterns of illegitimacy in different areas the historian may be able to discover the social mechanisms underlying illegitimacy in past time. It is hoped that the investigation of Swedish patterns will contribute towards a comparison of this form of social deviance in pre-industrial society.

In order to investigate long-term trends one must establish the reliability of sources used and part of the chapter is concerned with this sort of criticism. Swedish church records of the early modern period are not particularly good but, with caution, they can be used. Critical appreciation of the statistical sources provides the methodological basis of the chapter. It should, however, be remembered that the individual births, the fundamental material of this study, were in their way complex moments for both parents and community.

1 Illegitimacy in Swedish historical literature

The considerable body of Swedish literature dealing with illegitimacy in its historical setting may be divided into two kinds: the *legal historical* which deals with the treatment of illegitimate children and premarital sex relationships in both secular and ecclesiastical law; and the *demographical and sociological* which deals with the statistical evidence of high illegitimacy in Sweden since the beginning of the nineteenth century and attempts to isolate those factors which may have brought about a rise or fall in illegitimacy.

There are numerous legal historical studies of marriage and courtship customs in contravention of church law.[1] In Sweden the church had difficulty in making its point of view accepted. Perhaps the most telling example of this difficulty is the fact that the religious marriage ceremony never became the sole determinant of an approved husband-wife relationship. Instead the betrothal, which could occur in various forms outside church regulations, determined the legitimacy of children born before the marriage had taken place. The famous Swedish biologist, Carl Linneus, remarked during one of his travels that 'consensus non ceremoniae faciunt matrimonium.'[2]

But neither the church nor the state recognized a common law marriage and if betrothal did not lead to marriage those children born to the betrothed couple were illegitimate. The church could, of course, impose fines for fornication before marriage and for similar offences, but it never succeeded entirely in its demand that children born out of wedlock to engaged couples were bastards and consequently subject to a number of legal disabilities. Historians who have contrasted civil law with church law have come to the conclusion that the clan-based society of the early and even the late medieval period attached no particular onus to the child born out of wedlock nor to the mother of the child. What was, however, legally indispensable was the existence of some sort of stable relationship between the man and the woman: if this condition was not satisfied a child was, indeed, illegitimate. This distinction had quite remarkable consequences in that many children which in other cultures were bastards were legitimate in Sweden. Witness the obituary of the unwed mother of several children from Lye in Gotland: '25 January 1752 Cecilia Paulsdotter died. . . . She had three children, the middle one born under promise of marriage, but on her fiancé's absence in Karlskrona she let herself be bedded again, as in the first instance, and thus had two bastards and one legitimate child, but was never married.'[3] These distinctions are significant when illegitimacy is inferred and not explicitly stated in the source material. Similar distinctions will be treated when we come to terminology and the critique of sources.

Demographic and sociological studies go back to the middle of the nineteenth century. Swedish demographers and social commentators have been acutely embarrassed by the extremely high rate of illegitimate births recorded in Sweden as compared with other European countries. They were distressed by the general practice of measuring the moral condition of an area by the illegitimacy rate, for this made Stockholm the vilest of European capitals. Comparisons of various national illegitimacy rates began in the middle of the nineteenth century with the first publication of the Swedish Bureau of Statistics and were repeated in Agardh's and Ljungberg's patriotic economic-statistical survey of Sweden;

1. See Lizzie Carlsson, *Jag giver dig min dotter! Trolovning och äktenskap i den svenska kvinnans äldre historia* (1965–72). G. Bäärhielm, 'Utomäktenskapliga barns ställning' (1934). P-E. Wallén, 'Oäkta barn' (1968). Arthur Thomson, *Hävdande under äktenskapslöfte* (1967). A different type of study is Birgit Persson's work (not yet published) on the demographic consequences of the infanticide decree of 1778.
2. Bertil Gullander, *Linné på Gotland* (1971), p. 56. Orvar Löfgren, 'Family and household among Scandinavian peasants: an exploratory essay' (1974), pp. 32 ff.
3. Burial register, 25 January 1752, parish of Lye, Landsarkiv in Visby.

Gustav Sundbärg reiterated these comments at the beginning of the present century and continued with the same methods of presentation.[4]

Illegitimacy was treated as a grave aberration and as a symptom of moral degeneracy. These demographers were, nevertheless, aware that in commenting on the rate of illegitimacy they had to take into consideration the number of unmarried women at risk, the rate of marriage, the sex ratio and other demographic parameters. Importance was also attached to non-demographic factors. Sundbärg emphasized the effect of rising alcoholism on the higher number of illegitimates in the first half of the nineteenth century. Agardh and Ljungberg stressed the declining inclination to marry and the increasing tendency to concubinage caused by economic depression during the 1830s and 1840s; in the *riksdag* some politicians insisted that the rising number of illegitimates was a consequence of the protection given to unmarried mothers by Gustav III's infanticide decree of 1778.[5] As early as the 1850s several writers pointed out that the religious revival caused the number and rate of illegitimates to decline. The Bureau of Statistics in its report for the quinquennium 1851–5 noted that one of the consequences of the recent religious movements in Norrbotton was that the number of illegitimates had decreased.

In 1941 a modern demographer, Hannes Hyrenius, published a study of the relationship of religious intensity with the declining propensity to illegitimacy and found a positive correlation at provincial and district levels. His work, however, is confined to contemporary conditions. A sociologist, C-E Mawe, interested in social control in past time, found in 1958 that in one forest parish on the border with Norway religious enthusiasm inside the established church caused a decline in the rate of both illegitimacy and premarital pregnancy. His statistical evidence derives from parish records for the years 1770–1910: the period of religious enthusiasm covered the decades of the 1800s and 1810s. So far investigation into the relationship between religiosity and morality has been considered for areas which experienced high religious fervour and low illegitimacy, but no one has yet reversed the proposition and considered areas of traditionally stern sexual morality which were also centres of religious fervour. Such areas as Halland, Smaland and Norrbotton, where the religious revival of the nineteenth century is supposed to have been responsible for low illegitimacy, already had very low illegitimacy before this religious revival began.[6]

There is some evidence of an illegitimacy prone sub-society in Sweden.[7] Within the agrarian society there was a traditional group called 'travellers'

4. See *Bidrag till Sveriges officiella statistik: A. Befolkningsstatistik* (1857), pp. 42ff. C. A. Agardh and E. Ljungberg. *Försök till en statsekonomisk statistik öfver Sverige* III, part 3 (1859), pp. 59 ff. (This work is actually semi-official: Ljungberg was from 1854 secretary of a commission to improve the organization of statistics in Sweden.) G. Sundbärg, *Die Bevölkeringsstatistik Schwedens, 1750–1900; einige Hauptresultate* (1907).

5. During the eighteenth century the argument was often put forward that pregnant unmarried women committed abortion or exposed their newly born children because of the condemnation by church and neighbours. Contemporaries thought that Sweden's population growth was seriously limited by these practices. The Infanticide Decree of 1778 was meant to ameliorate the condition of unmarried pregnant women and so give incentive not to abort or expose the child. Pregnant unmarried women were given the right to travel at will throughout the country and to give birth in full anonymity without risk of investigation. Birgit Persson, 'Att vara ogift mor på 1700- och 1800-talet' (1972), pp. 125 ff.

6. Compare, for instance, the regional trends given for 1750–73 by H. Gahn, *Moral-statistiska uppgifter i frihetstidens tabellverk: En demografisk studie* (1915). For the period 1851–6, see *Bidrag till Sveriges officiella statistik: A. Befolkningsstatistik*, pp. 45 ff. And for 1901–10 and 1928–33, see Hyrenius (1941). From the eighteenth to the twentieth century those provinces with the lowest illegitimacy are nearly always the same: Smaland, Halland, Norrbotton.

7. A. Heymowski, *Swedish 'travellers' and their ancestry: a social isolate or an ethnic minority?* (1969).

(*tattare*), who were subjected to discrimination and relegated to certain occupations; in some respects they resembled Central European gypsies. It has long been held that these 'travellers' formed a distinct racial group, but a sociologist, Adam Heymowski, has recently shown in an extensive genealogical study that these people were of Swedish national origin. The discovery within the 'traveller' group of a high propensity to illegitimacy and cohabitation outside marriage was an interesting by-product of this genealogical research.

2 Terminology

Swedish parish records use various terms to describe children born out of wedlock. The official term is *oäkta*, the exact translation of 'illegitimate'. Popularly, however, and even in parish records, these children were called *horungar* (whore children), which has the same pejorative implication as 'bastard'. The unwed mother was subject to considerable ostracism, which is reflected in the seventeenth-century practice of writing *kona* (wench) and *konebarn* (wench-child) in order to indicate illegitimacy, but in the eighteenth century this terminology was replaced by *kvinnsperson* (female person). Since illegitimates were not always unambiguously named in parish records, knowledge of the various terms is important. Certain parishes had special marks to indicate illegitimacy, a circle with a dot in it. *Nota Bene* in the margin, the Latin word *nothus* or the Greek *apator* could be used. Some ministers distinguished consistently between genuine illegitimates and children born to betrothed couples; in the latter case the word *tro* (troth) followed an entry (see many examples from the early seventeenth century in the register of births of Tillinge-Svinnegarn parishes, in the Landsarkiv in Uppsala). There is, however, no reason to believe this practice to have been universal. The one legitimate child of the never-married woman, mentioned earlier, was entered as illegitimate in the baptismal entry.

Laslett and Oosterveen (1973, p. 267) have remarked that illegitimate births must sometimes be inferred from baptismal entries. This also holds for Swedish sources. Entries such as 'Måns' sister Brita's child' or 'Peter Träfot's daughter's son' are taken to refer to illegitimates, though they are not specifically so named. Entries in parish account books, when available, often indicate that these women paid fines for fornication.[8] Usually the child's father is not named and a relative to the mother is appointed as guardian. When the child was adopted into a family the term 'illegitimate' no longer applied, even though the mother had paid a fine, for this payment arose from committing the sexual act and not from the child's birth.[9] One type of entry which at first glance could be inferred to be of an illegitimate but which is not is that where the mother is not named 'wife of', as is customary. When parish accounts are available, one may note that these women paid no fines for fornication and therefore one may assume that the minister forgot to enter the poor woman's wifely status.

3 Sources

The primary sources for this study of illegitimacy are parish records. The most useful are the birth or baptism registers which in Sweden become common in the late seventeenth century; there are, however, some parish registers which date

8. These entries are in the Register of births for Irsta parish, February 1631 and May 1638. For the fines in connection with these births, see Special Accounts, Irsta parish. All these records are in the Landsarkiv in Uppsala.
9. See Arthur Thomson, *Otidig sängelag* (1966).

from the first half of the century. Usually these books register births as well as baptisms so that still-births are also recorded. Other parish records are the account books to which we have already referred and which often give detailed information of fines paid by named individuals for breaking church regulations. Particularly valuable are the records of fines paid for 'going to bed too soon' (*otida sängelag*), that is premarital conception, or for fornication (*boleri*), when marriage did not follow or was impossible. There are even fines paid for broken engagements. But unfortunately the account books do not always specify the particular offences but merely give a lump sum for fines on the income side of the ledger.

The minutes of the parish meeting occasionally recorded non-monetary punishment meted out by the church council to sexual sinners. The usual punishment for fornication was to have the erring party sit on the repenter's stool, popularly called the fornicator's stool, facing the congregation at the front of the church. After the service the sinner, sometimes holding birch branches and bare backed, begged for absolution.[10] Additional material is the correspondence between the parish priest and the bishop which sometimes dealt with individuals who were known to be disreputable, and with cases of adultery which had been difficult to decide. Some parish records list known fornicators under the heading 'noteworthy events'. Apart from ecclesiastical material, there are the district records, but these are less valuable in enabling us to judge the magnitude of illegitimacy. Although seventeenth- and eighteenth-century court records deal with cases of fornication and many other contemporary types of sexual frailty, their use as a record of illegitimacy is limited. The most usual cases are those in which the father of a child has either refused to marry the mother or has contested parenthood, or those in which one or both parents are already married. Thus, for various reasons many parents of illegitimate children fail to appear in the court records.

A comparison of birth registers with parish account books reveals that, whereas all cases of illegitimacy and inferred illegitimacy in birth registers lead to some sort of clerical fine or punishment, individuals are punished who do not appear in church records. This becomes evident from a comparison of the account books of the parishes of Björskog, 1628–36, and Irsta, 1628–32, with the minutes of the parish meeting which list those condemned to sit in the repenter's stool in Tyresö church, 1706–7, and in Björskog church in 1721–7 and with the list of fornicators in Tyresö, 1685–7.[11] All these records appear to have been preserved accidentally. They include 33 individual cases of fornication of which only 21 can be identified in the birth and baptism registers. Moreover, correspondence between the minister in Tillinge-Svinnegarn and the archbishop also give the impression that there were more illegitimates than were recorded in the parish records.[12] Not all these cases of fornication need have led to the birth of an illegitimate child, but given the type of evidence necessary to prove fornication – namely, milk from the woman's breasts or a great number of witnesses – it is highly likely that nearly all persons punished for fornication actually did beget children.[13] Children born out

10. This repenter's stool which is not known in Denmark and Norway is very similar to that used in Scotland. Arthur Thomson, 'Från "horpall" till "tjuvpall" ' (1967), p. 11; Hilding Pleijel, *Svenska kyrkans historia. Karolinsk kyrkofromhet, pietism och hernhutism, 1680–1772* (1935), pp. 92 ff.

11. Noteworthy events, Björskog parish; special accounts. Irsta parish; noteworthy events and list of fornicators, Tyresö parish. All records in Landsarkiv, Uppsala.

12. Correspondence from Tillinge-Svinnegarn parishes, Uppsala Archbishopric's archive, I–II, Landsarkiv, Uppsala.

13. Preliminary investigations occurred at a parish meeting when either a council of six representatives or the entire congregation was present. R. Gullstrand, *Bidrag till den svenska sockensjälvstyrelsens historia under 1600-talet* (1923), pp. 78 ff.

of wedlock were not the only ones not to have been entered in parish registers: indeed it is improbable that all legitimate births were recorded. Births were written down on small slips of paper and entered in the baptism register at the end of the year, but often several years would pass before the baptism register was written up, during which time some slips might well have been lost (this is especially common in large parishes; see the register of births, Uppsala Cathedral parish). One often finds corrections in parish registers for persons who had ordered a written certificate and who had discovered that their births had not been registered. In the final analysis Swedish parish records underestimate the number of illegitimate births. But it is the only kind of homogeneous evidence available and within limits it can be used to indicate trends rather than actual numbers.

There is yet another complication in using Swedish records. It was very common during the seventeenth century to have two baptism registers, one for legitimate and one for illegitimate births (see the parish archives of Holy Trinity, Uppsala, and Tyresö, and Huddinge). Usually both have been kept but there are instances when the registers of illegitimate births have disappeared. This is not apparent until one attempts to calculate the number of illegitimates and discovers that of several thousand births not one is illegitimate, as is the case in Skultuna parish between 1622 and 1641 and in Skinnskatteberg between 1623 and 1635; and there were undoubtedly a great many others. In Skultuna there are even specific accounts for the years 1621–3 which give fines for 'whoredom'.

Quality as well as quantity of registration governs our research into illegitimacy. The quality is decidedly variable: we find on the one hand a bare entry of 'bastard' and on the other hand a full description such as: 'Anna, an illegitimate child born in Mellangården in Kyrkbyn; father, Anders Ersson, servant; mother Brita Persdotter, who gave birth to an illegitimate child for the second time'. Luckily the second type of entry is more usual but the frequent omission of surnames means that such issues as those of women giving birth to more than one illegitimate child cannot be effectively studied. In a large parish there might well be a dozen Brita Persdotters who cannot be distinguished one from the other. In towns surnames are common, but even there patronymics are the rule. Thus, a woman called Brita Ström one year may be called Brita Thomasdotter the next. Some problems can, however, be treated in some detail; these include the social classification of fathers of illegitimate children, the existence of cohabitation and concubinage in towns, the degree to which extra-marital pregnancy led to geographical mobility among women and the spread of illegitimate conceptions over the months of the year.

4 Areas

The selection of areas to be investigated was made subsequent to the determination of the value of parish records as sources for the registration of illegitimate births. Since these documents are so inadequate and it is impossible to allow for deficiencies of registration, it was decided that no attempt should be made at this stage to obtain trends representative of the nation as a whole. Indeed, our efforts were directed to finding a number of parishes with diversified economic and social structures. The east Swedish demographic area was selected because it had traditionally higher illegitimacy rates than other Swedish demographic areas. Parishes were chosen in which the percentage of self-sufficient farm families was minimal. Previous family reconstitution of Swedish parishes dominated by farm owners revealed a stem family structure which in Swedish conditions militated against people indulging in premarital, extra-marital and even marital sexual relations.[14]

The following selection criteria were used: the prevalence of large manors employing unmarried labourers, nearness to lines of communication, integration in market production and the presence of non-agricultural production; also the presence of soldiers and sailors. To this end the following parishes were chosen:

1 Irsta in Västmanland which is situated close to Västerås, a market town which also has several large manors, especially Gäddeholm. Parish records date from 1627.
2 Tillinge with Svinnegarn in Uppland which lies just outside the market town of Enköping and which specializes in vegetable growing for the Stockholm market. Several large estates, especially Haga. This is the area which Hyrenius found, at the beginning of the twentieth century, to have the highest illegitimacy rate in the country. Church records begin in 1613, though Svinnegarn has separate records for 1695–1710.
3 Björskog in Västmanland which lies between two expanding market towns, Arboga and Köping, both specializing in iron. There was an important contingent of 'allotment' soldiers present, dating from the time when Karl XI had his main residence in an adjacent parish. A major highway from west Sweden to Stockholm passes through the parish. Church records begin in 1626.
4 Skultuna in Västmanland, somewhat north of Västerås with an economy based on bronze metal working and forges. It was a rural industrial parish with a strong foreign, mostly German, element. Church records begin in 1622, but do not register illegitimates until 1641.
5 Skinnskatteberg in northern Västmanland, a large forest parish in the heart of a mining district. There were many mines and foundries with copper and iron production of some importance. There was some agriculture but insufficient for the needs of the population. Both the population and the area of the parish were very large. Parish records begin in 1623 but do not register illegitimates until 1636.
6 The university and cathedral city of Uppsala. Two parishes were studied: firstly that of the Cathedral where the records begin officially in 1694, but records covering the period 1654–63 are preserved in the archives of a nearby parish; and secondly that of Holy Trinity, situated in an area serving a farm district to the west and the south, but in which townsmen are also recorded. Holy Trinity records begin in 1665. One reason for selecting Uppsala is that during the eighteenth century a study of the number of births including figures on illegitimacy was published as an exploratory exercise prior to the establishment of the Bureau of Statistics. We have found that these figures need minor corrections and additions.

14. In Alskog in Gotland, which has been treated by family reconstitution techniques, considerable sexual restraint was present both within and outside marriage. This does not mean that all stem family systems necessarily lead to depressed illegitimacy. In Alskog birth control was widespread so the number of sexually mature unmarried persons who did not inherit was very small. Some aspects of this community are treated in D. Gaunt, 'Family planning and the pre-industrial society: some Swedish evidence' (1973). See also the Central Statistical Bureau's investigation, 'Utom äktensskapet födda barn' (1914), pp. 28 ff., where they establish a connection between areas dominated by smallholdings and owner-operators with low illegitimacy.

Uppsala was an important administrative and university town but was also significant as a market for the very fertile farm area surrounding it.[15]

7 Tyresö with Dalarö just to the south and east of Stockholm. The economy was divided between large estates and fishing in the archipelago with marketing outlets in Stockholm. During the latter part of the seventeenth century a considerable manufacturing industry was established at the palace of Tyresö: this included a paper mill, a brick works and a cloth factory serving the military. Dalarö was important as a shipping port and it was from here that Swedish armies were transported to foreign parts; there were several inns in the port area. Its importance as a naval base declined in the late seventeenth century when the main fleet was transferred to Karlskrona. Church records begin in 1634 but Dalarö was separated from Tyresö by the 1680s, its own records starting in 1690.

8 Huddinge is a suburban parish to the southwest of Stockholm. A major highway passes through the parish on the way south. There was considerable inland transport and ferrying activity as well as several large manors. By studying this parish it was hoped to ascertain the indirect influence of Stockholm city on the surrounding areas.

5 Results

When the Swedish national statistics began to be compiled in the middle of the eighteenth century the ratios of births outside wedlock to all live births varied between 2.4 per cent and 2.9 per cent in the late 1780s and in the 1790s this percentage increased rapidly. The trend is even stronger if one relates the number of illegitimate births to the number of unmarried women at risk. Whereas in the period 1751–90 there were fewer than 20 illegitimate births yearly per thousand unmarried women aged 20–45, this figure rose from just over 20 in the 1790s to well over 30 in the 1820s; after this time the rate of increase slackened slightly. There is no reason to question the reality of these trends, although it may be possible to adjust the figures slightly upwards.[16]

However, it is still possible to discover what the situation was like in the period preceding the establishment, in 1747, of a special department of population statistics. Was illegitimacy before this time so low that the trend we see so clearly in the subsequent period reveals that sexual relations were then being transformed, perhaps by the commercialization of agriculture and the pauperization of rural areas between 1770 and 1850? Or was there a temporary decline in the propensity towards illegitimate births in the mid 1700s which later regained its original strength?

Table 13.1 shows the variations in the illegitimacy ratio for the nine east Swedish districts selected for diversity of socio-economic structure. Up till the 1660s illegitimacy was relatively high, ranging between 3.9 per cent and 5.9 per cent of all live births. The trend was, however, already downwards. These figures were not matched nationally before the turn of the eighteenth and nineteenth centuries. Unfortunately the statistical evidence is not altogether convincing and

15. Per Elvius, 'Førtekning uppå Barnens årliga antal som äro födde uti U . . . stad under de sist förflutne 50 åren' (1744), pp. 293 ff.

16. See Central Statistical Bureau (1914), table 1. For frequency figures consult *Historisk statistik. Befolkningsstatistik, 1720–1967* (1969), tables 28 and 30. These frequency calculations are suspect as they are based on extrapolations of regional age-sex pyramids from a later period. Gahn (1915) made a comparison of officially recorded illegitimacy and the relevant parish records. He found a clear under-registration in the mid eighteenth century.

Table 13.1: Illegitimacy ratios in nine Swedish districts, 1610–1750

Decade	All births	Illegitimate births Named	Inferred	Total	Ratio (%)
1610–19	304	14	4	18	5.9
1620–29	570	29	3	32	5.6
1630–39	1178	54	7	61	5.2
1640–49	1406	57	4	61	4.3
1650–59	1094	40	3	43	3.9
1660–69	2142	63	5	68	3.2
1670–79	2101	66	1	67	3.2
1680–89	2202	60	4	64	2.9
1690–99	2963	70	3	73	2.5
1700–09	3602	100	7	107	3.0
1710–19	3803	114	9	123	3.2
1720–29	4288	114	2	116	2.7
1730–39	4333	127	7	134	3.1
1740–49	4688	149	20	169	3.6
TOTAL	34674	1057	79	1136	3.27

Note: Every parish save Huddinge outside Stockholm had a lower than average illegitimacy ratio during the 1690s. In most cases the ratios were well below average, as may be seen from table 13.2.

probably never will be, given the poor quality of the first Swedish parish records. From the 1660s the illegitimacy ratio remained more or less stable at about 3 per cent. There was a marked decline in the 1690s, but an increase after that date. This rise was confined to Uppsala town and all other areas had a stable illegitimacy ratio of about 2 per cent. At the end of the period, during the 1740s the ratio began the climb which continued into the next century.

We have no proof of a definite connection between birth and illegitimacy rates, but during the 1690s there was a considerable drop in both rates for the whole of Sweden. In one east Swedish parish birth rates well below 20 per thousand have been calculated for the decade.[17] The period from the start of the Swedish-Danish war in 1675 to the end of the Great Northern War in 1721 is characterized by a low birth rate. This low rate was accentuated by famine towards the end of the 1690s and by plague in the years around 1710. In this investigation birth rates have not been considered since this would require knowledge of the total population during each decade. However, in the majority of parishes the total number of births per year during this decade was perceptibly lower than the average for each parish. We hope these data will enable us to make reasonably reliable judgements, while realizing that they will not be as accurate as those based on national birth rates.

The introduction of political absolutism in the 1680s had certain ecclesiastical consequences which accentuated the decrease in illegitimacies which had begun in the mid seventeenth century. Some of these changes in church organization can be likened to those which took place during the English Puritan Revolution. Unity and orthodoxy were the order of the day; special attention was given to punishment of sexual immorality, swearing, breach of the Sabbath, etc. The official crackdown on immorality can be dated from the Church Law of 1686 and the Church Manual of 1693, which stressed a stern disciplining of sinners. The

17. Nils and Inga Friberg, *350 års befolkningsutveckling i Mälardalen Tillberga* (1972), p. 28. In 1697 the birth rate was 10 per thousand and in 1709 it was 15 per thousand.

Table 13.2: Illegitimacy ratios in nine Swedish districts during the 1690s

Parish	Average	1690s	Birth rate
Björskog	3.3	3.2	normal
Uppsala, Holy Trinity	3.5	2.6	normal
Huddinge	4.5	6.3	low
Irsta	3.2	1.4	low
Skinnskatteberg	1.9	0.6	low
Skultuna	2.2	2.0	low
Tillinge-Svinnegarn	3.0	1.3	low
Tyresö-Dalarö	3.2	0.7	low
Uppsala, Cathedral	5.2	3.5	low

authority of the minister and church council was increased. Provincial governors were authorized to control the zeal of local ministers. From this time on the stocks began to be used in disciplinary cases. This period of strict morality continued until 1741, whereafter the use of the repenter's stool for common fornication was forbidden.[18]

It is surprising that the figures obtained are not very much greater. It is generally held that illegitimacy was common in Sweden since time out of mind, because the practice was subject only to mild sanctions. Such statements are made frequently by modern statisticians and social theorists attempting to interpret the stubbornly high rate of illegitimacy in modern times. The percentage of Swedish children born out of wedlock between 1610 and 1750 is relatively greater than in some other parts of Europe, notably in France. Laslett and Oosterveen have obtained an illegitmacy ratio of 2.4 per cent in England for the period 1610–1750. During the same period 3.3 per cent of Swedish births can be termed illegitimate. But in Denmark ratios as high as 9–10 per cent have been recorded.[19]

Table 13.3 shows the differences in illegitimacy ratios between the various parishes investigated. As might be expected Uppsala Cathedral parish tops the list with 5.2 per cent, its semi-rural twin parish, Holy Trinity, had 3.8 per cent, Huddinge which was economically and socially within Stockholm's orbit even in the early modern period, recorded 4.5 per cent, while the capital itself, because it had drawn to it women made pregnant elsewhere, might well have had a ratio twice as great. The more agricultural parishes, Björskog and Irsta in Västmanland

18. For general tendencies see Pleijel. For details of the opposition to church discipline for fornicators, see A. Thomson, 'Fran "horpall" till "tjuvpall" ' (1967). Many lawyers and royal officials opposed the use of the repenter's stool as an inhumane and unnecessary punishment. Some of them argued that fear of public shame induced pregnant unmarried women to attempt abortion, expose babies, or in extreme cases take their own lives. Thomson notes such an argument from the 1730s on p. 24. The clergy, on the other hand, wished to continue its use. Arguments against the repenter's stool appeared during discussions on a new codification of Swedish law. See, W. Sjögren (ed.), *Förarbetena till Sveriges rikes lag 1686–1736. Lagkommissionens protokoll* II (1901), for the comments of an appeals judge in 1702 (p. 163). Behind this reasoning lay, of course, a fear of underpopulation. For the rule of the English Puritans in the 1650s and the low level of illegitimacy, see Keith Wrightson, chapter 6 above.

19. The English figure comes from a reworking of Laslett and Oosterveen (1973), table 2, p. 267. In France rural parishes commonly had less than 1 per cent illegitimacy during the eighteenth century. In the cities, however, illegitimacy was greater. Here in-migration from rural areas was important. J. Depauw, 'Amour illégitime à Nantes au XVIIIe siècle' (1972), pp. 1155 ff.; and F. Lebrun, 'Naissances illégitimes et abandons d'enfants en Anjou au XVIIIe siècle' (1972), pp. 1183 ff. G. Bang, *Kirkebogstudier. Bidrag till Dansk befolkningsstatistik og kulturhistorie i det 17. aarhundrede* (1906), pp. 67 ff. records for the period 1645–9 an overall illegitimacy rate for Denmark of 10.5 per cent which sinks to 8.2 per cent in 1670–4 and 6.2 per cent in 1695–9. By the late eighteenth century, according to the recent work of H. C. Johansen, Danish illegitimacy amounted to only 3.6 per cent of all births. There was, however, considerable variation between parishes. H. C. Johansen, *Befolkningsudvikling og familiestruktur i det 18. aarhundrede* (1975), pp. 102 ff.

and Tillinge-Svinnegarn in Upland had rather similar ratios: these ranged between 3.0 per cent and 3.25 per cent. Even Tyresö-Dalarö with its various manufacturing enterprises and port area also fell within this range. Surprising, however, are the low ratios obtained for the industrially isolated parishes, Skinnskatteberg and Skultuna, which had 1.9 per cent and 2.25 per cent respectively. These low figures may well reflect the rather disciplined nature of early modern foundry settlements. Industrial isolates recruited male labourers from a large area. The adult population was more predominantly male than in other areas, which allowed a greater percentage of women to marry. Thus a lower percentage of women ran the risk of producing illegitimate children.

Table 13.3: Illegitimacy ratios per selected district, Sweden, 1610–1750

Parish	Period	Years missing	Economic type	No. of bastards	No. of total births	Ratio
Björskog	1626–1749	0	market agric.	139	4177	3.30
Holy Trinity	1665–1749	17	agric. suburb	64	1799	3.55
Huddinge	1673–1749	0	suburb	79	1730	4.50
Irsta	1627–1749	2	market agric.	97	2984	3.25
Skinnskatteb.	1635–1749	1	mining/forest	139	7306	1.90
Skultuna	1664–1749	16	foundry/manuf.	63	2793	2.25
Tillinge & Svinnegarn	1613–1749	16	market agric.	158	5266	3.00
Tyresö & Dalarö	1634–1749	9	manuf./agric.	88	2719	3.25
Uppsala	1660–1749	32	admin./market	309	5900	5.20
				1136	34674	3.27

The illegitimacies studied here reflect premarital relationships between engaged couples only to a very small extent. While premarital intercourse was common even among farm owners in Sweden, engaged couples usually managed to be married before the child arrived. Of 1,136 illegitimate births recorded for these parishes one has reason to believe that only 53 or 4.5 per cent were born to betrothed couples; the other children were the result of less stable relationships.[20] There is, however, some evidence of cohabitation in Uppsala town, where the same couple had more than one illegitimate child, but this group is not large.

However, there is a problem with regard to the quality of birth entries since specific information is available for fathers but is very sparse for mothers: occasionally these are not even named. This prevents any estimate of the extent to which cohabitation occurred and of the prevalence of unwed mothers who had more than one bastard. There are instances of men who fathered illegitimate children of different mothers: 11 cases of several illegitimate children born of the same father within an eight-month period. Illegitimate conceptions depended upon, among others, climatic and religious circumstances. Table 13.4 shows the monthly distribution of births and conceptions for children born out of wedlock.

The figures for rural areas vary considerably; whereas the median is 64, the high is 95 (birth in April, conception in July), and the low is 38 (birth in August,

20. Gahn (1915) obtains a slightly higher ratio, 8.4 per cent in 1751–6 but the statistical base is very narrow.

Table 13.4: Rural-urban variations in month of conception of illegitimate children in nine Swedish districts, 1610–1750

Months		No. of births		Ranking		Legitimate
Birth	Conception	Rural	Urban	Rural	Urban	births
January	April	70	29	5	4	7
February	May	71	29	4	3	3
March	June	67	31	6	1	6
April	July	95	27	1	7	9
May	August	75	20	2	10	10
June	September	58	31	8	1	12
July	October	49	21	10	8	11
August	November	38	17	12	12	4
September	December	53	20	9	10	1
October	January	40	28	11	6	2
November	February	61	29	7	4	4
December	March	72	21	3	8	8
Total		749	304			
Mean		62	25			
Median		64	28.5			

conception in November).[21] In Uppsala, however, there was greater uniformity over the year. Illegitimacy in rural areas was obviously related to harvest festivities in July and August. Midsummer celebrations did not seem so important. It is interesting that November was a low period in both rural and urban parishes, but was, on the other hand, relatively popular for the conception of legitimate children. In general illegitimates were conceived in the warm months from April to August while the colder months did not allow privacy outdoors. Months with most legitimate conceptions – December, January and May – are quite different from those of illegitimate conceptions.

It is possible to say something about the occupational grouping of the fathers of illegitimate children, but it is difficult for the mothers as they nearly always appear simply as 'maid', 'wench' and the like. Occupational information is available for 523 or approximately half of the fathers. Table 13.5 gives a breakdown of this information. Before discussing the figures it should be noted that the landholding group (including cottars) is badly under-represented. The listing of occupations does little more than indicate the relatively young age groups which fathered illegitimate children. Groups such as manservant, student and apprentice indicate more the age than the social status of these individuals. It was very common for farmers' sons, especially those not likely to inherit, to work as servants and apprentices. University students possibly ought to be grouped with the (non-noble) gentry. One group, perhaps unique to Sweden, is that of soldiers and sailors who held allotments in rural areas and were well integrated into the agrarian society; the majority of them did not belong to the farm-inheriting community.

Conception of a child out of wedlock was good reason for young women to move elsewhere, either to parents or away from them.[22] There were many such

21. Depauw (1972 a) shows similar unevenness in conceptions in Nantes. The peaks there came in late spring and early autumn. See also *Statistika Meddelanden A:1* (1914), p. 43, in which the same ranking of months as for the rural areas is found for both the eighteenth and nineteenth centuries. Ranking for legitimate births relate to 1770–80 and are taken from *Bidrag till Sveriges officiella statistik*, p. 49.
22. This aspect is treated in Depauw (1972a) but especially in Lebrun's study of Angers (1972), p. 1185.

Table 13.5: Occupation of fathers of illegitimate children in nine Swedish districts, 1610–1750

Occupation	Number Rural	Urban	Total
Manservant	119	51	170
Soldier	81	45	126
Farmer	5	0	5
Student	5	43	48
Merchant	1	4	5
Craftsman/apprentice	50	58	108
Gentry	19	23	42
Nobility	6	6	12
Miscellaneous	8	9	17
			523

cases. At least 118, or 10 per cent, of unmarried mothers moved between coming pregnant and the time of birth of the child. Parishes on main lines of communication witnessed a disproportionate number of such movements: Björskog 23 of 139 and Huddinge 20 of 79. It is known that many pregnant unmarried women travelled to Stockholm to bear their children in anonymity, but parish records also show that pregnant maids serving in Stockholm moved back to their home parish.[23]

5 Conclusion

Swedish illegitimacy during the period 1610–1750 measured in percentage of births was 3.27 per cent, which is higher than in contemporary France or England but it is not dramatically high. This figure was arrived at by studying the church records of nine parishes (actually of eleven congregations). These were chosen for diversity of socio-economic structure. Because of under-registration this 3.27 per cent does not reflect the actual incidence of illegitimacy in these areas, but it does provide a reasonably reliable indicator of the regional trend in east Sweden.

Illegitimacy in Sweden, as in England, was high at the beginning of the seventeenth century. The ratio was often higher than 5 per cent. But in the second half of the seventeenth century a decline set in and continued into the next century. During this time illegitimacy stayed fairly constant at about 3 per cent, although in the 1690s a low level of 2.5 per cent was reached. The whole of this period is also marked by militant orthodoxy in the Swedish church and by low birth rates. In the 1740s illegitimacy began the rise which continued into the next century. Swedish national statistics began to be kept in 1749, just at the time when illegitimacy started its ascent from a relatively long period of a stable low level.

Agricultural areas had illegitimacy rates ranging between 3.0 per cent and 3.25 per cent. The administrative town, Uppsala, recorded 5.2 per cent, its immediate suburb, Holy Trinity, had 3.5 per cent, while the Stockholm suburb of Huddinge

23. A standard explanation of Stockholm's exceptionally high illegitimacy is the influx of women from rural areas. The evidence from maternity hospitals is clear on this point. Cf. *Sundhetscollegii underdåniga berättelse om medicinal-verket i riket* (1851), p. 181 (1852), pp. 62 ff. and B. Persson, 'Att vara ogift mor pa 1700- och 1800-talen' (1972), who shows that the real extent of this influx cannot be ascertained as many unmarried mothers used their legal right to anonymity. While it is clear that Stockholm figures record many children conceived elsewhere, movement of unwed mothers went in two directions.

had 4.5 per cent. The two isolated parishes in which metal working was the dominant occupation had relatively low rates of 1.9 per cent and 2.25 per cent.

Swedish illegitimacy did not reflect premarital relationships as very few parents of illegitimate children were engaged or became married. Pregnant unmarried mothers often moved out of the parish in which the child was conceived. A study of conception months for children born out of wedlock indicates that, at least in rural areas, conception often coincided with the traditional harvest festivals of late summer.

14

Illegitimacy and marriage in three Swedish parishes in the nineteenth century

Ann-Sofie Kälvemark

Premarital conception has recently been ascribed an important role in the history of European population development.[1] An increase in premarital pregnancies is assumed to result generally in lower ages at marriage for women, prolonging their fertile period in marriage and thus increasing general fertility. The assumption, implicit or explicit, is that premarital conception is a cause of marriage. At times it is even characterized as forced marriage, the force being the socially, legally or morally motivated pressure on the bridegroom to marry the pregnant woman.[2] Since these marriages cannot be postponed to a customary or more convenient time, the pregnant brides are on average younger than usual. If such is indeed the case, the relationship between an increase in premarital conceptions and an increase in general fertility is established.

Although this relationship may appear self-evident, it remains to be tested, and there are other possible interpretations of the role played by premarital pregnancies. Premarital sexual relationships may have been authorized, or at least, tolerated, not by the clerical ceremony of marriage but by the decision to marry, manifested in betrothal or other forms.[3] In these cases the effect of premarital conception on the age of the bride and consequently on general fertility would be insignificant or non-existent.

There is, however, another important factor to be taken into consideration. Those extra-marital pregnancies which did not result in marriage resulted in illegitimacy. The occurrence of illegitimacy may also have had a significant influence on marriage. The child may be seen as the cause of the marriage, if an unmarried mother is in a position to marry the father of her child. But the mother may also remain unmarried, socially and economically not desirable as a bride. In the latter case an increase in illegitimacy may actually result in a decrease in the marriage rate. The indirect consequence, provided that illegitimacy is common, would then be a decrease in fertility.

The relationship between premarital conception, illegitimacy and marriage is here tested on Swedish material from the nineteenth century. Some one thousand marriages from parishes with primitive farming structure and methods in three agricultural areas were investigated; the availability of suitable source material was the major factor in the choice of the time period.

1. J. D. Chambers, *Population, economy and society in pre-industrial England* (1972), pp. 74 ff. Edward Shorter, 'Female emancipation, birth control and fertility in European history' (1973).
2. See, for instance, E. Grebenik, 'The fertility of women with premarital conception in Great Britain' (1958). K. Horstmann, 'Schwangerschaft und eheschliessung' (1959). Harold T. Christensen, 'Cultural relativism and premarital sex norms' (1964). For Sweden, see H. Sjövall, 'Aktenskapets hausse och baisse: svensk nuptialitet, 1861–1971' (1973).
3. See, for instance, S. Croog, 'Aspects of the cultural background of premarital pregnancies in Denmark' (1951), p. 2. P. Laslett and K. Oosterveen, 'Long-term trends in bastardy in England' (1973).

Julita in Södermanland county in the Lake Mälar region will be the main subject of investigation. The parish was relatively large and had a population of nearly 3,000 in 1860. The population increased steadily from the beginning of the century, a nearly continuous high surplus of births being offset by constant migration losses.[4] Julita was almost completely dominated by four large estates, the land of which was mainly leased to farmers and crofters. The population was thus almost wholly dependent on the estates. A change to more rational large-scale farming did not take place until the 1870s.[5] Julita is situated in a homogeneous farming area, representative of the Lake Mälar region; neither towns nor industries are located in the surrounding district. In all, 703 marriages have been investigated during the period 1830–60.

Julita will be compared with two other parishes: Järna in Dalecarlia and Lillhärdal in Jämtland county.[6] Järna was dominated by well-to-do peasant proprietors, a remarkable feature being that the fields were never enclosed, and the area therefore consisted of a mixture of numerous small parcels of land. Lillhärdal is a very large, thinly populated parish in the north of Sweden, known for its special marriage customs, including night courtships. 243 marriages have been investigated in Järna for the period 1851–60 and 191 in Lillhärdal for the period 1880–99. There is no error due to missing information.[7]

Swedish population registration, which constitutes the major source for this study, needs some comment. Every parish has its own continuous population register (*husförhörslängd*), in which all persons were registered at the place where they were living, farm, village, and so on. Changes in the status of the person, such as in- and out-migration, births, marriages, deaths, are always registered. The destination of the migrant, internal as well as external, is given. The central register is complemented by registers of births, marriages, deaths, and for later periods, migrations (registers of migration prior to 1860 exist occasionally, even as early as the eighteenth century; for further information on Swedish population registration, see above, chapter 13). This system, theoretically at least, allows of the use of cohort studies, though it involves cumbersome and time-consuming work. During earlier periods migrants were required to state only their intended destination, but not their actual arrival at this destination, so that there might still be considerable losses due to the disappearance of these migrants. Thus there is always the risk of incomplete information, especially when the migrants moved into larger towns where registration was often unsatisfactory. The possibility of making a successful cohort of marriages has been the decisive factor in the choice of the time period: the material before 1830 turned out to be defective. Fortunately, the source material for Julita as well as that for the places to which the married couples migrated, mostly surrounding parishes, has proved to be quite good for the period after 1830. Only four couples out of an initial 707 are missing for Julita and the collected material may therefore be considered complete.

The vital information needed is date of marriage, date of birth of the first child and the bride's age at marriage. There are, of course, supplementary data such as

4. Every year summary statistics on the population development in the parishes were given to Tabellverket, the governmental office for statistics prior to 1860. The data given are size of population, number of births, deaths, marriages and so forth. These statistics thus provide an easy summary of population development.

5. Christer Andersson, 'Jordbruksomläggningen in Julita' (1974).

6. For the information on Järna and Lillhärdal I am much indebted to undergraduate students Maj-Britt Gassby and Ingegerd Bäckström who have kindly allowed me to use their material from 'Äktenskaps bildning i Järna, 1851–60' and 'Äktenskapsbildning i Lillhärdal, 1880–90' (1973).

7. The period chosen is somewhat unfortunate because of the rapid increase in bastardy in Jämtland county during the latter half of the nineteenth century. Source material has been decisive for the choice of the period.

occupational or social status, place of birth, place of residence when married, children before marriage, etc. The married couples have first been extracted from the register of marriages. Supplementary information has then been collected from the register of births and from the *husförhörslängd*, by means of which the couples were traced up to the birth of their first child. If no child was born within the marriage, the couple was traced up to age fifty for the woman. The marriages were then separated into different groups. The relevant group for this investigation consists of those couples where the woman marries for the first time. Other couples have, accordingly been excluded. These marriages were then separated into five groups:

1 Conventional marriages: the wife has no extra-marital children when she marries; no child is born within the first seven months of the marriage, but children are later born within the marriage.
2 Childless marriages: these have been placed in a separate group for the obvious reason that there is no possibility of premarital conception.
3 Premarital conception marriages: a child is born within the first seven months of the marriage. The time limit of seven months has been chosen so as to be certain that the couple was aware of the expected child, thus making this circumstance a possible cause of marriage (there is no information available on miscarriages).
4 Marriages with illegitimate children: the wife has given birth to a child out of wedlock before her first marriage.
5 Premarital conception marriages with illegitimate children: the wife has *both* an illegitimate child *and* expects a child when marrying. The group is small – 17 cases in all – but it still significantly affects the age structure of the premarital conception marriages as well as the marriages with illegitimate children and is therefore treated separately.

As stated, this analysis will concentrate first on Julita and then make comparisons with the other areas. What then, was the distribution of marriages within the different groups during the decades 1830–60?

Table 14.1: Marriages in Julita, 1830–60 (absolute and relative distribution)

	1830–40		1841–50		1851–60	
	No.	%	No.	%	No.	%
First marriages	211	87.2	188	92.1	255	93.4
Second marriages	31	12.8	16	7.9	18	6.6
Total no.	242	100.0	204	100.0	273	100.0
First marriages:						
Conventional marriages	120	56.9	101	53.7	123	48.2
Childless marriages	12	5.7	8	4.3	16	6.3
Premarital conception	60	28.4	59	31.4	78	30.6
Illegitimate children	16	7.6	14	7.5	30	11.8
Premarital conception + illegitimate children	3	1.4	6	3.2	8	3.1
Total:	211	100.0	188	100.0	273	100.0

One conclusion may be drawn immediately from the distribution in table 14.1. Premarital conception was common in Julita, common enough to make it almost a normal feature: one third of the brides marrying for the first time were pregnant. Were premarital sexual relationships accepted and tolerated? From the legal and official moral point of view obviously not. Every 'guilty' couple had to pay a fine to the church which was entered in the so-called 'special accounts' (*specialräkenskaper*) of the local church. The names of the couples were, however, not given, only their places of residence. The fines were usually one *riksdaler* and 16 *skilling*, which corresponded to about one month's pay for a farm hand. But in spite of these sanctions, premarital conceptions were numerous and it seems likely that they were, to some extent, popularly accepted. It is also clear that the chances of an unmarried mother marrying were fairly good. The increase of such marriages over time is probably due more to an increase in the number of illegitimate births than to a change in attitude towards the unmarried mother.[8] But it cannot be definitely established whether or not the child affected the mother's chances of making an economically and socially favourable match. There is another interesting feature. It seems likely that more than half of the women with illegitimate children married someone other than the father of their child. This has been definitely established in one case only, where the father mentioned in the register of births was someone other than the bridegroom. In most cases, however, the father is not mentioned in the register of births, but when there is a time difference of several years between the birth of the illegitimate child and the marriage, it seems unlikely that the mother married the child's father, especially if she had moved several times after the birth of the child.[9]

Table 14.2: Average age at marriage for women in Julita, 1830–60 (median and mean values)

	1830–40			1841–50			1851–60		
	No.	Median	Mean	No.	Median	Mean	No.	Median	Mean
Conventional marriages	120	23	23.9	101	24	24.6	123	25	26.1
Childless marriages	12	30	32.1	8	25–28	31.5	16	25	27.3
Premarital conception	60	23	23.6	59	24	23.9	78	24	24.2
Illegitimate children	16	28	31.9	114	28	29.5	30	29	29.3
Premarital conception + illegitimate children	3	–	–	6	–	–	8	27	26.5

Premarital conceptions were numerous in Julita. But what did they signify? Were they part of an accepted pattern of marriage, in spite of official sanctions, and did they therefore affect the brides' ages at marriage only to a relatively small degree or not at all? Or did they constitute an unintentional but compelling reason to marry, which might be suggested by the considerably lower age at marriage of

8. From 1851–60, 54 illegitimate children were born. During the same period 38 women with illegitimate children married. Since in some cases the women had no more than one illegitimate child, it is evident that the bastard child was no impediment to marriage.

9. Only in one case can cohabitation without marriage over a longer period be established: a woman who first gave birth to an illegitimate child, the father of which is mentioned in the register of births. After two years she had another child by the same man. This child was, however, not registered as illegitimate in the register of births, but as *trolovningsbarn*, i.e. child of an engaged couple. After another two years the parents were finally married, the woman being pregnant at marriage. One might call this an example of a gradual progress towards marriage, an exception rather than the rule.

pregnant brides? Is there a special age pattern for those women who had an illegitimate child at the time of their marriage? There is a slight difference between the average age of brides in conventional marriages and those pregnant at the time of marriage. The difference is most noticeable in the mean values and during the last period; indeed, for the last period the brides in conventional marriages seem to be younger than the pregnant ones (of the 123 conventional marriages in the period 1851–60, there are 12 when the husband was married for the second time).

But even if there is no significant difference between the groups, one may still observe a slight but interesting difference over time. The median age at marriage for conventional marriages and premarital conception marriages is 23 for the first decade, 24 for the second decade, and 25 and 24 for the last period. This might indicate a development towards higher ages at marriage for women in Julita generally, corresponding to a similar development on the national level. It is remarkable that this development seems to apply to the two groups. This underlines the inevitable conclusion: the absence of differences between the average ages for pregnant brides and brides in conventional marriages and their parallel development over time indicates that sexual relationships were an integral part of the marriage pattern in Julita and as a rule followed a decision to marry. In spite of secular and religious sanctions, marriage actually was not contracted by the church ceremony. Promise of marriage more or less authorized sexual relationship or the relationship itself was interpreted as a decision to marry.

Brides who had illegitimate children, on the other hand, differ clearly from the other groups, having a much higher average age at marriage. It would appear, therefore, that illegitimate births did not affect fertility very much, since premarital births seem to have postponed marriage. In childless marriages women also had a higher average age at marriage, probably reflecting a higher degree of sterility in more advanced age.

There is another possibility of defining more closely the concept of marriage in Julita. If pregnancy before marriage were considered disgraceful, the marriage could be expected to take place at an early stage of the pregnancy. If, on the other hand, it were considered a relatively normal event, there would be no great hurry to marry. This problem may be related to the general marriage pattern. At what time of the year did marriage usually take place? Did the premarital conception marriages follow the seasonal pattern of conventional marriages? One might conclude that the greater the difference, the greater was the pressure to marry early during the pregnancy.

The marriage pattern of Julita conforms on the whole with the general marriage pattern of the country, with most marriages taking place during the last three months of the year (see table 14.3). The overwhelming majority of conventional marriages in Julita took place during these three months. But the other groups also show a clear preference for the last quarter of the year. However, for all three groups the tendency to marry in the last quarter of the year declined during the period 1830–60. The first and third quarters of the year were clearly not favoured months for marrying. This was probably due to the period of Lent in the first quarter and to the harvest season in the third quarter. The second quarter of the year was not popular during the first two periods but became more so during the last period, possibly due to a change in marriage customs. Marriages with premarital conceptions and those with illegitimate children do differ from normal marriages, but not markedly, and especially not during the first two decades. This might indicate that it was customary to postpone marriage to conventional dates, which implies that social pressure was not such as to force a pregnant bride to marry quickly to avoid a scandal.

An investigation of the relationship between date of marriage and the remaining time of the pregnancy at marriage will further elucidate this problem.

Table 14.3: Dates of marriages in Julita, 1830–60 (absolute and percental numbers)

1830–40	Jan.	Feb.	Mar.	Apr.	May	Jun.	Jul.	Aug.	Sep.	Oct.	Nov.	Dec.	Total
1830–40													
Conventional marriages	1	1	1	3	–	1	3	–	–	56	43	11	120
Percent		2.5			3.3			2.5			91.7		100.0
Premarital conception	1	3	6	7	2	4	1	–	2	22	8	7	63
Percent		15.9			20.6			4.8			58.7		100.0
All first marriages	2	4	7	10	2	5	4	–	2	78	51	18	183
Percent		7.1			9.3			3.3			80.3		100.0
1841–50													
Conventional marriages	–	2	1	–	4	1	–	2	1	38	43	8	100
Percent		3.0			5.0			3.0			89.0		100.0
Premarital conception	1	4	6	3	3	3	1	1	2	13	22	6	65
Percent		16.9			13.8			6.2			63.1		100.0
All first marriages	1	6	7	3	7	4	1	3	3	51	65	14	165
Percent		8.3			8.3			4.2			78.8		100.0
1851–60													
Conventional marriages	1	3	2	9	4	3	2	5	9	53	43	3	139
Percent		4.3			11.5			11.5			72.7		100.0
Premarital conception	3	4	8	6	3	13	3	1	1	14	11	11	78
Percent		19.2			28.2			6.4			46.2		100.0
All first marriages	4	7	10	15	7	16	5	6	10	67	54	16	217
Percent	v	9.7			17.5			9.7			63.1		100.0

It is evident from table 14.4 that marriage did not as a rule take place immediately after the couple knew the woman was expecting a child. The median value lies between three and four months of remaining expectancy at marriage. As many as 25 brides had less than one month left of their pregnancy when they married. But there seems also to be a connection between the remaining time of pregnancy and time of marriage. This is most obvious for the fourth quarter when a great number of marriages took place after a period of scarcely any marriages at all. This might also, however, have been a consequence of the time of conception, many of the children having been born during the first and second quarters of the year which would make marriage during the last quarter of the year suitable. It is nevertheless possible that many marriages were postponed to the conventional period in spite of the bride being pregnant.

This is evident from the average remaining pregnancy time to birth for marriages during different months. The average remaining time is much shorter for October than for November. A number of marriages with premarital conception were probably postponed to the conventional month of October, whereas no such postponement is evident for November with its high average of remaining time to

Table 14.4: Remaining time of pregnancy in relation to time at marriage, Julita, 1830–60

Months								
1830–40	−1	−2	−3	−4	−5	−6	−7	Total
Jan.		1						1
Feb.	1			1	1			3
Mar.		3	1		2			6
Apr.	1	1	2	1	1	1		7
May		1		1				2
Jun.				3		1		4
Jul.			1					1
Aug.								–
Sep.	1	1						2
Oct.	3	5	2	6	4	2		22
Nov.		3	3		1		1	8
Dec.			4	2	1			7
Total	6	15	13	14	10	4	1	63
1841–50								
Jan.			1					1
Feb.	1		1	1		1		4
Mar.			1	1	2		2	6
Apr.	1				1		1	3
May	2				1			3
Jun.		2			1			3
Jul.			1					1
Aug			1					
Sep.				1		1		2
Oct.	3	2	3		3		2	13
Nov.	2	3	4	4	5	2	2	22
Dec.		2	2	1			1	6
Total	9	9	14	8	13	4	8	65
1851–60								
Jan.	2				1			3
Feb.			1	3				4
Mar.		3	2		3			8
Apr.	2		2	1	1			6
May.		1	1	1				3
Jun.	3	1	1	3	2	3		13
Jul.			1			1	1	3
Aug.			1					1
Sep.			1					1
Oct.	2	4	4		3	1		14
Nov.			1	2	4	2	2	11
Dec.	2	2	2	2	1	2		11
Total	11	11	17	12	15	9	3	78

births. The short average time for other parts of the year may be interpreted as a tendency to postpone marriage to conventional times when possible, but marrying also at less convenient times if only a short time remains before the birth of the child. A consideration of the relationship between time of marriage and remaining time to birth has shed more light on the part pregnancy played in the concept of marriage in Julita. It is clear that pregnancy was not considered so shameful as to hasten marriage, which was often postponed to the conventional time.

Table 14.5: Mean interval between marriage and birth of first child (premarital conception only), Julita

	Jan.	Feb.	Mar.	Apr.	May	Jun.	Jul.	Aug.	Sep.	Oct.	Nov.	Dec.
Days	53	90	83	69	77	95	149	67	61	81	135	87

The information for Julita will now be compared with that obtained for the two other parishes, Järna in Dalecalia and Lillhärdal in Härjedalen, on the main points of premarital conception, marriage with illegitimate children and variation in age between different groups. The classification is the same as that used for Julita with the exception of the 'overlapping cases', which here are found in the group labelled 'illegitimate children'. The rate of premarital pregnancy for Julita is about the same as that for Järna whereas it is somewhat lower for Lillhärdal. The greatest difference is to be found in the group with illegitimate children. This is very small in Järna, but it is the dominant group in Lillhärdal, comprising 38 per cent of all marriages, that is, considerably greater than that of conventional marriages. The marriage norms appear to be stricter in Järna than in the other parishes. This is underlined by the fact that, in contrast to Julita, the parents of illegitimate children married in every case, indicating effective social control. Moreover, illegitimate births were few in the parish (Gassby, 1973, pp. 6 ff. Thirteen of the children in the investigation were *trolovningsbarn*, children of engaged couples). An important factor in the marriage pattern in Järna, where the land was never enclosed, was evidently the consideration of the geographical position of the fields. The combined land owned by husband and wife should be adjacent (Gassby, 1973, p. 10). This form of land tenure may have lent weight to the social sanction against illegitimacy. Nevertheless, the number of premarital conceptions was as high as in Julita and the usual fines were paid by the guilty couples, who had their names listed in the special accounts (Gassby, 1973, p. 11).

Table 14.6: Marriages in Julita, Järna and Lillhärdal (absolute and relative numbers)

	Julita 1851–60[(a)]		Järna 1851–60		Lillhärdal 1880–99	
	No.	%	No.	%	No.	%
First marriages						
Conventional marriages	123	48.2	133	57.6	64	33.5
Premarital conception	78	30.6	67	29.0	50	26.2
Illegitimate children	38	14.9	17	7.4	73	38.2
Childless marriages	16	6.3	14	6.0	4	2.1
Total	255	100.0	231	100.0	191	100.0

[(a)] The period of 1851–60 is chosen to coincide with the period for Järna

Table 14.7: Average age at first marriage for women in Julita, Järna and Lillhärdal (median values)

	Julita 1851–60		Järna 1851–60		Lillhärdal 1880–99	
	No.	Median age	No.	Median age	No.	Median age
Conventional marriage	123	25	133	26	64	23
Premarital uconception	78	24	67	26	50	22
Illegitimate children	38	29	17	26	73	25
Childless marriages	16	27	14	31	4	–

The marriage pattern in Lillhärdal was of quite another type. The comparatively low number of premarital conceptions may be explained by the exceptionally high number of marriages with illegitimate children. In two thirds of the cases, the parents of the illegitimate child married each other, but in the rest, the mother married someone else (Bäckström, 1973, p. 3). This conforms with the situation in Julita where the illegitimate child was obviously not a hindrance to the mother in acquiring a marriage partner. The postponement of the marriage ceremony until after the birth of one or more children may be explained not only by custom but also by such factors as the size of the parish and the absence of roads. Distance may have been an influential factor, the incidence of marriages with illegitimate children increasing with distance from the church (Bäckström, 1973, p. 15).

Premarital conception does not appear to have affected age at first marriage very much in either of the parishes. Brides with illegitimate children show more variation in age, being older in Lillhärdal but of the same age as the other groups in Järna. Perhaps conformity in age may be seen as another indication of stricter social control, the birth of the child taking place just before the marriage.

Premarital conception and illegitimacy in connection with marriage thus show a somewhat different pattern in the three parishes here investigated and seem to mirror social, economic and traditional conditions. We have to deal not so much with different types of marriages as with different functions of the church ceremony of marriage. This ceremony, our main source for the study of nuptiality in the past, is the usual official means by which the marriage was contracted. But in fact marriage was often contracted by other means, such as betrothal, cohabitation and behaviour in accordance with local and traditional patterns of marriage. Because of the lack of conformity premarital conception and illegitimacy cannot be considered to have a uniform effect on patterns of marriage and fertility.

15

Illegitimacy and marriage in Stockholm in the nineteenth century

Margareta R. Matovic

In 1850 Stockholm was a city of some 93,000 inhabitants and had entered a stage of rapid expansion. The population trend during the 1840s and 1850s reveals several interesting phenomena, one of which is a decrease in the number of marriages. It is a well known fact that the number of marriages generally rose during periods of economic prosperity and fell during less prosperous years, but the question arises as to whether these low rates were the result solely of an economic slump. It is reasonable to assume that other factors also affected the marriage rate and in this connection it is interesting to note the high incidence of illegitimate births in Stockholm during this period. With a rate of 46 per cent during the five-year period 1851–5, Stockholm was second to Vienna's 49 per cent among European capitals.

A number of special conditions were responsible for this high percentage in Stockholm. In the first place, a large number of children born to engaged couples were registered as illegitimate (clergymen had debated for years whether they should be considered illegitimate or not). Children of engaged couples were often born into relationships similar to marriage, which seem to have been quite usual among the lower strata of Stockholm's population. These marriages of conscience or common law marriages were obviously seen as an alternative by those who for economic or other reasons wished to avoid a church marriage.

The American sociologist, Oscar Lewis, has found that unlegalized marriages are common in the so-called poverty cultures and appear most frequently during the early stages of industrialization. One hypothesis, therefore, is that there was a hidden structure of unlegalized marriages during the period 1830–50, but that after this time the tendency to legalize such marriages increased. There is evidence in support of this hypothesis in parish registers from the 1860s and 1870s, when a large number of recorded marriages appear to be simply legalizations of common law relationships begun years earlier. The decline in the number of illegitimate births during these latter decades also suggests an increased tendency to legalize both old and new relationships.

Against the background of the economic and social changes which Swedish society underwent from 1850 to 1880, the following question with regard to Stockholm must be asked:

1 Who married whom? That is to say, what was the connection between choice of partner and social background and between choice of partner and occupation? Were there status groups within the working class who were able to marry 'above their station' and thereby enter the middle class? What was the situation of women and especially of widows? What was the relationship between the occupation of the deceased husband and that of the prospective husband?

2 At what age did people marry in different social groups?
3 How did economic fluctuations affect the inclination to marry and the choice of partner?
4 How did the inclination to marry and the choice of partners among new arrivals in Stockholm compare with that of the city's native inhabitants?
5 What was the incidence of common law marriages prior to legal marriage ceremonies and what was the incidence of illegitimate children?

Parish registers have proved both interesting and valuable as source material. Additional important sources are the tax-census rolls, censuses, address directories and information from population statistics. Swedish clergymen began to register the inhabitants of their parishes in the early years of the seventeenth century. The civil authorities soon grasped the value of the registers as a means of control and a provision for parish registration was included in the ecclesiastical law of 1686. The parish registers include so-called ministerial books in which banns, marriages, baptisms and burials were recorded. In addition, the clergy maintained catechism registers in which all confirmed members of the parish were listed. After 1748 these catechism registers also listed the children of the parish. Parish registers were used to check the tax-census rolls. Annual taxes levied on individuals became general in Sweden after the 1620s, and the collection of these taxes made it expedient to register the entire population in order to determine the number of persons liable to pay the tax. The registration was carried out with great care, since it was designed to facilitate the conscription of soldiers as well as the collection of taxes. Registration of the entire population was conducted annually in November, and such information as the individual's name, address, occupation and income were entered in the so-called tax-census rolls.

Information has been extracted from the parish registers of Stockholm's eight parishes for the period 1860–72. The year 1860 has been chosen as a starting date because the source material for the 1850s is less reliable from a demographic point of view. The establishment of the Swedish Central Bureau of Statistics led to the compilation of more and better material in the shape of censuses and other statistics. The parish records used include the registers of banns and marriages and, to some extent, other material available in connection with the calling of banns. The registers of banns consist of the vicar's handwritten entries in registers printed for the purpose and the information they contain is based largely on the documents and other information submitted by each betrothed couple. These documents could include letters from their parish ministers, certificates of bachelor- or spinsterhood or of divorce, estate inventory deeds and, in some cases, personal recommendations from relatives and/or certificates of baptisms of premarital children. The vicar supplemented this information by interviewing the couple about their current address or addresses and about their occupations. Therefore the registers of banns provide extensive information about the couples. The marriage registers, on the other hand, served primarily to confirm the fact that the marriage ceremony had been performed.

Many problems have arisen because of the varying and independent manner in which individual clergymen kept their registers. The degree of accuracy and sense of responsibility varied, as did the personal interest in the couples concerned. It is difficult to say what norms guided the vicars in their recording of information, but the variations suggest that they had a great deal of liberty and that in some cases they could refrain from recording otherwise obligatory information. Because of these variations, the portrait of each parish painted by its registers is coloured by the vicar's character. Some vicars were careless, or perhaps one should say, radical enough to avoid invading their parishioners' private lives, while others were very careful about detail and conscientious in carrying out their moral duty and so kept a strict eye on their charges.

The parish registers have thus proved to be rich and interesting sources, as in the case of Maria Magdalena parish, or meagre and difficult to interpret, as in the case of Adolf Fredrik parish. In addition, the registers could vary considerably from year to year because the parish had received a new vicar who had a different conception of his duty. These variations make systematic treatment of the data difficult. When it comes to the recording of place of birth of marriage partners, for example, studies carried out for Katarina, St Nicholas and Ladugårdsland parishes, show that these were not recorded in about 10 per cent of the cases. One interesting phenomenon is the fact that failure to record personal data is more prevalent for certain social groups. Studies of these three parishes have shown that there are relatively more cases of unrecorded personal data for the middle and upper classes than for the lower classes. This may possibly be explained by the vicar's personal attitude towards different social groups, which determined his judgement and the extent of his zeal in recording information in the register of banns. Couples from well-to-do families were treated with greater latitude than those from the working or servant classes. Vicars often left out information about place and date of birth, address, character and religion for the so-called 'better' people and one may assume that in these cases the vicar was so convinced of the individual's standing and moral qualities that he felt such information was unnecessary.

When registering the banns the vicar had to note, among other things, the couple's character or *frejd*, as it is called in Swedish. *Frejd* had to do with reputation and standing and was, in fact, a general assessment of moral character. In practice it was the vicar's subjective evaluation of the person, embodied in the necessary letter of recommendation and thus in the statement of character entered in the register of banns. The letter of recommendation from the vicar of one's home parish was an obligatory document for the lower classes and it followed members of these classes from the cradle to the grave, thus providing the clergy with a major source of information about the parishioner's personal history. This recommendation included not only the usual personal data, but also statements on behaviour and morals, crimes committed and sentences received, time spent in prison, illegitimate children and, for women, information on any premarital relationships. The interrogation which the prospective couple seems to have been subjected to in the registering of banns must have been humiliating for many and may even have frightened some couples away. It is difficult to determine the methods which the clergy used to gather information about the private lives of their parishioners. Arbitrary prejudice played much too great a role in the assessment of a person's 'character' for it to be possible to classify and evaluate the statements which were recorded. Until 1865 a detailed statement was entered as to each person's 'character', but the penal code of 1864 allowed some relaxation of this registration. More and more clergymen began to neglect it entirely, indicating that such statements were no longer obligatory. The disappearance of the 'character' assessments from registers of banns deprives us of an interesting source of material: in spite of doubts about the individual clergyman's objectivity, the 'character' statement contained much valuable information about patterns of behaviour and they reflected a great deal of contemporary modes of thought.

Within the period 1860–72, the years 1864, 1868 and 1872 have been especially selected for investigation because of the interesting economic situation which developed during 1868 and 1872. Data concerning each couple have been recorded on forms embodying all the information available from the registers of banns and marriages and each individual was then classified according to a social stratification model devised by Uno Gustafson. Correct social stratification requires a uniform system of job assessment and Uno Gustafson's model consists of ten occupational classes, the first four of which form a sort of upper stratum whose members had independent and supervisory functions. Classes 5 to 10 represent the working class and servants, that is to say, a lower stratum whose members worked for wages in subordinate positions. These class groups can then be compared with the stratification in society as a whole, either parish by parish or for the whole city.

It has been difficult to classify women because of the profusion of titles applied to them and because of the social implications of these titles. The model used for men is not applicable to women since their titles are based on social background and their fathers' occupations. The usual female titles were *miss*, applied to daughters of the nobility, *honourable spinster*, *mademoiselle* and *demoiselle*, applied to daughters of professional people and the middle class, and *mamsell*, *maiden*, *housemaid* and *housekeeper*, all of which were applied to lower-class girls and women. It has also proved difficult to discover which women were wage earners since many working women hid behind titles which do not reveal their occupations. Checks of tax-census rolls and the banns documents have revealed that many women whose titles did not imply an occupation were in fact wage earners and continued to work after marriage. The reason why so many women preferred to give the impression that they did not work seems to be connected with the social status attached to not having to support oneself. This was especially prevalent among women who called themselves *maiden* and *mamsell* and who wished to be recorded as living with their parents. The apellation *housemaid* and *housekeeper* are more controversial since they are at one and the same time occupational designations and titles with negative implications: Whether a woman with one of these titles had a job or not remains unclear. According to the instructions to vicars for registering banns, a woman who had an illegitimate child or who had had premarital relationships was not to be given a negative classification, but was rather to be registered as *housemaid* or *housekeeper*. However, both *housemaid* and *housekeeper* have been taken as occupational designations since it is probable that unmarried women of the lower classes, and especially unmarried mothers, had to support themselves by means of some sort of employment.

The detailed studies carried out for the years 1864, 1868 and 1872 concern St Nicholas parish and are preparatory studies for a larger investigation to be carried out with the help of quantitative methods and computer processing. Furthermore, a broad study of the Stockholm sources is to be undertaken in order to obtain an idea of the inclination to marry, the choice of marriage partners, the forms of cohabitation and the extent of illegitimacy. The period 1860–1910 has been studied decade by decade by means of a random sample of the couples for whom banns were called and by recording the data on forms which would serve as the basis for computer analysis. In preparing the data a number of difficulties were encountered in developing a coding system for the entries in the registers of banns and in the selection of a representative group of couples which would enable one to carry out an analysis covering several types of questions. A total of some 93,000 weddings were celebrated in Stockholm during the period 1860–1910, that is, some 10,000–20,000 weddings per decade for the eight parishes under study. To begin with, 1,000 couples were selected from a total of 9,171 for whom banns were called during the decade 1860–9 in the hope that they would prove representative. Some 15 per cent of these had to be discarded because several of the registers of banns were incomplete. However, by using information from other sources the gap has been reduced to 10 per cent, a percentage low enough to accord future results an acceptable degree of probability.

Alongside this large-scale quantitative study, an intensive study of Adolf Fredrik parish during the year 1864 has been carried out. The incomplete parish registers, in particular the registers of banns, had to be supplemented by information from other sources, consisting of documents giving personal data, presented to the vicar at the registration of banns, as well as the tax-census rolls, which provide data on occupation, living quarters, personal income, eventual cohabitation and premarital children. The investigation has been very time-consuming and complicated since it has been necessary to obtain the original documents for each person and then to trace this person in the tax-census rolls. Of the 125 couples for whom banns were called in 1864, that is to say 250 people, 32 individuals (12.9 per cent) could not be traced. The remaining persons have been traced in the tax-census rolls for 1863, 1864 and 1865, so that their situations were evaluated not only for the year banns were called, but also for the years immediately prior to and immediately following that date. By correlating all sources it is hoped to obtain a complete picture of each individual's social and economic circumstances at the time banns were called and to shed light on his or her background and choice of marriage partner, and thus to lay the foundation for new hypotheses and future studies.

The registers of banns and the tax-census rolls are dissimilar sources since they have entirely different functions. They give us interesting glimpses of how people presented themselves when confronted by the census taker and by the vicar. The tax-census took place each November and it was in each individual's interest to portray himself in as humble a manner as possible in both economic and social matters. The registering of banns, on the other hand, was connected with a certain amount of status and people attempted to 'better' their position with regard to title and occupation. In some instances in the Adolf Fredrik material where the tax-census and the registering of banns took place at nearly the same time, one finds that, when registering the banns, men listed as 'ordinary laboureres' on the tax-census rolls called themselves 'carpenter', 'driver', and the like, while one 'mason's helper' called himself a 'mason' and a 'brewery worker' a 'beer distributor'. One cannot, therefore, identify the individual's exact occupation with any degree of certainty from these two sources. Likewise, it is necessary to exercise caution when treating the numerous entries of 'unemployed' in the tax-census rolls. But the differences in occupational designation, as shown in the above examples, are in most cases so small that they do not invalidate the classification of the Adolf Fredrik parishioners.

An estimate of the effect of economic fluctuations on the inclination to marry and on the choice of partners has been attempted for St Nicholas parish for the years 1864, 1868 and 1872. A study of the connection between age, choice of partner and social group showed that within classes 1 to 4, that is within the upper stratum, the overwhelming majority of men chose brides significantly younger than themselves. The males in classes 5 to 10 showed a different pattern: both in 1864, a year of normal economic conditions, and in 1872, which was a year of economic boom, the men of these classes chose brides both younger and older than themselves. But in 1868, a year marked by crop failures and industrial crisis, there was a clear tendency for the men to choose brides older than themselves. It is clear that within this parish, at least, working-class men preferred to marry older women during years of crisis and in many cases the difference in age was considerable. It seems reasonable to conclude that economic considerations had a certain influence since older women were often better situated both as regards housing and savings than were their younger sisters. Another interesting feature is that couples for whom banns were called in 1868 changed their minds more frequently and did not marry. This was true not only for St Nicholas parish, but also for the other seven parishes: whereas 2 per cent of the couples abstained from marriage in 1868, only 0.8 per cent did so in 1872. Of the 15 couples who abstained in St Nicholas parish in 1868, 9 did not give a reason for their decision. This could be interpreted to mean that couples avoided marriage as an economic burden.

It was normal for couples to give a common address when registering banns and in the majority of cases this meant that the couple had begun marital cohabitation much earlier. When, in addition, the woman was designated as an 'attached woman' or the legitimation of children was noted, it is clear that the couple was legitimizing a common law marriage. A study of St Nicholas parish revealed that 26 per cent of the couples registering banns in 1864 lived together; by 1868 the figure had increased to 34 per cent and by 1872 it had jumped to 43 per cent. This increase does not necessarily mean that the incidence of cohabitation was lower prior to 1864. On the contrary, it may have been just as high or even higher, while the inclination to legalize relationships was lower. Non-legalized marriages were most common among the working class and it is within this class that the increased tendency to legalize established relationships became evident towards the end of the 1860s and during the 1870s.

In those cases where the register of banns show a common address for the couple but nothing more, it is not clear whether one should conclude that the couple lived together in a marriage-like relationship. The detailed information about each couple's situation for Adolf Fredrik parish in 1864 has thrown some light on this problem. 46.5 per cent of all the couples had common addresses and 40 per cent of the total number shared a marriage-like relationship, leaving 6.5 per cent of the total number as questionable cases. Of the 40 per cent having marriage-like relationships, 60 per cent had premaritally born children, but only one third of the questionable 6.5 per cent had children born out of wedlock. Most of the common addresses in Adolf Fredrik parish therefore represent cases of premarital cohabitation and one may assume that such was the case for the whole of Stockholm. It is probable that engaged couples tried to conceal their premarital cohabitation and any children they might have had when registering the banns, but this was possible only when these children had been born outside the parish. The effective concealment of cohabitation and of illegitimate children depended on how thoroughly the vicar checked up on his parishioners. In many cases premarital children were boarded out: in Adolf Fredrik parish 12 of the 29 couples with premarital children 'picked up' their children after the wedding or within the course of the following year. Further investigation will show whether this was a widespread practice.

In Adolf Fredrik parish non-legalized marriages and premarital children were also most prevalent among the working class. On the other hand, only a few domestics cohabited and had children, probably because of the nature of their employment. Premarital children also existed in the upper social stratum, that is, in classes 1 to 4, but the material from St Nicholas and Adolf Fredrik parishes shows that it was not so common in these groups. In Adolf Fredrik 6 per cent of the couples from these groups lived together before the banns were called; in St Nicholas it was only 4 per cent. There were also a number of illegitimate children in these groups. Non-legalized marriages were most common among the lower middle classes where the so-called mamselle marriages were frequent: a middle-class man lived together with a woman from a lower social class, who, officially, was in charge of his house and who was called the *house-mamsell*. She was, in fact, his common law wife and maid, but she was given the status title of *mamselle*.

An example of such a relationship is that between August Strindberg's parents: his father kept a spice shop, while his much younger mother was a maid at an inn. She became the senior Strindberg's housekeeper and 'attached' woman and they lived together for five years and produced three children before their relationship was legalized. After the mother's death, Strindberg's father, typically enough, married a new house-mamsell, thirty years his junior. The idea that later age of marriage among the upper and middle classes was a result of the man waiting for a suitable economic position so that he could support a family is not sufficient explanation of the mamsell-marriages, where the men were often well off. The institution is probably the result of complicated economic and social factors: one could mention the situation of women in the labour market, the surplus of women in the lower classes and last but not least, the contemporary traditional attitude to women.

When studying non-legalized marriages by means of the registers of banns, one meets, of course, only those persons who legalized their premarital relationships through marriage and one learns nothing at all about the relationships which were never legalized or noted in any statistical material. It may be possible to fill this

Table 15.1: Cohabitation and illegitimacy in Stockholm, 1864 (in percentages)

PARISH	Common address	Cohabitation with premarital children	Separate dwelling but premarital children	Separate dwelling and illegitimate children[(a)]	Separate dwelling Deceased or abandoned children	No. of banns analysed
St Nicholas	23.6	0.9	–	0.9	0.9	106
Clara	27.7	–	0.7	2.2	0.7	137
Jacob & Johannes	40.4	0.7	–	2.2	1.5	136
Catharina	46.1	5.7	–	3.5	0.7	141
Maria	38.5	9.8	3.9	3.9	3.9	153
Kungsholms	27.9	9.3	–	–	–	43
Ladugårdslands	45.5	1.5	–	0.8	1.5	132
Adolf Fredrik	22.4	24	–	8.8	0.8	125
Mean	35.15	6.17	0.72	3.19	1.44	Total 973

(a) The woman has a child/children from an earlier relationship

Table 15.2: Common address, cohabitation and premarital children upon registration of banns in Stockholm,[a] 1860–69

%	Separate dwelling No children %	Separate dwelling Premarital children %	Separate dwelling Illegitimate children[b] %	Separate dwelling Children from former marriage %	Common address No children %	Cohabitation Premarital children %	Cohabitation Illegitimate children[b] %	Cohabitation Children from former marriage analysed	No. of banns
Upper class, administrative, commercial, bourgeoisie	81.36	–	–	6.78	10.17	1.69	–	–	59
Middle class	60.92	0.57	–	8.05	17.82	2.87	1.72	8.05	174
Lower middle class	56.48	–	0.93	7.41	27.78	1.85	1.85	3.70	108
Artisans & skilled workers	43.04	1.52	2.28	2.53	37.72	6.84	2.53	3.54	395
Unskilled workers	42.96	1.41	2.82	1.41	38.73	5.63	2.82	4.23	142
Servants	71.43	–	–	–	28.57	–	–	–	7
Others	56.67	–	3.33	3.33	30	3.33	–	3.33	30
Mean	51.15	0.98	1.64	4.26	30.82	4.81	2.08	4.26	Total 915

[a] Random sample of 1075 couples, 915 couples analysed, 160 couples inadequate information
[b] The woman has a child/children from an earlier relationship

gap by studying the censuses which began in 1860 and were held every ten years thereafter and by studying the tax-census rolls. But this would reveal only those who volunteered such information and the results of such a study would be very limited, hardly reflecting the incidence of common law marriages over longer periods of time.

An important question, of course, is just what made a couple decide to legalize a long-standing relationship. One thought which immediately comes to mind is that the woman's pregnancy may have been a significant cause, since it would make the couple's illegitimate relationship obvious to the neighbours. In Adolf Fredrik parish, however, it is clear that only a few of the women were pregnant when the banns were registered. Only 18 per cent of the women expected children within seven months of the calling of the banns, but half of these women already had premarital children and had obviously established a marriage-like relationship long before the actual event. It is clear that having children did not lead directly to a decision to marry in Adolf Fredrik parish.

Table 15.3: Common address, cohabitation and premarital children upon registration of banns in two Stockholm parishes, 1864

CLASS	Common address		Cohabitation		Cohabitation premarital children		Separate dwelling and illegitimate children[(a)]		Total no. of banns	
	AF	SN	AF	SN	AF	SN	AF	SN	AF	SN
0			1		1		2		4	2
1					1				4	1
2					2		1		5	3
3		2	1		1				5	18
4		1		1	1		1		7	15
5									1	
6	7	15	13	1	18	1	5	2	75	47
7		1			1				1	5
8		2			2		1		6	5
9	1	2	5		1		1		15	10
10					2				2	
Total	8 6.4%	23 21.7%	20 16%	2 1.9%	30 24%	1 0.9%	11 8.8%	2 1.9%	125	106

Social classes

0 unknown, not actively employed
1 self-employed in agriculture, forestry and gardening
2 self-employed in industry and handicraft
3 self-employed in commerce and the transport industry
4 senior officials and professions
5 workers in agriculture, forestry and gardening
6 workers in handicrafts, industry, commerce and transport
7 shop assistants, waiters etc.
8 assistants in public and private administration, office staff
9 servants
10 soldiers and non-commissioned officers

Note: Adolf Fredrik (AF) was a largely working-class parish, St Nicholas (SN) was an upper-class parish

[(a)] The woman has a child/children from an earlier relationship

In his study of Stockholm's social structure in 1890, Uno Gustafson reports results which suggest that social differences were very great. Among other things, he draws the conclusion that upper-class couples married considerably later than did those of the lower classes. The question is whether this was also true of the 1860s. We have determined the age at first marriage for 462 individuals in St Nicholas and Adolf Fredrik parishes for the year 1864. The average age at first marriage of men belonging to classes 1 to 4 was 31 years and for women 27 years, while that for men in classes 5 to 10 was 29 and for women 28 years. The figures reveal that the differences between the social groups was not very great and that the average age at first marriage was quite high in all classes. This picture agrees with Hajnal's finding that Scandinavia and especially Sweden were typical of Western European marriage patterns, with late marriages and a large percentage of unmarrieds. In spite of the limited results of the investigations to date, they suggest that changes in the age at first marraige occurred during the period up to 1890. It seems probable that the inclination to marry at an earlier age among the lower classes was stimulated by the economic and social changes which Stockholm experienced during the course of the thirty years from 1860 to 1890.

Table 15.4: Correlation between cohabitation and birthplace for the working class in Stockholm, 1860–9

Sample: 469 couples (from the random sample of 1075)
16 couples inadequate information

	Cohabitation		No cohabitation			
	No. of couples	%	No. of couples	%	No. of couples	%
Male partner born in Stockholm	31	6.84	11	2.43	42	9.27
Male partner born outside Stockholm	205	45.25	206	45.48	411	90.73

$X^2 = 7.812$

A one-tailed X^2-test results in a p-value of approximately 0.005 which supports the hypothesis that workers born in Stockholm were more inclined to premarital cohabitation than workers born in other parts of Sweden.

Table 15.5: Average age at marriage in Adolf Fredrik and St Nicholas parishes, Stockholm, 1864[(a)]

	First marriage		Later marriages (for one or the other party)	
Class	Men	Women	Men	Women
1–4	31	27	47	36
5–10	29	28	36	41

[(a)] Number of couples analysed = 231.

III North America, Jamaica and Japan

16

Illegitimacy and bridal pregnancy in colonial America

Robert V. Wells

In the past students who have found it worth while to comment on bastardy and bridal pregnancy in colonial America have fallen into four categories. Among the earliest to investigate these topics were historians like Bruce and Earle who touched briefly on bastardy and bridal pregnancy as part of their wide-ranging descriptions of colonial society.[1] More often, however, students have had particular reasons for wishing to deal with these topics. One such group includes those devoted to the study of Puritan New England who have sought to show (for a variety of motives) that, with regard to morals, the Puritans were less perfect and more human than they have often been portrayed as being.[2] Legal historians have also commented on sexual matters that came to the attention of the colonial courts. These studies have generally been limited to legal restrictions on and court procedures for dealing with sexual offenders, although a few have tried to place the colonists' treatment of sexual offenders in some sort of social context.[3] Finally, at least some students of family and population patterns in early America have concerned themselves with the extent of illegitimacy and prenuptial pregnancy in the colonies; but most of the time these topics have been only a minor part of some more general study.[4]

The existence of this surprising array of material on bastardy and bridal pregnancy together with my own research on Quaker families, legal codes and court records makes it possible, for the first time, to explore two important questions. First, how common were illegitimacy and bridal pregnancy in colonial America? The second, and probably more important question is: what was the social significance of bastardy and bridal pregnancy in colonial America? Before this latter question can be answered effectively, it is important to attempt to determine how frequently these phenomena occurred. In dealing with both

1. Philip A. Bruce, *Economic history of Virginia in the seventeenth century* II (1896), pp. 34–8, 109–13; Alice M. Earle, *Customs and fashions in old New England* (1893).

2. In chronological order these include Charles F. Adams 'Some phases of sexual morality and church discipline in colonial New England' (1891), pp. 477–516; Henry B. Parkes, 'Sexual morals and the great awakening' (1930), pp. 133–5; Henry B. Parkes, 'Morals and law enforcement in colonial New England' (1932), pp. 431–52; Edmund S. Morgan, 'The Puritans and sex' (1942), pp. 591–607; Emil Oberholzer, Jr, *Delinquent saints* (1956); Kai T. Erikson, *Wayward Puritans* (1966).

3. Two of the best studies by a legal historian are by David Flaherty. They include his *Privacy in colonial New England* (1972), and 'Law and the enforcement of morals in early America' (1971), pp. 203–56. Older studies which are helpful include Herbert W. K. Fitzroy, 'The punishment of crime in provincial Pennsylvania' (1936), pp. 242–69; Julius Goebel, Jr, and T. Raymond Naughton, *Law enforcement in colonial New York* (1944); Arthur P. Scott, *Criminal law in colonial Virginia* (1930); Raphael Semmes, *Crime and punishment in early Maryland* (1938); Harry B. and Grace M. Weiss, *An introduction to crime and punishment in colonial New Jersey* (1960).

4. The most obvious exception to this pattern is Daniel Scott Smith and Michael S. Hindus, 'Premarital pregnancy in America, 1640–1971: an overview and interpretation' (1975). The author would like to thank Professor Smith for making this available to him prior to publication. More typical are John Demos, 'Families in colonial Bristol, Rhode Island: an exercise in historical demography' (1968), pp. 40–57; Philip J. Greven, Jr, *Four generations* (1970), pp. 112–16; and Julia C. Spruill, *Women's life and work in the southern colonies* (1972), pp. 314–39.

questions the focus will be on those colonies which became the United States; a study including the Caribbean colonies is beyond the scope of this chapter.

It would obviously be desirable to measure the extent of illegitimacy in colonial America in precise quantitative terms. Unfortunately, difficulties arising both from definitions and from the sources make it impossible to be exact. Nonetheless, enough evidence is available to allow at least some conclusions to be drawn on a reasonably sure basis. Before presenting the data, however, it is necessary to consider the possible limits.

An illegitimate birth, unlike most demographic events, is one which has a definite social significance attached to it. For some reason it is deemed less desirable than a legitimate birth. Just what makes a birth illegitimate is decided by the society in which it occurs. Thus, it is possible for a birth in one society to be deemed legitimate, while a similar birth in any other society may be illegitimate. It is, therefore, important to examine just what the colonists considered to be illegitimate fertility.[5]

The most common form of illegitimate fertility in the colonies was bastardy, that is, the birth of a child to an unmarried woman. However, a child born in adultery might also be considered a bastard.[6] But, as might be expected, these cases were but rarely discovered. In the seventeenth century the colonists did not always draw a clear distinction between bastardy, adultery, premarital pregnancy and premarital intercourse. All these offences were frequently brought into court under the general term of fornication. By the eighteenth century the differences were recognized and the courts became almost exclusively concerned with bastardy, leaving the other offences to the churches.

The nature of colonial American society raised at least two other issues about legitimate or illegitimate birth. The first of these is concerned with marriage patterns. Although the various colonies tried to institute formal marriage procedures, the settlers were not always willing or able to abide by the rules. For example, Rhode Island in 1647 passed a law requiring marriage to be performed by banns, with the approval of parents and at least one magistrate. Unless this procedure were followed the children of a union were to be considered illegitimate. In 1665 the colony felt it necessary to enforce this law, but at the same time recognized any common law marriages which had occurred before 1665 as valid. By 1698 the system had still to be perfected. In that year the colony decided to recognize as valid all marriages for which banns had been posted, but which had not been registered with a magistrate. This was done to prevent unscrupulous Rhode Islanders from seizing the property of children who had been declared illegitimate on the ground that their parents had not followed the marriage laws absolutely. The problem was finally resolved in 1733 by expanding the ways by which a marriage might take place.[7] The question of what constituted a legal

5. Although I have adopted no one particular conceptual framework, I have found the following works helpful in gaining an understanding of the social context of human sexual behaviour: Jessie Bernard, *The sex game: communication between the sexes* (1972); Kingsley Davis, 'Illegitimacy and the social structure' (1939), pp. 215–33; Kingsley Davis, 'Sexual Behavior' (1966), pp. 322–72; C. S. Ford and F. A. Beach, *Patterns of sexual behavior* (1951); Margaret Mead, 'Cultural determinants of sexual behavior' (1961), pp. 1433–79; Ira L. Reiss, *The social context of premarital sexual permissiveness* (1967). In addition, the special issues of the *Journal of Social Issues* 22 (1966), no. 2, and the *Annals of the American Academy of Political and Social Science* 376 (1968), dealing with sex in contemporary America, are helpful.

6. L. De Valinger, Jr (ed.), *Court records of Kent County, Delaware, 1680–1705* (1959), pp. 329–30.

7. J. R. Bartlett (ed.), *Records of the colony of Rhode Island and Providence plantations in New England* (1856–65) I, p. 187; II, pp. 102–5; III, p. 361; IV, pp. 395, 490.

marriage also perplexed the residents of colonies such as New York, Pennsylvania, Virginia and North Carolina.[8] Although we cannot be certain, the evidence suggests that the colonists took a fairly lenient view of who was married. Couples whose unions were lasting and who caused no problems for others seldom found themselves on trial for bastardy, even though the legality of their marriage might technically be questioned.

The fact that, by 1776, about 20 per cent of all Americans were black slaves raised other issues about legitimate fertility. We will return to this matter later, but two points must be noted here. First, although few slaves ever went through the legal requirements for a marriage, no white ever seems to have worried about whether or not black children were bastards. The reason for this is obvious: the only social condition that mattered was that the children of slaves were also slaves. The other point is that, in the opinion of many colonists, an inter-racial child was by definition illegitimate. Marriage between a white and a black was prohibited and their children were considered 'Spurious and Mixt Issue', and 'abominable mixtures'.[9]

Thus, the records that exist for colonial America on illegitimate fertility tend to focus on births to white women who were not living with a white man in some sort of ongoing, stable relationship. Although there is reason to believe that many other whites, and virtually all blacks who were parents could have been tried for bastardy, they seldom, if ever, were.

The problem of defining prenuptial pregnancy is much simpler. Obviously, this involves a pregnancy followed by a wedding and then a birth. Less clear, however, is how to measure this. At minimum one can take those first births occurring less than seven months after the wedding. However, some births which occurred within eight and nine months after the wedding must have been conceived before marriage, while a number of women presumably miscarried after they were married. In addition, some colonists seem to have accepted, if not approved, the custom of assuming that sexual privileges began with the promise to marry and not with the wedding itself.[10] Thus, to the extent that the colonists considered nuptials to begin with the engagement rather than with the wedding, counting the number of first births within seven months of the wedding as prenuptially conceived may do injustice to the colonial standards of morality.

There are two major groups of sources for the study of illegitimacy and bridal pregnancy in colonial America: legal documents and church records. Each of these groups can be divided into two categories. Legal documents include law codes and court records; church records consist of lists of births, marriages and deaths which have become familiar tools of demographic historians, and of documents of church discipline. It is important to note here just what we can and cannot learn from each type of record.

8. New York Historical Society, *Collections* II, (1811), pp. 361–4; Jack D. Marietta, 'Ecclesiastical discipline in the Society of Friends, 1682–1776' (1968), pp. 23–30; E. B. O'Callaghan (ed.), *Documents relative to the colonial history of the State of New York* III (1853), p. 253; John E. Semonche, 'Common law marriage in North Carolina: a study in legal history' (1965), pp. 320–49; W. W. Hening (ed.), *The statutes at large being a collection of all the laws of Virginia (1619–1792)* (1809–23) II, p. 51.

9. Bruce (1896) II, pp. 109–13; *The acts and resolves, public and private of the province of the Massachusetts Bay* (1869–1922) I, p. 578.

10. Many women defended themselves in court against charges of bastardy on the ground that they had believed a promise of marriage. For example, see Berthold Fernow (ed.), *The records of New Amsterdam from 1653 to 1674* (1897) III, pp. 190, 197, 251, 370, 377; IV, p. 104. See Smith and Hindus (1975) for an attempt to assess how common this custom was.

The strengths and weaknesses of the legal codes are perhaps most obvious. On the one hand they indicate those forms of sexual behaviour which the colonists felt ought to be limited, and note the penalties which were to be applied in each case. On the other hand, the codes offer no help in determining whether the norms defined in them were actually enforced. It is important to examine the legal codes of each and every colony if we are to understand the diversity of treatment of bastardy or premarital pregnancy. However, before discussing the legal codes in detail, we must consider the quantitative data.

Court records are much more helpful sources for determining how frequently colonists were actually punished for bastardy and premarital pregnancy. Many such documents deal with cases of illegitimate sexual behaviour and these can easily be counted and categorized.[11] Nonetheless, caution must be exercised in the use of these documents. First of all, there is no way of telling what proportion of sexual offenders were caught and brought to trial. Indeed, the records suggest considerable variation from colony to colony. For example, in York County, Maine, between 1711 and 1718, and in Prince Georges County, Maryland, between 1697 and 1699 the numbers of persons brought to trial for bastardy were 11 and 12, respectively. On the other hand, the number of persons tried for fornication (almost exclusively premarital pregnancy) amounted to 62 in Maine but only *one* in Maryland (Allen, 1964; Smith and Crowl, 1964). In New England, punishment of premarital fornication by the courts which had been common in the seventeenth century declined over time until it had almost disappeared by 1750 (Parker, 1932, pp. 442–3).

Unless the court records are read with caution, they can be very misleading as to the extent of bastardy and bridal pregnancy in the colonies. In Virginia in the 1630s, the records of one county court note eleven cases dealing with sexual misbehaviour. On closer examination, however, five of those cases prove to be slanders (the slanderer was punished severely), while four involved premarital intercourse, and there was one case each of bastardy and what appears to be a common law marriage (Ames, 1954). The York County, Maine, records similarly give an impression of much more sexual activity outside marriage than there actually was. For any one case an indictment, postponement and trial might appear in the record. Often the indictments and trials of the man and woman involved occurred at different times, even if the couple were married. And finally, at least some of the accused were found innocent. Thus, while 73 persons were actually indicted and brought to trial in York County, there were only 43 cases in which bastardy or fornication was judged to have occurred (Allen, 1964). In contrast to Virginia and Maine, New York colonial records probably understate the extent of bastardy and premarital pregnancy. The evidence suggests that New Yorkers often ignored the opportunity to prosecute pregnant brides and let the justices of the peace deal with bastardy out of court. The result was that, in the eighteenth century, most New York courts were dealing only with appeals to the decisions of the justices of the peace (Goebel and Naughton, 1944, pp. 102–5, 264–71).

11. Most of the studies listed in notes 2 and 3 made extensive use of court records. In addition, I have personally examined the following court records: L. de Valinger (ed.), *Kent County, Delaware*; Neal W. Allen, Jr (ed.), *Province and court records of Maine, V, York County, Maine, 1711–1718* (1964); Susie M. Ames (ed.), *County court records of Accomack-Northampton, Virginia, 1632–1640* (1954); J. H. Smith and P. A. Crowl (eds), *Court records of Prince Georges County, Maryland, 1696–1699* (1964).

Supplementary to the records produced by the state are church documents, the most important of which record disciplinary action taken against wayward members. Such lists can be used not only to count the frequency of a given offence, but also to determine why that particular action was considered inappropriate by the church. But these documents too are limited in their use. Since efforts to establish state churches in the colonies were generally ineffective, the records of any one church cannot be considered to cover the entire population of a given community. (The only exceptions might be in seventeenth-century New England. But there civil authorities dealt with sexual misbehaviour while the churches were still strong.) Another difficulty is the fact that churches in the various colonies seem to have experienced ebbs and flows of moral concern, in part stimulated by shifting patterns of civil enforcement, but also influenced by reform movements within the religious bodies themselves.[12] In addition, church records are helpful in studying behaviour which was considered sinful (fornication), but offer little information on acts which were illegal (bastardy).

Finally, at least some information regarding illegitimacy and bridal pregnancy is available in the lists of births, marriages and deaths which were kept by many colonial churches, and which were supplemented by civil lists in parts of New England. This is obtained quite simply by comparing birth dates of children with the marriage dates of their parents. However, it is important to keep in mind that birth records of illegitimate or 'early' children might have been left out of such lists since the actions we are interested in studying often may have resulted in temporary or permanent excommunication (or disownment as the Friends called it). Thus, variations in the incidence of sexual misbehaviour may reflect real changes, or they may be the result of changes in the rigour of discipline associated with a particular offence.

Because of the shortcomings inherent in the material it would seem best to regard the available data as establishing minimum levels. Unfortunately, it is impossible to determine, at present, how far below the real levels these minimum indices of bastardy and prenuptial pregnancy fall. The evidence for premarital pregnancy is fuller and probably more accurate. Daniel Scott Smith and Michael Hindus (1975) have summed up most of what we know about bridal pregnancy in the colonial period. The most important point to emerge from this study is the fact that the proportion of brides in the colonies who were pregnant at the time of their marriage rose steadily throughout the entire colonial period. Before 1680, there data show only 3.3 per cent of all brides had children within six months of their wedding. Between 1761 and 1800, the proportion of pregnant brides had risen to 16.7 per cent. For brides whose first children arrived within nine months of marriage, the corresponding change was from 8.1 per cent to 33.0 per cent. Although the amount of premarital pregnancy seems to have varied considerably from one community to another, the trend in all parts of the colonies was the same. It is important to note that Smith and Hindus offer convincing evidence that the increased tendency for brides to be pregnant at the time of their marriage was real, and not the result of some change in definition or record-keeping.

At first glance my own study of middle colony Quaker families seems at odds with the Smith and Hindus results. Of 271 Quaker brides whose marriages and childbearing occurred mostly in the eighteenth and early nineteenth centuries,

12. Parkes (1930), pp. 134–5; Oberholzer (1956), p. 130; Marietta (1968), pp. 136–56. Moral reform occasionally had an impact on civil records, Scott (1930), p. 262.

only 3.7 per cent had a child within seven months of marrying, and 11.1 per cent had a baby less than nine months after their marriage. This may be explained by the fact that these Quakers seem to have been among the first Americans to practise deliberate family limitation, and that low fertility within marriage is often associated with low incidences of bridal pregnancy and bastardy.[13] In addition, Smith and Hindus observed that close ties with a religious group tended to reduce the probability of the bride pregnant at the time of her marriage.

Unfortunately, the evidence on illegitimacy is far less complete. But what there is suggests that, while bastardy was not very common in the colonies, it, too, tended to increase throughout the seventeenth and eighteenth centuries. The same Quaker families we have just considered fit into this pattern. Out of a total of 1,542 recorded births, only six occurred before the parents were wed, which gives a ratio of only 3.9 illegitimate births per thousand live births. Interestingly, these all occurred after 1780. If the number of illegitimate births is compared to all live Quaker births after 1780, then the ratio of illegitimate births jumps to 9.7 per thousand. It is tempting to view this change as the result of a relaxation in attitude towards illegitimacy on the part of the Quakers. But Marietta (1968, pp. 136–7) has shown that the Friends became stricter rather than easier in enforcing discipline after 1750.

Evidence from elsewhere in the colonies is limited, but it tends to support the conclusions reached with regard to the Quakers. In Middlesex County, Massachusetts, there were 129 *single* women presented to the courts for fornication between 1761 and 1770. Assuming that each of these women only ended up in court if she had a child, there would have been about 10 illegitimate births per thousand live births if, as is also assumed, the 33,700 residents of Middlesex County had the relatively low birth rate of 40 per thousand.[14] Similarly, evidence collected by Parkes suggests that only 70–95 cases of bastardy a year occurred in ten of the fourteen counties in Connecticut and Massachusetts in the 1730s. If we assume that the population of these counties accounted for the same proportion of the total population of the colonies as they did in the 1760s, and if we further assume that the population had doubled in about thirty years then, if the birth rate were no more than 40 per thousand, there would have been only 13–18 bastards born out of every thousand live births. Here, as among the Quakers, bastardy seems to have increased toward the end of the eighteenth century (Parker, 1932, pp. 442–3). Using the same conservative figure for the birth rate, the number of bastardy cases in York County, Virginia, between 1645 and 1731 would suggest a ratio of illegitimate to all live births which was very close to that of Massachusetts and Connecticut in the 1730s (Scott, 1930, p. 281, records 73 cases of bastardy in 86 years). In Prince Georges County, Maryland, a comparable estimate suggests about 26 bastards were born for every thousand live births between 1696 and 1699; but in the Dutch church in Albany, New York, only one of the over one thousand births registered between 1693 and 1707 was clearly a bastard.[15]

Two conclusions may be drawn from this quantitative evidence. The first is that illegitimacy, whatever its general social consequence may have been, did not have a profound demographic impact. This is suggested not only by the evidence

13. Robert V. Wells, 'Family size and fertility and control in eighteenth-century America' (1971), pp. 73–82; Peter Laslett and Karla Oosterveen, 'Long-term trends in bastardy in England' (1973), p. 256.
14. George E. Howard, *A History of Matrimonial Institutions* II (1904), p. 193.
15. Smith and Crowl (1964); Joel Munsell, *The annals of Albany* III (1852), pp. 61–113.

presented here, but also by the fact that the level of childbearing within colonial marriages was so high as to account for almost the whole birth rate.[16] However, we should remember that many colonial 'marriages' could have been considered invalid and that the children could have been recorded as bastards. The second conclusion is that both premarital pregnancy and illegitimacy seem to have become more common in the eighteenth century than they were in the seventeenth, although it is impossible to measure the increase.

In the present state of our knowledge the most convincing explanation of this change is that the ability and, possibly the desire of colonial parents to control the sexual behaviour of their children declined in the eighteenth century. Smith and Hindus (1975) have attributed at least part of the increase in bridal pregnancy to such a change. It is tempting to associate the decline in parental control with increased geographic mobility. This may have worked in several ways. First, as both Philip Greven (1970) and Kenneth Lockridge (1970) have shown, the eighteenth century saw a greater tendency for children to leave home, thus removing themselves from close supervision. The Quaker families which have been studied also showed increased mobility among children at the very time that illegitimacy was increasing. Greater mobility, rising sexual misbehaviour, and decreased parental authority may well have been interconnected.

Two suggestions may be offered as to how increased mobility may have produced more illegitimacy and bridal pregnancy. First, in the seventeenth century many colonial communities were isolated villages settled by few families. Since most colonies adopted the strict standards of the Church of England regarding incest, this would have limited the number of available marriage partners. But as mobility increased and people moved in and out of towns and villages, the numbers of prospective partners would have increased significantly, as would the problems of parental control. The second point is closely related. Sexual customs are culturally determined and may involve subtle nuances of expression (see n. 5 above). Thus, as mobility increased, so too would the chance of two people meeting who did not fully understand the courtship customs one of the other. In such a situation there was a greater possibility of accidentally exceeding social limits. It is interesting that many Quakers attributed the increase in sexual misconduct among eighteenth-century Friends to greater contact with outsiders; confusion over the purpose of 'bundling' in New England may have led to unintended pregnancies, especially as outsiders began to come into that region.[17]

We must now examine the role illegitimacy and bridal pregnancy played in colonial society. The most important point to note is that in the course of two centuries the Americans changed their view of bastardy and bridal pregnancy. In the early days their dominant concern was the punishment of sin and the protection of the family. Later the economic implications of the problem became more important. Thus the colonists first adopted the practices of the English ecclesiastical courts and only later instituted parts of Elizabethan Poor Law. This change can be traced in the law codes of most colonies, but Connecticut, New York and Virginia will be considered in detail.

In Connecticut, legislation was passed before 1650 which established that the sin of fornication, but not any results of that sin, should be punished. This aimed

16. Wells (1971) pp. 81–2; Donald Bogue, *Principles of Demography* (1969), p. 662.
17. Marietta (1968), pp. 137–42; Henry R. Styles, *Bundling: its origin, progress and decline in America* (1871).

at ensuring not only the purity of the colony, but also its stability. Since the residents of Connecticut felt that 'the prosperity and well-being of Commonwealths doth much depend upon the well government and ordering of particular families', they took steps to ensure that fornicators either married if they could, or were severely punished if one or more of the participants was already wed.[18] Not until 1673 was there legislation which dealt with bastardy as a separate offence. Then it was treated as an economic matter with the prime concern financial support for the child.[19] The eighteenth century saw a continued preoccupation with bastardy in the laws while penalties for fornication were steadily reduced.[20]

After the English conquest of New York in 1664, the first laws, passed in 1665, linked fornication with such 'abominable sins' as swearing, drunkenness, Sabbath breaking, profaneness, and adultery;[21] but the first law which dealt with the civil offence of bastardy was not passed until 1774, although long before that time the justices of the peace were treating bastardy in accordance with Elizabethan Poor Law (*Colonial laws of New York* V, pp. 689–92; Goebel and Naughton, 1944, pp. 101–5, 264–71). Bastardy in New York, as in Connecticut, was a matter of economic rather than moral concern.

In Virginia also the control of sexual misconduct reflects a concern to eradicate sin. Although the first law dealing directly with fornication was not passed until 1643, the ministers and churchwardens had been instructed by the first meeting of the burgesses in 1619 to 'seeke to presente all ungodly disorders'.[22] Clearly fornication was included in all this ungodliness, for early court records show that the churchwardens were diligent in seeking out that particular 'disorder'.[23] By the late seventeenth century Virginia laws were distinguishing quite clearly between the 'sin' of fornication and the crime of bastardy: the punishments inflicted on fornicators were gradually reduced and those aimed at the parents of bastards were increasingly concerned with ensuring that the economic support of the child would not fall on the parish.[24]

Although governments in the American colonies gradually lost interest in prosecuting sexual sinners so long as the children of sin were financially cared for, the churches remained concerned with the punishment of sin. As prosecutions for fornication decreased in court records so they increased in church records. One particularly interesting church record is that of Plymouth, Massachusetts where fornicators were occasionally pursued by mail for several years after the offence so that the church might maintain its purity. The church felt it had a duty to 'look after church-children that lived elsewhere', who were guilty of 'a scandalous sin' of 'committing folly . . . before marriage'.[25] About the time that the Plymouth

18. *The Code of 1650 of the general court of Connecticut*, pp. 28, 48, 92. For some helpful insights on how bastardy and bridal pregnancy might threaten the family, see Smith and Hindus (1975); and Bernard Farber, *Guardians of virtue: Salem families in 1800* (1972), pp. 58–60.

19. *The laws of Connecticut: 1673* (1865), p. 6.

20. *Connecticut laws, 1715*, p. 7; *Connecticut acts and laws, with charter* (1750), p. 78.

21. *The colonial laws of New York from the Year 1664 to the Revolution* (1894–6) II, pp. 26, 35.

22. Hening, I, pp. 240, 253; Susan M. Kingsbury (ed.), *The records of the Virginia Company of London* III (1933), p. 172.

23. H. R. McIlwaine (ed.), *Minutes of the council and general court of colonial Virgina* (1925), p. 155; Ames (1954), *passim*. The same situation occurred in Massachusetts where a biblically based law passed in 1642 merely codified the practice of the preceding twelve years; see George L. Haskins, *Law and authority in early Massachusetts* (1970), pp. 137, 153, 269.

24. Hening, I, pp. 240, 253, 433, 438, 552; II, pp. 51, 114–15, 167, 168; III, pp. 74, 139–40, 361; VI, pp. 361–70, VIII, pp. 135–6, 374–7. In addition parts of the following works are helpful in tracing out this change: H. R. McIlwaine (ed.), *Journals of the House of Burgesses of Virginia* (1906–15). Cf. Scott (1930), pp. 252–4.

25. *Plymouth church records, 1620–1859* I (1920), pp. 197, 252, 263, 265, 269, 330.

congregation began to track down fornicators, memorials were being sent to the General Assembly of Massachusetts by clergy protesting that 'Incentives to Lewdness' were leading to a decline in purity, which in turn was threatening, 'the errand of our Fathers into this wilderness'. Behaviour such as fornication (or worse), 'a shameful sin, much increasing among us, to the great dishonor of Godde', had to be punished 'to prevent those abominable confusions for which defiled lands vomit out their inhabitants'.[26] The same concern can be found outside Massachusetts. In New Jersey residents worried about the sin of uncleanness, one of the 'heinous transgressions for which God Almighty afflicts a land', while in Quaker Pennsylvania action was urged against fornication and adultery 'for the preservation of virtue, chastity and purity among the inhabitants'.[27] Even the bishop of London, under whose control the Anglican churches in the colonies fell, felt it necessary to complain about the decline of morals in the colonies. In 1727 he urged enforcement of laws against 'enormous Crimes and Vices' such as fornication, swearing and drunkenness. It should be noted that when the Board of Trade forwarded his recommendations the 'enormous Crimes and Vices' had shrunk to mere 'Vices'.[28] During the seventeenth and eighteenth centuries a significant change undoubtedly took place in the colonists' treatment of illegitimacy and bridal pregnancy: from treating both as serious sins the former was ultimately dealt with as a civil problem and the latter as a matter of moderate concern to religious groups, but not to the state.

Virtually all students of colonial America have noted that servants frequently appeared in law codes and court proceedings. As might be expected, however, the records from those colonies in which servants were common pay far more attention to their misbehaviour than do the documents from colonies where servitude was rare. In New England, where servants were relatively rare, the majority of cases appearing in the courts before 1750 were for premarital pregnancy; little mention was made of servants in the law codes of that region.[29] In contrast, the overwhelming majority of cases brought into the southern courts involved servants, and there legislation dealing specifically with the sexual misconduct of servants was common.[30]

At issue, with regard to servants, was first of all the challenge to a master's control which sexual misbehaviour implied. More important, however, from the master's standpoint was the economic loss sustained if a female servant was unable to work for part of her time in bondage. The solution to the problem was simple. A female servant had her time in bondage extended to cover both lost time and whatever embarrassment her master experienced. If the father of a bastard was also a servant, his time was extended to pay for the upkeep of the child. In Virginia, if the father of a bastard was the mother's master, her extra time was served under another master (Hening, II, p. 167). This provision was added to the law when it became clear that some masters were deliberately getting their

26. *Acts and resolves of Massachusetts* VII, p. 537; VIII, pp. 50–2; N.B. Shurtleff (ed.), *Records of the Governor and Company of the Massachusetts Bay in New England* (1853–4) IV, pp. 2, 143.

27. Aaron Leaming and Jacob Spicer, *The grants, concessions and original constitutions of the Province of New Jersey*, (1758), pp. 527–8; *The charters and acts of assembly of the Province of Pennsylvania* (1762), p. 21.

28. William Whitehead, *et al.* (eds), *Documents relating to the colonial history of the State of New Jersey* (1880–1906) V, pp. 159–63.

29. Parkes (1932), p. 442; Allen (1964). For a discussion of servants in the colonies see Abbot E. Smith, *Colonists in bondage* (1947).

30. Scott (1930), p. 281; Semmes (1938), pp. 174–206; Ames (1954), p. li; Smith and Crowl (1964), pp. lvi–lvii; Hening, II, pp. 167–70; *A collection of all the public acts of assembly of the Province of North Carolina: now in force and use* (1752), p. 79; Laws of Maryland at large (1765), chapter 44, section 30.

female servants pregnant to keep them in bondage. At the same time the Virginians were unwilling to let such women go free, because they feared that that would offer incentive to female servants to get pregnant and blame it on the master.

Finally, one important aspect of illegitimacy related to the presence of both whites and blacks in the colonies. Although there is little evidence that miscegenation was ever widely practised, the laws designed to control inter-racial sex were much harsher than the laws dealing with bastardy and fornication among whites.[31] (The white colonists appear not to have been at all concerned that most childbearing among the black slaves would have been considered illegitimate by English standards.) Laws prohibiting inter-racial sex are to be found in colonies which had few slaves, as well as in colonies where slavery was common. The earliest indication of white disapproval of inter-racial sex occurred in 1630 in Virginia when one, Hugh Davis, was soundly whipped 'for abusing himself to the dishonor of God and shame of Christians, by defiling his body in lying with a Negro' (Hening, I, p. 146). In 1662, the punishment given to a white fornicating with a slave was made twice that legally required for fornication between whites (Hening, II, p. 170). Between 1691 and 1741, Virginia, Massachusetts, Maryland, Pennsylvania, and North Carolina, in that order, passed harsh laws, which were strictly enforced to keep whites and black apart sexually.[32]

Although the details varied, these acts all forbade marriage between whites and blacks. The minister presiding over such a union was subject to punishment and the inter-racial fornicators were harshly dealt with: double fines or whippings were ordered, servitude and banishment might be imposed if free persons were involved. Mulatto bastards were put out to service for thirty years, white bastards for twenty years. The revulsion white colonists felt toward miscegenation is evident from their rhetoric, in which the children 'of such unnatural and inordinate Copulations' were considered at best 'spurious issue' and at worst 'abominable mixtures'. But in fairness to the colonists, we should note that racial prejudice was not universal. Some mulatto bastards were born without unusual penalties being levied on their parents, and by the second half of the eighteenth century there is evidence that some Virginians realized such children should not be punished for the errors of their parents (Allen, 1964, p. 126, Smith and Crowl, 1964, *passim*; Hening, VIII, pp. 135–6). Nevertheless, it is safe to say that racism led most colonists to consider a child born of white and black parents, married or not, as somehow more threatening to society than children born out of wedlock to parents of the same race.

The punishment which an individual received depended in the first place on the time and place in which he or she lived. In Connecticut, for example, individuals living before 1650 were subject to the law against fornication which allowed the court to decide whether marriage, fines, whipping or some combination of these was best suited to the case. By 1715 bastardy had become a distinct offence with regular procedures established to provide support for the child, and a new law on fornication eliminated forced marriage as an option of the court and established a maximum fine of £5, and ten stripes for whippings (*Code of Connecticut*, p. 48; *Connecticut laws*, 1715, p. 7). But in Maryland the punishment for

31. Perhaps the best treatment of interracial sex in early America is Winthrop Jordon, *White over black* (1968), *passim*, but especially pp. 136–78; also J. Blasingame, *The slave community* (1972), pp. 78–94.
32. Hening, III, pp. 86–7; *Acts and resolves of Massachusetts* I, p. 578; *Laws of Maryland*, chapter 44, sections 25–8; *Acts of Pennsylvania*, pp. 110–11; *Acts of North Carolina* pp, 58–9, 69–70.

fornication in 1694 was a fine of £1 or 400 pounds of tobacco. Five years later the courts of that colony were given the option of ordering up to 39 lashes in place of fines. By 1715 the law provided for increased fines or whipping 'till the Blood do appear', unless 39 stripes were inflicted first. By the end of the eighteenth century the trend to harsher punishment had been reversed in Connecticut and the law on fornication was limited to ensuring support for the bastard. The law on bastardy in Maryland underwent a similar evolution. In 1694 the main concern was to ensure that a servant woman having a bastard should name a man who might support the child. By 1715 physical punishments were threatened to force confessions, but by 1749 all whippings were eliminated and the focus was entirely on providing support for the child.[33] In the Quaker colonies of New Jersey and Pennsylvania early, lenient legislation was replaced in the eighteenth century by harsher penalties designed to stamp out sexual misconduct (Leaming and Spicer, pp. 83, 244–5, 284–5; Fitzroy (1936), pp. 242–69).

The treatment of individuals brought before the court for sexual offences differed for men and women: in cases of bastardy the man was made financially responsible for the upkeep of the child and the woman was punished for erring, either by paying a fine, being whipped or, in the case of servants, by having to serve extra time. Court records indicate that these distinctions were observed, though in Maryland there seems to have been far greater diligence in punishing female offenders than males. But in cases of premarital pregnancy men and women were either given identical penalities, or were both allowed to escape punishment (Smith and Crowl, 1964; Allen, 1964). Punishment of sexual offences varied with social status: servants, slaves and free persons received different penalties. And within the free population wealthy and influential individuals involved in bastardy or bridal pregnancy seem often to have received lighter punishments or no punishment at all (Flaherty, 1972, p. 216; Munsell, III, pp. 10, 17; McIlwaine, *Journals* II, pp. 894–5). Finally, an individual was, to some extent, subject to the whim of the judges. Persons found guilty of the same offence at the same session were occasionally given different penalties. Over a period of five years the maximum penalty given for a particular offence by a particular court might be three times the minimum (Allen, 1964; Smith and Crowl, 1964; Ames, 1954; Valinger, 1959). Sometimes unusually stiff penalties were given to persistent offenders or persons having mulatto bastards. But in other cases more unusual circumstances were cited to justify exceptional punishment. At least one Massachusetts resident claimed he had been unfairly treated because the judges were relatives of the woman in the case (*Acts and resolves of Massachusetts* XIV, p. 470). Social utility seems to have been the motive when a Virginia court gave one man the option of providing a ferryboat in place of forty lashes for fornication and bastardy (Ames, 1954, p. 129).

Just as the penalty for bastardy or bridal pregnancy varied, so too did the response of individuals to their punishment. The majority seem to have accepted their fate quietly, taken their punishment, and resumed their place in the community. These people seem to have understood that they had violated social norms and regretted doing so. Most were even willing to undergo the ritual public humiliation by which society kept the boundaries of acceptable behaviour clear

33. Smith and Crowl (1964), p. xlvi; *Laws of Maryland, 1715*, chapter 27; *1749*, chapter 12; *Laws of Maryland made since 1763*, (1787), chapter 13.

and readmitted wayward members.[34] At least one foreign observer, who did not understand what was involved, felt that such public humiliations was a 'barbarity' (quoted in Flaherty, 1972, p. 160). There is little evidence that the majority of the colonists shared this view. Although they might not have considered their punishment a 'barbarity', some colonists refused to accept their fate gracefully. Among the most interesting resisters were those who continually and flagrantly violated social norms.[35] Close examination of both court and church records makes it clear that some individuals appeared regularly for a variety of offences (Allen, 1964; Smith and Crowl, 1964; Ames, 1954; Valinger, 1959; Marietta, 1968, pp. 51–3). Such people seem to have been continually at odds with their neighbours. Others violated social standards with a flair which bordered on contempt. Few were as bold as the couple who engaged in sexual intercourse on Boston Common in 1702, but a number of persons attempted intercourse in public. One Maryland couple was seen with her hand 'in his breeches' and his hand 'in her placket'. The man in this incident had previously told an acquaintance to leave the room in which the three were, because he wanted 'to swive Susan' (Flaherty, 1972, pp. 79–83; Semmes, 1938, pp. 182–3).

Resisters often challenged the judgement of society with regard to themselves even though they may have accepted that bastardy and bridal pregnancy generally needed to be controlled. One of the most obvious acts of resistance was flight, which occasionally involved jail break and posses in hot pursuit, but generally the guilty party simply disappeared quietly (one of the most colourful flights is in Allen, 1964, pp. 156–8). It is impossible to determine the number of persons, both men and women, actually fleeing punishment, but in the eighteenth century several colonies passed laws regulating the movement of persons suspected of bastardy. In 1732 the inhabitants of Purrysburg, South Carolina, found it necessary to request that a formal government be established since, in the absence of civil authority, 'many lewd Women had and did come there to be delivered of their bastard Children.'[36] (We have seen earlier how the Plymouth church in Massachusetts was forced to pursue some of its erring members by mail.) Some offenders brazened it out and resorted to physical violence. One Maine man threatened to bury an axe in the head of the constable who came to arrest him. In Pennsylvania a woman together with her two brothers and a sister, all armed with knives and staves, confronted the constable and a group of women who had been sent to examine her and threatened to 'have their hearts blood' if they did not leave: the accused was suspected of causing the violent death of her bastard child (Allen, 1964, p. 176; Fitzroy, 1936, pp. 267–8). Infanticide may have become common in the eighteenth century, for virtually every colony passed legislation declaring that, unless witnesses would swear to a stillbirth, the mother of a dead bastard would be presumed guilty of murder (see any of the law codes cited above; Parker, 1932, p. 450). Abortion, too must have been attempted on occasion, but the extent of the practice is, at this point, largely unknown.[37]

34. These behaviour patterns are clearest in the church records: see for example, *Plymouth church records, passim*; Marietta (1968); Flaherty (1972), pp. 156–60; Fitzroy (1936), pp. 265–6; 'Diary of Cotton Mather' (1911), p. 177.

35. Erikson (1966), pp. 3–29, discusses the creation of deviant sub-cultures. For some interesting insights into sub-cultures of sexual deviants, see Reiss (1967); Smith and Hindus (1975); and Laslett and Oosterveen (1973), pp. 280–4.

36. *Acts of Pennsylvania*, p. 21; Hening, IV, p. 213; J. H. Easterby (ed.), *The colonial records of South Carolina: the journal of the Commons House of Assembly, September 10 1746–June 13 1747* (1958), p. 57.

37. Semmes (1938), pp. 175–6, 203; R. Sauer, 'Attitudes to abortion in America, 1800–1973' (1974), p. 53.

Legal appeal was the last means used to escape punishment for bastardy or bridal pregnancy. The bases for such appeals were extraordinarily varied, reflecting both the colonists' imagination and the way in which the legal system worked. Women occasionally defended themselves on the ground that the man had promised marriage. There is the interesting case of a law suit, lasting two years, for support of a bastard, which was settled in the woman's favour because she had a written promise that the man would marry her, 'on enjoying her virginity' (Fernow, III, pp. 190, 197; IV, p. 104; for a similar case, see III, pp. 370, 377). More often, however, it was the man who appealed, because the bastardy laws were as concerned in finding someone to pay for the child as in establishing who was the father of the bastard. The Pennsylvania statute of 1705 recognized this when it provided that any man '*legally convicted* to be the *reputed* Father of the Bastard' (my italics) should pay for the upkeep (*Acts of Pennsylvania*, p. 21). As a result miscarriage of justice did occur. Thus, men appealed against their convictions on such grounds as the child was a mulatto, the judges were relatives of the woman, the woman was a whore, and the legal procedures for establishing paternity had not been properly followed.[38] One of the appeals on procedure was quashed when testimony was introduced quoting the guilty party as having admitted 'I f--d her once, but I minded my pullbacks. I sware I did not get it' (Wroth and Zobel, 1965, p. 334). Apparently the judges were dubious about the efficacy of coitus interruptus as a means of birth control. Occasionally appeals were directed towards the mode of punishment rather than its justice. A few men offered to take their bastards into their homes instead of paying support to the mother. If a mother refused such an offer she ran the risk of having her support cut off (Munsell, III, pp. 10, 17).

There remains the question: how were bastards treated in colonial America? Evidence on this subject is scanty, but what there is suggests that, by and large, the colonists were unwilling to punish children for the sins of their parents. In Virginia and Rhode Island, for example, the inability of bastards to inherit property seems to have been more the exception than the rule (O'Callaghan, III, p. 253; Bartlett, I, p. 187; II, pp. 102–5; III, p. 361). The long indentures for mulatto bastards around 1700 were brought into line with indentures for white bastards after 1750 (Hening, VIII, pp. 135–6). Finally, both William Franklin, the last royal governor of New Jersey, and Alexander Hamilton were able to achieve political eminence in the second half of the eighteenth century despite the fact that their parents were not legally married.

In conclusion three points stand out. First, both bastardy and bridal pregnancy appear to have been relatively rare in colonial America, so that control over sexual behaviour must have been fairly strong. Second, colonial America cannot be treated as one whole: variations in attitudes towards and frequency of sexual misbehaviour occurred over time and from one colony to another. Finally, the shift from religious to secular values and the increasing emphasis on black slaves in the colonies profoundly affected the way Americans responded to the problems of illegitimacy and bridal pregnancy in the seventeenth and eighteenth centuries.

38. *Acts and resolves of Massachusetts* XII, p. 283; XIV, p. 470; L. K. Wroth and H. B. Zobel (eds), *Legal papers of John Adams* I (1965), pp. 319–34.

17

The long cycle in American illegitimacy and prenuptial pregnancy

Daniel Scott Smith

The history of American illegitimacy and prenuptial pregnancy intertwines with broader themes in the development of American society.[1] These subjects are an integral part of both demographic and family history, two fields of growing interest to American historians. The level and trend in non-marital conceptions have great relevance for three central topics in the 'new social history': the study of blacks, women and communities. Sex itself, a matter of recurrent popular interest and one historians have recently begun to study, has been the major concern of recent work. Despite the relevance of the subject, the literature on American historical illegitimacy and prenuptial pregnancy remains scarce. With the exception of the past half century, the fundamental quantitative data are scattered and of uncertain quality. Missing too are the careful qualitative micro-studies illuminating the cultural and social contexts of non-marital fertility among the disparate groups composing the American population.

The central purpose of this chapter is therefore simple: to summarize what is currently known and thus to provide a base for future studies. The opening section presents the general interpretation of the long cycle in American and West European non-marital conceptions. The second part reviews the available data and their limitations for periods following and preceding the existence of national estimates. The final section discusses the two most distinctive American patterns: the level and trend in black illegitimacy and the early decline in white non-marital fertility in the first half of the nineteenth century.

1 Non-marital conceptions and the history of sexual behaviour

What must seem striking, particularly to demographers, is the extent to which historians have interpreted the history of illegitimacy and prenuptial pregnancy not as topics in demographic history but as proxy indicators for the history of sexual behaviour. Equally surprising to historians, perhaps, is the separation of the subject from particular historical times and places and its location within the framework of social theories purporting to explain, or describe, the long evolution of Western society from traditional to modern to post-modern.[2]

The non-demographic emphasis of recent historical work can be explained on practical grounds. Since marriage has been the principal and often nearly exclusive context of childbearing in Western societies, the study of illegitimacy and prenuptial pregnancy is marginal from the strictly demographic point of view.

1. In this chapter illegitimacy will refer to birth outside wedlock, prenuptial pregnancy to non-maritally conceived children born after marriage, and non-marital conception or fertility to both illegitimacy and prenuptial pregnancy.
2. Daniel Scott Smith and Michael S. Hindus, 'Premarital pregnancy in America, 1640–1971: an overview and interpretation' (1975), pp. 537–70. Edward Shorter, *The making of the modern family* (1975); and especially his 'Illegitimacy, sexual revolution and social change in Europe, 1750–1900' (1971), pp. 237–72; and his 'Female emancipation, birth control and fertility in European history' (1973), pp. 605–40.

The determinants of nuptiality and marital fertility are obviously more central to the analysis of population growth rates. The inferential step from measured illegitimacy and prenuptial pregnancy to sexual behaviour raises questions about the complex set of variables intervening between coitus and birth. Most important are variations in the level of fecundity, the incidence of abortion, and the use and effectiveness of contraception. At present evidence on the intervening variables is very limited for all but the most recent period in American history; very likely we will never have convincing quantitative data. Nevertheless, it does appear that the major surges in non-marital conceptions, in the eighteenth century and in recent decades, can only be attributed to increases in the proportion of females having sexual intercourse before marriage.[3] The intervening variables of contraception and abortion are doubtless more important in explaining the dampening and decline of non-marital fertility.[4] Sexual history will never be based on hard evidence, such as is available for the history of prices or the history of political parties. Yet the demographic proxies permit the historian to make inferences based on differences in behaviour. This approach seems clearly superior to relying on the pronouncements of ministers, reformers, and government bureaucrats.

There are several reasons why recent historians have adopted a long-run, sociological approach to the history of sex and non-marital conception. Most significant is the fact that sexual behaviour is deeply rooted in psychology and closely related to the institution of the family. Since both psychological and familial changes are relatively gradual compared to other kinds of historical changes, they should be looked at in a long-run perspective. In addition, a growing number of historians are now interested in questions of the long sweep of social history, in the lack of continuity in the history of Western societies, and in that amorphous body of social thought usually labelled 'modernization theory'. Finally, the history of sexual behaviour is in its initial stage: scholarly progress in new fields is stimulated both by the slow accretion of detailed studies and by the development and subsequent qualification and refutation of bold generalizations.

Although based on American and European data respectively, the Smith-Hindus and Shorter versions of the history of sexual behaviour share the same general framework. The two periods of rapid increase in premarital sexual activity are linked to shifts throughout society, from traditional to modern in the first instance, and from modern to post-modern in the second. Both interpretations stress the weakening of social and familial controls during the upsurges. Beyond this broad framework disagreement over fact and interpretation emerges. Part of this divergence is historical: in America prenuptial pregnancy declines after 1800, in Europe the drop comes more than half a century later. More controversial is Shorter's deduction that a new sense of female autonomy, generated by experience in market relationships, led to greater illegitimacy during the first sexual revolution in eighteenth- and nineteenth-century Europe.[5]

At this point there is no satisfactory answer to questions of motivation in the history of sexual behaviour. It seems to me that both Shorter and his critics

3. For a discussion of the basis of this inference, see Daniel Scott Smith, 'The dating of the American sexual revolution: evidence and interpretation' (1973).

4. Kingsley Davis and Judith Blake, 'Social structure and fertility: an analytic approach' (1956), pp. 211–35. Edward Shorter, John Knodel and Etienne van de Walle, 'The decline of non-marital fertility in Europe, 1880–1940' (1971), pp. 375–93.

5. Louise A. Tilly, Joan W. Scott and Miriam Cohen, 'Women's work and European fertility patterns' (1976), pp. 417–76, attack Shorter's lack of evidence and provide an alternative social and economic analysis.

present too rational and narrowly economic interpretations of the propensity to engage in sexual intercourse before marriage. More crucial are the underlying cultural ideas about male and female sexuality. In the early New England religious context, for example, women were viewed with some suspicion as being sexually closer to nature than to humanity. As social and familial controls over sex collapsed in eighteenth-century New England, young women may have been vulnerable to exploitation; they also may not have been passive and instrumental in their sexual behaviour. More definitive conclusions are possible concerning the differential incidence of premarital sex and prenuptial pregnancy. In contrast to the current American pattern, for example, there was much greater variation in prenuptial pregnancy by class and much less variation by female age at marriage in eighteenth-century Hingham, Massachusetts. The shift in these differentials reflects a larger change from a lineal to a conjugal family structure.[6] Although the interpretation of the history of sexual behaviour is surprisingly developed, these theories and speculations depend on a varied body of demographic and other evidence that demands scrutiny and explication.

2 Trends and their measurement

Like all demography, the history of non-marital conception is inescapably quantitative at its core. The incidence, variation over time, and differentials over social and geographic space must be established before historians can be confident about any interpretation. Numbers are thus inevitable but they are potentially deceptive. The numerical base for the history of American prenuptial pregnancy and illegitimacy has serious gaps and limitations. Special characteristics of American society aggravate the normal problems of data reliability. Throughout its history America has lacked either religious uniformity and an active religious bureaucracy or a well organized and inquisitive state. The federal system is merely one illustration of this tradition. Even today humanitarian concerns prevent ten states, including the large ones of California, New York, and Massachusetts, from directly collecting illegitimacy statistics. The reporting of vital events in American history has always had a strong voluntaristic element. Although governments have been concerned with illegitimacy, their interest has been primarily fiscal (tempered by humanitarianism) rather than statistical. The easily counted events in American history tend to be those belonging to people who 'counted' at the time; these are not the people most likely to conceive children out of wedlock.

For these reasons prenuptial pregnancy ratios more precisely chart trends in American non-marital conception than do figures on illegitimacy. These two indicators are, however, positively correlated over time (for a review of evidence on this point, see Smith and Hindus, 1975, note 2, p. 539). Since a sizable fraction of newly married couples migrate before their first child is born, and since nominal linkage of flawed records must necessarily be imperfect, prenuptial pregnancy ratios are to be regarded as indices (for a review of methodological problems see Smith, 'Dating of the American sexual revolution', pp. 323–7). The calculation of illegitimacy ratios, on the other hand, does not depend on the availability of marriage data or on record linkages. Defined as the quotient of illegitimate births divided by all births in a period, the illegitimacy ratios are

6. Smith and Hindus (1975), tables 1, 2, pp. 542–3. See also Daniel Scott Smith, 'Parental power and marriage patterns: an analysis of historical trends in Hingham, Massachusetts' (1973), pp. 419–28.

strongly influenced by both the level of marital fertility and the incidence of marriage in a population. To obtain the more precise illegitimacy rate, the number of illegitimate children must be divided by the number of unmarried women of fecund age. Unfortunately information of the marital status of the American population is scarce before the late nineteenth century.

3 Illegitimacy since 1920

Table 17.1 reports the official estimates of illegitimacy ratios by age and race. Also provided are the revisions of Phillips Cutright, and for 1965 and 1970, the estimates of June Sklar and Beth Berkov. The Cutright figures correct for both overall birth under-registration and the underestimation of the number of unmarried women. Incorporating data from the larger non-reporting states, the Sklar-Berkov calculations include separated women in the group at risk to bear an illegitimate child. Although the estimates differ, the disagreements are small, most important, the trends are not affected by the revisions. Since the three series rest on the same basic data, all would be distorted by the under-reporting or misreporting of illegitimate births. In recent years, at least, concealment of misreporting of legitimacy status does not appear to be a factor of any importance.[7]

Two generalizations leap from table 17.1: change in American illegitimacy has not been linear, and the levels of white and non-white illegitimacy are so different that separate historical analyses are required. Yet the trends in white and non-white illegitimacy are not radically different.

Between 1920 and 1940 illegitimacy rates declined slightly from what was already a low level by comparative standards. During the next two decades the non-white illegitimacy rate surged by 177 per cent before stabilizing. Over the thirty years from 1940 the white rate boomed by 283 per cent. The rate for all races climbed 99 per cent in the 1940s, 53 per cent in the 1950s, and 22 per cent in the 1960s; for whites over the three decades the increases were more constant: 69 per cent, 51 per cent, and 50 per cent. Not until abortion became more widely available did the white rate stabilize and after that declined.[8]

Despite the peaking in the illegitimacy rate, rapidly declining marital fertility and a rising age at marriage produced a major increase in the proportion of babies classified as illegitimate. Between 1965 and 1973 the white and non-white illegitimacy ratios rose 61.4 per cent and 58.2 per cent respectively; at the same time the white rate increased by less than 3 per cent and the non-white rate fell by 14 per cent. By contrast, the overall illegitimacy rate increased 204 per cent between 1940 and 1960 while the ratio climbed by only 39 per cent. These seemingly paradoxical differences underscore the importance of the indicator selected to measure the phenomenon of illegitimacy.

In recent years much of the discussion concerning American illegitimacy has focused on teenagers. Public policy considerations – the relative lack of access of young women to methods of fertility control – explain this emphasis. The

7. Phillips Cutright, 'Illegitimacy in the United States: 1920–1968' (1972), pp. 429–33. Not all scholars agree with the apparent reliability of current illegitimacy data. See the comment by Kingsley Davis, 'The American family in relation to demographic change' (1972), note 25, p. 262. Also James E. Teele and William M. Schmidt, 'Illegitimacy and race: national and local trends' (1970), pp. 127–44, and the discussion of the Teele and Schmidt paper, pp. 145–50.

8. See the interesting analysis comparing states with liberal and conservative abortion laws by June Sklar and Beth Berkov, 'Abortion, illegitimacy and the American birth rate' (1974), pp. 909–15.

Table 17.1: Trends in American illegitimacy, 1920–73

Year	Per 1000 unmarried women aged 15–44 Official	Cutright	Sklar-Berkov	Per 1000 live births Ratio	Per 1000 unmarried women 15–19	20–4	25–9	30–4	35–9	40–4
	A *Total*									
1920	–	8.7	–	29.3 [a]	–	–	–	–	–	–
1930	–	7.8	–	34.7 [a]	–	–	–	–	–	–
1940	7.1	8.0	–	37.9 [b]	7.4	9.5	7.2	5.1	3.4	1.2
1950	14.1	14.5	–	39.8 [b]	12.6	21.3	19.9	13.3	7.2	2.0
1960	21.6	21.7	–	52.7 [b]	15.3	39.7	45.1	27.8	14.1	3.6
1965	23.5	23.4	22.2	77.4 [b]	16.7	39.9	49.3	37.5	17.4	4.5
1970	26.4	–	25.7	106.9 [b]	22.4	38.4	37.0	27.1	13.3	3.6
1973	24.5	–	–	129.8 [b]	22.9	31.8	30.0	20.5	10.8	3.0
	B *White*									
1920	–	4.4	–	15.0 [a]	–	–	–	–	–	–
1930	–	4.3	–	18.6 [a]	–	–	–	–	–	–
1940	3.6	3.9	–	19.5 [b]	3.3	5.7	4.0	2.5	1.7	0.7
1950	6.1	6.1	–	17.5 [b]	5.1	10.0	8.7	5.9	3.2	0.9
1960	9.2	9.3	–	22.9 [b]	6.6	18.2	18.2	10.8	3.9 [c]	
1965	11.6	11.5	11.7	39.6 [b]	7.9	22.1	24.3	16.6	4.9 [c]	
1970	13.8	–	14.5	56.6 [b]	10.9	22.5	21.1	14.2	4.4 [c]	
1973	11.9	–	–	63.9 [b]	10.7	15.6	16.1	10.7	5.9	1.7
	C *Non-white*									
1920	–	41.5	–	125.0 [a]	–	–	–	–	–	–
1930	–	31.6	–	141.1 [a]	–	–	–	–	–	–
1940	35.6	39.1	–	168.3 [b]	42.5	46.1	32.5	23.4	13.2	5.0
1950	71.2	68.9	–	179.6 [b]	68.5	105.4	94.2	63.5	31.3	8.7
1960	98.3	90.2	–	215.8 [b]	76.5	166.5	171.8	104.0	35.6 [c]	
1965	97.6	94.4	72.3	263.2 [b]	75.8	152.6	164.7	137.8	39.0 [c]	
1970	89.9	–	75.1	349.3 [b]	90.8	121.0	93.8	69.8	21.7 [c]	
1973	84.2	–	–	416.9 [b]	89.7	108.9	82.4	56.4	26.2	7.2
	Negro only									
1970	95.5	–	–	375.8	96.9	131.5	100.9	71.8	21.7 [c]	
1973	89.5	–	–	457.5	96.0	117.2	86.0	58.1	27.4	7.7

[a] Cutright, 'Illegitimacy in the United States' (1972), table 1, p. 383.
[b] Official estimates.
[c] Age-group 35–44.

Source: Official estimates from US National Center for Health Statistics (1968), tables B, D, pp. 4, 8; (1974), table 11, p. 11; (1975), table 11, p. 11. Cutright, 'Illegitimacy in the United States' (1972), tables 1, 2, pp. 383, 384. Sklar and Berkov 'Abortion, illegitimacy, and the American birth rate' (1974), table 1, p. 910.

paradoxical but important difference between the illegitimacy rate and ratio clarifies the problem. While the rate for 15–19-year-old females has been lower than for women between 20 and 35, and while the increases in teenage illegitimacy rates have been less than for older women, illegitimacy ratios for teenagers are very much higher than for older women (see table 17.2). Slightly less than half of all illegitimate babies born in 1940 (47.6 per cent) and slightly more than half in 1973 (53.0 per cent) were teenage mothers. As a social welfare problem teenage illegitimacy looms large in America. Furthermore, the share of the 15–19-year-old group in the total illegitimate fertility rate is relatively high in the American population. For 1940, 1950, and 1960 the average share of the total rate of the 15–19-year-old group was 17 per cent. In each of the three years a hypothetical single woman would have 0.19, 0.39 and 0.72 children respectively between her fifteenth and forty-fifth birthdays. In two culturally similar countries with generally parallel fertility histories, the teenage shares were 12.5 per cent (Canada) and 7.5 per cent (Australia).[9]

Table 17.2: Change in official age-specific illegitimacy ratios and rates, 1940–73

Age group	Illegitimacy ratios per 1000 births 1940	1973	Absolute change	Percent change	Illegitimacy rate per 1000 unmarried females Rate 1973	Percent change in rate 1940–73
−15	644.8	847.5	202.7	31.4	–	–
15–19	134.7	339.2	204.5	151.8	22.9	209.4
20–4	36.8	108.2	71.4	194.0	31.8	234.7
25–9	16.3	48.5	32.2	197.5	30.0	316.7
30–4	13.0	50.0	37.0	284.6	20.5	302.0
35–9	14.9	64.7	49.8	334.2	10.8	217.6
40–4	15.0	76.9	61.9	412.7	3.0	150.0
15–44	37.9	129.8	91.9	242.5	24.5	245.1

Source: See table 17.1.

4 Prenuptial pregnancy since 1900

A government publication allows us to bring data on prenuptial and illegitimate births of ever-married women through the marriage cohort of the latter half of the 1960s. Twice before, in August 1959 and June 1965, the Current Population Survey of the Bureau of the Census asked large national samples of ever-married women to report their month and year of first marriage and first birth. What is most important about table 17.3 is the consistency between the prenuptial pregnancy rates and the illegitimacy rates given in table 17.1.

Little change in white prenuptial pregnancy is evident before the end of the Second World War. After an especially sharp increase in the 1955–64 decade, the rate has levelled off for the marriage cohort of the late 1960s. Although the prenuptial pregnancy rates for non-whites or negroes are substantially higher, the patterns over time are similar.

Can survey data on prenuptial conception be trusted? For the period after 1960 the CPS figure is close to estimates obtained by record linkage. A computer linkage of first birth records to first marriages for Lake County (Gary), Indiana, for 1962–7 produced estimates that 23.7 per cent and 54.6 per cent of white and negro legitimate first births were premaritally conceived.[10] Some 20.4 per cent of brides marrying before thirty in Whatcom County (Bellingham), Washington, in 1968 were pregnant at marriage.[11] Tracing Massachusetts birth records of 1966–8

9. Although the total illegitimate fertility rate lacks realism since most mothers of illegitimate children later marry, it does remove the effect of age-distribution on the summary rate. For Canadian trends of data, see Jacques Henripin, *Trends and factors of fertility in Canada*, (1972), table 11.7, p. 329. The Australian data are from K. G. Basavarajappa, 'Premarital pregnancies and ex-nuptial births in Australia, 1911–1966' (1968), table B, p. 144.
10. Alan M. Sear, 'Premarital pregnancy: a record linkage analysis' (1973), table 4, p. 150.
11. Warner S. Tillack, Carl W. Tyler. Rick Paguette, and Phillip H. Jones, 'A study of premarital pregnancy' (1972), table 1, p. 677.

Table 17.3: Current population survey estimates of premaritally conceived first births per thousand first marriages, 1900–1909 to 1965–9

	NEGROES OR NON-WHITES			WHITES				
	1971 survey Negroes		1959 survey Non-whites	1971 survey		1965 survey		1959 survey
First marriage cohort	Before marriage	Within 8 months	Within 8 months	Before marriage	Within 8 months	Before marriage	Within 8 months	Within 8 months
1965–9	315	538	–	49	203	–	–	–
1960–4	322	529	–	42	195	36	205	–
1955–9	–	–	–	34	160	37	183	160
1950–9	258	443	413	–	–	–	–	–
1950–4	–	–	–	31	112	25	130	119
1945–9	–	–	–	31	99	23	108	103
1940–9	190	314	294	–	–	–	–	–
1940–4	–	–	–	27	83	22	87	80
1935–9	–	–	–	25	93	–	–	86
1930–9	141	238	255	–	–	–	–	–
1930–4	–	–	–	26	90	–	–	90
1925–9	–	–	–	–	–	–	–	81
1920–9	–	–	218	–	–	–	–	–
1920–4	–	–	–	–	–	–	–	83
1910–19	–	–	207	–	–	–	–	89
1900–1909	–	–	118	–	–	–	–	74

Source: 1971: US Bureau of the Census (1974). table 17, p. 53. 1965: US Bureau of the Census (1969), tables 17, 18, pp. 39–41. 1959: US Bureau of the Census (1961), table 16, p. 38.

back to marriage records in the state and neighbouring states generated an estimate that 24.0 per cent of white and 38.7 per cent of non-white legitimate first births were conceived before marriage.[12] The National Natality Survey of a sample of mothers of 1964–6 births produced estimates that 19.5 per cent and 41.6 per cent of white and non-white first births came within eight months of marriage.[13] Although the samples, methods, and coverage are not identical, the general agreement of these studies with the CPS figure is encouraging.[14]

Local record linkage studies for periods before 1940 produce consistently higher figures than recorded in the retrospective CPS surveys. In an earlier essay I suggested the possibility that some of the older women surveyed in 1959 may have covered up the fact of a pregnancy before marriage (Smith, 'Dating of the American sexual revolution', table 3 and pp. 324–7). There is, however, no consistent shift in table 17.3 towards more 'conservative' responses for the same marriage cohorts sampled in both 1959 and 1971. An increased use of contraceptives in premarital relations may have produced a decline in prenuptial pregnancy during the first four decades of the twentieth century. Ryder has estimated indirectly that the interval between marriage and first birth increased markedly

12. Elizabeth Murphy Whelan, 'Illegitimate and premaritally conceived first births in Massachusetts, 1966–68' (1972), table 6, p. 18.

13. US National Center for Health Statistics, 'Interval between first marriage and legitimate first birth, United States, 1964–66' (1970), supplement, table 2, p. 2.

14. The only qualitatively different estimate of prenuptial pregnancy, based on the 1960 census figure of births within three calendar quarters of marriage, overstates the level by incorporating early post-marital conceptions. Davis (1972), table 6, p. 252.

between the birth cohort of *c*.1896–1900 and *c*.1921–5.[15] International comparison also points to declining non-marital fertility during the early decades of the twentieth century.[16] Until more local record linkage studies are available for the first four decades of this century, we cannot be very certain about the trend or level. It does appear that these years were not ones of marked change.

A comparative perspective is instructive for understanding the post-war period as well. During the 1950s the English speaking populations, in order, New Zealand, United States, Australia, England and Wales and Scotland, led a group of 23 developed nations in increases in illegitimacy rates. Gains in illegitimacy during the 1950s were positively correlated with lower rates of economic growth and, more directly, with increases in marital fertility and decreases in the age at marriage.[17]

This pattern tempts one to generalize that increases in marriage and general fertility rates might typically be associated with rising non-marital fertility. Legitimate and illegitimate fertility are, after all, similar phenomena, and each should react to changes which alter the environment and conditions for childbearing. This generalization is consistent with the absence of psychological peculiarities of unwed mothers, and with what might be labelled a 'social realism' in contrast to a 'social problems' approach to illegitimacy.

General patterns, however, are not rules, at least for changes in the short run. During the 1960s the American economy boomed, marital fertility fell, and the age at marriage rose. White illegitimate fertility rates continued to climb. Despite similarities, illegitimate fertility does differ to some extent in origins from legitimate childbearing. It is part of the history of sexual behaviour as well as of demographic history. During the 1960s premarital sexual experience probably increased more rapidly than in any previous decade in American history (Smith, 'Dating the American sexual revolution', pp. 331–2). The general congruence of the post-war experience of English speaking nations also cannot be extended into the 1960s and 1970s. The Australian illegitimacy rate, for example, jumped 36 per cent (from 21.0 to 28.6), while rates in the United States were finally stabilizing.[18] Not just an aspect of the histories of fertility and sexual behaviour, the history of illegitimacy is also illustrative of history generally, i.e., perversely dependent on the peculiarities of specific time and place.

5 Prenuptial pregnancy before 1920

The themes of general congruence with international patterns and specific American divergence also mark the course of non-marital fertility in the era before national estimates. The data problem for this earlier period is unfortunately not one of reconciling conflicting trends and reporting on possible distortions in the estimates. The most difficult problem is finding any data on illegitimacy valid enough to discuss. Since prenuptial pregnancy and illegitimacy trends are positively correlated, I focused on the former in my earlier work; the data from the Smith-Hindus article appear in table 17.4.

Before 1800 the trend is clear and roughly consistent with the experience of early modern England and France. Very low ratios marked mid-

15. Norman B. Ryder, 'The emergence of a modern fertility pattern: United States, 1911–66' (1969), p. 121.
16. Shorter, Knodel and van de Walle (1971); Shirley F. Hartley, 'The amazing rise of illegitimacy in Great Britain' (1966), pp. 533–44.
17. Phillips Cutright, 'Economic events and illegitimacy in developed countries' (1971), pp. 33–53.
18. *Official yearbook of Australia*, no. 59 (1973), p. 171.

Table 17.4: White American premarital pregnancy ratios from local record-linkage studies

Marriage period	No. of marriages[a]	Percent of first births born within: 6 months of marriage	8½ months of marriage	9 months of marriage
–1680	663	3.3	6.8	8.1
1681–1720	1156	6.7	14.1	12.1[a]
1721–60	1442	9.9	21.2	22.5
1761–1800	1097	16.7	27.2	33.0
1801–40	616	10.3	17.7	23.7
1841–80	572	5.8	9.6	12.6
1881–1910	119	15.1	23.3	24.4

[a] Number of marriages based on samples traced to or reporting on nine-month interval from marriage. The anomalous nine-month figure for 1681–1720 comes from a sample with a low ratio (Salem, Mass.) reporting at this interval but not for the 6 and 8½ month intervals.

Source: Smith and Hindus (1975), appendix I (summary), p. 561.

seventeenth-century New England, but prenuptial pregnancy increased towards the end of the century and accelerated during the second quarter of the eighteenth century. Following a decline from 1800 to the Civil War, prenuptial pregnancy ratios rose until the early years of the twentieth century.

How representative and reliable are the data in table 17.4? Although the Smith-Hindus series is designated as representative of the experience of white Americans, it is heavily biased toward rural New England population samples. One town, Hingham, Massachusetts, supplies over a third of the cases in table 17.4. New England is the most religious, homogeneous, stable, and documented region in early American history. Seventeenth-century Chesapeake society, on the other hand, was seriously disrupted by very high mortality and immigration. And in late seventeenth-century Somerset County, Maryland, some 18 per cent and 27 per cent of first children arrived within six and eight and a half months of marriage respectively.[19] Despite this higher rate in the seventeenth century, the eighteenth-century increase in New England ratios is paralleled by increases in two Virginia parishes and in Middle Colony Dutch reformed churches.

While the eighteenth-century increase seems firmly established, the relevant data for the nineteenth century are both more scattered and more deficient. During the first four decades of the nineteenth century, town vital registration deteriorated in New England. By the early 1840s over two thirds of all births in Massachusetts went unrecorded by the town.[20] The increased mobility of the population also results in a smaller proportion of marriages being traceable to a first birth. Unfortunately from the point of view of testing Shorter's linkage of capitalism and proletarianization to increased premarital sexual activity, we have no data at present for a large urban-industrial area in the nineteenth century. A very small and questionable sample for one industrial town (Willimantic, Connnecticut) provides the highest rates for any nineteenth-century American sample. Clearly more record linkage studies are needed. Yet we can have some confidence in a substantial decline in prenuptial pregnancy in the nineteenth

19. Russell R. Menard, 'The demography of Somerset County, Maryland: a preliminary report' (1975), table 17. I wish to thank Professor Menard for allowing me to cite his paper. For demographic conditions in the Chesapeake, see especially Lorena Walsh and Russell Menard, 'Death in the Chesapeake: two life tables for men in early colonial Maryland' (1974), pp. 211–27.

20. Robert Gutman, 'The birth statistics of Massachusetts during the nineteenth century' (1956), pp. 69–94.

century. When registration in Massachusetts improved (82 per cent complete in 1850, 95 per cent complete by 1880), the prenuptial pregnancy ratios are substantially below the eighteenth-century peaks.

Although the cultural diversity introduced by the waves of immigration in the nineteenth century perhaps makes comparison with the eighteenth century somewhat beside the point, the Smith-Hindus series does have the advantage of being heavily weighted with Protestant populations having colonial ancestry. It is likely that the Yankee population of New England and elsewhere led in the reduction of prenuptial pregnancy just as it did in general fertility. A commentator on an 1827 bundling conviction in the *Bloomington* (Indiana) *Gazette* noted, for example, that 'it is hoped this decision will put a stop to this indecent manner of sparking so common among youngsters of Ohio, Pennsylvania and Carolina.'[21] The attempts of nineteenth-century Yankees to force their pietistic values and behaviour on more traditional ethnocultural groups powerfully shaped the structure of political conflict in the northern states.[22]

The increases in prenuptial pregnancy in the second half of the nineteenth century and early twentieth century (evident in every sample in the Smith-Hindus series: Hingham, and Lexington, Mass., Willimantic, Conn., and Washentaw County, Michigan), may be attributable, at least in part, to generally improving birth registration.[23] In fact, the trend and level of prenuptial pregnancy between 1860 and 1940 are the most uncertain section in the three centuries of data. One may guess and speculate, as I have (Smith, 'Dating of the American sexual revolution'), but one must hope that future research will make the picture much clearer.

6 Illegitimacy before 1920

The available data on illegitimacy trends correspond to the trends in prenuptial pregnancy during the eighteenth and nineteenth centuries. Yet the records are exceedingly problematic. In early American records bastards are more likely to be found in court records than in either town or church vital registers. Only three of 1,509 births in the late seventeenth-century Somerset County, Maryland, parish register were listed as illegitimate; for the same years the court records reveal a total of 87 (Menard, 1975, tables 15, 16). In his study of the colonial period (above, chapter 16), Robert Wells calculates illegitimacy ratios ranging from 1 to 26 per thousand births. Although ratios tended to increase over the colonial period, Wells concludes that they were quite low by comparative standards. The increase is consistent with the better documented boom in prenuptial pregnancy during the eighteenth century. Similarly one can conclude that late eighteenth-century illegitimacy rates were substantially higher than those of a century later. What must certainly be a low estimate of the illegitimacy rate for Middlesex County, Massachusetts, in 1764 is more than double the rate for Connecticut in 1900 and for the native-born population of Massachusetts in 1890 (see table 17.5).

Table 17.5 also re-emphasizes the importance of distinguishing between the illegitimacy ratio and the illegitimacy rate. The illegitimacy ratios for the late

21. R. Carlyle Buley, *The old northwest: pioneer period, 1815–1840* (1950), I, pp. 375–6.
22. Richard J. Jensen, *The winning of the midwest: social and political conflict, 1888–1896* (1971).
23. A more recent study of the farm population of Montgomery County, Indiana, also points to an increase in prenuptial pregnancy around 1900. Some 21.2 per cent of first births to 1901–15 marriages came within 8½ months of marriage compared to 16.8 per cent for marriages between 1882 and 1900. Donald H. Parkerson, 'The sensuous farmer: premarital pregnancy in Montgomery County, Indiana' (1975).

Table 17.5: Estimated illegitimacy ratios and rates for eighteenth- and nineteenth-century predominantly white populations

Population and period	Illegitimate births per 1000 total births	Illegitimate births per 1000 unmarried women, 15–44
Middlesex County, Massachusetts, 1764[(a)]	10	4.6–5.6
Massachusetts, 1890[(b)]		
Total population	21	3.8
Native-born	21	2.6
Foreign-born	20	6.3
1861–70	8	–
1871–80	14	–
1881–90	19	–
Connecticut, 1900[(c)]	10	2.0
Michigan, 1890[(d)]	9	2.4
United States whites, 1920[(e)]	15	4.4
England and Wales[(f)]		
1861–70	61	18.2
1871–80	50	15.1
1881–90	47	12.6

(a) The number of illegitimacy cases was counted from the court records by George E. Howard, *A history of matrimonial insitutions* (1904) II, p. 193. Assuming a birth rate of 40 per thousand Wells, chapter 16 above, calculated an illegitimacy ratio of 10 per thousand. The Middlesex County ratio of women 16–44 to all women over 16 in 1800 was assumed for 1764. Two per cent of all females were estimated to be 15 years old from Coale and Demeny (1966), p. 92, assuming GRR=3.00, Mortality level 10. The proportion unmarried between 15 and 44 was alternatively estimated at one third and two fifths of all women from the 1774 Connecticut and 1773 New Hampshire figures. See Yasuba (1962), table IV–6, p. 111.
(b) Illegitimacy figures are from Massachusetts, *Registration reports* for various years. The estimate of unmarried women and total births comes from Spengler (1930), tables P, Q, R, and S, pp. 62–3.
(c) Illegitimacy figure is average for 1897–1903 from Connecticut, Bureau of Vital Statistics, *59th Registration Report* (1907), table I, p. 12, and table XXI, p. 270. Unmarried women from Spengler (1930), pp. 62–3.
(d) Illegitimacy estimate for Michigan in 1890 is from Michigan, *Vital statistics of Michigan, 1895*, table 30, p. 109. Unmarried women from US Department of the Interior (1895) pt I, p. 852.
(e) US 1920, from table 17.1 above.
(f) Hartley (1966), table 1, p. 537.

nineteenth century are higher for the Massachusetts county in 1764. Declining marital fertility and increasing spinsterhood in nineteenth-century Massachusetts are incoporated into the ratio, but these factors obscure the underlying non-marital behaviour expressed in the rate.[24] Compared to England and Wales, illegitimacy ratios for the three states (Massachusetts, Connecticut, and Michigan) with pre-1900 series reported by state vital registration agencies are quite low. This comparison suggests again the distinctive character of the American experience in the nineteenth century. Both the early decline in prenuptial pregnancy and the strikingly low illegitimacy ratios and rates point to the need for an explanation of American uniqueness.

24. Yasukichi Yasuba, *Birth rates of the white population in the United States, 1800–1860* (1961), pp. 108–20. Peter Uhlenberg, 'A study of cohort life cycles: cohorts of native-born Massachusetts women, 1830–1920' (1969), pp. 407–20.

If anything the magnitude of the decline in illegitimacy during the nineteenth century is understated. Just what percentage of bastardy cases found their way into the courts of Middlesex County during the 1760s is unknown; common sense tells us that all the guilty are not prosecuted, and an estimate of the legitimation ratio (the proportion of non-maritally conceived births born after marriage) tends to confirm that suspicion. With a wide range of assumptions (from 25 per cent to 33 per cent pregnant at first marriage, a marriage rate of 8 to 10 per thousand population), the proportion of non-maritally conceived births legitimated by the marriage of their parents ranges from 82 per cent to 90 per cent. In recent years only 60 per cent of white first non-maritally conceived children in the United States have been born after marriage.[25] Although some evidence points to a higher out-of-wedlock legitimation ratio for late colonial New England,[26] the calculated ratio is still very high. One must presume therefore that the actual number of illegitimate children was considerably higher than the total to be located in the court records.

Given the deficient recording of illegitimacy in American demographic records, it is doubtful whether scholars will ever be very certain concerning the magnitude of the phenomenon. The court records of the colonies remain, however, a rich and relatively unexploited source for the analysis of the qualitative meanings of nonmarital fertility.

7 Distinctive American patterns

Two distinctive features stand out in the American record of illegitimacy and prenuptial pregnancy: the early nineteenth-century decline in white non-marital fertility, and the considerably higher level of black illegitimacy and prenuptial pregnancy. Both phenomena demand more research, and here I will only sketch the dimensions of the problems. In principle, of course, any or all of the intermediate variables between premarital coitus and illegitimacy or prenuptial conception might be involved in the early fall in non-marital fertility. Since the available demographic data suggest that both illegitimacy and prenuptial pregnancy declined during the nineteenth century, the pattern cannot be explained away by a shift from one to the other. What are obvious alternatives from the perspective of the single pregnant woman are not alternatives at the societal level.

Evidence also points away from a hypothesis of declining fecundity, although this area too needs further study. The proportion of childless women does increase slightly during the nineteenth century. Yet only 7.7 per cent of ever-married women born in the 1835–9 period were childless.[27] Furthermore, increasing childlessness continued into the late nineteenth and early twentieth centuries. This increase may be partially attributed to a slightly later age at first marriage or the use of contraception in the early years of marriage. There are no indications of a decline in nutritional levels during the first half of the nineteenth century. The heights of soldiers, a proxy for nutritional intake during childhood, were identical in the Revolutionary and Civil Wars. Although there may be some medical causes of greater infertility during the course of the nineteenth century, a

25. Cutright, 'Illegitimacy in the United States', p. 405. Reynolds Farley and Albert I. Hermalin, 'Family stability: a comparison of trends between blacks and whites' (1971), p. 13.
26. Smith and Hindus (1975), pp. 544–5. In Hingham wealthier men who impregnated poorer women later married them; community pressure did not allow men to abandon their responsibilities.
27. Wilson H. Grabill, Clyde V. Kiser, and Pascal K. Whelpton, *The fertility of American women* (1958), table 9.

small change cannot explain the large drop in illegitimacy and prenuptial pregnancy.

We are left, then, with the alternatives of a decreased incidence of premarital coitus or the increased use of contraception and/or induced abortion in premarital relations. Behind the argument for the impact of contraception and abortion are the parallel decline in marital fertility and the theory that the dynamic forces of the nineteenth century, rapid economic development, social differentiation, and spatial mobility, either disrupted traditional means of social control or inspired a 'wish to be free', especially among young females.[28] The effects of the disruptive forces, it was argued in an earlier essay, were limited to the transition period of collapse of traditional society in the second half of the eighteenth century (Smith and Hindus, 1975, especially pp. 556–60). This viewpoint is generally confirmed by the impressive compilation and interpretation of quantitative indicators by David Hackett Fischer.[29] The early decades of the nineteenth century were ones of reintegration, not disintegration. Furthermore, the psychosocial impact of nineteenth-century ideology was in the direction of control and autonomy, not liberation and expressiveness.[30] Social and ideological changes during the early nineteenth century point not to a continued high incidence of premarital sex but to increasing sexual restraint. Conclusions from literary sources are, of course, no substitute for direct evidence.

More convincing is the straightforward linking of the control of fertility within marriage (almost certainly by such methods as withdrawal) and the decline of illegitimacy and prenuptial pregnancy. There is no inevitable connection between marital and non-marital contraceptive use. At the same time as French marital fertility was declining in the first half of the nineteenth century, illegitimacy and prenuptial pregnancy were increasing. In the French case, however, fertility rates for young married women did not decline. In Hingham Massachusetts, on the other hand, the fertility of newly married women in the mid nineteenth century was well below that of eighteenth-century women. On average 15 per cent of newly married women between 1721 and 1800 became pregnant in each of the first three months after marriage; in the 1841–60 marriage cohort, the probability of conception was less than half as great (0.072) in the first three months of marriage. This decrease must be primarily due to the use of contraception early in marriage; thus it is likely that unmarried couples also controlled their fertility.

Withdrawal was doubtless the most common practice. It certainly was the method most frequently denounced by moralists in advice manuals. And scattered evidence suggests that the method was practised, if not sanctioned, during the eighteenth century. In her divorce proceedings in 1710 Mrs Abigail Emery of Newbury, Massachusetts, accused her husband of Onan's 'abominable sin', which he engaged in because 'he feared the charge of children.'[31] Although John Harrington of Marlborough, Massachusetts 'minded [his] pullbacks' in the famous bastardy case of 1771, he was still convicted of fathering Ann Josselyn's bastard child.[32] With the decline of religious values to a specialized and limited

28. The phrase comes from the book by Fred Weinstein and Gerald M. Platt, *The wish to be free: society, psyche, and value chance* (1969).
29. David Hackett Fischer, *America: a social history* I, *The Main Lines of the Subject, 1650–1975*.
30. For details see Daniel Scott Smith, 'Family limitation, sexual control and domestic feminism in Victorian America' (1973), pp. 40–57; for a more general view, see Charles E. Rosenberg, 'Sexuality, class and role in nineteenth-century America' (1973), pp. 131–53.
31. Nancy F. Cott, 'Eighteenth-century family and social life revealed in Massachusetts divorce records' (1976).
32. L. Kinvin Wroth and Hiller B. Zobel (eds), *The legal papers of John Adams* (1965), III, pp. 329–34.

part of American motivation, withdrawal became a useful rather than a deviant act. Although the incidence of abortion is unknown and probably unknowable, it may have been a significant practice, particularly in the urban areas of the northeast.[33] To some extent, then, the decline in prenuptial pregnancy and illegitimacy was caused by conscious interference with the fertility consequences of sexual intercourse.

Equally strong evidence exists for a declining incidence of premarital intercourse during the first half of the nineteenth century. The practice of bundling, a style of courtship with obvious erotic possibilities and possible fertility consequences, disappeared.[34] Courtship became more decorous and distant. Although religion no longer dominated American culture, participation in church activities accelerated during the ante-bellum period. Most significant were the greater involvement of adolescents and the early conversions of females. Current survey research links premarital restraint to active religious involvement; and religion in nineteenth-century America meant moral behaviour, not other-worldly concerns. Ministers did not particularly focus on sexual misconduct in their sermons; rather, drinking, gambling, and slander seemed more dangerous and pervasive to the clergy. Finally, foreign travellers tended to remark on the good morals and premarital restraint of American young people.

Altogether this evidence points to a decrease in premarital sexual intercourse. Despite Shorter's (1975, p. 334) comment that 'I don't believe [it] at all',[35] one must explain how late eighteenth-century prenuptial pregnancy rates could be as high as the incidence of premarital sexual experience that women born in the late nineteenth century reported to the pioneer surveyors of sex (Smith, 'Dating of the American sexual revolution', table 5, p. 329, summarizes these studies). The Whig interpretation of sexual history is as misguided as the belief in an onward-and-upward march of democratic institutions. Perhaps, as Shorter insists, it should have happened. In the very long run there must be some positive connection between economic freedom and sexual freedom. In the shorter run, in the first half of the nineteenth century in America, the progress of economic individualism was linked to the growth of premarital sexual restraint.

The second major distinctive aspect of the history of American illegitimacy and prenuptial pregnancy involves the experience of the black population, before and after slavery. Controversy abounds, much is still poorly understood, and several important studies are in progress. Since the controversial 1965 report of the politician and social scientist, Daniel Patrick Moynihan, both historians and sociologists have devoted considerable attention to the experience of the black family in American history.[36] Following Frazier's classic work, Moynihan cited as 'roots of the problem' of 'Negro family breakdown', slavery, post-Reconstruction discrimination and racism, and the rending impact of urbanization.[37] The principal result of the researches of the past decade has been to

33. R. Sauer, 'Attitudes to abortion in America, 1800–1973' (1974), pp. 53–67. Over three quarters of prenuptial conceptions of the highly educated Kinsey sample were terminated by induced abortion. Paul H. Gebhard *et al.*, *Pregnancy, birth and abortion* (1966), table 27, p. 77. Abortion was a surprisingly open matter in the early twentieth century; see George B. Mangold, 'Children born out of wedlock' (1921), pp. 81–2.

34. Henry Reed Stiles, *Bundling: its origins, progress and decline in America* (1871). Paul Faler, 'Cultural aspects of the industrial revolution: Lynn, Massachusetts shoemakers and industrial morality, 1826–1860' (1973), p. 371.

35. One must realize, however, that Victorian ideology was not so much anti sex as pro conjugal love. Carl N. Degler, 'What ought to be and what was: women's sexuality in the nineteenth century' (1974), pp. 1467–90, provides a useful corrective to the works of the intellectual historians.

36. For the report and the reactions, see Lee Rainwater and William L. Yancey (eds), *The Moynihan Report and the politics of controversy* (1967).

37. E. Franklin Frazier, *The negro family in the United States* (1966).

destroy all the 'myths' about the subject, leaving varying fragments of truth in each.

Demographically and familially the American slave experience was unique. Early in the eighteenth century a native born slave population emerged in the Chesapeake with surprisingly high fertility and moderate mortality.[38] Both a cause and a consequence of these demographic rates, a two-parent family pattern developed in the slave population.[39] Despite this modal structure in practice, the slave family not only lacked legal sanction, but was also vulnerable and subject to disruption by masters. Although the family functioned as a means of social control for the master and had great psychological importance for the slaves, the family as an institution lacked certainty and economic power. Norms, sexual or otherwise, rest on certainty and are enforced by power. Neither prudish nor promiscuous, premarital sexual behaviour reflected family and communal regulation as well as the absence of the property considerations so important to peasant communities elsewhere.[40] Indeed, the situation of the black population both during and after slavery is so different that the more relevant comparisons should be with other black populations in the New World. Religion, stratification, the role of the family, the key variables in an analysis of illegitimacy, are, of course, quite different for the American white and black populations. Since most of my information for whites pertains not to the South but to New England, little historical comparison from my data is possible or relevant.

It is not even very clear that history is especially important for understanding the evolution of black patterns. In the post-Reconstruction rural South economic discrimination and powerlessness of the black population persisted. No data on black illegitimacy or prenuptial pregnancy exist for this period. The proportion of male-headed families provides something of an index of family stability; although affected by mortality and migration, this measure should presumably be correlated with the incidence of illegitimacy.[41] Given the legacy of slavery and the failure of Reconstruction to provide blacks with a viable economic base, the proportion of two-parent households in post-bellum America is remarkably high. In various southern locales, between 1865 and 1880, some 70–87 per cent of black families had an adult male head. Similar percentages are reported for Boston in 1880, and for cities in the Ohio River Valley between 1860 and 1880. Despite economic depression and growing segregation, no marked trends developed; in the 1930 census 85 per cent of non-white families were headed by males.[42]

38. Russell R. Menard, 'The Maryland slave population, 1658 to 1730: a demographic profile of blacks in four counties' (1975), pp. 29–54.

39. Stanley L. Engerman, 'Some economic and demographic comparisons of slavery in the United States and the British West Indies' (1976), provides a valuable review of comparative patterns.

40. This cursory summary ignores the complexities and controversies surrounding the history of the black family. I found the following most useful: Reynolds Farley, *Growth of the black population: a study of demographic trends* (1970); Eugene D. Genovese, *Roll, Jordan, roll: the world the slaves made* (1972), pp. 77–103; Herbert Gutman and Richard Sutch, 'The slave family: protected agent of capitalist masters or victim of the slave trade', and 'Victorians all? the sexual mores and conduct of slaves and their masters' (1976), pp. 94–162.

41. The focus of the Moynihan Report on the variable of female-headed families, a supposed indicator of matriarchy or matrifocality, has unfortunately led historians into a narrow approach to the history of the black family. In refuting the straw man of the Moynihan Report, historians have neglected many important topics. See Herbert Gutman (1970).

42. Herbert G. Gutman, 'Le phénomène invisible: la composition de la famille et du foyer noirs après la Guerre de Sécession' (1972), table 1, p. 1207. Paul J. Lammermeier, 'The urban black family of the nineteenth century: a study of black family structure in the Ohio Valley, 1850–1880' (1973), table 2, p. 443. Elizabeth H. Pleck, 'The two-parent household: black family structure in late nineteenth-century Boston' (1972), pp. 1–31; Farley and Hermalin (1971), table 3, p. 6. See also Crandall A. Shifflett, 'The household composition of rural black families: Louisa County, Virginia, 1880' (1975), pp. 235–60.

Despite this historical pattern of higher illegitimacy levels and a higher incidence of female-headed families among blacks, history seems of little relevance to the current situation of black families. Before the Second World War legitimate classification of birth and male-headed families are the overwhelmingly modal patterns for both blacks and whites; they remain majority patterns for blacks in current data. Neither the post-war increase in black illegitimacy nor the rising proportion of female-headed families have important origins in inter-generational relationships. If there were a historical 'tradition' involved, one would expect the lines of transmission between generations to be stronger.[43]

The argument that urbanization is a major source of distinctive black patterns is also rather weakly supported. Not only do teenage southern females of both races not differ from girls in other regions with respect to premarital sexual experience, but the differences between metropolitan and non-metropolitan areas are quite small.[44] Within the South in 1960, rural and urban non-white illegitimacy rates are identical.[45] Since the 1940s a larger proportion of non-metropolitan ever-married non-white or negro women bore their first child before marriage than women living in metropolitan areas. As with the 'historical legacy of slavery' argument, the urbanization hypothesis is, at best, a very partial one.[46]

A similar conclusion may also be advanced for the effects of improvement of health conditions, better living standards, a younger age at menarche, and the control of venereal disease on legitimate and illegitimate black fertility.[47] Although trends in childlessness do roughly correspond to the incidence of venereal disease over time, the regional and educational differentials in fertility do not correspond to variations in the incidence of the disease. Furthermore, the fecundity impairment associated with venereal disease does not appear to be of sufficient magnitude to account for observed trends in non-white childlessness or illegitimate fertility.[48]

The very limited truth in each argument leaves, of course, the question of how the trend and level in black illegitimacy may be explained. The higher level compared to the white population is best attributed to the long existing differentials in the economic situation between the races. This is a situational difference, not a product of a culture of poverty or a culture associated with race. An explanation of the trend rests on the general congruence of white and non-white

43. On the question of inter-generational transmission see Jerold Heiss, 'On the transmission of marital instability in black families' (1972), pp. 82–92. Clark E. Vincent, C. Allen Haney and Carl M. Cochrane, 'Familial and generational patterns of illegitimacy' (1969), pp. 659–67. Beverly and Otis Dudley Duncan, 'Family stability and occupational success' (1969), table 1, p. 275. And Peter Blau and Otis Dudley Duncan, *The American occupational structure* (1967), pp. 331–7. Phillips Cutright and Omer Galle, 'The effect of illegitimacy on United States general fertility rates and population growth' (1973), pp. 515–26, demonstrate that women with non-marital fertility experience do not have more children than average.

44. John F. Kantner and Melvin Zelnik, 'Sexual experience of young unmarried women in the United States' (1972), tables 6 and 7, p. 13.

45. Cutright, 'Illegitimacy', table 27, p. 412. For state differentials in 1960, see Irene B. and Conrad Taeuber, *People of the United States in the twentieth century* (1971), pp. 424–8.

46. US Bureau of the Census, *Current population report* (1969), table 18, p. 41; (1974), table 21, p. 60. The best historical study suggesting the destructive impact of urban life on black family structure is Frank F. Furstenberg, Jr, Theodore Hershberg, and John Modell, 'The origins of the female-headed black family: the impact of the urban experience' (1975), pp. 211–34.

47. Cutright, 'Illegitimacy', pp. 392–400. Also Cutright, 'The teenage sexual revolution and the myth of an abstinent past' (1972), pp. 26–9, calculates that 90 per cent of the increase in non-white illegitimacy rates of 15–19 year olds may be attributed to better health conditions in 1968 compared to 1940. His ingenious calculation assumes that one fetal death averts one illegitimate birth. The fallacy of this assumption is demonstrated by Nathan Keyfitz, 'How birth control affects births' (1971), pp. 109–21.

48. On the role of health conditions see Farley (1970), pp. 206–45; for an important critique of this interpretation see Joseph A. McFalls, Jr, 'Impact of VD on the fertility of the US black population 1880–1950' (1973), pp. 2–19.

trends. The great unexplained residual in non-marital fertility increase results from changes in attitudes and behaviour toward marriage and premarital sexual intercourse.[49] Rather small changes in the proportion of the population which is sexually active are translated into large increases in the illegitimacy rate (this is the central and valuable argument of Cutright, 'Teenage sexual revolution'). Pointing to a changing climate of values is not much of an explanation, and perhaps it would be more honest to admit that these changes are poorly understood. The current levels of black illegitimacy are not deeply rooted historically, in recent demographic or econimic trends, or in the value oreintation of the black population. Indeed, a continued decline in the black illegitimacy rate is likely for the near future.[50]

8 Conclusion

These indefinite conclusions mean that an adequate history of American illegitimacy and prenuptial pregnancy is a future goal, not an accomplished fact. Scattered data, bold calculations, and suggestive possibilities are no substitute for more hard information and systematic research. Very badly needed are prenuptial pregnancy studies which trace births to migrant couples; colony and state indices of vital records make this feasible. The completeness of vital registration needs to be explored; here the nineteenth century is the most obscure. Perhaps most importantly, the qualitative aspects of the subject, the social control of sex and non-marital conception and the social and cultural contexts of the phenomena among the diverse groups in the American population, demand the attention of historians and historical demographers. As promised, this chapter suggests a beginning, not a final conclusion.

49. For evidence on the recent reduction of the age of entry into premarital sexual relations of both US whites and blacks, see Melvin Zelnik and John F. Kantner, 'The probability of premarital intercourse' (1972), table 3, p. 340.
50. Marcia J. Kramer, 'Legal abortion among New York City residents: an analysis according to socio-economic and demographic characteristics' (1975), pp. 128–37. For the impact of abortion on illegitimacy in California see June Sklar and Beth Berkov, 'Teenage family formation in postwar America' (1974), pp. 80–90. Note, however, the debate on why illegitimacy continues in an era of easy abortion between Sklar-Berkov and Phillips Cutright and Frank F. Furstenberg, Jr, in *Family Planning Perspectives*, 6 (1974), pp. 127–35.

18

Illegitimacy in Jamaica

Shirley Foster Hartley

Jamaica, the country registering the highest illegitimacy rates and ratios in the world, was discovered by Columbus and settled first by the Spanish and later by the English. After centuries of slavery and colonial rule, Jamaica achieved political independence from Great Britain in 1962. Although still a developing nation, Jamaica has a well trained indigenous leadership and a professional corps. It has made giant strides in education, in economic development and in urbanization. Yet the country continues to produce the world's highest proportion of births out of wedlock. The paradox is evident. When asked by the interviewers from their own society, people of all classes say that 'marriage is best', affirming the universal 'principle of legitimacy'.[1] But marriage rates in Jamaica are among the lowest in the world, and illegitimacy ranges from 70 per cent to 74 per cent of all births, a ratio which is the highest among 70 countries of the world that report such information. With 189.5 illegitimate births per thousand unmarried women in the childbearing ages, Jamaica also stands highest among 46 countries whose data permit calculation of the general illegitimate fertility rate.[2] The number of births out of wedlock almost doubled between 1943 and 1964.

How does one account for these different rates of increase in the three measures of illegitimacy? What is there about the mating patterns and family structure that year after year so high a proportion of births are produced outside legal marital units? A number of authors have suggested that consensual unions are simply the non-legal equivalent of marriage and that, therefore, illegitimacy may be such in name only. Yet a variety of evidence indicates that consensual unions, in which a man and a woman live together, with their children, are rarely stable, long-lasting or legalized later in life.

The main purpose of this chapter is to call in question simplistic explanations of the Jamaican pattern (these have already been ruled out in a larger international study[3]), and to suggest the need for a more unified, historical, social structural and cultural analysis. As Johnson and Cutright (1973) suggest, we need to explain such patterns 'in historical terms (how the patterns of sexual behaviour outside legal marriage began), as well as in contemporary terms (why they persist)'. We will, therefore, focus first on the origin and then on the persistence of the Jamaican pattern.

1 Early Spanish rule

Columbus discovered Jamaica on his second voyage to the New World, 3 May 1494. For the whole of the sixteenth century and the first half of the seventeenth

1. Bronislaw Malinowski, 'Parenthood: the basis of social structure' (1930), pp. 113–68.
2. Shirley Foster Hartley, 'Comparative differences and changes in levels of illegitimacy' (1969).
3. Shirley Foster Hartley, *Illegitimacy* (1975).

century the island was occupied by the Spanish. After an unsuccessful search for gold the conquerors turned to grazing and agriculture for a living and used the indigenous Arawak Indians as slave labourers – used them so badly that within a century and a half the entire original population was exterminated. Few African slaves were brought to Jamaica prior to 1518 but from that date onwards the organized slave trade between Africa and the West Indies flourished, and the number of blacks in Jamaica grew as the Arawak Indians were decimated.[4] The first available population count covers the year 1611, when negroes, both slaves and free, were listed as 4 per cent of the 1,510 population. The Arawak Indians, described by early explorers as an 'abundant population with numerous little villages' were listed as only 74 in number, or less than 5 per cent of the total.

2 English colonial rule and slavery

The English under the leadership of Oliver Cromwell, the Protector, set out to capture all the Spanish possessions in the Caribbean. After a series of defeats on other islands, they began to occupy Jamaica in May 1665; as they moved slowly inland most of the Spanish left for Cuba, taking their slaves with them. Sailors, troops and eventually new settlers from England, Scotland, Ireland, and from the other Caribbean islands began planting subsistence crops. Since not all were voluntary immigrants (some were criminal and political prisoners, others youths or indentured servants), motivation to produce was uneven, and agricultural success was long in coming. The death rate from both starvation and disease was high in the early years, leading to prompt requests to Cromwell for permission to import a fresh supply of African slaves (Gardner, pp. 27–43).

Between 1655 and 1808 approximately 750,000 slaves from West Africa were brought into Jamaica in excess of those exported in the slave trade.[5] By 1673 those of African ancestry constituted over half the rapidly growing population. Whites never again comprised a large proportion of the population (see table 18.1). During this period slaves were listed together with cattle as the 'stock of the plantations'.[6] Breeding of the 'stock' was considered less practical than the purchase of full-grown slaves, that is, until the importation of slaves was ended. It should be noted that if, over a period of 150 years, the excess of slaves imported over those exported was anything like 750,000, deaths must have been very high and would have greatly exceeded birth replacements among the slave population, for by 1793 only about 35 per cent of the net numbers of imports appear in the island estimates of all blacks and coloureds (table 18.1).

On slave plantations the work routine and living conditions allowed little freedom for affectional bonds or family life. The work day began at 5 or 6 a.m. and ended at 5.30 p.m. or later during the harvest (Gardner, p. 387). Housing was described as wretched, one-room hovels made of four posts with mud and wattle sides, thatched roofs and a mud floor. By a law of 1736 marriage was forbidden to white bond servants and even to overseers, as well as to the slaves (bond servants were infrequently given permission to marry by the masters, but only under stringent conditions and penalties; Gardner, p. 96). Therefore, sexual connections of all but a very small minority of white males were of the non-marital type.

4. W. J. Gardner, *A history of Jamaica* (1909), pp. 7–10. Some estimates indicate that most of the Indians were wiped out within fifty years of the Spanish occupation.
5. Wendell Bell, *Jamaican leaders* (1964), p. 6.
6. Douglas Hall, 'Slaves and slavery in the British West Indies' (1962), pp. 305–18.

Table 18.1: Percentage distribution of the population of Jamaica by race, 1673–1960

Year	Black and coloured		White	Chinese[a]	East Indian[a]	Others	Total no. (in thousands)
1673	55		45	–	–	–	17.2
1696	84		21	–	–	–	(46.4)[b]
1736	85		8	–	–	–	(94.2)
1775	95		6	–	–	–	(209.6)
1788	88		6	–	–	–	(291.4)
1793	90		10	–	–	–	291.4
	Black	Coloured					
1844	77.7	18.1	4.2	–	–	–	377.4
1861	78.5	18.4	3.1	–	–	0.1	441.3
1871	77.6	19.8	2.6	–	–	–	506.2
1881	76.5	18.9	2.4	0.1	1.9	0.2	580.8
1891	76.4	19.1	2.3	0.1	1.6	0.6	639.5
1911	75.8	19.6	1.9	0.3	2.1	0.3	831.4
1921	77.0	18.3	1.7	0.4	2.2	0.4	858.1
1943	78.1	17.5	1.1	1.0	2.1	0.2	1237.1
1960	76.8	14.6	0.9	1.2	3.4	3.1	1609.8

[a] In 1943 and 1960 the Afro-Chinese and the Afro-East Indians, who might have been earlier included among the coloured, are counted among the Chinese and East Indian respectively.
[b] Numbers in parentheses are census estimates which do not equal the sum of the racial components.

Note: The percentages given from 1673 through 1793 are from data compiled by Broom (1954), p. 116; those given from 1844 through 1943 are from Roberts (1957), p. 65; those given for 1960 are from *West Indies population census* p. 1. (NB 1808, slave trade outlawed; 1838, abolition of slavery.)

The female slave was merely a thing to be used by the whites, marriage was never considered, but children were inevitable.[7] Livingston claims that vicious slave drivers rarely conceded that slaves might be human beings, except for the sexual use of the women who had no personal rights. They were at the command of any white man who looked at them. Overseers were 'expected to keep concubines. . . . Slaves "copied" the vices of their superiors because they were more apparent and easier to appropriate than their virtues.'[8] The black or coloured woman who attached herself to the more powerful white class had at least the hope of attaining eventual freedom for herself and/or her child. By the time of the first census of 1844 (table 18.1), something like 70,000 persons, or 18 per cent of the population, had been produced by the sexual matings of white males with black, or later coloured (mixed) females. The system of concubinage was a direct result of the inferiority of the non-white under the slave system. (It has been estimated that only about 40 per cent of the slave imports were female, but I have seen no good evidence on this point, nor do we know of differential mortality among the sexes. However, if women were relatively rare, one might expect that their value, at least as sexual partners and reproductive potential, would increase.)

Among 'head negroes', those who were slave drivers or skilled craftsmen, there is some evidence that polygamy, of African origin, was allowed. In 1801, a Mr Edwards claimed that 'in Jamaica, on a moderate computation, not less than ten thousand of such as are called Head Negroes possessed from two to four wives.'[9]

7. S. J. and E. F. Hurwitz, *Jamaica: a historical portrait* (1971), p. 63.
8. William P. Livingston, *Black Jamaica* (1900), p. 22.
9. Quoted in Edward Braithwaite, *The development of Creole society in Jamaica, 1770–1820* (1971), p. 215.

If women comprised less than half the population, polygamy on so large a scale would have increased their relative scarcity as mates. Among the field slaves the highly systematized polygamous patterns of Africa were replaced by promiscuous intercourse, by keeper relationships which were dissolved at will, and in some cases by faithful concubinage. The 'husband' was not an essential part of the slave family. As long as his 'wife' and children were the property of another, they were not dependent on him for maintenance. They received their allowances directly from the master. 'As M. J. Smith has pointed out, *the children were neither legitimate nor illegitimate – they were the lawful property of the mother's owner*' (emphasis mine).[10]

While arguing that slavery and the family life of slaves was not as bad in the southern United States as has often been portrayed, Fogel and Engerman (1974, pp. 155–6) suggest that conditions in the West Indies were quite different:

> During most of the eighteenth century, masters in colonies such as Jamaica, discouraged family formation and high fertility rates, preferring to buy adult slaves in Africa rather than to rear them. It was general policy to maintain an imbalance between the sexes with men outnumbering women by a ratio of 4 to 3. To further reduce the basis for stable families, planters encouraged polygamy among slaves by rewarding favored men with second and third wives. Thus, for the remainder of the population, the male-female ratio was about 13 to 8. So large a disproportion between the sexes was bound to encourage sexual activity outside of the family and to reduce fertility.

However, evidence from the three plantations studied in detail by B. W. Higman indicates that males there were in the minority throughout the period for which data are available, 1817 through 1832. At Shettlewood Pen the sex ratio reached its lowest at 62 to 64 males per hundred females while crude birth rates were *higher* than for the other plantations with sex ratios of 89 to 101.[11] Thus, we cannot draw conclusions about sexual activity or fertility from the knowledge of the sex ratios alone.

While on the one hand planters were charged with neglect of breeding, Carley claims that the healthiest and strongest types among the slaves were actually valued for breeding purposes.[12] It may have been that breeding was successful but that infant (and fetal) mortality inhibited successful replacement of the population. In 1788 infant mortality was reckoned at about one half the number of children born to slave women (Goveia, 1965, p. 124).

> The care given to infants was quite poor compared with the South[ern US]. Mothers were not encouraged to nurse their children; the southern practice of a 40 to 50 per cent reduction of the workload of nursing mothers was not imitated in Jamaica. Further evidence of the neglect of pregnant women is to be found in the high rate of stillbirths. On one of the leading Jamaican plantations, 75 out of 345 births over a four-year period were stillborn. It has also been charged that abortion was both encouraged and widely practised [Fogel and Engerman, 1974, p. 156; see also Hurwitz and Hurwitz, 1971, p. 79].

10. Elsa V. Goveia, *Slave society in the British Leeward Islands at the end of the eighteenth century* (1965), pp. 217, 234.
11. B. W. Higman, 'Household structure and fertility on Jamaican slave plantations: a nineteenth-century example' (1973), p. 529. See also Anthony Marino, 'Family fertility and sex ratios in the British Caribbean' (1970, for an excellent analysis of sex ratio differences since 1881.
12. Mary Manning Carley, *Jamaica, the old and the new* (1963), p. 108.

Although there may have been some instability of sexual unions which might reduce conceptions from the maximum obtainable, the pattern of sexual use of females by all males – black, coloured, bond servants, overseers, and whites in general – would lead this author to assume that birth rates could not have been low through sexual abstinence.[13] Rather, it would seem likely that impaired health conditions of the women, the high probability of sterility due to venereal disease, and infant and childhood mortality were the main conditions restricting the natural increase of the population.

3 The decline of slavery

In Britain the Society for the Abolition of the Slave Trade instigated a number of improvements in the legal position of slaves. As early as 1781, the Jamaican Assembly passed a law forbidding the mutilation of one's own slave (Gardner, p. 215). The effectiveness of the law was doubtful, because evidence by a slave against a white man was not admissible in court. Continuing reports of atrocities and rising public consciousness led to a law being passed in England which stopped slave vessels being cleared in any British port after March 1808. Slavery continued, but no new slaves arrived from Africa to replenish dwindling stocks. For the first time, continuance of the system required successful breeding. Although we have little direct evidence, population estimates indicate that for 51 years, from 1793 to 1844, the numerical increase in total population was little more than it had been in the previous 18-year period.[14]

> With the cutting off of manpower supplies from Africa, it became necessary to look more carefully after the health and fertility of the resident black workforce. One day per fortnight (Mondays), except during crop time, and in addition to the Christmas, Easter and Whitsun holidays, was to be given to the slaves so that they could attend their provision grounds. They were not to be worked on Sundays, except, of course, when the canes were being brought in. Bounties were to be paid to overseers to encourage 'breeding women', and females (queen bees) with six living children, whether their own or adopted, were to be exempted from hard labour. . . . Public slave whippings were cut down to ten lashes if the owner or overseer was not or could not be present to witness, and to not more than the Mosaic thirty-nine otherwise [Braithwaite, 1971, p. 293].

New slave laws passed by the Jamaican House of Assembly in December 1826 specified provisions under which the marriage of slaves might be performed. The clause exempting mothers with six children from hard labour may have been aimed at promoting fertility and/or making the system more acceptable. Abstracts of sections pertinent to our study follow.[15]

13. Fogel and Engerman assume abstinence to be the main cause of infertility among most of the childless (about 25 per cent of all) slave women in the Southern US. Yet, there are several unexamined alternatives to abstinence as a cause of childlessness. See H. Gutman, *Slavery and the numbers game* (1975).

14. Before the slave trade ended, from 1775 to 1793, imports led to rapid population increase, averaging about 2 per cent per year. The period 1793 to 1844 includes 15 years of legal slave importation and 36 years of its prohibition. Overall, the 51-year population increase averaged about half of one per cent per year. Thus, although the pace of population growth slowed, the numbers did not decline. We cannot tell the relative contribution of births and deaths, but we know that immigration must have been reduced later in this period.

15. Bernard Martin Senior, *Jamaica* (1969), pp. 141 ff.

Sec. 4: That marriages of slaves are to be solemnized without fee or reward; but the ceremony is only to take place between parties who shall have satisfied the clergyman of the parish that they possess a proper knowledge of the nature and obligation of such a contract, and produce such proofs that they have sanction of their owner, or of his legal representative, for the performance of the ceremony.

Sec. 33: That any person committing rape on a female slave shall suffer death without benefit of clergy.

Sec. 130: That the evidence of slaves shall be admitted in certain cases; provided a certificate of baptism be produced and that the slave understands the obligation of an oath. But no free person shall be convicted but on evidence of two slaves, who shall be examined apart, and the complaint made within 12 months and after 1st May 1827.

Thus, over three hundred years had passed between the introduction of African slaves into Jamaica and the introduction of laws which would *allow* marriage among slaves if the owner approved, would allow some rights to mothers, and would penalize the rape of a female slave. Although the latter may have been difficult to enforce, slaves had at least some recourse to the courts as persons.

We must now consider whether there was, at this time, a change in household structure and mating patterns as established under slavery. In an analysis of detailed household registrations, B. W. Higman identified 13 different household types for the three Seaford plantations in the year 1825. At that point in time about 40 per cent of the households and almost 50 per cent of the people enumerated lived in units approximating an elementary family (Higman, 1973, pp. 534–8). Triennial counts of male and female slaves from 1817 to 1832, with births and deaths occurring during each three year period, indicate a more or less consistent natural decrease in the 958 slaves counted in 1817. Of all births registered, 14 per cent died at an age of over 10 days but under 2 years and 10 months. Since mothers at that time received 13 shillings and 4 pence for each birth surviving at least 9 days, it is likely that most surviving births were registered. However, estimates of infant mortality within the first 9 days range between 25 per cent and 50 per cent of all live births (Higman, 1973, p. 545).

Although Higman concludes from household composition available only for 1825 that the data 'may be suggestive of early casual mating followed by relatively stable monogamy', he had no time data to indicate 'stability' of household units, no evidence of the actual sexual relationships, the paternity of the children in the household or the duration of co-residential arrangements. In fact, his computation of age-specific fertility over the years 1817–25 and 1825–32 demonstrates that women living with men in 1825 (household types 4, 5 and 12) were no more likely to produce children than those without men in the household (Higman, 1973, pp. 547–8). These data imply an independence of sexual and housing arrangements. Between 1825 and 1827 there were three marriages of couples who had been living together in 1825. It is not clear whether these had any relationship to the newly legalized status of slave marriage or whether any of the other 90 households that could have involved a nuclear family (male and female with or without children) in 1825 might have religious or legal sanction. Detailed information for these three estates does not indicate any overwhelming change of slave status with the imposition of new laws. It does appear that there were at least five older, higher-status male slaves at Old Montpelier who were polygamous. On the same plantation evidence indicates that white men fathered children of slave women out of all proportion to their own small number (Higman, 1973, p. 534).

4 Emancipation of the slaves

After years of discussion and some compromise in parliament, the act abolishing slavery in all parts of the British Empire was passed on 28 August 1833. The abolition was accompanied by an outright grant of 20 million pounds sterling as compensation to slave owners in the colonies. But the law required that each colony should draw up its own emancipation act acceptable to the British government before indemnity would be paid (Hurwitz and Hurwitz, 1971, p. 119). Jamaican slaves were finally given legal freedom in August 1838. The British, however, left the details of implementing the act wholly in the hands of the Jamaican ruling class, whose values and attitudes towards blacks had not changed with the law. With 'freedom' many ex-slaves were forced to leave the only home they had ever known. They had no rights to the land, even though they and generations of their ancestors had cultivated and improved their individual slave plots. Squatter settlements around Kingston and Spanish Town swelled, while ex-slaves searched for odd jobs and survival. Many continued to work on plantations as the only way of life they had ever known.

Emancipation did mean that such marriages as had been performed by missionaries could be made legal merely by recording the act in the office of the island secretary. Within four years some 3,000 marriages were performed by Baptist missionaries alone (Gardner, p. 415). Many thousands of marriages were celebrated by people who had lived together for years. Even so, these represented only a small proportion of the total population. According to Livingston, the young entered sexual unions at puberty, with 'respect and affection struggling up through animal passion' only gradually (Livingston, p. 113). When missionaries preached parental responsibility and launched campaigns against customs such as concubinage and illegitimacy, they spoke an unfamiliar 'language' not easily understood by people who had adapted to generations of slavery by pretending acquiescence to the white man's ways. Many of the abstractions preached by the Christian missionaries made little sense under the actual conditions of life. Most blacks still lived like animals, crowded together in wretched hovels.[16]

Although there were few changes in living conditions with emancipation, improved conditions of life did follow a change in government in 1886. A small uprising at Morant Bay in 1865 had been overdramatized and cruelly suppressed. Playing on the fears of the Jamaican legislature, controlled by the planters, the then governor, Eyre, persuaded the elected legislators to resign and return control to a strong governor representing the British crown. A newly appointed governor with the power to circumvent the old leadership began making real improvements in police protection, health care, schools and in the registration of births and deaths (Hurwitz and Hurwitz, 1971, chapter 7). At the first official islandwide registration of births in 1878, 59.3 per cent of all newborn infants were recorded as illegitimate. 'To meet illegitimacy, an act was passed providing for

16. But see James M. Phillippo, *Jamaica, its past and present state*, for an account of new villages built by freed slaves with the help of the Baptist mission. It was said that at least in these villages marriage was idealized.

the determination of the putative father and the affiliation of the children. But the initiative was left to the mother and the cost of the process prevented her resorting to it. The law became practically a dead letter' (Livingston, p. 97). In the ninety years of recording births the percentage out of wedlock has ranged from 58 to 74. At the census of 1881 only 29 per cent of the female population aged 15 and over were married. In 1960 it was even lower at 27 per cent.

5 Trends in illegitimacy

Not only the number but also the proportion of births out of wedlock has increased steadily as the total population has increased. (Absolute numbers are important for the calculation of the indicators of illegitimacy: the ratio and the rate.) From the first official registration of births in 1878 until the most recent report in 1964, there has been a slow but steady rise from 59 per cent to 74 per cent in the ratio or proportion of all children born out of wedlock (see table 18.2). No other nation reports such high ratios. Caution is always advisable in the use of such statistics, allowing for some under-registration, inaccurate reporting, etc. However, for a developing nation, Jamaican data are good.[17] In 1957 Professor George Roberts of the University of the West Indies suggested that the reliability has not been out by more than 3.2 per cent since 1891. The general illegitimacy rate, indicated in the last column of table 18.2, shows the number of illegitimate births per thousand unmarried women in the childbearing ages, 15 to 44. Although the rate is not available for every year, between the 1943 and 1960 censuses there was almost a 70 per cent increase in the propensity of unmarried women to produce children out of wedlock. With about 190 births for every thousand unmarried women in 1960, this means that for unmarried women in the thirty-year childbearing span almost one in five was producing an illegitimate birth (later we will examine the age-specific rates as these vary for five-year groupings of mothers; table 18.3). The illegitimacy rate in 1960 was almost as high as the legitimate fertility rate of the same year and higher than the legitimate rates of earlier years.

It is too early to know whether independence from Britain in 1962 and complete control of their country by Jamaicans will change the long history of childbearing outside marriage (for a review of the research into consequences of childbearing out of wedlock see Hartley, 1974, chapter 1). Without improvements in the stability of family life and the socialization of the young, 'the widening gap between the majority of poor Jamaicans and the rest'[18] may continue to reduce the possibilities of human development. It would appear that a pattern of social disorganization, once established, is subject to the laws of inertia. That is, the historical pattern will remain in its prior state unless acted upon by some superior force. Better education, urbanization, economic development, democracy and improved communication seem not, as yet, to have acted as that force for change.

17. Experience in census-taking dates back to 1844, and although the under-enumeration was probably great, the Jamaican attempt was based upon and profited from the British census of 1841. An eighth census was taken in Jamaica in 1943 and a ninth in 1960. Details from the tenth census was not available for this presentation. Few countries in the world, developed or underdeveloped, have a longer experience with the collection of demographic information (*International Population Census* 1968).
18. James Mau, *Social change and images of the future* (1968), p. 116.

Table 18.2: Numbers, ratios and rates of illegitimate births in Jamaica, 1878–1964

Period	No.[a]	Ratio[b]	Rate[c]
		%	
1878		59.3	
1881–5	12996 (av/yr)	58.9	
1886–90	13698 (av/yr)	60.38	
1891–5	15613 (av/yr)	60.64	
1896–1900	17705 (av/yr)	62.62	
1901–5	19888 (av/yr)	64.47	
1906–10	19589 (av/yr)	62.44	
1911–15	21105 (av/yr)	65.34	
1916–20	21618 (av/yr)	69.23	
1921–5	23170 (av/yr)	71.63	
1926–30	25170 (av/yr)	72.14	
1931–5	25538 (av/yr)	71.85	
1936	26201	71.66	
1937	25200	71.28	
1938	26957	70.99	
1939	26294	70.16	
1940	25429	69.74	
1941	26375	69.71	
1942	28091	69.93	
1943	27484[d]	69.81	114.76
1944	28959	69.33	
1945	26125	68.83	
1946	27028	67.71	
1947	29690	68.62	
1948	28608[d]	68.09	113.47
1949	30191	68.81	
1950	32344	69.75	
1951	33992	70.2	
1952	33994	70.1	
1953	36190[d]	70.9	139.03
1954	38412	71.6	
1955	39944	71.6	
1956	41831	71.9	
1957	43540	72.0	168.24
1958	45484	71.6	
1959	46122	72.2	
1960	49493	72.4	189.53
1961	48068	72.7	
1962	47412	73.0	
1963	48746	73.6	
1964	50675	74.13	

(a) The number is that of illegitimate live births, not including stillbirths.
(b) Illegitimate births as a percentage of all live births.
(c) Illegitimate live births per thousand unmarried women, aged 15–44.
(d) These numbers exclude births to women under age 15 and over age 44.

Source: Ratios for 1881 to 1944 were obtained from *Jamaica, Quarterly Digest of Statistics* (1947), p. 2. Ratios for 1945 to 1964 and numbers from *Annual Report on Jamaica* for each year from 1947 to 1965, pages varying for each year. For the sources for illegitimacy rates, see table 18.3.

We must examine some of these social structural and cultural influences in the light of the available demographic data most closely concerned with illegitimate fertility. These are:

1 patterns of marital and non-marital union;
2 avoidance of births out of wedlock;
3 prenuptial pregnancy.

6 Patterns of marital and non-marital union

Few nations in the world have such a high proportion of women outside legal marital unions during the childbearing years as does Jamaica. The historical pattern persists. Three-quarters of the women aged 15–44 reported themselves unmarried in the 1943 and 1960 censuses. Only 1 per cent of 15–19 year olds, and 10 per cent of 20–24 year olds reported themselves married. Marriage is not merely postponed: half the women are still unmarried at age 40–44. A high proportion of unmarried women in the childbearing ages is not necessarily accompanied by high rates or ratios of illegitimacy. Both Jamaica and Japan have a high average age at marriage, but Japan records only 1 per cent of all births as illegitimate while Jamaica reports over 99 per cent of women aged 15–19 are unmarried, yet illegitimate births to that age group are 800 times higher in Jamaica than in Japan. The illegitimacy rate for 15–19 year olds was 0.17 for Japan in 1964 and 135.4 for Jamaica in 1957 (latest available).

The above data refer to the condition of being in or outside legally registered marital unions. It has often been claimed that in Jamaica and in the Caribbean in general, consensual or common law unions are the 'functional equivalent' or a 'functional alternative' to legal marriage.[19] If this is the case, then it might be more appropriate to include people who are living together in consensual unions with legal marriages, to transfer 'nominally illegitimate' births within these unions to the legitimate group and compute new rates of legitimate and illegitimate fertility. The overriding issue, therefore, is to decide if the consensual union in Jamaica is the equivalent of marriage. But this raises a series of further questions. If we define consensual union, as Roberts does (1957, p. 294), as 'the continuous association of two given mates', how do we define 'continuous'? What evidence is there that 'the basic characteristic of the common law union is its transient nature . . . transitional between the other two types' (Roberts, 1957, p. 294)? What evidence is there that persons join in common law relationships, have children, rear them and marry in later years?

Rather than joining into a consensual union and then having children, the time order for many mothers is reversed. The percentage distribution of mothers in the 1960 census according to union status is revealing: of all mothers in the youngest age group, 15–19 years of age, 67 per cent said they had never lived with a partner. Even in the next older age group, 20–24, 42 per cent of the mothers had never lived with a partner (Francis, 1963, pp. 5–16). In those proportions, at least, motherhood preceded any arrangement for living with a man. There was time

19. Many authors use the term 'common law' union interchangeably with consensual or living unions or concubinage. This is incorrect if it refers merely to sexual household unions, not to the seven or more years continuity, public commitment and legally enforceable rights and duties specified under English common law. F. M. Henriques, *Family and colour in Jamaica* (1952); George W. Roberts, *The population of Jamaica* (1957); O. C. Francis, *The people of modern Jamaica* (1963).

during pregnancy and immediately following birth, but before the census, to enter into a consensual union, but only a minority of women did this. Asked how they happened to enter into consensual unions, 12 of 15 women in Blake's (1961) sample said their first experience of living with a partner was precipitated by pregnancy. Thirty-three out of 49 women said they later entered into a union because of the burden of child care and the need for help. Respondents in a much larger survey mentioned a variety of reasons for entering into consensual union: some did not like the surreptitious nature of visiting relations, some suggested that the woman could perform cooking and laundry services in return for the man's support, some thought authority over children was more secure and a full 40 per cent said they began living with a man because of pregnancy or childbirth.[20] Consensual union, then, is often the consequence rather than the cause of pregnancy out of wedlock.

One might expect long-term, stable associations where people enter into consensual unions and have children, particularly in view of the fact that childbearing comes early and of the fact that most women in the 40–44 age group are still unmarried. There is a potential of 20 to 25 years of stability within consensual unions. Yet, the respondents in Judith Blake's study (1961, pp. 31–2) reported a median of only 3.6 years for all consensual unions. Half the unmarried women (whose average age was 31.7 years) said they had had three or more unions; 35 per cent of the male respondents reported 15 or more unions. In their very large survey Stycos and Back found that the most common form of sexual union was the 'visiting' type. Not counting those of less than three months' duration, the median was only 1.2 years for visiting unions and 3.5 years for cohabiting unions, with an average of one to two years between those unions that lasted at least three months. Simey (1946) and Henriques (1952) attempted to equate legal and consensual unions: they found themselves developing distinct types, each related to length of time (or stability?) with three years somewhat arbitrarily chosen to designate those in 'faithful concubinage'. But the time factor, whether it be one year or three or twenty, tell us nothing about the commitment or fidelity of partners. The essential distinction is between cohabiting relations that can be broken merely at the will of either party, and those which require legal or religious sanction (Stycos and Back, 1964, p. 84).

If transition from consensual union to marriage were frequent, the average age at marriage would be close to the average age at the transition. But Roberts reports that the average age of common law legitimation was six years higher for females and eight years higher for males than the average age for all marriages. It is true that common law unions decrease rapidly after age 39, but that is no reason to suppose that most or even many end in legal union. Rather, the period of rapid dissolution of common law unions is also the period of a rapid rise in the category 'no longer living with husband or common law partner'. We know from the census that divorces and marital separations are rare, with widowhood generally occurring past the childbearing years. The main increases in the proportions married occur in the 25–34 age groups with small increases after age 34 (Francis, 1963, pp. 5–12). A pattern of common law unions that become formal marriages late in life seems to be less likely than a pattern in which most females enter into sexual association with men. Some of them are, indeed, likely to marry and the others gamble on the possibility that 'transient' unions may lead to marriage.

20. J. M. Stycos and K. W. Back, *The control of human fertility in Jamaica* (1964), pp. 91 ff.

In a survey of 1,359 currently mated lower-class Jamaican women, Stycos and Back (1964, p. 132) found that 60 per cent of the 411 women who were married between age 15 and 40 reported that the marriage occurred without a prior common law relationship, although some had had a 'visiting' relationship; of 560 women aged 30–40 who had had common law relationships only one in five resulted in marriage. If women who were between unions had been included in the survey, the probabilities of marriage following such unions would obviously have been lower still. In a report on mating patterns in Trinidad, Roberts and Braithwaite found that:

> Marriage is more often entered at the first stage of the mating pattern. Two and one half times as many women began in a marital union as enter one later by way of a common law union. Of the ever-married, 48.6 per cent entered without previous 'visiting' or 'common law' unions. 30.7 per cent entered in the second stage, 21.7 per cent in the third stage, but we do not know how many partners in each of the later two were needed before marriage was contracted. At any stage it was far less likely that 'visiting' or 'common law' unions would end in marriage than in some non-marital state.[21]

If marriage were largely the culmination of unions long existent in common law form, where children had been born and cared for in a stable situation, we would find very few first and early parity births occurring within marriage. Census details (Francis, 1963), indicate that the distribution of mothers by number of children born is a normal one, because the many high parity married mothers limit the proportions possible at low parity (e.g. 15 per cent of married mothers reported ten or more children and 15 per cent reported one child). The inference which has to be drawn from the evidence we have quoted seems to be as follows: even though a portion of common law unions do, as we would expect, end in marriage, the living arrangement is neither the functional equivalent of, nor an intermediate stage between, single or 'visiting' status and legal marriage. We must continue, therefore, to view births recorded as illegitimate as indicating a real, not merely a nominal, difference in life situation from that indicated by births recorded as legitimate. Women who are not legally married, whether or not in consensual union, are the group at risk of conceiving and bearing illegitimate children.

7 Conception, contraception and abortion

The probability of conception is related to the age at entry into sexual unions, the frequency of coitus and the use or non-use of a variety of possible contraceptives and to the fecundity (or ability to conceive) of the partners. These have changed over time in Jamaica. The average age of first coitus was reported to be 16 or 17 years of age for the 1,359 female respondents of Stycos and Back (1964, p. 26). One fifth reported their first sexual intercourse at age 14. A larger proportion (76 per cent) of the young women had entered one or more ongoing sexual unions by age 19 than had been true for each older age group (p. 126). Thus, frequency or regularity of coitus seems to have increased over time, at least for the younger age group.

21. G. W. Roberts and L. Braithwaite, 'A gross mating table for a West Indian population' (1961).

Contraception could, of course, limit the number of conceptions from early and continuing non-marital relationships. Limiting conceptions, however, requires the desire to do so, the knowledge, availability and use of effective contraception. The desire for small families seems to be apparent in every survey of Jamaican women. Richard J. Udry (1973, pp. 365–71) has computed that, if women limited births to the number they say they want, Jamaican crude birth rates would have been only about one third of those actually reported. Knowledge of the possibility of birth control seems to be almost universal, at least in the recognition that 'there are people who do something to keep themselves from having too many children' (Stycos and Back, 1964, p. 36). Most respondents have heard of specific methods as well, but effective knowledge of various methods is less common, especially in the rural areas. Stycos and Back (p. 43) conclude that a 'large portion of the lower-class population has a very meagre range of total knowledge of birth control methods.' From our examination of illegitimacy ratios and rates, it is clear that Jamaicans have not developed the combination of favourable motivation, knowledge and use of effective contraception among the unmarried that would inhibit the production of children out of wedlock.

Abortion is the last method of avoiding illegitimate birth. We know that it has been used in European and Latin American countries during the early stages of fertility control,[22] and is more likely to be used by single than married women in proportion to their numbers or in proportion to the number of pregnancies.[23] But in Jamaica abortion is universally damned by respondents (Blake, 1961, p. 199; Stycos and Back, 1964, p. 41). Although 30 per cent of the 1,359 women asked could spontaneously mention abortion as a means of birth control and 94 per cent of those asked directly claimed awareness of abortion, only 2 per cent regarded its use favourably and 55 per cent unfavourably. Those who said they knew the method well were twice as likely to say they disliked it because they thought it harmful than because they thought it sinful or immoral (Stycos and Back, 1964, pp. 40–62).

8 Prenuptial pregnancy

In many societies large proportions of those who conceive out of wedlock marry before childbirth and thereby avoid illegitimacy. In the United States (at least from 1950 to 1970) and in England and Wales (at least from 1938 to 1970) something like 55 per cent to 70 per cent of all prenuptial pregnancies that resulted in a live birth have been legalized by marriage before birth (Hartley, 1975, chapter 8). The studies of the past history of illegitimacy in Western Europe elsewhere in this volume show that large proportions of women could be pregnant before marriage with low or very low rates and ratios of illegitimacy. In Jamaica, on the other hand, it is clear from a variety of evidence that pregnancy is not generally an impetus to marriage. Among mothers aged 15–19, no more than 5 per cent and among mothers 20–24, 16 per cent, could have been births prenuptially conceived but legitimated by marriage before the birth of the child (Hartley, 1969, p. 152). Even after birth not many Jamaican children are legitimized by

22. D. V. Glass and E. Grebenik, *The trend and patterns of fertility in Great Britain* (1954), pp. 38–144; Lawrence Lader, *Abortion* (1966); Henry P. David, *Family planning and abortion in the socialist countries of central and eastern Europe* (1970); Mariano B. Requena, 'The problem of induced abortion in Latin America' (1968), pp. 785–99.
23. Christopher Tietze, 'Two years' experience with a liberal abortion law: its impact on fertility trends in New York City' (1973); Registrar General, Great Britain, *Statistical review of England and Wales, supplement on abortion* (1973).

marriage of their parents. Although some authors suggest that the women like their independence and freedom, when asked, nine out of ten of the women respondents in common law unions said that they hoped to marry their present mate (Stycos and Back, 1964, p. 90). We have already seen that the probability of that outcome is not very great.

9 Fecundity and illegitimate fertility rates

Fecundity or the ability to conceive and bear children, seems to have changed over time in Jamaica. General improvements in public health and nutrition lead us to expect improved fecundity. There is evidence, moreover, to indicate a decline in sterility or partial sterility resulting from the recent control of venereal diseases. Indeed, in the 1943 census, almost 20 per cent of the women completing the childbearing period reported that they had never had a child. A rise in fertility during the 1950s occurred in conjunction with a campaign to control venereal disease and an actual decline in syphilitic deaths.[24] From reports of Kingston hospital tests in the mid thirties Tekse reports 42 per cent to 45 per cent of admissions had syphilitic indications. Authorities advised that gonorrhoea was believed to be present in from 60 per cent to 90 per cent of female cases (Tekse, 1968, pp. 12–13). As sterility of the unmarried was reduced, the probability of conception and birth out of wedlock was increased.

It is clear from the very high numbers, ratios and rates of illegitimates that the means of avoiding births out of wedlock are seldom used in Jamaica (Hartley, 1975). Neither universal and early marriage, nor avoidance of non-marital coitus, nor consistent use of effective contraception, nor abortion, nor marriage during pregnancy have been effectively used to reduce illegitimacy. On the contrary, the age-specific rates listed in table 18.3 indicate that for every age group there has been an increasing tendency for unmarried women to produce children. The

Table 18.3: Age-specific illegitimate fertility rates in Jamaica

Age	1943	1948	1953	1957	1960	% difference 1957 as a % of 1948
15–19		90.91	105.17	135.40		148.9 (10-year period)
20–4		185.21	222.91	247.99		133.9
25–9		147.88	192.88	228.68		154.6
30–4		97.12	130.51	162.72		167.5
35–9		63.49	73.94	99.67		156.9
40–4		21.09	23.88	30.23		143.3
15–44	114.76	113.47	139.03	168.24	189.53	165.2 (1960 as a % of 1943)

Note: Rates are the number of births per thousand unmarried women in each age-group for the year.

Source: Calculations from raw data on legitimate and total births by age of mother, reported in UN *Demographic Yearbook* (1954), pp. 297 and 266; (1959), pp. 249 and 274; (1965), pp. 555 and 306. For number and proportions of women in the childbearing years and percentage unmarried at specific ages, *Estimates of intercensal population by age and sex* (1964) were used.

24. Kalman Tekse, *A study of fertility in Jamaica* (1968), p. 12.

number of illegitimate births per thousand unmarried women actually went up (for the five-year age groupings from something between 33 per cent and 67 per cent in the ten years 1948 to 1957). For unmarried women in the thirty-year childbearing span from age 15–44 there was a 65 per cent increase in the rate between 1943 and 1960. By 1960 the rate was almost as high as the legitimate fertility rate though it probably will not continue to rise. Even if all women had been unmarried and all births had been out of wedlock, the illegitimacy rate would have been only a few points higher at 195.81.

In a larger, more detailed study I have calculated the precise effects of changes in the number, the age distribution of females, the proportions unmarried at each age, the age-specific legitimate and illegitimate fertility rates in order to learn which ones had been most influential in the changing illegitimacy measures over time.[25] For Jamaica the entire rise in illegitimacy ratios and in crude birth rates from 1948 to 1957 is explained by the increases in the age-specific illegitimacy rates. If those rates had remained stable as in 1948, the illegitimacy ratio would not have increased, but would have declined to 63.9 per cent of all births. The crude birth rate for 1957 would have been 30.5 instead of rising to 38.1.

10. Social and cultural influences

Space allows only a brief review of some of the social-structural and cultural variables frequently cited as relevant to the study of illegitimacy.

Residence in towns or in the countryside may mean many different things to people of different age, sex or marital status at different periods in history. The urban influence on illegitimacy is neither clear cut nor unidirectional. Cities in their early stages of growth are likely to exhibit unique age and sex structures, different probabilities of marriage, different probabilities of participating in non-marital sexual relations, access to the information and tools of contraception, greater availability of medical clinics for the control of venereal disease, less pressure to marry during pregnancy and different access to and acceptance of abortion. It is the complex interplay of these factors that produces more or less illegitimacy over time in urban as against rural areas.

The proportion of the population living in the Kingston-St Andrews metropolis grew from 25 per cent to 30 per cent between 1960 and 1970. (Data for smaller cities are not separated from their county reports.) Although the Kingston marriage rate is two to three times higher than that of other parishes and the birth rate is about one third higher than that of other areas (Jamaica, Department of Statistics, 1972), by 1970–1 births out of wedlock were 83–85 per cent of all births, far above the national ratio. Yet from 1941–5, illegitimate births in Kingston had been only 61 per cent of the total (Roberts, 1957, p. 290).

Status differences are referred to by all authors on the subject of illegitimacy in Jamaica. Not only does marriage confer higher status, but persons of higher status are generally more strongly committed to marriage and legitimate children. The most commonly used indicators of social class are educational level, income and occupation. The educational level of women is directly related to the likelihood of marriage for each age grouping. In a society in which most women are available for sexual relations, a woman must undoubtedly have other qualities,

25. See George W. Barclay, *Techniques of population analysis* (1958); or Hartley (1969), for details of the standardization procedure.

such as appearance, education or status, to attract a man to a legally binding commitment. And the men better able to afford the accompaniments to the wedding ceremony, said to be of great importance in Jamaica, are those of middle or upper class standing.

Income inequalities in Jamaica are higher than in most countries for which the data are obtainable. In 1958, the lowest 60 per cent of income units received only 19 per cent of total income.[26] In 1954 a sample survey of household expenditures in Kingston led to estimates that 30 per cent of all households had weekly incomes of less than 2 Jamaican pounds while 15 per cent had 15 Jamaican pounds or more per week (Mau, 1968, p. 29). A variety of data indicate that the female-headed households are most likely to have the lowest incomes. Women working in agriculture, textiles, laundry and dry cleaning, in domestic work, or the higglers who have stalls in the Coronation Market seem to earn in one week about what an unskilled man would earn in one day. On this lower income the women are likely to have several mouths to feed.

However, Edith Clarke (1966) has shown that class should not be viewed merely in terms of income, at any rate in three very different communities in Jamaica. The relatively high wages earned in 'Sugartown' in eight months of employment were most often squandered in a short period of affluence. The large movements of people retarded the potential for social organization with the result that marriages were a small proportion of all connections, and instability of sexual unions was very high. In 'Orange Grove', on the other hand, where annual incomes were lower than in 'Sugartown', there was a good proportion of middle-class families in terms of stability planning for the future, and family and community organization. Marriages in 'Orange Grove' represented 80 per cent of all unions and concubinage was for the disesteemed poor. Similarly Stycos and Back (1964, pp. 329–30) found that both occupation and residence are independently related to marital status: Mountain regions and St Ann had twice as high a proportion of married at age 30–34 as other areas. Farmers were two to three times more likely to be married than agricultural labourers. These findings tend to concur with Goode's conclusions (1961, pp. 910–25) that villages with high social and cultural integration have low illegitimacy.

Both religious affiliation and higher levels of attendance at church are related to higher proportions married. When both partners are Catholic or both are Protestant, the couple is more likely to be married than to participate in common law or visiting types of unions (Stycos and Back, 1964, pp. 329–39). These factors again would be indicative of the stability of individuals and their integration into a social group that placed some value on the religious and legal basis of family life over alternative mating patterns. Moreover, group relationships involve the possibilities of sanctions, formal and informal, even such simple ones as personal approval or disapproval.

Neither concubinage nor the consensual union is recognized in the Jamaican legal code, which provides no safeguards for the woman. The man is not liable for her support or maintenance. However, the maintenance and bastardy laws of Jamaica do make a man liable for the support of his illegitimate children, provided they are under age, but the operation of the law presents so many practical difficulties that it is seldom invoked. When sanctions against fathers

26. A. Ahiram, 'Income distribution in Jamaica, 1958' (1964), p. 337. See also Donald McLeod, 'The personal income tax in Jamaica' (1969).

prove ineffectual, the state does, generally, step in to offer some positive support to the 'wholly destitute' mother and her children. Under the Poor Law of 1889, a person must be propertyless and unable to earn a living in order to obtain assistance. In practice the law has been tempered so that a widowed or unmarried mother with three or more children may obtain relief.

One cannot hope to specify all the informal sanctions and influences governing human social behaviour. Nevertheless, we must examine some of the more obvious rewards and punishments attached to the bearing of children out of wedlock. In the slave period rewards for childbearing went to the slave owner, and in the early years incentives paid for slave births went to the plantation overseer, not to the parents. Later, the mother, acting as agent of the slave owner, received some allowance for caring for the child. Since slave owners might sell individuals at any time it was to their advantage to forbid marriage. The pattern of human relationships developed over hundreds of years of slavery was not wiped out by emancipation, and it is questionable whether the system of rewards and punishments has changed in such a way as to make marriage and childbearing within marriage more attractive than casual sexual relationships outside marriage.

We know that in the Blake study over 80 per cent of both male and female respondents claimed that 'marriage is best.' Yet, young girls are often pregnant before they have a chance to think about marriage. Since so many are involved in childbearing outside marriage, community criticism cannot be very great. And in a tropical country where breadfruit, bananas, oranges, papayas, etc., are plentiful, an additional child, at least in the rural areas is not much expense or bother. Nevertheless, with each child the woman becomes more and more dependent on the favours of men. Where sexual intercourse is engaged in freely by most of the women in the population, at least one of the motives for marriage does not exist for the men. If a particular woman does not want to play the game the men have others from whom to choose: the alternatives for the woman, however, are extremely limited. Women are behaving as though they believed that visiting or consensual unions were merely stages in the transition from the single to the married state. In fact, the prevalence of visiting and consensual unions may minimize the chances of marriage by reducing the motivation and rewards within marriage for the male. The worst effect of the situation we have described are felt by the children of these non-marital unions, a full 70 per cent of all those born in Jamaica. Shifted to grandmother, back to mother, to any other relative that will accept them for a time, they often bear the brunt of attacks by their mother's various male partners and by step-siblings. It is not surprising that psychological tests find adult Jamaicans to be 'dependent and mistrustful'.[27]

11 Conclusion

In conclusion we list some of the more obvious points of conflict for Jamaicans with the implications for family disorganization obvious in the contradictions. They are based on responses of Jamaicans to questions posed by Jamaicans and compared with actual behaviour reported by Jamaican statisticians.

27. Madeline Kerr, *Personality and conflict in Jamaica* (1951).

1 An early average age of 16–17 for females at first sexual union exists alongside a late ideal age for marriage (on average the late twenties).
2 A widespread pronouncement that 'marriage is best' is combined with one of the lowest marriage rates in the world.
3 A stated preference for virginity is accompanied by a campaign to eliminate the condition.
4 A relatively small ideal family size of three or fewer children is accompanied by knowledge of different methods of birth control. Yet Jamaica has one of the world's highest birth rates (38–40 per thousand over the past ten years), one of the highest illegitimacy rates and ratios and a very large average family size. Only 31 per cent of the same group of males who state their ideal family size to be three or fewer children approve of any of the various means of birth control.
5 Men seem generally unwilling to take responsibility for the physical and financial support of their own offspring by miscellaneous alliances and are even more reluctant to care for the children of the wife or concubine from previous unions. So the child is shuttled from person to person and has to fend for himself. There is little opportunity for the children to develop their intellectual potentialities, their creativity or individuality.

Our study of Jamaica has revealed a nation with a history of slavery extending over some three hundred years: slavery which prohibited marriage and legal family relationships but encouraged breeding. Now, even 135 years after the emancipation of slaves, there have been few alterations in the patterning of mating behaviour and child care. And as there are no effective social controls to reduce the number of births out of wedlock, the country registers the highest illegitimacy rates and ratios in the world.

19

Illegitimacy in Japan

Akira Hayami

Illegitimacy in Japan has not, until recently, been the subject of academic study. National statistics were not collected before the beginning of the twentieth century, and only fragmentary and disorganized data are available for the period prior to the late nineteenth century.

Before the Meiji Restoration of 1868 there was no clear distinction between legitimate and illegitimate children. Concubinage was a recognized practice among the wealthy and upper classes and in farming communities sexual relationship before marriage was an accepted custom. The imperial house was no exception. The Taisho Emperor, who succeeded in 1912 and founded the present dynasty, was a child of the last Meiji Emperor by a concubine. Thus it is fair to say that Japanese society has traditionally been tolerant of illegitimacy. There is not even an appropriate word in the traditional Japanese language for an illegitimate child. It is possible to indicate that someone is the child of a concubine, but there is no Japanese equivalent of the English word 'bastard'.

The distinction between *kosei* (legitimate) and *shisei* (illegitimate) in the statistics of the Meiji period is the result of the introduction, after the Restoration, of European philosophy and systems of registration, which required the creation of new terms to translate Western concepts. Prior to the Restoration, therefore, public documents do not distinguish between these two categories: in the *shūmon aratamechō* (registers of religious faith) there is neither a categorical nor a terminological distinction between legitimate and illegitimate children in any household. It is, however, possible to count the number of children born to unmarried parents, or to widows or widowers, though, strictly speaking, one should not conclude that these children were illegitimate: quite frequently a couple married after they had had a child. In the present study those children who appear in the *shūmon aratamechō* as having only one parent are classed as illegitimate. Taking these children as a percentage of the total number of births, calculated from the best available material[1] (an unusually detailed set of registers for a single village, complete for a continuous period of one hundred years), we discover that of 503 males born in the period 1773–1869, 34 or 6.8 per cent, and of 490 females, 35 or 7.1 per cent fall into this category. These figures are the only statistics available to date and represent, in my opinion, the lower limit of the illegitimacy ratio in Tokugawa Japan.

The first illegitimacy statistics taken in the post-Restoration period were prepared by the government of Metropolitan Tokyo in 1878.[2] According to these figures, of 29,755 live births in that year, 791 were illegitimate. The proportion of

1. *Shūmon aratamechō* of Nishijo-mura, Anpachi-gun, Mino-nokuni, 1773–1869. See Akira Hayami, 'Labor migration in a pre-industrial society: a study tracing the life histories of the inhabitants of a village' (1973).
2. Naikaku Tōkei Kyoku (Bureau of Statistics), *Ishin igo teikoku tōkei zairyō isan* (Imperial statistical data since the Restoration) IV (1913).

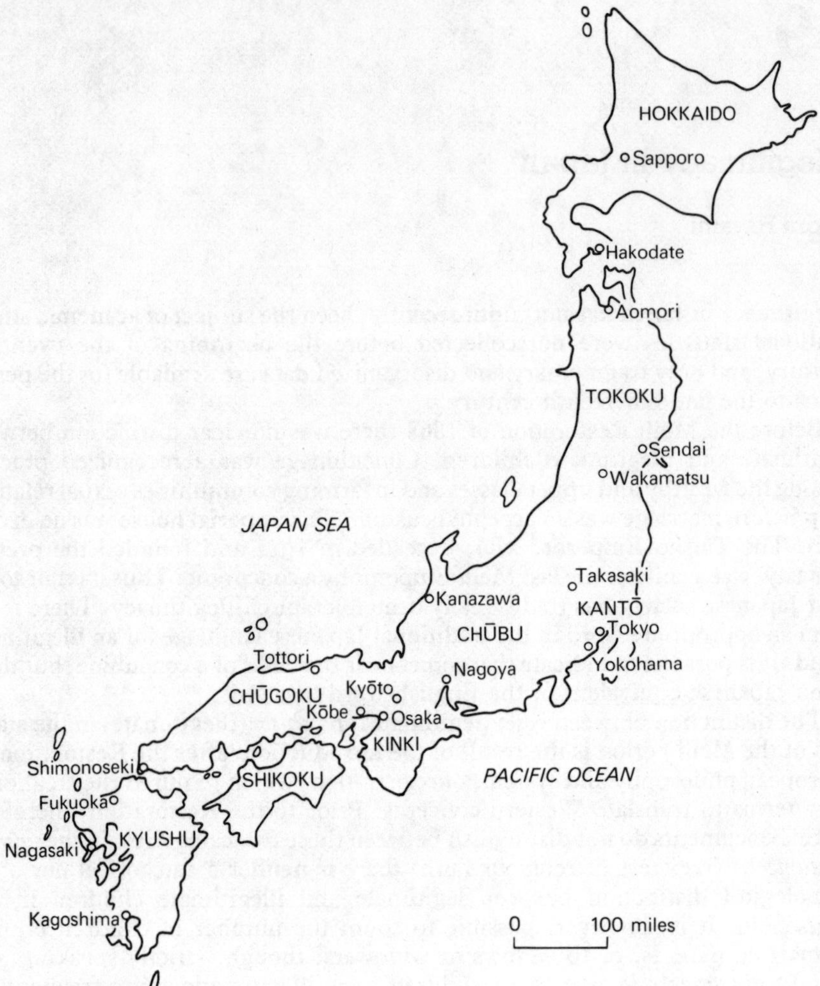

Fig. 19.1 Main districts and cities in Japan

illegitimate births (the illegitimacy ratio) in this 1878 sample is 2.7 per cent. This percentage must be on the low side because the illegitimacy ratio rises over the succeeding years. The ratio climbs sharply to 8.9 per cent in 1887, then reaches, after minor fluctuations, a high of 10.0 per cent in 1897. Such an increase is almost certainly due to the gradual improvement in the technique of gathering information. The same observation applies to metropolitan Osaka, for which we have the next earliest set of statistics. Taking later changes into consideration, the illegitimacy ratio of 7.2 per cent in 1881 is too low. The ratios of 17.5 per cent in 1888, and 19.6 per cent in 1897, are far more plausible. Thus the ratios for the early 1880s are unreliable and should not be used as a basis for research.

Table 19.1 shows the illegitimacy ratios in 1887 and 1897 for which years the statistics may be accepted as accurate, for those *fu* (metropolitan cities) and *ken* (prefectures) where survey data were taken. Out of 47 *fu* and *ken*, data exist for 19,

Table 19.1: Illegitimacy ratio by *ken* or *fu*, Japan, 1887 and 1897

Ken or Fu	1887	1897
	%	%
Aomori-ken	2.7	3.9
Akita-ken	3.4	–
Iwate-ken	2.4	–
Miyagi-ken	3.4	–
Fukushima-ken	3.9	–
Tochigi-ken	3.2	–
Saitama-ken	2.3	3.4
Tōkyō-fu	8.9	9.9
Kanagawa-ken	3.6	5.9
Toyama-ken	2.1	3.4
Fukui-ken	3.9	–
Yamanashi-ken	–	2.7
Shizuoka-ken	2.5	–
Ōsaka-fu	14.9	19.6
Wakayama-ken	2.6	–
Tottori-ken	9.7	10.1
Kōchi-ken	5.4	6.8
Saga-ken	1.8	3.4
Nagasaki-ken	4.5	–
Kumamoto-ken	1.7	3.9
Kagoshima-ken	–	5.4
Total	6.7	8.1

Note: Ken and *fu* are local administrative units created after the Restoration. The three most urbanized prefectures, Tokyo, Kyoto and Osaka, were called *fu*, usually rendered 'metropolis', all others, *ken*.

or about 40 per cent for 1887 and 12, about 25 per cent for 1897. The average national illegitimacy ratio indicated by these is 8.1 per cent for 1897, a ratio quite compatible with the ratio of 8.8 per cent in the more reliable registration system of 1900.[3] Table 19.1 shows that the ratio rose over the ten-year period in all the prefectures studied. At the same time there are clear regional variations: illegitimacy ratios are highest in Osaka, Tottori and Tokyo and lowest in the prefectures north of Tokyo, or west and south of Tottori.

Urban statistics for this period present us with a different picture. In table 19.2 the 54 cities with populations of more than 25,000 in 1897 are arranged in order of illegitimacy ratios: the very wide range of ratios is immediately obvious. Hakodate, the highest, has an illegitimacy ratio 14 times that of Kagoshima, the lowest. Twelve of the top 20 cities are in Kinki, Chūgoku and Shikoku districts. The other 8 in the top 20 are all, except Wakamatsu and Takasaki, major cities of over 100,000 inhabitants. The ratios for Takasaki and Wakamatsu are unusually high in 1897, but if one were to substitute the average ratios for the five years 1892–6 these two places would fall below the top 20, so that it would appear that their 1897 ratios and rankings are the result of survey errors. The more sparsely populated districts of Tohoku in the north and Kyūshū in the southwest, on the other hand, show low ratios. Except for Nagasaki and Wakamatsu the highest ratios are 8.3 per cent in Aomori in the north and 8.5 per cent in Fukuoka in the south. It should be noted that eight of the lowest ranking twenty cities are in these two districts.

3. Shirley F. Hartley, 'The decline of illegitimacy in Japan' 1970, table 1.

Table 19.2: Illegitimacy ratio in cities over 25000 inhabitants, Japan, 1897

		%			%
1	Hakodate (Hokkaido)	43.2	28	Nagano (Nagano)	8.7
2	Sakai (Osaka)	25.2	29	Maebashi (Gumma)	8.6
3	Shimonoseki (Yamaguchi)	24.7	30	Niigata (Niigata)	8.6
4	Nara (Nara)	23.7	31	Fukuoka (Fukuoka)	8.5
5	Okayama (Okayama)	23.6	32	Tsu (Mie)	8.4
6	Osaka (Osaka)	22.5	33	Aomori (Aomori)	8.3
7	Sapporo (Hokkaido)	21.7	34	Hiroshima (Hiroshima)	8.0
8	Kobe (Hyōgo)	21.3	35	Sendai (Miyagi)	7.8
9	Takamatsu (Kagawa)	19.0	36	Toyama (Toyama)	7.4
10	Wakamatsu (Fukushima)	18.3	37	Yamagata (Yamagata)	7.3
11	Matsue (Shimane)	18.0	38	Fukui (Fukui)	7.1
12	Tottori (Tottori)	17.8	39	Chiba (Chiba)	6.9
13	Ōtsu (Shiga)	17.2	40	Naha (Okinawa)	6.8
14	Takasaki (Gumma)	17.2	41	Kōfu (Yamanashi)	6.5
15	Kyoto (Kyoto)	16.7	42	Akita (Akita)	6.4
16	Nagoya (Aichi)	16.6	43	Ujiyamada (Mie)	6.2
17	Nagasaki (Nagasaki)	15.7	44	Kumamoto (Kumamoto)	5.8
18	Yokohama (Kanagawa)	15.1	45	Utsunomiya (Tochigi)	5.8
19	Kōchi (Kōchi)	14.1	46	Mito (Ibaraki)	5.6
20	Tokyo (Tokyo)	13.1	47	Shizuoka (Shizuoka)	5.3
21	Gifu (Gifu)	12.7	48	Morioka (Iwate)	5.3
22	Wakayama (Wakayama)	12.7	49	Kurume (Fukuoka)	4.2
23	Himeji (Hyōgo)	11.0	50	Takaoka (Toyama)	4.0
24	Matsumoto (Nagano)	10.8	51	Yonezawa (Yamagata)	3.7
25	Tokushima (Tokushima)	10.7	52	Saga (Saga)	3.6
26	Matsuyama (Ehime)	9.4	53	Hirosaki (Aomori)	3.2
27	Kanazawa (Ishikawa)	9.3	54	Kagoshima (Kagoshima)	3.1

The following observations may therefore be made on the data in table 19.2:

1 The ratio is high in the Osaka-dominated Kinki district, as far east as the Nagoya region, and in western Honshū and Shikoku.
2 Tokyo, the capital and largest city, shows a high ratio.
3 Cities in the newly colonized island of Hokkaido are also very high.
4 Port towns like Yokohama, Shimonoseki and Nagasaki have quite high ratios.

To amplify this picture a calculation has been made of the coefficient of correlation between the ratio and the distance from Osaka for all cities in table 19.2, except those in Hokkaido. A correlation of $r = 0.54$ was obtained. Confining the calculation to the cities under observation (1), the correlation is $r = 0.70$, which is within the significant limit. A city's illegitimacy ratio is therefore generally inversely proportional to its distance from Osaka.

In contrasting the illegitimacy ratios of urban and rural areas we find the urban ratios to be generally higher. Material which provides such data is scarce, but table 19.3 shows the ratios in urban and rural areas for 1887 and 1897 where they are available. In those prefectures which have towns to which observations (2) to (4) apply, the ratios are much higher in the towns than in the rural areas:

	1887	1897
Tokyo	1.9 ×	2.6 ×
Kanagawa	4.1 ×	3.1 ×
Nagasaki	6.2 ×	–

Table 19.3: Illegitimacy ratio by urban and rural areas, Japan, 1887 and 1897

	1887		1897	
	Urban	Rural	Urban	Rural
	%	%	%	%
Aomori-ken	1.3	2.8	3.2	3.9
Akita-ken	5.0	3.4		
Iwate-ken	1.9	2.4		
Miyagi-ken	6.2	3.1		
Tōkyō-fu	10.3	5.3	13.1	5.1
Kanagawa-ken	11.9	2.8	15.1	4.8
Toyama-ken	2.6	2.1	7.4	3.1
Fukui-ken	7.3	4.1	7.1	5.0
Shizuoka-ken	3.7	2.5		
Ōsaka-fu	20.2	12.7	22.7	17.3
Wakayama-ken	7.2	2.2		
Tottori-ken	15.1	9.4	17.7	9.6
Kōchi-ken	5.0	5.5	14.1	6.5
Saga-ken	1.5	1.8	3.6	3.4
Nagasaki-ken	22.9	3.7		
Kumamoto-ken	2.2	1.7	5.8	3.9
Total	10.3	3.5	13.2	3.9

But in the other prefectures the differences in illegitimacy ratios in urban and rural areas are much smaller, averaging only 1.5 times in 1887. This pattern is confirmed by the high coefficient of correlation between urban and rural illegitimacy ratios in these prefectures: $r = 0.94$ in 1887 and $r = 0.92$ in 1897. These prefectures have an extremely high positive correlation between illegitimacy ratios in urban and rural areas. However, in Tokyo, Kanagawa and Nagasaki, which have towns to which observations (2) to (4) are applicable, though the rural ratios are low, the urban ratios are very high. The ratios in these cities are clearly determined independently from the ratios in the surrounding rural districts.

The regional variations in rural illegitimacy ratios in table 19.3 can be explained in the same manner as was applied in observation (1) for table 19.2. That is, for the prefectures considered in table 19.3, the illegitimacy ratios are inversely proportional to the distance of the seats of the prefectural government from Osaka with a coefficient of correlation of $r = 0.68$.

Certain conclusions may be drawn; but the question is, first of all, how to interpret the correlation of the illegitimacy ratio with distance from Osaka. Osaka was the centre of commerce and finance in Tokugawa Japan and the operations of the market economy were focused on that city.[4] The markets for rice, the staple commodity, and for other products were there. Highly sophisticated commercial, financial and credit institutions were all based and developed in Osaka. This was a city of half a million commercially minded individuals, in complete contrast to the political city of Edo, dominated by samurai-bureaucrats (the population in Edo after 1700 is estimated at around 500,000 samurais and 500,000 commoners. The samurai population of Osaka, on the other hand seems to have been about 10 per cent). Compared with Edo, Osaka was less steeped in Confucian ethics, more secular and more realistic. These factors seem to have contributed to a higher illegitimacy ratio in Osaka and the surrounding areas. After the Meiji Restoration

4. William B. Hauser, *Economic institutional change in Tokugawa* (1974), chapter 2.

Osaka rapidly lost its unique position. For, whereas in the Tokugawa period rice as a means of paying taxes had flowed through Osaka from all parts of Japan, the land tax was now paid in cash and Osaka's storehouses no longer bulged with rice. The introduction of steam power made possible direct, nationwide transport links between producing and consuming districts and this affected adversely the position of Osaka as a supplier of goods to Edo, now renamed Tokyo.

The late nineteenth century witnessed the rapid disappearence of the pattern and mode of life of Tokugawa Japan because of modernization, industrialization and urbanization. In Tokyo, the capital, in port cities like Yokohama, Kobe, Shimonoseki and Nagasaki, in the two newly developed cities of Hokkaido and Kobe, which were all centres respectively of modern transport and industry, the army and the administration, higher illegitimacy ratios kept pace with these modern developments, and produced the regional patterns described above. After 1900 the illegitimacy ratio began to decline and it is, therefore, of interest to discover the peak years of illegitimacy. The data for the years 1887–97 give interesting regional differences in the peak years. Complete data for the entire period are available for only eleven prefectures. In Osaka, Tottori and Tokyo, where the ratios are high, the peak came early in the years 1890–4. By contrast, in the other prefectures, with lower ratios, the peak ratios are in the later years, 1895–7. The same relationship appears in the cities. In eight Kinki cities the average peak year is 1892. In ten cities in Tohoku and Hyūshū the average peak year is 1895, three years later. In cities, especially those Kinki cities with the highest ratios, illegitimacy had reached its peak and begun to decline at the end of the nineteenth century. For other cities and rural districts there is only very scant data for the whole eleven years, but there is evidence that in these areas the illegitimacy ratio did not peak until the beginning of the twentieth century.

It is commonly assumed that a rising illegitimacy ratio is the usual concomitant of industrialization and urbanization in almost all countries. In Japan, on the contrary, the ratio clearly decreased as industrialization and urbanization progressed. It is not possible to predict how long this decrease will continue, but as the ratio is now less than one per cent, an asymptotic effect and probably a future rebound may be anticipated.

However, the declining illegitimacy ratio as industrialization progressed in Japan must also be set against the high illegitimacy ratio in pre-industrial Japan. To explain this decrease is a task for the future, requiring more detailed analysis. It is hoped that closer examination of *shūmon aratamechō* and other registers of residents in the cities will help to explain the high illegitimacy ratios of pre-industrial Japan.

Bibliography

Place of publication is London unless otherwise stated. The following abbreviations have been used:

ASR	*American Sociological Review*
Annales DH	*Annales de démographie historique*
Annales ESC	*Annales d'économies, sociétés et civilisations*
FPP	*Family Planning Perspectives*
JIH	*Journal of Interdisciplinary History*
JMF	*Journal of Marriage and the Family*
LPS	*Local Population Studies*
PS	*Population Studies*
SB	*Social Biology*

Adams, C. F.: 'Some phases of sexual morality and church discipline in colonial New England', *Proceedings of the Massachusetts Historical Society*, 2nd series, 6 (1891).

Agardh, C. A.: *Försök till en statsekonomisk statistik öfver Sverige III*, part 3 (Karlstad, 1859).

d'Angeville, A.: *Essai sur la statistique de la population Française*, new edn ed. E. LeRoy Ladurie (Paris, 1969).

Arensberg, C. M. and Kimball, S. T.: *Family and community in Ireland* (1940), 2nd edn (Harvard, 1968).

Ashby, A. W.: 'One hundred years of poor law administration in a Warwickshire village', chapter 6 in *Oxford studies in social and legal history* (Oxford, 1912).

Atkinson, J. C.: *Forty years in a moorland parish* (1891).

Bäärhielm, G.: 'Utomäktenskapliga barns ställning', *Minneskrift ägnad 1734 års lag II* (Stockholm, 1934).

Back, K. W. and Stycos, J. M.: *The control of human fertility in Jamaica* (New York, 1964).

de Balzac, H.: *Le Lys dans la vallée* (Paris, 1966).

Bang, G.: *Kirkebogstudier. Bidrag till Dansk befolkningsstatistik og kulturhistorie i det 17. aarhundrede* (Copenhagen, 1906).

Barclay, G. W.: *Techniques of population analysis* (New York, 1958).

Bardet, Jean-Pierre: 'Enfants abandonnés et enfants assistés à Rouen dans la seconde moitié du XVIII siècle', in *Hommage à Marcel Reinhard*, Société de démographie historique (Paris, 1973).

Barnes, J. A.: 'Class and committees in a Norwegian island parish', *Human relations* VII, 1 (February 1954).

Basavarajappa, K. G.: 'Premarital pregnancies and ex-nuptial births in Australia, 1911–1966', *Australian and New Zealand Journal of Sociology* 4 (October 1968), pp. 126–45.

Beach, F. A. and Ford, C. S.: *Patterns of sexual behaviour* (New York, 1951).

Beechey, F. C.: 'The Irish in York, 1845–1875', unpublished PhD dissertation (University of York, 1977); see also under Finnegan.

Becker, H. S.: *Outsiders: studies in the sociology of deviance* (New York, 1963).
Becon, Thomas: *Catechism* (1560).
Bell, Wendell: *Jamaican leaders* (Berkeley, 1964).
Bennett, H. S.: *Life on the English manor: a study of peasant conditions, 1150–1400* (Cambridge, 1937).
Berkov, B. and Sklar, J.: 'Teenage family formation in postwar America', *FPP* 6 (spring 1974).
'Abortion, illegitimacy and the American birth rate', *Science* 185, no. 4155 (September 1974).
Bernard, J.: *The sex game* (New York, 1972).
Berques, H.: *La prevention des naissances dans la famille* (Paris, 1960).
Blackstone, William: *Commentaries on the laws of England*, 12th edn (1796).
Blake, J.: *Family structure in Jamaica: the social context of reproduction* (New York, 1961).
Blake, J. and Davis, K.: 'Social structure and fertility: an analytic framework', *Economic development and cultural change* IV (April 1956).
Blasingame, J.: *The slave community* (1972).
Blau, P. and Dudley Duncan, O.: *The American occupational structure* (New York, 1967).
Blayo, Y.: 'La population de la France, chapitre III – natalité, fecondité', *Population* 29 (1974), pp. 51–81.
'Mouvement naturel de la population française de 1740 à 1829', *Population* 25 (1970), pp. 15–64.
Blayo, Y. and Henry, L.: 'Données démographiques sur la Bretagne et l'Anjou de 1740 à 1829', *Annales DH* (1967), pp. 91–171.
Blayo, Y. with Blayo, C.: 'L'illegitimité en France en 1800 et en 1968', in *Ve Colloque National de Demographie du Centre National de la Recherche Scientifique* 935 (1976), pp. 221–6.
Bogue, D.: *Principles of demography* (New York, 1969).
Boissevain, J.: *Friends of friends: networks, manipulators and coalitions* (Oxford, 1974).
Boorde, Andrew: *The breviarie of health* (1575).
Boswell, James: *The life of Samuel Johnson . . . to which is added the journal of a tour to the Hebrides*, ed. P. Fitzgerald (1897).
Bothuan, R.: *Etude sur l'économie, la vie sociale et démographique de la paroisse de Plougastel au XVIIIe siècle* (Brest, 1967).
Bowden, P.: 'Statistical appendix', in Joan Thirsk (ed.), *The agrarian history of England and Wales* IV, *1500–1640* (Cambridge, 1967).
Boyd, K.: 'The theological presuppositions of Scottish church pronouncements on sex, marriage and the family, 1850–1914', unpublished PhD thesis (University of Edinburgh, 1973).
Bradley, L.: 'Common-law marriage: a possible cause of under-registration', *LPS* 11 (1973).
Braithwaite, E.: *The development of Creole society in Jamaica, 1770–1820* (Oxford, 1971).
Brinkworth, E. R.: 'The study and use of archdeacon's court records, illustrated from Oxford records, 1566–1759', *Transactions of the Royal Historical Society*, 4th series, XXV (1943).
(ed.): *The archdeacon's court; liber actorum, 1584*, 2 vols, Oxford Record Series XXIII (1942), XXIX (1946).
Brinton, C.: *French revolutionary legislation on illegitimacy, 1798–1804* (Cambridge, Mass., 1936).
Broom, L.: 'The social differentiation of Jamaica', *ASR* 19 (1954), pp. 115–25.
Bulloch, J. and Drummond, A. C.: *The church in Victorian Scotland, 1843–1874* (Edinburgh, 1975).
Burgière, André: 'De Malthus à Max Weber: le mariage tardif et l'esprit de l'entreprise', *Annales ESC* (1972), pp. 1128–38.
Burn, Richard: *Ecclesiastical law*, 5th edn (1763).
Burton, Thomas: *Diary*, ed. J. T. Rutt, 4 vols (1828).

Carley, M. M.: *Jamaica, the old and the new* (1963).
Carter, Ian: 'Illegitimate births, and illegitimate inferences', *Scottish Journal of Sociology* 1 (1977), pp. 125–35.
Caspard, Pierre: 'Conceptions prénuptiales et développement du capitalisme dans la Principauté de Neuchâtel, 1678–1820', *Annales ESC* 4 (1974).
Chalmers, T.: *The Christian and civic economy of large towns*, vol. III in his *Works* (Glasgow, 1838–42).
Chambers, J. D.: *Population, economy and society in pre-industrial England* (Oxford, 1972).
Chamoux, A.: 'L'enfance abandonnée à Reims à la fin du XVIIIe siècle', *Annales DH* (1973), pp. 263–85.
'Mise en nourrice et mortalité des enfants légitimes', *Annales DH* (1973).
Charbonneau, H.: *Tourouvre-au-Perche au XVII et XVIIIe siècles* (Paris, 1970).
Chaunu, P. *et al.*: in E. de Bouard (ed.), *Histoire de la Normandie* (Toulouse, 1970).
Chevalier, L.: *Classes labourieuses et classes dangereuses à Paris pendant la première moitié du XIXe siècle* (Paris, 1958).
Christensen, H. T.: 'Cultural relativism and premarital sex norms', *ASR* 25, 1 (1960), pp. 31–9.
Clark, P.: 'The migrant in Kentish towns, 1580–1640', in P. Clark and P. Slack (eds), *Crisis and order in English towns, 1500–1640* (1972).
'Eighteenth-century migrations: some problems of quantitative analysis', in P. Clark *et al.*, *Poverty and social policy, 1750–1870* (Milton Keynes, 1974).
Clarke, E.: *My mother who fathered me* (1957).
Coale, A. J.: 'The decline of fertility in Europe from the French Revolution World War II', in S. J. Behrman, L. Corsa and R. Freedman (eds), *Fertility and family planning: a world view* (Ann Arbor, 1969).
Coale, A. J. and Demeny, P.: *Regional model life tables and stable populations* (Princeton, 1966).
Coale, A. J., Anderson, B. A. and Härm, E.: *Human fertility in Russia since the nineteenth century* (1979).
Coale, A. J. and Treadway, Roy: 'A summary of changing fertility in the provinces of Europe (unpublished paper prepared for the Summary Conference on European Fertility, Princeton, New Jersey, 23–27 July 1979).
Cochrane, C. M., Haney, C. A. and Vincent, C. E.: 'Familial and generational patterns of illegitimacy' *JMF* 31 (1969).
The Code of Napoleon . . . literally translated from the original and official edition by a barrister of the Inner Temple (New York, 1841).
Comfort, A.: *The anxiety makers* (1967).
Connell, K. H.: *Irish peasant society* (Oxford, 1968).
Connolly, S. J.: 'The chastity of the Irish reconsidered', unpublished typescript (Cambridge Group, 1978).
'Illegitimacy and pre-nuptial pregnancy in Ireland before 1864: the evidence of some Catholic parish registers', *Irish economic and social history* IV (1979).
Cooke, R.: *A white sheet* (1629).
Cornwall, J.: 'Evidence of population mobility in the seventeenth century', *Bulletin of the Institute of Historical Research* XL (1967).
Corsie, E. A.: 'Domestic servants in selected parishes of Edinburgh, 1871–91', MA thesis (University of Edinburgh, 1975).
Cott, N. F.: 'Eighteenth-century family and social life revealed in Massachusetts divorce records', *Journal of Social History* (fall 1976).
Cox, J. C.: *The parish registers of England* (1910).
Cramond, W.: *Illegitimacy in Banffshire* (Banff, 1888).
Croix, A.: *Nantes et le pays nantais au XVIe siècle* (Paris, 1974).
Croog, S.: 'Aspects of the cultural background of premarital pregnancy in Denmark', *Social Forces* 30 (1951).

Crum, F. S.: 'The birth rate in Massachusetts, 1850–90', *Quarterly Journal of Economics* XI (1897).
Cutright, P.: 'Economic events and illegitimacy in developed countries', *Journal of Comparative Family Studies* II (1971).
'Teenage sexual revolution and the myth of an abstinent past', *FPP* 4 (1972).
'Illegitimacy in the United States, 1920–68', in R. Parke Jr and C. F. Westoff (eds), *Demographic and social aspects of population growth* (Washington, 1972).
'Illegitimacy and income supplements', *Joint Economic Committee US Congress, Studies in Public Welfare* 12 (Washington, 1973).
Cutright, P. and Galle, O.: 'The effect of illegitimacy on United States general fertility rates and population growth', *PS* XXVII (November 1973).
Cutright, P. and Johnson, D. R.: 'Problems in the analysis of Latin American illegitimacy', in M. Armer and A. Grimshaw (eds), *Methodological problems in comparative sociology* (New York, 1973).

Dalton, M.: *The countrey justice* (1622).
David, H. P.: *Family planning and abortion in the socialist countries of central and eastern Europe* (New York, 1970).
Davidson, M. and Grabill, W. H.: 'Marriage, fertility and child-spacing, June 1965', *Current population reports* series P–20, 186 (1969).
Davis, K.: 'Illegitimacy and the social structure', *American Journal of Sociology* 45 (1939), reprinted in William J. Goode (ed.), *Readings on the family and society* (New Jersey, 1964).
'The forms of illegitimacy', *SF* 18 (1939).
Human society (New York, 1948).
'Sexual behaviour', in R. K. Merton and R. Nisbet (eds), *Contemporary social problems*, 2nd edn (New York, 1966).
'The American family in relation to demographic change', in R. Parke Jr and C. Westoff (eds), *Demographic and social aspects of population growth* (Washington, 1972).
Davis, N. Z.: 'The reasons of misrule: youth group and charivaris in 16th century France', *Past and Present* 50 (1971).
Degler, C. N.: 'What ought to be and what was: women's sexuality in the nineteenth century', *American Historical Review* 79 (1974).
Delaselle, C.: 'Les enfants abandonnés à Paris au XVIIIe siècle', *Annales ESC* (January/February 1975).
Demos, J.: 'Families in colonial Bristol, Rhode Island: an exercise in historical demography', *William and Mary Quarterly*, 3rd series, 25 (1968).
Deniel, R.: 'La population d'un village du nord de la France, Sainghin-en-Mélantois, de 1665 à 1851', *Population* 20 (1965).
Depauw, J.: 'Amour illégitime et société à Nantes au XVIIIe siècle', *Annales ESC* 4 (1972).
'Immigration féminine, professions féminines et structures urbaines à Nantes au XVIIIe siècle', *Enquêtes et documents, Centre de Recherches sur l'Histoire de la France Atlantique* II (Fontenay-le-Comte, 1972).
Diderot, Denis: *Supplement au voyage de Bougainville* (Paris, 1966).
Dixon, R. B.: 'Explaining cross-cultural variations in age at marriage and proportions never marrying', *PS* XXV (1971).
Downame, John: *Foure treatises tending to disswade all christians from foure no lesse hainous than common sinnes; namely swearing, drunkenness, whoredome and briberie* (1609).
Drake, M.: *Population and society in Norway, 1735–1865* (Cambridge, 1969).
Dreyer-Roos, S.: *La population strasbourgeoise sous l'Ancien Regime 1681–1789* (Strasbourg, 1969).
Dudley Duncan, B. and O.: 'Family stability and occupational success', *Social Problems* 16 (1969).
Dunlop, John Graham: *The autobiography of John Graham Dunlop* (1932).

Dupâquier, J. and Charlot, E.: 'Mouvement annuel de la population de la ville de Paris de 1670 à 1821', *Annales DH* (1967).

Earle, A. M.: *Customs and fashions in old New England* (New York, 1893).
Elvius, P.: 'Förtekning uppå Barnens årliga antal, som äro födde uti U . . . stad under de sist förflutne 50 åren', *Kungl. Swenska Wetenskaps Academiens handlingar* 5 (Stockholm, 1744).
Engels, F.: *The origin of the family, private property and the state* (1884), English translation (1940).
Engerman, S. L.: 'Some economic and demographic comparisons of slavery in the United States and the British West Indies', *Economic History Review*, 2nd series, XXLX, no. 2 (1976).
Erikson, K. T.: *Wayward puritans: a study in the sociology of deviance* (New York, 1966).
Eversley, D. E. C.: 'Exploitation of Anglican parish registers by aggregative analysis', in E. A. Wrigley (ed.), *Introduction to English historical demography* (1966).
Ewen, C. L. (ed.): *Witch hunting and witch trials* (1929).

Fairchilds, Cissie: 'Female sexual attitudes and the rise of illegitimacy', *JIH* VIII, 4 and IX, 2 (1978, a reply to Flandrin, 1978).
Faler, P.: 'Cultural aspects of the Industrial Revolution: Lynn, Massachusetts shoemakers and industrial morality, 1826–1860', *Labour history* 15 (1974).
Farber, B.: *Guardians of virtue: Salem families in 1800* (New York, 1972).
Farley, R.: *Growth of the black population: a study of demographic trends* (Chicago, 1970).
Farley, R. and Hermalin, A. I.: 'Family stability: a comparison of trends between blacks and whites', *ASR* 36 (1971).
Festy, P.: 'Extra-marital fertility and its occurrence in stable unions; recent trends in Western Europe', paper presented at 2nd European population seminar, the Netherlands (1978).
Finnegan, Frances: *Poverty and prostitution* (Cambridge, 1979); see also under Beechey.
Flaherty, D.: 'Law and the enforcement of morals in early America', *Perspectives in American history* V (1971).
Privacy in colonial New England (Charlottesville, 1972).
Flandrin, J. L.: 'Mariage tardif et vie sexuelle: discussions et hypothèses de recherche', *Annales ESC* 27 (1972).
'L'attitude à l'égard du petit enfant et les conduites sexuelles dans la civilisation occidentale', *Annales DH* (1973), pp. 143–210.
Les amours paysannes (Paris, 1975).
Familles, parenté, maison, sexualité dans l'ancienne société (Paris, 1976), English translation by R. Southern, *Families in former times: kinship, household and sexuality* (Cambridge, 1979).
'A case of naivete in the use of statistics', *JIH* IX, 2 (1978).
Flinn, M. W. *et al.*: *Scottish population history from the seventeenth century to the nineteen-thirties* (Cambridge, 1977).
Fogel, R. W. and Engerman, S. L.: *Time on the cross* (Boston, 1974).
Forbes, T. R.: *Chronicle from Aldgate: life and death in Shakespeare's London* (Yale, 1971).
Ford, T.: *Reformation sure and steadfast* (1641).
Forster, R. and Ranum, O.: *Family and society: selections from 'Annales'* (Baltimore, 1976).
Fortes, Meyer: 'Parenthood, marriage and fertility in West Africa' *Journal of Development Studies*, special issue on population and development, 14, 4 (1978).
Francis, O. C.: *The people of modern Jamaica* (Jamaica, 1963).
Frazier, E. F.: *The negro family in the United States* (Chicago, 1966).
Friberg, N. and I.: *350 års befolkningsutveckling i Mälardalen, Tillberga* (Stockholm, 1972).
Frykman, Jonas: 'Sexual intercourse and social norms: a study of illegitimate births in Sweden, 1831–1933', *Ethnologica Scandinavia* (1975).
Horan i bondesamhället (Lund, 1977), English summary, pp. 220–9.

von Fürer-Haimendorf, C.: *Sherpas of Nepal* (1964).
Furstenberg, F. F. Jr, Herschberg, T. and Modell, J.: 'The origins of the female-headed black family: the impact of the urban experience', *JIH* VI, 2 (autumn 1975).

Gahn, H.: *Moral-statistika uppgifter i frihetstidens tabellverk. En demografisk studie* (Uppsala, 1915).
Ganiage, J.: *Trois villages de l'Ile de France au XVIIIe siècle* (Paris, 1963).
Gandy. G. N.: 'Illegitimacy in a handloom weaving community: fertility patterns in Culcheth, Lancs., 1781–1860'. D.Phil dissertation (University of Oxford, 1978).
Garden, M.: *Lyon et les Lyonnais au XVIIIe siècle* (Paris, 1970).
Gaunt, David: 'Family planning and the pre-industrial society: some Swedish evidence', in K. Ågren *et al.* (eds), *Aristocrats, farmers and proletarians: essays in Swedish demographic history* (Uppsala, 1973).
Gautier, E. and Henry, L.: *La population de Crulai, paroisse Normande* (Paris, 1958).
Gebhard, P. H. *et al.*: *Pregnancy, birth and abortion* (New York, 1966).
Genovese, E. D.: *Roll, Jordan, roll: the world the slaves made* (New York, 1974).
Gibson, E.: *Codex Juris Ecclesiastici Anglicani* (1713).
Gill, Derek: *Illegitimacy, sexuality and the status of women* (Oxford, 1977).
Gillis, John R.: *Youth and history* (New York, 1974).
Glass, D. V.: *Numbering the people* (Farnborough, 1973).
Glass, D. V. and Grebenik, E.: *The trend and patterns of fertility in Great Britain* (1954).
Gleason, G. H.: *The justices of the peace in England, 1558–1640* (Oxford, 1969).
Godolphin, J.: *Reportorium canonicum* (1678).
Goode, William J.: 'Illegitimacy in the Caribbean social structure', *ASR* 25 (1960), pp. 21–5.
'Illegitimacy, anomie, and cultural penetration', *ASR* (1961).
The family (Englewood Cliffs, 1964).
World revolution and family patterns (New York, 1963).
Goody, Jack: *Production and reproduction: a comparative study of the domestic domain* (Cambridge, 1976).
Gorer, Geoffrey: *Himalayan village: an account of the Lepachas of Sikkim*, 2nd edn (1967).
Gough, Richard: *Antiquityes and memoyres of the parish of Myddle* (1875).
Govea, E. V.: *Slave society in the British Leeward Islands at the end of the eighteenth century* (New Haven, 1965).
Grabill, W. H., Kiser, C. V. and Whelpton, P. K.: *The fertility of American women* (New York, 1958); see also under US Bureau of the Census.
Grebenik, E.: 'The fertility of women with premarital conception in Great Britain', *Bulletin de l'institut international de statistique* 36 (1958).
Greven, P. J.: *Four generations* (New York, 1970).
Griffiths, E.: *The two books of homilies* (Oxford, 1859).
Gulliver, P. H.: *Neighbours and networks: the idiom of kinship in social action among the Ndendeuli of Tanzania* (Berkeley, 1971).
Gutman, H. G.: 'Le phenomène invisible: la composition de la famille et du foyer noirs après la guerre de secession', *Annales ESC* 27 (July-October 1972).
'The birth statistics of Massachusetts during the nineteenth century', *PS* 10 (July 1956), pp. 69–93.
Gutman, H. G. and Sutch, R.: 'The slave family: protected agent of capitalist masters or victim of the slave trade', and 'Victorians all? The sexual mores and conduct of slaves and their masters', in P. A. David *et al.*, *Reckoning with slavery: a critical study in the quantitative history of American negro slavery* (New York, 1976).

Hair, P. E. H.: 'Bridal pregnancy in earlier rural England in earlier centuries', *PS* 20 (1966), pp. 233–43.
'Bridal pregnancy in earlier rural England further examined', *PS* 24 (1970), pp. 59–70.
Before the bawdy court (New York, 1972).

Hajnal, John: 'European marriage patterns in perspective', in D. V. Glass and D. E. C. Eversley (eds), *Population in history* (1965).
Harrison, D.: 'The culture of poverty in Coconut village, Trinidad, a critique', *Sociological Review* 24 (1976).
Hartley, Marie, and Ingilby, Joan: *Yorkshire village* (1953).
Hartley, S. F.: 'The amazing rise of illegitimacy in Great Britain', *Social Forces* 44 (June 1966).
'Illegitimacy among married women in England and Wales', *JMF* 31, 4 (1969).
'The decline of illegitimacy in Japan', *Social Problems* 18 (1970).
Illegitimacy (Berkeley, 1975).
Haskins, G. L.: *Law and authority in early Massachusetts* (New York, 1960).
Hauser, W. B.: *Economic institutional change in Tokugawa Japan* (Cambridge, 1974).
Hayami, A.: 'Labour migration in a pre-industrial society: a study tracing the life histories of the inhabitants of a village', *Keio Economic Studies* X, 2 (1973).
Heiss, J.: 'On the transmission of marital instability in black families', *ASR* 37 (February 1972).
Hélin, E.: 'Une sollicitude ambiguë: l'évacuation des enfants abandonnés', *Annales DH* (1973), pp. 225–9.
Henderson, G. D.: *The Scottish ruling elder* (1935).
Henripin, J.: *Trends and factors of fertility in Canada* (Ottawa, 1972).
Henriques, F. M.: *Family and colour in Jamaica* (1953).
Henriques, U. R. Q.: 'Bastardy and the new poor law', *Past and present* 37 (1967).
Henry, L.: 'Some data on natural fertility, *Eugenics Quarterly* 8 (1961).
Henry, L. and Houdaille, J.: 'Fécondité des mariages dans la quart nord-ouest de la France de 1670 à 1829', *Population* 28 (1973).
Heymowski, A.: *Swedish 'travellers' and their ancestry: a social isolate or an ethnic minority?* (Uppsala, 1969).
Higman, B. W.: 'Household structure and fertility on Jamaican slave plantations: a nineteenth-century example', *PS* 27, 3 (1973).
Hill, Christopher: *Puritanism and revolution* (1958), reprint (1962).
Hindelang, H.: 'Die eheliche und uneheliche Fruchtbarkeit mit besonderere Berücksichtigung Bayerns', *Beiträge zur Statistik Bayern* Heft 71 (Munich, 1909).
Hindus, M. S. and Smith, D. Scott: 'Premarital pregnancy in America, 1640–1971: an overview and interpretation', *JIH* V (winter 1975).
Homans, G. C.: *English villagers in the thirteenth century* (Cambridge, Mass., 1941).
Hopkirk, Mary: *Nobody wanted Sam* (1949).
Horstmann, K.: 'Schwangerschaft und Eheschliessung', International Population Conference (Vienna, 1959).
Houlbrooke, R. A.: 'Church courts and people in the diocese of Norwich, 1519–70', unpublished DPhil. thesis (University of Oxford, 1970).
Howard, G. E.: *A history of matrimonial institutions* (Chicago, 1904).
Hull, F.: 'Agriculture and rural society in Essex, 1540–1640', unpublished PhD thesis (University of London, 1950).
Hyrenius, H.: *Studier rörande den utomäktenskapliga fruktsamhetens regionala variationer* (Lund, 1941).

Imhof, A. E.: *Einführung in die historische Demographie* (Munich, 1977).

Johansen, H. C.: *Befolkningsudvikling og familiestruktur i det 18 aarhundrede* (Odense, 1975).
Johnson, D. R. and Cutright, P.: 'Problems in the analysis of Latin American illegitimacy', in M. Armer and A. Grimshaw (eds), *Comparative social research* (New York, 1973).
Jones, J. B. H.: 'Puritanism and moral legislation before the Civil War', MA thesis (University of Wales, 1954).

Jordan, W.: *White over black, American attitudes towards the negro, 1550–1812* (Chapel Hill, 1968).

Kantner, J. F. and Zelnik, M.: 'The probability of premarital intercourse', *Social Science Research* 1 (1972).
'Sexual experience of young unmarried women in the United States', *FPP* 4 (October 1972).
Kennedy, R. E.: *The Irish: emigration, marriage and fertility* (Berkeley, 1973).
Kent, J. R.: 'Attitudes of members of the House of Commons to the regulation of "personal conduct" in late Elizabethan and early Stuart England', *Bulletin of the Institute of Historical Research* XLVI (1973).
Keyfitz, N.: 'How birth control affects births', *SB* 18 (June 1971).
Knodel, John: 'Law, marriage and illegitimacy in nineteenth-century Germany', *PS* 20 (1967).
The decline of fertility in Germany, 1871–1939 (Princeton, 1974).
Knodel, John: see Shorter, E.
Köllman, W.: 'The population of Germany in the age of industrialism', in H. Moller (ed.): *Population movements in modern European history* (New York, 1964).
Kussmaul, Anne: 'Servants in husbandry in early modern England', unpublished PhD thesis (University of Toronto, 1978).

Lacey, W. K.: *The family in classical Greece* (1968).
Lader, L.: *Abortion* (Boston, 1966).
Lallemand, L.: *Histoire des enfants abandonnés* (Paris, 1885).
Lammermeier, P. J.: 'The urban black family of the nineteenth century: a study of black family structure in the Ohio valley, 1850–1880', *JMF* 35 (August 1973).
Lasat, J-C. and Videau, J.: *Données de démographie regionale*, Les collections de l'INSEE 23 (1969).
Laslett, P.: *The world we have lost*, 2nd edn, reprint (1979).
'Philippe Ariés and la famille', *Encounter* (February 1976).
Family life and illicit love in earlier generations (Cambridge, 1977).
'Illegitimate fertility and the matrimonial market', paper presented to the conference of the International Union for the Scientific Study of Population on 'Nuptiality and fertility, plural marriage and illegitimate fertility in historical demography', Kristiansund, Norway, September 1979.
Laslett, P. with Harrison, J.: 'Clayworth and Cogenhoe', in H. E. Bell and R. L. Ollard (eds), *Historical essays, 1600–1750, presented to David Ogg* (1963).
Laslett, P. with Oosterveen, K.: 'Long-term trends in bastardy in England', *PS* 27, 2 (July 1973).
Laslett, P. with Wachter, K. W., Hammel, E. A. *et al.*: *Statistical studies in historical social structure* (New York and London, 1978).
Lawrence, W.: *Diary*, ed. G. E. Aylmer (Beaminster, 1961).
Leach, E. R.: *Pul Eliya, a village in Ceylon* (Cambridge, 1961).
Lebrun, F.: 'Naissances illégitimes et abandons d'enfants en Anjou au XVIIIe siècle', *Annales, ESC* (July/October 1972).
Lee, R. D. (ed.): *Population patterns in the past* (Princeton, 1977).
Leffingwell, Albert: *Illegitimacy and the influence of seasons upon conduct* (1892), reprint (New York, 1976).
Legouis, Emile: *William Wordsworth and Annette Vallon* (1922).
LeRoy Ladurie, E.: *Une sire de Gouberville, gentilhomme campagnard du Cotentin de 1553 à 1562* (La Haye, 1972).
Montaillou, village occitan de 1294 à 1324 (Paris, 1975), English translation by Barbara Bray (1978).
Levasseur, E.: *La population française* (Paris, 1891).

Levine, David: *Family formation in an age of nascent capitalism* (New York and London, 1977).
Levine, David: see Wrightson, K.
Lewinsohn, Richard: *A history of sexual customs* (1958).
Lindner, F.: *Die uneheliche Geburten als Socialphänomen* (Leipzig, 1900).
List, A. C. C.: *The two phases of the social evil* (Edinburgh, 1861).
Livi Bacci, Massimo: *A century of Portuguese fertility* (Princeton, 1971).
A history of Italian fertility (Princeton, 1977).
Livingston, W. P.: *Black Jamaica* (1899).
Lockridge, K.: *A New England town: the first hundred years, Dedham, Mass., 1636–1736* (New York, 1970).
Löfgren, Orvar: 'Family and household among Scandinavian peasants', *Ethnologica Scandinavica* (1974).
Logan, W.: *The great social evil* (1871).
Lottin, Alain: 'Naissances illégitimes et filles-mères à Lille au XVIIIe siècle', *Revue de l'histoire moderne et contemporaine* (1970).

McArdle, Frank: *Altopascio: a study in Tuscan rural society, 1587–1784* (Cambridge, 1978).
McFalls, J. A.: 'Impact of VD on the fertility of the United States black population, 1880–1950', *SB* 20 (March 1973).
Macfarlane, Alan D. J.: 'The regulation of marital and sexual relationships in seventeenth-century England', unpublished MPhil. thesis (University of London, 1968).
The diary of Ralph Josselin, 1616–1683, British Academy Records of Social and Economic History, new series, III (Oxford, 1976).
'Historical anthropology', *Cambridge Anthropology* 3, 3 (1977).
Macfarlane, Alan D. J. with Harrison, S. and Jardine, C.: *Reconstructing historical communities* (Cambridge, 1977).
Mackenroth, G.: *Bevölkerungslehre, Theorie, Sociologie und Statistik der Bevölkerung* (Berlin-Göttingen-Heidelberg, 1953).
Maclaren, A. A.: 'Presbyterianism and the working class in a mid nineteenth-century city', *Scottish Historical Review* XLVI (1967).
McLaren, D.: 'The marriage act of 1653', *PS* 28, 2 (1974).
Malcolmson, R. W.: 'Infanticide in the eighteenth century', in J. S. Cockburn (ed.), *Crime in England, 1550–1800* (1977).
Malinowski, Bronislaw: 'Parenthood: the basis of social structure', in V. F. Calverton and S. D. Schmalhausen (eds), *The new generation* (New York, 1930).
Sex and repression in savage society (1927), reprint (1960).
Mangold, G. B.: 'Children born out of wedlock', *University of Missouri studies: Social Science Series* III (Columbia, 1921).
Marchant, R. A.: *The church under the law: justice, administration and discipline in the diocese of York, 1560–1640* (Cambridge, 1969).
Marcus, Stephen: *The other Victorians* (New York, 1964).
Marietta, J. D.: 'Ecclesiastical discipline in the Society of Friends, 1682–1776', unpublished PhD thesis (Stanford University, 1968).
Marshall, Dorothy: *The English poor in the eighteenth century* (1926).
Mather, Cotton: *Diary*, *Massachusetts Historical Society Collections*, 7th series, 7 (1911).
Mau, J.: *Social change and images of the future* (Cambridge, Mass., 1968).
Mawe, C-E.: *Studier i den sociala kontrollen i Östmark* (Uppsala, 1958).
Mayhew, H.: *London labour and the London poor* (1861).
Mead, M.: 'Cultural determinants of sexual behaviour', in W. C. Young (ed.), *Sex and the internal secretions* (1961).
Menard, R. R.: 'The Maryland slave population, 1658 to 1730: a demographic profile of blacks in four counties', *William and Mary Quarterly*, 3rd series, 32 (1975).

Menard, R. R. with Walsh, L.: 'Death in the Chesapeake: two life tables for men in early colonial Maryland', *Maryland Historical Magazine* LXIX (1974).
Mercier, R.: *L'enfant dans la société du XVIIIe siècle* (Paris, 1961).
Mitchell, Joseph: *Reminiscences of my life in the Highlands*, new edn ed. I. Robertson (Newton Abbot, 1971).
Mitterauer, Michael: Familienformen u. Illegitimität in ländlichen Gebieten Österreichs, *Archiv für Sozialgeschichte* (1979).
Mohammed El Kordi: *Bayeux au XVIIe et XVIIIe siècles: contribution à l'histoire urbaine de la France* (Paris, 1970).
Molinier, A.: 'Enfants trouvés, enfants abandonnés et enfants illégitimes en Languedoc au XVIIe et XVIIIe siécles', in *Hommage à Marcel Reinhard* (Paris, 1973).
Mitchell, J. C.: *Social networks in urban situations: analyses of personal relationships in Central African towns* (Manchester, 1969).
Mols, R.: *Introduction à la démographie historique des villes d'Europe du XIVe au XVIIIe siècles*, 3 vols (Louvain, 1954).
Moore, M. J.: 'Fertility histories and birth expectations of American woman, June 1971', *Current Population Reports*, series P-20 (1974).
Morgan, E. S.: 'The puritans and sex', *New England Quarterly* 15 (1942).
Moryson, Fynes: *An itinerary* (Glasgow, 1907–8).

Newman-Brown, W.: 'The receipt of poor relief and the life-cycle in Aldenham, Hertfordshire, 1630–1680', in R. M. Smith (ed.) *Land, kinship and life cycle* (1980).
Noordam, D. J.: 'Ongehuwde moeders en onwettige kindern in Maashuis', *Holland* 4 (August 1977).

Oberholzer, Emil Jr: *Delinquent saints* (New York, 1956).

Parkerson, D. H.: 'The sensuous farmer: premarital pregnancy in Montgomery County, Indiana', unpublished paper (University of Illinois, 1975).
Parkes, H. B.: 'Sexual morals and the great awakening', *New England Quarterly* 3 (1930).
'Morals and law enforcement in colonial New England', *New England Quarterly* 5 (1932), pp. 431–51.
Pearce, David, and Farid, Samir: 'Illegitimate births: changing patterns', *Population Trends* (autumn 1977).
Persson, B.: 'Att vara ogift mor på 1700- och 1800-talet', in K. Westman Berg (ed.), *Könsdiskriminering förr och nu* (Stockholm, 1972).
Phelps-Brown, E. H. and Hopkins, S. V.: 'Seven centuries of the prices of consumables compared with builders' wage rates', *Economica* 92 (1956).
Phillippo, J. M.: *Jamaica, its past and present state* (1843), reprint (1969).
Pinchbeck, Ivy: 'Social attitudes to the problem of illegitimacy', *British Journal of Sociology* 5 (1954).
'The state and the child in sixteenth-century England', *British Journal of Sociology* 7, 4 (1956).
Pleck, E. H.: 'The two-parent household: black family structure in late nineteenth-century Boston', *Journal of Social History* VI (1972).
Pleijel, H.: *Svenska kyrkans historia – Karolinsk kyrkofromhet, pietism och herrnhutism, 1680–1772* (Stockholm, 1935).
Prenger, G.: *Die Unehelichkeit im Königreich Sachsen* (Leipzig, 1913).
Prinzing, F.: 'Die uneheliche Fruchtbarkeit in Deutschland', *Zeitschrift für Sozialwissenschaft* 5 (1902).
'Uneheliche Geburten', in J. Conrad *et al.* (eds), *Handwörterburch der Staatswissenschaften* (Jena, 1911).

Quaife, G. R.: 'The consenting spinster in a peasant society: aspects of premarital sex in "puritan" Somerset', *Journal of Social History* (winter 1977), pp. 228–44.

Quaife, G. R.: *Wanton wenches and wayward wives* (1979).

Rainwater, L. and Yancey, W. L. (eds): *The Moynihan report and the politics of controversy* (Cambridge, Mass., 1967).

Rauhe, C.: *Die unehelichen Geburten als Sozialphänomen* (Munich, 1912).

Rawson, Beryl: 'Roman concubinage and other de facto marriages', *Transactions of the American Philological Association* 104 (1974).

Rees, T.: *Miscellaneous papers on subjects relating to Wales* (1867).

Registrar General (of England and Wales): *Annual reports* 1–83 (1839–1920), succeeded by *Statistical reviews* (annual, 1920 on); especially 5th report (1843), 6th (1844), 8th (1847), 17th (1856) and 72nd (1909).

Population trends, Office for Population Censuses and Surveys (1975 on); see also under Pearce and Farid.

Registrar General for Scotland: *Detailed reports* (1855, 1856, 1859).

Reiss, I. L.: *The social context of premarital permissiveness* (New York, 1967).

Requena, M. B.: 'The problem of induced abortion in Latin America', *Demography* 5, 2 (1968).

Richardson, R. C.: *Puritanism in northwest England: a regional study of the diocese of Chester to 1642* (Manchester, 1972).

Roberts, G. W.: *The population of Jamaica* (Cambridge, 1957).

Roberts, R.: *The classic slum* (Manchester, 1971).

Rock, Paul: *Deviant behaviour* (1973).

Rosenberg, C. E.: 'Sexuality, class and role in nineteenth-century America', *American Quarterly* XXV (1973), pp. 131–53.

Rossiaud, J.: 'Prostitution, youth and society, in the towns of southeastern France in the fifteenth century', in R. Forster and O. Ranum (eds), *Deviants and the abandoned in French society*, essays translated from *Annales ESC* (Baltimore, 1978).

Rousseau, J. J.: *Correspondence générale* VI (Paris, 1924–34).

Les confessions (Paris, 1969).

Ryder, N. B.: 'The emergence of a modern fertility pattern: United States, 1911–66', in S. J. Behrman *et al.* (eds), *Fertility and family planning: a world view* (Ann Arbor, 1969).

Sauer, R.: 'Attitudes to abortion in America, 1800–1973', *PS* XXVIII (March, 1974).

Savatier, J.: 'L'évolution de la condition juridique des enfants naturels en droit français', in *Première journée d'études juridiques Jean Dabin* (Brussels, 1965).

Scammell, J.: 'Freedom and marriage in medieval England', *Economic History Review* XXVII, 4 (1974).

Schmidt, W. M. and Teele, J. E.: 'Illegitimacy and race: national and local trends', in C. V. Kiser (ed), *Demographic aspects of the black community* XLVII (1970).

Schofield, R. S.: 'Age specific mobility in an eighteenth-century rural English parish', *Annales D H* (1970).

Schofield, R. S. and Berry, B. M.: 'Age at baptism in pre-industrial England', *PS* XXV (1971).

Scott Smith, D.: 'Parental power and marriage patterns: an analysis of historical trends in Hingham, Massachusetts', *JMF* XXXV (1973); see also under Hindus, M. S.

'The dating of the American sexual revolution: evidence and interpretation', in M. Gordon (ed), *The American family in social-historical perspective* (New York, 1973).

'Family limitation, sexual control and domestic feminism in Victorian America', *Feminist Studies* 1 (1973).

Sear, A. M.: 'Premarital pregnancy: a record linkage analysis', *SB* 20 (June 1973).

Semonche, J. E.: 'Common-law marriage in North Carolina: a study in legal history', *American Journal of Legal History* 9 (1965).

Senior, B. M.: *Jamaica, as it was, as it is, and as it may be* (New York, 1835), reprinted (1969).

Seton George: *The causes of illegitimacy, particularly in Scotland* (Edinburgh, 1860).

Shaffer, J. W.: 'Family, class and young women: occupational expectations in nineteenth-century Paris', *Journal of Family History* 3, 1 (1978).

Sheehan M. M.: 'The formation and stability of marriage in fourteenth-century England: evidence of an Ely register', *Medieval Studies* 33 (1971).

Shifflett, C. A.: 'The household composition of rural black families: Louisa County, Virginia, 1880', *JIH* VI (1975).

Shorter, E.: 'Illegitimacy, sexual revolution and social change in modern Europe', *JIH* II (1971).

'Sexual change and illegitimacy: the European experience', in R. Bezucha (ed.), *Modern European social history* (Lexington, 1972).

'Female emancipation, birth control and fertility in European history', *American Historical Review* 78 (1973).

The making of the modern family (New York, 1975).

Shorter, E., with Knodel, John and van de Walle, E., 'The decline of non-marital fertility in Europe, 1880–1940', *PS* 25 (1971).

Smith, A. E.: *Colonists in bondage* (Chapel Hill, 1947).

Smith, R. M.: 'English peasant life-cycles, and socio-economic networks', unpublished PhD thesis (University of Cambridge, 1974).

'Population and its geography in England, 1500–1730', in R. Butlin and R. Dodgshon (eds), *An historical geography of England and Wales* (1978).

'Some reflections on the evidence for the origins of the European marriage pattern', in *The sociology of the family*, ed. C. Harris, monographs of the *Sociological Review* 28 (1980).

(ed.), *Land, Kinship and Lifecycle* (forthcoming).

Smith, W. A.: *Lewisana, or life in the Outer Hebrides* (1874), 2nd edn (1886).

Smout, T. C.: 'Illegitimacy – a reply', *Scottish Journal of Sociology* 2 (1977).

Sogner, Sølvi: 'Illegitimacy in old rural society: some reflections on the problem arising from two Norwegian family reconstitution studies', in S. Åkerman, H. C. Johansen, and David Gaunt (eds), *Chance and change* (Odense, 1978).

Sole, J.: 'Passion charnelle et société urbaine d'ancien régime: amour vénal, amour libre et amour fou à Grenoble au milieu du règne de Louis XIV', *Actes du colloque de Nice* (1969).

Souden, D. C.: 'Movers and stayers in family reconstitution populations, 1600–1780' in M. Kitch (ed.), *Migration in pre-industrial England* (1980).

Spruil, J. C.: *Women's life and work in the southern colonies* (New York, 1972).

Spufford, M.: *Contrasting communities: English villagers in the sixteenth and seventeenth centuries* (Cambridge, 1974).

Stone, Lawrence: *The family, sex and marriage in England, 1500–1800* (1977).

Strachan, J. M.: 'Immorality of Scotland', *Scotsman*, 20 May, 2 and 7 June (1870).

Stubbes, Philip: *The anatomie of abuses* (1585).

Styles, H. R.: *Bundling: its origins, progress and decline in America* (Albany, 1871).

Sundbärg, G.: *Die Bevolkerungsstatistik Schwedens, 1750–1900, einige Hauptresultate* (Stockholm, 1907), reprint (1970).

Swinburne, Henry: *A treatise of spousals or marriage contracts* (1686).

A briefe treatise of testaments and last willes 5th edn (1728).

Syme, Sir Ronald: 'Bastards in the Roman aristocracy', *Proceedings of the American Philosophical Society* 104, 3 (1960).

Tait, W.: *Magdalenism, an inquiry into the extent, causes and consequences of prostitution in Edinburgh*, 2nd edn (Edinburgh, 1842).

Taylor, C. C.: 'Population Studies in 17th-Century and 18th-Century Wiltshire', *Wiltshire Archaeological and Natural History Magazine*, LX (1965).
Teitelbaum, Michael S.: *Fertility decline in Britain*, unpublished typescript (1977).
Tekse, K.: *A study of fertility in Jamaica*, Department of Statistics, Jamaica (1968).
Thomas, D. S.: *Social aspects of the trade cycle* (1925).
Thomas, K.: *Religion and the decline of magic: studies in popular beliefs in sixteenth and seventeenth century England* (1971).
Thompson, E. P.: *The making of the English working class* (1963).
Thompson, Flora: *Lark rise to Candleford* (Oxford, 1945).
Thomson, A.: *Otidig sängelag* (Stockholm, 1966).
Hävdande under äktenskapslöfte (Lund, 1967).
'Fran "horpall" till "tjuvpall" ', *Saga och sed* 5 (1967), pp. 5–51.
Tietze, C.: 'Probability of pregnancy resulting from a single unprotected coitus', *Fertility and Sterility* 11, 5 1960).
'Two years experience with a liberal abortion law: its impact on fertility trends in New York City', *FPP* 5 (1973).
Tillack, W. S., Tyler, C. W., Paguette, R. and Jones, P. H.: 'A study of premarital pregnancy', *American Journal of Public Health* 62 (May 1972).
Tilly, C.: *An urban world* (Boston, 1974).
Tilly, C. Scott, J. W. and Cohen, M.: 'Women's work and European fertility patterns', *JIH* VI (1976).
Tomasson, R. F.: 'Premarital sexual permissiveness and illegitimacy in the Nordic countries', *Comparative Studies in Society and History* 18, 2 (1976).

United Nations: *Demographic yearbooks* (1948 on); especially *Study of discrimination against persons born out of wedlock* (1967).
United States, Bureau of the Census: 'Marriage, fertility and childspacing, August 1959', by Wilson H. Grabill and Robert Parke Jr (Washington, 1961).
186, 'Marriage, fertility and childspacing, June 1965', by Wilson H. Grabill and Maria Davidson (Washington, 1969).
263, 'Fertility histories and birth expectations of American women, June 1971', by Wilson H. Grabill and Maurice J. Moore (Washington, 1974).
United States, National Center for Health Statistics: 'Summary report, final natality statistics', *Monthly Vital Statistics Report* 22, 12 (March 1974), and 23, 11 (January 1975).
'Interval between first marriage and legitimate first birth, United States, 1964–66', *Monthly Vital Statistics Report* 12, 12 (1970).

Valentine, J.: 'Illegitimacy in Aberdeen and the other large towns of Scotland', *Report of the British Association for the Advancement of Science* (1859).
Valmary, P.: 'Familles paysannes au XVIIIe siècle en Bas-Quercy', *Institut national d'Etudes démographiques*, cahier 45 (1965).
Vann, Richard T.: Review of E. Shorter in *Journal of Family History* 1, 1 (1976), pp. 106–17.

van de Walle, E.: *The female population of France in the nineteenth century: a reconstruction of 82 departments* (Princeton, 1974).
van de Walle, E.: see Shorter, E.
Wallen, P-E.: 'Oäkta barn', *Kulturhistorisktlexicon för nordisk medeltid* XIII (Malmö, 1968).
Wardlaw, R.: *Lectures on female prostitution* (Glasgow, 1842).
Wells, R. V.: 'Family size and fertility control in eighteenth-century America', *PS* 25 (1971).
Westermarck, Edward: *The history of human marriage* (1921).

Whelan, E. M.: 'Illegitimate and premaritally conceived first births in Massachusetts, 1966–68', *SB* (1972).
Wrightson, K.: 'Infanticide in earlier seventeenth-century England', *LPS* 15 (1975).
'The Puritan reformation of manners, with special reference to the counties of Lancashire and Essex, 1640–1660', unpublished PhD thesis (University of Cambridge, 1974).
Wrightson, K. and Walter, J.: 'Dearth and the social order in early modern England', *Past and Present* 71 (1976).
Wrightson, K. and Levine, D.: *Poverty and piety in an English village, Terling, 1525–1700* (New York, 1979).
Wrigley, E. A.: *Industrial growth and population change* (Cambridge, 1961).
(ed.) *An introduction to historical demography* (1966).
'Family limitation in pre-industrial England', *Economic History Review*, 2nd series, XIX (1966).
'Age at marriage in early modern England', *Proceedings of XIII International Congress of the Genealogical and Heraldic Sciences* (1976).
'The changing occupational structure of Colyton over two centuries', *LPS* 18 (1977).
'Births and baptisms: the use of Anglican baptism registers as a source of information about the number of births in England before the beginning of civil registration', *PS* 31, 2 (1977).

Yasuba, Y.: *Birth rates of the white population in the United States, 1800–1860* (Baltimore, 1962).

Zink, A.: *Azereix: la vie d'une communauté rurale à la fin du XVIIIe siècle* (Paris, 1969).

Index

Arrangement: alphabetical, word-by-word.
Abbreviations used: *p* means passim, scattered references; *n* means note (reference to notes is only made when the entry is unlikely to be inferred from the text. Note numbers have not been specified).
Figures in **bold type** indicate whole chapters or sections.

Aachen, Germany (*maps*, 291, 293, 299), 292
abandonment, *see* foundlings
Abbaretz, France, 24, 249
Aberdeen, 41*n*, 46, 204, 205
Aberdeenshire (*maps*, 42–5), 199, 200, 206
abortion, 52, 72, **76–7**, 207; in Sweden, 315*n*; in America, 360, 363, 365, 374, 375; in Jamaica, 382, 391, 392
acknowledgement of paternity: in England, 73–4, 101, 105, 107, 119, 120; in Scotland, 204–5, 213, 215, 216; in France, 259, **264–8**, 269, 273; in Sweden, 316; in America, 361; in Jamaica, 394–6*p*; *see also* naming of bastards, parents of bastards *and* putative fathers
Act (1650), against adultery, incest and fornication, 181
Act (1624), to prevent murdering of bastards, 77
Adolf Fredrik parish, Stockholm, 338, 340–2*p*, 344, 345
affiliation orders, 122
Africa and Africans, 5*n*, 74–5, 167*n*, 380–4*p*
Agardh and Ljunberg's economic-statistical survey of Sweden (1859), 314
age at bastard bearing, compared with age at marriage and first birth in marriage, 55, 92–3, 107–8, 130–2, 161, 162, 191
age at marriage and bastardy trends, 11, 369; in England, ix–x*p*, 20–2, 24, 50, 54–9*p*, 84, 158–62*p*; in Scotland, 202–3, 212; in France, 273–5*p*; in Sweden, 330–1*p*, 335, 342; in America, 365, 369; in Jamaica, 388; in Japan, 388
age at marriage of bastard bearers, 105–6, 129–30
Ain, France, 253, 254
Akita, Japan, 399, 400, 401
Albany, New York, 354
Alcester, Warwicks. (*map*, 70), 21, 23, 87–91*p*, 159–62*p*, 164, 233–4*p*; detailed case study, **94–120*p***
alcohol and the bastardy prone: in England, 168, 169, 173, 179; in Scotland, 200, 228, 231, 245; in Sweden, 315
Aldenham, Herts. (*map*, 70), 21, 23, 87–91*p*, 159–62*p*, 164, 234, 236; detailed case study, **94–120*p***
'*alias*' (double surname), 82–3*p*, 104–5, 118–19*p*, 145–8*p*; *see also* naming of bastards
Allen, Neal W. (1964), studies of Colonial America, 352, 358, 359, 360
Alps, France, 251
Alskog, Sweden, 319*n*
Alvie, Scotland, 210
America (*now* United States; *see also* Caribbean, Latin America), 2, 9–11*p*, 27–8, 59, 218, 226, 231–2, 286; bastardy among blacks, xi, 5, 7, 351, 358, 361, 365–8*p*, 375–8*p*; illegitimacy and bridal pregnancy in Colonial, **349–61**; The long cycle of illegitimacy and prenuptial pregnancy in, **362–78**; compared with Jamaica, 382, 391; *see also* New England *and* individual states, counties and towns
Angers, France, 251, 324*n*
Angus (*maps*, 42–5), 202
Anhalt, Germany (*maps*, 291, 293, 299), 290
Anjou, France, 25*n*, 250–1, 322*n*
Aomori, Japan (*map*, 398), 399, 400, 401
Aquitaine, France, 250, 251
Arboga, Sweden, 319
Ardèche, France, 251
Argyll (*maps*, 42–5), 209
Arnsberg, Germany (*maps*, 291, 293, 299), 308
Ash, Kent (*map*, 70), 23, 51, **141–57**, 224, 230, 233
Ashby, A. W. (1912), cited on bastardy in a Warwickshire village, 72, 73
attitudes of clergy: in England, 72, 75, 120, 141–51*p*, 172–3*p*, 177–86*p*, 224–5*p*; in Scotland, 41, 192–3*p*, 198–9*p*, 201–2*p*, 206–8*p*, 210–16*p*; towards reporting bastardy, 48–51*p*, 79–81, 141, 144, 149–50*p*, 177–8*p*, 337–8*p*, *see also* Christianity, church discipline, religious beliefs *and* individual denominations
attitudes to bastardy, 4, 49, 224, 225, 239–40, 277, 313; in England, 49–50, 71–85*p*, 119, 141, 151, 156–9*p*, 175–9*p*; in Scotland,

attitudes to bastardy (*contd*)
192–216*p*; in France, 249, 259, 262, 264–5; in Sweden, 314–16*p*, 330–4*p*, in America, 349–51*p*, 355–61*p*, 369; in Jamaica, 381, 385, 395; in Japan, 49, 397; *see also* attitudes of clergy, marriage attitudes and practices, moralists *and* rules of respectability
Auchbrek, Scotland, 200
Aurich, Germany (*maps*, 291, 293, 299), 294, 295, 298, 304, 306, 307
Australia, 367, 369
Austria, 3*n*, 9*n*, 26–28*p*, 41, 46, 54, 61, 239
Autun, France, 261
Ayrshire (*maps*, 42–5), 46
Azereix, France, 250

Balzac, Honoré de, cited on theme of putting children out to nurse in France, 262
Banbury, Oxon (*map*, 70), 21, 23, 63, 87–90*p*, 159–62*p*, 164, 229; detailed case study, 122–34, 140
Banffshire (*maps*, 42–5), 46, 47, 199–207*p*, 210, 215–16*p*
baptism of bastards, ix, 48–9, 52, 78–9, 119, 183, 235; *see also* inferred bastardy
Barra, Scotland, 210
Bas-Quercy, France, 250
'bastard' as a term of abuse, 49, 75, 85, 316
bastardy defined, *see* definition and concepts of bastardy
'bastardy principals', 163–9*p*, 174, 241–6*p*
bastardy prone sub-society, hypothesis of, x–xiv*p*, 49, 61, 71, 81–4*p*, 158, 181; evidence from family reconstitution studies, 112–19*p*, 133–40*p*, 151–6*p*, 163, 167–9*p*, 174; detailed discussion of, 217–46, in Sweden, 315–16
Bautzen, Germany (*maps*, 291, 293, 299), 296
Bavaria, Germany (*map*, 291), 285, 288, 290, 292, 294–8*p*, 300, 307
Beauvais, France, 250
Becker, Michael, as an example of a libertine, 145, 230
Bede's *Ecclesiastical History*, derivation of 'sparrow' metaphor from, 218
Bedfordshire, 34, 39, 66; *see also* Campton/Shefford *and* Southill
Belgium, 25, 28, 46, 48
Berkshire, 30, 34, 66
Berlin (*maps*, 291, 293, 299), 287–90*p*, 294–5*p*, 298, 300–4*p*, 306–7*p*
Berwickshire (*maps*, 42–5), 200, 203
Bethnal Green, London, 63, 64
betrothal, *see* courtship customs
Birkenfeld, Germany (*maps*, 291, 293, 299), 289
Birstall, Yorks, 101*n*
birth control, *see* contraception
Bjorskog, Sweden, 317, 319, 322, 323, 325
blacks, bastardy among: in America, xi, 5, 7, 351, 358, 361, 365–8*p*; in Caribbean and Jamaica, xi, 5, 379–96*p*; *see also* inter-caste unions
Blackstone, William (1973), cited on legitimacy, 8*n*
Blake, Judith, study of Jamaican family structure (1961), cited 389, 391, 395
Blayo, Yves, on illegitimate births in France, 278–83; cited, 26, 31
Bolton, Lancs., 184–6*p*
Bolton, Percy, Yorks (*map*, 70), 86–7*p*
bondage system, 200, 203, 214, 357, 358, 380; *see also* servants *and* slavery
Boorde, Andrew (16th-century doctor), cited on abortion, 77
Bordeaux, France, 255
Borders of Scotland, 47, 203, 206, 214–15*p*; *see also* individual counties and parishes
Boston, Mass., 360, 376 and *n*
Boswell, James: on Dr Johnson, 214*n*; as a libertine, 231
bothy system, 201, 202, 208, 210, 211, 215, 216
Bottesford, Leics. (*map*, 70), 21, 88, 159–62*p*, 164
Bouches-du-Rhône, France, 251, 271
Boughton, Kent, 146–7
Bourg, France, 254
Braithwaite, E. (1971), on Creole society in Jamaica, quoted, 383
Brampton/Longtown, Cumb., 63
Brandenburg, Germany (*map*, 291), 298
Branfield, Suffolk, 48
Bremen, Germany (*maps*, 291, 293), 290
Breslau, Germany (*maps*, 291, 293, 299), 302, 308
bridal pregnancy, *see* prenuptial pregnancy
Bristol, Rhode Island, 349*n*
Bristol, Somerset, 63
Britain, x, 2, 41, 48, 71, 84, 369*n*; relationship with Jamaica, 379–86*p*; *see also* individual countries
Brittany, France, 250, 251, 254–7*p*; 261, 280
Bruce, Philip A. (19th-century American historian), cited on bastardy and bridal pregnancy, 349
Brunswick, Germany (Braunschweig; *maps*, 291, 293), 289, 290, 294, 295, 298
Buckinghamshire, 30, 34, 66
bundling custom, 59*n*, 211–13*p*, 355, 371, 375
Burgundy, France, 250, 259, 261
Burn, Richard, cited on legal situation relating to bastardy, in *Ecclesiastical Law* (1788), 73, 74
Burnham-on-Crouch, Essex (*map*, 70), 188–90
Burns, Robert: as a libertine, 193, 231; quoted, 231
Bury, Lancs., 180, 185
Bute, Isle of, *maps*, 42–5

Caithness (*maps*, 42–5), 47, 48, 201, 202
California, 364, 378*n*
Calvados, France, 251

Camberwell, London, 63
Cambridge, 60, 63
Cambridge Group for the History of Population and Social Structure: background to and current bastardy research by, ix, x, xiii, 19, 73, 78, **86–157**; comparison of Earls Colne reconstitution with findings of, 71; data sources from reconstitution studies, 21, 23, 109, 159; statistical analysis on locality persistence by James Oeppen of, 33, 65–8; Wilson's work on prenuptial pregnancy, 55*n*; *see also* references to individuals of the group
Cambridgeshire, 30, 34, 60; *see also* Cambridge, Wilburton *and* Willingham
Campton/Shefford, Beds. (*map*, 70), 21, 23, 87–8*p*, 94–5*p*, 97, 99–100*p*, 102, 234
Canada, 367
Canterbury, Kent (*map*, 70), 141, 146*n*, 147, 150
Caribbean, 5, 29, 31*n*, 350, 380; *see also* Jamaica *and* Trinidad
Carolina, 371; North, 351, 357*n*, 358*n*, South, 360
Carter, Ian (1977), cited on works of Christopher Smout, 41*n*, 192*n*
category of illegitimates, 7–8, 72, 166–7, 188–190*p*, 312; *see also* definition and concepts of bastardy *and* 'Principle of Legitimacy'
Cathedral parish, Uppsala, 319, 322, 323
Catholicism, influence of, 61, 149, 209, 210, 249, 257, 394
Chalmers, Thomas (19th-century commentator), cited on sexual behaviour in towns, 199
Chalons-sur-Marne, France, 250
Chemoux, A. (1973), illegitimacy figures for 18th-century France cited, 252, 253, 257*n*
Champagne, France, 261
Charlot, E. and J. Dupaquier (1966), figures on foundlings in 18th-century France cited, 251, 252, 253
chaumer system, 202, 203, 215
Chemnitz, Germany, 288, 312
Chesapeake, Maryland, 370, 376
Cheshire, 24*n*, 30, 35, 75*n*, 180*n*, 181; *see also* Prestbury
Chevalier, Louis (1958), cited on 19th-century Paris, 269
Chiba, Japan, 400
childwyte, 49, 242, 244, 245
Chinese, in Jamaica, 381
Chislet, Kent, 157
Christianity, influence of, xiv, 6–11*p*, 60, 177, 192–3*p*, 224–5*p*, 385; *see also* attitudes of clergy, church discipline, religious beliefs *and* individual denominations
Chūgoku, Japan (*map*, 398), 399
church discipline: in England, 49, 72–85*p*, 162–74*p*, 178–90*p*, 235, 241; in Scotland, 192–3; in Sweden, 314, 317, 330, 334; in America, 351, 353, 356–7, 360; *see also* attitudes of clergy, Christianity, religious beliefs *and* individual denominations
cities, illegitimacy in: England, 26, 63–4*p*; Scotland, 41, 47; Europe, 62, 64, 285, 393; France, 26, 249, 351–5*p*, 261–2*p*, 276–7, 282–3; Germany, 287–9*p*, 296–7*p*, 301–12*p*; Sweden, 319–20, 322, 325, 336–45*p*; Japan, 399–402*p*; *see also* urbanization
civil registration: England and Wales, ix–x*p*, 8, 13, 16–18*p*, 28–37*p*, 53, 63–4; *see also* Registrar General's Reports
Clackmannan, *maps*, 42–5
Clare parish, Stockholm, 342
Clarke, Edith (1957), cited on Jamaica, 394
Clayworth, Notts. (*map*, 70), 225
Coale, Ansley: cited on European fertility pattern, 36; data on Russian locality persistence of illegitimacy from, 38; development of demographic indices of fertility by, 270*n*, 286, 288
Code Napoléon, 8*n*, 264–6
cohabitation, *see* consensual unions
Colchester, Essex, 76
Coll, Scotland, 210
Cologne, Germany (Köln; *maps*, 291, 293, 299), 302
Colyford, Devon, 94, 119
Colyton, Devon (*map*, 70), 17*n*, 21, 23, 86–93*p*, 159–62*p*, 164, 223, 229*n*, 233–4*p*; detailed case study, **94–120*p***
common law marriage, *see* consensual unions
concubinage, 9, 56, 72, 231; France, 269, 271; Sweden, 315, 318; Jamaica, 381, 382, 385, 394; Japan, 397; *see also* consensual unions
Coniston, Lancs., 94
Connecticut, 354, 355–6, 358, 359, 370, 371, 372
Connell, K. H., cited on Irish respect for chastity in *Irish Peasant Society* (1968), 209
consensual unions, xiv, 10–11*p*, 56, 72, 224, 239, 312; England, 75, 82, 110, 120, 134, 145–56*p*, 166, 174, 187; Scotland, 206; France, 249, 268–9*p*, 272–3*p*, 277; Sweden, 314, 316, 318, 323, 330*n*, 335, 336–45*p*; America, 350–2*p*; Jamaica, 379, 384, 385, **388–90**, 394, 395; *see also* concubinage
contraception in: England, 37, 52–3; Europe, 29, 300; France, 260, 271, 277; Sweden, 319*n*; America, 361, 363, 365, 368, 373, 374; Jamaica, 391, 392; *see also* family limitation
Cornwall, 30, 34, 66
Cotentin, France, 249
court records: England, 72–84*p*, 162–74*p*, 177–90*p*, 241, 242; Sweden, 314, 317; America, 351–61*p*, 371–4*p*; ecclesiastical, *see* church discipline
courtship, 'interrupted', 57, 92, 108, 131, 161, 187–91*p*, 220, 223, 230
courtship customs, 2, 10, 40, 53–61*p*, 64, 176; England, 88, 166, 171–4*p*, 188–91*p*; Scotland, 192–3*p*, 206–8*p*, 211–14*p*; Sweden, 314, 327–35*p*, 336–45*p*; America, 351, 355, 371, 375; *see also* courtship intensity hypothesis *and* courtship, 'interrupted'

courtship intensity hypothesis, xi, 9, 41, 53–61, 225–6
Cramond, W. (19th-century commentator), cited on Scottish illegitimacy, 200–2*n*, 206*n*, 208, 210; quoted, 207
Creech, William (18th-century commentator), cited on Scottish statistics, 194
Croix, Alain (1974), cited on 16th-century Nantes, 8*n*, 24*n*, 250*n*, 256
Cromwell, Thomas (Henry VIII's Vicar General), cited on requirement to keep parish registers (1538), 48
Croy, Scotland, 210
Crulai, France, 250
Culcheth, Lancs., xiii
Cullen, Scotland, 200
cultural patterns, and bastardy, 27, 40, 53–4*p*, 59, 64, 355; *see also* locality patterns, regional patterns *and* temporal patterns
Cumberland, 30, 35, 63, 66
Cutright, Phillips, cited on illegitimacy in the United States, 365–6*p*, 373*n*, 377–8*p*; *see also* Johnson, D. R. and P. Cutright
cutty stool, see repenter's stool
Czechoslovaks in Germany, 285, 292

Dalecarlia, Sweden, 328, 334, 335
d'Angeville, A. (1969), figures on illegitimacy in 19th-century France cited, 251–6*p*
Danzig, Germany (*maps*, 291, 293, 299), 301–2
data reliability in England: 4–29*p*, 31–4*p*, 48–53*p*, 77–81*p*, 224–5; from reconstitution studies, 95–120*p*, 122, 125, 141–50*p*, 163*n*; in Interregnum, 176, 181–9*p*; for network analysis, 241, 243, 244
data reliability outside England: in France, 249–55*p*, 266–7; in Germany, 292; in Sweden, 313, 317–21*p*, 328, 337–8, 340; in America, 352–3*p*, 362, 364–8*p*, 370–3*p*, 378; in Jamaica, 386; in Japan, 397–9*p*
Davis, Kingsley: as inaugurator of sociological study of bastardy in 'Illegitimacy and the social structure' (1939), 1, 71 (quoted); on category of illegitimates from 'The forms of illegitimacy' (1939), 7; other references, 350*n*, 363*n*, 368*n*
Davis, Natalie Z. (1971), study of youth and peer groups cited, xii
declarations of pregnancy (*déclarations de grossesse*), 187, 254, 255
Dedham, Essex, 79, 183
definition and concepts of bastardy, 5–10*p*, 41, 73–4*p*, 264–5, 350–1, 382, 397; *see also* category of illegitimates and 'Principle of Legitimacy'
Delaware, 350*n*
Denmark, 46, 322, 327*n*
Depauw, J. (1972), cited on bastardy in Nantes, 255, 256, 262, 324*n*
Derbyshire, 30, 35
deviancy, definition of, 227
deviancy and bastardy, 1–2, 61, 72, 84, 148; the bastardy prone sub-society, 218, 227, 228, 230, 245; *see also* sexual non-conformism
Devon, 24*n*, 30, 34, 66, 94, 181; *see also* Colyford, Colyton, Hartland *and* Hemyock
diaries as sources, 76, 79–83*p*, 171*n*, 172*n*, 179, 182*n*, 184*n*
Dinan, France, 255, 261
distance from church related to marriage practice, 335
Dorset, 30, 34, 66
double surname, see '*alias*'
Drake, Michael (1969), cited on illegitimacy and living-in farm service, 84
Dresden, Germany (*maps*, 291, 293, 299), 288, 296, 302, 312
Dumfriesshire (*maps*, 42–5), 47, 199, 200, 210
Dunbartonshire (*maps*, 42–5), 209
Dundee, 197, 205
Dunlop, John (autobiography, 1932), quoted on 19th-century Scottish brothels, 198
Durham, 30, 35, 66

Earlie, Alice M. (19th-century historian), on Colonial America, 349
Earls Colne, Essex (*map*, 70), 71, 85, 184, 221*n*, 230, 233; case study, 79–83
Earsden, Northumb., 21, 23
Easingwold, Yorks., 23
East Lothian (*maps*, 42–5), 200–3*p*, 205, 210, 214
Ecclesiastical History (Bede), derivation of 'sparrow' metaphor from, 218
economic conditions, and effects on bastardy, 369; in England, 37, 57–9*p*, 89–93*p*, 160–2, 170–5, 176, 189–91; in Scotland, 195, 209, 214–16*p*; in Ireland, 206; in France, 260, 262, 274, 275, 277; in Sweden, 315, 320–5*p*, 334–5*p*, 336; in America, 355–7*p*, 369, 375–7*p*; *see also* incomes, occupations, Poor Laws, poverty *and* status, socio-economic
Edderton, Scotland, 210
Edinburgh, 46, 47, 194–8*p*, 204, 205
Egypt, 60
élites: social control by, 3, 58, 60, 158, 162, 172–5*p*, 223–5*p*; sexual conduct of, 7*n*, 56, 58, 76, 193–9*p*, 224*n*, 230–2; *see also* social asymmetry, *and* status, socio-economic
England (*map*, 70), ix–x*p*, 2, 4, 7–11*p*, 261, 265; bastardy trends over time and space, 12–41, 65–8, 83–5; reliability of records, 48–53, 78–9; courtship hypothesis, 53–65; legal and social attitudes to bastardy, 73–8; in 16th and 17th centuries, 158–91; bastardy prone society, 81–3, 217–46; compared with Sweden, 321, 325, 327*n*; *see also* Midland England, Southern England, *and* individual counties
England and Wales, 8, 12–18*p*, 28–9*p*, 34–5, 48, 59*n*, 63–8*p*, 369, 391; *see also* England *and* Wales
Enköping, Sweden, 319

Essex, 30, 32, 34, 76–8*p*, 170–2*p*, 177–87*p*, 222; *see also* Burnham, Colchester, Dedham, Earls Colne, Great Totham, Great Waltham, Hatfield Peverel, Leaden Rothing, Sandon *and* Terling
Europe (*map*, 12), xi–xiii*n p*, 2*n*, 4, 6, 74, 268, 391; general fertility trends over time and space, **7–12, 25–9***p*, **36–40***p*, 46–8*p*, 50, 151*n*, 284–5; courtship hypothesis, 53, 58–9; social control, 60, 62, 64; and the bastardy prone sub-society, 221, 240; Germany and, 300, 310, 312; Sweden and, 327, 336, 345, America and, 362, 363; *see also* individual countries
examinations of bastard bearers, 75–7*p*, 120, 167, 181, 187
extra-marital conception, 8–9, 54, 58, 330, 362–4*p*, 369, 373; *see also* measuring illegitimacy *and* prenuptial pregnancy

Fairchilds, Cissie (1978), cited on social symmetry and asymmetry, 56*n*
family: attitudes to bastards, 4, 81, 84, 120; cohesion and control, xiii, 1–5*p*, 37, 61–2*p*, 93, 221; in literature, xii, xiii, 61; in France, 258–62*p*; in America, 355, 376; in Jamaica, 380–4*p*, 394, 395; *see also* parental control *and* social control
Family life and illicit love in earlier generations (Laslett, 1977): findings on bastardy over time cited, x, 4*n*, 19, 97, 123, 156, 176*n*; concept of bastardy prone sub-society cited, 141*n*, 151; *see also* Laslett, Peter; 'Long term trends in bastardy in England' *and The World we have lost*
family limitation, 258, 260, 262, 354; *see also* contraception
family reconstitution studies, 19–23*p*, 26*n*, 85, **86–140, 141–57, 158–70**, 318–19; for study of bastardy prone sub-society, 217*n*, 219*n*, 234, 236–8
fertility, relationship between legitimate and illegitimate, 327, 369; England, ix, **12–29, 32–41**, 57, **65–8**, 217–18; from reconstitution studies, 86, 92–3, 107, 149, 151, 237; Scotland, 43–5, 47; France, **270–5**; Germany, 287–8; Sweden, 321, 331; America, 365, 369, 373–4; Jamaica, 386, 393, 396
fertility testing through courtship, 57, 206, 214
Fife (*maps*, 42–5), 202
Finnegan, Frances (1979), study on whores of York cited, 227–8, 232
Flandrin, Jean-Louis: various works on the history of sexuality cited, xii, 2*n*, 25, 56, 59*n*, 260; quoted on 18th-century foundlings, 254
Flinn, Michael (*et al.*, 1977), contributions to the study of Scottish population history acknowledged, 41, 44, 192*n*
Fogel, R. W. and S. L. Engermen (1974), cited on conditions of slavery in Jamaica, 383*n*; quoted, 382
fornicator's stool, *see* repenter's stool
Forty years in a moorland parish (Rev. C. J. Atkinson, 1891), evidence of tolerance towards bastardy in rural society from, 76
Fougères, France, 255, 261
foundlings (*enfants trouvés*), x, xii*n*, 78, 127, **249–61***p*, 265–7*p*, 274–6*p*, 278–93*p*
framework knitters and bastardy, xiii, 87, 88, 95
France (*maps*, 272–4, 276, 279–80), x, xiii*n*, 2, 4*n*, 8*n*, 64, 187; fertility trends, 15, 22, 24–7*p*, 31, 46; courtship model, 54, 55, 59*n*; bastardy prone sub-society, 222, 228–9, 231, 232; illegitimates and foundlings in pre-industrial, **249–63**; illegitimacy during 19th century, **264–77**; illegitimate births from 1740 to 1829 and in the 1960s, **278–83**; compared with Sweden, 322, 325*n*; compared with America, 369, 374; *see also* individual *départements*, towns and parishes
Francis, O. C. (1963), statistics on modern Jamaica cited, 389, 390
Frankfurt-am-Main, Germany, 301–2*p*
Fukui, Japan, 399, 400, 401
Fukuoka, Japan (*map*, 398), 399, 400
Fukishima, Japan, 399

Gahn, H. (1915), cited on 18th-century Swedish illegitimacy, 315*n*, 320*n*, 323*n*
Gainsborough, Lincs. (*map*, 70), 21, 23, 87–8*p*, 94–5*p*, 97, 99–100*p*, 102, 234
Gandy, G. N. (1978), study of marriage practices among handloom knitters of Culcheth cited, xiii
Garden, M. (1970), study on 18th-century Lyons cited, 259
Gardner, W. J. (1909), cited on history of Jamaica, 380, 383, 385
Gaunt, David, on illegitimacy in 17th- and 18th-century East Sweden, **313–26**; cited, 26
Gedling, Notts. (*map*, 70), 21, 23, 87–8*p*, 94–5*p*, 97, 99, 101, 103
geographical size of parish, 88, 243
Germany (*maps*, 291, 293, 299), x, 27–8*p*, 31, 38–40*p*, 47–8*p*, 61, 68, 75; urban and rural illegitimacy, **284–312**; *see also* individual states, provinces, areas and towns
Gerrard, Dr (19th-century Banff), quoted on attitudes of bastard begetters, 202–3
Gers, France, 251
Gifu, Japan, 400
Gillis, John R. (1974), study on youth and history cited, xii
Gironde, France, 271
Glasgow, 47, 194, 198, 205
Glenelg, Scotland, 210, 211
Glenshiel, Scotland, 210
Gloucestershire, 24*n*, 30–1, 34, 66
godparents, required for baptism of bastards, 183, 235
Goebel and Naughton (1944), cited on Colonial New York court records, 352, 356
Goode, William J.: analysis of illegitimacy by types cited, 72; theory of social control cited, 84*n*,

Goode, William J. (*contd*)
 394; use of illegitimacy ratios in *The Family* (1964) cited, 287
Goody, Jack (1976), concept of 'divergent devolution' in relation to marriage codes cited, 9
Gotland, Sweden, 314, 319*n*
Goubert, P, cited on bastardy and economic change, 84; incidental references, 250*n*, 259
Gough, Richard (chronicler of Myddle), quoted, 231, 235
Great Britain, *see* Britain
Great Totham, Essex, 79
Great Waltham, Essex, 183–4
Greece, Ancient, 7 and *n*, 9*n*, 10
Greenock, Scotland, 205, 209
Grenoble, France, 257, 258
Greven, Philip (1970), cited on children leaving home and parental control in 18th-century America, 355
Gustafson, Uno, his social stratification model used by Matovic for 19th-cent. Stockholm, 339

Hajnal, John, 'European marriage patterns in perspective' (1965) cited, 11, 345
Hakodate, Japan, (*map*, 398), 399, 400
Halland, Sweden, 315
Hamburg, Germany (*maps*, 291, 293), 290, 294–5*p*, 302, 307
Hampshire, 30, 34, 66
Hanover, Germany (*maps*, 291, 293, 299), 46, 294–5*p*, 298, 302, 304, 307
Hanseatic Cities of Germany, 290, 298
'harbouring', as an offence, 235
Hardwicke's Marriage Act (1753), 51, 148, 152
Harefield, Middlesex, 235
Harris, Scotland, 204
Harrison, J. R., findings of Prestbury study (in Laslett and Oosterveen, 1973) cited, 24*n*, 61, 145
Hartland, Devon (*map*, 70), 21, 23, 63, 87–90*p*, 92*n*, 105*n*, 159–62*p*, 164, 236; detailed case study, **122–40**
Hartley, Shirley Foster: *Illegitimacy* (1975) cited as standard demographic source, xi, 41; on illegitimacy in Jamaica, **379–96**; other references, 265*n*, 369*n*, 372, 391
Haslingden, Lancs., 186
Hatfield Peverel, Essex, 77
Hawkshead, Lancs. (*map*, 70), 21, 23, 87–91*p*, 159–62*p*, 164, 234, 237–8; detailed case study, **94–120*p***
Hayami, Akira, on illegitimacy in Japan, **397–402**; cited, 6
Hearth Tax Assessment (1671), 170
Hemyock, Devon (*map*, 70), 87–8*p*, 94–5*p*, 97, 99, 101, 103
Hening, W. (1809–23), cited on laws of Virginia, 356–8*p*
Henriques, F. M. (1952), cited on types on legal and consensual unions in Jamaica, 388–9*p*
hereditary illegitimacy, 2, 83, 119, 210, 218–26*p*, 236–8*p*, 377
Herefordshire, 29, 30, 34, 66
Hertfordshire, 30, 34, 39, 66; *see also* Aldenham
Hesse, Germany (*map*, 291), 289, 298, 309
Heymowski, Adam (1969), cited on 'travellers' and bastardy prone, 316
Highlands of Scotland, 47, 193*n*, 197, 201–2*p*, 206, 208–15*p*; *see also* individual counties and parishes
Higman, B. (1973), cited on family and household structure in 19th-century Jamaican slave plantations, 382, 384, 385
Hill, Christopher, review of *Family life and illicit love in earlier generations* commented on, 51*n*
Himeji (Hyogo), Japan, 400
Hindelang, H. (1909), study of German fertility cited, 296, 297, 307, 311; quoted on effects of imbalance of sex-ratio, 306
Hindus, M. and D. Scott Smith, 'Premarital pregnancy in America 1640–1971' (1975), cited, 349, 351, 353–5*p*, 362–78*p*
Hingham, Mass., 364, 370, 371, 373*n*, 374
Hirosaki (Aomori), Japan, 400
Hiroshima, Japan, 400
Hochstadt, Steven, *see* Knodel, John and Steven Hochstadt
Hokkaido, Japan (*map*, 398), 400, 402
Holy Trinity parish, Uppsala, 318, 319, 323
hospital records, as sources, 78, 194, 197, 249, 254–60*p*, 274–6*p*, 292
housing conditions and bastardy, 2, 170, 190–1, 201–3, 215; *see also* living-in farm service
Huddinge, Sweden, 318, 320, 322, 323, 325–6
Hungary, 64
Huntingdonshire, 30, 34, 39, 66
Hurwitz, S. J. and E. F. (1971), cited on history of Jamaica, 381, 382, 385
Hutterites and high marital fertility, 286, 288
Hyrenius, Hannes (1941), analysis of relationships between religion and illegitimacy, 315

Iceland, 26–7, 41
Ile-de-France, 251, 259
Ille-et-Vilaine, France, 250, 251
'Illegitimacy a study in morals' (Albert Leffingwell, 1892), cited, 2, 11, 29, 72
immigration, effects of, 29, 31*n*, 209, 257, 371; *see also* migration and mobility
incomes, and bastardy, 57, 81, 92, 98, 170–1, 274–7*p*, 340, 393–4*p*; *see also* economic conditions and bastardy *and* status, socio-economic
index of illegitimate fertility (I_h): described, 11*n*, 270, 286; Europe, 12, 28; France, **270–7*p***; Germany, **286–311*p***
India, 29
Indiana, 367, 371

industrialization, and bastardy trends, xii, 6; England, 27, 29, 87–8, 94–5, 122; Scotland, 44, 199; Europe, 26, 263, 284; France, 275, 277; Germany, 284, 311; Japan, 402; Switzerland, 25*n*; *see also* 'modernization' theory *and* urbanization
infant mortality, 3, 103, 120, 126, 258–61*p*, 233, 382–4*p*; *see also* infanticide
infanticide, 52, 72, 77–8, 207, 258, 315, 360; *see also* infant mortality
inferred bastardy, 141, 142, 163*n*, 314, 316, 321; *see also* baptism of bastards
inheritance rights of bastards, 9, 62; England, 73, 85, 120; France, 264–5, 268, 277; Sweden, 319*n*, 324; America, 361; *see also* property ownership and attitudes to bastardy *and* wills
inter-caste unions, 7, 351, 358, 381, 385
Interregnum, illegitimacy during, 25, 51*n*, 79–81, 125, 172–3, **176–91**
Inveravon, Scotland, 200
Inverness-shire (*maps*, 42–5), 200, 210
Ireland and Irish, xii*n*, 48, 59, 177*n*, 214, 228, 380; in Scotland, 198, 201, 205–6, 208–10*p*
Irsta, Sweden, 316*n*, 317, 319, 322, 323
Isère, France, 251
Isigny, France, 250
Islam, influence of, xi, 60
Islands of Scotland, 47, 209–12*p*, 214–16*p*; *see also* individual islands and parishes
Islay, Scotland, 210
Italy, x, 28, 37–40*p*, 68
Iwate, Japan, 399, 400, 401

Jacob and Johannes parish, Stockholm, 342
Jamaica, xi, **379–96**; under Colonial rule 379–86; marriage practices, 388–90; prenuptial pregnancy, 391–2, bastardy trends, 386–7, 392–3; social and cultural influences, 393–6; *see also* individual towns
Jämtland, Sweden, 328, 334, 335
Japan (*map*, 398), xi, xii*n*, 6, 31, 39, 388, 397–40; *see also* individual administrative units, districts and towns
Jargeau, France, 250
Järna, Sweden, 328, 334, 335
Johnson D. R. and P. Cutright (1973), cited on need for historical analysis of sexual behaviour, 379
Johnson, Dr Samuel, quoted on attitudes to chastity of women, 75, 214
Josselin, Ralph (17th-century vicar of Earls Colne), records on bastardy from diary cited, 79–83*p*, 171*n*, 172*n*, 179, 182*n*
Julita, Sweden, 22, **328–35*p***
Jura, France, 260

Kagoshima, Japan (*map*, 398), 399, 400
Kälvemark, Ann-Sofie, 228*n*; on illegitimacy and marriage in 19th-century, Sweden, 327–35; findings cited, 22, 55, 62
Kanagawa, Japan, 399, 400, 401
Kanazawa, Japan (*map*, 398), 400
Karlskrone, Sweden, 320
Katarina parish, Stockholm, 338, 342
Kent, England, 30, 34, 46, 66, 150*n*; *see also* Ash, Boughton, Canterbury, Chislet, Rye *and* Sittingbourne
Kent county, Delaware, 350*n*
Kincardine (*maps*, 42–5), 199, 200
Kingston, Jamaica, 385, 392, 393
Kinki, Japan (*map*, 398), 399, 400, 402
Kinross-shire, *maps*, 42–5
kinship, 3, 5, 62, 72, 83–4*p*, 165–8*p*, 187, 213; among bastardy prone, 217, 219*n*, 222, 239, 241–6*p*; *see also* family, 'bastardy principals', name sets *and* network analysis
Kirkcudbrightshire (*maps*, 42–5), 47, 199
Kirkmichael, Scotland, 200
Knodel, John, studies cited, 38, 273*n*, 286–90*p*, 292, 301; *see also* Shorter, Edward, John Knodel and E. van de Walle
Knodel, John and Steven Hochstadt, on urban and rural illegitimacy in Imperial Germany, **284–312**; cited, 15, 31
Kobe, Japan (*map*, 398), 400, 402
Kochi, Japan, 399, 400, 401
Kofu (Yamanashi), Japan, 400
Königsberg, Germany (*maps*, 291, 293, 299), 302
Konstanz, Germany (*maps*, 291, 293, 299), 39
Köping, Sweden, 319
Kumamoto, Japan, 399, 400, 401
Kungsholms parish, Stockholm, 342
Kurume (Fukuoka), Japan, 400
Kussmaul, Anne (1978), study on the link between illegitimacy ratios and levels of servants in 19th-century English counties cited, 56
Kyoto, Japan (*map*, 398), 400
Kyūshū, Japan (*map*, 398), 399, 402

Labourers and bastardy, 112–13, 118, 119, 132–3, 163, 170, 171
Ladugårdslands parish, Stockholm, 338, 342
Lairg, Scotland, 210
Lake County, Indiana, 367
Lallemand, L. (1885), cited on Paris foundlings, 254
Lambeth, London, 63
Lanarkshire (*maps*, 42–5), 201, 206
Lancashire, 24*n*, 30, 35, 177, 179–81*p*, 183–7*p*, 222; *see also* Bolton, Bury, Coniston, Culcheth, Haslingden, Hawkshead, Liverpool, Manchester, Preston, Rochdale, Tunstall, Whitworth *and* Wigan
Landes, France, 251
Languedoc, France, 250
Lannion, France, 261
Lark Rise to Candleford (Flora Thompson, 1945), evidence of tolerance towards bastardy in rural society from, 76

Laslett, Peter: introduction to the comparative history of bastardy, **1–65**; the bastardy prone sub-society, **217–40**; *see also Family life and illicit love in earlier generations*, 'Long term trends in bastardy in England' *and The World we have lost*
Laslett, Peter and Karla Oosterveen, *see* 'Long Term trends in bastardy in England'
Latin America, 75, 268, 391
Laval, France, 261
Lawrence, William (17th-century diarist) cited on 'staine of bastardy', 76
Leaden Rothing, Essex, 76
Leffingwell, Albert and 'Illegitimacy a study in morals' (1892) cited, 2, 11, 29, 72
legal codes, American, *see under* legislation on bastardy
legislation on bastardy: English, 73–5, 77–8, 177–81*p*; French, 8*n*, **264–6**; Swedish, 321–2; American, 349–52*p*, 355–61*p*, Jamaican, 385–6, 394–5; *see also childwyte*, church discipline, court records, harbouring *and* marriage Acts and Laws
legitimation of bastards by marriage, 56, 57; in England, 73–4; in France, 265, 268, 271–7*p*; in Sweden, 329, 337, 341, 342, 344; in America, 350; in Jamaica, 379, 385, 388, 389; *see also* marriage chances of bastard bearers
Le Havre, France, 251
Le Puy, France, 255
Leicestershire, 10, 30, 34, 66; *see also* Bottesford *and* Shepshed
Leipzig, Germany (*maps*, 291, 293, 299), 288, 296, 302, 312
Leith, Scotland, 46, 205
Léon, France, 250
Lesbury, Northumb. (*map*, 70), 224
Levasseur, E. (1891), cited on French illegitimacy, 269, 270, 276
Levine, David: cited on repeaterdom, 87–8, 233*n*; cited on relation between age of unmarried mothers and age at marriage, 92–3; cited on 19th-century decline in bastardy, 98; *see also* Levine, David and Keith Wrightson
Levine, David and Keith Wrightson, on the social context of illegitimacy in early modern England, **158–75**; findings on age at marriage and illegitimacy trends cited, 22, 107; findings on local controls cited, 53; findings on bastardy prone cited, 82, 225*n*, 229, 230; use of network analysis cited, 241–5*p*; *see also* Levine, David *and* Wrightson, Keith
Lewis, Oscar (American sociologist), cited on relation between poverty and consensual unions, 336
Lewis, island of, 193, 194, 204, 211–14*p*
Lexington, Mass., 371
libertines, 58, 60, 194–8*p*, 230–2*p*, 258–9
Liège, France, 261
Lille, France, 26*n*
Lillhärdal, Sweden, 328, 334, 335
Lincoln, 61*n*
Lincolnshire, 17*n*, 30, 35; *see also* Gainsborough *and* Lincoln
Linneus, Carl (Swedish biologist), on marriage and courtship customs in Sweden, quoted, 314
List, Alfred C. C. (19th-century Scottish moralist), quoted, 196
literacy, education and bastardy, 2, 200, 256, 393–4
literature, bastardy in, xii, xiii, 1–4*p*, 61, 217; England, 75–6, 168; Scotland, 41, 42, 46, 48, **192–216*p***; France, 265; Sweden, 313–16*p*; America, 349, 362, 374
Liverpool, 63
Livi Bacci, M. (1977), cited on technique for estimating proportions never married, 22*n*
living-in farm service, 29, 84, 196, 210; *see also* bothy system and chaumer system
locality patterns, 10–11*p*, 54, 64, 220, 224; France, 250, 251, 257; Germany, x, 297, 303, 311; Sweden, 325, 326, 335–6; *see also* locality persistence *and* village controls
locality persistence, of legitimate and illegitimate fertility, xiv, 2; England, **29–40**, 54, 59, 60, 63, 220, 221; Europe, 37–39, 48; Scotland, **41–8**; *see also* locality patterns, locality persistence values, social control and village controls
locality persistence values, **32–40**, **43–8**; space-time analysis of variance in, 33, 36–7, **65–8**
Lochcarron, Scotland, 210
Lockridge, Kenneth (1970), cited on children leaving home and parental control in 18th-century America, 355
Logan, William (19th-century Scottish doctor), cited, 194*n*, 197; quoted, 198
Loire, France, 251
Loiret, France, 250
London, 30, 34, 46–7*p*, 63–7*p*, 89, 209; foundlings in, xii*n*, 78; migration to, 31*n*, 89, 166*n*
'Long term trends in bastardy in England' (Peter Laslett and Karla Oosterveen, 1973), findings on illegitimacy in English history cited, 4*n*, 17*n*, 19*n*, 96*n*, 123, 176, 327*n*; on repeaterdom, 86, 87; and compared with reconstitution studies, 123, 142–5*p*, 159; and compared with other countries, 24*n*, 284*n*, 316, 354*n*; quoted, 277; *see also Family life and illicit love in earlier generations* and *The World we have lost*
Lot, France, 251
Lowlands of Scotland, 194, 199–200*p*, 202–3*p*, 206–8*p*, 210–12*p*, 214–16*p*; *see also* individual counties and parishes
Lübeck, Germany (*maps*, 291, 293), 289, 290
Luneburg, Germany (*maps*, 291, 293, 299), 304
Lye, Sweden, 314

Lynn, Mass., 375*n*
Lyons, France, 253, 255, 259, 260, 282

Macfarlane, Alan, on illegitimacy and illegitimates in English history, **73–85**; cited, 4, 51*n*, 178, 179*n*, 224, 230, 235*n*
Maebashi (Gunima), Japan, 400
Maine, 352, 360
Maine-et-Loire, France, 250, 251
maintenance of bastards: England, 72–5*p*, 84, 105, 120, 129, 156, 177–9*p*; France, 253; America, 356, 359, 361; Jamaica, 382, 394–5, 396; *see also* Poor Laws
Malinowski, Bronislaw (1930), on the 'Principle of Legitimacy', cited, 5–8*n*, 62, 72, 379; quoted, 5
Manchester, 63, 64, 180, 181, 184
manorial court rolls, 85, 162*n*, 188*n*, 236, 241–2*p*, 244–5*p*
Maria parish, Stockholm, 338, 342
Marietta, J. D. (1968), on Quakers in America, 354, 360
Marlborough, Mass., 374
Marriage Act (1653), 149, 184, 186
Marriage Acts and Laws, 7–11*p*; English, 51, 148–9, 152, 184, 186, 235; French, 249, German, 292, 299; Swedish, 314; American, 10–11, 350–1, 358; Jamaican, 380, 383–5*p*
marriage age, *see* age at marriage
marriage attitudes and practices: general, ix–xiv*p*, 3, 7–12*p*, 22, **53–62**, 176, 222; England, 71–2, 89, 105–6*p*, 130, 140, 148–51*p*, 169–74*p*, 189–91*p*; France, 249, 267–77*p*; Sweden, 314–16, **327–35*p***, **336–45*p***; America, 350–1, 373–4, 378; Jamaica, 379, 388–96*p*; Japan, 397; *see also* concubinage, consensual unions, courtship customs, polygamy *and* proportions never marrying
marriage chances of bastard bearers, 6–7, 327; England, 75, 83, 85, 92, 105–7*p*, 129–30*p*, 245; Scotland, 194, 207; Sweden, 330, 335
marriage definition, xiv, 9, 10, 178, 184; *see also* definitions and concepts of bastardy
Marriage Duty Act (1694), 51
Maryland, 349*n*, 352, 357–60*p*, 370, 371, 376*n*
Massachusetts, 351*n*, 354, 356–61*p*, 364, 367–8, 370–6*p*
Matovic, Margareta, on illegitimacy and marriage in Stockholm in the 19th century, **336–45**
Matsue (Shimane), Japan, 400
Matsumoto (Nagano), Japan, 400
Matsuyama (Ehine), Japan, 400
Mawe, C. E. (1958), cited on relation between bastardy and religiosity in Sweden, 315
Mayence, France, 253
measuring illegitimacy, 8, 11*n*, 13–15, 29, 32, 51; France, **270–7**; Germany, **285–9**; America, 364–5, 371–3; *see also* index of illegitimate fetility, rates of illegitimacy *and* ratios of illegitimacy
Methley, Yorks., 21, 23
Meyer, Jean, on illegitimates and foundlings in pre-industrial France, **249–63**; cited, 24*n*, 26*n*
Michigan, 371, 372
micro-localism, 47, 48, 59–60, 63, 217, 220, *see also* locality patterns, locality presistence *and* village controls
Mid Lothian (*maps*, 42–5), 201, 210, 214
Middlesex, England, 34, 66, 67; *see also* Harefield
Middlesex County, Mass., 354, 371, 373
Midland England, 64*n*, 98, 122; *see also* individual counties
migration and mobility in Britain, 85, 105, 120, 134, 139–40, 235; general levels, 81, 105, 110, 151, 165–6, 215, 219, 243; of bastard bearers, 86, **88–92**, 105–7, 110, 129–30, 219, 235; of bastardy prone, 222, 223, 236, 238; repeaterdom and, 88–91, 234–6; effects on records, 37, 101–3, 110, 126–7, 150, 156; *see also* immigration
migration and mobility outside Britain: Europe, 285, France, 253, 254, 257, 258, 261–3; Germany, 308–11*p*; Sweden, 315*n*, 318, 324–5, 326, 328; America, 355, 360, 364, 370, 376, 378; *see also* immigration
Milizac, France, 250
miscegenation, *see* inter-caste unions
Mito (Ibaraki), Japan, 400
Mitterauer, M. (1979), cited on sexual nonconformism in Austria, 26*n*, 239
Miyagi, Japan, 399, 400, 401
mobility, *see* migration and mobility
'modernization' theory, 6, 26*n*, 27–8, 284, 363, 402, *see also* industrialization, sexual revolution theory *and* urbanization
Molinier, A. (1973), cited on foundlings and bastards in Languedoc, 250, 255
Mols, R. (1955), cited on bastardy trends in French towns, 255
Monigaff, Scotland, 206
Monmouthshire, 30, 35, 66
Montgomery County, Indiana, 371
moralists, on bastardy, 1–3*p*, 5, 41, 62, 168, 188, 192–216*p*
Morant Bay, Jamaica, 385
Moray (*maps*, 42–5), 47, 199
Morbihan, France, 253
mortality of bastards, 3, 103, 120, 126; and foundlings in France, 258–61*p*, 263; Jamaica, 263, 382–4*p*; *see also* infanticide *and* infant mortality
Moryson, Fynes (1908), cited on marriage chances of non-virgins in Germany, 75
Moynihan, Daniel Patrick and the *Moynihan Report* (1965), on experience of blacks in America cited, 375
Mull, island of, 210

Munich, Germany, 288, 301, 302
Myddle, Salop (*map*, 70), 231, 235

Nagano, Japan, 400
Nagasaki, Japan (*map*, 398), 399, 400–2*p*
Nagoya, Japan (*map*, 398), 400
Naha (Okinawa), Japan, 400
Nairnshire (*maps*, 42–5), 47
name sets, **113–18**, 122, **133–40**, **152–6**, 236–8, *see also* 'alias', naming of bastards *and* network analysis
naming of bastards, 85, 101, 104, 145–8*p*, 222, 277; *see also* 'alias', name sets *and* network analysis
Nantes, France, 249–51*p*, 254–6*p*, 262, 322*n*, 324*n*; 17th-century records, 8*n*, 22, 24
Nara, Japan, 400
Neckarkreis, Germany (*maps*, 291, 293, 299), 294, 295, 298
Nepal, 72*n*
Netherlands, 28
network analysis, for the study of bastardy, **163–9**, 219*n*, 229, **236–8**, **240–6**
Neuchâtel, Switzerland, 25*n*
New England, 173, 349, 352–3*p*, 355, 357, 370, 371; *see also* individual states
New Jersey, 349*n*, 357, 359, 361
New York (*formerly* New Amsterdam), xiv, 11, 349*n*, 351–2*p*, 354–6*p*, 364, 378*n*, 391*n*
New Zealand, 369
Newbury, Mass., 374
Newcastle-upon-Tyne, 8*n*, 63
Newman, Anthea, on an evaluation of bastardy recordings in an East Kent parish, **141–57**; cited, x, 110, 233
Niederbayern, Germany (*maps*, 291, 293, 299), 292
Nièvre, France, 251
Niigata, Japan, 400
Nivernais, France, 259
Nord, France, 251
Norfolk, 30, 32, 34, 39, 46, 66; *see also* Norwich
Normandy, France, 250, 261
Norrbotton, Sweden, 315
North America, *see* America
North and West versus South and East, differences in European illegitimacy levels, 11–12; *see also* regional patterns
Northamptonshire, 30, 34
Northumberland, 30, 35; *see also* Earsden, Lesbury *and* Newcastle
Norway, 26*n*, 46, 56, and *n*, 167*n*, 315
Norwich, Norfolk, 63, 77*n*, 81
Nottingham, 63
Nottinghamshire, 29–30, 35, 48, 61*n*, 63, 66, 88; *see also* Clayworth *and* Gedling

Oberbayern, Germany (*maps*, 291, 293, 299), 292
occupations, and bastardy, 81; England, 87–8*p*, 93–5*p*, **110–13***p*, 119–20*p*, **132–3***p*, 163–4*p*, 170–1*p*; Scotland, 194–216*p*; Sweden, 323–5*p*, 339–45*p*; Jamaica, 393–4; *see also* status, socio-economic
Oeppen, James (and Kenneth Wachter), on space-time analysis of variance in levels of legitimate and illegitimate fertility, **65–8**; cited, 33–9*p*
Ohio, 371, 376
Okayama, Japan, 400
Old Montpelier, Jamaica, 385
Oldenburg, Germany (*maps*, 291, 293, 299), 289, 290, 294, 295, 298
Oosterveen, Karla, cited as originator of concept of bastardy prone sub-society, x; *see also* 'Long term trends in bastardy in England' *and* Oosterveen, Karla and Richard M. Smith
Oosterveen, Karla and Richard M. Smith, on bastardy and the family reconstitution studies of Colyton, Aldenham, Alcester and Hawkshead, **94–121**; cited, 76, 145
'Orange Grove', Jamaica, 394
Orkney Isles (*maps*, 42–5), 46, 199–205*p*, 210–12*p*
Osaka, Japan (*map*, 398), 398–402*p*
Osnabrück, Germany (*maps*, 291, 293, 299), 298
Otsu (Shiga), Japan, 400
Oxfordshire, 34, 66; *see also* Banbury

Paisley, Scotland, 205
Pakistan, 29
parental control, xiii, 1, 166, 169, 199–216*p*, 355; *see also* family *and* social control
parents of bastards, identification and description, **103–10**, **127–31**; *see also* acknowledgement of paternity, name sets, naming of bastards, network analysis *and* putative fathers
Paris, 26*n*, 46, 61, 267–9*p*; foundlings and illegitimates in 19th century, 251–6*p*, 258–62*p*, 274, 276; illegitimacy trends, 278, 279–83*p*
parish registers in England, ix–x, 12–26*p*, 31–2*p*, 48–53, 72–85*p*; used in reconstitution studies, 86–93*p*, 94–120*p*, 122–40*p*, 141–57*p*, 158–70*p*, 182–9*p*; evidence of bastardy prone sub-society in, 217–20*p*, 222, 224–5, 230, 233–40*p*; *see also* data reliability
parish registers outside England: in France, 8*n*, 22–5*p*, 249–51*p*, 254–5*p*; in Sweden, 313–26*p*, 327–35*p*, 336–45*p*; in America, 351, 353, 354, 370, 371; in Japan, 397
Parks, H. B. (1930, 1932), cited on illegitimacy in Colonial America, 352, 354, 357
Pas-de-Calais, France, 251
Peeblesshire, *maps*, 42–5
Pennsylvania, 349*n*, 351, 357–61*p*, 371
Perth, Scotland, 46, 205

Perthshire (*maps*, 42–5), 200, 202
Picardy, France, 261
Ploudalmezau, France, 250
Plougastel, France, 261
Plymouth, Mass., 356–7, 360*n*
Poland and Poles, 4*n*, 285, 292, 298
polygamy, 381–2, 385
Pomerania, Germany (*map*, 291), 298
Poor Laws: accounts as sources, 72, 113, 120, 150, 156, 241; effects of enactment, 13, 92, 98, 120, 151, 172–5*p*, 191; overseers as parish notables, 105, 172–4*p*, 191, 230, 235; in America, 355; in Jamaica, 395; *see also* poverty
Poplar, London, 63
Portugal, 27, 33, 38–41*p*, 48, 68
Posen, Germany (*maps*, 291, 293, 299), 292, 298
poverty and bastardy, 2, 236; in England, 81–5*p*, 113, 117–19*p*, 164–5*p*, 168, 170–5*p*, 179; in France, 259–60; *see also* incomes, occupations, Poor Laws *and* status, socio-economic
pre-marital chastity, 59, 75, 193, 209, 213–14, 375; *see also* courtship customs *and* rules of respectability
prenuptial pregnancy, xiv, 2, 8, 327
prenuptial pregnancy in Britain: in England, 7–12*p*, 20–5*p*, 49*n*, 50, 52–7*p*, 61, 141, 219–20*p*, 227; in parish reconstitution studies, 98, 103, 108–9*p*, 125, 131–2, 158, 161–6*p*, 174, 188–90*p*; in Scotland, 49*n*, 204, 206, 208, 211–16*p*; in Ireland, 48*n*
prenuptial pregnancy outside Britain: in Europe, 25–6*p*; in France, 271, 272; in Sweden, 317, 323, **329–35***p*, **340–4***p*; in America, **349–61***p*, **362–78***p*; in Jamaica, 391–2
Presbyterians, 180, 182, 183, 185, 212
Prestbury, Cheshire, 24*n*, 61, 145
Presteigne, Radnor, 63
Preston, Lancs., 183
Prince Georges County, Maryland, 352, 354
'Principle of Legitimacy' (Malinowski), 5–8*n*, 62, 72, 379; *see also* category of illegitimates *and* definitions and concepts of bastardy
Prinzing, F. (1902, 1911), cited on effects on bastardy of imbalance of sex-ratio in Imperial Germany, 307
proletarianization, *see* Poor Laws, poverty *and* status, socio-economic
property ownership and attitudes to bastardy, 9, 58, 62; England, 75, 81, 190; Scotland, 214; Sweden, 318–19, 324, 334; Jamaica, 385; *see also* inheritance rights of bastards
proportions never marrying, 11–12*p*, 22, 57, 71, 84–5*p*, 372, 388
prostitution: in England, 79, 82, 152, 169, 191, 219–21*p*, 227–31*p*; in Scotland, 192, 194–201*p*, 205, 214, 216; in France, 258
Provence, France, 281
Prussia, Germany (*map*, 291), 46, 284–5*p*, 287–8*p*, 290–2*p*, 294–8*p*, 300, 302–9*p*
public penance, 74, 178, 192–3, 317, 322, 359–60
Puritans and bastardy levels, 25, 51*n*, 79, 81, 122*n*, 173, **176–86**; Sweden compared with England, 313, 321–2; in America, 349
putative fathers, 75, 101*n*, 107, 119, 361; *see also* acknowledgement of paternity *and* parents of bastards
Pyrenees, France, 4*n*, 49, 251

Quaife, G. R. (1979), cited on study of sexual history in 17th-century Somerset, xiii
Quakers, 349, 353–4, 355, 357, 359
quarter sessions records, as sources, 72–84*p*, 162–74*p*, 177–90*p*, 241, 242

Radnorshire, 63
Raploch, Scotland, 209
rates of illegitimacy: general, 13–17*p*, 286–7*p*, 365–6, 371–2; England, 16–17, 32–40*p*, 65–8*p*; Scotland, 42, 44, 45; Germany, 287–9*p*; Sweden, 320; America, 365–7*p*, 371–2*p*, 377–8*p*; Jamaica, 379, 386–8*p*, 391–3*p*, 396; Japan, 388
ratios of illegitimacy, usage and shortcomings, 14–15, 29, 43, 51, 270, 273, 285–7*p*, 364–5, 371–2
ratios of illegitimacy in Britain: in England, 13–32*p*, 48, 51, 158–62*p*, 176, 190–1*p*, 232–3; as a % of first births, 54–5; parishes in reconstitution studies, 96–9*p*, 123–6*p*, 142–3*p*, 163–5*p*; in Scotland, 42–4*p*, 199–200*p*, 202–5*p*, 207–14*p*; relation to repeaterdom, 232–4, 239
ratios of illegitimacy outside Britain: Europe, 24–7*p*; France, 24–6*p*, 249–57*p*, 270, 275, 278–83; Germany, 287–8*p*; Sweden, 320–6*p*; America, 354, 365–7*p*, 371–2*p*; Jamaica, 379, 386–7, 391, 393, 396; Japan, 388, 397–402*p*
recording of illegitimacy not allowed, for social reasons, 53, 364
regional patterns, of bastardy, 3, 313; England, **29–31**, 54, 88, 220; Scotland, 47, 199–216*p*; Europe, 11–12; France, 250–1*p*, 271–7, 278–81; Germany, 284, **292–3**, **298–301**, 303–6*p*, 309–11*p*; America, 361; Japan, 399–402*p*; *see also* locality patterns
Registrar General's Reports: England and Wales, 13–15, 30–5*p*, 63–4; Scotland, 41, 196, 199–204*p*, *see also* civil registration
Reims, France, 257
religious beliefs, and bastardy: Britain, 2, 29, 61, 180, 194; France, 257, 262; Sweden, 313–15*p*, 323; America, 361, 364, 375, 376; Jamaica, 394; *see also* attitudes of clergy, Christianity, church discipline *and* individual denominations
Renfrewshire (*maps*, 42–5), 209

Rennes, France, 254, 255, 257–9*p*, 261
repeaterdom, *see* repetitive bastard-bearing
repenter's stool (cutty stool *or* fornicator's stool), 192–3, 317, 322
repetitive bastard-bearing: evidence from English parish studies, 82–3*p*, 86–91*p*, 98–101, 108, 125–6, 143–4, 152, 166–9*p*, 181–9*p*; and the bastardy prone sub-society, 49, 55, 217–20*p*, 222, 224, 228, 232–8, 245–6*p*; in Sweden, 323
revolutions, effects of, 31, 39, 256, 263, 264, *see also* Puritans *and* wars
Rhin, Bas, France, 251
Rhineland, Germany (*map*, 291), 290*n*, 309; valley, 298
Rhode Island, 349*n*, 350, 361
Rhône, France, 229, 253, 271, 280
Rickinghall, Suffolk (*map*, 70), 236, 242–5
Rickman's interest in ecclesiastical registration of bastardy cited, 13
Roberts, George W. (1957), cited on Jamaica marriage and illegitimacy, 388, 389, 393; *see also* Roberts, G. W. and L. Braithwaite
Roberts, G. W. and L. Braithwaite (1961), on mating patterns in Trinidad, quoted, 390
Rochdale, Lancs. (*map*, 70), 185–6
Rock, Paul (1973), cited on definition of deviancy, 227
'rogue' counties, xiii, 30–2, 39–40, 47, 48, 66–7
Roman Empire, 1, 10
Rose's Burial Act (1812), 98, 113
Ross and Cromarty (*maps*, 42–5), 199–201*p*, 203, 206, 210, 212–13*p*
Rouen, France, 282
Rousseau, Jean Jacques: as a libertine, 259; cited on merits of suckling children, 260–2*p*
Roxburgh (*maps*, 42–5), 207
Ruhr valley, Germany, 284, 298
rules of respectability, 6–8*p*, 58–9*p*, 193–5*p*, 225; *see also* attitudes to bastardy *and* social control
rural bastardy levels, *see* urban-rural patterns of bastardy
Russia and Russians, 31, 38–9*p*, 64, 262
Rutland, 30, 35, 39, 66
Rye, Kent, 153

Sachsen-Meiningen, Germany, 289
Saga, Japan, 399, 400, 401
St Ann, Jamaica, 394
St Brieuc, France, 261
St Lambert des Levées, France, 250
St Malo, France, 26*n*, 250, 254, 256, 257
St Nicholas parish, Stockholm, 338–42*p*, 344–5*p*
Saint-Sernin, France, 250
St Similien parish, Nantes, 24, 249
Saint-Viger, France, 250
Saitama, Japan, 399
Sakai (Osaka), Japan, 400
Sandon, Essex, 182
Sâone, Haut, France, 251
Sapporo, Japan (*map*, 398), 400
Saxony, Germany (*map*, 291), 289–90*p*, 294–8*p*, 307, 312
Scandinavia, x, 2, 27–8*p*, 41, 56, 59*n*, 261, 345, *see also* individual countries
Schleswig-Holstein, Germany (*maps*, 291, 293, 299), 298
Schofield, Roger: cited on proprotions never marrying, 22; mobility study by, 166*n*
Scotland (*maps*, 42–5), x, 49*n*, 56, 63, 369, 380; general fertility trends, 22, 27, 28; locality persistence over time, 4, 33, 38, 39, 41–8, 68; aspects of sexual behaviour in 19th century, 192–216; bastardy prone sub-society, 217, 223*n*, 227, 230; *see also* Borders, Highlands, Islands, Lowlands *and* individual counties and parishes
Scott Smith, Daniel, on American illegitimacy and prenuptial pregnancy, 362–78; cited, 27; *see also* Hindus, M. and D. Scott Smith
Seafield, Scotland, 200
Seaford plantations, Jamaica, 384
seasons and their influences on conception, 2*n*, 52, 57, 318, 323–4, 326, 331–4
Seine, France, 251, 267, 272
Selkirkshire, *maps*, 42–5
Sendai, Japan (*map*, 398), 400
Serbia, xiii*n*
Serignan, France, 250
servants and bastardy levels, 56, 75, 84, 218, 231, 235; evidence from English parishes, 105–7*p*, 112–13*p*, 118–19*p*, 129, 163–7*p*, 176, 187; Scotland, 195–7*p*, 204–6*p*, 210; France, 262, 265; Sweden, 338, 339, 342–4*p*; America, 357, 359; *see also* bondage system *and* slavery
Seton, George (19th-century Scottish commentator) quoted, on causes of illegitimacy, 206, 210
settlement laws and papers, 92, 120, 150, 191, 235, 292, 299
sex-ratios, imbalance of, 205, 306–8, 310, 315, 323, 342, 381, 382
sexual intercourse outside marriage, 51, 72, 78, 178; *see also* courtship customs, extra marital conception, marriage attitudes and practices, prenuptial pregnancy *and* rules of respectability
sexual nonconformism, bastardy in the study of, x–xiv*p*, 1–2*p*, 11, 22, 27–9*p*, 37, 52–62*p*; *see also* bastardy prone sub-society *and* deviancy and bastardy
sexual revolution, theory of, xii, 26–9, 158, 363–4*p*, 369, 374–5*p*, 378
Shakespeare, William, quotation from Edmund's apology for bastardy in *King Lear*, 277
Shepshed, Leics. (*map*, 70), 21, 23, 87–8*p*, 159–62*p*, 164

Shetland Isles (*maps*, 42–5), 197, 199–201*p*, 203–5*p*, 210–13*p*
Shettlewood Pen, Jamaica, 382
shielings and courtship, 211, 212
Shikoku, Japan (*map*, 398) 399, 400
Shimonoseki, Japan (*map*, 398), 400, 402
Shizuoka, Japan, 399, 400, 401
Shoreditch, London, 63
Shorter, Edward (studies on sexual history and theory of a 'sexual revolution'), cited, xii, 2*n*, 26*n*, 263, 362*n*, 375; quoted, 158; *see also* Shorter, Edward, John Knodel, and E. van de Walle
Shorter, Edward, John Knodel and E. van de Walle, *The decline of non-marital fertility in Europe* (1971), findings cited, 2*n*, 268, 271, 284, 300, 312, 363, 369; European map reproduced and discussed, 11–12; statistics reproduced and discussed, 28–9; theory of 'modernization' discussed, 284, 363–4, 370
Shropshire, 29, 30, 34, 66; *see also* Myddle *and* Wem
Sigmaringen, Germany (*maps*, 291, 293, 299), 298, 300, 304, 306
Sikkim, 76*n*
Silesia, Germany (*map*, 291), 292, 298
singletons, 91, 100–1, 117, 125, 187, 218, 220; *see also* 'sparrows'
Sittingbourne, Kent, 143
Skinnskatteberg, Sweden, 318, 319, 322, 323, 326
Sklar, J. and B. Berkov (1974): cited on abortion and illegitimacy in America, 365*n*, 378; estimates of illegitimacy rates cited, 365, 366
Skultuna, Sweden, 318–19*p*, 322–3*p*, 326
Skye, Isle of, 210
slavery, 358, 361, 375–6, 379–85*p*, 395; *see also* bondage system *and* servants
Smaland, Sweden, 315
Smith, J. H. and P. A. Crowl (1964), cited on courts of Colonial America, 352, 358–60*p*
Smith, Richard M., 59*n*; on introduction to family reconstitution and the study of bastardy, **86–93**; cited on repeaterdom and migration, 233*n*, 234; on network analysis in relation to the bastardy prone sub-society, **240–5**; cited on network analysis, 229, 236; *see also* Oosterveen, Karla and Richard M. Smith
Smout, Christopher, on aspects of sexual behaviour in 19th-century Scotland, **192–216**; cited, 41, 84, 217, 230
social asymmetry, 55, 56, 80, 166, 187, 230–1; Scotland, 194–8*p*; France, 258, 259, 265; Sweden, 236, 342; Jamaica, 381
social control, illegitimacy as a problem of, xii, xiii, 1–7p, 60–2*p*, 158, 285; England, 72, 84, 169–75*p*, 176–91*p*; Germany, 306, 310, 311; Sweden, 334, 335; America, 363, 364, 374; Jamaica, 386, 395, 396; *see also* family, parental control *and* village controls
Södermanland, Sweden, 328–35*p*
Sogner, Sølvi (1978), study of Norway cited, 26*n*, 56*n*, 57*n*
Solé, J. (1969), cited on prostitution in Grenoble, 258
Somerset, England, xiii, 24*n*, 30, 34, 66; *see also* Bristol
Somerset County, Maryland, 370, 371
Somme, France, 272
Souden, David (1979), work on migration patterns cited, 89–92
sources for study of bastardy in Britain, xi–xii, 42–53, 72–9*p*, 85, 120–2, 162–3*p*; for 17th century, 170–5*p*, 177–90*p*; for Scotland, 192–216*p*; for study of bastardy prone, 217, 222, 227, 236; for network analysis, 240–4*p*; *see also* parish registers
sources for study of bastardy outside Britain: France, 249–55*p*, 266–70*p*, 274, 276, 277–8*p*, 282; Germany, 289–92, 294, 298, 305–7*p*, 309, 311–12; Sweden, 313–20*p*, 327–9*p*, 335, 337–40*p*, 344; America, 351–3, 362–73*p*, 376–8*p*; Jamaica, 384–94*p*; Japan, 397–402*p*
Southern England, 64*n*, 143; *see also* individual counties
Southill, Beds., 234
space-time analysis of variance of fertility levels, 33, **36–40**, 45–7, **65–8**
Spain, 25, 39
Spandau, Germany, 308
Spanish Town, Jamaica, 385
'sparrows', 157, 218–20*p*, 222–4*p*, 228, 235, 245; *see also* Bede *and* singletons
Spufford, Margaret (1974), methods for studying 16th- and 17th-century sources adopted by Levine and Wrightson, 170*n*, 171
Sri-Lanka, 72*n*
Stade, Germany (*maps*, 291, 293, 299), 304
Staffordshire, 30, 34
status, socio-economic, and bastardy, 29, 49, 56–8*p*, 75, 81–5*p*; evidence from English parish studies, 81–3, 106, 117, 119, **162–75*p***, 179, 187; Scotland, **193–216*p***; in relation to bastardy proneness, **223–32*p***, 243–5*p*; Germany, 308, 312; Sweden, 336–45*p*; America, 359, 370; Jamaica, 380–1, 393–4; *see also* economic conditions, élites, occupations, poverty *and* social asymmetry
Stepney, London, 63
Stewart, Susan, on reconstitution studies of Banbury and Hartland, **122–40**
Stirlingshire (*maps*, 42–5), 209
Stockholm (county), 317, 318, 320, 322, 323, 325–6
Stockholm (city), 314, 319, 320, 325; illegitimacy and marriage in the 19th century, **336–45**
Stone, Lawrence: Trevelyan lecture (1975) cited, xii; *The Family, sex and marriage in*

Stone, Lawrence (*contd*)
England 1500-1800 (1977) cited, 2*n*, 59*n*, 221*n*, 231*n*
Strachan, Dr J. M. of Dollar, articles in *Scotsman* (1870) on Scottish immorality cited, 200*n*, 204–9*p*, 212
Stranraer, Scotland, 198, 209
Strasbourg, France, 257
Stubbes, Philip (16th century), cited on consequences for bastardy levels of raising the age of marriage compulsorily, 84
Stycos, J. M. and K. W. Back (1964), survey of fertility in Jamaica cited, 381–92*p*, 394
Styria, Austria, 61
Subsidy Assessment (1524), 170
Suffolk, 30–2*p*, 34, 242*n*; *see also* Branfield *and* Rickinghall
'Sugartown', Jamaica, 394
Sundbärg, G. (1970), cited on Swedish illegitimacy statistics, 315
Sundt, Eilert, pioneer of Scandinavian studies cited, 56–8*p*
Surrey, 30, 34, 66, 67
Sussex, 30, 34, 66
Sutherland (*maps*, 42–5), 47, 200, 202, 210
Sweden, x, 1*n*, 26–8*p*, 38–41*p*, 46, 68, 222, 228–9*p*; 17th and 18th centuries, **313–26**; 19th century, **327–35**, **336–45**; *see also* individual areas, towns and parishes
Swinburne, Henry, 17th-century authority on English marriage processes, quoted, 10, 73, 178
Switzerland, 25*n*, 28

Tait, William (19th-century Scottish doctor), on Scottish prostitution, 197, 205; quoted, 195, 197, 198
Takamatsu (Kagawa), Japan, 400
Takaoka (Toyama), Japan, 400
Takasaki, Japan (*map*, 398), 399, 400
Talavera, Spain, 25
Teitelbaum, Michael (1977), cited on British fertility, 41*n*, 47, 48*n*, 59*n*
temporal patterns, in bastardy, ix–xiv*p*, 2–3, 49, 53, 54, 59, 60, **65–8**; in Britain, **12–29**, **33–40**, **41–8**, 220; in Europe, **24–9*p***, 33, **37–41**, 284, 369; in France, **278–83*p***; in Germany, **294–8**, 299, 300, 301; in Sweden, 320–2*p*, 325; in America, 354, 355, 358–9, 361, **364–7**, **370–8**; in Jamaica, 379, 386, 392; in Japan, 398, 399, 402
Tenon, Jacques (18th-century French surgeon), figures on Paris bastardy cited, 252–4*p*
Terling, Essex (*map*, 70), 21, 23, 25, 82, 88, 180, 189; detailed case study, **158–75*p***; bastardy prone sub-society, 225*n*, 233, 236, 241–4*p*
textile industries and bastardy, 83, 88–9*p*, 94, 262, 275, 277; *see also* framework knitters *and* weavers
The World we have lost, (P. Laslett, 1971), cited, 176*n*, 177*n*, 188, 191
Thezels, France, 250
Thomson, Reverend Charles (19th-century Scotland), objecting to the bothy system, quoted, 201–2
Thüringen, Germany (*maps*, 291, 293, 299), 289, 296, 297
Tillinge-Svinnegarn, Sweden, 316, 317, 319, 322, 323
Tochigi, Japan, 399
Tokuku, Japan (*map*, 398), 399, 402
Tokushima, Japan, 400
Tokyo (*formerly* Edo; *map*, 398), 397, 399–402*p*
Tomintoul, Scotland, 200, 210
Tongue, Scotland, 210
Tottori, Japan, (*map*, 398), 399–402*p*
Toulouse, France, 255, 257
Tourouvre-au-Perche, France, 250, 251*n*
towns, bastardy in, *see* urban-rural patterns of bastardy *and* urbanization
Toyama, Japan, 399, 400, 401
'travellers' and vagrants, 105, 230, 235, 315–16, *see also* migration and mobility
Trevières, France, 250
Trinidad, 390
Troumeauville, France, 250
Tsu (Mie), Japan, 400
Tunstall, Lancs., 17*n*
Tyresö/Dalarö, Sweden, 317, 318, 320, 322, 323

Udry, Richard J. (1973), cited on Jamaican fertility, 391
Ujiyamada (Mie), Japan, 400
undeclared bastardy, *see* inferred bastardy
under-registration of bastardy, *see* data reliability
United States, *see* America
Uppsala (county), Sweden, 316, 317, 319, 322, 323
Uppsala (city), Sweden, 318–24*p*
urban-rural patterns of bastardy, 59, 64; England, **62–4**, 123–5, 151; Scotland, 41, 199, 201, 205–6, 214; France, 26, 249–51*p*, 253–7*p*, 262–3*p*, 274–6*p*, **279–81**; Germany, ix, **284–312*p***; Sweden, 321–6*p*; America, 377; Jamaica, 393; Japan, 400–2*p*; *see also* urbanization
urbanization, and bastardy trends, xii, 27, 284, 285; Scotland, 44, 47, 195; France, 251, 258, 274–7*p*; Germany, 305–6, 310–11; America, 375–7*p*; Jamaica, 379, 386, 393; Japan, 402; *see also* industrialization and 'modernization' theory
Utsunomiya (Tochigi), Japan, 400

Valentine, James (19th-century commentator), cited on illegitimacy in Scottish towns, 204, 205

van de Walle, Etienne, on illegitimacy in 19th-century France, **264–77**; cited, 15; *see also* Shorter, Edward, John Knodel and E. van de Walle
van den Broeke, C., cited on illegitimacy and prenuptial pregnancy in Belgium, 25
Västeras, Sweden, 319
Västmanland, Sweden, 316n, 317–19p, 322, 323, 325, 326
venereal disease, 83, 194–7p, 221n, 228, 377, 383, 392–3p
Victorian: bastardy trends, 13, 17–19, 29–31, 63–4; morals and moralists, 2, 7, 192–216p; prostitution, **193–9**, **227–9**; Scotland, 41, **192–216p**; servants, 56; urban–rural patterns, 64
Vienna, Austria, 336
village controls, 49, 53, 83, 170–5p, 176–91p, 394; *see also* locality patterns *and* social controls
Virginia, 349n, 351, 352, 354–9p, 361, 370, 376n
Vitré, France, 255, 261
Vivarais, France, 260

Wachter, Kenneth, contributions to space-time analysis of variance in levels of legitimate and illegitimate fertility, **65–8**; cited, 33, 39
Wakamatsu, Japan (*map*, 398), 399, 400
Wakayama, Japan, 399, 400, 401
Wales, 63, 64n, 123, 201, 209; *see also* England and Wales *and* individual counties and parishes
Wardlaw, Ralph, (19th-century moralist), cited on female prostitution and disease, 194, 195, 197; quoted, 193
wars, effects of, 31, 98, 149, 293–4p, 321, 373; *see also* revolutions
Warwickshire, 24n, 30, 31n, 34; *see also* Alcester
Washentaw County, Mich., 371
Weavers, 82, 94, 153
Wells, Robert, on illegitimacy and bridal pregnancy in Colonial America, **349–61**; cited, 7, 11, 371
Wem, Salop, 86, 87, 234, 235
West Indies, 380, 382; *see also* Caribbean, Jamaica *and* Trinidad
West Lothian (*maps*, 42–5), 47, 201, 210, 214
Westmorland, 30, 31, 35, 66
Westphalia, Germany (*map*, 291), 290n, 298, 309
wet nurses, use of, 78, 249, 258–63p
Whatcom County, Washington State, 367
Whitechapel, London, 63, 64
Whitworth, Lancs., 186
Wiesbaden, Germany (*maps*, 291, 293, 299), 308
Wigan, Lancs., 63
Wigton, Cumb., 63
Wigtownshire (*maps*, 42–5), 199–201p, 203, 205–6p, 210, 215
Wilburton, Cambs., 235
Willimantic, Conn., 370, 371
Willingham, Cambs., 21, 23
wills as sources, 72–3p, 85, 120, 162n, 165, 168, 240–1
Wilson, Christopher, current reserach on prenuptial pregnancy cited, 55n, 57n, 61
Wiltshire, ixn, 34, 66
Worcestershire, 30, 34, 66
Wordsworth, William, as a member of the bastardy prone sub-society?, 231
Wrightson, Keith: on the nadir of English illegitimacy in the 17th century, **176–91**; findings cited, 25, 51n, 53, 76, 81, 108, 224; *see also* Levine, David and Keith Wrightson
Wrigley, E. A., various demographic studies cited, 59n, 101, 103, 177n, 285n, 309; on age at marriage, 105, 140; on Colyton, 112, 113, 159

Yamagata, Japan, 400
Yamanashi, Japan, 399
Yokohama, Japan (*map*, 398), 400, 402
Yonezawa (Yamagata), Japan, 400
York, England (*map*, 70), 74, 227–9p
York County, Maine, 352
York County, Virginia, 354
Yorkshire, 24n, 29, 30, 35, 66, 85n; *see also* Birstall, Bolton Percy, Easingwold, Methley *and* York